# PRIVATE
# NETWORKS
# PUBLIC
# OBJECTIVES

# PRIVATE
# NETWORKS
# PUBLIC
# OBJECTIVES

*Edited by*

## ELI NOAM

*Columbia Institute for Tele-Information*
*Columbia Business School*
*New York, USA*

## AINE NÍSHÚILLEABHÁIN

*INSEAD*
*Fontainebleau Cedex, France*

1996

ELSEVIER

AMSTERDAM • LAUSANNE • NEW YORK • OXFORD • SHANNON • TOKYO

ELSEVIER SCIENCE B.V.
Sara Burgerhartstraat 25
P.O. Box 211, 1000 AE  Amsterdam, The Netherlands

ISBN: 0 444 82549 5

Printed in The Netherlands.

# CONTENTS

# Contributing Authors

*Sandra Braman*, Research Assistant Professor at the Institute of Communications Research, University of Illinois-Urbana, has been conducting research in the area of macro-level effects of the use of new information technologies and their policy implications for 15 years. She has published almost three dozen book chapters and articles, and is currently working on two books: *The Information Regime*, which analyzes commonalities in the information policy approaches of three domains of international relations (trade, defense, and agriculture), and *Information Policy and Power*, which presents a framework for the analysis of information policy.

*Graciela Chichilnisky* is Professor of Economics at Columbia. She co-founded Financial Tele-Communications Ltd. (FITEL - an international telecommunications firm) with Geoffrey Heal, and served as its Chairperson and Chief Executive. She is currently working on a decentralized tele-communications system for global custody of international securities. Her most recent books, co-authored with Geoffrey Heal, are *The Evolving International Economy* and *Oil in the International Economy*.

*David J. Gabel* is currently an Associate Professor of Economics at Queens College, and has been teaching there since 1987. Before teaching he worked for the New York State Consumer Protection Board and American Telephone and Telegraph Company. Prof. Gabel is widely published, most recently his paper *Federalism: An Historical Perspective*, in *Crossing Lines: American Regulatory Federalism and the Telecommunications Infrastructure*, edited by Paul Teske. His forthcoming publications include *Opening Networks to Competition: The Regulation and Pricing Access*, editing with David Weiman, and *Current Issues in the Pricing of Voice Telephone Services,* in *Telecommunications Policy*, August, 1995. He recived his BA from Boston University, Magna Cum Laude with a distinction in History in 1976, an MS in economics from University of Wisconsin at Madison in 1982, and his PhD in Economics also from the University of Wisconsin at Madison in 1987.

*Shane Michael Greenstein* has been an Assistant Professor of Economics at the University of Illinois at Urbana/Champaign in the Department of Economics since 1990, and before that taught at Stanford University. He has articles forthcoming in the June 1996 issue of the *Rand Journal of Economics*, and chapters in several books, including *The Mosaic of Economic Growth*, edited by Gavin Wright and Ralph Landau, *The Economics of New Products*, edited by Tim Bresnahan and Robert J. Gordon, and *Colliding Worlds: The Convergence of Computers, Telecommunications and Consumer Electronics*, edited by David Yoffie. He received a Bachelor of Arts in Economics from the University of California at Berkeley, and his PhD in Economics from Stanford University.

*Allen S. Hammond, IV,* is a Professor of Law at the New York Law School, where he has been teaching since 1989, before that he taught at several schools, including Howard University and the Syracuse University College of Law. In the *University of Pennsylvania Law Review*, in the Summer of 1994 his paper, *Private Networks, Public Speech: Constitutional Speech Dimensions of Access to Private Networks*, Volume 55, Number 4. Forthcoming publications include *Regulating the Multi-Media Chimera: Electronic Speech Rights in the Era of Media Convergence*, in *Rutgers Computer and Technology Law Journal*, Volume 21, No. 1 Spring 1995, and the *Casebook on Communications and Entertainment Law*. He received his Bachelor of Arts from Grinnell College in 1972, his Juris Doctor from University of Pennsylvania School of Law in 1975, and his Master of Arts in Communications from the Annenberg School of Communications, University of Pennsylvania, 1977.

*Koichiro Hayashi* is the Group Vice President of Multimedia Promotion Headquarters of Nippon Telegraph and Telephone Corporation. Since joining NTT in 1963, he has held a variety of senior management positions, and prior to assuming his present position in August 1995, he was the President of NTT America, Inc., a wholly-owned subsidary of NTT. He is widely published, and his two most recent works are *Universal Service*, about the original principle of universal service in telecommunications, and *Information Superhighway, Now and Future*, with Dr. John N. Latta. He recieved his Bachelors degree in Law from Tokyo University in 1963, and his PhD in Economics for Kyoto University in 1991.

*Brian Kahin* directs the Information Infrastructure Project in the Science, Technology and Public Policy Program at Harvard's John F. Kennedy School of Government, where he also lectures on law, technology and public policy. He has edited several volumes on infrastructure, including *Building Information Infrastructure* (1992), *Public Access to the Internet* (1995), *Standards Policy for Information Infractructure* (1995), and *The Information Infrastructure Sourcebook* (1993-). In addition, Mr. Kahin serves as General Counsel for the Interactive Multimedia Association and directs the Association's intellectual property activities.

*Richard A. Kramer* is a high technology analyst for Kleinwort Benson, a stockbrocker based in London. Previously he worked at Nortel in England, and before that he worked as Assistant Director at the Columbia Institute for Tele-Information. He has also worked for a videotex joint venture company and as a consultant to a number of non-profit communications groups. He holds degrees from Columbia University and the University of Pennsylvania. His papers include "Investment and Structural Trends in Multinational Services," (CITI,1993) and "To Strategies and the Emergence of a Global Oligopoly," (CITI,1992) both with Áine M. NíShúilleabháin.

*Dale Lehman* is Associate Professor of Economics at Fort Lewis College. He has taught at 10 universities and consulted and published widely in the telecommunications and information industries. His expertise is in market structure analysis, demand modeling and public policy analysis.

*William H. Lehr* is Assistant Professor at Columbia Business School. His current research examines advances in information technology and the effects on competitive dynamics and industry structure. Lehr holds undergraduate and masters degrees in chemical engineering from the University of Pennsylvania, and an MBA from the Wharton School of Business. He received his PhD in economics from Stanford. Major publications and papers include *Standardization: Understanding the Process, Voluntary Standards and Industry Competition: Two Case Studies, Voluntary Standards, Multiple Markets, Standards Institutions, and Industry Structure*, and (with Roger Noll) *ISDN and the Small User: Regulatory Policy Issues*.

*Robin Mansell* is a Professor and Director of the Centre for Information and Communication Technologies at the Science Policy Research Unit, University of Sussex. Her research focuses on the social and economic impact of advanced information and communication technologies and services. She has worked as an academic and consultant in Canada, the United States and Europe on issues of European and international policy. She is the author of many scholarly articles and reports including *The New Telecommunications: A Political Economy of Network Evolution*, Sage, 1993; *Communication by Design: The Politics of Information and Communication Technologies* (editor and contributor with Roger Silverstone), Oxford University Press, forthcoming March 1996.

*Bruce W. McConnell* is Chief of Information Policy and Technology at the Office of Information and Regulatory Affairs, Office of Management and Budget, where he assumed the position in 1992, and has been at the office since 1985. His office is heavily involved with oversight of the acquisition of information technology resources by government agencies, and helps to implement the administration's plans to encourage the development of the National Information Infrastructure (NII). He received a Bachelor of Science in mechanical engineering from Stanford University in 1971, and a Masters of Public Administration from the University of Washington in 1985.

*Terrence P. McGarty* is the President of The Telemarc Group, Inc., a company he founded in 1984 and which invests in and manages several high tech start up ventures. He was also a founder of Telemarc Telecommunications, Inc., a Personal Communications Services System Operator, holding the experimental license for Boston, the first national experimental network license for PCS. He is the author of four books, including *Business Plans that win Venture Capital*, and over seventy five professional papers that cover topics ranging from medical imaging to telecommunications. He holds a PhD in Electrical Engineering and two other degrees from the Massachusetts Institute of Technology and previously studied medicine in the joint Harvard/MIT program.

*Michael Meyerson* is a Professor of Law at the University of Baltimore School of Law. He has written widely on communications and modern technology. His articles have appeared in Notre Dame Law Review, Georgia Law Review, University of Miami Law Review, Washington & Lee Law Review, Harvard Journal of Law and Technology, Stanford Journal of International Law, and Hastings Law School's COMM/ENT. He has co-authored *Cable Television and Other Nonbroadcast Media* (Clark Boardman), with Daniel Brenner and Monroe Price.

*Milton Mueller* is an Assistant Professor at Rutgers University in the Department of Communications in the School of Communications, Information, and Library Science. He taught at the University of Nebraska at Omaha and was a Research Assistant at the International Center for Telecommunications Management. He is the author of several books and many articles. His most recent book is *Universal Service: Competition, Interconnection and Monopoly in the Making of the American Telephone System* from MIT Press. His paper *Universal Service as an Appropriability Problem: A New Framework for Analysis* in *Toward a Competitive Telecommunications Industry: Selected Papers from the 1994 Telecommunications Policy Research Conference*, edited by Gerald Brook. Dr. Mueller received his BA in Animation and Filmmaking from Columbia College in Chicago, and his MA and PhD, both in Communications from the Annenberg School of Communications at the University of Pennsylvania.

*Áine M. NíShúilleabháin* is a PHD candidate in France at INSEAD. She previously served as Associate Director of the Columbia Institute for Tele-Information from 1993-1994. She is a telecommunications analyst specializing in strategic business development, investment, and structural trends in the European, Asia-Pacific, and US markets. Her publications include "Monopolistic Competition in European Telecommunications: Emerging Global Players," (London: Euro CPR); *European VANS Markets: 1992; Far East Telecom Operators: 1993; Asia-Pacific VANS Markets: 1993*, (Northern Business Information/McGraw Hill). She also previously served as the Assistant Director of CITI from 1990-1992, and holds degrees from Dublin University and the University of Pennsylvania.

*Eli M. Noam* is professor of Finance and Economics at the Columbia University Graduate School of Business and Director of the Columbia Institute for Tele-Information. He has also served as Public Service Commissioner engaged in the telecommunications and energy regulation of New York State. His publications include over a dozen books and about 200 articles on domestic and international telecommunications, television, information and regulation subjects. His recent books include *Telecommunications in the Pacific Basin*, ed. (Oxford, 1994) and *Asymmetric Deregulation*, ed. (Ablex, 1994). Forthcoming books include are *Telecommunications in Africa*, *Telecommunications in Latin America* and *Telecommunications in Western Asia*. He is a member of the New York and Washington D.C. bars, a licensed radio amateur Advanced Class, and a commercially rated pilot.

*Richard E. Nohe* is Director, Corporate Affairs for NTT America, Inc., where he is responsible for research, business development and government relations. During 1996 he will be on a leave of absence for one year, joining the Brookings Institution's Congressional Fellows Program to work in the U.S. Congress. Previously, Mr. Nohe was researcher at the Columbia Institute for Tele-Information (CITI) at Columbia University's Graduate School for Business. Before that, he directed live evening newscasts at WRDW-TV, a CBS affiliate. Mr. Nohe holds a B.A. in English from Augusta College, a Master of Professional Studies from the Interactive Telecommunications Program at New York University, and a J.D. from the evening program at New York Law School.

*A. Michael Noll* is Professor of Communications at the Annenberg School for Communication at the University of Southern California. Before teaching at the Annenberg School, he was involved in industry. For nearly 15 years he performed basic research at Bell Labs at Murray Hill, and from 1977 to 1984 worked in the AT&T Consumer Products and Marketing Department where he performed technical evaluations and identified opportunities for new products and services. He is the author of three books on telecommunication electronics, telephone systems and television, and is a frequent author of op-ed pieces. He recieved his Bachelor of Science in Electrical Engineering from Newark College of Engineering in 1961, his Masters from New York University in 1963 and his PhD from Polytechnic Institute of Brooklyn in 1971.

*David P. Reed* is a Senior Advisor, Strategic Planning, with Cable Television Laboratories, Inc. In this position, he is responsible for developing projects that address issues of immediate interest to member companies. Before his current position, he served three years in the Federal Communication Commission as a Telecommunications Policy Analyst in the Office of Plans and Policy, where he worked on video dialtone, personal communications services, and spectrum auction policies. He authored OPP Working Paper #28, *Putting It All Together: The Cost Structure of PCS*. He holds three degrees: a Bachelor of Science in Electrical Engineering from Colorado State University, a Masters of Science in Electrical Engineering from Carnegie Mellon, and a PhD from the Department of Engineering and Public Policy at Carnegie Mellon University.

*Anthony Michael Rutkowski* is the Vice President of Internet Business Development for General Magic, Inc. Before this he served as the Executive Director of the Internet Society and previously served as its Vice-President and founding trustee for two years. Before that, he was the Director of Technology Assessment in the Strategic Planning Group of Sprint International, and the International Telecommunication Union. He is active in IEEE, ABA and numerous other forums, he has authored or contributed to several books, written more than 100 published articles and reports. He has testified by request to the U.S. Congress and government agencies on many occasions, and remains a visible and prolific analyst-writer - appearing at many industry forums. He has received a B.S. in Electrical Engineering from the Florida Insitute of Technology and a J.D. from American University.

*Rohan Samarjiva* is an Associate Professor at the Department of Communication at the Ohio State University in Columbus, Ohio, and is the president of the Communication Technology Policy Section of the International Association for Mass Communication Research. His research interests are political economy and policy aspects of emerging communication technologies. His publications have appeared in the *Journal of Communication, Media, Culture and Society, Telecommunications Policy, The Information Society, Gazette* and *Communication Yearbook*, among others. Samarjiva is founding associate editor of the new Sage journal, *New Media: Technology, Society, Culture.* He holds PhD and MA degrees from Simon Fraser University, Canada, and is an Attorney-at-Law in Sri Lanka.

*Paul Teske* is Associate Professor of Political Science at the State University of New York at Stony Brook. He has analyzed telecommunications policy for the New Jersey Board of Public Utilities, the New York City Department of Telecommunications, the New York State

Telephone Association, Teleport Communications Group, and the U.S. Congressional Office of Technology Assessment. He is the author of several journal articles on regulation and telecommunications. Teske wrote the 1990 book *After Divestiture: The Political Economy of State Regulation.* He also is co-author (with Mark Schneider) of the 1995 book *Public Entrepreneurs: Agents for Change in Local Government*, and edited the recent volume *American Regulatory Federalism & Telecommunications Infrastructure.* He holds PhD and MPA degrees in Public Affairs from Princeton University's Woodrow Wilson School and a BA with highest honors in Economics from the University of North Carolina at Chapel Hill.

**Dennis L. Weisman** is currently an Assistant Professor of Economics at Kansas State University and a member of the graduate faculty. He has over ten years experience in the telecommunications industry in the areas of regulation and business strategy development. Dr. Weisman's work has appeared in the *Journal of Regulatory Economics*, the *Yale Journal of Economics, The Journal of Policy Analysis and Management*, and the *Federal Communications Law Journal.* He is also the co-author of a book for the MIT Press and the American Enterprise Institute entitled *Designing Incentive Regulation for the Telecommunications Industry.* He holds a PhD in economics from the University of Florida in 1993, an MA in economics from the University of Colorado, 1981, and a BA in mathematics and economics from the University of Colorado in 1979, Magna Cum Laude in economics.

**Martin B.H. Weiss** is an Associate Professor of Telecommunications and is Co-Director of the Telecommunications Program at the University of Pittsburgh. His principal research activities have focussed on the issues surrounding the development and adoption of technical compatibility standards. He is also interested in telecommunications policy, information policy, telecommunications services, and network management. From 1978 to 1981, he was a Member of the Technical Staff at Bell Laboratories; from 1983 to 1985, he was a Member of the Technical Staff at the MITRE Corp; and from 1985 to 1987 he was a Senior Consultant with Deloitte, Haskins, and Sells. His most recent work is forthcoming in *Telecommunications Policy* (coauthored with William H. Lehr) "The Political Economy of Congestion Charges and Settlements in Packet Networks."

**Steven S. Wildman** is an Associate Professor at Northwestern University in the Department of Communication Studies, and is also Director of the Program in Telecommunications Science, Management and Policy. Previously he taught at the University of California at Los Angeles and was a consultant for the Rand Corporation. Recently he has authored *Video Economics* with Bruce M. Owen. Several papers are forthcoming, *Network Programming and Off-Network Syndication Profits: Strategic Links and Implications for Television Policy* with K. Robinson in *Journal of Media Economics* and *Trade Liberalization and Policy for Media Industries* in the *Canadian Journal of Communication.* Prof. Wildman received his BA in Economics from Wabash College in 1971, and his MA and PhD, both in economics, from Stanford University in 1977 and 1980, respectively.

**Ken Zita** is a Managing Partner at Network Dynamics, of which he is a co-founder. Currently he has been involved with the European Bank for Reconstruction and Development for evaluation of overlay networks in areas like Uzbekistan and Russia, and for the investment in and reconstruction of the telecommunications sector in Moldova. He has written for many publications, including *The Economist*, the *Asian Wall Street Journal* and *The Far Eastern Economic Review*. He is also the authors of *The Economist's* special report on *Modernising China's Telecommunications*, and has presented papers before the U.S. Congress Joint Economic Committee. He recieved his Bachelor of Arts in the Philosophy of Science with High Honors from Wesleyan University in Connecticut.

# Introduction

## Eli M. Noam and Áine NíShúilleabháin

Telecommunications today are shaped by the twin dynamics of technical integration on the one hand, and institutional diversification on the other. To some extent these diametric tendencies serve as substitutes. Networks can be upgraded through more powerful integration - as in the case of narrow and integrated broadband networks (ISDN and IBN) - with attendant economies of scope and scale[1] or through a diversification of providers that creates choice and efficiency.

Throughout the twentieth century, telecommunication networks around the world tended to be centralized state-government run operations. But as the century comes to a close, the privatization of ownership of national networks is well underway. This process has received much attention, even if the reality of privatization often still left government in control. Yet there is a second type of privatization that has been less noted--the "use-privatization" in the form of private and closed-user group networks not accessible to the general public. This type of privatization has been a quieter process but of arguably greater long-term significance. It is based on networks that are private although not necessarily privately-owned or even separate from the shared public switched network. They may be fashioned from state-owned segments (as in the Ministry-run networks of the People's Republic of China) or they may be used by the state (as in the case of the US government's giant FTS-2000 system). They may serve a single organization, or a group of them, such as in the case of clearing networks of financial institutions.

An analogy may clarify the distinction. Whereas ownership-privatization corresponds to transferring shares in a state-run railroad to private shareholders, use-privatization compares to admitting private automobiles and taxis on highways as alternatives to buses. Arguably, ownership changes of the Long Island Railroad, Conrail, or Amtrak had but a minor impact on New York City, whereas mass marketing of the private automobile bore enormous impact on its city scape, metropolitan growth patterns, employment distribution, and demography.

The trend toward private segmented networking began to gather momentum in the latter part of the 1970s and has continued to accelerate. Although these were typically perceived as special arrangements on the margins of the regular system, this began to change. In 1980, for example, virtually 100 percent of US network investment was made by public network carriers. By 1986 this had dropped to 66 percent. The rest was made by users themselves and by providers of private network arrangements.

In addition to intra-organizational networks, there emerged private shared networks operated by domestic and international value-added network (VAN) service providers (these are discussed in Part Seven of this volume). First to develop were networks linking financial institutions - the US payment netting systems FEDWIRE and CHIPS, their UK and Japanese counterparts CHAPS and CHATS, and the international fund transfer network SWIFT.[2] Inter-Airline networks too, were at the forefront, notably SITA.[3] These were followed by horizontal networks serving travel agents, insurance companies, and advertising agencies. Next to develop were vertical industry networks such as those of General Motors and General Electric linking suppliers, dealers, insurers, transportation entities, and financial intermediaries across geographically-dispersed locations. Such private shared value-added service networks were complemented by domestic and international VANs promoted by the public telecommunications operators (PTOs or TOs) in reaction to the private efforts and also as revenue-generators for the longer term. The National Science Foundation, having assumed direct responsibility for the research community's computer networking infrastructure in 1986, funded the backbone of the early Internet whose host-computer population continues to double annually, with 10 million hosts exceeded in 1996. The Internet is an electively-open[4] public-private shared ensemble of far-flung autonomous private and public networks. The trend toward use-differentiation of public- and privately-accessible components means that the economic and policy issues addressed in this volume address most Internet-specific debates.

Private networks began as dedicated voice circuits leased from the monopoly telephone company. More complex arrangements rapidly evolved, expanding in range to incorporate transport on other domestic and foreign carriers, both established ones and new entrants. They introduced internal switching capacity and offered the potential for varied traffic routing with associated cost-reductions. They also permitted circuit-sharing among PBX[5]-interconnected users: these were the market precursors of virtual (i.e. logically-managed) private network services offered by public carriers that combined the economies of scale of general ("public") networks with the flexibility and control of separate access-controlled "private" sub-networks. Thus the distinction between switched public network and non-switched (fixed) dedicated private network began to erode. Enterprise networks selling excess capacity to others, and the emergence of private shared networks transformed into public entities[6] compounded the tendency.

With the emergence of alternative transmission systems - starting with the US Federal Communications Commission's (FCC) *Above 890* decision permitting alternative infrastructure government for intra-organizational private line - it became increasingly possible for users and systems integrators to aggregate capacity. Thus private networks based upon economy and efficiency of available bandwidth, and functional rather than territorial in character, began to proliferate. Estimates for numbers of existing private networks per country at any point in time vary wildly and no telephone company - least of all within the US - claims definitive knowledge of the scope of such activity within its operating territory.[7] For over a decade, however, the international internetworking sectors -- enterprise, private shared network/(I)VAN, and Internet -- have been adopting similar practices: interconnecting digital PBXs, mainframes, minicomputers, and PCS via combinations of leased-lines, packet-switching capability and more advanced transmission modes, and protocols ensuring interoperability at critical points. (The basic difference between the three sectors is organizational and — from the perspective of this volume — a matter of the relative openness of controlled infrastructures.) Extrapolating from these trends, the future portends the popularization of "Personal Networks" (PNs) beginning with the US, Western Europe and Japan.

**Overview of this Volume**

The chapters of this volume spring from a two-year research project initiated by Columbia University's Institute for Tele-Information (CITI). The project was supported by CITI affiliate NTT of Japan, joined by Telia of Sweden, with full program responsibility and implementation by CITI. We are grateful for their support.

The aim of the project was to:

- model and explain the reason for various networking arrangements - public, private, hybrid, group, intra-organizational, virtual, etc.;
- project the evolution of the telecommunications network into a pluralistic federation of subnetworks;
- analyze the economics of private networks, and the technological options and network configurations available to providers both of public and private capacity;
- examine the policy implications of use-privatization for social objectives traditionally incorporated in public networks, such as technical compatibility; universal service; common carriage; privacy; consumer protection; service quality; urban/rural service similarity; ability to fashion national and international policies.

Through its various contributors, this volume addresses the future of telecommunications and information systems, and the maintenance of traditional public objectives within the emerging network of networks.

**I. Taxonomy: Defining the Network Environment**

Our working definition of private networks is based not upon physical separateness (which would exclude software-defined networks), or on ownership and institutional designation. Rather, private networks are characterized by user control of access, terms of usage, and internal pricing.[8] This definition does not position centrally competition via alternative physical facilities but rather the establishment of restricted networking arrangements by corporate and other user group organizations.

The first chapters, by Terrence McGarty and Tony Rutkowski, aim to minimize terminological confusion associated with networks. Networks differ along numerous dimensions, including intra- vs inter-organizational; intra- vs inter-premises; public-carrier, user, or third-party provisioned; resale- or facilities-based; and hybrid or virtual.

Tony Rutkowski highlights the historical notions of openness but contemporaneous definitional lacunae with regard to private networking enshrined in international administrative treaties. Rutkowski, defining networks as 'interoperating arrays of information objects' supporting shared information processing among multiple entities, argues that the impossibility of their consistent characterization based upon the designations 'public' or 'private' requires a shift of definitional focus to the information objects themselves. Most useful are the indices of object-publicness (origins of provision, access availability, ownership, control, and financing) which follow. Several subsequent chapters assume these distinctions without explicit clarification. Expanding, Terrence McGarty develops a taxonomy of networks to clarify some of the boundaries distinguishing public and private systems. By analyzing the 'genetics' of network, he divided them into two species: hierarchal networks like the RBOCs and distributive networks similar to the LANs in many offices.

This description is then used to illustrate how networks will increase its move to the distributed met work, because of the economics of the situation.

## II. History and Recent Developments

Part Two of this volume covers the evolution of private networking from the turn of the century to today's complex blurring of software functionality controlled by network providers and user-customers. Eli Noam attempts a broad interpretation of the formation and transformation of networks, contextualizing their growth and institutional forms against a backdrop of competing theories of network evolution. His model of evolution and internal dynamics implies that a network coalition, left to itself under majority-rule principles, would expand beyond the size that would hold in the event of equal treatment of each subscriber. With arbitrage and user choice (both destabilizing the redistributive mechanisms), the pro-expansion policy characteristic of cost-sharing arrangements creates pressures for the construction of alternative network arrangements. In fact the very success of network expansion in terms of cost-minimization and universal service bears the seeds of its own demise, hence the "tragedy" implied by this chapter's title. David Gabel analyzes the historical rivalry between AT&T and Western Union which demonstrates that technological innovation without flexibility is no guarantor of success.

The contributions of Milton Mueller and Paul Teske address the pragmatics of drawing analytic boundaries against the backdrop of private-networking activities. Mueller's analysis of the extent of private networking in the US distinguishes between the single (e.g. PBX- or LAN-based) and multi-site network: whereas the latter is in decline due to the multiplication of software defined networks and wireless technologies the former increases both in number and complexity. Teske provides a useful overview of federal and state trends in US government networking and suggests that too little attention has generally been paid to their contributions to national infrastructure (the Internet's unanticipated expansion obviously provides the supreme exemplar).

## III. The Economics of Private Networks

Sandra Braman introduces Part Three by tracing out the wider boundaries of networking as defined by organizational and legal structures. Beyond the immediately-visible contributions of public support for the information infrastructure to their private counterparts, her paper examines four levels of reciprocal influence inherent in the evolution of organizational form, legal transformation, emergence of the network economy, and increased societal complexity. William Lehr investigates plausible outcomes arising from models of service quality alongside various network-development scenarios based on fragmentation of infrastructure control. His work provides clear justification for mounting concern -- visible today in industry fora -- to ensure affordable reliability levels in ever-more-decentralized operating environments. As Martin Elton noted, various ceilings exist that define those levels of quality for which network user-groups are willing to pay.

Graciela Chichilnisky begins with the observation that economic fundamentals in network services markets may be precisely opposed in character to those predicted by classic textbook examples. Her chapter examines the formation of user-coalitions capable of exploiting network externalities which they induce on others, thus surmounting the network start-up problem. Shane Greenstein examines those conditions under which decentralized network systems converge toward standardization. In the short run (and assuming stable market structure), standards coordinate contemporaneously and largely anticipated market behavior which reduces interconnection costs. In the long run standardization has a significant impact upon technical change.

## IV. Interoperability: Technical

The next two chapters address network interoperation and ongoing technical developments. Martin Weiss proposes a theory of standards and regulation centered on the notion of entropy. This has its policy implications since excessive market entropy underpins more expensive and less manageable purchasing processes whilst inadequate levels also introduce disadvantages - hence the scenario where lax regulation and tighter controls might effectively constrain fluctuations within desired limits.

David Reed explores unbundling of physical and logical elements within the advanced intelligent network environment as a conceptual and practical matter. New costs deriving from unbundling should be set against the benefits of more open access conditions.

## V. Interoperability: Economic and Legal

Part Five of the volume focuses on legal and economic issues raised by use-privatization and those access constraints which result. Robin Mansell's case studies of European electronic trading networks suggest that user-community pressure for increased access to advanced applications and infrastructure is unlikely to be strong where such adjustment conflict with such economic interests as network security and flexibility (i.e. the fundamental motivations underlying initial establishment of such private entities). Dale Lehman and Dennis Weisman indicate what an efficient set of incentives for private network interconnection with public systems might look like. Michael Meyerson analyses the constitutional and antitrust issues pertaining to group networks. In the final part of this section Al Hammond addresses the legal side of network interoperability.

## VI. Interoperability: Domestic and International Policy

The succeeding group of articles address policy concerns. Rohan Samarjiva develops a framework for analyzing the consumer and privacy implications of use-privatization. Brian Kahin and Bruce McConnell trace the twenty-year evolution of the Internet from its origins in the Advanced Research Projects Agency (ARPA) of the US Department of Defense through the NREN (National Research and Education Network) of 1989 and culminating in recent part- privatization and commercialization of various components. The historical paradigm has been that of partial public funding of autonomous internetworks. However, as Internet service-demand increases and the TCP/IP protocol enjoys widespread adoption, the nonprofit user segment lag their commercial counterparts in elaborating clear service and growth strategies. In fact, those opportunities afforded the nonprofit sector remain somewhat limited by current 'acceptable use' policies, which may require modification to preserve the balance of networking power.

Steven Wildman explores prospective productivity benefits contingent upon exploitation of private networking capabilities, concluding that these are potentially large and justify considerable IT investment. Michael Noll's chapter examines network security and reliability within the decentralized network environments: in particular common channel-signaling and the additional vulnerability this implies, which in turn requires technological, procedural and cooperative solutions enhancing network reliability.

## VII. International Studies: Toward the Future

Áine NíShúilleabháin analyzes the adaptation of private networking capabilities to the public network environment by telecommunications operators (TOs) in Europe, North America, Asia-Pacific, and Latin America as well as the emerging global networking market. Koichiro Hayashi and Richard Nohe share the view that the trend towards privatization of telecom operators blurs the distinction between public and private networks and raises questions about the hybrid networks of the future. Their article compares infrastructure and private-network developments in the US with those of Japan where the marketplace is more strictly segmented. In view of rapid multiplication of both private and hybrid networking arrangements these authors dismiss the possibility of single-carrier dominance of a major telecommunications or computing market.

Ken Zita's paper addresses large-user networking options in Asia where regional corporate - i.e. private - networks were until recently a necessity. The competitive response of (former, in some cases) monopoly public-service providers to basic-service revenue erosion has been to introduce a range of so-called managed network services. However despite aggressive supply-side push by carriers in this direction, traditional private-line networks still dominate corporate communications across the region. Richard Kramer discusses whether the infrastructure monopoly can survive as a concept or practical matter. Finally, Eli Noam analyzes the public network's evolution into a pluralistic federation of subnetworks, and thus to a "system of systems" operating on top of a "network of networks."

Many other excellent papers were part of the Columbia project but had to be excluded because of length constraints. The collaborative study of this subject continues as the evolution of networks continue. Questions evolve, driven in part by the growth of wireless communications, by the steady march of operator privatization worldwide, by the growing clarity surrounding the convergence of voice and data communications, and in particular by the explosion of computer networking. The richness of the networking environment has also increased exponentially with the emergence of scores of new service providers (the new service-territory which is the Internet provides a crucial stimulus), as well as software and internetworking competitors within the equipment industry. These companies continue to redefine the boundaries of networks, both public and private, as leading-edge technology is insistently layered on today's solutions. The goalposts marking technology performance thus advance apace, and so to does the digitalization of human interaction.

Particular thanks are due to the to Project Advisory Board members who participated in several meetings during 1991-93 (complete list in Appendix A); to NTT and Dr. Koichiro Hayashi and to Telia and Dr. Bertil Thorngren in particular; to Douglas Conn who helped launch and manage the project; and Alex Wolfson and John Kollar - respectively CITI Associate Director and Project Manager for Private Networks - whose contributions have been important throughout.

# ENDNOTES

[1] See an earlier book of the Columbia Institute for Tele-Information, Martin. J. C. Elton (ed.) *Integrated Broadband Networks* (Elsevier, 1994).

[2] This Belgian cooperative society is owned by 2,313 member banks in 105 operating countries. SWIFT in 1994 claimed 40,139 users defined as financial (including non-bank) institutions allowed to use the SWIFT network.

[3] Societe Internationale de Telecommunications Aeronautiques, a cooperative venture involving 550 (mostly airline) members. The SITA Global Network (SGN) comprises 500 nodes supporting voice and data communications in 130 countries in 1994. The overlay High-Speed Network (transmission backbone) reached an additional 208 nodes.

[4] It is possible to partition or otherwise circumscribe unauthorized access to so-called secure parts - such as the US Department of Defense's MilNet - of the internetwork.

[5] Private Branch Exchange, typically used to support in-house customized voice-and-data systems.

[6] In the following decades numerous facilities-based carriers emerged offering transmission capacity internationally (Cable & Wireless, PanAmSat), nationally (MCI, Sprint, Wiltel), regionally (Frontier, Allnet, LDDS), locally (MFS, Teleport Communications, Bay Area Teleport, IntelCom, and major cable providers).

[7] In 1991, Gartner Group estimated the numbers of private networks in Europe as follows: Portugal 100; Greece and Iceland 200; Austria and Norway 300; Denmark 400; Finland and the Netherlands 450; Switzerland 500; Belgium 550; Sweden 600; Spain 800; Italy 1400; Germany 1500; France 2000; and the UK 4500.

[8] Such control may be delegated to a carrier or systems integrator.

# PRIVATE NETWORKS ADVISORY BOARD*

*Europe*

**Cor Berben**; Head of Section; Regulatory Conditions on Access to Networks & Services/ONP, DG XIII/D; European Commission
**Lleven De Poorter**; Director, Corporate Planning; SWIFT
**Patricia M. Dinneen**; Head of Strategy, North America; British Telecom
**L. Daniel O'Neill**; Special Advisor; SITA
**Francois Petit**; Director, Business Development; Alcatel N.V.
**Jonathon Solomon**; Director, Corporate Business Development; Cable & Wireless
**Bertil Thorngren**; Director, Head of Corporate Planning; Televerket (Telia)

*Japan*

**Yasukuni Kotaka**; Vice President, Engineering Administrations; NEC
**Nobuhiko Shimasaki**; Tokai U
**Motojiro Shiromizu** and others; Executive Director, General Manager Communications Systems; Fujitsu
**Hideaki Toda** and others; Executive Vice President, International Affairs, NTT

*\*note: Affiliations listed were at the time of the project.*

PRIVATE NETWORKS PUBLIC OBJECTIVES
E. Noam and A. NíShúilleabháin (Editors)
© 1996 Elsevier Science B.V. All rights reserved.

# Taxonomy: Defining the Network Environment

## A Taxonomy of Networks: Is it Public or Not?

Anthony M. Rutkowski

## 1. HISTORY

### 1.1. International

The terms "public" and "private" in telecommunications instruments can be traced back to the very earliest international agreements. Indeed, the first multilateral treaty for telecommunications begins with the preamble "With the intention of enabling both public and private traffic..."[1]

In this context, the term "public" in the preamble is synonymous with "State," while "private" has the connotation of non-State messages. However, the Dresden Convention also introduces another notion regarding public access that has subsequently emerged as a key concept. Article 6 states that "The use of the telegraphs of the Union Governments shall be open to all, without any exceptions."

Several years later when the Conference de Paris adopted the 1865 Convention, hereafter call the Paris Convention, that established the International Telegraph Union, a three-fold distinction is made between *dépêches d'État, dépêches de service*, and *dépêches privées*. *Dépêches de service* are basically messages relating to running the network. The Paris Convention also uses the term "private" in the context of states dealing with *compagnie privée* owning and/or operating an interconnecting telegraph network.

The Paris Convention enshrined the notion of "open-to-the-public" in Article 4 which obliges that "The contracting High Parties recognize for all persons the right of correspondence by means of international telegraphs." The Convention also obliges states in their important cities to maintain "offices open to the public" during certain hours.

It is worth noting that when an international regime for radio communication first began to emerge in 1903, the whole issue of public versus private was effectively sidestepped. Private sector entrepreneurs had already effectively established private telecommunications networks and services. By taking a facilities-based approach which involved sovereign states licensing radio station operators, there was no need to deal with the question of "private networks" as long as the stations were licensed to operate in the respective countries. In practice, this potential leak of revenue-earning public correspondence traffic was partially plugged through a special supplementary group of international Radio Regulations.

This concept of a private company -- either owning facilities or operating a network -- has remained essentially unchanged since 1865. It is now embedded in the 1982 Nairobi Convention currently in force:

*Private Operating* Agency: Any individual or company or corporation, other than a governmental establishment or agency, which operates a telecommunication installation intended for an international telecommunication service or capable of causing harmful interference with such a service.

*Recognized Private Operating* Agency: Any private operating agency, as defined above, which operates a public correspondence or broadcasting service and upon which the obligations provided for in Article 44 of the Convention are imposed by the Member in whose territory the head office of the agency is situated, or by the Member which has authorized this operating agency to establish and operate a telecommunication service on its territory.[2]

Similarly, the concept public access became metamorphosed into phrases such as "making services...generally available to the public" as well as "the right of the public to correspond by means of the international service of public correspondence."[3]

The concept of what today is often regarded as a "private network" does not even arise in the international treaty instruments until the 1973 Telegraph Regulations, where it is noted under an article dealing with "services offered to users" that:

"Administrations or recognized private operating agency(ies) may, subject to the applicable national law, provide telex, photo telegraph, data transmission and/or other telegraph services and may place international circuits at the exclusive disposal of users in those relations where circuits remain available after the needs of the public telecommunication services have been satisfied."[4]

This 1973 provision was superseded at the 1988 WATTC by the famous Article dealing with "special arrangements" where it is recognized that:

"a) ...Subject to national laws, Members may allow administrations or recognized private operating agency(ies) or other organizations or persons enter into such special mutual arrangement with Members, administrations, or recognized private operating agency(ies) or other organizations or persons that are so allowed in another country for the establishment, operation, and use of special telecommunication networks, systems and services, in order to meet specialized international telecommunication needs within and/or between the territories of the Members concerned, and including, as necessary, those financial, technical, or operating conditions to be observed."

This provision explicitly allowed for the first time in international law the establishment of internetworks on a global scale. It is particularly notable for purposes of this study, that the undefined term "specialized networks" is the term employed, as opposed to "private networks." This fortuitously sidesteps the quagmire of attempting to deal with any kind of public-private dichotomy. Indeed, there is nothing to prevent a specialized network from providing any kind of service or capability to the public, if it is allowed under national law.

## 1.2. U.S. Domestic

It is beyond the scope of this study to present a historical overview on the use of the terms "public" and "private" in U.S. domestic telecommunications law. It's fair to say, however, that by the time of the adoption of the Communications Act of 1934, the U.S. model with respect to private networks was similar to the international models -- if for no other reason that the U.S. obligated itself to follow many of the international treaty provisions.

The differences largely arose from an early willingness at the outset of availability of the technology to allow:

- Extensive intra-corporate radio-based networks
- Extensive computer networks
- The emergence of distinctions between "basic public" and other kinds of telecommunications networks and services that remained outside the scope of regulation
- A shift toward dealing with public carrier networks as facilities or "tools" rather than an exclusive service-based approach
- The application of modular open architecture approaches to allow access to resources that were part of public common carrier networks

Another factor of major importance is the traditional distrust of "bigness" -- especially monopolies public or private. Antitrust concerns are a fundamental part of American culture. Indeed, it is amazing that the AT&T monopoly held as long as it did. The emergence of digital technologies, however, effectively spelled the end of the monopoly era in telecommunications. There is no "natural monopoly" in today's information-telecommunication world.

## 2. DOMINANT CARRIERS AND PUBLIC OBLIGATIONS

The primary problems of "public" communications policy today fall into two areas involving market distortions. Each area begs a distinct question:

- How do you continue to deal with organizations -- public or private -- that acquired their facilities and their market share based on public largesse in granting them monopoly privileges?
- How do you continue to deal with organizations that operate under legal obligations to provide certain kinds of telecommunication capabilities they might not otherwise provide?

Today, practically all our telecommunications "regulatory" activities worldwide focus on one or both of these questions.

These problems have a special relevance for this study, because they arise out of legal, social, and government policy concerns, not from technical ones. Whatever *indicia* are fashioned for "public" must be directly relevant to the two major policy problems above.

However, the information systems/digital technology is not going to make this an easy task. In any kind of exacting sense the task is impossible. There are no magic solutions, no opportunities to do things with smoke and mirrors. The variables are too numerous and complex, with all kinds of entrenched interests.

On the other hand, there may be opportunities to encourage shared models. There are some good examples already with various "open network" regulatory approaches at national, regional, and global levels. The trick will be to avoid details that are either technology dependent or have anti-competitive trap doors, or have the potential to be used in anti-competitive ways. The OS model and many of its siblings are a good example of all three.

A.D. Little's Hugh Small raised a very significant point at the Financial Times Conference by noting that the time is ripe for "building in" opportunities for competition in many of the facilities and network models being constructed. In the same sense, it is also possible to build in some solutions to the primary problems raised above by developing some good, widely shared models.

## 3. THE INFORMATION ARRAY MODEL

Today's networking world can be described as a combination of physical facilities and virtual everything. It's virtual reality riding on top of a web of glass. The classical old link and node definitions have no relevance. Dave Farber, who heads the University of Pennsylvania's Distributed Systems Lab, describes what he calls the emerging "National Backbone." The national (if not international) fiber grid is simply conceptualized as a big, distributed computer bus.

We're not there yet, but it's where we're heading. Bob Kahn's Gigabit Testbeds are already presenting lots of interesting options. Any model that this study develops must accommodate this emerging environment if the model is to be useful.

Along these lines, for purposes of developing a network taxonomy for parsing things public and private, the following definition of *network* might be useful:

> A network is an interoperating array of information objects whose prime function is to allow the sharing of information and information processes among multiple objects.

This model is also useful, if a bit abstract, because it's similar to the approaches actually being taken by information systems people trying to deal with their own boundary problems. Its beauty is the elementary simplicity. You can apply it to everything from three tin-cans with strings to knowbots(R) traversing the Internet.

An *information object* is simply a discrete, definable information function that can be used or acted upon. Basic service elements can be regarded as information objects. A computer file can be an information object. So if you create a network, you are simply establishing a known structured relationship among information objects -- an architecture -- through which the objects can interoperate.

It is further useful to elaborate some of the basic properties of such a network:

> Networks are scalable, nettable, and capable of multiple gateways in both physical and logical dimensions.

*Scalable* means basically that you can make the network bigger, following a similar architecture. *Nettable* means that you can embed one network within another network. *Multiple gateways* mean that you can have separate networks that have multiple means dedicated to avenues of interoperation between them.

This network model is useful because information objects can be characterized being "public" or "private" to varying degrees. This shifts the problem away from dealing with public or private networks -- which is a basically hopeless, if not meaningless, task -- and focuses instead on individual information objects. In a sense, the FCC did the same thing in the Computer III Inquiry with the concept of Basic Service Elements (BSEs). BSEs are defined public information objects that are made available through networks. This model doesn't worry about characterizing the networks themselves.

Of course, if a network exists somewhere and is not connected to anything else, and all the information objects are purely private, then the network could comfortably be characterized as private. Relatively few networks in this world are so simple and bounded.

## 4. PUBLIC INDICIA

Ultimately, however it is necessary to begin dealing with the properties that make an information object "public." Private can simply be regarded as whatever is left, i.e., non-public.

Five prominent properties seem relevant for the purposes of the study:

*Who provides it?* In other words, who makes the information available? If it is a public body that makes it available, or a non-public body operating under an obligation established by a public body, then the object can be said to be at least partially public. Under old legal regimes this property was very important.

*Who can access it?* In other words, who can effect communication with the object. If this can be done anonymously, i.e., by anyone, then the object can be said to be at least partially public. For example, anonymous File Transfer Protocol (FTP) servers on the Internet are usually regarded as having these public qualities.

In our increasingly complex information infrastructure environment, this property of access may be the most significant one. Another way of portraying accessibility is connectivity; and connectivity is a big issue today. It was one of the more interesting new requirements embedded in the new International Telecommunication Regulations adopted by WATTC '88. Connectivity might become the new "public" good. In a sense, government already overtly funds connectivity. The big policy question however is how much connectivity is enough?

*Who owns it?* In other words, who has title. This can involve ownership of real physical property, or of intellectual property. If a public body owns the object, or if it is in the public domain, the object is at least partially public. The characterization becomes more difficult when you attempt to deal with the issue of acquisition of facilities (and customers) arising from former public largesse? One could even argue that where the property is subject to government regulation, that at least some of the rights of use have been effectively ceded to the government.

*Who controls it?* This is one step beyond access. It involves giving the object instruction if it is involved in an information process; or moving, or altering it if it is pure information. Once the object is accessed, what can be done with it?

This property is made more complex because there can be widely varying degrees of control. There may also be a time factor. Control for how long? In complex network management processes, there may also be different priority levels invoked under failure conditions. In the case of a simple information file, read/write permissions are a good example of different kinds of control. In electronic news networks today, editors of monitors frequently exercise control functions over distribution capabilities. Stodolsky's INET '91 presentation, for example, examines the public policy options and considerations underlying this aspect of control.

Generally, if the control of an information object is anonymously equal, it can be regarded as public. Real world environments, however, are fairly complex. The providers or owners of objects usually exercise some control, and objects necessarily exist under the control of operating or network management systems.

*Who pays for it?* Information objects and their array in networks have associated economic costs. If those costs are borne by or otherwise underwritten by public bodies, the object may be described at least partially as public.

The National Science Foundation, for example, pays for all the information objects associated with a major Internet backbone. The Department of Defense pays for MilNet. The General Services Administration pays for FTS-2000. The Swiss federal government and cantons similarly pay for SWITCH. This property is obviously rather tempered by other properties in determining the overall characterization of the object or network as public or not.

## 5. CONCLUSIONS

The use of the term "public" with respect to telecommunication or to information communication networks is highly complex. To even attempt to make a characterization in all but the most simple situations, it is useful to proceed through a two-step analytical process.

First the network architecture must be examined and be parsed into an array of information objects. Each one of those objects must then be examined in light of face properties: who provides it, who can access it, who owns it, who controls it, and who pays for it. On the basis of the combined aggregate of all the results, it is possible to say that the object has a certain "public index figure." For example, on a scale of one to one hundred, a central office telephone switching object might rate a 70.

It seems, however, that the continued use of the term "public" only has meaning today with respect to residual historical developments (regulation of dominant carriers, international legal obligations, etc), potential disputes over unfair trade practices, or the striving for a meaningful, current public good like the promotion of connectivity.

In these contexts, it seems necessary to focus more on information objects than networks because of the essential impossibility today to characterize most networks as public in any kind of consistent or definitive way. In addition, there may be individual information objects that represent such an important public asset, that they should be protected with a high "public index factor."

# ENDNOTES

[1] *see* State Treaty Between Austria, Prussia, Bavaria, and Saxony of 25 July 1850 (official ITU translation), generally referred to as the Dresden Convention.

[2] *See* nos. 2008 and 2009, International Telecommunication Convention, Nairobi, 1982.

[3] *See ibid* nos. 15 and 131.

[4] *See* no. 8, Telegraph Regulations, 1973, International Treaty.

PRIVATE NETWORKS PUBLIC OBJECTIVES
E. Noam and A. NíShúilleabháin (Editors)

9

# The Morphology and Taxonomy of Networks

Terrence P. McGarty

## 1. INTRODUCTION

Networks provide for the interconnection of a wide base of users and empower the users in the interexchange of information. The users, in most cases involved with the creation of economic value, employ the network resource as a means to, among other rational processes, increase revenue, decrease expenses, or increase market share. The equation on the part of the consumer of the network resource is a simple economic equation: is there more revenue or less expenses -- namely, is profit increased? Therefore, the choice of a network, be it public or private, is an economic choice. This paper attempts to show that the underlying economics of that choice are going through dramatic change. The change is precipitated by a fundamental change in the underlying structure of networks, driven not just by architectural and regulatory changes, but by more fundamental changes driven by technologies. These changes are, in many ways, beyond the control of the current players in the field, be they carriers or regulators. These changes are reforming and distorting all of the tools that we as policy makers have used in determining the social and political consequences of the policies we develop. It is the intent of this paper to outline some of these concepts of change.

The paper will focus on private networks. Prof. Eli M. Noam defines these as:

> "a network whose access is under the control of the closed user group or the user directly, albeit some of these control functions may be delegated to a carrier. The user controls access, exit, and internal pricing. "[1]

This paper addresses five specific questions as they relate to private networks:

> (i) What are the evolutionary paths that these networks are taking, and what affect might these paths have on the strategies of carriers, equipment makers, and large users?
> (ii) How does a commercial entity gain a competitive advantage in a private network, and what is the value creation equation that provides the compelling reason for gaining an advantage? What are the specific sources of value creation? Is it possible that non-standardized networks can result in dis-economies?
> (iii) Can private networks migrate to the consumer or residential user?
> (iv) What is the impact of private networks on the value of information?
> (v) How can one measure, unequivocally, the economic value that specialized and customized networks provide to an economic entity in terms of value creation and innovation?

Our approach to answering these questions is fivefold:

(i) Networks are characterized in terms of their basic elements, called their morphology or appearance. We then take these shape characteristics and cluster them in a taxonomy, or classification, of networks.

(ii) The fundamental underlying differences in these networks and demonstrate that there is an essential genetic difference between the basic two types -- hierarchical and distributed. Fundamentally, hierarchical networks possess significant scale economies, whereas distributed networks have minimal scale economies. This fact, the basic difference in the DNA of networks, is critical in determining the answers to all of the questions posed.

(iii) Using the paradigm of Darwinian Selection to show that fundamental forces will move to the selection of one of the two network types over the other, and that this selection is critical for policy makers to understand.

(iv) A specific example of how this change is effecting policy is discussed -- the NPRM on PCS/PCN, 1.8-2.0 GHz band for Personal Communications Systems. We argue, based upon current filings, that the change is upon us and will have a significant impact on network designers, users, and policy makers.

(v) Combining these facts with the concept of value in a economic entity we discuss how private networks play a key role in the development of value.

This paper presents the fourth step in an evolving understanding of networks, information, and economic value creation.[2] It presents for the first time the basic realization that networks are conceptualizable within the context of an organic entity, and thus the approach to deconstructing the dynamics of such evolution is achievable and strikes at the heart of policy making.

## 2. NETWORKS: MORPHOLOGY AND TAXONOMY

Networks, as currently viewed by users, designers, and policy makers are NOT evolved from a common ancestor. Rather, there are at least two different network concepts in use today that are genetically different and isolated. That genetic isolation gives rise to dramatically different evolutionary paths, and dictates that the hierarchical system that we are most familiar with is doomed to extinction. The genetic material of distributed networks, new to the scene due to dramatic changes in technology, are anticipated to survive. The distributed genetic material of networks behave dramatically differently, and policy makers in particular must recognize this. For example, scale economies disappear in such a structure, and thus all of the policy analyses based upon these issues are no longer applicable.

This section begins with a taxonomical and morphological analysis of networks in general. The approach is first phonetic, relating to externalities, and later discusses the differences that are at the heart of network differences.

### 2.1. Elements
There are four architectural elements in the telecommunications network. These elements are the control functions, the transport function, the interconnect function, and the interface function. It should be noted that these functions have evolved over the years in content and

content and complexity. We view these elements in the context of a communications network that must support the current most advanced concepts in communications. Details of each are described below:

*Control:* Control elements in an architecture provide for such functions as management, error detection, restoral, billing, inventory management, and diagnostics. Currently, the voice network provides these functions on a centralized basis, although in the last five years there have evolved network management, control schema, and products that allow for the custom control and management of their own networks. Companies such as IBM, AT&T, and NYNEX have developed network management systems that move the control from the network to the customer.[3] On the sub-network side, companies such as NET, Timeplex, Novell, 3-COM, and others have done similar implementations for local area networks, data multiplexers, and other elements. Centralized network control is no longer necessary and, in fact, may not be the most efficient way to control a network.

What is important, however, is that network control providing the above functions be an essential element of either a public or private network. Thus, as we consider network evolution, this element or set of functions must be included.

Control has now been made to be flexible and movable. The control function is probably the most critical in the changes that have been viewed in the context of an architecture. In existing networks, the control is centralized, but in newer networks, the control is distributed and empowered to the end users. The users can now reconfigure, add, move, and increase the capacity of their network.

Let us briefly describe how the control function can now be distributed. Consider a large corporate network consisting of computers, LANs, PBXs, and smart multiplexers, as well as a backbone fiber transport function. Each of these elements has its own control facility for management and restoral. Each has the capability to reroute traffic from one location to another, while the routing systems are programmed into the system as a whole. On top of these sub-element control functions is built another layer of control that views the network as a holistic entity. This form of control has been termed a manager of managers. It monitors all of the sub-net elements and takes control if necessary. It is embodied in several independent controllers, each having the capability of taking control from a remote network. This form of organic network control has evolved in recent years and is now common in many corporate networks.

In addition, this concept of the organic network was described in detail by Huber in the Department of Justice report to the U.S. Justice Department during the first Triennial Review of the MFJ.[4]

*Transport:* The transport element is provided by the underlying transport fabric, whether that be a twisted pair of copper wires, fiber optic cable, a radio, or other means. Transport should not be confused with other elements of the network. Transport is merely the provision of physical means to move information, in some form, from one point to another. It is generally expressed as bits per second(bps), or in terms of bandwidth. Bandwidth as a transport construct is the most enabling. Transport does not encompass the need to change the information or to make any other enhancement to the information.

It has been recognized that the horizontal scale economies of all of the network elements, including, but not limited to transport, were actually diseconomies of scale in the market. In the current network environment, the issue of transport and its enabling capacity has arisen again. This was caused by the introduction of fiber. Fiber may be divided for the user in terms of bits per second, or bandwidth.

The fiber optic repeaters are not there solely as a result of fiber constraints on transport. They are also there because they enforce the voice regime of the voice-based world view. The repeaters do not repeat data rates, they repeat framing sequences based on 64 Kbps voice frames. Thus any work station must use 64 Kbps as the underlying data fabric.

In contrast, dark fiber is the provisioning of an optical fiber to be used as the end user sees fit. It is the world view analog of the LAN. The LAN provides co-axial bandwidth of several hundred MHZ whereas the fiber provides the bandwidth of GHz to TeraHz.

*Interconnect:* The interconnect element of the architecture describes how the different users are connected to one another or to any of the resources connected to the network and is synonymous with switching. Interconnection assumes that there is an addressing scheme, a management scheme for the addresses, and a scheme to allow one user to address, locate and connect to any other user.

Interconnection has in the past been provided by the Central Office switches. As it shall be discussed, this implementation of an architectural element was based on certain limitations of the transport element. With the change in the transport element of structures allowing greater bandwidth, the switching needs have changed. Specifically, distributed systems and scale economies of the distributed architectures allow for interconnectivity controlled by the CPE and not the Central Office. As will be shown later, with the advent of Local Area Networks and CATV voice communications are the ones using distributed interconnectivity elements.

This argument for interconnection, combined with transport and control (namely horizontal integration) was valid in 1970. It is not, however, valid today. They are separable functions, and scale economies are in the hands of the CPE manufacturers not the network providers. In effect, there exists no monopoly in interconnect as a result of these technology changes. This is a dramatic change from 1971 and Kahn's analysis.

There are three general views of interconnection that are valid today: the Telephone Company, the Computer Scientist, and the User:

The Telephone Company view is based on the assumption of voice-based transport with universal service and the assumption of the inseparability of interconnect and control.

The Computer Scientist view is based upon the assumption that the network, as transport, is totally unreliable, and that computer hardware and software must be used in extremis to handle each data packet. Furthermore, the Computer Scientist's view of the network is one where timeliness is secondary to control. The Computer Scientist's view has been epitomized in the quote, "Every Packet is an Adventure." This is said with glee as each data packet is sent out across the network, and through the best hacking the Computer Scientist saves the packet from the perils of Scylla and Charybdis.

The third view is that of the User, who is interested in developing an interconnect capability that meets his or her needs and minimizes cost. This is minimization of both obsolescence and cost strategy. Processing costs and capacity costs are declining every year. An investment must try to follow the curve. In a hierarchical view of interconnect, such as a large centrally switched network, the changes occur once every few years. The lost cost and performance efficiency can become significant. In contrast, in an end user controlled environment, with a fully distributed architecture, the lost efficiency is minimized as technology advances.

*Interface:* The interfaces are the end users connection to the transport element. The interface element provides for the conversion from the end user information stream to the information streams that are used in the transport form of the network. For example, the telephone interface for voice is the analog conversion device.

We have divided the network elements into these four categories to demonstrate that there are clearly four distinct and separable areas for growth and policy formation. Issues of regulation, due to potential monopolist control, are always a concern, but it will be demonstrated that in all four areas there are economies in market disaggregation.

## 2.2. Network Morphological Elements

In order to develop a network taxonomy, and in order to provide a Key for the taxonomy in determining which network fits where, it is first necessary to identify the network's morphological elements. Consider the work of Linneaus in characterizing plants. After many centuries of naturalists' identifying differing plants it became quite clear that there were several key characteristics that were used for the identification and differentiation of plants. These characteristics were related to the morphology and appearance of each species. Thus for plants, we look at the leaves, the flowers, the fruits, the shoots, the roots, and the seeds. These represent the elements necessary for the morphological structure.

In describing any network we have the following four major elements: control, interconnect, interface, and transport. They are like the elements in plants of flower, fruit, seed, shoot, and root. Each may have added subtleties in their structure but they represent the first high level differentiators of the network morphology. We now define these elements in detail. We then proceed to further differentiate these elements to a depth adequate for the development of a taxonomy for segmentation.

*Control:* Control functions in a network describe all of those functions necessary for the operations, administration, and maintenance of a network. It includes such functions as network management, network restoral, billing, inventory management, and network reconfiguration.

*Interconnect:* The interconnect functions describe all of those functions that are necessary for the identification, selection, processing, and support of all user-to-user connections on a network. Interconnection assumes an addressing scheme, a management scheme for the addresses, and a means for one user to address and connect to any other user including the determination of where that user is and how to locate them.

*Interface:* The interfaces are the connection between the end user and the transport element. The interface includes all of the functionality necessary for the user.

*Transport:* This element characterizes the physical and electronic means of transporting the information from one location to another. Transport focuses on the point to point means of the network.

We add a fifth element, namely the user as a means to help differentiate the ultimate use of the network as a means to allow for partitioning along the lines of use. Thus:

*User:* This is the end user of the network. The user may or may not be a human, and as a user has needs to be met in terms of the network structure. For example, the user may be a software process which may be configured in a client server mode, and as such the set of users may be the clients and a single server.

We will now begin to describe each of these areas out in further detail. Our approach is to develop a morphological structure that provides detail on general structural elements leaving the specific choice of the element to the lowest level. A morphology has no repetition of low level element choices. Each is independent. In addition, each choice is descriptive and is not exclusive.

The morphological approach is as follows. Each element, E.k, has a set of sub elements, E.k.j. In turn, each of these may be subdivided into other elements, E.k.j.n, until the final step is a descriptor of a sub element. A descriptor, D.k.j.n is a positive, inclusive statement of that sub element. For example a flower may have sepals, petals, stamen, and pistil. The sepals have venation. The venation may be parallel, pinnate, or palmate. The characteristics or descriptors are parallel, pinnate, or palmate. They are positive statements. It is unacceptable in a morphology to have parallel and nonparallel. The latter must be descriptive and inclusive in a class.

In a morphology, a complete classification is the set of all descriptors, {D.k.j.n:k=1,..K, j=1..J,n=1..N}. We must be certain that the set partitions the space of all known networks into classes that are separate. Hence, only the same network may have the same descriptor set.

## 2.2.1. Users

We begin the development with the user division since in many cases it is the end user who ultimately defines the network. For example, the current focus is on the users being processes, processors, or data files. Rarely in the current environment do we see the human being as a specific user. In the current stage of development of networks, there is a stronger trend toward the user being the main user of the network.

The elements that further define the set of users are as follows:

*Type:* The type of user characterizes the nature of the end user or end user set. The end user may be a human, a data file, a process, or a processor.
*Time:* The time element describes the nature of the connection as perceived by the end user. Depending on the user, the time element may have multiple options. The descriptors for this type are as follows:
    *Simultaneous:* All users are communicating at the same time.
    *Displaced:* Some users are not in the same time frame and, moreover, there are a disparate set of these time frames.
    *Shifted:* Time frames are equally shifted.
*Transaction:* This element describes the nature of the interaction between the users. Specifically it may be:
    *Shared:* All users may randomly access the services.
    *Sequenced:* A protocol of control from one user to another exists.
    *Directed:* Control is forced from a single point.
*Set:* The set of users may be homogeneous or inhomogeneous. If the set is homogeneous then the descriptor of type is definitive. If the set is inhomogeneous, then the descriptor of type must be expanded.

Thus the user element can be fully characterized by the descriptor set:

$$\{D.1.1.n_1, \ D.1.2.n_2, \ D.1.3.n_3, \ D.1.4.n_4\} \tag{1}$$

where D.i.j characterizes the specific descriptor sequence and the $n_k$ characterizes the specific dichotomous ending.

### 2.2.2. Interconnect

Interconnect in the broadest sense describes the totality of how the users are brought together in a shared community for the purpose of communicating. As stated before, communications is the ability to change the state of one user or another in the linkages of the total process. Interconnection is the establishment and maintenance of the infrastructures that are required for the maintenance of these paths of communication.

In a similar fashion, we can describe the interconnect sub-elements as follows;

*Location:* The location of the interconnect agents or elements are the first item in the morphology deconstruction in this area. The location reflects the nature of the network as well as the world view of the designers. The following are the specific descriptors.

*Fully Distributed:* Each user of the network has access to and control over its own interconnect facility, which in turn may act autonomously in the network.

*Intra-Netted:* Interconnecting is done on a clustered basis with a collection of users in a closed and geographically compact community, each having access to a server that facilitates all of the network connections in an autonomous fashion.

*Regional:* Interconnecting is performed on the basis of a closed user group that is loosely connected geographically. A system provides a local switching node that is itself autonomous.

*Centralized:* In this configuration, the interconnecting is performed by a single element, that controls and directs all switching.

*Hierarchical:* A hierarchical network is one in which the interconnection or switching is hierarchically distributed, in that each element may switch to a certain degree, possibly locally, but the broader the reach of the switching, the higher in the network switch levels the switching or interconnection must go. The current public switched network is an example.

*Addressing:* This is a key factor in the overall operations of the interconnect function. Specifically, addressing permits the naming of any node and the location of that node or user for access of the interconnect function. Addressing has two characteristics. The first is the geographical nature of addressing that states where, physically, in the network the addressing may be used and effected. The second in the temporal factor of addressing that relates to the issue of whether the addresses themselves are static or dynamic. Specifically, with dynamic addressing we change the address from time to time. Adaptive addressing changes addresses based upon other factors.

(i) Physical Addressing:

*Local:* This type of addressing allows for addresses to be local to a select user group. There is no way to address a foreign user entity.

*Universal:* This allows for global addressing of any user on the network.

*Serialized:* This approach allows for addressing of groups, then sub groups and then ultimately down to selected end user communities.

(ii) Temporal Addressing:

*Static:* In this addressing system all addresses are kept constant with time.

*Dynamic:* In this scheme, addresses are changeable with time occurring to some prearranged system or protocol.

*Adaptive:* Adaptive addressing goes beyond dynamic addressing in that it responds not only to time and place, but also to other exogenous factors in the end user or network operating factors. An adaptive addressing scheme may change addresses depending on other factors.

*Selection:* This element of interconnect focuses on the issue of how the interconnect process is managed. Specifically, there are two currently observed descriptors: random and assigned.

*Random:* This system is based upon an algorithm or protocol, but the result depends on factors that are random.

*Assigned:* This is a preassigned system, where knowing the state of the network at any one time determines the connection path.

*Performance:* The performance determinant addresses the issue of the quality of service delivered. The quality may be judged along several axes. The following are the current set of determinants.

*Time:* This factor relates to the time of setup or other such factors.

*Signal:* This relates to the quality level of the voice signal, or the data or image signals.

*Delay:* This is the characterization of the delay in the network.

*Blocking:* This is the characterization of the blocking in the interconnect.

*Links:* The link element or descriptor of the interconnect function relates to the types of interconnect that are employed. Specifically, is the interconnect a physical interconnection, a virtual interconnection, or a relational one? The reader is referred to Tannenbaum for the full detail on these approaches. At a higher level each is described below:

*Physical:* This is a defined and measurable physical path between all interconnections and users.

*Virtual:* This is a path that is created on the basis of signaling vectors between all of the users. Although not a physical path, it is an algorithmically defined path that is reconstructible at any instant from the state of the network.

*Relational:* This is a fully random path built upon relations between users in the network. It depends upon states of the users and the network, unlike the virtual path that depends solely upon the state of the network.

*Setup:* This is the final descriptor of the interconnect element. It represents the nature of the interconnect signaling, as separate from or a part of the communication channel from user to user. The two forms are as follows:

*In Band:* ALL signaling in the same path as the user to user communications in all layers of the communication channel, physical or logical.

*Out of Band:* Signaling takes different physical and/or logical paths.

### 2.2.3. Interface

Interface describes the nature of the interaction between the user and the interfaces and transport. Interface describes the elements that allow for the users to take maximum advantage of the others users' interface needs.

There are five descriptors of the interface level:

*Modality:* This descriptor describes the nature of the information flowing to or from the user. There are the following types: Video, Voice, Text, Data, and Image. In addition to the above simple descriptors, there are a set of compound descriptors that reflect a multimedia environment. We develop those through a concatenation of the above descriptors.

*Multiplicity:* This descriptor indicates the nature of the number of end users connected to a single interface. Simply stated there may be one or many.

*Integratability:* This descriptor indicates the temporal, spatial, or logical nature of the interface. In the simple temporal case, we can envision the interface operating in asynchronous mode with timing shared by all of the users. In a spatial synchronous mode, we can envision all of the users sharing a common virtual spatial reference, even though all of the users may have different screens with different aspect ratios and other such factors. Logical synchronicity describes the ability to assure the cohesiveness of the information presented in the display interface. In a similar fashion, asynchronous integrability reflects the fact that there is no overall timing of the events and that they follow a system of one to one arrangements. The third level is sub-synchronous wherein some may be synchronized while others are not.

*Conversationality:* This describes the nature of the interface and its users as it relates to the sessions that may be created on the network. The interface may range from the shared, or party-line, method, to the conversational systems common in multimedia communications, to a private line, and finally into a fully secure link.

*Links:* This descriptor indicates the number of links that are supported per interface.

### 2.2.4. Control

Control is the broadest element in the morphology of networks. The issue of control may span from who owns and operates the network to how, specifically, the network is managed as a living and operating entity.

*Management:* Who, specifically, owns and operates the network. It is essentially the legal control part of the network.

*Users-Direct:* Each user has direct control over the network.

*Users-Indirect:* Each user has an influence on the network, but the control is indirectly applied.

*Shared:* Users share in a pooling fashion the control over the network.

*Public:* There is a publicly accepted control point for the network. Such is the case for the public switched network.

*Private:* This is a network provided on a private basis. Control is in the hands of a private entity.

*Maintenance:* The philosophy behind the real time control of the network. It describes how the network is managed and maintained as an operating entity. Several possible, and currently recognized descriptors are possible:

*Centralized:* Controlled by a single entity.

*Sectored:* Broken into segments that are controlled by separate entities divided by geography, or function, or some other such factor.

*Distributed:* A fully distributed and autonomous function.

*Scope:* The scope element describes the breadth of elements that are performed by the network as it is functioning in its operational management role. The functions may include some of the following descriptors.

*Inventory*
*Maintenance*

These are the major descriptors of the control function. All too often designers have not focused on the control descriptors as an element in the network morphology. In this paper, we have presented several key control descriptors, and are quick to point out that there may be more discovered as control becomes a more significant factor in the design of a network.

### 2.2.5. Transport
Transport is the set of elements that relate to the underlying means of movement of the communications signals from one point to another. In its simplest sense, it represents the media of movement and the specific signals that are used to make that movement possible. In the context of the IS model (Tannenbaum) these represent the lowest three levels, Levels, one to three.

*Medium:* The medium characterizes the lowest level of transport, referring to the specific transport vehicle. In the following list we refer to fiber, radio, and other specific means of transport.

*Method:* The method or means of transporting the signal. There are two general descriptors that, in turn, have more specificity. They are analog and digital, in all their known variations.

*Mode:* The characteristics of the level three elements of keeping links in the network in operation. The two major ways of doing it to date are synchronous and asynchronous.

### 2.3. Network Taxonomy
Having developed the morphological concepts in networks, in this section we plan to develop the concept of taxonomies' use of these morphological elements. As with any taxonomical development, the choice is somewhat arbitrary, especially as we begin at the highest level. The work of Sokal and Sneath in taxonomical classification may be referred to, and it is their work that has influenced our current approach. If we recall plant taxonomies, the division is first along the lines of seed bearing and non-seed bearing plants. Then the division in the seed bearing branch are those with fruit (flowering plants) and those without (conifers). The same issues are present with networks. What factor do we start with that is as important as seeds and then flowers or fruits? The issue of taxonomy based on highest level of morphological division is critical.

In the development of a taxonomy, we begin with the available morphologies and generally attempt to generate taxa based upon the highest level of differentiators. As we have discussed before, we have presented architectural variants and infrastructure variants. These were developed at the highest level without any benefit of the morphology that we have also developed.

The concept of genera and species in plant taxonomy is a statement that says that there are sets of common elements that are in collections of different networks and that this collection is common to sub-classes of such networks.

Networks have evolved over time and some types no longer exist. Most step-by-step voice networks are no longer in existence. They have been superseded by cross-bar and then electronic switching systems. The question may be asked -- what is the evolutionary past of the local area network? The reason for this question is to not only understand the past, but also to recognize that the past is the prologue to the future, and to project possible network evolutionary trends.

As in plant taxonomy, there is a set of hierarchical relationships among networks. The collection of networks at lower levels, such as genera and species, can be concatenated upwards into the taxa.

## 3. NETWORK GENETIC STRUCTURE

The previous section discussed the phenotypic characteristics of networks. We focused on external observables and allowed classification of networks based upon these characteristics. A similar approach is taken in the plant and animal world. Phenotypic characters are used, for the most part, to classify species, genus, families, etc. In contrast, there is in the plant and animal world an underlying genotype. This genotype is driven by the genetic material of the species. The gene is what expresses the phenotype characters. The basis of the gene is the carbon in the DNA. We argue that a similar approach can be applied to networks -- that we can deconstruct the genotypes of certain broad classes based on silicon rather than carbon. This argument is in its earliest stages of development, but its usefulness in evaluating the evolution of networks appears to be significant.

In the analysis that we have developed, the genetic makeup is driven by the difference in technology as well as by the difference in world view.[5] The genetic makeup of the network therefore is composed of the following:

> (i) *World View*: The world view is based upon the paradigm or example from which all development proceeds. RBOCs still are working from the hierarchical voice-based approach of Vail and Bell. Distributed systems evolve from the LAN technology of the late sixties and early seventies, driven by the desire to put as much investment into software as possible.
>
> (ii) *Technology*: The hierarchical networks are still replacing relays and operators. The view towards software in these networks is based upon minimal intelligence at the home terminal, and maximum control at the central switch. Distributed systems anticipate uncertainty, assume intelligent end-user devices, and move toward emphasis on software. They assume that silicon costs will continue to decrease.
>
> (iii) *Organization*: The distributed inclination is toward empowering the end-user. The control is distributed and interconnected also. The hierarchical network is typified by an RBOC with strong central control, excessive overhead, and large fixed costs.[6]

Clearly there is a difference between the structure of a hierarchical network and a distributed. We shall detail this in the next section.

## 4. THE SELECTION PROCESS

The selection process employs Darwin's idea of natural selection -- survival of the fittest -- to networks. Policy must follow this concept and not fight it. At best, by fighting the Darwinian path, policy will delay, but not change, evolution. The genetically more fit network will be the survivor. Fitness relates to the overall value chain impact of all users of a network. The fitness quotient of an environment of a network is predicated upon the users of the network, and on the competitive advantage that the use of such a network provides.

From an evolutionary perspective, each species has a set of phenotypic characteristics that allow it to handle the challenges of its environment.[7] These phenotypes are a reflection of its basic genetic materials. Species are generally closely related in an evolutionary sense, and as we ascend to genus, families, divisions, and classes, we see a decrease in relationship. We also see that members of those classes, for example, demonstrate differing abilities to handle changes in their environment.

Consider two simple examples: oaks and grasses. Oaks are in the class of plants called dicots. They are woody and take twenty years to go to seed. If their environment changes quickly in that period they will not go to seed and will perish. Thus oaks, mighty oaks, have an Achilles heel in their requirement of long-term stability. Grasses are monocots, a more recent evolutionary class. They grow from year to year, go to seed many times in a year, are propagated by the wind, and are very insensitive to water, sun, cold, and other factors. One need think no further than the friendly crab grass. They spread by runners in a highly distributed fashion in their local domain. They are highly flexible and have shown rapid rates of genetic mutations. The survival of a species and its evolution depend upon two factors -- its basic genetic makeup, and the change that the environment has with respect to how the species can cope. Thus for networks we can address these two issues and reflect a conclusion. Let us consider the two different classes of networks; hierarchical and distributed.

(i) *Genetic Makeup*
   *Hierarchical:* As described above, it is a rigid, centralized, and control-oriented system.
   *Distributed:* This is software directed, user-empowered and allows for full flexibility.
(ii) *Environmental Stresses*
   *Hierarchical:* This system cannot readily reorient itself for change.
   *Distributed:* This is a highly flexible organism readily adaptable to change.

When we compare these two factors for the two network classes, we argue that the survivor will be the one that matches the changes in the environment with its underlying genetic makeup. It seems clear from this preliminary study that a fully distributed architecture will have a better chance of surviving because of its underlying flexibility to adapt to its enviroment and because of its flexibility to mutate to meet the needs of the user.

## 5. CURRENT NETWORK EXAMPLE

A current example of networks that exemplify the characteristics discussed in this paper are those presently being developed in the PCN/PCS arena. This new network architecture offers several interesting and timely examples of where policy must recognize the essential changes in networks. We argue that the FCC has failed to do so in its current filings, and that it is basing its current policy positions on assumptions consistent with hierarchical networks but totally inconsistent with distributed networks. In this section we work through this example and provide a list of the key policy issue that must be reconsidered in light of this evolutionary change.

The FCC has released a Notice of Public Rule Making (NPRM) in the area of Personal Communications Services (PCS). This new and innovative form of networking will be the first national network that will be based upon a distributed architecture, at least as proposed by some of the contenders. This architecture consists of the following elements:

*Radio Frequency Transport:* In this case the 1.8-2.0 GHz bands will be allocated for transmission. As we have stated, this open bandwidth approach, like dark fiber and coaxial LANs, opens up many dimensions for new networking operations.

*CDMA Switching and Interconnect:* One of the proposed technologies for switching is Code Division Multiple Access (CDMA) which would allow many users to access the same frequency band by giving each user an access code that is mathematically and electronically orthogonal to all other users. By using extensive, and distributed processing power, both in cell sites, and more importantly, in the end-user's terminal, a fully distributed switching fabric is established.

*Distributed Network Control:* The control of these networks is based not only on the control at some central facility but, more importantly, is based upon control at the user's terminal.

*Interface with Complexity but Low Cost:* The end-user's terminals enough processing capability so that they can be reprogrammed, in some cases by downloading new software to them. The net result is that the network can change in a real-time and organic fashion.

This new network configuration has several innovative features. There is a current mind-set among many of the cellular carriers that it is important to keep the minutes of use up, and that the revenue for minutes of use must also be held constant. In contrast, most consumer-oriented companies recognize that success is determined by gaining market share and that share, once lost, is extremely costly to regain. In the current cellular market, most players are in a game of limited price competition, and the stabilization of share along standard duopolist lines of controlling market growth while retaining profitability through price management. Penetration of the total market has been gradual and the relative share has be held at 50% each. With the increase in additional carriers in the 1.8GHz band, this will change significantly. The new objective will be to maximize market share through the rapid increase of market penetration. Penetration increases mean that market share is obtained through the acquisition of new, untapped, customers, and not through the buying away of an old customer base. The means to achieve this new and rapid market penetration increase is a three pronged strategy: price, quality, and accessibility.

The price of the set and the service must be dropped to a critical point to make it readily accessible. This is clearly the success point of the VCR strategy when penetration blossomed at a $300 price point. The same price points are there for the wireless market. The quality of the set and the service must meet a minimal level of expectation. Systems such as those in Hong Kong were the first to recognize and implement this approach. Systems such as those in New York have failed. The difference is in the penetration in these two markets: 8% for Hong Kong and 2% for New York. Accessibility means that the customer can get both the set and service with minimal effort. Thus, even a short trip to a store, or the need for installation, or the process of additional credit approval is counter-productive.

In short, the success of the new players in attaining and retaining the growing market share is to create a system with a low barrier to entry and a high barrier to exit. In essence, low entry barriers imply low costs and ease of access; high exit barriers mean high service quality and low fixed and predictable costs. The overall strategy is one where there should be no ambiguity of expectations on either side.

The main driver in gaining increased penetration is the ability to reduce the costs to the consumer to a critical level. That level and the way in which it is priced is critical to customer acceptance. At best, the service may present a package of benefits to the consumer.

However, these benefits are not needs. There is a distinct difference. Benefits may be cost justified, even understood to be important, but are displayable. Needs have taken a life unto themselves. The need can become less cost-sensitive after it has been established.

Thus the pricing for new wireless services, must follow the low barrier to entry approach. As such, if the service is provided on a fixed-price basis, independent of the level of local usage, then there is not the fear of the "meter ticking." Thus the recommendation is the provision of service at $30 or less per month for unlimited local usage. In fact, recent tests have shown that users will actually give up their local telephone service at this price level and use wireless alone.

Price is only part of the equation. The service must be profitable. Thus the fully loaded costs must be reduced dramatically. It has been shown that wireless systems are predominantly variable in cost and that they have limited fixed cost structures. Thus the strategy to reduce costs is simple: increase productivity. There are no significant scale economies. One cannot reduce costs by increasing volume.[8] Thus the imbedded carriers at 800 MHZ have the same advantage or disadvantage as any other player in the market. There are no economies of scale and thus there can be no ability to dominate the market by having initial presence. Market power is attained through pricing, and pricing through performance.

If one believes that dramatic penetration is achievable at $30 per month per customer for unlimited local usage, then a profitable operation can be developed wherein the fully loaded expenses are $300 per year per customer or less. Moreover there are four strategies that help achieve this goal. They fall clearly into the four areas of acquisition, retention, operations, and depreciation.

Our four point strategy for success in this business is as follows:

(1) Separate the set from the service and market, and sell the service through cost-effective channels used by other service entities, such as direct mail, telemarketing, etc.

(2) Reduce turnover through the development of brand loyalty, quality service, and effective customer support. Balance customer expectations with those of the delivered service. Manage, monitor, and match the customer perceptions with systems performance.

(3) Automate all operations as much as possible, from the initial design to the daily upkeep. Use controllable variable expenses that may be outsourced to minimize unit costs.

(4) Utilize the most frequency and power efficient technology to maximize the cost per unit spectrum per customer. This currently calls for the adoption of CDMA technology rather than other digital or analog systems. Use controllable variable costs where appropriate. Co-location in central offices will eliminate the need for MTSOs, or cellular switches.

The details of how this four point strategy may be implemented, and detail the implementation impacts, have been developed elsewhere.[9]

The current wireless technology, as embodied in the cellular communications systems, is composed of several key technological elements. Specifically they are the Cell Sites, the MTSO (Mobile Telephone Switching Office), and whatever connections or management systems are in place. The connections between the cell sites and the MTSOs are digital circuits carrying the voice signals. It should be emphasized that the MSTO is necessary for the purpose of establishing the connection between a time-varying wireless circuit and a fixed twisted pair circuit. In addition, it should be noted that a MTSO is an historical artifact, representing a pre-divestiture barrier between the wireless circuit and the switched network. With Signaling System 7, such a barrier is no longer needed. It will be argued that with co-location, the switched network can be turned into a fixed "Backplane" for the wireless interconnection fabric.

The MTSOs are interconnected via the Public Switched Telephone Network (PSTN) of the local carrier. The local carrier receives a set of digital circuits, and their signaling information, for interconnection with other non-cellular users.

MTSO operations are comparable to a small central office of an average local carrier. Software maintenance and switch control are the typical functions performed. The additional costs of an MTSO are the carrier charges from the MTSO to the PSTN, a Class 5 Central Office. These charges are ongoing and consist of a fixed charge plus a variable element. Specifically, under the current tariffs, the cost is about $0.11 per minute per voice call. This includes an amortization of many charges from the local telephone company. It is not a marginal cost price of access costs and switch costs only. In fact, on a per line basis, the cost for carrier access charges are the dominant cost per subscriber. Specifically, charges of $0.70 per minute for cellular include the $0.11 cost. Some systems cost as high as $0.24 depending on the LATA interconnect permitted.

A dramatic change is occurring with the move to co-location and to unbundled marginal cost pricing on an equitable basis. Simply put this means that anyone may gain switch access alone, without an allocation for the plant cost and priced at the same level as the telephone company, (namely at the marginal price); and it also means that a wireless company may co-locate their equipment in the telephone company central office. The Qualcomm QTSO is such an architecture where the cells are intelligent and an adjunct processor, the QTSO, is placed in the central office. This will eliminate the need for a MTSO, shorten the access lines, reduce the access line costs, and increase overall system reliability. It will, in effect, put the wireless company in the wireless radio business and keep it out of the telephone switching business.

In extremis, this old paradigm uses design philosophies that select optimal cell sites and result in fights to access the right piece of real estate. The old paradigm takes extensive time to select and install, and yields a large value for the cell life cycle cost factor.

The new paradigm is driven by the desire to be flexible and to drive the cell allocation and utilization in a fashion that maximizes the Net Present Value of the business. It clearly is a system approach that does not follow the old book. The new paradigm is characterized in three key ways:

> *(1) Flexibility of design and layout.* Using sophisticated design tools, sub-optimal sites are chosen based upon a life cycle cost methodology.
> *(2) Maximization of NPV of Business.* The costs of leases, service care, and upkeep are critical. The system uses a dynamic network management and control system that dynamically measures the field strength of the system via sensors in the field, and from this generates a feedback to the cell sites to optimize performance. This allows for a fully automated optimization of the cell operation in a holistic fashion. It focuses on reducing the operations side of the life cycle costs. It does

this by allowing for maintenance and repair dispatching on a more orderly basis, allowing for the management and control of spares and inventory, and allowing for the changes in cells when new ones are added, or in the event of environmental propagation changes.

*(3) User measurement with the intent to maximize customer perception.* By having the *in situ* measurement devices not only can we adjust the cells to meet system performance factors, but we can also adapt and manage the system to meet the necessary customer perception factors.

In this section we have focused on several key technical factors that will result in cost reduction. These are:

*Co-Location:* Eliminates MTSO and reduces the per line access charge.
*Network Management:* Reduces the up-front planning costs and reduces the ongoing maintenance and repair costs. Improves performance and customer reception.
*CDMA Digital:* Increases the number of cells and thus reduces depreciation. Makes for simpler planning.

Let us now consider the implications of these changes in the economics of these new systems. Specifically, we shall comment on each network element.

(i) *Transport*: The transport in this case is radio. It can range from being free, as in a lottery, to being a large fixed up front amount, as in an auction, to a variable amount as in a CATV system. In contrast to the wireline RBOC, business transport costs are controlled by policy, not by rational economics. Let us defer this item for the moment.

(ii) *Interconnect*: The switching is done via the CDMA code network using the handset along with the cell sites. There are two types of cells, larger full cells, and smaller re-radiators or microcells. The larger cells are driven by capacity. A typical cell can handle 400 voice trunks, or a possible 40,000 customers. It may cost $1 million. Unlike analog cellular, CDMA requires only one MTSO for coverage rather than the forty or fifty. The re-rads are low cost and handle problems of coverage.

(iii) *Interface*: The handset is fully variable in cost, and available to each purchasing customer.

(iv) *Control*: The control is integrated into both the cell site and the handsets.

Thus, if we look at the economics of the new wireless technologies we note that the capital and expenses are composed of fixed and variable amounts. Specifically:

$$C = C_F + C_V \tag{2}$$

$$E = E_F + E_V \tag{3}$$

Where we have C for capital and E for the operating expenses. It has been shown elsewhere that for this business $E_F$ is small and can be disregarded. Thus E is all variable. Now consider depreciation, D:

$$D = D_F + D_V \tag{4}$$

It can readily be shown that fixed depreciation depends on fixed capital. Thus let us focus on capital. As we have shown the capital consists of the cell sites and the re-rads. If we assume that 2.5% of the users are active at any time in the busiest hours, then a 400 channel cell site can handle 10,000 users. This means that the scale increment is 10,000. If we also assume that a cell can handle a 3 mile radius or about 30 square miles, then using re-rads, 1,500 square miles requires one cell plus 50 re-rads. A cell costs $1 million and the re-rads cost $20,000 each. This means that the first 10,000 customers will cost $2 million. Therefore, the fixed costs are $2 million capital.

Let us now contrast this for analog cellular. Each cell can handle only 40 channels, and a new cell is required per coverage site. Thus, despite the 40 cell capacity, 50 cell sites are needed to cover 1500 square miles. Each cell site costs the same $1 million. 2,000 channels are provided at affixed capital of $50 million. Thus the scale increment is 50,000 customers, and the fixed capital is ten times higher. This does not include the added fixed cost of the MTSO.

Therefore, we can show that the marginal costs, $Co_M$, approach the average costs, $Co_A$, in a very small time frame for the new wireless system. Therefore, we argue that there are *de minimus* scale economies.

This new technology will result in the following new policy observations:

(i) *Lack Of Scale*: The *de minimus* scale economies in these distributed networks mean that the arguments from the theory of monopolistic pricing no longer apply. There is no basis for monopoly, there are no barriers to entry, and there are de minimus barriers to exit. Policy makers should re-evaluate their basic premises and review the results. In particular, the FCC should use the PCS NPRM as the first vehicle to open up this new line of insight. Lehman and Weisman argue from the premise of significant fixed and imbedded costs. They further argue on the basis of an existing infrastructure. The author has argued before that telecommunication, due to the rapid change in technology, is not equipped to be an infrastructure and that, based on the argument herein, the scale issues negate all of the proposed policy recommendations.

(ii) *Rate of Change*: Technology is now allowing change to occur in a more fluid fashion. Silicon, although not really free, is extremely low in cost. The continuing cost is in the software development. In this new CDMA world, the projected prices for the neccessary chip is in the tens of dollars range and decreasing. The entire handset will, in five years, be below $200. It will be the software that will lead the change in the network.

(iii) *Openness versus Standards*: Standards are a way to ensure a form of universal service. Standards are arrived at by a slow and litigious process and hope to result in a single result. Pressed by the technology change, however, the standard is often out of date or excessively compromised. The net result is that coalitions, not standards, are the way of the future. The direction of policy should be to strengthen coalitions, and not enforce standards.

(iv) *Coalitions Versus Regulation*: Coalitions are the alternative to regulation. Regulation can be a control in a monopolistic market to ensure public good. In a free and openly competitive market this no longer holds. The ability to commodify service offerings, and the change from high fixed cost structures, requires a re-evaluation of the regulation assumptions and a clear statement of them.

## 6. VALUE CREATION WITH NETWORKS

Value creation in a network has been a matter of study by both academics and users over the past ten years. For the purpose of this paper, we shall consider value creation as the ability to take any economic entity and to add to that entity a capability with a network that will change the value of that entity in some measurable fashion. The concept of value that we shall use will be that of the net present value of the business entity. We can then readily show that the value is decomposable into revenue, expense, and capital elements, and that this value can also be manipulated via tax or fiscal policy.

### 6.1. Value Measures

All too frequently analysts will use a change in productivity in a business to attempt to show some amorphous competitive advantage. We argue, however, that there exists a clear and simple approach, deployable on the unit business scale, that demonstrates all of these elements in full and complete analytical detail and is subsequently measurable in any market environment.

The value of a business is defined as the net present value of the business based solely upon its long term cash flows. Specifically, if $R(k)$ is the revenue from the business for the k year, $E(k)$, the expenses of the business for the k year, and $C(k)$ the capital expenditures for the business for the k year, then, assuming *de minimus* effects of working capital and an all equity financing scheme, the year's cash flow is:

$$CF(k) = R(k) - E(k) - C(k) \tag{5}$$

The net present value, or value, is defined as the discounted sum of these cash flows. The discounting used is the cost of capital for this entity.[10] Thus the value of business entity I is:

$$V(I) = CF(1)/(1+m) + \ldots \ldots + CF(n)/(1+m^n) \tag{6}$$

where n is the business investment time horizon, and there is no salvage value to the business.[11]

### 6.2. Value Creation

Now consider a business entity that has a value, $V(I,b)$, where we denote b as before the use of the new networking technology. Similarly we denote a as after, and the value as $V(I,a)$. Let us consider a business that has revenue and expenses but has no capital. The extension to capital is trivial. Let us first begin with revenue.

The revenue of a business with a single product is considered. Let us assume that the product has a unit price of p and that there is a demand elasticity that says the demand for the product at p is $q(p)$. Let us assume that we know this function. Let us also assume that:

$$q(p_1) > q(p_0) \text{ for all } p_1 > p_0 \tag{7}$$

Now let the T be the total market base. The addressable market is the demographic percentage of T, namely $D(T)$. The feasible market is the psychographic percentage of $D(T)$, namely $P(D(T))$. The adoption percentage of the feasible market is the target market, namely

A(P(D(T))), equals the target market, TM.  Finally, the actual units sold are based on share, S, and are total units, TU, where:

$$TU = q = S(TM) = S(A(P(D(T)))) \qquad (8)$$

Recall that S, A, P and D, depend on p.  Some of these factors also depend on other intangible factors such as brand recognition, advertising, etc.  In general in a commodity market, all things being equal, price is the sole determinator.  Therefore, market size depends solely on price, and price on cost.  Therefore, we argue that we can neglect the revenue side in this case and focus solely on the expense side.

The expenses of a business can be broken down into the expenses for a set of processes. If we view a business in the Porter context of its value chain, that chain is composed of a set of supportive processes.  These processes may be engineering, marketing, sales, customer service, inventory, administration, etc.  Let us assume that such processes are identifiable and that the business is a collection of these.  Thus the expense for the business is:

$$E = E(1) + E(2) + \ldots\ldots + E(n) \qquad (9)$$

Now E(I) is the expense associated with a single process.  It can be expressed, if properly decomposed into the product of a revenue driver (RD), a productivity factor (PF), and a unit cost (UC).  For example, a sales force has as the revenue driver the number of new customers.  The productivity factor is the number of new customers per year per sales person. The unit cost is the expense per sales person.  Thus the sales expense is:

$$E(Sales)^{12} = RD(Sales)\ PF(Sales)\ UC(Sales) \qquad (10)$$

To reduce the cost we can do three things.  First, we can reduce the number of new customers.  This is not at all appropriate and thus is not done.  Second, we can increase the productivity and thus reduce the productivity factor.  This can be done by more effective targeting of the sales force through telemarketing, inbound 800 number services etc.  Third, we can reduce the salary of the salesforce.  This third factor is probably the worst; salespeople are motivated by money.  If anything the compensation should be increased to further increase productivity.  Thus, in this case we can see how sales productivity is targeted by better acquisition of customers.

Thus networks can reduce costs in several ways: eliminating processes, reducing unit costs, reducing the productivity factor, or in some cases reducing the revenue driver.  This can be shown in the examples discussed in the next section.

### 6.3. Value Creation Examples
In this section we will show that there are several common examples of cases where the use of a network has clearly created value for the firm in many ways.

#### Case 1: American Airlines
American Airlines has developed a significant competitive advantage in the use of their private network and their SABRE reservation system.  It was, and is, a strategic tool based on networking and the control of information.  It allows for ease of access to all products and

28

in a way has commoditized the market. This concept of commodicization was first used in airlines, so that competition was essential to be based upon the most efficient carrier. The distortions in this market are due to the fact that the owners of such airlines as TWA, Continental, USAir, the late Eastern and Pan Am have been the U.S.Government through the bankruptcy courts. This distortion has, through a policy position, distorted the normal market efficiencies. One can argue that this is a paradigm for what could happen in private networks if the government subsidizes via policy the RBOC positions.[13]

### Case 2: Federal Express

Federal Express has market share based on end user accessibility. Their network keeps costs down and share up. The private network that they use tracks all items from beginning to end, and suffers a fairly low, although not zero, error rate. They have a fully integrated satellite, radio, and land line network system.

### Case 3: Healthcare

In the area of health care, McGarty and Sununu[14] have shown that the use of private networks can reduce the costs of health care provision by 20%. The test that these figures were based upon were performed in Boston.[15]

## 7. CONCLUSIONS

We began this paper with a definition of private networks that essentially stated that they were a collection of networking elements, wherein the power to manage them lay in the hands of their users. The two forces that have enabled this have been deregulation as well as technology. We further went on with a discussion that stated that although networks have all the same physically viewable characteristics, they were in some sense genetically different. Hierarchical or RBOC type networks were fundamentally and genetically different from Distributed or LAN type networks. This concept of genetic difference was based upon an ability to adapt by the different network.

Although we began this metaphorical analysis in the attempt to demonstrate limited relationships, we soon found that the underlying relationships Darwin saw in natural species are also fundamental to man-made species like networks. This strengthening of the metaphor allows us to use the observations and techniques to answer the questions posed earlier.

*(i) What are the evolutionary paths that these networks are taking, and what are the implications that these paths will have on the strategies of carriers, equipment makers, and large users?*

The evolutionary paths of networks are first determined by recognizing the two types of networks that have evolved: hierarchical and distributed. Further, it is based upon observing that the new paradigm of "silicon is free" makes the survival of distributed networks highly favorable, and the survival of hierarchical networks problematic. Users will migrate towards value increasing network solutions. If the distributed technology tends towards that end, as it has been argued, then that is where the users will go.

*(ii) How does a commercial entity gain a competitive advantage in a private network and what is the value creation equation that provides the compelling reason for making such a choice?*

*What are the specific sources of value creation? Is it possible that non-standardized networks can result in diseconomies?*

A commercial entity is concerned, if it is a rational business entity, with value creation and value increase. Value in this context is an increase in the net present value of the firm. This value can be increased by increasing revenues, decreasing expenses, or decreasing capital flow, or any combination of these elements. The specific sources of value creation can be determined by examining the microstructure of a business, understanding process and productivity flow, and showing how the network improves each. Non-standardized networks are essentially the silicon version of biodiversity in the carbon world. More silicon gene flow from non-standardized networks will allow for the ability to adapt to rapid change in a business environment. Looking at today's business networks one sees an amalgam of different interconnections, each selected for optimal performance. It is specious at best to assume that a business entity may stand still and optimize its entire operation. Business is run on a continuim of sub-optimum choices.

*(iii) Can private networks migrate to the consumer or residential user?*

Value creation is measurable and demonstrable from the perspective of the business entity. It is not the case for the consumer. The consumer is in one sense an irrational entity whose maximization and choices are, on an individual basis, unpredictable and unanalyzable. All that said, however, the PCS example presented in the paper clearly shows the potential for migration to the end user as consumer. The major driving factors for consumer penetration is access and cost. The lower the entry cost the better the opportunity.

*(iv) What is the impact of private networks on the value of information?*

Information has value only in its ability to change something. That change results in a change in the operations of the economic business entities that we have discussed herein. This change therefore results in a measurable change in the value of the company. The issue of information and private networks is therefore a coupled concept. Information will have an effect in an entity. The change will be proportional to the cost of gathering the information and its timeliness. If a private network changes those factors, then the network, per se, creates value, in addition to the information. We have discussed this in our discussion of examples in the paper.

*(v) Can one measure, unequivocally, the economic value that specialized and customized networks provide to an economic entity in terms of value creation and innovation?*

Value creation was definitively described for any economic entity as the change in net present value of the firm. The impact of the network in creating value can therefore be measured as we have discussed.

These five questions were posed in the context of the paper, to focus the effort on the impact of private networks on business entities. More importantly, however, this paper provides a broader view of the evolution of networks, and a reevaluation of the underlying assumptions that have been at the heart of policymakers. In particular, the fact that distributed networks using today's technology can have *de minimus* scale economies. This one fact is the major observation that should be made by policy makers. Many of the companion papers, such as Lehman and Weisman[16] or Oniki,[17] all assume significant fixed costs and *de minimus* variable costs. The opposite will occur and in certain cases is only true for the distributed network. Thus, because of the economic imperative, business will be converging more and more on distributed private networks, to the detriment of the Hierarchical RBOC type network. Regulation, to the contrary, will slow this process but not stop it.

## REFERENCES

Blackwood, M.A., and A. Girschick, *Theory of Games and Statistical Decisions*, New York: Wiley, 1954.

de Sola Pool, I., *Technologies Without Barriers*, Cambridge, MA: Harvard University Press, 1990.

de Sola Pool, I., *The Social Impact of the Telephone*, Cambridge, MA: MIT Press, 1977.

Dertouzos, M.L., and J. Moses, *The Computer Age*, Cambridge, MA: MIT Press, 1979.

Dugan, D.J., and R. Stannard, "Barriers to Marginal Cost Pricing in Regulated Telecommunications," *Public Utilities Fortnightly*, vol 116, No 11, pp 43-50, Nov. 1985.

Futuyama, D.J., *Evolutionary Biology*, Sunderland, MA: Sinauer, 1986.

Harvey, P.H., and M.D. Pagel, *The Comparative Method in Evolutionary Biology*, Oxford: Oxford, 1991.

Henderson, J.M., and R.E. Quandt, *Microeconomic Theory*, New York: McGraw Hill, 1980.

Hopper, M., "Rattling SABRE-New Ways to Compete on Information," *Harvard Business Review*, No. 3, pp.118-125, 1990.

Huber, P.W., *The Geodesic Network*, Washington D.C.: U.S. Department of Justice, January, 1987.

Kahin, B., "The NREN as a Quasi-Public Network: Access, Use, and Pricing," J.F. Kennedy School of Government, Harvard University, W.P.#90-01, Feb., 1990.

Kahn, A.E., *The Economics of Regulation*, Cambridge, MA: MIT Press, 1989.

Lehman, D.E., and D.L. Weisman, "Access Charges for Private Networks Interconnecting with Public Systems," this volume, pp. 193-210.

Mandelbaum, R., and P.A. Mandelbaum, "The Strategic Future of Mid Level Networks," J.F. Kennedy School of Government, Harvard University, Working Paper, October, 1990.

McGarty, T.P., *Business Plans*, New York: J. Wiley,1989.

McGarty, T.P., and G.J. Clancey, "Cable Based Metro Area Networks," *IEEE Journal on Selected Areas in Communication*, Vol 1, No 5, pp 816-831, Nov 1983.

McGarty, T.P., "Growth of EFT Networks," *Cashflow*, pp 25-28, Nov. 1981.

McGarty, T.P., and L.L. Ball, "Network Management and Control Systems," IEEE NOMS Conference, 1988.

McGarty, T.P., "Local Area Wideband Data Communications Networks," EASCON, 1982.

McGarty, T.P., and M. Sununu, "Applications of Multi-Media Communications Systems to Health Care Management," HIMSS Conference, San Francisco, Feb. 1991.

McGarty, T.P., "Multimedia Communications in Diagnostic Imaging," *Investigative Radiology*, April, 1991.

McGarty, T.P., and R. Veith, "Hybrid Cable and Telephone Networks," IEEE CompCon, 1983.

McGarty, T.P., and S.J. McGarty, "Impacts of Consumer Demands on CATV Local Loop Communications," IEEE ICC, 1983.

McGarty T.P., "Multimedia Communications Systems," *IMAGING*, Nov. 1990.

McGarty, T.P., "Multimedia Communications Architectures," SPIE Optical Communications Conference, Boston, MA, September, 1991.

McGarty, T.P., "Alternative Networking Architectures; Pricing, Policy and Competition, Information Infrastructures for the 1990s," Harvard University, J.F. Kennedy School of Government, Nov. 1990.

McGarty, T.P., and S.J. McGarty, "Information Architectures and Infrastructures; Value Creation and Transfer," 19th Annual Telecommunications Policy Research Conference, Solomons Islands, MD, September, 1991.

McGarty, T.P., "Wireless Communications Economics," Carnegie Mellon University, ATI Conference, June,1992.

Noam, E. M., "The Tragedy of the Common Network: Theory for the Formation and Breakdown of Public Telecommunications," this volume, pp. 51-64.

Oniki, H., and R. Stevenson, "Efficiency and Productivity of Public and Private Networks of NTT," Twentieth Telecommunication Policy Research Conference, September, 1992.

Porter, M., *Competitive Advantage*, New York: Free Press, 1985.

Porter, M., *Competitive Strategy*, New York: Free Press, 1980.

Porter, M., *The Competitive Advantage of Nations*, New York: Free Press, 1990.

Shubik, M., *A Game Theoretic Approach to Political Economy*,Cambridge, MA: MIT Press, 1987.

Shubik, M., *Game Theory in the Social Sciences*, Cambridge, MA: MIT Press, 1984.

Spulber, D.F., *Regulation and Markets*, Cambridge, MA: MIT Press, 1990.

Stace, C.A., *Plant Taxonomy and Biosystematics*, London: Arnold, 1989.

Telmarc Telecommunications Inc., Pioneers Preference, FCC Gen Docket 90-314, PP 76, May 4, 1992.

Telmarc Telecommunications Inc., Pioneers Preference, Reply to Comments, FCC Gen Docket 90-314, PP 76, June 25, 1992.

Telmarc Telecommunications Inc., NPRM Response, FCC Gen Docket 92-333, November 9, 1992.

Vickers, R., T. Vilmansen, "The Evolution of Telecommunications Technology," IEEE Proceedings, vol. 74, No. 9, pp 1231-1245, Sept 1986.

West, E.H., et al, "Design, Operation, and Maintenance of a Multi Firm Shared Private Network," IEEE MONECH Conference, pp.80 - 82, 1987.

Winograd, T., and F. Flores, *Understanding Computers and Cognition*, Reading, MA: Addison Wesley, 1987.

## ENDNOTES

[1] E. Noam, private correspondence to the author. This is based on a general consensus of the opinions of several authors during the 1991-1992 year at the Columbia Institute for Tele-Information (CITI) conferences.

[2] There are three previous papers that have been developing the theme of networks and their evolution. The first, Alternative Network Architectures, was presented at Harvard in the fall of 1990. It introduced the concept of world view in networks and the ability to deconstruct the intent from the results of the

32

design. The second paper, Information Infrastructures, presented at the 19th TPRC, developed the value concept of information in the context of a network. The third was Morphology and Taxonomy of Networks which developed the concept that there are fundamental organic differences in Networks that result from basic evolutionary differences.

[3.] McGarty, T.P. and L.L. Ball, "Network Management and Control Systems," IEEE NOMS Conference, 1988.

[4.] See Huber, P.W., *The Geodesic Network*, Washington, DC: U.S. Department of Justice, January, 1987.

[5.] The Author has argued in "Alternative Network Architectures" that world view is the driving factor in the analysis and deconstruction of networks. This world view is developed based upon a paradigm or example used to drive all development. It has been shown in that paper that the RBOC world view is that of a hierarchical voice based centrally controlled network. Suffice it to say that any attempt by any one of the seven RBOCs to break from that mold has resulted in failure. In fact their operations of cellular carriers follow that mold religiously.

[6.] The current staff reductions in the RBOCs is a sign that they are recognizing that their cost infrastructure is much too high. Take NYNEX as an example. They have 26,000 management employees and another 52,000 craft for 13 million access lines. That means one management per 500 and one craft per 250. In contrast in the new wireless systems the ratio is an order of magnitude better. This means that by eliminating high fixed organizational mindsets the costs can be driven down.

[7.] From an evolutionary perspective each species as a result of its genetic structure presents the outside world with certain phenotypes or characteristics (see Futuyama). The world in turn presents conditions for survival. Survival of the fittest then is the matching of species phenotypes to the conditions of the environments. Those that do not match well die off and those that match grow and survive. This is all based on the concept of a fitness function namely a measure of how easily a species can reproduce. If we view reproduction as a measure of success then distributed systems are cockroaches!

[8.] See the Telmarc Telecommunications Inc. filings with the FCC, especially the NPRM response. In the NPRM response, Telmarc includes a detailed model of the wireless communications business, and it is based upon this model that the lack of scale is demonstrated. There has been no other model to date that has been developed to demonstrate this. It should be noted that the Telmarc model relies heavily on the QUALCOMM technology.

[9.] See the paper by McGarty on Wireless Network Economics. This paper details the results in this paper and constructs a demand and business model based on extensive experience in the industry.

[10.] See McGarty, Business Plans. The author details the selection process for the choice of the costs of capital as well as details the model that is developed in this section. The model is based upon what is called a "tops down" and "bottoms up" approach to the business.

[11.] The restraint placed upon this model can be readily eliminated by including a market for salvage, impacts of financing, impacts of fiscal policy, and all other issues. We have shown this elsewhere and are in this paper focusing only on the essential features.

[12.] E(Sales) = Number of New Customers*(1/ Number of New Customers per Salesman)*Expense per Salesman

[13.] See the paper by Hopper. The author of this paper is a Senior Vice President of AMR, the parent of American, and the person responsible for the development and operation of the system. Hopper presents one of the most compelling arguments for information systems and private networks.

[14.] McGarty, T.P., and M. Sununu, "Applications of Multi-Media Communications Systems to Health Care Management," HIMSS Conference, San Francisco, Feb. 1991.

[15.] McGarty and Sununu performed a detailed several month study at several Boston hospitals evaluating the impact on costs with the use of a private network base multimedia communications system. The paper details the results in the context of process flow as has been developed in this paper.

[16.] Lehman, D.E., and D.L. Weisman, "Access Charges for Private Networks Interconnecting With Public Systems."

[17.] Oniki, H. and R. Stevenson, "Efficiency and Productivity of Public and Private Networks of NTT."

PRIVATE NETWORKS PUBLIC OBJECTIVES
E. Noam and A. NíShúilleabháin (Editors)

History and Recent Developments

# Private Telecommunications Networks: An Historical Perspective

David Gabel

## 1. INTRODUCTION

Joseph Schumpeter has argued that the life-span of monopolies were limited by the "creative destruction" forces of capitalism. For a period of time, a firm may be able to dominate an industry and earn monopoly profits. As other firms become aware of these profit opportunities, they are attracted to the industry. Through the process of innovation, the entrant may displace the first dominant firm and earn monopoly profits. In turn, the second dominant firm's high earnings will attract rivals to the industry.[1]

This mode of analysis has been used to explain the centrifugal forces operating in the telecommunications industry. In U.S. v. AT&T[2], the defendant argued that, due to the regulatory objectives of promoting universal service, the prices for some business communications services had been kept above the economic cost-of-service. High prices were set for business customers in order to provide a subsidy to residential customers.[3] According to AT&T, private telecommunications networks, as well as specialized common carriers, established service because of these regulatory distortions. If Bell had been free to establish subsidy-free rates, the firm believed that it could have continued to serve the entire telecommunications market at a lower cost than in its currently fragmented form.[4]

Eli Noam has argued that the same forces are currently pulling apart the network. In his paper on the "Tragedy of the Commons," he shows how subsidies can drive business customers off the common network. In order to avoid burdensome subsidies, large business customers have an incentive to establish private networks.[5] Noam's results are driven by the assumption of a U shaped cost curve and declining marginal utility.[6] Using this framework, Noam argues that because of subsidies, the initial customers of the network will eventually leave the network and form a second, or additional networks. They leave the first network because the marginal benefit of adding on marginal customers is less than the marginal cost. This results in a reduction of the welfare of the initial network customers and they are therefore better off establishing their own network. If not for the subsidies following from the initial customers to the customers who later join the network, there would be no need to establish this second network. The decision to establish a second network is "The Tragedy of the Common Network." If the network did not expand beyond the size where marginal private benefit equaled marginal private cost, there would be no incentive to form the second network. In his "Tragedy of the Commons" paper, Noam treats customers as a homogeneous body.[7] Noam has also addressed the development of private networks in a second paper, "The Public Telecommunications Network: A Concept in Transition."[8] In that paper he argued that it was the diverse demands of the service economy that made it impossible to sustain a monopoly, public network. Private networks were formed because they provide the type of diversity that could not be provided through the traditional PTT complex.

The presentation made by Noam in the "Transition" paper was more compelling, and I argue below, more accurately reflects the forces that currently and historically have pulled apart the public network. The emergence of new networks has less to do with subsidies than it does with changes in the macro economy, the organizational structure of firms, and the ability of the incumbent telecommunications firms to install new technology that meets the needs of large users.

As the starting point for this paper, I review the formation of some of the nation's first alternative private networks. These networks were largely perceived by information intensive sectors of the economy as a superior means for transferring information between business units. The private networks provided a superior mode of communications for large businesses, and played a large role in the demise of Western Union. I show that the substitution of private networks for the public telegraph system of Western Union fits within Schumpeter's vision that an innovative entrant would constrain the long-term earning power of a monopolist, such as Western Union. In section three, I provide data on the size of the private line market prior to the divestiture of AT&T, as well as on the market shares of the competitive suppliers. In section four of the paper, I review some of the factors which led to the formation of private networks during the post-World War II era. Finally, in section five, I offer some propositions regarding the formation and demise of networks.

## 2. TELEGRAPH SERVICES AND THE EMERGENCE OF THE MULTI-UNIT FIRM

The expansive territorial span of the United States was an initial barrier to the development of large scale industrial enterprises in the United States. While the nation's population was growing rapidly during the first half of the nineteenth century, its dispersion over a wide territory limited the ability of firms to engage in large scale manufacturing. Costly transportation and communication technologies made it expensive for a firm to exploit the economies of scale available in existing manufacturing technologies. A necessary condition for the growth of large scale manufacturing was the development of technologies that lowered the cost of serving multiple markets.[9] In the two decades prior to the Civil War, three key technologies, canals, railroads and the telegraph, played a role in the take-off of the economy. The canals and railroads lowered transportation costs and increased the nation's access to coal, an inexpensive energy source.[10] Paralleling many of the nation's railroads was the nation's first high-speed information network, the telegraph. The telegraph improved the ability of firms to coordinate marketing and production activities in different localities, helped tie together the nation's banking and financial markets, and provided instant access to price information on the nation's commodity markets.[11]

In 1876 coordination of market activities was further enhanced by the invention of the telephone. Initially though, the impact on the nation was limited; business customers perceived few uses for Alexander Graham Bell's invention. The telephone was initially perceived as a poor substitute for the telegraph because it did not offer a written record for commercial transactions. Few saw how it could be used to coordinate market activities or for social purposes.[12] The lack of vision by the first managers and subscribers can be partly attributed to the limitations of the technology. Until the first switchboard was installed in 1878, telephony was conducted on a point to point basis (mesh network). Typically customers ordered connections between their homes and businesses or between an office and a factory; it was hard to envision how universal coverage would be achieved.[13]

The development of the switchboard in 1878 radically changed the prospects of the industry. The deployment of the switchboard lowered the cost of service because the star topology reduced the amount of wire that was need for connecting subscribers and increased the possibility of sharing supporting structures, such as pole brackets. Furthermore, switchboards radically expanded the number of customers that could be reached. No longer were customers limited to calling customers with whom they had a direct connection. The increased calling area increased the value of service and this, in turn, stimulated demand.[14]

The public rapidly accepted the telephone. According to the Bureau of the Census, "By 1899 telephony...not only had surpassed telegraphy in physical and financial magnitude, but by its very growth had seriously restricted the expansion of" telegraphy.[15] The telephone gained almost complete control of the local telecommunications market. It was the preferred mode of communication within cities because it was more rapid, and less expensive. The telegraph operated at a cost disadvantage because of the need to use Morse telegraph operators on either end of the circuit. Telephony was less labor intensive, and consequently quickly became the dominant telecommunications technology for intra-city traffic.[16]

Telephony also quickly dominated the long-distance market. By 1902 there were 120,704,844 long-distance telephone messages, nearly thirty million more than the number of telegraph messages. Only when a written record was required, or a long-distance communication for which the cost of telephony exceeded that of telegraphy, did the older technology sustain a competitive edge.[17] The nation's leading long-distance telephone company, AT&T, did not limit its services to telephony. As early as 1879, Bell was marketing private line telegraph service, in competition with Western Union, to the nation's largest industrial, banking, and financial firms.[18] Before the invention of the telephone, large users of the telegraph network requested and obtained private line service.[19] Private line telegraph service was primarily used by four classes of customers: railroads, the press, industrial customers, and the financial community. The bankers and brokers were the largest customer group; in 1912 they accounted for 80 per cent of the private line business.[20] The private wire business was concentrated in the Northeast and Mid-West,[21] the regions of the nation with the greatest industrial and commercial development.

According to the Interstate Commerce Commission, the largest private network was leased to a banking and brokerage house. The system connected New York to important regional centers in both the United States and Canada:

> [The private-wire network] leased by a banking and brokerage house, operated four circuits from New York, N.Y. via four different routes to Chicago, Ill,, and one circuit thence through Salt Lake City, Utah, to San Francisco, Cal. At Salt Lake City there were connected a circuit running through Butte, Mont. and Seattle, Wash., to Vancouver, British Columbia. Another part of this same system extended from Chicago north St. Paul, Minn. to Winnipeg, Manitoba, and south through Memphis, Tenn., to New Orleans, La. There were numerous short wires connecting with the circuits above described, and a large number of terminal and intermediate drops.[22]

The bankers and brokers used the service primarily for exchange trading. When the wire was not being used for this purpose, market and other types of news was transmitted. Some private line networks were just used to transmit information. The familiar stock ticker and paper tape was used to widely distribute information on the volume of trading and the price of the transactions. One of the larger private networks was owned and operated by the New York Stock Exchange. The network had about one thousand ticker machines in operation, and according to the Bureau of Census, "[t]his system sent out over the tape nearly thirteen million separate impressions in 1901-2, and over seventy-five thousand on some days, while it required about fifty tons of paper to keep the tickers supplied with reels of narrow tape."[23]

Industrial firms used the private lines mainly for coordinating activity between the different branches of the multi-unit firm.[24] As with the bankers, the industrialists believed that a private line provided benefits that were not available on the public network. Their networks provided extra privacy, something both parties desired in order to protect trade secrets. The Interstate Commerce Commission pointed out in 1918 that the superior quality of a private network was also of crucial importance to industrial firms:

> It is said that the matter transmitted over some industrial wires is of so technical a nature that the accuracy of service over the public wires can not be depended upon. Telegraphic discussions of chemical formulae and artistic designs are instances cited as possible over private wires, but impossible, at least in the view of the [industrialists], over public wires. Abolishment of private wires would make it necessary to conduct such discussion by mail, it is said.[25]

Other advantages of private wires included: higher quality and transmission speeds, as well as the carriers' commitment to restore service first on private lines on which there was an outage due to down lines. In order to obtain the best personnel, The lessees of private lines hired highly skilled telegraph operators. These operators received a premium which was up to fifty-percent higher than the wage paid to the less-skilled operators on the public telegraph network. It was because of the superior service, rather than cost savings, that most customers obtained the private line service.[26] Private lines were used by the "wire services" to distribute news stories and market quotations to the thousands of newspapers around the nation.[27] The railroads obtained private line service through the construction of stand-alone systems. The rail lines needed a network that could be used to coordinate the flow of traffic throughout the nation. Information was transferred along the lines to insure that trains were safely spaced apart, to convey arrival and departure times, and to coordinate the shipment of freight.

The telegraph companies found it costly to provide the high-grade of service needed in the railroad business. Postal Telegraph, the nation's second largest telegraph company, decided that because the service requirements of the railroads was "too exacting," to not serve them. The other large carrier, Western Union, did not operate lines in all of the rural areas covered by the rail system. Since the services available from the public telegraph companies was limited in quality and geographical coverage, the railroads decided to build their own private networks.[28]

While private line networks were used to provide both telephone and telegraph services, the latter service was far more common.[29] AT&T only marketed its private line telegraph service to large users. Providing telegraph service to the public would have required the firm to hire workers for coding and decoding messages, as well as delivering messages. AT&T chose to only sell its telegraph service to customers with sufficiently large needs that they could afford to hire their own telegraph operators. While initially the market for this service was limited, the refinement of the telegraph printer around 1910 made the service more widely available.[30]

There were no technological barriers that hindered AT&T's provision of telegraph service. The same transmission lines used for switched message calls could be employed for telegraph service. Because of the similarity in transmission technologies, AT&T had some concern that Western Union would retaliate and enter the toll telephone business. Since, within city limits, the telegraph lines were not as ubiquitous as telephone lines, the threat would have been expensive to carry out. Absent the construction of its own telephone exchanges, Western Union would have had to ally itself with the Independent telephone companies that were competing with AT&T. While Western Union threatened to reciprocate and provide private line toll telephone service, the threat did not deter AT&T from expanding its offerings of private line telegraph services.[31] The competition between Western Union and AT&T for telegraph service illustrates three important concepts regarding private and public networks: the role of subsidies, technological innovation, and network design.

The first private networks were established to satisfy the customers desires for better service (speed, accuracy, privacy, and access to remote locations), rather than in response to regulatory distortions (the telegraph industry was not regulated during these years). It was inefficient for the public network to be designed to meet the more demanding needs of large users. The uses made of private networks by the financial community, newspapers, and manufacturers, illustrate that the rapid growth of private networks prior to the Great Depression was not a "Tragedy." Instead, private networks were an economically efficient response to the needs of the information intensive sectors of the economy.

Second, consistent with the Schumpeterian theory of transient dominance, new technologies eroded the power of the dominant firm, Western Union. The telephone company was able to exploit economies of scope between telephone and telegraph service, and this provided them with some cost advantages. As early as 1910, Bell was fond of pointing out that if telephone and telegraph communication was provided over the same trunk facilities, "one telephone circuit of two wires" could also be used to provide "at least four telegraph circuits." By user intercity facilities for both voice and messages, Bell believed that significant cost savings were realized.[32]

Third, AT&T was able to quickly capture the local message market because telephone facilities were more ubiquitous within a city. Western Union could not compete in AT&T's market until it changed the way its facilities were designed. Instead of locating operator facilities at one or only a few locations in a city, Western Union would have had to spread its operations throughout the town. This would have been an expensive course to pursue.

## 3. FACILITIES USED FOR PRIVATE NETWORKS

The relative importance of private line telegraph service varied accross firms. For the nation's two largest telephone companies, Western Union and Postal Telegraph and Cable, private line systems provided less than ten percent of their revenues. By as early as 1914, AT&T, which had somewhat of a cost advantage because of economies of scope with telephone service, had captured a majority of the private wire telegraph business. Tables One and Two show the mileage and revenues controlled by the three largest suppliers of private Morse telegraph service.

| Morse-service mileage: 1914[33] Table One | | | | |
|---|---|---|---|---|
| | in private wire service | in public wire service | totals | percent private wire |
| Western Union | 47,969 | 926,504 | 972,473 | 4.93% |
| Postal | 17,283 | 245,695 | 262,978 | 6.57% |
| Bell Company | 140,477 | 500,000 | 640,477 | 21.93% |
| total | 205,729 | 1,672,199 | 1,877,928 | 10.96% |

Sources: Federal Communications Commission, *The Investigation of the Telephone Industry*, 1939, p.129 and *Statistics of Communication's Common Carriers*, Federal Commission's annual report.

| Morse-service annual revenues: 1914[34] Table Two | | | | |
|---|---|---|---|---|
| | private wire service | public wire service | totals | percent private wire |
| Western Union | $1,084,837 | 38,640,009 | 39,724,847 | 2.73% |
| Postal | 626,034 | 7,851,769 | 8,477,804 | 7.38% |
| Bell Company | 2,218,638 | 9,411,423 | 11,630,061 | 19.08% |
| total | 3,929,510 | 55,903,203 | 59,832,713 | 6.57% |

Ten years earlier, Bell had only about twenty-eight percent of the business. Bell's expansion between 1904 and 1914 was partly at the expense of the telegraph companies; during the same ten years, the private line revenues of the telegraph companies declined. The business of providing private lines for telegraph operations remained an area of rapid growth for AT&T until the Great Depression. Fifteen years later, in 1929, the miles of Bell's private telegraph lines had increased to 1,200,000 miles. By that time though, the composition of the leases had changed. While in 1914 80% of leases were taken by bankers and brokers, in 1929, 33% of the mileage was rented by newspapers and press associations.

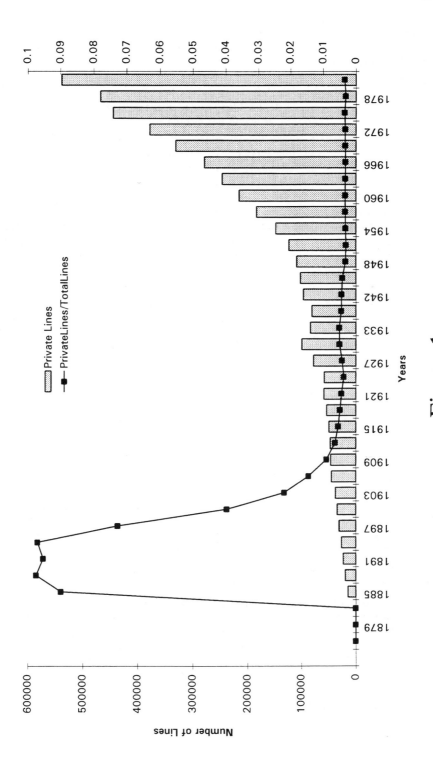

Figure 1

The growth in importance of leased lines to presses is attributable in part to the introduction in 1925 of telephotograph service. This new service was used by newspapers and wire services to transmit photographs and facsimiles.[35]

Figure One shows the growth in the number of private line circuits between 1885 and 1981. The vertical axis on the left shows the number of private telephone lines as measured by the common carriers. The value likely excludes private lines that were not supplied by common carriers. Therefore, it would not include private lines on private networks. The right-side vertical axis shows the percentage of total common carrier lines that were accounted for by private line service. During the early years of telephony, private line service accounted for approximately ten percent of the installed lines. The ratio was high because telephony was marketed primarily to business customers, and switched service was in its infancy stage. While private line service was available from the beginning of AT&T's operations, switched service was not introduced until 1878. The large dip in the percentage of private line phones after 1897 is attributable to the growth of residential service. When AT&T's patents expired in 1894, rival telephone companies rapidly entered the market and targeted the neglected residential community. The competition led to a rapid growth in the number of residential subscribers, and a comparatiavely slow growth in the number of private lines.

The data series stops in 1981. After the divestiture of AT&T in January 1984, the Federal Communications Commission stopped reporting the number of private line loops. Private line service was made part of a larger reporting category, special access lines, and this new category included some switched services, such as interexchange carrier access.

## 4. FORMATION OF PRIVATE NETWORKS IN THE POST WORLD WAR II ERA

There has been a proliferation of private networks during the post-World War II era. In many ways the recently constructed private networks were established for the same reasons that were crucial during the first thirty years of telephony: security, the need for central management to coordinate and monitor activities in different units of the firm, the need to reach remote areas, and, more generally, the "failure" of the common carriers "to meet the new or specialized consumer demands in the market place."[36]

Immediately after World War II, a large part of the demand for new services was related to the growth of commercial television. AT&T was unable to provide the networks with ubiquitous or cost effective intercity transmission facilities. Since the facilities available through AT&T were unsatisfactory, the networks set up private, microwave systems.[37]

The other principle factor driving the demand for private line networks was the growth of the data processing industry. As the cost of processing dropped, operating systems that provided real-time solutions to problems became more common, and electronic mail communications took-off, the need for data communication lines increased.[38] The public switched network was not capable of providing the quality transmission lines that were needed for high speed data and video transmission.[39]

In the late 1950's, the shortcomings of the public switched network were discussed extensively in the FCC docket "Above 890."[40] A decade later, as the problems persisted, the data processing industry provided the common carriers with a list of ten ways in which service could be improved. The list included the speed of connection and disconnection, as well as the associated billing period; a greater variety of bandwidth and transmission speeds;

a reduction in the error rates; improved circuit testing procedures; and the deployment of a digital data transmission network.[41] Today, 30 years after "Above 890," large business customers have many of the same complaints about the public switched network. The users have established private networks, or obtained service from alternative local exchange carriers, because of quality-of-service and cost considerations.[42]

During the post-World War II era there has been a major change in the type of technology used in the public switched network. While manual switching systems were widely deployed in the 1940s, by 1990 the switching was largely completed by computer controlled equipment.[43] Similar modernization activity has occurred with interoffice facilities--coaxial, N and copper carrier systems have been replaced with T-carrier and fiber optics. With respect to the local loop, loaded lines were initially an impediment to the provision of high-speed data services. Loaded cables pairs have been largely eliminated from the loops located near large business customers.[44]

Despite these changes in facilities, large users still express their dissatisfaction with the service provided by the public switched telephone network. In part this is the result of the slow pace in which the public switched telephone network operators have deployed new technology. For example, during the 1970s the Bell Systems leading product in the PBX market was the analog, Dimension Private Branch Exchange (PBX). While the Dimension PBX was satisfactory for the majority of users, it was cumbersome for data transmission. Consequently many customers chose to buy digital PBXs from other suppliers. According to Temin, AT&T's decision to market the analog technology reflected the internal management style of the firm during the 1970s. The deployment of technology was determined by engineering criteria, rather than market objectives. The engineers controlled the operations of the Bell System, and they believed that digital consumer premise technology should not be deployed until the national network was converted from analog to digital technology.[45]

While more rapid deployment of digital technology would have allowed the Bell System to maintain its market share in the customer premise market, a more fundamental problem for the local exchange carriers (LECs) is the design of the exchange switching machines. The architecture of the switches limits the ability of the public switched telephone network operators to compete in the market for high-speed and video services. Data and video services have fundamentally different usage patterns that voice telephony. When only voice telephony was provided on the public switched network, engineers assumed that during the peak-demand period each customer placed one call that lasted for three to five minutes.[46] High-speed data services often involve short-bursts of information, perhaps 15 to 20 seconds in length. The number of per customer data connections during the system busy-hour is significantly larger than one. At the other extreme, some data transmissions, as well as video, will involve connections that last for the full system busy-hour.[47]

The switching network has been designed to satisfy the needs of voice telephony. The deployment of a switch that is used for voice, video and high-speed data transmission will increase the variance of usage patterns. In order to provide these three services through the same public switching nodes, there must be fundamental changes in the current design of the switching machines.[48] To date, the exchange public switched telephone network operators have not been able to obtain a switch that economically provides all three services. Consequently their current offerings of high-speed switched data services are offered through auxiliary machines, such as the Stromberg-Carlson Metropolitan Area Network or AT&T's Broadband Service 2000 Switch.[49]

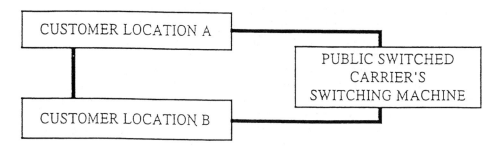

The lack of a switching machine that can economically provide switched voice, high-speed data and video services explains in part why customers find it cost efficient to establish a private network. Due to the unavailability of a multi-purpose switch, public switched telephone network operators are unable to obtain a competitive advantage by exploiting economies-of-scope.[50] Since a local exchange carrier uses separate switching equipment for non-voice services, users may find it more economical to rely on private services. By constructing a private network, transmission costs may be reduced, as well as switching costs.

To transmit data between customer locations, the firm can either use a private, direct link (A to B), or use the public switched telephone network operator's switching machine. While the direct link involves a shorter distance, it may be cheaper to use the public switched telephone network operator's facilities. The cost of using the shared facilities could be less than the cost of constructing a private network. But when the public switched telephone network operator has to install special switching equipment for high-speed data services, there are few customers who will share the responsibility of recovering the fixed cost of the auxiliary switching equipment. This will raise the unit cost of obtaining high-speed data services from the public switched telephone network . Until the demand for high-speed data and video services broadens, agile niche suppliers may be able to provide non-voice services at a lower cost than public switched telephone network operators. While a local exchange company could also install direct facilities between locations A and B, the speed at which these large firms are able to respond to customers needs is notably slower than the entrants. But if the demand for these products broaden, the telephone companies marketing position will improve because of economies of scale.

### 4.1. Will We See A Repeat of Western Union's Demise?

In the preceding section I argued that a market developed for specialized carriers because of the technical limitations of today's switching technologies, and because it was costly to redesign the existing switched network to provide new services. The inability of the incumbent to rapidly adopt to technological changes raises the specter that today's telephone public switched telephone network will go through the same Schumpeterian destructive phase experienced by Western Union. Unable to obtain high speed data service over the public switched network, customers will obtain service from the new suppliers.

Private digital networks are capable of providing voice services. Currently, they are used to provide intracompany voice communications and to obtain access to long-distance carriers. The economics of telephony suggest that it is unlikely that private networks will expand into marketing voice services on a common carriage basis. While private carriers have access to customers where conduit is readily available, in less densely populated areas providing duplicate loop facilities is difficult. In order to establish a second exchange network, the carrier would have to obtain a permit from the city for burying its cables. This is a formidable barrier-to-entry and is most likely to be overcome by cable companies since they already pass ninety percent of American households.

The ability of cable companies to introduce a rival telecommunications network is quite dependent on the pricing of interconnection. If a second exchange network is established, it lowers the percentage of customers who are served by a given switching machine. For example, if a city is initially served by one switch, all exchange calls originate and terminate on the same switch. If a new carrier enters the market, the percentage of exchange calls between switches will no longer be zero. The cost of these switching interoffice calls is, at the minimum, twice as expensive as the cost of an intra-office call.[51] If rates are established to reflect the cost of connecting competing exchange switches, customers will have an economic incentive to migrate to one firm. By relying on one firm, the cost penalty of additional interoffice calls is avoided. For example, after interconnection of competing telephone service was ordered in Lacrosse, Wisconsin in 1913, almost all customers moved onto one system in order to avoid the penalty associated with interoffice calls. The Wisconsin Railroad Commission had determined that the cost of an interoffice call was five cents and that cost should be recovered from the originating party. There was no charge for intra-office calls.[52]

In summary, just as the ubiquitous local telephone exchange gave AT&T a first-mover advantage over Western Union at the start of the twentieth century, the public switched telephone network operators continue to have an important advantage today. While specialized common carriers and private networks will be able to serve niche markets, the core voice market of the public switched telephone network is not contestable at this point in time.

## 5. CONCLUSION

As illustrated by the rivalry between AT&T and Western Union, new technology can lead to the rapid demise of a dominant firm. But the adoption of superior technology is not a sufficient condition for successful entry. Today's private data and voice networks may be based on technologically that is more advanced than the LECs' facilities, but the entrants are only a limited threat to the public switched telephone network's core, voice exchange services. The history of telecommunications networks in the United States suggests that regulation may have been a "boogy-man" used to explain the growth of private networks. While subsidies from business to residential customers, if they do exist, may have played a role in the growth of private networks, the origin is more based in the heterogeneity of user needs, and the inability of the incumbent firm to rapidly adjust its network to efficiently meet the demands of all customer groups. The problems faced by the LECs are conceptually similar to the challenge faced by Western Union prior to the advent of regulation. Once committed to a particular architecture and mode of doing business, it is cumbersome to modify the network so that the new technology may be rapidly deployed.

46

## ENDNOTES

[1.]See pp. 85-106, Joseph Schumpeter, *Capitalism, Socialism and Democracy* New York: Harper & Row, 1942.

[2.]Civil Action No. 74-1698 (D.D.C.)

[3.]American Telephone and Telegraph, "Defendants' Third Statement of Contentions and Proof," United States v. American Telephone and Telegraph, pp. 15, and 361-381, March 10, 1980.

[4.]Ibid., pp. 35, 2097-2136.

[5.]Eli Noam, "The Tragedy of the Common Network: Theory for the Formation and Breakdown of Public Telecommunications," in this volume, pp. 51-64. A private network is a set of telecommunication facilities which is not available for public use. Conversely, a public network, or common carriage, is "a public offering to provide for hire facilities...whereby all members of the public who choose to employ such facilities may communicate or transmit intelligence of their own design or choosing." National Association of Regulatory Utility Commissioners v. F.C.C. 525 F.2d 630, 641 (D.C. Cir.) cert. denied, 425 U.S. 999 (1976).

[6.]Of course, the assumption of a U shaped cost curve is not crucial; all that matters is that at some point the marginal benefit of an additional network customer is less than the marginal cost.

[7.]Noam does allow for a variation in the number of lines used by a subscriber, but otherwise treats them as homogeneous.

[8.]Eli M. Noam, "The Public Telecommunications Network: A Concept in Transition," 37 *Journal of Communications* 30 1987.

[9.]See pp. 49, 75, Alfred Chandler, *The Visible Hand: The Managerial Revolution in American Business*, Cambridge: Harvard University Press, 1977.

[10.]Ibid.

[11.]Ibid.

[12.]See, p. 11, Robert W. Garnet, *The Telephone Enterprise: The Evolution of the Bell System's Horizontal Structure, 1876-1909*, John Hopkins University Press, 1985 and pp. 32-61, Claude S. Fischer, "Touch Someone: the Telephone Industry Discovers Sociability," *Technology and Culture*, v.29, 1988.

[13.]Garnet, pp. 15-16, 20.

[14.]Garnet, pp. 20-21.

[15.]Department of Commerce and Labor, *Telephones and Telegraphs: 1902* Washington: Government Printing Office, 1902, p.3.

[16.]Ibid., p.99.

[17.]Ibid.

[18.]See p.734, M.D. Fagan, ed., *History of Engineering and Science in the Bell System: The Early Years (1875-1925)*, Homdal, New Jersey: Bell Telephone Laboratories, 1975.

[19.]Similar to today's software controlled private line services, the subscribers to private line services rarely had exclusive control over a wire between two points. Instead, the subscriber had exclusive access to the circuit for the hours negotiated in a contract. Subscribers to private line service could not use the dedicated line service during the system peak demand hours of 10 to 12 A.M. Interstate Commerce Commission, "Private Wire Contracts," 50 ICC (1918) 731, 734-736.

[20.]The meat packing and steel industries accounted for the next largest block of business, approximately nine percent. The bankers and brokers accounted for a smaller proportion of the private telephone lines-- 27 per cent.
Ibid. p. 738. The difference was likely due to the need for a written record of the financial transactions.

[21.]Ibid., p. 738.

[22.]Ibid., pp. 738-39.

[23.]See p. 104, Department of Commerce and Labor, Bureau of the Census, *Telephones and Telegraphs: 1902*, Washington: Government Printing Office, 1906.

[24.]Interstate Commerce Commission, "Private Wire Contracts," 50 ICC (1918) 731, 740-1.

[25.]Ibid., p. 742. The larger private industrial networks typically connected the firm's headquarters with its manufacturing plans and distributing stations. Smaller private industrial networks were used primarily to connect headquarters with a factory. Ibid., p. 740. The industrial firms considered only about five percent of this intracompany traffic to be of sufficiency urgency that they would have used public wires if private systems were not available. For the remaining 95%, if private wires were not available, the firms would have substituted the mail. Ibid., p. 741.

[26.]Ibid., 742-3, 749.

[27.]Green to Stockton, February 25, 1888, Box 1217, AT&TCA.

[28.]AT&T, "Third Statement," pp.540-1; and N.A., quoting Postal Company, December 1909, in "Western Union Telegraph Company--Statistics--1912," ATT, box 20.
    Even though the railroad companies found public telegraph service to be of unacceptable quality, they did recognize the advantages of sharing some facilities. The railroads allowed the telegraph companies to use their right-of-way for the stringing of poles. In 1902, 72.4% of the telegraph companies' wires were strung alongside of railroad tracks. See p. 104, Department of Commerce and Labor, Bureau of the Census, *Telephones and Telegraphs: 1902*, Washington: Government Printing Office, 1906.

[29.]Interstate Commerce Commission, "Private Wire Contracts," 50 ICC (1918) 731, 736.

[30.]See pp. 738-39, 743-44, Fagan, *Engineering and Science in the Bell System.*

[31.]H. Stone/J. Hudson, March 28, 1995, "Private Line Rates in Chicago," box 1284, ATT.

[32.]N.A., December 1909, in "Western Union Telegraph Company--Statistics--1912," ATT, box 20.
    There is some evidence to suggest that similar economies-of-scope can be achieved today in the telephone and entertainment industries. James Cornford and Andrew Gillespie have estimated that in the United Kingdom, the addition of cable telephony to an entertainment network raises capital costs by 28% but increases revenues around 91%, p.594 "Cable Systems, Telephony and Local Economic Development in the UK," *Telecommunications Policy*, November 1993.

48

[33.]Interstate Commerce Commission, "Private Wire Contracts," 50 ICC (1918) 731, 735. The Commission noted that the Bell value of 500,000 was composed of "250,000 miles of telephone circuits, each of two wire, making 500,000 miles available for superimposed Morse service, although not so used at present time."

[34.]Ibid. The Bell revenue is from the long-distance portion of AT&T and does not include any revenue obtained from the local, Bell operating companies. The $9,411,423 in Bell revenue was "[n]ot Morse service, but included for purposes of comparison." Ibid.

[35.]See pp. 9-10, James M. Herring and Gerald C. Gross, *Telecommunications: Economics and Regulation*, New York: McGraw-Hill, 1936. While the data presented in Table One excluded data for the Bell Operating Companies, it is not clear if Herring and Gross's data excludes or includes these operations.

[36.]See, for example, Plaintiff's Third Statement of Contentions and Proof, in United States v. American Telephone and Telegraph, 74-1698 (D.D.C), p. 86 (quote); "Comments of Microwave Communications, Inc." in "Regulatory and Policy Problems Presented by the Interdependence of Computer and Communication Services and Facilities," FCC Docket No. 16979 (hereafter "Computer I,"), March 5, 1968, p. 26-28; Federal Communications Commission, "In the Matter of Allocation of Frequencies in the Bands Above 890 Mc," 27 FCC 359, 377-9 (1959); and Stanford Research Institute, "Policy Issues Presented by the Interdependence of Computer and Communications Services," Report No. 7379B-1 (1969), pp. 25-29.

[37.]Plaintiff's Third Statement of Contentions and Proof, January 10, 1980, pp. 90-110.

[38.]MCI, "Comments," p.1; "Response of U.S. Department of Justice," Computer I, March 5, 1968, p.2; Stanford Research Institute, "Decision Analysis of the FCC Computer Inquiry Responses," Report No. 7379B-3 (1969), p.13 and "Analysis of Policy Issues in the Responses to the FCC Computer Inquiry," Report No. 7379B-2, p. 115-6.

[39.]MCI, "Comments," p.27.

[40.]FCC, "Allocation of Microwave Frequencies Above 890 Mc.," pp. 364-379. For example, the Electronics Industries Association stated that potential uses of private microwave systems included firms "which require highly specialized communications circuits which are not readily or economically obtainable over wire communications systems..." Ibid., p. 378.

[41.]Stanford Research Institute, "Analysis of Policy Issues," p.47.

[42.]See, Eli M. Noam, "The Public Telecommunications Network: A Concept in Transition," 37 *Journal of Communications*, 30, 1987; p. 2137, John M. Griffiths, "ISDN Network Terminating Equipment," 30 *IEEE Transactions on Communications* 1982; p. 43, Roger G. Noll, "The Future of Telecommunications Regulation," in *Telecommunications Regulation Today and Tomorrow*, ed. Eli M. Noam 1983; Re Pacific Bell, 69 PUR4th 225, 236 1985; and Jane L. Racster, Michael D. Wong, and Jean-Michael Guldmann, "The Bypass Issue: An Emerging Form of Competition in the Telephone Industry," National Regulatory Research Institute, 84-17 1984.

[43.]See table 25, Federal Communications Commission, *Statistics of the Communications Industry in the United States*, Washington: Government Printing Office, 1949.

[44.]Byrne, Coburn, Mazzoni, Aughenbaugh, and Duffany, "Positioning the Subscriber Loop Network for Digital Services," 30 *IEEE Transactions on Communications* 2006 1982.

[45.]See p.150, Peter Temin with Louis Galambos, *The Fall of the Bell System: A Study in Prices and Politics*, Cambridge: Cambridge University Press, 1987.

MCI believed that its original success in the transmission market would derive from its ability to quickly respond to customer needs in niche markets. As a new firm, they would not have to give "consideration to the preservation of other forms of types of service." MCI, "Comments of MCI," p.8.

[46.]Peak-hour usage is one of the primary criteria used to determine the amount of switching equipment needed to serve customers.

[47.]Kenneth F. Giesken, "ISDN Features Require New Capabilities in Digital Switching Systems," 3 *IEEE Journal of Telecommunications Networks* 19-28 1984.

[48.]Ibid., p. 20.

[49.]See p. 4, 96, "Bell Atlantic Set to Rollout Offerings Similar to SMDS," *Network World*, October 14, 1991 and p. 35, "PacBell Gives SMDS Thumbs-Up," *Communications Week*, October 14, 1991.

[50.]Economies of scope exist if

$$C(Q_1,0) + C(0,Q_2) > C(Q_1,Q_2) \tag{50.1}$$

where $Q_1$ = the output of product one; $Q_2$ = the output of product two. The equation merely states that it is cheaper to have product one and two produced by a single firm [$C(Q_1,Q_2)$], than by having separate firms produce product one and two [$C(Q_1,0) + C(0,Q_2)$].

[51.]Switching costs will double, at a minimum, because of the use of two machines. The available cost data suggests that the cost penalty is much higher. See p. 53, David Gabel, "Deregulation: Should the Local
Telephone Market be Next?," *New England Law Review* 24 1989.

[52.]Ibid., p.55.

PRIVATE NETWORKS PUBLIC OBJECTIVES
E. Noam and A. NíShúilleabháin (Editors)
© 1996 Elsevier Science B.V. All rights reserved.                                    51


The Tragedy of the Common Network: Theory for the Formation and Breakdown of Public Telecommunications

Eli M. Noam

## I. INTRODUCTION[1]

Recent years, have witnessed major transformation in telecommunications industry structure, from monopoly to an increasingly diversified environment. Because many of the changes originated in the United States, they are often viewed as the product of particularly American business interests and ideology. But more recently, several other industrialized countries have begun to adopt similar policies, or at least to discuss changes that previously seemed unthinkable.[2]

These developments raise the question whether the change has explanations that are more fundamental than the nature of the respective governments in power. Of course, there are unique aspects to any country, and they will keep national telecommunications system to some extent distinct. But the variations should not obscure central themes that repeat themselves elsewhere.

Unfortunately, there has been little attempt at a broader-gauged interpretation of the formation and transformation of networks that can explain the dynamics of change.[3] To provide such analysis is the aim of this essay.

## 2. THEORIES FOR THE EMERGENCE OF MULTIPLE NETWORKS

A number of explanations have been offered for the demise of monopoly in telecommunications. There are four major types of theories with different drivers: technology, politics, non-sustainability, and market structure.

The *technological* explanations stress new transmission options that lowers entry barriers, and the merging of telecommunications and computing which undermines monopoly power.[4] But these observations are not adequate explanations. The same technologies are available anywhere on the globe, and certainly in the developed world, yet their impact on network structure has been highly varied, providing no evidence for a technological determinism at work. Technology offers the precondition for necessary but not sufficient institutional change.

*Political* explanations use the perspective of countervailing powers, arguing that in the information age, a telecommunications monopoly becomes too powerful so that its scope needs to be limited by a governmental structural policy to establish competition. The problem with this view is that the creation of a multiplicity of carriers is not the only policy option. Alternatives might well be a stricter nationalization, or more effective regulation, or a size-reduction along geographical and/or functional lines while maintaining monopoly. Thus, it is not clear why the introduction of competition should be the result of monopoly power.

Another view is that a monopoly, even if efficient across its multiple products, cannot protect itself from entry into some lines of business, especially in the presence of rate regulation. This view is essentially that of an economic *non-sustainability* theory.[5] This can explain the emergence of entrants for new products of a multi-product firm, but it does not adequately cover competition in traditional core markets of a telecommunications monopolist, unless one accepts restrictive assumptions.[6]

Another type of explanation is the classical industrial organizational view. It postulates that monopoly structure leads to inefficiency in performance, and hence eventually to the entry of competition. Yet this view is at tension with the reality of network performance in those countries where structural changes in networks are most rapid. If inefficiency were the causal force for rival entry, Egypt or Mexico (to use two examples) should have introduced competition long before the U.S. and Japan, which had arguably the most advanced and ubiquitous networks in the world even before embarking on their liberalizing policies.

It has always exasperated the proponents of the traditional network system to be told that their problem was inefficiency. This clashed with their observations of economies of scale, benefits of long-term technological planning, and effectiveness of end-to-end responsibility.

Thus, none of these theories for the emergence of multiple networks provides an adequate explanation.

In contrast, this paper advances an alternative view based on the dynamics of group formation. Its explanation is not based on the *failure* of the existing monopoly system. To the contrary, the breakdown of monopoly is due to its very *success* in advancing telephone service and in making it universal and essential. But as the network expands, political group dynamics take place, leading to overexpansion, redistribution, and instability. This creates increasing incentives to exit from the "sharing coalition" of the network, and to an eventual 'tipping' of the network from a stable single coalition to a system of separate sub-coalitions.

This view of the effectiveness of monopoly, yet of its success undermining its own foundations is basically Schumpeterian. From the monopoly's perspective, it is deeply pessimistic, because it implies that the harder their efforts and the greater their success, the closer the end to their special status is at hand. Like in a Greek tragedy, their preventive actions only assure their doom.

## 3. A MODEL OF NETWORKS

### 3.1. The basic model[7]

One can look at a network as a *cost sharing arrangement* between several users. Let the total cost of a network serving n subscribers be given by C(n).

n assumes that users are homogenous. (Of course, some network participants are much larger than others, but that poses no problem if one defines a large organization to consist of multiple members of type n, e.g., telephone lines or terminals rather than subscriptions. Later, we will drop that assumption.)

Let an individual's utility be given by u(P,n), where P is the price for network usage, and n are the number of network members. We assume network externalities to exist, ($\delta u/\delta n > 0$), though at a declining rate, i.e. a subscriber is better off the more other members there are on the network, *ceteris paribus* (including network performance and price).[8] Price is also a function of network size, since cost is shared by network uses. For simplicity, utility is expressed in monetary units:

$$u = u(P) + u(n) = -P(n) + u(n) \qquad (1)$$

We assume that the network membership is priced at average cost, i.e. that users share costs equally.[9] (This assumption will be dropped later.) This can be shown schematically in figure 1, where $u(n)$ is steadily increasing, though at a declining rate, and $P = AC = C(n)/n$ is declining, at least at first.

Figure 1
Stages in Network Expansion

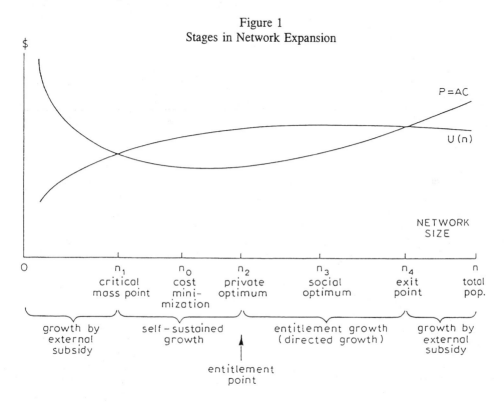

## 3.2. Critical mass

Subscribers might find it attractive to join a well-sized network to share costs, while the number of subscribers n adds to utility. This can be seen in Figure 1, where the utility of joining a network rises at first. Conversely, where the network is small, average cost is high, and externalities small. In that range, below a "critical mass" point $n_1$, a network will not be feasible, unless supported by external sources. We define critical mass as the smallest number of users such that a user is as well off as a non-user $u(n) = P(n)$.[10]

To reach $n_1$ requires a subsidy of sorts, either by government or by the network operator's willingness to accept losses in the early growth phases of operations. The strategic problem is to identify in advance a situation in which such a break-even point $n_1$ will be reached within the range $n < N$, where $N$ = total population, and within the range of demand. Possibly, such a point does not exist, and subsidies would have to be permanent in order to keep the network from imploding. We will return to the critical mass issue later in subsection 3.10.

### 3.3. Private Optimum

Through the cost-sharing phases of network growth, the earlier network users can lower their cost by adding members. However, average cost increases in the range beyond the point $n_0$ where $AC = f'(n)$.

Beyond $n_0$ expansion becomes unattractive for cost reasons; new subscribers, for example because they are in more remote locations with lesser population density, are more costly to serve. However, some further expansion would be accepted by the network members since newcomers beyond the low cost point would still add to utility. The optimal point $n_2$ is given where the equation holds:

$$u'(n) = (1/n) \ [C'(n) - C(n)/n] \tag{2}$$

This is the case in the range of increasing AC $((C'(n) > AC)$, since $u'(n)$ is positive). If they are given the ability to exclude, existing subscribers would not accept network members beyond $n_2$, the private optimum.[11]

### 3.4. Social optimum

From a societal point of view, however, the optimal network size in an equal price system tends to diverge from the private optimum.

Assume social welfare given by the sums of utilities[12]

$$W = n[u(P(n)) + u(n)] = n[-C(n)/n + u(n)] \tag{3}$$

so that its derivative

$$(dW/dn) = -C'(n) + n \ u'(n) + u(n) = 0 \tag{4}$$

$$u'(n) = (1/n) \ [C'(n) - u(n)] \tag{5}$$

Marginal cost equals the incremental user's utility, plus the existing n user's marginal utility. Since $u(n) > C(n)/n$ below the a point of intersection $n_4$ in Figure 1, social optimum $n_3$ is greater than private optimum $n_2$. (It should be noted that the same size will be chosen by an unconstrained monopolist that sets the price at $P = u(n_3)$ to exhaust consumer surplus.)

### 3.5. Entitlement Point and Universal Service Obligation

The discrepancy of private and social optimum leads to government intervention, normally known as a "universal service" policy.

To understand the politics of government-directed network expansion, let us assume a political decision mechanism in which the majority rules the single network. As a first case, assume that private optimum size $n_2 < N/2$, which means that there are more people outside than inside the network, while there are positive net benefits, i.e., $u(n_2) - AC(n_2) > 0$. A majority consisting of $N - n_2$ network outsiders would therefore outvote the $n_2$ network insiders, and require the opening of the network to additional members. This would be the case up to the point where network size reaches $N/2$, at which point the network insiders have grown to a majority and will resist further growth. Beyond $N/2$ then (or where $n_2 \geq N/2$ and a majority against expansion exists from the beginning) a politically directed growth will occur if the coalition of network insiders can be split by aligning the remaining outsiders

N/2 with some of the insiders who are offered a more favorable share of cost, i.e., by price-discrimination, especially in the allocation of the fixed cost. It will be shown in sections 8 and 9 that this coalition formation will lead to an over-expansion of the network.

Politically directed growth beyond private optimum $n_2$ can be termed an "entitlement growth" because it is based on political arguments of *rights* to participate in the network where average net benefits are positive (encouraging attempts of entry) while marginal net average benefits are negative, leading to attempts at exclusion. In economic terms, the argument is made to expand the network at least to where $C'(n) = P = u(n)$, leaving fixed costs to be distributed unequally, for example, by a Ramsey pricing rule. When the marginal private net benefits are positive, there is no need to resort to the language of entitlements, since growth is self-sustaining and sought by network insiders. It is only beyond that point that entitlements, rights, and universal service rights (i.e. obligations by the network) become an issue. We thus define $n_2$ as the "entitlement point."

This way of analyzing entitlements serves to clarify the often-considered question: for which services will universal service be extended? Using the analysis, the answer is that it will be for those services that

(a)  have grown beyond minimum critical mass and
(b)  have reached, through self-sustained growth, a private optimum, beyond which further growth is not internally generated because *marginal* average net benefits are zero, but where
(c)  average net benefits are positive (and therefore encourage demand for entry), and
(d)  the number of those excluded is sufficiently large to lead to an opening by political means.

### 3.6.  Exit From the Network

There may well be a point where the network is expanded by government requirement to an extent that, given its increasing cost, a user is better off by not participating. We define $n_4$ as the "exit point," i.e., the largest n such that an indifference exists between dropping off the network and sharing in the cost of supporting the expanded network.

$$u(n) = u(P). \tag{6}$$

It is possible that this exit point lies beyond the total population, $n_4 > N$. But this seems not likely under an average-pricing scheme, because the last subscribers may impose a heavy burden on the rest of subscribers. Thus, assuming $n_4 < N$, a government's aim to establish a truly universal service is normally infeasible without resorting to a subsidy mechanism or price discrimination. In other words, a universal service policy is dependent on a redistributive policy.

### 3.7.  Political Price Setting and Redistribution

We have so far assumed that universal service is something imposed externally by government. In this section, however, it will be shown that the *internal* dynamics of network members will take the network towards expansion beyond private and social optimum, and towards its own disintegration.

As has been shown above, a network will cease to grow on its own after private optimum $n_2$. But this conclusion was based on a pricing scheme of equal cost shares. Yet there is no reason why such equality of cost shares would persist if they are allocated through a decision mechanism that permits the majority of network users to impose higher cost shares on the minority. (This assumes that no arbitrage is possible.) Unequal prices and a departure from cost could be rationalized benignly as merely "value of service" pricing, i.e. higher prices for the users who value telephone greatly.

Suppose for purposes of the model that decisions are made through voting by all network members.[13] Let us assume at this stage that all users are of equal size (or that voting takes place according to the number of lines a subscriber uses, which is the same thing) and that early network users have lower demand elasticity for network use. The determinative vote is provided by the median voter located at $n/2$. A majority would not wish to have its benefits diluted by a number of beneficiaries larger than necessary. This is the principle of the "minimal winning coalition." Its size would be $n/2 + 1$.

A majority will establish itself such that it will benefit maximally from the minority. The minority that can be maximally burdened are the users with less elastic demand for telephone service, which are the early subscribers. But there is a limit to the burden. It is given by the utility $u(n)$ and a factor $k(n)$ to account for users' inability to adjust to a sudden absence of service in the short and middle term. K account for the assymmetry in entry and exit. Once one becomes a member of a network, the desirability of leaving it is larger than the utility of joining had been originally and if price gets pushed above $u(n)$ minority + $k(n)$, subscribers would drop off. The majority bears the rest of the cost. The minority's price $P_B$ will be such that $P_B = u(n_2) + k(n_2)$. The majority's price will then be[14]

$$P_A = (2/n_2)C(n_2) - u(n_2) - k(n_2) \qquad (7)$$

This then is the redistributory outcome, assuming no discrimination within majority and minority, and a fixed network size $n_2$.

## 3.8. Monopoly and Expansion

But such redistribution and size are not a stable equilibrium, for several reasons. As prices to the minority are pushed up to the limit and beyond, there are now incentives for the minority network members to exit the network and form new ones in which they would not bear the redistributory burden. This exit would deprive the majority of the source of its subsidy and is therefore undesirable to it. The way for the majority to prevent this "cream-skimming" or "cherry-picking" is to prohibit the establishment of another network. There are also incentives for arbitrage from low price to high price users. This, too, requires prohibition and enforcement. Thus, a monopoly system and the prevention of arbitrage become essential to the stability of the system.

At the same time, and importantly, the model predicts that the network is unstable insofar as it will expand beyond $n_2$ as shown in figure 2. For the majority, there is added marginal utility from added network members, while much of its cost is borne by the minority. The majority will therefore seek expansion. Initially, the majority would admit new members up to the point $n_5$ where marginal utility to its members is equal to the marginal price to them, subject to the maximum price extractable from the minority. But this is not the end of the story. With expansion to $n_5$, the majority is now $n_5/2$ rather than $n_2/2$, i.e. larger than before, and it can also tax a larger minority ($n_s/2$) than before. Hence, the expansion process would take place again, leading to a point $n'_s > n_s$. This process would continue, until an equilibrium would be reached at the point where a majority member maximizes welfare, $W_A$.

$$(du/dn) = o, \text{ where } W_A = u(n) - P_A \tag{8}$$

substituting from (7), we have

$$(du/dn) = u(n) - (2/n)C(n) + u(n) + k(n) \tag{9}$$

$$(dw/dn) = 2u'(n)-(2nC'(n)-C(n)/n^2) + k'(n) = 0 \tag{10}$$

This expression is positive at the private optimum $n_2$, leading to an optimum size

$$n5 > n2 \tag{11}$$

Figure 2
Redistribution in Networks

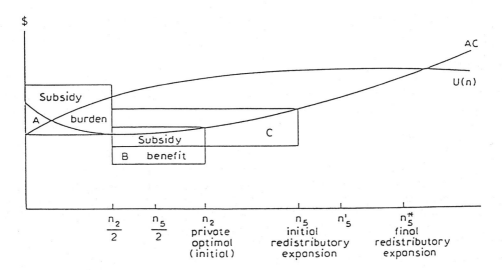

The difference in size varies with k. The greater the cost of dropping off the only network, the larger the network will become through redistribution. Protective rules of monopoly create a high k, and so does the greater dependency on network participation. However, if in the process $n_s/2$ becomes larger than the critical mass point $n_1$ (defined by $u(n1) = (c(n1)/n1))$ they could drop off and create a new network.

58

### 3.9. Network Tipping[15]

As this process of expansion takes place, the minority is growing, too. The likelihood that its size increases beyond the point of critical mass $n_1$ is increased, and the utility of its members, given the burden of subsidy, may well be below that of membership in a smaller but non-subsidizing alternative network. Suppose there are no legal barriers to the formation of a new network. In that case, a user's choice menu is to stay, to drop off altogether, or to join a new network association. Assume that the new network would have the same cost characteristics as the traditional network has. (In fact, it may well have a lower cost function for each given size if there has been accumulated monopolistic inefficiency in the existing network and rent-seeking behavior by various associated groups.)

Then, minority coalition members would find themselves to be better off in a new network B, and they would consider such a network, abandoning the old one. The only problem is that of transition discontinuity. A new network, in its early phases, would be a money-losing proposition up to its critical mass point $n'_1$.

The majority may attempt to alleviate these pressures to exit by reducing the redistributory burden and thus keeping the minority from dropping out. But that means the network size $n_5$ would not be optimal to the majority anymore, and members would have to be forced out. And this, in turn, would reduce its majority, so that it would have to drop the subsidizing burden from at least some minority members as the $n/2$ point separating the majority from the minority shifts leftwards.

This means either higher burdens on the shrinking minority — frustrating the purpose of bribing it into staying — or still less benefits for the majority if it wants to keep the network from fragmenting. Such a disequilibrium process will continue up to the point where the minority is too small to create a self-supporting new network. One might call this the effect of *potential exit* by the minority, and it results in a lessened redistribution.

### 3.10. Unequal User Size

We have assumed so far that network voters are of equal size. In reality however, some users are much larger in terms of lines n than others. The minority's position would be further weakened if voting were governed by a principle of "one subscriber, one vote" rather than the "one line, one vote" previously assumed.

Suppose users are ordered according to size on Figure 1; in other words, the largest users are those that have joined the network first. This is not unrealistic, since users with great needs for telecommunications are likely to have been the first to acquire a telephone, and early subscribers had the longest time to expand usage. Let us further represent the distribution of lines n for a user v by where $A > 0$, $a \geq 1$

$$n = Av^{-a} \tag{12}$$

The median voter (or median account) is $v/2$ and its preferences govern. But the network size provided by the users arrayed to the left of such median user is larger than those to the right. They are given by

$$n_m = A \int_{n/2}^{n} v^{-a} dv = \left( \frac{A}{1-a} \right) \left( 1 - \frac{n}{2^{1-a}} \right) \tag{13}$$

$n_m$, the median account, is to the right of $n/2$ in Figure 1. In other words, the median voter whose preferences govern is at a network size greater than the median point of the network size. The more the distribution of lines is skewed, (the larger the coefficients A and a) the further to the right is $n_m$. And the more skewed the distribution, the more likely is it that the voting minority will reach, by itself, a size beyond the critical mass point.

### 3.11. Interconnection

The process of unraveling of the existing network would commence even earlier if a new network has the right to interconnect into the previous one, because in that case it would enjoy the externality benefits of a larger reach $n_A + n_B$, while not being subject to redistributory burden. This is why interconnectivity is a critical issue for the establishment of alternative networks, as the historical examples demonstrate, from the *Kingsbury Commitment* in 1913[16] to *Execunet* in 1977[17] and today's *ONA*[18] and New York's *collocation*[19] proceedings.

Since the benefits of network reach remain minority subscribers', exit decision becomes strictly price-driven, and takes place if utility plays no role, price reach remains the same through interconnection.

Would there exist, for any sub-network, internal redistribution based on coalitions? Once the possibility of exit is established, each burdened sub-group could join another network. Thus, internal redistribution will happen only if a network is unique to its users.

Network interconnection means that the network still centers around as a society-wide concept of interconnected users. But it consists now of *multiple* subnetworks that are linked to each other. Each of these subnetworks has its own cost-sharing arrangements, with some mutual interconnection charges. Interconnection facilitates the emergence of new networks. It lowers entry barriers. On the other hand, it may reduce competition by establishing cooperative linkages instead of end-to-end rivalry.[20] Interconnection is a useful concept, because it responds to the often-made claim that a single network is necessary for universal reach. This is clearly incorrect. Interaction does not usually require institutional integrations, and this was one of Adam Smith's major insights. Otherwise, we would have only one large bank for all financial transactions.But as the next section will show, it also may lead to market failure in the establishment of the original network.

### 3.12. Subsidies for Reaching Critical Mass

We have mentioned before that waiting for demand to materialize prior to the introduction of a network or network service may not be the optimal private or public network policy. Demand is a function of price and benefits, both of which are in turn functions of the size of the network. Hence, early development of a network may require internal or external support in order to reach critical mass.

This suggests the need, in some circumstances, to subsidize the early stages of the network—up to the critical mass point $n_1$—when the user externalities are still low but cost shares high. These subsidies could come either from the network provider or its membership as a start-up investment, or from an external source such as a government as an investment in "infrastructure," a concept centered around externalities. The question now is how the internal support is affected by the emergence of a system of multiple networks.

The private start-up investment in a new form of network is predicated on an expectation of eventual break-even and subsequent positive net benefits to members. But if one can expect the establishment of additional networks, which would keep network size close to $n_1$, there would be only small (or no) net benefits realized by the initial entrants to offset their earlier investment. This would be further aggravated by interconnection rights, because a new network could make immediate use of the positive network externalities of the membership of the existing network that were achieved by the latter's investment. Hence, it is less likely that the initial risk would be undertaken if a loss were entirely borne by the initial network participants while the benefits would be shared with other entrants who would be able to interconnect and thus immediately gain the externality benefits of the existing network users, but without contributing to their cost-sharing. The implication is that in an environment of multiple networks which can interconnect, less start-up investment would be undertaken. It pays to be second. A situation of market failure exists.

How could one offset this tendency if it is deemed undesirable? Patents are one solution. Where a service is innovative but not patentable, one might create a "regulatory patent" for a limited period of protection. Similarly, interconnection rights might be deferred for a period, or joint introductions be planned that eliminate the first entrant penalty. But these measures would also reduce the usefulness of alternative networks, and could hence lead to the dynamics of political expansion, redistribution, and break-up described in earlier section.

It is quite possible, moreover, that none of these measures would be as effective in generating the investment support in the way that a monopoly network would that can reap all future benefits. This would mean that the private and social benefits of networks in the range between $n_1$ and $n_4$ would not be realized. In such a situation, there may be a role for direct outside support, such as by a government subsidy. This may strike one at first as paradoxical. Shouldn't a competitive system of multiple networks be *less* in need of government involvement than a monopoly? But just as the subsidies to individual network users that were previously *internally* generated by other network users will have to be raised *externally* (through the normal mechanism of taxation and allocation) if at least some users are still to be supported, so might subsidies to the start-up of a network as a whole have to be provided externally, also through taxation and allocation, where network externalities as well as start-up costs are high enough to make the establishment of a network desirable.

### 3.13. Social Welfare and Multiple Networks

If network associations can control their memberships, stratification is inevitable. They will seek those members who will provide them with the greatest externality benefits -- those that have many actual or potential contacts with. Furthermore, they will want to admit low-cost, high volume, good risk customers as club members. Thus, different affinity-group networks and different average costs will emerge.

But what about social welfare in such a differentiated system? The traditional fear is that the loss of some cost-sharing and externalities brought by a second network would reduce social welfare. But the news is not necessarily bad. Where the network was at $n_3$ or substantially larger than the socially optimal size $n_4$, the fracture of the network could increase social welfare, depending on the cost and utility functions, if cost closer to $n_0$ is reached. Where mutual interconnection is assured, one can keep the externalities benefits (and even increase them) while moving down the cost curve towards a lower AC. Furthermore, the cost curves themselves are likely to be lower with the ensuing competition.

The welfare implications of the formation of collective consumption and production arrangements is something analyzed by theorists of clubs.[21] The club analysis, applied to networks, can show:

1. Given mobility of choice, different groups will cluster together in different associations according to quality, size, price, interaction, and ease of internal decision-making. The economically optimal association size need not encompass the entire population.[22]

   Optimal group size will vary according to the dimension to be optimized. Optimal group size depends on the ratio of marginal utilities for different dimensions, set equal to the ratio of transformation in production, and is in turn related to size.[23] But this does not imply that one should keep networks non-ubiquitous and unequal. Financial transfers can be used.

However:

2. It is generally not Pareto-efficient to attempt income transfer by integrating diverse groups and imposing varying cost shares according to some equity criteria. It is more efficient to allow sub-groups to form their own associations and then re-distribute by imposing charges on some groups and distribute to others. The set of possible utility distributions among separate groups dominates (weakly) the set of such distributions among integrated groups. User group separation with direct transfer is more efficient than the indirect method of enforced togetherness with different cost shares. In other words, differentiated networks plus taxation or another system of revenue shifting such as access and interconnection charges, is more efficient than monopoly and internal redistribution.

## 4. CONCLUSION

The analysis of the model means that a network coalition, left to itself under majority-rule principles, would expand beyond the size that would hold under rules of equal treatment of each subscriber. Such an arrangement can be stable only as long as arbitrage is prevented, as long as the minority cannot exercise political power in other ways, and, most importantly, as long as it has no choice but to stay within the burdensome network arrangement.

But beyond that point, the pro-expansion policy creates incentives to form alternative networks. And the more successful network policy is in terms of achieving universal service and "affordable rates," the greater the pressures for fracture of the network. Hence, the very success of network expansion bears the seed of its own demise. This is what we can call the "tragedy of the common network," in the Greek drama sense of unavoidable doom, and borrowing from the title of G. Hardin's classic article "The Tragedy of the Commons"[24] on the depletion of environmental resources.[25] In the case of telecommunications the tragedy is that the breakdown of the common network is not caused by the failure of the system but rather from its very success -- the spread of service across society and the transformation of a convenience into a necessity.

62

## ENDNOTES

[1.] I am grateful to Bruce Greenwald and Julianne Nelson for their helpful comments.

[2.] The United Kingdom, for example, has created a telecommunications duopoly and allowed Mercury to compete with a privatized British Telecom for local and long-distance service; Germany has removed its telecommunications operator, Deutsche Bundespost, from the Ministry of Posts and Telegraphs, leaving the latter a regulatory role only; Japan privatized its telecommunications monopoly service provider, NTT, and has allowed entry into all telecommunications sectors, including local service, under various conditions; and the European Community has called for the separation of regulatory and operations functions for all member states, and has mandated a liberalized entry policy for value-added services. See generally, Eli M. Noam, *Telecommunications in Europe*, New York: Oxford University Press, 1991.

[3.] One attempt was a US Department of Justice report on the post-divestiture network. Huber, Peter, *The Geodesic Network*, Washington D.C.: U.S. Government Printing Office, 1987. Another approach is that of Koichiro Hayashi of NTT. "The Economies of Networking - Implications for Telecommunications Liberalization," paper presented at the IIC Conference, Washington, D.C., Sept. 1988.

[4.] See, for example, Ithiel de Sola Pool, *Technologies of Freedom*, Cambridge Mass.: Harvard University Press, 1983 ("This development [diminishing importance of distance to cost], along with the development of multiple technologies of communication and of cheap microprocessors, will foster a trend toward pluralistic and competitive communication systems." p. 229); George Gilder, *Microcosm: The Quantum Revolution in Economics and Technology*, New York: Simon & Schuster, 1989; J.S. Mayo, "The Evolution of Information Technologies," in *Information Technology and Social Transformation*, B.R. Guile, ed., Washington, DC: National Acadamy Press, 1985; S.F. Starr, "New communications technologies and civic culture in the USSR," Paper presented at the Center for International Affairs, Harvard University, October 1987 (arguing technological options and convergence of data processing and transmission made pluralization inevitable even in centrally planned economies).

[5.] Baumol, William J., Panzar, John C., and Willig, Robert D., *Contestable Markets and the Theory of Industry Structure*, New York: Harcourt Brace Jovanovich, 1982.

[6.] Shepherd, William, "Concepts of Competition and Efficient Policy in the Telecommunications Sector," in Eli M. Noam, ed., *Telecommunications Today and Tomorrow*, New York: Harcourt Brace Jovanovich, 1983.

[7.] I will follow the analysis in Noam, Eli, "The Next Stage in Telecommunications Evolution: The Pluralistic Network," paper presented at the Pacific Telecommunications Conference, Japan, October 1988. For sections 1-4, I adapt part of the methodology of my colleague Geoffrey Heal, "The Economics of Networks," Columbia University, unpublished paper, 1989, for which I am indebted.

The model of the present paper can also be used for "standards coalitions" rather than "network coalitions." For the literature on standards, see David, Paul A., "Some new standards for the economists of standardization in the information age," in P. Dasgupta and P.L. Stoneman, eds., *Economic policy and technological performance*, Cambridge, U.K.: Cambridge University Press, 1987b.

[8.] For convexity, assume u(c,P,1) > u(c,P,o), i.e. the first user has positive benefits even if no one else is on the network. Network externalities are discussed in Brown, Stephen and David Sibley, *The Theory of Public Utility Pricing*, Cambridge University Press, 1986. See also W.W. Sharkey, *The Theory of Natural Monopoly*, Cambridge, U.K.: Cambridge University Press, 1982.

[9.] More completely, if a user's budget y goes toward network access P and other goods x (with $P_x = 1$)

$$y = P + x \tag{9.1}$$

Then u = u(n,y-P)  With average cost pricing, thus becomes the indirect utility function

$$u = u(n, y - (C(n))/n) = u(n) + y - (c(n))/n \tag{9.2}$$

if utility is expressed in monetary units.

[10.]Heal defines it, similarly, as

$$u (y/p - [F + f(n)]/np; n) = u(y/p; 0). \tag{10.1}$$

See also, David Allen, "Net telecommunications service: Network externalities and critical mass," *Telecommunications Policy*, September, 1988, pp. 257-271.

[11.]This is not to suggest that such self-restriction in size actually exists. Almost always, there is a governmental requirement for expansion instead of genuine self-government of users. An example is Bolivia, where local subscribers are members of cooperatives, and have resisted an expansion that reduces the value of the their membership shares.

[12.]We assume that the utility off network is equal to income y of the budget constraint.

$$u(o,x) = y \tag{12.1}$$

[13.]This analysis should not suggest that a self-governing and voting mechanism exists in reality (although it exists for telephone cooperatives in Finland and the US), but rather to understand the pressures and dynamics that are transmitted to the governmental institutions which embody the different user interests.

[14.]We use in the following the continuous n/2 rather than the discrete (n/2) - 1 and (n/2) +1.

[15.]The terminology of "tipping" is due to Schelling, Thomas, *Micromotives and Macrobehavior*, New York: W.W. Norton, 1978.

[16.]Letter of Nathan C. Kingsbury, vice-president of AT&T, to James McReynolds, U.S. Attorney General, dated December 19, 1913 (AT&T agreed to connect independent telephone companies to the AT&T network, among other provisions, as a compromise to avoid antitrust litigation).

[17.]MCI Telecommunications Corp. v. FCC, 561 F.2d 365 (D.C. Cir. 1977) (*Execunet I*); see also, *MCI Telecommunications Corp. v. FCC*, 580 F.2d 590 (D.C. Cir.) (*Execunet II*), *cert. denied*, 439 U.S. 980 (1978).

[18.]Third Computer Inquiry, 104 FCC 2d 958 (1986), *modified*, 2 FCC Rcd 3035 (1987), *further reconsid. denied*, 3 FCC Rad 1135, *vacated and remanded*, California v. FCC, 905 F.2d 1217 (9th Cir. 1990).

[19.]Opinion No. 89-12, *Opinion and Order Concerning Regulatory Response to Competition*, Case 29469, New York State Public Service Commission, issued May 16, 1989, at 24-29.

[20.]Mueller, Milton, "Interconnection Policy and Network Economics," paper presented at Telecommunications Policy Research Conference, Airlie, Virginia, Oct. 31, 1988.

[21.]Schelling, Thomas C., *Models of Segregation*, Santa Monica: Rand, 1969. Buchanan, James M, and Tullock, Gordon, *The Calculus of Consent*, Ann Arbor, Mich.: The University of Michigan Press, 1965. Tullock, Gordon, "Public Decisions as Public Goods," *Journal of Political Economy*, no. 179: no. 4: 913-918, July-Aug. 1971. Rothenberg, Jerome, "Inadvertent Distributional Impacts in the Provision of Public Services to Individuals" in Grieson, Ronald, ed., *Public and Urban Economics*, Lexington, Mass.: Lexington Books, 1976. Tiebout, Charles, "A Pure Theory of Local Expenditures," *Journal of Political Economy*, 64: no. 5:414-424,

1956. McGuire, Martin, "Private Good Clubs and Public Good Clubs: Economic Models of Group Formation," *Swedish Journal of Economics,* 74: no.1: 84-99, 1972.

[22.]The results discussed would not hold if the marginal costs of new network participants drops continuously more than their marginal benefits to an existing network user. The latter is unlikely since marginal cost, beyond a certain range, is either flat or very slowly decreasing, or in fact increasing.

[23.]Buchanan, *op. cit.*, p. 4,5.

[24.]Hardin, Garrett, "The Tragedy of the Commons," *Science*, vol. 162, Dec. 13, 1968.

[25.]Tragedy is used in the sense of Alfred North Whitehead: "The essence of traumatic tragedy is not unhappiness. It resides in the solemnity of the remorseless working of things."

PRIVATE NETWORKS PUBLIC OBJECTIVES
E. Noam and A. NíShúilleabháin (Editors)
© 1996 Elsevier Science B.V. All rights reserved.

The User-Driven Network: The Present Extent of Private Networking in the United States

Milton Mueller

## 1. INTRODUCTION

One of the most far-reaching consequences of deregulating telecommunications equipment and services is the ability of businesses to build and operate their own communication systems. Private networking can be viewed as both a cause and a consequence of telecommunications liberalization. The existence of large users with their own distinct communications needs and information equipment put pressure on regulators to open up the telecommunications marketplace. The subsequent liberalization of ownership and interconnection arrangements in turn made it easier for companies to develop their own networks. This has resulted in a tremendous shift in the network's center of gravity, from the center to the periphery. Initiative and innovation now are more likely to come from the end user, and more specifically from the capabilities of privately-owned customer premises equipment, than from the operators of public networks.

How far has private networking gone in the United States? There is little quantitative information about this, because private networks by definition are created by unregulated entities exempt from the reporting requirements which allow us to track the investment and usage of common carrier networks. Worse yet, the categories used to count investment reflect a separation between the worlds of telecommunications and computers that may have existed decades ago, but is no longer valid. This paper draws on a variety of data sources to provide some rough proportional estimates of the present extent of private networking in the United States.

Macroeconomic data suggests that something important is happening, although it is unable to define just what it is. Robert Crandall discovered a divergence between the total consumption of telecommunications equipment in the U.S. and the investment of the common carriers. Using aggregate statistics from the Commerce Department, the Census Bureau, the FCC, and the United States Telephone Association, he found a 162% increase in overall consumption of telecommunications equipment, but only a 64% increase in the common carriers' capital expenditures. Crandall locates a large part of the growth in equipment in the specific category "Nonbroadcast Communication Equipment," which includes fiber optic equipment, satellite equipment, and point-to-point radio. He also discovered a large surge in central office switching equipment and carrier line equipment. He concludes that "rapid growth in the sale of this equipment indicates a growing importance of newer technologies in building private and common carriage systems."[1]

This conclusion, while suggestive, does not move us any closer to a quantification of private networking's impact, because the data do not distinguish between new networks which are carriers of other people's traffic and truly *private* networks. Some of the growth is accounted for by new interexchange carriers, information service providers, and other entities that represent new service providers rather than user-driven privatization. Crandall's data could simply be a measure of the growth in supply created by a more diverse and competitive environment. A deeper problem is that "telecommunications equipment" is probably the wrong place to look for the growth of private networking. As we shall see, the area in which private users are taking the greatest initiative is in new applications of computer and information processing technologies to the management of their organizational communications. Such investments probably show up in entirely different categories.

## 2. SOME DEFINITIONS AND DISTINCTIONS

The phenomenon of private networking must be understood within the framework of the theory of the firm. This theory posits two distinct methods for a company to acquire what it needs for its operations. One is to purchase it from an outside producer, via a market transaction. The other is to produce it itself. The structure of the firm and of the industry is determined by the extent to which "markets" or "hierarchies" turn out to be the most efficient choice. The relevance to our topic should be obvious. When we ask why firms engage in private networking as opposed to relying on common carriers, we are asking why they choose to rely on internal hierarchies rather than market transactions with outside suppliers to supply their communication needs. The crux of the public/private distinction is that in private networks, a firm produces its own network services by combining intermediate inputs into a final product (a telecommunications network service). Although it may order facilities, services, and equipment from outside suppliers, the real responsibility for assembling and operating the network is *internalized*.

The theory of the firm outlines several reasons why firms might rely on themselves instead of a market transaction to supply a needed service. None of them appear to fit the case of networks very well, however. The aspect of the theory that comes closest to our needs is that of *asset-specificity*, wherein the network can be viewed as a highly specialized product customized to the needs of a specific user. The theory's explanation of why firms exert direct control over custom-made inputs focuses on vertical integration as a way of avoiding opportunistic behavior on the part of a supplier. In the case of telecommunications networks, however, protection against opportunism does not appear to be the main consideration; rather, it is a combination of cost savings and the telephone company's inability to offer sufficiently customized or advanced products. Most telephone companies have proven to be unwilling or unable to create optimal combinations of intermediate inputs suited to the specific needs of firms; or if they do, the costs are higher than if the firm does it for itself. Many firms have discovered that they can reap substantial economic and strategic benefits by taking over network ownership or management, or both.

Stigler's[2] and Williamson's[3] theory of the life cycle of the firm posits a general trend toward vertical *dis*integration as an industry grows. Does internalization of network management represent more integration or more disintegration? There is an apparent paradox here. The vertical disintegration of the end-to-end service of the traditional public network is accompanied by a growing number of firms integrating forward into the assembly and management of networks. Management-internalization thus could be seen as a reversion to a less specialized market structure, because functions that once were hired out are now being supplied internally. At the same time, privatization goes hand-in-hand with the disintegration of the telecommunications system into its piece-parts, and the growth of pluralism and specialization in the component markets. If multiple firms can make decisions regarding intermediate network inputs independently, then multiple suppliers, competition, technological variation, and specialization in the intermediate market will be supported. The privatization of management feeds upon and reinforces the breakup of the end-to-end network into its component parts, and encourages proliferation of the suppliers of those component parts. Hence, in the long run, use-privatization leads to much greater specialization in telecommunications services and facilities even though it internalizes or integrates the network management function.

Once "internalization of network management" is accepted as the distinction between public and private networks there is no reason to assume *a priori* that the network "private sector" will continue to grow at the expense of the "public sector" indefinitely. Internalization may be simply a temporary response to the uncertainties of deploying new technology, or to the inadequacies of the POTS-based telephone companies and the pricing distortions of regulated monopoly. Network management functions that are now internalized may migrate back to third-party providers as the telecommunications industry becomes more competitive, flexible, integrated, and experienced in the ways of telematics. CitiBank doesn't want to be one of the world's biggest telecommunications companies; it has to be because no existing third-party firm has the geographic scope or expertise needed to handle its special communications needs any better than it handles them itself. Most private networks have emerged to meet new or extremely specialized communications needs. On the other hand, it is also possible that fundamental changes in technology and economics *will* result in the permanent privatization of many network capabilities. Hence the issue of quantification becomes important. How often does private networking occur, and in which direction is the trend?

## 3. TWO TYPES OF PRIVATE NETWORKING

In the course of attempting to quantify private networking I found it necessary to introduce a distinction between two very different kinds of private networks. Let us call them "Type A" private networks and "Type B" private networks. The distinction turns on whether the network is *confined to the user's own premises* (Type A), or is *distributed across multiple sites* (Type B). With Type A private networks, the user organization takes control of network management and equipment selection on its own premises, but relies primarily on the public system for communication links to outside points (including remote office sites of the same organization). With a Type B private network, the privatization of network management is extended to multiple sites via privately owned or dedicated transmission facilities.

Type A private networks are user-driven facilities for intrapremises telecommunication. They are owned, managed and maintained by the user or leased from a third party contractor, but not from the telephone company. LANs and PBXs are the fundamental examples of Type A private networks, but the category also can include larger networks formed by fiber, copper, or radio linkages connecting buildings on a corporate or university campus. The transmission facilities of Type A networks, however, do not cross public rights of way; they are limited in scope to the user's contiguous territory. They may either be closed, stand-alone networks (like a typical LAN), or have an outlet to the public switched network (like a typical PBX). If they are interconnected, however, traffic to other sites must be delivered over the public network for it to qualify as a Type A private network.

Type B private networks use *either* owned *or* dedicated transmission facilities to connect customer-owned telecommunication or information processing facilities on more than one office site. In a Type B private network, the transmission facilities need not be owned by the user, but the end-to-end communications paths must be dedicated exclusively to the user. An example is a closed, intracorporate voice network that uses IXC leased lines to connect privately owned PBXs in geographically dispersed office sites. Another example would be a data network using VSAT technology to connect data terminals owned by a company in multiple office sites. The primary difference between Type B and Type A private networks is that the Type B user's networking responsibilities extend beyond its own building or office complex. Generally speaking (and recognizing that the boundaries can be porous) Type B networks are not accessible via the public network. Of course, it is possible for a single organization to have both Type A and Type B private networks. For example, a company with a nationwide Type B data network might also own separate LANs and PBXs. Software Defined Networks do *not* count as Type B private networks, or as private networks at all, for two reasons: first, they involve shared use of a public carrier's switched transmission facilities; second, the management of the traffic flow is handled primarily by the carrier, not the user.

One can nit-pick at this distinction, particularly when large users employ complex mixtures of public, Type A, and Type B facilities. But the distinction is real and important nevertheless. As we shall see, it corresponds to two distinct categories of network privatization, categories with quantifiably distinct characteristics and trends. Type A and Type B private networks are appropriate for very different classes of users, have different effects upon the public network, and reveal different trends. On the whole, the picture of network privatization that we get from making the distinction is far clearer than the one we get when we ignore it.

With this framework in mind, I set out to quantify the extent of private networking in the United States. This was done with no funding support, so the methods are crude and the estimates are very rough. Nevertheless, the results are clear enough to enable some basic conclusions to be drawn.

## 4. QUANTIFYING TYPE B PRIVATE NETWORKING

When "private networks" are discussed in the course of CITI conferences, most people appear to have Type B private networks in mind. They are thinking of large, geographically distributed, closed user networks, exemplified by SITA or the FTS 2000 network. Sometimes we are left with the implication that these large private networks threaten to outstrip the public system in size, resources, or technological leverage. But there is surprisingly little quantitative information about such private networks. How many are there? How do they compare in size to the common carrier networks? Are they growing or shrinking in number?

Consulting organizations and industry associations have conducted surveys of large corporate telecommunications users, but they are not very useful from this standpoint.[4]

Generally, these surveys are not constructed to facilitate a comparison between the size of the private networks *vis a vis* the public network. They simply monitor the behavior and attitudes of corporate networkers. They rarely introduce a distinction between public and private facilities, so that the information they derive applies as much to large corporate users' consumption of public network service as it does to their management of private networks.

The paper's approach to quantification is based on the study of a microcosm. Because counting and measuring the number of Type B private networks in the U.S. was simply impossible given the time and resources available to the author, we limited our study to the state of Nebraska. Nebraska is a small state, but it has a sophisticated telecommunications sector and a closely-knit community of telecommunications managers. This made it possible for us to identify all of the actual or potential Type B private networks in the state, and to directly administer a survey to them. The rationale behind this approach is simple. Through reports to the public utility commission we know the size of the public switched network in the state along various dimensions: plant, route miles, stations, etc. If we can identify most or all of the Type B networks in the state and acquire comparable information about them, we can derive an empirical estimate of the proportions of public and private networking that is valid in at least one geographic area. One can have any opinion one likes about the generalizability of this evidence, but this much is certain: one case is one more than we have now.

Even in this limited context there are still significant gaps in the data. Our survey required busy telecommunication managers to give us a raft of details about their capital expenditures, operating budgets, future plans, number of terminals and sites, etc. Many were cooperative, but some simply refused. Some of those who cooperated were unable to answer some of our questions.

Figure 1
Capital Investment of Type B Private Networks vs. Public Carriers

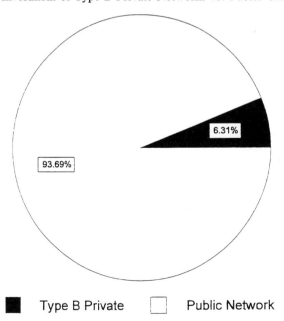

There were 232 establishments in Nebraska with 250 or more employees in 1989 (Figure 1). Of that number, we estimate that approximately 25, or 11 percent, managed Type B private telecommunication networks. We were able to obtain survey information from 16 of them. (Table 1) The largest of these networks, in terms of the value of the capital equipment they owned, were associated with a class of business known as "right of way" companies: railroads, power utilities, and pipelines. These companies were much more likely to own rather than lease transmission capacity. They accounted for 65% of the book value of equipment, and 88% of the fiber and microwave route miles.

Table 1

| Establishment | Employ | # Sites | Type | # Voice | # Data | Val $m | %V | %D |
|---|---|---|---|---|---|---|---|---|
| 1. Union Pac RR | 12000 | 85 | voi + data | 7500 | 2500 | $34.50 | 80% | 95% |
| 2. NPPD | 2256 | 28 | voi + data | 1350 | 375 | $12.00 | 70% | 85% |
| 3. OPPD | 2482 | 24 | voi + data | 3444 | 1500 | $25.39 | 75% | 75% |
| 4. State DAS | 16000 | 400 | data | 0 | 8500 | $6.00 | 0% | 95% |
| 5. UNL | | 3 | data | 0 | 2000 | $3.00 | 0% | 80% |
| 6. UNO/UNMC | 6000 | 3 | voi + data | 6000 | 1800 | $2.10 | 2% | 80% |
| 7. Creighton Univ | 2000 | 2 | data | 0 | 500 | $1.30 | 0% | 75% |
| <the next five | | | voi + data | | | | | |
| respondents | | | data | | | | | |
| combined to | 8816 | 602 | data | 5984 | 6301 | $10.92 | 3% | 77% |
| maintain | | | data | | | | | |
| confidentiality | | | data | | | | | |
| <the next four | | | data | | | | | |
| respondents | | | data | | | | | |
| combined to | 3500 | 37 | data | | 2374 | $15.99 | 8% | 87% |
| maintain | | | data | | | | | |
| confidentiality | | | data | | | | | |
| 17. Marriott | | | | | | | | |
| 18. Lincoln Elec. | | | | | | | | |
| 19. Peo Nat Gas | | | | | | | | |
| 20. Peter Kiewit | | | no data | | | | | |
| 21. GSA-feds | | | | | | | | |
| 22. Offutt AFB | | | | | | | | |
| 23. ConAgra | | | | | | | | |
| 24. Woodmen | | | | | | | | |
| | | | | | | | | |
| TOTALS | 53054 | 1184 | | 24278 | 25850 | $111.20 | | |

The second largest category was government. This included the state Department of Communication, a branch of the Division of Administrative Services (DAS), and the University of Nebraska system, which includes two campuses in Lincoln, the University of Nebraska at Omaha, the University of Nebraska Medical Center, and the Peter Kiewit Conference Center. We did not attempt to count the state Educational Television Network

(ETV) because of its status as a broadcast network. Unfortunately, we were unable to obtain information about the federal government network or the network at the Offutt Air Force Base. Federal government offices in the state utilize the FTS 2000 private network, but the GSA was unable to give us any useful information about its size in Nebraska. Each federal agency orders capacity from it independently, making information gathering most difficult. The military, of course, was concerned with the security implications.

Financial service companies and banks were the third category. Many had private data networks, but they were smaller and more dependent on leased facilities from public carriers. One bank, however, had just installed a private radio system to replace leased lines as the basis of its ATM network. See Figure 2 for a chart of the relative proportions of each sector.

The Type B networks which answered our survey linked 24,278 voice terminals and 25,850 data terminals in the state. By way of comparison, the state's local exchange carriers serve a total of 887,988 access lines, 215,966 of which were business access lines, in 1991. The 24,278 voice terminals served by Type B nets represents 2.73% of all access lines and 11.24% of all business access lines in the state. Of course, there is no way to know exactly how many data terminals are linked via the public network, so a comparison on that dimension cannot be made.

Figure 2
Type B Private Networks in Nebraska: Share of Capital Investment

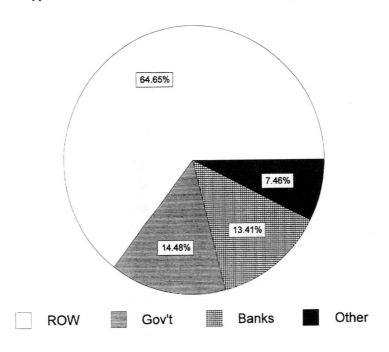

Five of the sixteen responding Type B networks had voice capabilities, while the remainder were primarily data networks. The last two columns in Table 1 represents the network manager's estimate of how much of the organization's voice (%V) and data (%D) traffic is carried by the private network. Private voice networks typically serve intra-organizational voice communication only and thus carry a lower percentage of the traffic generated by the organization than data networks. For example, the University of Nebraska at Omaha's Type B network consists of a privately owned fiber cable linking the UNO campus with the Medical Center and a downtown conference center. While the network carries an estimated 80% of the data generated by the organization, only 2% of its voice traffic is confined to that network.

The combined book value of the surveyed Type B networks was equal to approximately $111.2 million. This is 6.31% of the total plant in service of the state's local exchange and interexchange carriers (Figure 1). This number might go up to all of 8% if the missing networks were included. Although of course there is no way to be sure of the size of the missing data points, we are sure that we do have information for the largest networks. Type B networks which rely on leased lines for transmission simply are not very capital-intensive relative to the public network, even if, as is the case with the state government, a large number of terminals are served.

Table 2
Attitudes and Plans of Type B Network Managers

Ranking of Motives for Type B Private Networking

| Motive | 1st | 2nd | 3rd | 4th |
|---|---|---|---|---|
| Cost Savings | 56% | 11% | 33% | 0 |
| Control of Network Management | 22% | 33% | 45% | 0 |
| Inability to get desired service from carriers | 11% | 33% | 23% | 33% |
| Security | 11% | 22% | 0 | 67% |

Type B Private Networks: Trends

| Since 1945 | | Future Plans | |
|---|---|---|---|
| More Private | 10 (62%) | More Private | 2 (12.5%) |
| More Public | 3 (19%) | More Public | 6 (37.5%) |
| Same | 3 (19%) | Same | 8 (50%) |

Plan a Shift to SDN?

| Yes | 7 (44%) | No | 9 (56%) |
|---|---|---|---|

We asked the network managers a series of questions about private vs. public networking (Table 2). Four motives for private networking were presented to the respondents and they were asked to rank order them. Cost savings was ranked first most frequently; "Security" was ranked last the most often (by two-thirds of the respondents). Control of network management was important, but not overwhelmingly so; two respondents ranked it first and three ranked it second in importance. The aggregation of the responses conceals very different attitudes among managers, however.

When asked to indicate "how [their] company's reliance on its Type B private network has changed since 1985," almost two thirds answered that they thought they had moved toward "more reliance on [their] private network." When asked about future trends, however, half (50%) said they expected things to remain at the same level. Of the remainder, 37.5% thought they would rely more on public networks and 12.5% thought they would rely more on private networks. Those who expected to rely more on private networks were also those with the largest investments in privately owned transmission facilities.

We also asked respondents whether they planned to shift some of their voice or data traffic which is now on a Type B private network to a Software Defined Network in the future. A significant number planned to do so: 44% said "Yes" and 56% answered "No." The Yes's tended to be the Type B networkers who relied more on leased rather than owned facilities. Our Nebraska survey discovered that 7 of 40 businesses (17.5%) with 100 or more employees were using SDN for voice and/or data communication. Many of these companies were large users who otherwise would have been prime candidates for Type B private networks: United Parcel, Vickers (a large manufacturing firm), ConAgra, as well as the state government. Coincidentally, perhaps, information derived from the AT&T Network Operations Center in Bedminster, New Jersey indicates that SDN traffic accounts for 17% of the calls on AT&T's switched interexchange network.

The story of the state government's network strategy is a good illustration of the motives underlying the trend towards SDN. In 1985-86, the state used its own network constructed of FX and WATS lines for voice and data communication. This saved money but created heavy managerial burdens. According to state communications director Bill Miller, the staff was responsible for tracking down service outages, and spent one and a half weeks each month running algorithms to optimize the cost efficiency of its facilities. An impetus for change was created when AT&T announced that it was withdrawing its Telpak tariff in 1986. The withdrawal of Telpak would have raised the state's costs by 100%. In 1987 the state temporarily outsourced its voice services to Lintel Long Distance. Then in 1989 it signed a five year contract with AT&T for a software defined network. The SDN gives them dedicated links to seven locations in the state, and uses shared facilities to all other points. Under the SDN contract, the state Communications Division re-markets long distance service to city governments, high schools, and other state agencies. (The withdrawal of the Telpak tariff also prompted the state's Educational Television network to shift from microwave to satellite facilities.)

How representative is this experience? In this case there is some national data to draw upon: The National Association of State Telecommunications Directors' 1991 Membership Survey. The survey contains some information about private networking by states, although unfortunately its definitions and data categories are not compatible with the framework of this study. According to the NASTD survey, many state telecommunication directors are facing budget restrictions and heavy pressures to cut costs. Twenty-six of thirty-five responding states reported using "private networks under bulk tariffs" as a "step their organization has taken to control expenditures in the last two years." This was second only to "increased cost monitoring" as the most frequently cited cost-controlling measure. Unfortunately, "private networks under bulk tariffs" was not defined by the survey, and it is clear that the term was interpreted by many states in a way which *includes* software defined networks. Nebraska, for example, is listed as one of the states which has shifted toward "private" networking when in fact it has moved in the opposite direction. An establishment which is migrating to SDN from a privately managed network based on leased lines, is moving *away* from user-driven privatization toward greater facilities sharing and fewer management responsibilities.

Table 3

|  | Fiber | Copper | Microwave | Cellular | Combined |
|---|---|---|---|---|---|
| Own 75-100% | 6 | 3 | 14 | 5 | 5 |
| Lease 75-100% | 22 | 19 | 14 | 9 | 11 |
| Mixed (25-75% O&L) | 3 | 7 | 1 | 0 | 15 |
| Total States Responding | 31 | 29 | 29 | 14 | 31 |

| Future Trends | Lease | Own |
|---|---|---|
| Totals: | 18 (75%) | 6 (25%) |

| States with an existing preference for ownership (5) | Kentucky, Massachusetts, South Carolina, Texas, Utah |
|---|---|
| States now mixed or oriented toward leasing but planning to move toward more ownership (3) | Mississippi, Tennessee, Wyoming |
| States now oriented toward owning but planning to move toward more leasing (0) | none |
| States now mixed but planning to move toward more leasing (10) | Alabama, Arizona, Colorado, Connecticut,, Louisiana, Maryland, Montana, New Mexico, Ohio, Pennsylvania |

The NASTD survey contains some interesting information about ownership patterns (Table 3). It is clear that states are using a complex mixture of owned and leased facilities, but some patterns emerge. Copper and fiber facilities are more likely to be leased than owned. (22 states lease 75-100% of their fiber capacity, and only six states own 100% of their fiber networks.) The pattern for microwave networks, on the other hand, is more balanced. Fourteen states own 75% or more of their microwave facilities, while fourteen states lease 75-100% of them. Copper facilities are also more often leased than owned; nineteen states lease 90% or more of their facilities, three states own 75% or more, and seven states mix owned and leased facilities near a 50-50 balance. If the ownership-leasing patterns for each of the four media are combined, we find only five states with an across-the board preference for ownership, less than half of the number of states (eleven) which consistently lease. Fifteen states maintain a mixture.

The predominant future direction seems to be toward leasing rather than ownership. However, as was the case with the Nebraska Type B networks, systems which have already made a commitment to ownership are more likely to continue that trend. Eighteen of thirty responding states said that they would move toward leasing rather than owning in the future. Six said they would move toward ownership. Six said they would maintain a mix of owned and leased facilities. Many states cited the budget contraints of the past few years as the reasons for favoring leasing over ownership.

In conclusion, an analysis of Type B private networking reveals the following measurements and trends. Large, distributed private networks are rare; only 11% of the larger businesses and only 1.4% of all establishments with fifty or more employees have them. Within the category of Type B networks, there are two distinct types: those based on owned transmission facilities and those based on leased transmission facilities. Type B networks based on leasing are not totally disappearing, but in the voice world there is a distinct trend toward outsourcing management responsibilities and achieving sharing economies via SDNs. In the past, cost savings available via leased lines prompted large users to assume network management responsibilities; today, cost considerations are driving them *away* from Type B private networks. Most ownership-based private networks, on the other hand, plan to intensify their usage of their private facilities and continue down the path of ownership. The primary economic impediment to ownership-based Type B networks is not just the investment in communications equipment itself, but access to rights of way. That is why right of way companies have the most extensive private networks and also why most growth in such private networks is likely to occur via applications of radio, or applications of fiber with minimal right of way issues, such as intra-campus or point-to-point links between two office sites.

Type B private networking began primarily as a response to the pricing distortions of regulation, particularly the underpricing of dedicated lines that occurred with AT&T's first predatory responses to competition in that market in the 1970s. Although there are other, less directly cost-related reasons for Type B private networking, those motivations affect a relatively small and specialized portion of the business world.

## 5. TYPE A PRIVATE NETWORKS

The real growth in private networking is occurring on a much smaller scale. The growth of workplace PCs, distributed computing, and voice processing technology is increasingly turning the office into the site of an internal private network. In order to avail themselves of the full range of computer products and services, business managers are constructing intra-organizational networks and assuming responsibility for network management functions.  By the same token, the product and software markets are evolving in ways that make it progressively easier and less costly for businesses to assume this function.

Type A private networking is a product of the deregulation and detariffing of customer premises equipment in the 1970s.  It represents a permanent and cumulative revolution in the relationship between users and the public network.  For decades, the telephone companies' control of access and transport gave them leverage over the type of terminal equipment that could be used in the home and the office.  Now the tables are turned; CPE deregulation and privatization lead to enormous diversity and specialization in equipment and processes at the customer end.  Consequently, end-user equipment increasingly drives the kind of access and transport services offered by the public network.

In order to quantify Type A private networking, we drew on nationwide data regarding LAN and PBX markets and on our own survey of forty Nebraska businesses.

## 5.1. LANs

Local Area Networks are proliferating at an extraordinary pace.  In Nebraska in 1991, 78% of all establishments with more than 100 employees had installed one or more LANs.  Since 1986, the number of installations has grown by 800%, and the number more than doubled in the last two years alone.

Table 4[5]
Number of PCs in Use, 1986-1991

| Year | Total PCs in Use (millions) | Workplace PCs (millions) | Workplace PCs Networked (%) |
|------|------|------|------|
| 1986 | 13.834* | 9.148** | 06%** |
| 1987 | 18.121* | 12.279** | 13%** |
| 1988 | 23.208* | 16.976** | 18%** |
| 1989 | 33.058* | 21.984** | 26%** |
| 1990 | 43.164*** | 28.920*** | 33%*** |
| 1991 | 53.731*** | 36.000*** | 45%*** |

The growth of LANs is propelled by the increasingly universal adoption of personal computers as an essential facility for many desk jobs.  Table 4 shows the steady growth in the number of PCs in use.  Table 5 lists the number of desk jobs in various sectors and the degree of PC penetration. Whereas in 1984 there was one PC in the office for every 18 desk workers, in 1989 there was one for every three workers. By 1996, one estimate says there will be 9 computers in the office for every 10 deskworkers.[6]

Following closely behind the spread of PCs has been a growth in networked or distributed computing. Bellcore estimated that the number of LANs grew from 20,000 in 1983 to 800,000 in 1988. Dataquest estimates show that from 1989 to 1993 there will be a 24% CAGR in unit sales and a 39.5% CAGR in installed base. A conservative estimate of the number of LANs in 1991 would be 2.5 million.[7] In Nebraska, however, we found a growth rate for LANs that greatly exceeded the national estimates (Table 6).

Table 5[8]
Computers in the Office (1989)

| Sector | Deskworkers | PCs | PCs per Worker |
|---|---|---|---|
| Finance, Insurance, Real Est. | 5,896 | 1,360 | 0.23 |
| Business & Legal Services | 5,549 | 1,925 | 0.35 |
| Retail Trade | 4,516 | 672 | 0.15 |
| Other Services | 3,836 | 873 | 0.23 |
| Transport, Utilities | 3,103 | 763 | 0.25 |
| Manufacturing (durable) | 3,100 | 977 | 0.32 |
| Educational Services | 2,917 | 4,288 | 1.47 |
| Health Services | 2,699 | 539 | 0.20 |
| Wholesale Trade | 2,588 | 711 | 0.28 |
| Manufacturing (non-durable) | 2,179 | 598 | 0.27 |
| Agriculture, Mining, Construction | 2,118 | 598 | 0.28 |
| State/Local Government | 2,022 | 421 | 0.21 |
| Federal Government | 654 | 255 | 0.39 |
| Total | 41,178 | 13,981 | 0.34 |

The significance of this growth goes well beyond the diffusion of specific technologies. It is part of a profound change in the balance of public and private networking. A LAN is unambiguously a private network. The user owns the server and wiring, maintains the network, and makes all the choices about software, features, topology, media, and access. The technology and software associated with PCs and LANs have put private networking within the reach of all but the smallest businesses. The increasingly universal adoption of PCS and LANs indicates the complete privatization of intra-premise data networking.

Table 6[9]
LAN Growth, Survey of 40 Nebraska Buisnesses

| Year | Number of LANs |
|---|---|
| Before 1985 | 9 |
| 1986 - 1987 | 36 |
| 1988 - 1989 | 118 |
| 1990 - 1991 | 286 |

LANs per Company, Surveys of 1500 LAN Users

| | Size of Company in ($ Millions) | | | |
|---|---|---|---|---|
| AVG# LANs | $1-5 | $5-100 | $100-1,000 | $ > 1,000 |
| in Use | 4 | 6 | 15 | 67 |

   Telecommunication common carriers are responding to the growth of LANs by targeting the LAN interconnect market. High speed data communication standards such as frame relay, MDS, FDDI, and ATM are working their way to the market. A new offering by Teleport known as LANLINK is a particularly telling example of a public carrier's response to the growth of Type A private networking in data communication. LANLINK improves the speed and efficiency of LAN-LAN connections over the customary leased DS1 services, and also provides bridging functionality, sparing LAN users the need to invest in equipment. (Bridges typically represent an investment of $4,000 - $20,000.) If LANLINK can be taken as typical of how public carriers will respond to LANs, it supports the thesis of this paper in two ways. First, the common carriers are conceding the *intra-premise* LAN market to private users; the carriers are only going after the *interconnect* market, which is currently served by leased lines, i.e. by Type B arrangements. Second, the telephone companies--even innovative ones like Teleport--are behind the curve. They are trying to catch up to a market which was created by Type A private networking, rather than creating a new market themselves. Teleport's nationwide deployment of a LAN interconnect service will not be available until the first quarter of 1993, at the earliest. Developments in the public network are thus lagging behind developments in Type A private networking by four or five years. This gives users enough time to establish a substantial installed base.

## 5.2. PBXs

A PBX is a Type A private network for voice rather than data services. Voice networking went through the cycle of privatization and response by public carriers a decade earlier than the data communications market, so the results may be a harbinger of what is to come in the LAN market. In the early and mid-1980s, the features available via PBXs generally exceeded what was available from the telephone companies. PBX manufacturers beat the public carriers in bringing digital capabilities to the market, and often offered cost savings as well. PBXs thus grew rapidly during the latter half of the 1970s. Growth has since leveled off as the telephone companies have developed a competitive response in Centrex and the market has been saturated.

Table 7 shows the number of lines served by PBX, Key systems (KTS) and Centrex from 1982 to 1991. While the private share of voice business lines is no longer growing, there is no substantial reversal of the privatization of voice networking, either. Rather, the market has stabilized at a level in which PBXs and Key systems have captured a substantial share (43-45%) of multiline business telecommunications. Since 1985, Centrex's share of business lines relative to PBXs and KTS has grown by only 1.7%. If the comparison is extended to 1982, Centrex's share has barely changed. The biggest increase in relative share of business lines has been in Key systems (KTS), which grew from 40% in 1982 to 46% in 1991. As a piece of telephone equipment which is usually purchased by the user, Key systems represent small Type A facilities.

Table 7[10]
Installed Base: PBX, KTS, and Centrex, 1982-1992 (millions of lines)

| Year | PBX Base (% of total) | KTS Base (% of total) | Centrex Base (% of total) | Total Base |
|---|---|---|---|---|
| 1982 | 20.5 (48%) | 16.8 (40%) | 5.0 (12%) | 42.4 |
| 1983 | 22.8 (50%) | 18.2 (40%) | 5.0 (10%) | 46.0 |
| 1984 | 24.1 (49%) | 20.2 (41%) | 5.0 (10%) | 49.3 |
| 1985 | 24.9 (48%) | 22.2 (43%) | 4.9 (9%) | 52.1 |
| 1986 | 25.7 (47%) | 24.4 (45%) | 4.8 (8%) | 54.8 |
| 1987 | 26.5 (45%) | 26.7 (46%) | 5.3 (9%) | 58.6 |
| 1988 | 27.3 (44%) | 28.6 (46%) | 5.8 (10%) | 61.7 |
| 1989 | 28.0 (43%) | 30.6 (47%) | 6.4 (10%) | 65.0 |
| 1990 | 28.2 (43%) | 30.3 (46%) | 7.0 (11%) | 65.5 |
| 1991 | 28.4 (43%) | 30.3 (46%) | 7.4 (11%) | 66.1 |

State Governments: Dominant Direction, PBX vs. Centrex[11]

|  | PBX | Centrex | Both |
|---|---|---|---|
| Number of States | 13 | 14 | 2 |

Table 8[12]
Voice Processing Equipment Growth

|  | Year | Revenues($mill) | Growth Rate |
|---|---|---|---|
| Voice Messaging | 1989 | 646 | 52% |
|  | 1990 | 852 | 32% |
|  | 1991 | 991 | 16% |
| Voice Response | 1989 | 355 | 52% |
|  | 1990 | 423 | 19% |
|  | 1991 | 484 | 15% |

The thesis that private CPE is holding on to a stable share of business lines was supported by both the Nebraska survey and the NASTD survey of state governments. Table 8 shows that of twenty-nine states responding, thirteen said that PBX would be the dominant direction in the future, fourteen said that Centrex would be the dominant direction, and two states said that they would be expected to play an equal role.

### 5.3. Voice Processing and Computer-Telephone Integration.

While growth rates for PBXs and Key systems are flat, other developments indicate that Type A private networking will continue to play a major role in the voice arena, and may even expand dramatically. Features such as voice messaging, call accounting systems, and automatic call distribution systems (ACD) further blur the line between voice and data, and give managers important new functions which are critical to the way office communications take place. In 1991, voice messaging and voice response sales grew by 15% and 16% respectively, despite a recession which slowed the growth in PBX, KTS, and Centrex lines to less than 1%.(See Table 8) The introduction of wireless data communications and wireless PBXs should stimulate a new round of privately-developed CPE purchases as managers search for new on-premise networking solutions. Here again, advanced wireless features will be available to users via CPE purchases using unlicensed frequencies long before public carriers bring PCS or similar services to the market.

Computer-Telephone Integration (CTI) has been defined as the functional integration of human agents and telephone network capabilities, voice and data switching, office computing, and voice processing. The long term future of Type A private networking will be determined by who takes the initiative in implementing the integration of office voice and data capabilities. If it is the telephone companies, then Type A private networking will decline. If, as seems much more likely, this transition will take place via the mediation of equipment vendors (both switch manufacturers and computer manufacturers), software providers, and system integrators, then Type A private networking will take over voice and data functions as quickly as LANs are currently taking over intra-premise computer networking.

Type A networking will probably always remain privatized for the following reasons. Studies of information distribution within organizations consistently show that about 90% of the non-voice information generated by an organization stays within the confines of a single building or cluster of buildings. Half of the information generated by a work unit stays within that unit; another 25% is shared with peer departments; e.g., in a division. Another 15% goes to higher levels of management within the building or complex. Altogether, only 10% goes outside, to remote corporate headquarters, customers, suppliers, or government agencies.[13] The concentration of information flow within the premises of the organization makes it more likely that the managers of the organization will exert direct control over the configuration and technology of intra-premise networks. They will view internal communications not as a homogeneous service like voice telephony to be consumed from an outside supplier, but as a heterogeneous set of functions which they must specify and configure to suit the specific purposes of the organization. Configuring internal information flows is as much a part of the management task as establishing the physical layout of an assembly line or the arrangement of offices in the building.

## 6. "HIGHWAYS" OR "PLUMBING:" SOME CONCLUDING COMMENTS

My object has been to define the phenomenon of network privatization more precisely by assembling quantitative information about two distinct types of private networking. As we have seen, the large scale, distributed private network is a significant phenomenon, but is confined to about 10% of the largest businesses. All indications are that the proportion of businesses which develop Type B private networks will remain stable or decline. There are many defections owing to the growth of SDNs, but also some additions due to applications of radio technology.

If our concept of private networking is focused more narrowly on what businesses are doing *within their own premises*, however, we find that the country's data communications are in the process of being taken over completely by users for themselves. In voice communication, the business line market appears to have stabilized at a level of about one third privatized. The analysis above suggested that intra-premise or Type A private networking will continue to ratchet upwards, as managers exert direct control over the configuration of their office communications systems. A lot depends on how far the integration of voice and data goes and how it is handled by equipment manufacturers. Public carriers are responding to these markets, but their service offerings tend to lag behind by several years and to stop at the building door. They are positioned to connect different Type A facilities, but not to reverse the privatization of intra-office systems.

We need a metaphor or model for this new relationship between public and private networks. Many speak in grand terms of network "confederations" and "electronic highways." I propose a humbler but more accurate analogy. The appropriate model is not highways but *plumbing*. In plumbing systems there is a large-scale public infrastructure for general distribution, but the domain of these public utilities basically stops at the building

82

premises. Once inside the building, the owner controls the equipment choices and configuration. It's up to the user how many showers, toilets and sinks there will be, whether the pipes will be PVC, copper, or galvanized, how well they are insulated. If the pipe leaks, the owner has to contract for the repairs. So it will be with the network of the future. I see users taking almost complete control of the character of the network within buildings and office complexes, with public carriers being forced to provide an increasingly heterogeneous set of services in order to be capable of linking up these diversely equipped sites. Public networks retain powerful--indeed, insurmountable--advantages outside the premises due to the high transactions costs and other entry barriers associated with the use of public rights of way, and because of the significant economies of scale in shared transmission.

I like the plumbing metaphor because it is less pretentious than the highway metaphor and a lot more realistic. Anyone who has struggled with a printer that can't be accessed because of protocol conflicts or wiring problems between devices on a LAN knows that the process has a lot more in common with a clogged toilet than the Tennessee Valley Authority. The common mistake is to view the process of transformation from the perspective of the telephone companies and their competitors. In reality, the end users, and particularly their ability to purchase telecommunications *equipment* uniquely configured to suit their needs, are the real drivers of change.

**ENDNOTES**

[1] Robert W. Crandall, *After the Breakup: U.S. Telecommunications in a More Competitive Era*, The Brookings Institution, Washington DC, 1991.

[2] Stigler, George, "The Division of Labor is Limited by the Extent of the Market," *Journal of Political Economy,* 59:185, 1951.

[3] Williamson, Oliver, *Markets and Heirarchies: Analysis and Antitrust Implications*, New York: Free Press, 1975.

[4] International Communications Association 1990 Survey.

[5] Sources: * U.S. Bureau of the Census; ** Statistical Abstract of the United States, 1991; *** Technology Futures, Inc., *Local Area Network Interconnection.*

[6] Technology Forecasting, Inc. *Local Area Networks*, 1992, p. 41.

[7] Technology Forecasting, Inc., *Local Area Networks*, 1992, p23-24.

[8] Source: U.S. Bureau of the Census.

[9] Source, *Communications Week*, November 18, 1991, p.7.

[10] Source: Northern Business Information (NBI) estimates.

[11] Source: NASTD 1991 Membership Survey.

[12] Source: Vanguard Communications, U.S. Industrial Outlook, 1991.

[13] Stallings, William, *The Business Guide to Local Area Networks*, Carmerl, IN: H.W. Sams, 1991 p.15.

PRIVATE NETWORKS PUBLIC OBJECTIVES
E. Noam and A. NíShúilleabháin (Editors)
© 1996 Elsevier Science B.V. All rights reserved.

# When the Public Goes Private

Paul Teske

## 1. INTRODUCTION - GOVERNMENT AS USER

The federal government is by far the largest single employer in the United States. In addition, more than one in seven working Americans are employed by state or local governments. Government workers make up a very large percentage of employment in the American economy, and in other nations. Not surprisingly, then, a very large share of telecommunications usage is generated by government at all levels. A broader conception of the public sector, including public universities, public health care facilities, libraries, and other related public and not-for-profit enterprises, makes public sector choices even more important to telecommunications providers. Government choices about usage privatization, especially in establishing private networks, are important simply in terms of the scale of the government enterprise. As Kettl[1] noted about FTS 2000: "The very size of the government's contract made it unlike any other player in the market."

Such choices are also important if we ask whether or not governments should act *differently* than private enterprises in establishing private networks. If broader government policy aims to encourage innovation in technology and the expansion of network facilities to all citizens, then governments may develop their own networks differently than would profit-making enterprises. In this paper I consider the choices governments have made, the factors that have contributed to those choices, and the effects of those decisions.

American federal and state governments are relatively sophisticated users of information technology. For example, recent data show that the federal government has the highest ratio of computers to deskworkers, even compare to business access to computers, while state governments are equal to business and local governments trail behind business.[2] As service operations that specialize in information rather than the production of physical goods, governments must use information technology to their advantage.

Several governments have established private networks to consolidate traffic on one network to achieve cost savings by avoiding access charges. Sometimes governments actually own all or part of a network, including switches and lines, but most often they lease facilities or services from telephone providers.

The degree of ownership varies greatly. The federal government now buys services in long-term contracts with AT&T and US Sprint in its FTS 2000 network. Many state governments have similar contracts; in 1989, according to Caudle and Marchand[3], state governments leased their complete systems in Florida, Texas, Connecticut, Maryland, Montana, and New Hampshire. Oklahoma and South Carolina own their government networks. Many states utilize mixed networks; for example, Washington state owns its network switches but not the lines, and Colorado owns only the Denver portion of its network. Caudle and Marchand[4] note: "The decision to own or lease has been a difficult one in most states. Changing user demands, rate structures, and needed management skills do not facilitate clear-cut decision-making."

## 2. WHY THE PUBLIC GOES PRIVATE

There are several justifications for establishing separate government networks of some type. Cost advantages are probably most important, especially in an era of government deficits. As with other private networks, government users may be able to avoid subsidizing other users by negotiating volume prices that are closer to the costs of service provision. Many government officials view the pursuit of cost savings as their duty. However, these decisions ignore the possibility that citizens, who are also residential ratepayers, may lose money over the longer run, if the state private network does not provide "economic" bypass. Given the size of some large government networks, their bypass may be economic. However, some critics[5] have argued that FTS 2000, the largest government network, actually may not be saving money relative to the volume discount rates now routinely given to large users.

Second, some governments establish their own networks to enhance security and privacy for sensitive operations. This is most obviously justifiable for national intelligence gathering organizations like the CIA and the FBI, and may also be important for state criminal justice organizations, such as New York CRIMNET, and perhaps, too, for social service or health providers.

Third, some governments have developed a single large network because they realized that several of their agencies were already developing separate networks. For example, Oregon had twenty separate government agency networks. Caudle and Marchand[6] note: "There still remains a multitude of disparate voice, video, and data networks controlled by state agencies." If each agency made different choices about providers, services, and standards, interconnection might become difficult, and some governments hope that a large unified network will allow them to coordinate and control all telecommunications operations.

Fourth, private government networks may provide special features, or "functionality", that can not easily be provided without private networks. Redundancy is one such feature. Often private networks retain an "option demand" to use shared network facilities should their own system fail. Or, with new technology and attention to this issue, extra redundancy may be built-into the separate government networks from the start, as Iowa has done with its TIM system.[7]

Fifth, governments may develop private networks to provide a strategic advantage, by delivering services to their clients more effectively. Internet is an example of a subsidized network aimed at improving the flow of research and development communications. Networks that are built explicitly with client service in mind may achieve more cost savings, productivity and service quality than can purchasing services from an existing network. This includes providing direct services, such as motor vehicle registration, as well as providing access to state databases. Education is the most important example; at 93% of total costs, education is the most labor-intensive services in our economy.[8] The OTA[9] notes: "educational institutions . . . as large users of communications services -- often ranking second only to State government -- exert considerable market power." Sometimes education networks utilize separate facilities, in other cases, as in Maine, they are constructed as part of public networks.

Many of these reasons for private government networks parallel those for private corporations. Opposing these arguments is the "taxpayers are also ratepayers" perspective that shortrun savings to government from private networks may lead to long run cost increases for telephone ratepayers. Whether or not this is accurate, such an argument does *not* have political salience, as cost savings are immediate and traceable to individual political actions, while rate increases are longer term and less traceable. A more important argument against "the public going private" is that the external benefits of extending a larger network that other users can utilize may be substantial, particularly in rural areas that might otherwise not be modernized quickly. This is an infrastructure justification with parallels to public transportation choices to provide government highway, railway or airline service to rural areas to stimulate other economic and social benefits for the people of that region and those who wish to contact them.

Next I examine some significant federal, state, and local government choices about private networks in more detail.

## 3. THE FEDERAL GOVERNMENT AND FTS 2000

FTS 2000 is the largest private telecommunications network in the world and the largest non-defense government contract. The two firms that won the contract, AT&T with 60% of the business, and US Sprint with 40%, can earn up to $25 billion in revenue over ten years. When completed, the network will serve 1.3 million federal employees all over the U.S., using over 300,000 miles of fiber optics. American defense agencies across the world are served by a separate network operated by the Defense Communications Agency, which spends more than $ 3 billion annually.[10]

Prior to FTS 2000, the U.S. General Services Administration managed telecommunications by purchasing equipment and leasing lines at a time when there was no real telecommunications competition. Since 1963, for long distance services the government used AT&T's Tel-Pak services. That network, although larger than the 17 largest private business telephone systems combined,[11] only provided basic direct dial service and low speed data transfer. Over time, many agencies left the GSA system and paid more for better services with other providers. FTS 2000 was intended to reduce this risk of technological obsolescence.

Kettl[12] argues that the GSA had three options: (1) to incrementally improve the old system, (2) to design and purchase a new system, or (3) to develop a competitive bidding process. Even with the decision to contract, however, the contracting process itself became very controversial, with an original plan to have one winning bidder that could achieve economies of scale. Congress, particularly Texas Democratic Representative Jack Brooks, encouraged a procurement split to benefit more than one firm. The bidding process itself featured several accusations of illegal information passage to bidders.

FTS 2000 began service in October 1989, serving twenty-nine agencies. It can provide many advanced services, including conference calling for up to forty-eight different locations at once, video conferencing, electronic mail, high speed fax, protocol conversion, and packet switching. The contract allows AT&T and Sprint to sell services to their assigned agencies; the more services they sell, the more revenue they can generate.

In addition to new services that can increase productivity and improve employee monitoring, FTS 2000 can save agencies money. Compared to the old system, FTS 2000 has already saved an estimated $500 million.

In addition to the procurement problems, recent concerns focus on whether FTS 2000 is really saving money. While the comparable historic cost savings noted above are accurate, as volume discounts for large private users have expanded, however, the General Accounting Office[13] has argued that the federal government could have saved about $ 150 million more *without* using FTS 2000. Criticism also focused on the fact that US Sprint, the more expensive provider, has received more than its prescribed 40% share. All of these concerns have attracted Congressional attention and hearings.

The Congressionally-endorsed concept of requiring all agencies to use FTS 2000 became controversial after a 1991 failure of AT&T service in New York that slowed critical airport communications. To provide improved reliability, the Federal Aviation Administration wanted to establish its own separate network. After Congressional hearings in 1991, the FAA was allowed an exception to go outside the network for extra reliability.

Current and future issues for FTS 2000 include whether it will be exclusively an internal government network, or whether it will be used to provide electronic services to the citizenry, whether the next contract will operate similarly, or with more competitors, and whether most agencies should be required to use FTS 2000.

### 3.1. The Federal Government and the Internet

The Internet connects computer users and has become *the* shining example of a successful public private network. Originally developed by the Defense Department's Advanced Research Projects Administration as ARPANET, for military use and to test packet switching technology, the backbones of the Internet were extended by NSF (through NSFnet, started in 1986) and other federal agencies to universities and research facilities. It has grown into "the network of networks," as many users begin to realize its vast potential. As of the end of 1992, the Internet included 6,000 member *networks* and over 5 million *users* in over 100 nations.

Internet is subsidized by the federal government, either directly through the NSFnet backbone, or through grants to users. Through 1992, the network backbone was supported by $ 29 million from NSF, $ 13 million from the state of Michigan, and $ 60 million from IBM and MCI. Large subscribers connect on a flat fee basis so that for most actual users there is no usage charge, a fact which has contributed to its rapid growth. Apart from basic interconnection rules established by consensus by the Internet Society, the Internet Architecture Board, and the Internet Engineering Task Force, the Internet runs itself.[14]

The Internet is increasingly used as an example of what a "national information superhighway" could be, or is sometimes discussed as already being that facility. President Clinton has proposed developing the Internet into NREN, the National Research and Education Network.[15] After years of quiet growth in one segment of the economy, the Internet now receives substantial publicity and attention.

### 4. STATE GOVERNMENT NETWORKS

The fifty state governments are major players in telecommunications. In 1989, researchers from Syracuse University found that several states had already developed extensive networks and many more were following. They note: "For the most part, the new networks take advantage of the existing infrastructure or are building the networks in stages."[16]

A few states, including New York, Texas, Florida, North Carolina, Ohio, Michigan, Pennsylvania, Indiana, and Wisconsin, have advanced networks that connect government, universities, and commercial businesses. New York provides a useful case study, as its governmental agencies have utilized more than 8 networks -- including CAPNET, EMPIRENET, LINCS, CRIMNET, LOTTERYNET, SUNYNET, SUNYSAT, and NYSERNET.

New York has developed state private networks to cut costs and to improve reliability. The state spends over $200 million annually on telecommunications services.[17] EMPIRENET and CAPNET are used by most state agencies, except Criminal Justice (CRIMNET) and the universities, which have their own systems.

CAPNET, a state owned and managed network started in 1987, links sixty-five buildings within an eight to ten mile radius of Albany, with 600 miles of fiber optic lines and a 35,000 line PBX. CAPNET provides the largest nation's packet switching system, except for FTS 2000, to 6,000 users. Blunt[18] notes: "unlike CAPNET, EMPIRENET is a service contract, i.e., the state owns no assets." EMPIRENET, started in 1988, connects 12,000 lines in agency offices across the state.[19] EMPIRENET will save $ 150 million over five years, compared to the previous networks. Agency users pay for bandwidth utilized rather than per mile charges. The state Lottery had maintained its own leased network to link 7,000 statewide agents, but switched to EMPIRENET to save money.

CRIMNET, started in 1989, links state criminal justice agencies, including the state police, the courts, criminal corrections, probation, and motor vehicles, and is funded by their respective budgets. To maintain network control and better confidentiality, these agencies chose not to join EMPIRENET.[20] The large bandwidth saves money and allows experiments with video conferencing and facsimile-sent fingerprints.

The state's educational and research networks include SUNYNET, NYSERNET and SUNYSAT. SUNYNET, started nearly 20 years ago to link data terminals to central SUNY administration, now links the thirty-two SUNY colleges and universities.[21] SUNYNET is funded partly by the central administration and partly by each campus. SUNYSAT provides satellite up and downlinks to each campus, and is operated by NYSERNET. As a high-speed data network, NYSERNET has a broader role: to link together universities, supercomputers, research facilities and labs, medical centers, and libraries in New York, to promote research and educational exchange. NYSERNET is funded by the state government, the National Science Foundation, and the network providers, New York Telephone and Rochester Telephone.

In 1992, representatives of all of New York State networks developed cooperative opportunities for mutual advancement to the next level of technology.[22] They considered how better to leverage these networks into economic development for the state. They proposed to: "Utilize the state's considerable public and private educational community to converge their existing data, video, and voice networks into an expanded, integrated 'open digital highway.' Merge this new 'Educational' network with state government's EMPIRENET."[23]

Several other states have developed major private network systems. Indiana's Intelenet provides data, video, and voice services for government agencies, including local governments and education, and aggregates government user demand to achieve volume discounts for long distance services. Minnesota's STARS (State Telecommunications Access and Routing System) network, links statewide public users and is supported by the Department of Administration and the Higher Education Advisory Council. Richter[24] notes

88

that the assistant commissioner of administration "described the state's role in telecommunications development as equivalent to "the prime tenant in a new office building. When the public sector moves in, the private companies are attracted, too."

In other, particularly rural, states, governments self-consciously use the extension of their services, including education, to promote network and facility upgrading that can benefit other users and stimulate private sector development in that region. Essentially, some states use their own network needs to stimulate a telecommunications "industrial policy." Such a strategy may have significant external benefits for their private economies if these upgraded network pieces are accessible to private sector users. Fulton[25] notes: "In the meantime [waiting for ISDN], states have a quicker, more effective tool for exploiting the economic development potential of fiber optics: themselves. Aside from home entertainment, the largest future markets for telecommunications technology in rural areas are governments."

Maine has offered free access to state rights-of-way to provide carriers with incentives to extend networks. Seven campuses of the state university are linked by an interactive video network that transmits courses to 200 schools. State Planning Director Richard Silkman notes: "If you run fiber optics out there [to rural areas], you have a guaranteed market -- the university. What we're hoping to be able to do is stimulate demand on the business side of those facilities."[26]

Wyoming and Georgia government officials note that they could extend their own networks to remote parts of the state, but the private sector spillovers are more positive if they contract with the local exchange carrier. Richter[27] found that: "Georgia's decision to implement a state-of-the-art digital network stemmed partly from officials' desire to benefit the state as a whole, both public and private sectors." And Wyoming's Telecommunications Administrator argued: "Quite frankly, we could build our own network here to get to the far reaches of the state, but we recognized that we as the lead customer in the state should try to push the telecommunications industry as far as possible, with us as the prime user."[28] To pursue its telecommunications industrial policy, Nebraska uses state government procurement as a lever.

## 5. LOCAL GOVERNMENT NETWORKS

Local governments in the U.S. vary in size, from the very populous, like New York City, to the tens of thousands of smaller villages and towns across the country. Obviously, their telecommunications needs and capabilities vary widely. Here, I briefly present two extreme cases of private telecommunications networks -- New York City and Bloomsburg, Pennsylvania.

New York City is larger in population than all but a few states and is much more dense. Private communications networks in New York City, particularly for Wall Street firms, are the most advanced in the world. The city government has added to its own extensive private data and voice networks by striking a deal with a competitive provider, Metropolitan Fiber Systems (MFS), a firm that wanted to enter the market for private communications access. In 1990, City government and MFS completed a franchise agreement for MFS to install and operate a voice/data fiber optic system. In return for this right, MFS pays a franchise fee to and provides city government exclusive use of a share of the fiber optics put into their network at a cost 25% below their lowest volume discount. Thus, through its franchising and rights-of-way power, New York City expanded its own private network substantially, and at a very low cost.[29]

Bloomsburg, Pennsylvania, is a rural town of about 10,000 people and rests toward the other extreme of the telecommunications spectrum from New York City. Bloomsburg does share with New York a desire to encourage businesses that use telecommunications intensively to enter and remain in their community. Thus, a town analysis determined that lack of access to a interexchange carrier point-of-presence was limiting their telecommunications options. Along with their branch of the state university, Bloomsburg is bypassing the public switched network, with a microwave link to a point-of-presence in Harrisburg. Thus, even small governments are considering various forms of private networks and network bypass for reasons of service improvement or cost reduction.

## 6. TRENDS IN AMERICAN GOVERNMENT NETWORKS

Until telecommunications carriers are given more pricing flexibility, and perhaps beyond then as well, more governments may pursue the option of private telecommunications networks. Such networks are already well established at the national government level, by all state governments, by most large cities, and increasingly by smaller and more moderate sized communities. Once these networks are installed, especially if they utilize owned rather than leased facilities, governments are not likely to abandon them easily. Thus, the public may go private more often and may stay private, unless their technology becomes outdated quickly.

The exceptions occur when governments believe that their choices to implement purely private networks harm their public network providers, and thus their own competitive position as a location for business growth and expansion. Some states have already recognized this issue and are developing policy accordingly. Other governments believe that technology will change so fast that leasing facilities or "virtual networks" is the more appropriate and flexible response.

Perhaps a more important trend will be the interconnection policies of government networks with other networks, especially as telecommunications service delivery functions advance. Networks could easily and more productively provide motor vehicle licensing and registration, building department records, voter registration, and a range of other governmental functions. Such linkages to their "clients" may become the most important influences over government network choices. Increased interconnection will greatly enhance the importance of privacy concerns. Who should have access to which government data and in what form?[30] A related question becomes, what is the best funding mechanism for access to such data and services?[31] Higher user prices will discourage small users, which harms the basic premise, but low user prices may not cover costs and will send uncertain signals about public acceptance of the technology.

## 7. CONCLUSIONS

As with private businesses, cost savings are one of the most important reasons for the public to go private. Functionality, confidentiality, reliability, and control issues are also influential. An increasingly important trend is governments' moving from use of their networks only for internal communication toward use for external client services.

While it is too early to make final judgments about government networks, initial successes have largely come from cost savings over previous arrangements. For example, despite controversy, Kettl[32] argues: "FTS 2000 was a huge success in many important

90

respects." Missed opportunities from some of these networks are less obvious; many governments have not attempted to develop a better telecommunications infrastructure for economic development. But the evidence is not yet in for those that have. As gateways to providing better government-citizen interactions, the experiments are only just beginning.

The Internet has "snuck up" on many analysts to become the most interesting and important governmentally-supported network. As it grows beyond its initial role for universities and the research community, it becomes less of a private network, and more of a publicly-accessible network of networks with amazing potential.

## REFERENCES

Arnum, Eric. "The Internet Dilemma: Freeway or Tollway?" *Business Communications Review,* December 28, 1992.

Blunt, Charles, Sharon Dawes, and John Philippo. *Transitioning New York In the Information Age: Telecommunications - A Vital Infrastructure for the New York.* Report prepared for the New York State Forum for Information Resource Management, 1993.

Caudle, Sharon, and Donald Marchand. *Managing Information Resources: New Directions in State Government.* Syracuse University, 1989.

Fulton, William. "Getting the Wire to the Sticks." *Governing*, August 1989.

General Accounting Office of the United States. *FTS 2000: GSA Must Resolve Critical Pricing Issues.* IMTEC-91-79 September, 1991.

Hart, Jeffrey, Robert Reed, and Francois Bar. "The Building of the Internet: Implications for the Future of Broadband Networks." *Telecommunications Policy*, 666-81, Nov. 1992.

Katz, James and Richard Graveman, "Privacy Issues of a National Research and Education Network." *Telematics and Informatics* 8: 71, 1991.

Kettl, Donald, *Sharing Power: Public Governance and Private Markets.* Washington, D.C.: Brookings Institution, 1993.

McClure, Charles, Ann Bishop, Philip Doty, and Howard Rosenbaum, *The National Research and Education Network (NREN): Research and Policy Perspectives.* Norwood, N.J.: Ablex Publishing Corporation, 1991.

Office of Technology Assessment, *Rural America at the Crossroads: Networking for the Future: Summary.* Washington, D.C., 1991.

Perelman, Lewis. "A New Learning Enterprise." In *Business Week* supplement, "The Technology Revolution Comes to Education," December 3, 1990.

Richter, M.J. "Telecommunications: A Telecompetitive World." *Governing*, September, 1990.

Richter, M.J., "Staying Connected: Disaster Recovery for Government Telecommunications." *Governing*, September 1991.

Schmandt, Jurgen, Frederick Williams, and Robert Wilson, *Telecommunications Policy and Economic Development: The New State Role*, Praeger Press, 1991.

Slye, W. Russel "Federal Government Use of Telecommunications." In *NTIA Telecom 2000: Charting the Course for A New Century.* U.S. Department of Commerce. Washington, D.C.: Government Printing Office, 1988.

Teske, Paul and John Gebosky. "Local Telecommunications Competitors: Strategy and Policy." *Telecommunications Policy*, October, 1991.

# ENDNOTES

[1.]Kettl, Donald. 1993. *Sharing Power: Public Governance and Private Markets*. Washington, D.C.: Brookings Institution.

[2.]From 1989 statistics from the Gartner Group on the number of *deskworkers* per computer, by SIC code, the U.S. average is 2.94. The most computerized group is the federal government with a figure of 2.56. The next categories (by SIC code) are business and legal services 2.88; durable goods manufacturing 3.17; agriculture, mining and construction 3.55; wholesale trade 3.63; non-durable manufacturing 3.65; *state government 3.79*; transportation and public utilities 4.07; finance, insurance and real estate 4.33; services other than health and education 4.55; health 5.0; *local government 6.10*; and retail services 6.71.

[3.]Caudle, Sharon and Donald Marchand. *Managing Information Resources: New Directions in State Government*. Syracuse University, 1989.

[4.]Page 61, Ibid.

[5.]General Accounting Office of the United States. *FTS 2000: GSA Must Resolve Critical Pricing Issues*. IMTEC-91-79 September, 1991.

[6.]Page 61, Caudle, Sharon and Donald Marchand. *Managing Information Resources: New Directions in State Government*. Syracuse University, 1989.

[7.]Pages 49-50, Richter, M.J., "Staying Connected: Disaster Recovery for Government Telecommunications." *Governing*, September, 1991.

[8.]Page 16ED, Perelman, Lewis. "A New Learning Enterprise." In *Business Week* supplement, The Technology Revolution Comes to Education, December 3, 1990.

[9.]Page 25, Office of Technology Assessment. *Rural America at the Crossroads: Networking for the Future: Summary*. Washington, D.C., 1991.

[10.]Page 357, Slye, W. Russel. "Federal Government Use of Telecommunications." In *NTIA Telecom 2000: Charting the Course for A New Century*. U.S. Department of Commerce. Washington, D.C.: Government Printing Office, 1988.

[11.]Page 68, Kettl, Donald., *Sharing Power: Public Governance and Private Markets*. Washington, D.C.: Brookings Institution, 1993.

[12.]Page 72, Ibid.

[13.]General Accounting Office of the United States. *FTS 2000: GSA Must Resolve Critical Pricing Issues*. IMTEC-91-79 September, 1991.

[14.]Hart, Jeffrey, Robert Reed and Francois Bar. "The Building of the Internet: Implications for the Future of Broadband Networks." *Telecommunications Policy* November, 1992: 666-81.

[15.]McClure, Charles, Ann Bishop, Philip Doty, and Howard Rosenbaum. *The National Research and Education Network (NREN): Research and Policy Perspectives*. Norwood, N.J.: Ablex Publishing Corporation, 1991.

[16.]Page 61, Caudle, Sharon and Donald Marchand, *Managing Information Resources: New Directions in State Government*. Syracuse University, 1989.

[17] Schmandt, Jurgen, Frederick Williams, and Robert Wilson. *Telecommunications Policy and Economic Development: The New State Role*. Praeger Press and Blunt, 1989; Charles, Sharon Dawes, and John Philippo. *Transitioning New York In the Information Age: Telecommunications - A Vital Infrastructure for the New York*, 1993. Report prepared for the New York State Forum for Information Resource Management.

[18] Page 111, Blunt, Charles, Sharon Dawes, and John Philippo. *Transitioning New York In the Information Age: Telecommunications - A Vital Infrastructure for the New York*. Report prepared for the New York State Forum for Information Resource Management, 1993.

[19] EMPIRENET uses leased services from Eastern Microwave for interLATA service, NY Tel for local connections, and IBM for management software.

[20] CRIMNET includes a 56 kb backbone, with over 300 circuits over 12 T1 nodes in all major cities of the state. The T1 lines are leased from a variety of providers, including AT&T, Sprint, and Eastern Microwave, and the local circuits are provided by local telephone companies like NY Tel and Rochester.

[21] In 1989 a T1 backbone ring was installed to provide 56 kb data service.

[22] Blunt, Charles, Sharon Dawes, and John Philippo. *Transitioning New York In the Information Age: Telecommunications - A Vital Infrastructure for the New York*. Report prepared for the New York State Forum for Information Resource Management, 1993.

[23] Page iii, Ibid.

[24] Page 21A, Richter, M.J. "Telecommunications: A Telecompetitive World." *Governing*, September, 1990.

[25] Page 42, Fulton, William. "Getting the Wire to the Sticks." *Governing*, August, 1989.

[26] Page 42, Ibid.

[27] Page 17A, Richter, M.J. "Telecommunications: A Telecompetitive World." *Governing*, September, 1990.

[28] Page 18A, Ibid.

[29] Teske, Paul and John Gebosky. "Local Telecommunications Competitors: Strategy and Policy." *Telecommunications Policy* October, 1991.

[30] Katz, James and Richard Graveman. "Privacy Issues of a National Research and Education Network." *Telematics and Informatics* 8: 71, 1991.

[31] Arnum, Eric. "The Internet Dilemma: Freeway or Tollway?," *Business Communications Review* December: 28, 1992.

[32] Page 94, Kettl, Donald. *Sharing Power: Public Governance and Private Markets*. Washington, D.C.: Brookings Institution, 1993.

PRIVATE NETWORKS PUBLIC OBJECTIVES
E. Noam and A. NíShúilleabháin (Editors)
93

# The Economics of Private Networks

## The *Filière Electronique*: Contributions of Public Networks to Private Networks

Sandra Braman

## 1. INTRODUCTION

As we negotiate with each other the "material" of the network -- the fibers and the wavelengths, the standards and the protocols -- we are also negotiating with each other how to live as individuals, communities, societies, states, and as a global community. A telecommunications network is not only comprised of the lines and nodes of the physical infrastructure; it is also the very stuff of the organizations and societies that use it; network society is civil society as well.

Two things flow from this: First, in addition to the kinds of economic issues normally addressed in policy-making and -analysis processes, macro-level and society-wide matters are also pertinent to the question of what public investment in the telecommunications infrastructure means to private networks. It is important to look not only at the economic policy, but also at how the economy operates; and not only the economic, but the social, political, cultural, and ecological issues as well.

Second, while we have the habit of thinking about network issues as if they are stand alone, and can adequately be analyzed in that way, in today's environment this is not valid. The network is meaningless and cannot be understood separate from the web of social relations -- including those expressed in industrial form -- that is dependent upon, occurs within, and would operate quite differently without, the net. The Europeans have acknowledged this by using the phrase *filière électronique* to describe both the network and the institutions and web of social relations the net enables. (The term was coined in the 1982 Farnoux report to the French government and has since been taken up by a number of analysts.[1])

Looking at the question of the relationship between public and private networks from this perspective, four macro-level effects of the use of the net provide a context in which to understand ways in which public support for the net contributes to private networks:

(1) Evolution of organizational form.
(2) Transformation of the law.
(3) Emergence of the network economy.
(4) Increase in complexity and turbulence.

This chapter examines these very fundamental and contextual contributions by public networks to their private counterparts. By examining each of these four characteristics of this stage of the information society, we get a sense of the self-reflexivity of the processes by which we design, build, and regulate nets both public and private, and of the multi-dimensionality of the effort. In building the net, we are at the same time constituting our societies, our political cultures, our economy, and ourselves.

## 2. EVOLUTION OF ORGANIZATIONAL FORM

Over the past couple of decades we have come to understand organizations primarily as information systems.[2] From this perspective, it is clear why the introduction of new information technologies not only stimulates shifts in the nature of organizations, but actually makes possible the evolution of new organizational forms. Transnational corporations have been the most aggressive in taking advantage of the new possibilities, and it is from studying them that we are learning the most about what the emergent possibilities are.

Among the characteristics of organizations that the net -- whether funded privately or publicly -- makes possible are:

- Much more flexibility in determining how centralized and decentralized decision-making will be. While with earlier technologies, decisions about degree of centralization had to be made once, and for the organization as a whole, under network conditions such decisions need not be fixed in stone, nor fixed in one way for the entire organization. Some areas of organizational life can be made individually for each level of organization and communication.
- Increased capacity for collocation of general and local knowledge. Incorporating local knowledge -- knowledge of the particularities of circumstances into decision-making processes designed around taking advantage of more systematic, general knowledge.
- Boundary permeability. Historically relationships between corporations were largely across the transactional boundary of the marketplace. While these relationships between organizations may have been long-lived and significant to all parties involved, they were also fairly stable in form and generally involved interactions only at one point of the processes of production and distribution describing each party's activities. Today a multiplicity of types of relationships between organizations, long-term commitments over multiple dimensions -- what might be termed shared responsibilities for a single production process, and flexibility in reassignment of tasks -- make the boundary between organizations more permeable and harder to define than previously.
- Ability to control a higher level of articulation of the organizational and informational structures. The first stage of the information society,[3] which introduced the telegraph and telephone, made it possible to control agents at a distance, and therefore permitted existing types of organizations to grow larger, and to spread over greater distance. During the second stage, organizations took advantage of these types of possibilities to become global, and we saw, therefore, during the middle of the 20th century, the development of the multinational corporation, dependent upon the range of information technologies for functioning. With the addition of intelligence and greater capacity in the network, which we are seeing in this third stage of the information society, organizations now have the ability to control organizations with both high levels of internal differentiation as

well as geographic spread. This aspect of the network, of course, can also be problematic, as is discussed in the section on complexity and turbulence to follow.

Public investment in the telecommunications infrastructure enables private sector organizations to take advantage of the possibilities for organizational change that the net makes possible. Corporate networks that are closed to the public immediately limit their ability to participate in an information economy so significantly characterized by network relationships that it is coming to be known as the network economy. Placing such a horizon on the possibilities of organizational evolution will simultaneously damage competitiveness in a world in which, according to many network economists[4] cooperation and coordination are as important as -- and therefore critical to -- competition. Heavy public sector investment in the network, conversely, extends the range of possibilities available to all in terms of the range of organizational alternatives that become open.

One result of the evolution of organizational form is that the very boundary between what is public and what is private is shifting. In the policy making domain, this has been acknowledged in the emergence of the term "policy networks," describing the mutating interdependencies between the two.[5]

## 3. TRANSFORMATION OF THE LAW

The use of new information technologies has stimulated processes that have lead to changes in the nature of the law as well. While some changes are due to the uses of new information technologies by the legal and judicial system itself, others derive from efforts to conduct business and other social activities in an environment to which the law rarely applies, and with which it with difficulty copes. Because of the convergence of technologies, often multiple, and potentially radically different, sets of laws or regulations may concurrently, though conflictingly, apply to the same message or communication process. The consequences include constant litigation in practice, frustration on the part of regulatory systems incapable of dealing with the subject of their regulation, judicial systems that acknowledge their inability to understand the empirical realities that provide the "facts" of the case, and national and international legal and regulatory systems that do not provide guidance or conflict resolution under today's conditions.

The law has responded to these problems in a variety of ways.

1)  The law is moving away from the nation-state. Because so many of the information and communication processes and products in the information economy are international or global in nature, nation-state law is rarely sufficient. As transactions, agreements and conflicts move to the international arena, so does the law. Adding fuel to this process is the interest of large legal firms serving the interests of their clients, now mostly important transnational corporations, who are also less interested in serving the social, cultural, and political goals of national law than in pursuing their own goals, and thus, are happy to move to the international arena as appropriate.[6] A variety of theories to justify this move have been put forward, including the argument that international law -- ideally the General Agreements on Tariffs and Trade (GATT) -- is today our true constitutional venue, since the dangers that most threaten us are those that come from international trade, not from church and state (with the nature of the state itself undergoing radical changes).[7]

2) Laws of different jurisdictions are coming into harmonization. With the increase in the movement of information, goods, and people internationally, it has become clear that ease in transactions is facilitated when regulatory and legal systems are coordinated with each other, meaning their fundamental structures and the types of categories in use are the same. (It is harmonization of accounting systems that is one of the ultimate goals of the discussion of trade in services under the General Agreements under Tariffs and Trade [GATT]). Increasingly, as in the efforts to build the European Community and the North American Free Trade Agreement (NAFTA), regional and international law in effect supplants national or local law.[8]

3) Contract law is playing a more important role. Dezalay[9] brilliantly has pointed out ways in which contract law is beginning to lead to development of law in other areas. When there is no existing or appropriate national or international law for a particular situation in the information economy, or when existing law is so self-contradictory regarding the matter at hand as to be problematic, contracts provide far more flexibility and the capacity to tailor agreements to the particulars of the information economy. They also, of course, provide some additional privacy barriers.

4) Algorithmic decision-making procedures are increasingly replacing cognitive (that is, human) decision-making procedures within the law. The critical significance of this shift is indicated by the fact that several different types of cases have presented this as a constitutional problem to the US Supreme Court. Differences in the type of surveillance, and therefore of control, is the pertinent form of information collection for algorithmic decision-making procedures, with the interest on statistical probabilities rather than the particularities of individual circumstances. Tribe[10] argues that, by definition, constitutional decision-making in any context is NOT appropriate for treatment with algorithmic decision-making procedures. Algorithmic decision-making procedures work with established categories and relationships within and between them, while it is the very point of constitutional decision-making to establish categories and determine the relationships with and between them.

5) Katsh[11] has elaborated for us the ways in which the use of computerized databases has made it possible to be far more aggressive in constructing new lines of precedent -- and, therefore, of argument. Locating (or creating) a line of argument by tracing it through cases in which pertinent (or appropriate) positions have been taken has historically been an extremely time-consuming matter; as a consequence, lines of precedent become essentially boiler-plate as the significant streams of cases in particular areas emerge. With the enormous reduction in the cost of developing new lines of precedent, greater creativity is possible.

6) The use of new information technologies has also introduced some new alternatives to regulation, and a variety of legal techniques not previously available.[12] This is occurring at the same time that the study of the sociology of the law is becoming aware of the relationship between particular cultural and social features and the type of legal system that develops around them.[13]

It may well be here, in the reshaping of the legal environment, that public investment in the building of an information infrastructure means the most to the development of private networks, for it is here that the use of networks by those outside of, as well as within, specific organizations provides the flux through which and from which private networks variously resolve themselves as they constitute and reconstitute themselves.

## 4. THE EMERGENCE OF THE NETWORK ECONOMY

Antonelli[14] argues that harmonized information flows have now replaced the market as the key coordinating mechanism for the market. Grabher and others today are exploring the nature of what has come to be called the network firm, as we explore what appear to be some qualitatively different characteristics of the information economy.

This is a particularly important area from the perspective of private networks, since the implication of the emergence of the network economy is that a greater number of types of information than previously have to be gathered, analyzed, and incorporated into decision-making processes. Judgments about when and how moves are successful operate under some different rules. Pertinent features of the network economy include:

1) Identification of the long-term project rather than the firm or industry as the basic unit of analysis. Complexity interdependent relationships among organizations -- both private sector and public sector -- mean that valid analyses of economic processes need to take networked groups of firms together. From the perspective of the individual organization, the implication is that the synergies generated through the networked activities should be incorporated into the valuation of a firm's worth, the economic benefits of particular processes, etc.

2) The addition of cooperation and coordination to competition as central economic dynamics. Because interdependence is a key feature of the network economy, prizing competition may not always be the most appropriate approach, and in many circumstances is even counter-productive.

3) An expansion of the types of capital available to include what has come to be called intellectual capital. Additional types of information resources appear through the lens of an information or network economy, rather than from the perspective of the emphases of an industrial economy. Currently this is most visible and publicly debated in the confoundingly difficult area of intellectual property rights.

In this area, the contribution of public investments toward private networks can not be overstated. Public networks enable the operations of the network economy, create the environment in which those involved in private networks work, and offer (and encourage) new modes of operation.

## 4. INCREASE IN COMPLEXITY AND TURBULENCE

As with any other conceptual or material tool, we have begun[15] to find everywhere the concepts of complexity and turbulence. The number of linkages, possible routes, types of processing, and numbers of messages and bits of data being transmitted through the global information infrastructure have so increased that, in fact, the complexity of our activities has increased to the point that we experience many of our social processes as turbulent, and sometimes chaotic. Beck[16] describes our condition, as a consequence, as a *Risk Society*, in which we are more probabilistically concerned about dangers in the future than we are, as historically, we were driven by the past. Beck's work provides crucial insights into the social, political, and cultural effects of living in an environment in which the casual chains are so long both in terms of number of steps and, sometimes, in time, that we can no longer, in many cases, validly determine casual relations. Among the consequences to which Beck points are impacts on morality when responsibility can no longer reasonably be assigned, and of the inclination to move towards non-rational modes of explanation when cause and effect no longer are determinable. Sabel[17] and Rosenau[18] have been looking at complexity and turbulence within the economy.

The study of complexity and turbulence has spread across the entire range of social sciences in recent years.[19] This work largely focuses on ways of coping with complexity and surviving turbulent and chaotic conditions. (This emerging discipline has been going under different names according to disciplinary home, choice of conceptual emphasis, etc.. It includes second order cybernetics, complex systems theory, self-organizing systems theory, chaos theory, and analyses of punctuated equilibria.) What has been learned that is pertinent to understanding the relationships between public support for the net and private networks includes:

1) Mutually beneficial processes and positive feedback are at least as important as competitive processes and negative feedback. This has implications for research, as well as linkages with the characteristics of the network economy. Ideally, systems are so characterized by their participation in and contributions to such processes that they may be described as co-evolutionary.

2) A focus on the deviation-amplifying effects of casual processes. Generally we have treated small differences in initial starting conditions for casual processes as trivial, but we are learning through the study of chaos that seemingly trivial differences at the beginning of processes can yield significantly different outcomes. In telecommunications terms, Antonelli[20] is talking about this when he describes the way in which random small events in networks can have significant and long-lasting effects.

3) An emphasis on process rather than on the product or the achieving of a fixed state. Healthy systems are today understood to be constantly undergoing self-renewal, or autopoisis, rather than always seeking to achieve or return to an equilibrious state. There are implications for organizations here as they define both their missions and their structures and working procedures.

4) Healthy systems are characterized by autopoitis -- self-organizing -- activity by their constituent elements. For this to happen, two types of collocation are significant: collocation of general knowledge with specific, or local, knowledge; and collocation of knowledge with decision-making power. Both of these are made possible far more easily than ever before by the particular characteristics of the net.

5) In times of turbulence, there is both a need for deviance, experimentation, development of alternatives in all domains, and a higher likelihood of success for experiments that respond intelligently to shifts in the environment. The implication for the relationships between public and private networks is clear: the richer the network environment, the greater the opportunities for the experimentation that is most likely to identify the paths to success in this environment. To this end, participants in private networks -- or those who would like to be -- should appreciate as much public support for development of the information infrastructure as possible.

The increase in complexity and turbulence, and what we are learning about how to deal with them, are pertinent to the relationships between public support for networks and private networks because they provide policy guidelines -- for both the public and the private sectors. On the part of the public sector, it should be a goal to attempt to maximize interactions that take advantage of complexity and turbulence perceived as opportunities, rather than designing a system in which their now-endemic conditions are approached more sympathetically.

## 6. CONCLUSIONS

Taking a macro-level view of the nature of the net lets us see ways, beyond the most immediately visible economic contributions of public support, for the information infrastructure to benefit private networks. While less easily calculable, far more important contributions are in the shaping of an environment in which private networks may establish themselves, and develop the networked relationships within the net that will determine their long-term viability. These efforts are self-reflexive in that each effort itself alters the conditions under which economic activities operate. Simultaneously, they are the conditions under which communities and societies find themselves, and in which we carry out our political lives. While the emphasis here has been on the economic implications of the macro-level effects discussed, the intertwining with other areas of social life is key to understanding ways in which the public and private building of networks itself shifts the very social environment in which those networks are embedded. Thus, we are examining not the net, but the *filière électronique*; and through the *filière électronique* we are shaping ourselves as a civil society.

## REFERENCES

Antonelli, C. (Ed), *The Economics of Information Networks*, Amsterdam: North-Holland, 1992.

Archer, M., *Culture and Agency: The Place of Culture in Social Theory*, Cambridge: Cambridge University Press, 1988.

Beck, U. (trans. Mark Ritter), *The Risk Society: Towards a New Modernity*, Newbury Park, CA: Sage Publications, 1992.

Braman, S., "Harmonization of systems: The third stage of the information society," *Journal of Communication*, 43(3), pp. 133-140, 1993.

Braman, S., "Trade and information policy," *Media, Culture, and Society*, 12, pp. 361-385, 1990.

Cass, R.A., "The perils of positive thinking: Constitutional interpretation and the negative first amendment thinking," *UCLA Law Review*, 34(5-6), pp. 1405-1491, 1987.

Degreene, K.B., *The Adaptive Organization: Anticipation and Mangement of Crises*, New York: Wiley Interscience, 1982.

Dezalay, Y., "Putting justice 'into play' on the global market: Law, lawyers, accountants and the competition for legal services," *Tidskrift fur Rattssociologi*, 6(1-2), pp. 9-67, 1989.

Dezalay, Y., "The BIG BANG and the law: The internationalization and restructuration of the legal field," *Theory, Culture, and Society*, 7, pp. 279-293, 1990.

Dyson, K. & Humphreys, P. (Eds), *The Politics of the Communications Revolution in Western Europe*, London: Frank Cass, 1986.

Grabher, G., *The Embedded Firm: on the Socioeconomics of Industrial Networks*, New York: Routledge, 1993.

Guerin-Calvert, M. & Wildman, S.S. (Eds), *Electronic Services Networks: A Business and Public Policy Challenge*, Washington, DC: Annenberg, 1991.

Haas, E.B., *When Knowledge is Power: Three Models of Change in International Organizations*, Berkeley: University of California Press, 1990.

Jantsch, E., *The Self-Organizing Universe*, New York: Pergamon Press, 1989.

Jordan, G. & Schubert, K., "A preliminary ordering of policy network labels," *European Journal of Political Research*, 21, pp. 7-27, 1992.

Karpf, J., "Competition between types of regulation: The impact of computerization of law," 8th European Conference of Critical Legal Studies, Budapest, October 1989.

Katsh, E, *The Electronic Media and the Transformation of the Law*, New York: Oxford University Press, 1989.

Mattelart, A., and Cesta, Y.S. (trans. D. Bruxton), *Technology, Culture, and Communication*, Amsterdam: North Holland, 1985.

Mitnick, R.M., *The Political Economy of Regulation, Creating, Designing, And Removing Regulatory Forms*, New York: Columbia University Press, 1980.

Morgan, G., *Images Of Organizations*, Beverly Hills: Sage, 1986.

Pekelis, A.H., "Legal techniques and political ideologies: A comparative study," In R. Bendix (Ed.), *State and Society: a Reader in Comparative Political Sociology*, pp.355-377, Boston: Little, Brown & Co., 1968.

Petersmann, E., *Constitutional Functions and Constitutional Problems of International Economic Law*, Fribourg, Switzerland: University of California Press, 1991.

Tribe, L.H., "Constitutional Calculus: Equal Justice or Economic Efficiency?" *Harvard Law Review*, 98, pp. 592-621, 1985.

van Waarden, F., "Dimensions and types of policy networks," *European Journal of Political Research*, 21, pp.29-52, 1992.

Zeleny, M.(Ed), *Autopoiesis, Dissipative Structures, and Spontaneous Social Orders*, Boulder CO: AAAS Selected Symposium, 1980.

## ENDNOTES

[1.] See: Dyson, K. & Humphreys, P,(Eds), *The Politics of the Communications Revolution in Western Europe*, London: Frank Cass, 1986 and Mattelart, A., & Cesta, Y.S., *Technology, Culture, and Communication*, trans. D. Bruxton, Amsterdam: North Holland, 1985.

[2.] Haas, E.B., *When Knowledge is Power: Three Models of Change in International Organizations*, Berkeley: University of California Press, 1990 and Morgan, G., *Images of Organizations*, Beverly Hills: Sage, 1986.

[3.] Braman, S., "Harmonization of systems: The third stage of the information society," *Journal of Communication*, 43(3), pp. 133-140, 1993.

[4.] See: Antonelli, C. (Ed), *The Economics of Information Networks*, Amsterdam: North-Holland, 1992; Grabher, G., *The Embedded Firm: on the Socioeconomics of Industrial Networks*, New York: Routledge, 1993, or Guerin-Calvert, M. & Wildman, S.S. (Eds), *Electronic Services Networks: A Business and Public Policy Challange*, Washington, DC: Annenburg, 1991.

[5] Jordan, G. & Schubert, K., "A preliminary ordering of policy network labels," *European Journal of Political Research*, 21, pp.7-27, 1992; van Waarden, F., "Dimensions and types of policy networks," *European Journal of Political Research*, 21, pp.29-52, 1992.

[6] Dezalay, Y, "Putting justice 'into play' on the global market: Law, lawyers, accountants and the competition for legal services," *Tidskrift Fur Rattssociologi*, 6(1-2), pp.9-67, 1989 and Dezalay, Y., "The Big Bang and the law: The internationalization and restructuration of the legal field," *Theory, Culture, and Society*, 7, pp.279-293, 1990.

[7] See: Cass, R.A., "The perils of positive thinking: Constitutional interpretation and the negative first amendment thinking," *UCLA Law Review*, 34(5-6), pp.1405-1491, 1987 and Petersmann, E., *Constitutional Functions and Constitutional Problems of International Economic Law*, Fribourg, Switzerland: University of California Press, 1991.

[8] Braman, S., "Trade and information policy," *Media, Culture, and Society*, 12, pp.361-385, 1990.

[9] Dezalay, Y, "Putting justice 'into play' on the global market: Law, lawyers, accountants and the competition for legal services," *Tidskrift Fur Rattssociologi*, 6(1-2), pp.9-67, 1989, Dezalay, Y., "The Big Bang and the law: The internationalization and restructuration of the legal field," *Theory, Culture, and Society*, 7, pp.279-293, 1990.

[10] Tribe, L.H., "Constitutional Calculus: Equal Justice or Economic Efficiency?" *Harvard Law Review*, 98, pp. 592-621, 1985.

[11] Katsh, E, *The Electronic Media and the Transformation of the Law*, New York: Oxford University Press, 1989.

[12] Karpf, J., "Competition between types of regulation: The impact of computerization of law," 8th European Conference of Critical Legal Studies, Budapest, October 1989.

[13] Mitnick, R.M., *The Political Economy of Regulation, Creating, Designing, and Remocing Regulatory Forms*, New York: Columbia University Press, 1980 and Pekelis, A.H., "Legal techniques and political ideologies: A comparative study," In R. Bendix (Ed.), *State and Society: A Reader in Comparative Political Sociology*, pp.355-377, Boston: Little, Brown & Co, 1968.

[14] Antonelli, C. (Ed), *The Economics of Information Networks*, Amsterdam: North-Holland, 1992.

[15] Fractal mathematics, the foundation of studies of complexity and turbulence, developed only recently partially because of the requirement for massive mathematical manipulations only made possible through use of a computer.

[16] Beck, U. (trans. Mark Ritter), *The Risk Society: Towards a New Modernity*, Newbury Park, CA: Sage Publications, 1992.

[17] See Sabel, C. "Moebius-strip Organizations and Open Labor Markets: Come Consequences of the Reintegration of Conception and Execution in a Volatile Economy," in P. Bordieu & J. Coleman (eds.), *Social Theory for a Changing Society*, pp. 23-54, Boulder: Westview Press, 1991.

[18] See Rosenau, J., "A Pre-theory Revisisted? World Politics in an Era of Cascading Interdependence," *International Studies Quarterly*, 28(3), pp. 245-306, 1984.

[19] Archer, M., *Culture and Agency: The Place of Culture in Social Theory*, Cambridge: Cambridge University Press, 1988; Degreene, K.B., *The Adaptive Organization: Anticipation and Management of Crises*, New York: Wiley Interscience, 1982; Jantsch, E., *The Self-Organizing Universe*, New York:

Pergamon Press, 1989, Zeleny, M.(Ed), *Autopoiesis, Dissipative Structures, and Spontaneous Social Orders*, Boulder Co; AAAS Selected Symposium, 1980.

[20.]Antonelli, C. (Ed), *The Economics of Information Networks*, Amsterdam: North-Holland, 1992.

PRIVATE NETWORKS PUBLIC OBJECTIVES
E. Noam and A. NíShúilleabháin (Editors)
© 1996 Elsevier Science B.V. All rights reserved.

# Quality Choices in a Network of Networks

William Lehr

## 1. INTRODUCTION[1]

De-regulation, globalization, and rapid advances in technology are pushing us towards a world of virtual networks offering new, integrated services from a growing array of new service providers. The boundaries between public and private networks are blurring. Increasingly, we communicate via a patchwork mosaic of interconnected semi-autonomous sub-networks: a *network of networks*. In this new environment, the quality and reliability of our electronic communications infrastructure depends on the design decisions of each of the constituent sub-networks. Increasingly, these design decisions are being left to decentralized market forces. Can we rely on these forces to select the socially optimal level of quality?

Economists interested in the relationship between market structure and product quality have focused either on a monopolist's manipulation of quality to facilitate imperfect price discrimination[2] or oligopolistic quality differentiation to soften price competition.[3] The former research is applicable to the regulation of dominant carriers (e.g., AT&T or the Local Exchange Carriers (LECs)); while the latter may shed light on the effects of increased facilities-based competition (e.g., between AT&T and the other long distance companies, or between the LECs and alternative carriers such as Teleport or Metropolitan Fiber Systems). Further analysis of both of these circumstances is of great importance in assessing how the changes cited above will affect service quality. Both illustrate the potential inefficiency of market-based solutions: firms may either *under-* or *over*-invest in quality enhancements. Neither, however, considers what happens when control over the quality choice is decentralized. By assuming that the quality of *each* final good is chosen by a single agent, they ignore the coordination problem which confronts a network of networks.

This paper addresses this deficiency by presenting a model which shows how the fragmentation of network ownership and control creates a coordination problem which leads to inadequate investment incentives. The modelling perspective is quite abstract and ignores the messy details associated with engineering real-time, multimedia networks and the extremely difficult economic challenges of cost recovery and pricing in a broadband environment. The discussion of regulatory policies/politics is rather simplistic, and strong mathematical assumptions underlie the model's formulation (e.g., regarding the information available to decision-makers, the dimensionality of quality preferences, and the regularity of functions). The point of this exercise is to demonstrate how fundamental the basic coordination problem is. Even when much of the real world's complexity is stripped away, we are left with a difficult problem in collective choice which is not readily amenable to regulatory interventions. The principal lessons of this paper are cautionary. Although we should not expect a network of networks to adopt the first-best level of quality, traditional modes of direct intervention (via pricing regulations, penalties and/or minimum quality standards) may be worse. This conclusion may be obscured, but is unlikely to be reversed by a less abstract, more complex analysis.

In order to make the key features of the model and its results intelligible to non-economists, the discussion of technical details in the main body of the text is kept to a minimum.[4] Section 2 explains the formulation of the model in order to clarify the nature of the economic problem faced by a network of networks, and in order to relate the modelling abstraction to the real world situation. Section 3 presents the main conclusions which emerge from an analysis of the model. Section 4 addresses further extensions while Section 5 presents conclusions.

## 2. DESCRIPTION OF THE MODEL

The quality of communication services is inherently multidimensional in at least two important senses. First, we can measure quality in a variety of ways. For example, the quality of plain old telephone service depends on the level of line noise, the delay in establishing a connection, the probability of blocking or disruptions, and the flexibility/variety of service features. We may presume that all consumers would prefer higher quality along each of these dimensions, while differing in their willingness-to-pay for enhancements and in their willingness to trade off improvements along different quality dimensions. For example, voice telephony is intolerant of delays but (relatively) tolerant of bit errors, whereas certain data communications reflect opposite preferences. Thus, we should expect the willingness-to-pay for quality to vary systematically both across consumers and for each consumer based on the type of communication to be undertaken.

Appropriate product design and feature pricing strategies may exploit these multidimensional preferences in order to facilitate price discrimination. This can aid in recovering fixed costs and avoiding the deadweight losses associated with monopoly pricing (e.g., priority pricing to exploit variable tolerances for delay or special fees for data-reliable connections). Indeed, the desire to accommodate these diverse tastes is one of the forces which is fueling the emergence of semi-autonomous sub-networks. Since the focus of this paper is not pricing, let us ignore this type of multidimensionality and assume the quality of each sub-network can be represented by a scalar quality index, $x_i$.

The second sense in which quality is multidimensional arises because network services are a composite good. The effective *end-to-end* quality of service depends on the quality of each of the components which comprise the network. The quality of service in a network-of-networks will depend on the quality of each of the constituent sub-networks. Therefore, even if the quality of each sub-network may be described by a scalar index, $x_i$, the quality of the network of networks must be represented by a vector, $x \equiv (x_1, x_2 \ldots, x_N)$. To study the effects of decentralization of control over network design, I compare the choice of x when the quality of each of N interconnected sub-networks is chosen by a single agent with what happens when the sub-networks choose $x_i$ for $i = 1, 2, \ldots N$ independently. Let us assume that the net benefits which accrue to the network designers of the ith sub-network can be described by a utility function, $U^i(x)$, and define the social welfare function as the sum of the N utility functions,

$$W(x) = \Sigma_{i=1,N} U^i(x). \tag{1}$$

This formulation permits great flexibility in identifying the sub-networks, while suppressing the distinction between service providers and consumers. It purposefully ignores the role of market prices and the competition for subscribers, implicitly assuming that the aggregate effects for each network are captured by the network utility functions. Several economists have noted how the positive externalities associated with larger networks may encourage the coalescence of smaller networks.[5] Subscribers with heterogeneous tastes on smaller networks may be willing to compromise in order to adopt a common, compatible technology. Often, however, formation of a single, centrally-controlled network is neither economically feasible nor desirable. Preferences may be sufficiently heterogeneous or privacy/control may be important enough to outweigh the positive externalities of forming a single network, even though interconnection remains desirable.

This paper begins with the assumption that we have a network of interconnected sub-networks. Perhaps the simplest example to consider is the case of N private corporate networks which are interconnected via the Public Switched Telecommunications Network (PSTN). Within-firm calls occur "on-net" and, presumably, the quality of these calls need depend only on the quality of the corporate network (i.e., office wiring, the PBX, etcetera).[6] The quality of "internet" calls between firms is likely to depend on the quality of *at least* the qualities of the originating, terminating, and interconnecting networks. In general, the quality of service experienced by subscribers on one corporate network may be affected by the quality of all the other networks which are interconnected.

The interdependence of network qualities may be quite complex, depending on what aspect of quality and type of network we are considering. For example, modem communications occur at the minimum baud rate supported along the transmission path. Only improvements in the speed of networks at the minimum rate permit faster communications. With back-up power arrangements, the reliability of each of network may be higher when interconnected if failure probabilities are uncorrelated.[7] In a packet network, the expansion of buffering at any node in the network may increase the likelihood of successful communications between all nodes.

The socially efficient quality choice, $x^*$, occurs when a single agent chooses the vector x so as to maximize total surplus, $W(x)$. We may think of this as the *centralized* solution which would emerge if the sub-networks could costlessly coordinate their quality choices. If we exclude the possibility of external subsidies, then the centralized solution may require transfer payments among the sub-networks.

When control over quality choices is decentralized, we have an N-player game wherein each network attempts to set the quality of its network as a best reply to the independent choices of the other N-1 networks. A *decentralized* solution, $x^0$, is a Nash equilibrium to this game, wherein each network i chooses $x_i^0$ so as to maximize its net incremental willingness-to-pay for quality, $U^i(x)$. With suitable regularity conditions regarding the domain of x and the functional forms of the $U^i(x)$, we can guarantee existence of at least one centralized and one decentralized solution.[8] Additional assumptions allow us to assure that the solutions are in the interior of the domain of x and can be characterized by the following first order necessary conditions (FONC):[9]

*Centralized Solution:* $x^*$ solves $\partial W/\partial x_i = \partial U^i/\partial x_i + \Sigma_{j \neq i}\partial U^j/\partial x_i = 0 \; \forall i \in N$ (2)

*Decentralized (Nash) Solution:* $x^0$ solves $\partial U^i/\partial x_i = 0 \; \forall i \in N$ (3)

These two classes of solutions represent extremes. The centralized solution represents the ideal which could arise from perfect cooperation among the sub-networks. With efficient bargaining, perhaps during the stage when interconnection agreements are defined, it is conceivable that the sub-networks could agree to implement x* and arrange side-payments among networks as necessary. In a sense, this is what occurred in the Bell Telephone network before divestiture. Ma Bell invested in improving the quality of network switches to optimize the benefits from both long distance and local exchange services. Improvements in intermachine trunking improved the quality of long distance services directly and local services indirectly by expanding the capacity for alternate routing. Ma Bell's cost/benefit analysis could take into account the effect on the combined long distance/local exchange market of changes in the quality of any constituent component.

At the other extreme, the decentralized solution presumes that perfect transfer payment schemes are impossible and assumes that agents care only about their private benefits. Although this is perhaps too pessimistic a view of how these decisions will be made, it seems overly optimistic to presume that the centralized solution will prevail. For example, consider the potential implications for antitrust and the costs of monitoring and enforcing the necessary transfer payments were the Baby Bells and AT&T to seek to reach such an agreement.

Without a further parameterization of the $U^i$ it will be impossible to specify the magnitude of any welfare differences which may exist. The advantage of considering these two classes of solutions is their ability to highlight the coordination problem which arises when we decentralize network control.

## 3. COMPARISON OF THE CENTRALIZED AND DECENTRALIZED SOLUTIONS

A comparison of these two solutions yields four important conclusions:

(i)   The decentralized solutions are all sub-optimal;
(ii)  Symmetric quality is neither desirable nor likely;
(iii) The decentralized solution may provide either too much or too little quality; and,
(iv)  Regulatory remedies may be difficult to implement.

Each of these conclusions is discussed at greater length below.

### 3.1. The decentralized solutions are all sub-optimal
From a comparison of the FONCs for the two solutions (Eqn 2 and 3), it is clear that $x^*$ and $x^0$ will differ unless:

$$\Sigma_{j \neq i} \partial U^i / \partial x_i = 0 \; \forall i \in N. \tag{4}$$

This term measures the marginal externality imposed on other networks when network i improves its quality. In general, we would not expect this term to be zero and so should not expect a decentralized solution to be optimal. If the networks compete with each other and quality is costly to improve, then the externality might be negative. For example, the $U^i$ might refer to profit functions for competing service providers or for corporations which use information technology as a source of competitive advantage (e.g., American Express improves its private network to offer more detailed customer billing services then VISA). Quality improvements on a competing network reduce own profits.

The networks may face a version of a Prisoners' Dilemma: when qualities differ, customers switch to the higher quality; but once qualities are matched, market shares are balanced. Although each firm's profits may be maximized if both could commit to low quality, it may be a dominant strategy to invest in high quality. Although the gains to consumers from having higher quality services may more than offset the reduction in industry profits, this need not be the case.

If the externality is negative, then the decentralized solution might result in excess quality wherein every network sets higher quality than is optimal. In this case, it may even be desirable to have *maximum* quality standards. The notion that there could be too much investment in quality may strike readers as implausible, yet corporate and political decision processes might impose just such a bias. After all, how often does one hear of a politician or corporate information officer (CIO) campaigning for lower quality and reliability (even when advocated cost-cutting will be expected to have this effect)? The costs of too little quality are apparent to everyone who uses the network, while awareness of the costs of too much quality may be apparent only to those few with detailed knowledge of the network. This may make the costs of errors in selecting the optimal quality level asymmetric for the decision-maker, inducing a bias in favor of erring on the side of excessive quality.

The externality would be positive if networks weakly benefited from improvements in the quality of other networks. For example, if other networks invest to reduce line noise or blocking probabilities, then internet callers to those networks may experience higher quality communications without bearing the costs of those improvements. In most cases, it seems likely that improvements in component quality lead to improvements in system quality, at least weakly. (The opposite might be true if quality improvements in one network lead to changes in traffic patterns which harmed the quality of another network or service.)

The above discussion should convince the reader that it is premature to presume *a priori* that we know the sign of the quality externality. Moreover, it is possible that the externality effects may be positive on some networks and negative on others. And, until we are able to sign the aggregate externality, we cannot determine which direction remedial policies should seek to move market outcomes should we seek to intervene. In spite of these difficulties, however, we can be reasonably certain that the externality is non-zero at $x^*$, and hence, the first term in Equation 2 is also nonzero, which corresponds to the FONC for the decentralized solution. Therefore, the decentralized solution will not be optimal.

It is also worth noting that generally the decentralized solution will not be unique, and when multiple solutions exist, these are likely to be Pareto rankable.[10] Let $x^{0-Low}$ and $x^{0-high}$ refer to the choices of x among the set of decentralized equilibria which minimize and maximize W(x), respectively. Thus, $W(x^*)-W(x^{0-high})$ is the minimum and $W(x^*)-W(x^{0-low})$ is the maximum welfare loss associated with decentralization. If there are multiple equilibria which are Pareto rankable, then there is the added coordination problem of selecting $x^{0-high}$ rather than $x^{0-low}$. For example, let us relax several of our assumptions regarding the form of $U^i$ and suppose $U^i=min(x_1,...,x_N)$ such that the quality of communications depends on the minimum quality set by any network.[11] In that case every symmetric equilibrium with $x_i=x_j$, for $i,j \in N$ is a decentralized equilibrium, but only the one were $x_i=xmax$ for every network is socially efficient.

### 3.2. Symmetric quality is neither desirable nor likely

The previous example notwithstanding, we should not expect symmetric solutions for either the centralized or decentralized solutions to prevail in general. As noted earlier, customers are likely to differ in their willingness-to-pay for quality improvements based on differences in their traffic patterns. These heterogeneous tastes are reflected in differences in the $U^i$ functions. If these differ, then it is reasonable to expect it to be optimal for networks to set different levels of quality and, in the market equilibrium, we should expect heterogeneous quality choices.

If all of the subscribers had identical tastes and started from symmetric positions (e.g., regarding their installed base), then we might expect all of the networks to agree to adopt the identical level of quality. Even with identical tastes, however, the symmetric solution may not be optimal if quality investments are a public good. For example, it may be optimal for only one of the networks to invest in a back-up power supply which could be made available to whichever network's primary power supply failed. Each of the networks may prefer that it not be selected as the one to make the investment and yet strictly prefer that at least one network makes the investment.

In the more typical case where subscribers tastes for quality differ, the heterogeneity in network quality will make it more difficult for policy-makers to effect welfare-improving quality improvements. For example, a uniform minimum quality standard will not be able to support the optimal solution since it cannot be higher than the minimum quality network in the centralized solution $x^*$, and thus will not be binding on networks which are supposed to set higher quality standards.

### 3.3. The decentralized solution may provide either too much or too little quality.

As noted earlier, unless we can specify the sign of the externality, we cannot say whether the welfare loss results from too much or too little quality. However, even if we assume that the externality is weakly positive for every network, we can only conclude that quality is too low on average.[12] By this we mean that it cannot be the case that *every* network sets quality too high in the optimal solution; however, it may be the case that *some* networks set too high quality in the decentralized solution.[13] This could occur if quality choices are *strategic substitutes* rather than *strategic complements*.[14] For example, in a packet switching network, investments to increase buffering capacity in one network may make it less desirable to increase buffering capacity in another network since it does not matter where packets are buffered. In this case, quality investments would be strategic substitutes. Alternatively, if the speed of one network is improved it may increase the marginal advantages from increasing the speed of other networks, or quality investment may be strategic complements.[15] When quality investments are strategic complements and the externality is positive, then we can be sure that the decentralized solution results in too little investment in quality. Although this seems to be the presumption with which most would-be regulators begin, it is instructive to note that this result depends on a number of important assumptions.

### 3.4. Regulatory remedies may be difficult to implement

Once we recognize that the market process will adopt a sub-optimal solution, it is reasonable to consider potential regulatory remedies. First, it should be obvious that there will exist a system of penalties and subsidies which, in theory, could support the efficient solution. Penalty/subsidy functions of the form:

$$T^i(x_i) = \Sigma_{j \neq i} U^j(x_i, x^*_{-i}) - \Sigma_{j \neq i} U^j(x^*_i, x^*_{-i}) \tag{5}$$

will cause each of the networks to internalize the externality and will support the efficient solution.[16]

Although this penalty scheme is theoretically plausible, it may be extremely difficult to implement in practice. The regulator would need to know each of the network $U^i$ functions which would require detailed knowledge about both subscribers' willingness-to-pay and the costs of improving the quality of each network. Acquiring this information is likely to be quite expensive, if not impossible. The costs of implementation would represent a deadweight loss which might very well overwhelm the welfare loss which they were designed to correct.

Similarly, it may be possible to design a pricing scheme for interconnection or for terminating network messages which would support the optimal solution. Once again, however, these would require more detailed information than is likely to be available to regulators and there is no reason to expect the appropriate prices to arise naturally (e.g., via a tatonnement process). Traditional externality problems are often more readily amenable to price-based solutions because the externality is associated with a commodity good. In the model presented here, the incremental quality of different networks are not perfect substitutes which can be traded. It is important *which* network's quality is improved. The marginal externality associated with the quality of each network depends on traffic patterns which may be affected by pricing schemes, thereby further complicating the regulatory problem. Furthermore, pricing or penalty/subsidy schemes which do not accurately reflect network payoffs may result in an outcome which is worse then the worst decentralized solution, $x^{0\text{-low}}$.

Minimum quality standards (MQS) offer another regulatory alternative which are superficially appealing precisely because they are easy to implement and require less information. If the centralized solution is symmetric, then an MQS can support the optimal solution, but when tastes are heterogeneous and both centralized and decentralized solutions call for different network qualities, the effects of MQS are more complex.

If the decentralized equilibrium is unique, the externality is positive and qualities are strategic complements, then we know there exists an MQS which is welfare improving. One such MQS is equal to the minimum quality which is set by any network in the optimal solution. This has to be welfare improving because the above assumptions guarantee that each network chooses too low quality in the decentralized solution, so forcing the minimum quality network to assume its level will weakly increase the quality of every other network. Since we have assumed that the externality is positive, this benefits all networks in aggregate. An MQS which exceeds this level, however, may be worse than the worst decentralized solution.

Alternatively, if qualities are strategic substitutes then the gains from improving the quality of a lower quality network may be more than offset by reductions in the quality of a higher quality network. In this case, there may not exist a welfare enhancing MQS.

If there are multiple equilibria, then MQS which are not binding may be welfare improving in an ex ante sense. If the equilibria are locally separated, then an MQS which helps select a Pareto superior Nash equilibrium can yield important benefits and yet not be binding on any of the networks in the observed equilibrium. Therefore, it is wrong to presume that the existence of an MQS which is not binding has no effect. However, since the inferior equilibrium is not observed and we may not be sure that it would have been selected in any case, it may be difficult to assess the gains from such an MQS.

The difficulties of calculating the optimal MQS and the dangers of setting one so high that welfare actually declines should caution us against setting overly aggressive performance standards. On the other hand, the potential coordination benefits suggest that more modest standards may offer large gains which will be difficult to measure directly.

The generality of the preceding conclusions is both their greatest virtue and their greatest vice. They illustrate the fundamental nature of the coordination problem which results from decentralizing network control. In the next section, I present a very simple numerical example and discuss a variety of extensions to the basic model.

## 4. EXTENSIONS AND FURTHER QUESTIONS

The next two sub-sections present simple examples to further elucidate the preceding discussion, while the third sub-section presents initial speculations of how introducing uncertainty might further complicate matters.

### 4.1. Example #1: Linear Quality and Demand

Consider a situation where there are N private networks which are interconnected through the PSTN (the quality of which we will treat as a parameter) and let the $U^i$ have the following form:

$$U^i = A_i x_i + B_i \Sigma_{j \neq i} (\alpha(x_i + x_j) + \beta x_p) - C x_i^\delta \tag{6}$$

where $A_i$, $B_i$, $C$, $\alpha$, $\beta$ and $\delta$ are positive constants with $\delta > 1$. The first term corresponds to the value to subscribers of on-net calls, which increases as the quality of the network, $x_i$, increases. The second term corresponds to the value of internet calls. In this formulation, the quality of internet calls depends on the sum of the quality of the originating and terminating network, weighted by $\alpha$, and the quality of the PSTN, given by $x_p$, and weighted by $\beta$. The $(A_i, B_i)$-parameters capture taste differences among the networks for on-net and off-net calling. The last term is the cost of increasing quality and $\delta$ is assumed greater than 1 to assure that costs are strictly convex. The FONC for the decentralized and centralized solutions are:

$$\partial U^i / \partial x_i = 0 = A_i + \alpha(N-1)B_i - \delta C x^{\delta-1} \tag{7}$$

$$\partial W / \partial x_i = 0 = \partial U^i / \partial x_i + \alpha \Sigma_{j \neq i} B_j \tag{8}$$

which yield the following unique solutions:

$$x_i^0 = \{[A_i + \alpha(N-1)B_i]/\delta C\}^{1/(\delta-1)} \text{ and } x_i^* = \{[A_i + \alpha(N-1)B_i + \alpha(N\hat{B} - B_i)]/\delta C\}^{1/(\delta-1)} \tag{9}$$

where $\hat{B} = (1/N)\Sigma_i B_i$. We know that the solution is unique since the $U^i$ are strictly concave in $x_i$. Also, note that the decentralized solution provides too little quality ($x_i^0 < x_i^*$) since the externality is positive and quality is a strategic substitute, and that surplus is lower in the decentralized solution. Furthermore, note that unless the $A_i$ and $B_i$ are identical, asymmetric qualities are both optimal and a decentralized equilibrium. Finally, notice that the optimal and decentralized solutions do not depend on the quality of the PSTN and so changes in its quality, while welfare improving for the N private networks, would not influence their quality choices. These results are readily apparent by inspection of the two solutions.

Now, let us assume that costs are quadratic ($\delta=2$) and the networks are symmetric ($A_i=A$ and $B_i=B$). With these additional assumptions, the solutions simplify to:

$$x_i^0 = [A+\alpha(N-1)B]/2C \quad \text{and} \quad x_i^* = x_i^0+\alpha(N-1)B/2C \tag{10}$$

which allows us to obtain a simple expression for the magnitude of the welfare loss associated with decentralization:

$$W(x^*)-W(x^0) = \alpha^2N(N-1)^2B^2 \tag{11}$$

Notice that the welfare loss increases with the value placed on internet calling quite rapidly.

## 4.2. A second simple example: quality is the minimum of the network qualities

Now, consider a slightly different version of the above example with symmetric utilities and quadratic costs, where the $U^i$ have the following form:

$$U^i = Ax_i + B\Sigma_{j\neq i}\min(x_i,x_j,x_p) - Cx_i^2 \tag{12}$$

In this example, the quality of internet calls is no longer the weighted sum of the qualities of the interconnecting networks, but rather the minimum of the quality experienced on the end-to-end path from the originating and terminating networks. With this formulation, the payoffs are no longer continuously differentiable, but it is still the case that the externality is weakly positive and that quality choices are weakly strategic complements.

In order to derive the solutions, notice that even if a network expected all of the other networks to choose zero qualities, it would choose to set $x_i=A/2C>0$ because on-net calling would still be valuable; and, no network would ever choose quality greater than $(A+(N-1)B)/2C$, even if all of the other networks and the PSTN had arbitrarily high qualities. Therefore, the optimal centralized solution is for all networks to choose the $x_i$ equal to $A/2C$ if $x_p$ is less than $A/2C$; and, otherwise choose $x_i$ equal to the minimum of $x_p$ and $(A+(N-1)B)/2C$. Any symmetric solution where x is between $A/2C$ and the minimum of $x_p$ and $(A+(N-1)B)/2C$ is a decentralized solution. Thus, in this example, the optimal solution is also always a Nash equilibrium; however, it is only when the quality of the PSTN is sufficiently low ($x_p<A/2C$) that we can be sure the two solutions will coincide and there will not be a welfare loss associated with decentralization of network control. Once the PSTN's quality gets sufficiently high, there is a potential coordination problem associated with selecting one of the symmetric low quality equilibria.[17]

Finally, note that as the quality of the PSTN increases, the losses from failing to coordinate on the efficient solution increases. In a sense, quality choices become more "strategic." Ignoring bypass issues, when $x_p$ is sufficiently low, everyone agrees on the optimal solution and voluntary enforcement of the efficient outcome is easily achieved. As the network quality increases, however, externality issues become more important.[18] Whenever the quality-externalities become more important, both the efficiency losses from failing to enforce the centralized solution and the costs of enforcement[19] are likely to be larger. It is exactly under such circumstances that specialized institutional structures (e.g., voluntary standard setting bodies) may become important, especially if information asymmetries preclude effective use of more direct regulatory interventions (e.g., the government orders everyone to adopt $q^*$).

In the first example, quality investments are perfect substitutes -- improvements in any of the networks along the end-to-end path contribute to overall quality. The second example examines the case where quality is determined by the weakest link in the end-to-end chain. Which functional form better reflects reality is a question for the engineers, and surely depends on what one means by "quality." The first might correspond to a packet network where one's measure of quality is *average* end-to-end packet delay, while the second might be relevant if one is concerned with the *maximum* end-to-end delay. The former measure is important if one is interested in supporting asynchronous terminal sessions, while the latter is important if one wishes to support video or telephony.

### 4.3. Effect of Uncertainty

In all of the analyses above, I have assumed perfect information. As long as quality is *ex post* verifiable and it is possible to specify and enforce complete, contingent contracts, uncertainty should not represent a problem for implementation of the centralized solution. The presumption of ex post verifiability and enforcement may be reasonable for agreements governing quality attributes which are based on a large sample of (at least in principle) inexpensive observations. For example, delay until dial tone is received or line noise (bit error rates) seem amenable to low cost monitoring and successful contracting. Breach would be quickly detected. These sorts of situations are perhaps the easiest for regulators to address.

In contrast, network reliability -- interpreted as freedom from major disruptions -- offers a more difficult problem. Increased reliability is provided via back-up capacity. Since major network failures are (of necessity) a very infrequent occurrence, it may be much more difficult to reliably ascertain the quality of back-up systems ex ante. A moral hazard problem may arise if the probability of failure is low enough, the costs of unreliable back-up are great enough, and there are no criminal penalties available to deter breach ex ante. For example, in the absence of criminal penalties, a "fly-by-night" database network might agree to provide high-quality back-up services which would become operational in the event of a major system failure on connected sub-networks. The back-up provider could collect insurance premiums up front and declare bankruptcy if a major failure resulted in it breaching its contract.

From a modelling perspective, the effect of uncertainty would be likely to increase the multiplicity of equilibria since they would depend on participants' beliefs regarding true costs and benefits and each other's strategies. This seems likely to further complicate the coordination problem and thus the present analysis may be overly optimistic. On the other hand, if uncertainty is sufficiently severe we may be blissfully ignorant of just how far from the optimal outcome we are.

### 5. CONCLUSIONS

This paper presents a first step towards understanding how the fragmentation of control over our information infrastructure might affect the quality of service. The results suggest that we cannot remain comfortable that the market's *Invisible Hand* will guarantee a simple solution. In a network of interconnected sub-networks, each network will invest in improvements which will affect the interests of subscribers on other networks. The quality-externality may be positive or negative. There are likely to be a multiplicity of equilibria which will further complicate efforts to internalize the externality and make it resistant to simple regulatory remedies. Since tastes for quality are inherently heterogeneous, the optimal solution will involve heterogeneous qualities, which cannot be enforced with uniform quality standards. The present analysis assumes perfect information, but in more realistic situations, we might expect there to be significant uncertainty and asymmetric information which would hamper both public policy interventions and/or collective decision-making among the sub-networks. Although it is theoretically possible to support the optimal quality solution with centrally-administered subsidy/penalty schemes or pricing, implementing these in practice may be very difficult. Minimum quality standards, however, may be useful in precluding coordination on a Pareto inferior equilibrium, when there are multiple such equilibria.

Thus, the growing public concern regarding the effects on network quality of increased decentralization, deregulation and its attendant implications for industry structure appear warranted. Additional theoretical and empirical work is needed to help determine the magnitude of the potential threat. We need much better data on the costs and benefits of improving quality and reliability in our information infrastructure and how these are allocated among producers and consumers.

## REFERENCES

Besanko, D., Donnenfeld, S. and White, L., "The Multiproduct Firm, Quality Choice and Regulation," *The Journal of Industrial Economics*, vol. XXXVI, no. 4, 411-429, June 1988.

Bulow, J., Geanakoplos, J. and Klemperer, P., "Multimarket Oligopoly: Strategic Substitutes and Complements," *Journal of Political Economy*, 93, 488-511, 1985.

Gabszewicz, J. and J. Thisse "Price Competition, Quality and Income Disparities," *Journal of Economic Theory*, vol 20, 340-359, 1979.

Heal, G., "Economics of Networks," draft CITI Private Network Conference paper, Winter 1992.

Laffont, J. and J. Tirole, "The Regulation of Multiproduct Firms, Part I: Theory," *Journal of Public Economics*, vol 43, 1-36, 1990.

Laffont, J. and J. Tirole, "The Regulation of Multiproduct Firms, Part II: Applications to Competitive Environments and Policy Analysis," *Journal of Public Economics*, vol 43, 37-66, 1990.

Motta, M., "Endogenous Quality and Coordination of Decisions," Center for Operations Research and Econometrics Discussion Paper #9152, Universite Catholique de Louvain, Belgium, October 1991.

Schmalensee, R., "Market Structure, Durability, and Quality: A Selective Survey," *Economic Inquiry*, vol 17, 177-196, April 1979.

Shaked, A. and J. Sutton, "Relaxing Price Competition Through Product Differentiation," *Review of Economic Studies*, vol 49, 3-1, 1982.

Spence, M., "Monopoly, Quality and Regulation," *Bell Journal of Economics*, vol 6, no 2, 417-429, Autumn 1975.

## ENDNOTES

[1] I would like to thank Stan Besen, Niel Stolleman, Glen Woroch and participants in the Columbia Institute for Tele-Information's conference on *Private Networks and Public Objectives* on May 15, 1992, for helpful comments. All remaining errors are my own.

114

[2.] Besanko, D., Donnenfeld, S. and White, L., "The Multiproduct Firm, Quality Choice and Regulation," *The Journal of Industrial Economics*, vol. XXXVI, no. 4, June 1988, 411-429, Laffont, J. and J. Tirole, "The Regulation of Multiproduct Firms, Part I: Theory," *Journal of Public Economics*, vol 43 (1990a) 1-36, Laffont, J. and J. Tirole, "The Regulation of Multiproduct Firms, Part II: Applications to Competitive Environments and Policy Analysis," *Journal of Public Economics*, vol 43 (1990b) 37-66, Schmalensee, R., "Market Structure, Durability, and Quality: A Selective Survey," *Economic Inquiry*, vol 17, April 1979, 177-196 and Spence, M., "Monopoly, Quality and Regulation," *Bell Journal of Economics*, vol 6, no 2, Autumn 1975, 417-429.

[3.] Gabszewicz, J. and J. Thisse (1979) "Price Competition, Quality and Income Disparities," *Journal of Economic Theory*, vol 20, 340-359, Motta, M., "Endogenous Quality and Coordination of Decisions," Center for Operations Research and Econometrics Discussion Paper #9152, Universite Catholique de Louvain, Belgium, October 1991 and Shaked, A. and J. Sutton (1982) "Relaxing Price Competition Through Product Differentiation," *Review of Economic Studies*, vol 49, 3-14.

[4.] Interested readers are encouraged to see the working paper on which the present chapter is based entitled "Network Quality Choices in a Network of Networks," January 1992, CITI Working Paper #521.

[5.] Heal, G., "Economics of Networks", draft CITI Private Network Conference paper, Winter 1992.

[6.] In a world of virtual networks, building networks and Centrex services, even on-net calls may be routed across facilities whose quality is controlled independently.

[7.] Assume networks 1 and 2 provide mutual emergency back-up power such that either network fails only if both networks fail. This agreement improves the reliability of both networks if the probability failures are either negatively or uncorrelated; however, if they are positively correlated then reliability may decline. The latter could occur if failures propagate across networks.

[8.] To guarantee existence of a socially optimal *centralized* solution, $x^*$, define the domain of x such that the quality of sub-network i is a real scalar such that $0 \leq x_i \leq xmax < \infty$; and let each of the $U^i(x)$ be continuous on the domain of x. To guarantee the existence of a *decentralized* or Nash solution, further assume that the $U^i$ are concave in own-quality, $x_i$.

[9.] To allow characterization of the solutions by FONC, assume that the $U^i$ are twice continuously differentiable on x. To guarantee that the solutions $x^*$ and $x^N$ are interior, assume the following boundary conditions hold for each i: (i) $U^i_i(0,x_{-i}) \geq 0$ (normalization); (ii) $U^i_i(xmax,x_{-i}) < 0$ (guarantees never optimal nor equilibrium for any network to set $x_i=xmax$); and, (iii) $U^i_i(0,x_{-i}) > 0$ (guarantees never optimal to set quality of network i to zero). These assumptions are sufficient, but not necessary to guarantee the existence of interior solutions.

[10.] Even if the centralized solution is not unique, all solutions will yield the same total welfare. Assumption that $U^i$ is strictly concave in $x_i$ is sufficient to guarantee uniqueness of decentralized solution.

[11.] This example does not satisfy the assumptions made above regarding the form of $U^i$, (e.g., $U^i$ is not twice differentiable and $U^i(xmax,x) > 0$). It is useful because it clearly demonstrates the problem of multiple equilibria.

[12.] Formally, assume that $\partial U^i/\partial x_j \geq 0$ $\forall j \neq i$ and $\forall i$, $\exists j \neq i$ such that $\partial U^i/\partial x_j > 0$ so that for each network there is at least one other network which strictly benefits when network i improves its quality.

[13.] The proof is by counter-example.

[14.] Besanko, D., Donnenfeld, S. and White, L., "The Multiproduct Firm, Quality Choice and Regulation," *The Journal of Industrial Economics*, vol. XXXVI, no. 4, June 1988, 411-429.

[15.]Formally, $x_i$ and $x_j$ are strategic complements or substitutes if $\partial U^i/\partial x_i \partial x_j$ and $\partial U^i/\partial x_i \partial x_j$ are both weakly positive or negative, respectively.

[16.]Note that $\partial U^i/\partial x_i + \partial T^i/\partial x_i = \partial W/\partial x_i = 0$ at $x^*$.

[17.]Although an MQS can easily support the efficient outcome, this is not especially interesting since the example is so simple.

[18.]Free-riding is not really an issue in the symmetric case, but it could be in the asymmetric case where the $B_i$ differ.

[19.]One might expect monitoring/enforcement costs to be larger when the private gains from deviating from $q^*$ are larger according to the old adage "where there's a will, there's a way.."

PRIVATE NETWORKS PUBLIC OBJECTIVES
E. Noam and A. NíShúilleabháin (Editors)

# Network Evolution and Coalition Formation[1]

Graciela Chichilnisky

## 1. INTRODUCTION

International financial networks such as Euroclear, CEDEL, SWIFT, and Global Custody networks, are important factors in the rapid development of cross-border securities trading.[2] The value of the transactions going through these networks is high: more than US $4 billion worth of cross-border equities are transacted daily.

Network services exhibit two distinctive characteristics: (1) The willingness to pay increases with the level of activity, because the network is more valuable when it has more uses;[3] and (2) Unit costs decrease with the volume sold, because there are large fixed set-up costs.[4] Because of these characteristics the economic fundamentals of the market for network services can be opposite to what is predicted in classic textbook examples: the supply can be downward sloping, while the demand can increase with prices.[5] For these reasons the evolution of the market for network services can be very different from that of standard markets.

As global capital markets evolve the communications and administration of trading requires more complex and extensive networks. The emergence of the services needed to support global capital markets depends on the feasibility or the survival of the network service. A large "capital mass" of users may be necessary before a network producer "breaks even" i.e. achieves positive profits.[6] Once this critical mass is achieved, however, there are increasing profits to be obtained from each additional user. For this reason setting-up a network is often described as a "start-up" problem. This problem can be difficult to solve: Many potentially valuable networks fail to emerge or to survive. This paper argues that the formation of certain coalitions of users can solve this problem. The idea is that if no one can find smaller coalitions of users which produce strong positive externalities to each other, the size of the critical mass can be reduced, and the start-up problem can be overcome. The literature has not examined so far the formation of coalitions of users which can exploit the externalities which they induce on others. This is the main focus of the paper.

### 1.1. Network Coalitions

The formation of coalition of users can be crucial for the network's operation. Many international securities networks are organized into "clusters" of users (coalitions) who "communicate" with each other much more frequently than they do with the rest of the users. Examples are global custodians cross-border securities holdings. They use a network such as SWIFT and CEDEL to make and receive payments or other instructions with several thousand entitites across the world. In addition, these banks communicate routinely with about forty other banks worldwide, which are called their "subcustodians." Subcustodians handle the paper instruments, and administer and report on taxes and corporate actions in each country. Furthermore, the global custodians also have a network of clients, several hundreds on occasions, with whom they also communicate very frequently. Each communication is about a cross-order transaction of typically US $50,000 or more.

The bank has, therefore, two levels of network use: "infrequent use" to communicate with a large number of institutions across the world, and "frequent use" to communicate with a smaller group of institutions such as subcustodians or customers. The ability to communicate with the latter, i.e. at the "frequent use" level, is very valuable. Fewer parties of the second type are needed in the network for the user to reach the same level of benefit that the user derives from infrequent use. Therefore, if a cluster of users of the second type become network users, in practice the "critical mass" required to break even can be smaller.

## 1.2. The Network Evolution

With these practical applications in mind we formalize a network market with many users. Using game theory and dynamic stochastic analysis, we show how the network evolves. We define a critical mass, define stochastic process of coalition formation through time, and specify the long-run properties of the resulting network market.

We explore the formation of coalitions of users when the externalities produced by the players are heterogeneous, i.e. when there exist clusters of players which produce more externalities to each other than they do to the rest of the potential users. Proposition 12 and Corollary 13 establish that the gains from decentralization in this context, i.e. the gains from distinguishing those clusters and producing a cluster of networks rather than one big centralized network, are surprisingly large. We show below that the probability of success of the network *increases exponentially* with decreases in the size of the clusters. This may account for the actual network structure (clusters of users) that one observes in practice (e.g. global custody networks).

Proposition 12 and several examples explore the gains to decentralization formulated by calculating the stopping time until coalitions of critical mass are formed. This is financially important since until critical mass is reached, profits are negative. The critical mass of the network (Section 5) measures its economic feasibility in terms of the number of players which are required for positive profits and determines the number and the stability properties of Nash equilibrium of a network game (Sections 3 and 4, Propositions 8 and 9 and Corollaries 10 and 11). We show that the set of Nash equilibria are quite different under different information structures.

## 1.3. A Dynamic Network Game

With these applications in mind, we formalize the network market and study a dynamic game determining its dynamics and equilibria or steady states.

Users come into the network following a stochastic process. They may stay or leave depending on the economic incentives. There are large and small users; the former are informed about the externalities which they produce to other users, and the latter are not. Two scenarios are considered. In the first, the externalities between the users are homogeneous: all players within a certain group must simultaneously join the network in order for the critical mass to be achieved. A second scenario studies the expected length of time required to reach a critical mass of users with clusters of users which are heterogeneous in terms of the externalities they produce to each other. We prove the existence of solutions and the number of solutions under different characteristics of the users. We explore the characteristics of the critical mass and the difficulties of the start-up problem. We show in Proposition 12 that the probability of success (survival) of the network increases exponentially with decreases in the size of the clusters. Somewhat suprisingly, while the size of the clusters is all important, the number of clusters required to break even is almost irrelevant.

## 2. THE ECONOMICS OF INTERNATIONAL FINANCIAL NETWORKS

We focus on two main characteristics of international financial networks:

*Communications externalities:* The parties exchange information through the network. Thus the more parties that are accessible through the network, the more valuable the network's communicating ability is.

*Audit trails:* A historical record of each transaction must be kept. Audit trails are records of the messages sent, by whom, and when, and of the actions taken by the different parties with respect to each trade.

These characteristics motivate the following definitions:

Let $u_i(q_i,x)$ be the $i$ th user's utility from consuming a quantity $q_i$ of the network services or messages, and let $x$ be the number of users, indexed by the integers. The variable $q_i$ is either 0 or 1 depending on whether the network is used or not. Since the utility derived from using the network increases with the number of other users:

$$\frac{d}{dx} u_i(q_i, x) > 0 \tag{1}$$

Similarly, when there are no users the utility of using the network is zero:

$$u_i(q_i, 0) = 0 \tag{2}$$

Assume all users use the same amount of network services, and choose units of measurement so that the total quantity of network services consumed is equal to the number of users.[7] Let $u_i = u_j$ for all $i, j \in X = R^+$. Conditions (2.1) and (2.2) imply that users are willing to pay higher fees for the same network services when the network has more users, and that at zero network use, they will only wish to pay 1. Formally:

$$\frac{d}{dx} D(x) > 0 \tag{3}$$

and

$$D(0) = 0$$

where $D(x)$ is the $x$'s user "willingness to pay" for the network services, given that up to $x$ users are already using the network. The associated demand function is also denoted $D$.

In economic terms the network's data bases and switches are *fixed costs* in the provision of network services, since they must be incurred independently of the amount of network use. These costs are generally quite large and typically incurred once. This implies that the average cost of a message decreases with the number of messages, so that there are increasing returns to scale in the production of the network services. The average cost of a message typically decreases and goes to zero as the number of messages goes to infinity, which we now assume. This gives rise to an average cost curve denoted $C(x)$, satisfying:

$$\frac{d}{dx} C(x) < 0 \tag{4}$$

and

$$\lim_{x \to \infty} C(x) = 0 \tag{5}$$

We assume $C(x)$ that is continuous. The associated supply curve is denoted $S(p)$, where $p$ denotes price. The user's externalities lead to an upward sloping demand curve $D(x)$, while increasing returns in production lead to a downward sloping average cost curve $C(x)$. Diagram 1 illustrates.

Diagram 1

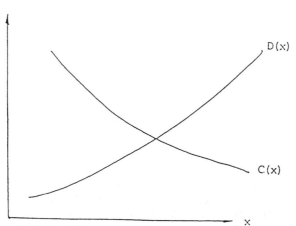

D(.) is willingness to pay; C(.) is average cost.

We are concerned here with the "start up problem"; therefore we assume that a producer's main concern is to break even in order to cover its fixed costs and operate with non-negative profits. An *Average Cost Pricing Equilibrium* is defined as a price-quantity vector at which the market clears, and producers charge at average cost. At such an equilibrium, producers break even:

*Observation:* Under conditions 2.1, 2.2, 2.3, 2.4, and 2.5, there is a unique market clearing average cost pricing equilibrium $(p^*,x^*)$ such that $x$ satisfies $D(x^*) = C(x^*)$ and $p^*=D(x^*)$. This equilibrium is unstable under either the *quantity adjustment process*

$$(2.6) \quad \dot{x} = \lambda(D(x) - C(x)), \text{ for a real number, } \lambda > 0, \tag{6}$$

or under the *Walrasian price adjustment process*

$(2.7)\, \dot{p} = \mu(ED(p))$, for a real number, $\mu > 0$, $\qquad\qquad$ (7)

where $ED(p)$ denotes the excess demand function $D^{-1}(p)-C^{-1}(p)$. This market clearing equilibrium is Pareto inefficient as it undersupplies network services: for all $\epsilon > 0$, $(p^*,x^*)$ is Pareto inferior to a non-market clearing allocation (a price - quantity vector) with quantity $x^* + \epsilon$ users and with prices defined by their willingness to pay $D(x^*+\epsilon)$. Producers charge according to the average cost curve $C(x^*+\epsilon)$.

Diagram 2

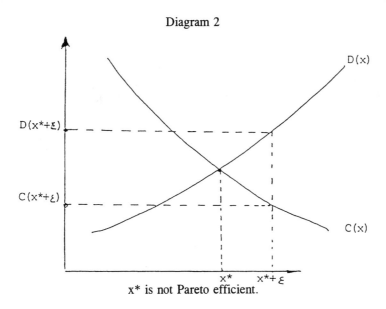

x* is not Pareto efficient.

A proof is given in the Appendix.

*Definition 1:* A *Critical Mass* of users is the *quantity* of users at which producers break even: the willingness to pay curve intersects the average cost curve.

A critical mass of users consumes a quantity of network services which is equal to that produced at the average cost pricing equilibrium. At this quantity of network services, each user's willingness to pay equals or exceeds average cost, leading to no loss or to a net gain to the user who joins the network. Below the critical mass the opposite is true, namely average costs exceed willingness to pay, so there is a net loss from using the network.

## 3. THE NETWORK GAME

We shall now consider strategic moves on the part of the users. Through time, users choose strategically whether to join the network or not, or whether to leave the network once joined. Over time, a typical user will join or leave the network several times. The user's strategic decisions lead to a level of network use, and therefore to an average cost and to a price they are willing to pay.

In order to simplify notation users are now indexed by the positive integers, i.e. $X = \{1,2,...\}$.[8]

122

A *Network Game G* is defined as follows. The *players* are all the potential network users in the set $X$. Each player $y \epsilon X$ has *two possible strategies*: to use the network or not to use it: if $\varphi(y)$ is player y's move, then $\varphi(y)$ is either 0 or 1. Through time a player may either join or leave the network, and may do so several times. The *quantity of network use* is the sum of the player's strategies:

$$x = \sum_y \varphi(y) \qquad (8)$$

Assuming that producers charge at average costs, the *payoff* to the players who use the network are their welfare gains (or losses), defined as the difference between two prices: the average cost and the willingness to pay. In other words: a player is better off the larger its willingness to pay in relation to the average cost which it pays for the service:

*Definition 2:*The *payoff* to the player who plays strategy 1 is the difference between the user's willingness to pay and the average costs computed at the sum of the players' strategies:

$$x = \sum_y \varphi(y), \quad i.e. \qquad (9)$$

$$P(\varphi) = D\left(\sum_y \varphi(y)\right) - C\left(\sum_y \varphi(y)\right) \qquad (10)$$

Diagram 3

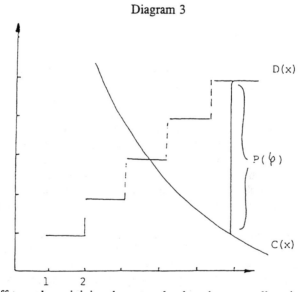

The payoff to a player joining the network when the game allocation is $\varphi$.

The payoff to the player who plays the strategy zero is zero, i.e. $P(0)=0$.

All players know the average costs and demand function, as well as the total number of users.

*Definition 3:* We define a large player as one who is aware of the impact of its strategy on prices, and acts accordingly.

*Definition 4:* A small player is one who acts as if it had no influence on prices.

Each player aims at maximizing payoffs. Denote the cardinality of the set of players $X$ by $X_{max}$, with $x^* < X_{max} < \infty$.

*Definition 5:* A game allocation[9] $\varphi^*$ is a Nash equilibrium when, for each player $x'$, $\varphi^*(x')$ is the optimal response of player $x'$ to the strategies played in $\varphi^*$ by all the others.[10]

*Definition 6:* An adjustment process is defined now as follows:

$$\varphi_{t+1} = \varphi_t^+ \tag{11}$$

where $\varphi_t^+$ is the optimal reaction to allocation $\varphi_t$, defined so that for each player $x$:

$$P(\varphi_t^+(x), \varphi_t^0(x)) = \max_\theta P(\theta, \varphi_t^0(x)) \tag{12}$$

Observe that a Nash Equilibrium is a *steady state* of this adjustment process, i.e. a game allocation $\varphi^*$ such that $(\varphi^*)^+ = \varphi^*$.

*Definition 7:* The *region of stability of a steady state* $\varphi^*$ denoted $S(\varphi^*)$, is the set of all game allocations $\varphi^0$ such that if the adjustment process start at one such allocation, then it will converge to the steady state $\varphi^*$. Formally $\varphi^0 \in S(\varphi^*)$ iff $\varphi_{t=0} = \varphi^0$ implies:

$$\lim_{t \to \infty} \varphi_t = \varphi^* \tag{13}$$

## 4. NASH EQUILIBRIA WITH SMALL AND LARGE PLAYERS

The steady states of the network are quite different when the traders are small as compared to when they are large. The following results are proven in the Appendix.

*Proposition 8:* When players are large, the network game $G$ has two Nash Equilibria, denoted $E_0$ and $E_{Xmax}$: the former has no network use, and the latter includes all users. Both equilibria are locally unique, and they are also locally stable according to the adjustment process (3.1). Once the usage of the network up to the critical mass minus one is reached, the adjustment process converges to the equilibrium $E_0$, so that the network does not survive. Once usage on or above the critical mass is achieved, this leads necessarily[11] to the equilibrium $E_{Xmax}$. The equilibrium $E_0$ is not Pareto efficient. The equilibrium $E_{Xmax}$ is Pareto efficient, but at $E_{Xmax}$ the market does not clear; there is an excess demand for network services.

*Proposition 9:* Assume that players are small, and that at the critical mass usage the costs equal the willingness to pay. Then the network game $G$ has as many Nash equilibria as the number of all combinations of players into subgroups of critical mass size, plus two i.e. $(Xmax_{x^*}) + 2$. The latter two are the Nash equilibria $E_0$ and $E_{Xmax}$ defined in Proposition 8. The Equilibrium $E_0$ is Pareto inferior. Once the number of users reaches the level of critical mass minus one, the network will converge to the equilibrium $E_0$. $E_{Xmax}$ is a Pareto efficient and stable Nash equilibrium, but the market does not clear at $E_{Xmax}$. Once the number of users equals or exceeds the critical mass plus one the network converges to the equilibrium $E_{Xmax}$. All the $(Xmax_{x^*})$ equilibria with a critical mass are unstable. Furthermore, if at the critical mass the willingness to pay exceeds the network costs, then there are only two Nash equilibria, $E_0$ and $E_{Xmax}$.

## 5. CRITICAL MASS

The results presented so far indicate the importance of the critical mass in determining the network's behaviour. The critical mass is the smallest number of users at which producers' profits cease to be negative. Below the critical mass, the network is not sustainable since firms make negative profits. The following corollaries show a negative correlation between the size of the critical mass and the ability of the network to converge to its Pareto Optimal position. They also show how fixed costs and the level of externalities can influence the size of the critical mass itself:

*Corollary 10:* The area of convergence to the Pareto Optimal Nash Equilibrium decreases as the critical mass increases.

*Proof:* This follows from Proposition 9.

*Corollary 11:* The critical mass of the network decreases when fixed costs decrease, or when the externalities among the users increase.

*Proof:* This follows from conditions 2.1, 2.2, 2.3, 2.4, and 2.5 of the function $C$ and $D$.

However important is the critical mass for both producers and users, it is an unstable position. If the critical mass is exceeded, usage will immediately increase towards the e Pareto Optimum, $E_{Xmax}$. If, however, the critical mass is not reached, usage will inevitably dwindle to zero, i.e. to the Pareto inferior equilibrium $E_0$. These are the conclusions we reach when examining the network usage problem as a non-cooperative game for the users. In order to reach a Pareto efficient solution, it is essential to reach the critical mass. This requires the simultaneous decision by at least $x^*$ users to join the network. A cooperative solution, namely the formation of a coalition, could resolve the problem and lead the economy towards the Pareto Optimal solution $E_{Xmax}$. The critical mass required for optimality, therefore calls for the formation of coalitions to resolve the network start up problem.

## 6. START-UP: A GAME OF COALITION FORMATION

The difficulty in reaching a Pareto efficient outcome resides in the formation of coalitions of the right size, at least a critical mass size. This is a necessary condition for the network to break even and thus to its commercial feasibility. This is called the network "start up" problem. The amount of time needed to reach a critical mass is crucial in the financial feasibility of the "start up." A common strategy[12] is to subsidize the first users until critical mass is reached and then charge according to monopoly pricing or any other feasible pricing rule. If such a strategy is followed, and $F$ represents fixed costs at each period $t$, then in financial terms the network must justify a maximum loss of $\$F$ per period during each time $t \geq 0$ period until a $T$ is reached at which $x(T) \geq x^*$. In other words, the network may have to justify a loss of up to:

$$ML = \sum_{t=0}^{T} F \lambda^{-t} \tag{14}$$

where $T$ satisfies $x(T) \geq x^*$, and $0 < \lambda < 1$ is a discount factor. Obviously, any strategy which minimizes $T$ makes the start up problem easier. In particular, considering the present discounted value of a stream of net revenue over an infinite time horizon, denoted $R$, the decision problem of the network manager is whether $R$ is smaller or exceeds $ML$ at an appropriate discount rate $\lambda$. This problem is obviously very sensitive to the value of $T$.

The following shows how $T$ may decrease dramatically when instead of aiming at the formation of one coalition of critical mass, we form several "locking" subcoalitions of smaller size. A possible rationale for seeking the formation of such subcoalitions is that the players are heterogeneous: they naturally divide into subgroups within which players produce stronger externalities to each other than they do to the rest of the network users. An example is provided by dividing the population of users in subsets of users which communicate more frequently with each other than with the rest of the network, or those subsets of users who share a common data base or node. Rohlfs[13] calls this phenomenon a "non-uniform calling pattern."

## 7. EXAMPLE 1: AN HETEROGENEOUS NETWORK WITH 6 PLAYERS

Consider a network with six users, indicated with the letters a to f. Users a, b and c form subcoalition I, and within this group users produce externalities of value 20 to each other. The same is true for users within subcoalition II, composed of users d, e, and f. The externalities produced by a member of subcoalition I to a member of subcoalition II are always equal to 2. Assume that externalities are symmetric, i.e. player $i$ produces the same externality on player $j$ as $j$ does on $i$. The average level of user 0 to user externalities in this network is $(20 \times 2 + 6)/5 \sim 9$. Assume for simplicity that average costs are constant $C(x) = 35$. Consider now the *willingness to pay* $D(x)$ as defined in Sections 1 and 2, averaged over all possible players. Formally, this is generated by the average externalities between the users so that $D(1)$ = average externality to any player of one other player being in the network. Then $D(1) \sim 9, D(2) \sim 18$ etc. Then we need at least four users to form a critical mass of the network, since $D(4) = 36 > 35$ while for any $x < 4, D(x) < 35$.

Note however that if any *two* users *within one group* agree simultaneously to use the network, their specific willingness to pay denoted $D*(a,b) = 40$ which exceeds the average willingness to pay for two players, $D(2) = 18$, is larger than average costs $= 35$. Thus, if two such users within one subcoalition agree simultaneously to use the network, their payoff exceeds average costs and thus in terms of the strategies defined for the game $G$, they will stay in the network. We indicate this by saying that these two players are "locked in." The formation of a "decentralized" critical mass, (consisting here of the two players in subcoalition I) depends then not only on the number of users but also on what users join the network at any one time. When users are heterogeneous, a critical mass could then be achieved much more quickly when there exist "clusters" of users with stronger externalities.

## 8. RANDOM COALITION FORMATION WITH HETEROGENEOUS USERS

With Example 1 in mind we seek to formalize the formation of users' coalitions by a dynamic game generated by a random process with memory. As in sections 1 and 2 there is a set $X$ of potential player indexed by integers, of cardinality $X_{max}$. Since users are heterogeneous, they produce different externalities to each other. Certain subsets $S_\gamma$ of $\beta$ players each (called subcoalitions of critical mass) are given initially. They consist of players who produce more externalities to each other if they use the network, than they would produce to others outside their subsets. Assume that the willingness to pay of each player in the set $S_\gamma$ when all others in $S_\gamma$ are in the network, matches or exceeds the average costs of serving the $\beta$ players in this subcoalition. Formally, let $e_{ij}$ denote the externality produced by

126

# Diagram 4

## A Heterogeneous Network with six Players

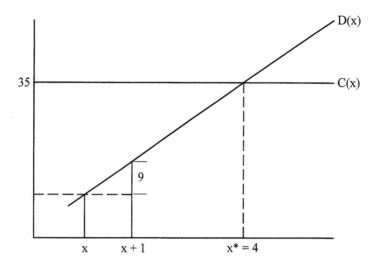

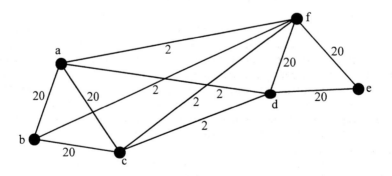

user $i$ on the user $j$ which we may assume is symmetric ($e_{ij}=e_{ji}$). Consider the average externality on the $j$ player, defined as:

$$e_j = \frac{1}{X_{max}} [ \sum_{i=1,\ldots,X_{max}, i \neq j} (e_{ij}) ] \tag{15}$$

This defines an average willingness to pay denoted $D(.)$, where $D(n+1)-D(n)=e$, or $D(n)=ne$ where $e$ is defined by:

$$e = \frac{1}{X_{max}} \sum j \, e_j \tag{16}$$

By the assumption made on the subcoalitions:

$$S_\gamma \text{ for each j in } S_\gamma \quad \sum_{i,j \in S_\gamma} e_{ij} \geq D(x^*) \tag{17}$$

where $x^*$ is the critical mass defined from the average costs $C(x)$, as in Section 2. There are $\alpha$ disjoint critical mass subcoalitions $S_\gamma$ with $\alpha \times \beta = x^* \leq X_{max}$.

At any time $t=0,1,2,\ldots$ each of the in $X$ players has an equal change of joining or not joining the network. The decision of each player to join the network or not at time $t$ is independent from the decisions of all other players at time $t$, and is also independent from the decision of this player at other times as well *except that* if at any time $t$ the $\beta$ members of one subcoalition $S_\gamma$ agree simultaneously to join the network, then their payoff meets the average costs and they are "locked in": for all $t \geq t'$ the payers in $S_\gamma$ remain in the network i.e. $\varphi(j)(t')=1 \forall t' \geq t, j \in S_\gamma$. The game continues with other players sometimes joining and sometimes leaving the network. Typically each player will join and leave the network several times. However, once locked into a subcoalition with a "critical mass," the player will remain locked in. The random game continues without the members of the subgroups who have agreed, i.e. with $k.\beta$. less players, where $k$ is the number of subgroups who have agreed at any time t. This random game formalizes the formation of coalitions in the network.

We study the expected numbers of periods until a critical mass of players $x^*$ have joined the network via subcoalitions $S_\gamma$ (denoted $ET$). We compare this with the expected number of periods needed for a critical mass $x^*$ of players to decide simultaneously (at any one time $t$) to join the network. The problem of finding a coalition of "average" critical mass ($x^*$) to make the network sustainable is then related to that of forming several smaller (decentralized) subcoalitions with total cardinality adding up to the average critical mass. We show that on average the speed with which the critical mass is reached with decentralized coalitions increases exponentially with decentralization (i.e. with the size of the subcoalitions) but it is surprisingly indifferent to the total number of such subcoalitions. This indifference is the source of decentralization efficiencies.

With this background, the random game of coalition formation is formalized mathematically as follows. At each trial $\alpha$ groups of $\beta$ fair coins are tossed, $\alpha \times \beta = x^*$. We stop as soon as every one of the groups of coins has come up all heads in at least one trial. We call this the formation of a $\alpha,\beta$- *decentralized coalition*, namely one made up of $\alpha$ subcoalitions of size $\beta$ each. We compare the expected number of trials $ET$ to form such a $\alpha,\beta$ decentralized coalition with the expected number of trials required for all coins to come up heads simultaneously. The latter is the expected number of trials required to reach a $\alpha,\beta$- *centralized coalition*, namely one coalition with $\alpha \times \beta$ members. The comparison measures the benefits of forming decentralized vs. centralized coalitions. Obviously, the expected number of trials is lower for the $\alpha\beta$- decentralized coalition. It is less obvious, however, that the speed gained is exponentially increasing with decreases in the size of the subcoalitions, i.e. the number $\alpha$, and is practically indifferent to the number $\beta$ of such subcoalitions[14]:

*Proposition 12:* We compare the expected number of trials $ET$ to form such a $\beta$ coalitions of $\alpha$ traders each, i.e. an $\alpha,\beta$- decentralized coalition, with the expected number of trials required for the formation of a coalition of size $\alpha\times\beta$, i.e. a $\alpha,\beta$ *centralized coalition.* The benefit of forming decentralized as opposed to centralized coalitions is exponentially increasing with decreases in the size of the subcoalitions, i.e. with the number $\alpha$, but is practically indifferent to the number $\beta$ of such subcoalitions. Formally: the expected number of periods needed to achieve a $\alpha,\beta$ decentralized coalition, $ET$, is approximately $2^\beta\log\alpha$, when $\alpha$ and $\beta$ are large. The speed gained is exponentially increasing with decreases in the size of the subcoalitions, i.e. with the number $\alpha$, but it is practically indifferent to the number $\beta$ of such subcoalition (the proof is in the appendix).

## 9. EXAMPLE 2. GAINS FROM DECENTRALIZING A NETWORK

Consider fifteen players, divided into three disjoint sets ($\alpha=3$) denoted subcoalitions $S_\gamma$ of five players each ($\beta=5$). Each player within a given subcoalition produces an externality worth eighteen to all other players in the same subcoalition. Each player in $S_\gamma$ produces an externality worth one to players in other subcoalitions $S_{\gamma'}$, for $\gamma'\neq\gamma$. *On average, the willingness to pay $D(.)$ increases by* $[(18\times4)+10]/15=82/15=5.5$. with each new user joining the network. Willingness to pay for each additional user (derived from the average externality) is therefore 5.5. For simplicity assume that average network costs $C(.)$ are constant $C(x) \equiv 71.8$. Since $14\times5.5\sim77$, and $13\times5.5\sim71.5<72$, the average critical mass $x^*$ required by the network to break even is 15 players, i.e. $x^*=X_{max}$. However, a subcoalition of all five players within one of the groups $S_\gamma$ produces sufficient externalities to each other to "lock in," since $18\times4=72>71.8$. As these five players pay the average costs the network breaks even. Each of the five users has a positive payoff, and thus an incentive to stay in the network.

Consider now the expected number $ET$ of trials until all three five player subcoalitions join the network, which is the Pareto efficient solution $E_{Xmax}$ of Propositions 8 and 9. By Proposition 12 this number is $ET\sim2^5\log3\sim59$. In contrast, the expected number of trials for an average critical mass of users (15) to join the network simultaneously, is $2^{15}\sim32,768$.

The following corollary formalizes the remarkable gains from following a decentralized approach to coalition formation:

*Corollary 13:* The ratio of the expected number of trials to reach critical mass with a $\alpha,\beta$ decentralized coalition to that required to reach it with $\alpha\times\beta$ centralized coalition is $\log\beta/2^{\beta(\alpha-1)}$.

## 10. PREVIOUS LITERATURE

While networks and their critical mass have been analyzed before, the literature has not examined so far the formation of coalitions of users which form to exploit the externalities which each user produces to the others. This is the main focus of the paper. The second focus is to explore heterogeneous externalities, and how exploiting them increases dramatically the economic feasibility of the network. Related literature on networks include Rohlfs,[15] Oren and Smith,[16] Katz and Shapiro,[17] Farrell and Saloner,[18] and Heal.[19] All of these works focus on different problems and look at them from different angles than ours. Oren and Smith[20] examine the critical mass issue but they occur on the effect of different pricing structures under the assumption that users maximize benefit minus costs and a monopoly supplier maximizes profits. Katz and Shapiro[21] develop an oligopoly model in which consumers value "compatibility" between products, which they call network externalities. They study a different set of problems: the social and private incentives for firms to produce compatible products, or to switch between compatible and incompatible products. Similarly, Farrell and Saloner[22] study the problem of benefits to consumers and firms from standardizing product. Heal[23] studies Nash equilibrium usage patterns of networks and their stability properties. All these works have some points in common with ours, because they consider user's externalities, the critical mass problem, and the non-cooperative equilibria strategies of users in joining or leaving a network. However, with the exception of Heal[24] none of these pieces examine the number of equilibria, nor their welfare properties in terms of Pareto efficiency. Nor do they consider the global stability properties of such games. None of these pieces, including Heal's,[25] study how the solutions vary with the size or knowledge of the players as is done here. Finally, none of these works analyzes the formation of coalitions involved in the "startup" or feasibility problem with heterogeneous users, nor the speed of convergence to a solution, which we do in order to compare centralized and decentralized networks. The interest of our formalization and results was anticipated in Rohlfs,[26] who proposes that it would be important to explore the "startup" problem as well as the differences introduced in its solution in networks with "non-uniform calling pattern."

## 11. APPENDIX

### 11.1. Observation in Section 5
*Proof:*This observation is easy to establish. Conditions 2.1, 2.2, 2.3, 2.4, and 2.5 imply that the intersection of the two curves $D(x)$ and $C(x)$ exists and is unique. The slopes of $C(x)$ and $D(x)$ imply that at any quantity lower than $x^*$, average cost prices exceed user's willingness to pay, leading to a drop in production under the quantity adjustment process (2.6). At quantities exceeding $x^*$ the willingness to pay exceeds average cost prices, leading to a tendency to increase output under the same adjustment process. Similar arguments are used to prove instability under the Walrasian price adjustment process in (2.7). It is immediate that $(p^*,x^*)$ is Pareto inferior to $(D(x^*+\epsilon),x^*+\epsilon)$: this follows from the properties of the demand and the average cost supply curves, since user's utilities increase with the difference between their willingness to pay and the average cost.

### 11.2. Proposition 8
*Proof:*Consider the game allocation $E_0$, where each player plays the 0 strategy, i.e. $\varphi(y)$ for all $y$ in $X$. For any given player $y_0$, $0=P(0,\varphi^0(y_0))>P(1,\varphi^0(y_0))$ because $P(1,\varphi^0(y_0))<0$ since:

$$\sum_y \varphi(y) < x^* \qquad (18)$$

so that average cost exceeds willingness to pay. Since this is true for all $y_0$ in $X$, $E_0$ is indeed a Nash Equilibrium. This Nash equilibrium is stable in the area of allocations where the sum of player's strategies does not exceed $x^*-1$. This is because at any game allocation $\varphi$ with:

$$\sum \varphi(y) < x^*-1 \tag{19}$$

a player who is not in the network receives a zero payoff, which cannot be improved by this player joining the network since, in the latter case, payoffs are negative or zero. On the other hand, a player who uses the network can increase its payoff by playing the 0 strategy instead, thus increasing its payoff from a negative number to zero. $E_0$ is therefore a Nash equilibrium and its region of stability consists of those allocation $\varphi$ satisfying:

$$\sum \varphi \leq x^*-1 \tag{20}$$

$E_0$ is Pareto inefficient. Consider now the network allocation $E_{Xmax}$ in which all players play the strategy 1, i.e., $\varphi(y)=1$ for all $y$. $E_{Xmax}$ is clearly a Nash equilibrium: since by assumption $x^*<X$, every player will play strategy 1 when all others use the network, as this leads to the maximum possible payoff, namely $D(X_{max})-C(X_{max})$. Consider now any allocation $\varphi$ where the sum of all player's strategies is larger than or equal to $x^*$. Then at this allocation the optimal strategy for any player who is not in the network (and therefore receives a zero payoff) is to join the network. Since payoffs are positive for network usage above $x^*$ and $x^*<X_{max}$, by joining the network this player increases its payoff to a positive number. Similarly, a player who uses the network at the allocation $\varphi$ cannot improve the payoff by playing the zero strategy, because a payoffs are larger than or equal to zero when the network usage is at or above $x^*$. This shows that the area of stability of the equilibrium $E_x$ contains all allocations with $\varphi$ with:

$$\sum \varphi(x) \geq x^* \tag{21}$$

It is immediate to see that the Nash Equilibrium $E_x$ is Pareto optimal, since at $E_x$ the maximum payoff $D(X_{max})-C(X_{max})$ is achieved.

## 11.3. Proposition 9

**Proof:** The allocations $E_0$ and $E_{Xmax}$ are both Nash equilibria: the proof is the same of that of Proposition 8. The regions of stability have now decreased, because small players do not believe that their use of the network will alter the price/willingness to pay relation, and therefore the payoffs. Any allocation where the network is used by a set of players of critical mass size, is now a Nash equilibrium. This follows from the fact that players are small: if a player uses the network when the total number of users equals the critical mass, then it does not use the network, and has therefore a zero payoff, it will not gain by joining the network because at the critical mass the payoff is the same, i.e. zero. Consider now the case where, at the critical mass, payoffs are positive.[27] Then no allocation where the numbers of payers equals the critical mass is a Nash equilibrium. This is because at such an allocation, the payoffs of joining the network are larger than those for not joining it for any player who is not already using the network.

## 11.4. Proposition 12

*Proof:* Define for any fixed $n>1$, the event $A_i=\{$The coins in group i have not come up heads in any of the first n trials$\}$. Then:

$$T>n = \bigcup_{i=1}^{\alpha} A_i \tag{22}$$

$$P(A_i) = (1 - (\tfrac{1}{2})^\beta)^n \tag{23}$$

$$P(T>n) = \sum_i P(A_i) - \sum_{i<j} P^2(A_i) + \sum_{i<j<k} P^3(A_i)\ldots \tag{24}$$

Letting $c=1-(1/2)^\beta$ we have:

$$P(T>n) = (\tbinom{\alpha}{1}) c^n - (\tbinom{\alpha}{2}) c^{2n} + (\tbinom{\alpha}{3}) c^{3n} \tag{25}$$

$$ET = 1 + P(T>1) + P(T>2) + \ldots \tag{26}$$

$$= 1 + (\tbinom{\alpha}{1})[c+c^2] - (\tbinom{\alpha}{2})[c^2+c^4](\tbinom{\alpha}{3})[c^3+c^6] \tag{27}$$

$$= 1 + (\tbinom{\alpha}{1})\frac{c}{(1-c)} - (\tbinom{\alpha}{2})\frac{c^2}{(1+c^2)} + (\tbinom{\alpha}{3})\frac{c^3}{(1-c^3)} - \ldots \tag{28}$$

or:

$$ET = 1 + (2^\beta-1)[(\tbinom{\alpha}{1}) - (\tbinom{\alpha}{2})\frac{c}{(1+c)} + (\tbinom{\alpha}{3})\frac{c^2}{(1+c+c^2)}] \tag{29}$$

If $\beta$ is large then $c>1$, and

$$ET \sim 2^\beta[(\tbinom{\alpha}{1}) - (\tbinom{\alpha}{2})/2 + (\tbinom{\alpha}{3})/3 \ldots + (-1)^{\alpha-1}(\tbinom{\alpha}{\alpha})/\alpha] \tag{30}$$

Now, for every $\alpha>1$:

$$\sum_{i=1}^{a} (-1)^{i+1}(\tbinom{\alpha}{i})/i = 1 + \tfrac{1}{2} + \ldots \frac{1}{a} \tag{31}$$

so that

$$(10.2) = 2^\beta[1 + \tfrac{1}{2} + \ldots \frac{1}{\alpha}] \sim 2^\beta \log \alpha \tag{32}$$

if $\alpha$ is also large.

## REFERENCES

Farrell, J. and G. Saloner, "Standardization, compatibility, and innovation," *Rand Journal of Economics*, Vol 16, No. 1, Spring 1985.

132

Heal, G.M., "Price and Market Share Dynamics in a Network Industry," Working Paper, Columbia University Graduate School of Business, New York, 1990.

Howell, M. and A. Cozzini,"International Equity Flows-1989 Edition," Salomon Brothers European Equity Research London, August 1989.

Katz, M. and C. Shapiro, "Network Externalities, Competition and Compatibility," *The American Economic Review*, Vol 75, No. 3, pp. 424-40, June 1985.

Oren, S. and S. Smith, "Critical Mass and tariff structure in electronic communications markets," *The Bell Journal of Economics*, 12, pp. 467-86, Autumn 1981.

Rohles, J., "A theory of interdependent demand for communication services," *The Bell Journal of Economics and Management Science*, Vol 5. No 1, pp. 16-37, Spring 1974.

## ENDNOTES

[1.] This paper was presented in seminars at the Department of Economics, Columbia University, February 1990, at the Economics Department, Stanford University, August 6, 1990, at the Economics Department of Harvard University September 1990, at the Computer Sciences Department of Yale University November 1990, at the Starr Center New York University May 1991, and at the first meeting of the Brown-Columbia-Hopkins Workshop in 1992. Herbert Robbins and Geoffrey Heal provided valuable comments and suggestions.

[2.] Cross-border securities are stocks or bonds which are held in custody or listed in the stock exchange of one country, and traded in another country.

[3.] This is called a "positive externality" across users.

[4.] This effect is called "increasing returns."

[5.] See the discussion below.

[6.] For example, McCaw Communications, which was sold recently for several US $billions to AT&T, never reached the break even point.

[7.] Because of this assumption and the fact that $q_i$ is either 0 or 1, the charges to each user are what is usually denoted "connect charges."

[8.] All properties of the model are preserved in discrete terms, except that now the average cost curve may or may not intersect the demand curve. Therefore the *critical mass* $x^*$ is now re-defined as the smallest quantity of users at which willingness to pay exceeds average costs, and we assume $x^* > 1$.

[9.] A *game allocation* is a function, $\varphi:X\ \{0,1\}$, i.e. an element of the set $\{0,1\}^X$, a sequence of 0's and 1's indexed by the set $X$.

[10.] i.e. $\varphi^*(x')$ maximizes the payoff to player $x'$, given the values of for all $\varphi^*(x)$ for all $x \in X, x \neq x'$. This is a standard concept of Nash equilibrium in non-cooperative games. For any game allocation $\varphi$, let $(\theta, \varphi^0(x))$ be the allocation with values equal to those of $\varphi$ everywhere except at $x$, and with $\varphi(x) = \theta$.

[11.] i.e. the region of stability $E_0$ is usage up to critical mass minus one.

[12.] Rohles, J., "A theory of interdependent demand for communication services," *The Bell Journal of Economics and Management Science*, Vol. 5 No. 1, pp. 16-37, Spring 1974; and Heal, G.M., "Price and Market Share Dynamics in a Network Industry," Working Paper, Columbia University Graduate School of Business, New York, 1990.

[13.]Rohles, J., "A theory of interdependent demand for communication services," *The Bell Journal of Economics and Management Science*, Vol. 5 No. 1, pp. 16-37, Spring 1974.

[14.]To simplify computations in the following we assume $x^*=X_{max}$. Obviously when $x^*<X_{max}$ both the decentralized process and the centralized process proceed faster to reach a coalition of average critical mass. This is because when $x^*<X_{max}$, the probability that $x^*$ coins come up simultaneously heads is strictly larger than the probability that all coins is a set of cardinality $x^*$ come up heads simultaneously. Similarly, the formation of $\alpha$ decentralized coalitions of $\beta$ players each summing up to cardinality $x^*$ within a larger group of cardinality $X_{max}>x^*$ is faster, so that the final result for $x<X_{max}$ is not significantly altered.

[15.]Rohles, J., "A theory of interdependent demand for communication services," *The Bell Journal of Economics and Management Science*, Vol. 5 No. 1, pp. 16-37, Spring 1974.

[16.]Oren, S. and S. Smith, "Critical Mass and tariff structure in electronic communications markets," *The Bell Journal of Economics*, 12, pp. 467-86, Autumn 1981.

[17.]Katz, M. and C. Shapiro, "Network Externalities, Competition and Compatibility," *The American Economic Review*, Vol. 75 No. 3, June 1985, pp. 424-40.

[18.]Farrell, J. and G. Saloner, "Standardization, compatibility, and innovation," *Rand Journal of Economics*, Vol. 16, No. 1, Spring 1985.

[19.]Heal, G.M., "Price and Market Share Dynamics in a Network Industry," Working Paper, Columbia University Graduate School of Business, New York, 1990.

[20.]Oren, S. and S. Smith, "Critical Mass and tariff structure in electronic communications markets," *The Bell Journal of Economics*, 12, pp. 467-86, Autumn 1981.

[21.]Katz, M. and C. Shapiro, "Network Externalities, Competition, and Compatibility," *The American Economic Review*, Vol 75. No. 3, pp. 424-40, June 1985.

[22.]Farrell, J. and G. Saloner, "Standardization, compatibility, and innovation," *Rand Journal of Economics*, Vol. 16 No. 1, Spring 1985.

[23.]Heal, G.M., "Price and Market Share Dynamics in a Network Industry," Working Paper, Columbia University Graduate School of Business, New York, 1990.

[24.]Ibid.

[25.]Ibid.

[26.]Rohlfs, J., "A theory of interdependent demand for a communication services," *The Bell Journal of Economics and Management Science*, Vol. 5 No. 1, pp. 16-37, Spring 1974.

[27.]Note that with this definition the critical mass payoffs could be strictly positive; for example this would occur in Diagram 3 if $C(x)$ goes between two horizontal steps of $D(x)$.

PRIVATE NETWORKS PUBLIC OBJECTIVES
E. Noam and A. NíShúilleabháin (Editors)

# Invisible Hand versus Invisible Advisors: Coordination Mechanisms in Economic Networks

Shane Greenstein

## 1. INTRODUCTION

The national information infrastructure today encompasses a broad spectrum of activities. Telephones, automatic-teller machines, computers, the Internet, local area networks (LANs), and supermarket scanners all play a part. It involves both simple and sophisticated equipment -- telephones, wireless communication devices, microprocessors, and thousands of miles of copper and fiber optic lines. Millions of highly skilled professionals maintain and operate this network, regularly modifying and upgrading it, customizing it to millions of uses.

This information infrastructure did not arise overnight, nor did it arise under the guidance of any single policy vision. A host of legal, economic, and historical factors shaped its development over most of this century. The processes were decentralized, usually market oriented, and seemingly too chaotic for any organization to control. Of course, some have tried to control it. AT&T, IBM, the Federal Communications Commission, and the Department of Defense are among those organizations who briefly, and sometimes successfully, coordinated the development of one component of the whole.

There is no single policy vision coordinating infrastructure development today. No centralized decision process could possibly guide such a complex engineering network. By default, decentralized market mechanisms, private firms, and standards development organizations (SDOs) are responsible for many technical standards within the information infrastructure. This state of affairs has grabbed the attention of many industry and academic observers, raising many novel issues. The primary purpose of this essay is to summarize and synthesize for the non-specialist the insights made by economists about the costs and benefits of relying on market-oriented mechanisms for decentralized network development. Economists have been concerned about these issues in the rather recent literature on network economics and standardization. This literature contains many useful insights, but not all of them are consistent with one another, nor do they all transparently synthesize into a single policy vision that is accessible to the non-specialist. Thus, extending this literature with an eye towards synthesis should have some value. A second purpose for this essay is to identify important issues that remain unaddressed and point towards the direction of answers.

Though the article will focus more on the development of interesting insights than the development of management strategies or public policy, I do not intend for this to be an abstract or impractical academic exercise. The paper will focus exclusively on important contemporary events and the development of tomorrow's information infrastructure. Insights about these events should be useful for the development of appropriate public policy and management strategy.

## 1.1. An overview

The bottom line of this paper is that standardization activity plays a dual role when technical decisions are made by decentralized market-oriented decisionmakers. These dual roles, as a coordinator and a constraint, show up both in short-run and long-run analysis. Analysis engenders so much confusion because both roles are not always recognized. Here is a brief summary of the paper's analysis:

In the short-run, when market structure is relatively stable, standards coordinate contemporary and anticipated market behavior. The costs of using a network of components usually decline because standardization reduces the costs of interconnection. Standards let component designers anticipate interconnection requirements and improve the part of the system in which they specialize. Standards permit system users to make investments in assets and be assured that the assets' value will not depreciate due to loss of connectivity. Yet this coordination benefit is not free. Standards limit the choices of users and vendors. Both users and vendors become locked-in to a set of technical constraints that they may change only at a high cost. Moreover, vendors recognize the strategic importance of locking users to a standard and spend considerable resources on manipulating their development.

In the long-run, the ultimate importance of standardization comes through its impact on technical change. This is because many parts of the information infrastructure have not reached the stasis associated with mature product markets. For example, standardization issues lie at the core of developments in digital cellular telephones, high-definition television, and large local area network communication protocols. In this setting standardization also plays a dual role as a constraint and as a coordinator. As coordinator, stable, functional, predictable standards can aid technical development in most markets. Yet, standards also lock-in users and suppliers. Lock-in is especially costly when technical possibilities change rapidly, removing previous costly technical constraints and imposing others. Thus, standards will constrain technical improvement, but that development will occur sooner and more development will occur along more components.

The analysis first sets the stage with relevant definitions and background. Then it presents a view of the market factors influencing standardization processes in the short-run, i.e., while industry structure is fixed. It follows with an analysis of market factors influencing standardization in the long-run, i.e., while industries evolve. It ends with a discussion of the role of SDOs in the short- and long-run. A short epilogue presents some closing remarks.

## 1.2. Definitions and distinctions

The difficulty with any analysis is that today's information infrastructure is a "network of networks." It consists of a hodge-podge of public and private telephone networks, the Internet, private LANs and WANs, mainframe and mini computing centers, and numerous communication bridges between various sub-networks. Telephone companies, computer hardware and software companies, satellite operators, the Federal Government, and virtually every user plays some role in this network.

Analysis breaks through this hodge-podge by focusing on one "economic network" at a time. An economic network is composed of all buyers and suppliers who have economic incentive to care about a system's technical features. This concern about technology arises from one of two simple economic factors. Either all users desire to communicate with one another, as in a traditional telephone network, or all users need electronic components to work with each other, as when an industry-wide network of buyers uses the same "standard bundle" -- the minimal set of components necessary to insure system performance.

Notice that the use of "network" here is not conventional (nor will it be throughout this paper). Economists view telecommunications networks as more than just the physical linkages and the electronic signals they comprise, indeed, more than just the physical equipment extant today. Economic relationships extend beyond physical boundaries of equipment. In other words, many buyers and sellers of the same information technology may not buy equipment or services from the same supplier, but they may be a subset of the same economic network if they use compatible equipment. Only when AT&T operated so much of the whole telephone network were the physical network and the economic network virtually synonymous.

All activity in an "economic network" is centered around interoperability: whether a component may serve as a sub-system within a larger arrangement of components. In the simplest case, compatibility-standards can define the physical fit of two components. Familiar examples are modular phone jacks on telephone cords and handsets, and compatible telephone switches. More complex are the standards that determine electronic communication channels. The need for these standards is obvious, since successfully filtering, transmitting and translating signals across telecommunication networks requires precise engineering. Similar needs arise in the design of circuitry between computers, their operating system and application software programs.

More generally, compatibility solves but one issue in a wider array of coordination problems. Most on-line commercial networks, such as Prodigy, Compuserve or America On-line, or the private networks of thousands of commercial organizations and thousands of private firms, are sophisticated electronic networks. These often involve on-line transaction processing, employ a mix of sophisticated telecommunications and computing equipment, and must operate reliably on a daily basis. Accomplishing this involves all the coordination activities associated with the successful management of a business enterprise. Products and services must be defined and tied to billing, output must be controlled and its quality assured, electronic signals must be routed without hesitation and so on. An organization must also plan and develop capital capacity and plan the requisite staffing to meet long run service needs. Sometimes these decisions involve coordinating actions within a single organization. More often then not, they involve coordinating decisions across divisions within the same company, or between upstream and downstream vendors, or between a vendor and a governmental regulator.

Economic research to date focuses primarily on the factors influencing the development of compatibility standards. This focus on the nexus of economics and technology is a bit narrow, since it virtually ignores the important organizational costs just mentioned. Nonetheless, this does not invalidate the merits of the analysis of compatibility, since interoperability is necessary for any coordination on any level. It simply means that standard analysis leaves aside lots of the messy details of coordinating organizations in practice. This review will try to point out where this hole matters and where it does not.

Finally, one other key is the economist's taxonomy of processes that develop standards. Unfettered market processes may develop standards as a *de facto* result of either a "sponsored" or an "unsponsored" market process. In a sponsored process, one or more entities, suppliers, or cooperative ventures, creates inducements for other economic decision-makers to adopt a particular set of technical specifications and become part of an economic network (e.g., pre-divestiture AT&T-sponsored telecommunication standards). An unsponsored process has no identified originator with a proprietary interest, yet follows well-documented specifications (e.g., the QWERTY keyboard). Voluntary industry self-regulation may also play a role when economic networks arise out of the deliberations of SDOs (e.g., IEEE). Of course, government bodies may also shape the development of economic networks (e.g, FCC). This review also try to point out when sponsorship matters and when it does not.

There is no compelling reason for government organizations to become involved in the development of every network. They often do so because important public policy issues are at stake, as when domestic and foreign firms use standardization as a competitive weapon. They often do not do so because exogenous forces, such as dramatic technical change, outstrip the ability of any administrative process to guide events and it may be easier to leave decisions to market participants. The question of when it is best to rely on a market process instead of an government decision making is an open and active topic of debate, since it usually swings on trade-offs between imperfect market processes and imperfect government intervention. This essay will touch on this issue below, but it will not be the primary focus.[1]

Instead, this article will first focus on one part of this debate: understanding the efficacy of relying on decentralized market-based decision making processes and private organizations -- i.e. with minimal government intervention. This is due mostly to space constraints, not any lack of interest. If the reader is interested, several other studies, referenced below, have largely addressed questions regarding government policies.

## 2. SHORT-RUN ANALYSIS: INVISIBLE HANDS?

Short-run and long-run analysis require different approaches. Short-run analysis presumes that the number of key decision makers (e.g., firms, potential users) is virtually fixed. This is not bad if many rigidities limit how many firms can feasibly produce for a market in the short run -- e.g., a firm's technical expertise, economies of scale, and various other competitive advantages associated with incumbency. By implication, short-run analysis is not appropriate for investigating how technical innovation influences the adoption of standards and the number of suppliers, and vice versa. In addition, since rigidities differ in importance in different markets, the appropriateness of this type of analysis will also differ by industry.

For short-run analysis it is convenient to distinguish between networks in which many suppliers provide related services, a few do, or only one dominates. These distinctions help organize insights about patterns of outcomes and the factors that produce them. Of course, it is not always obvious in practice which markets belong in which categories; Indeed, much controversy is essentially argument over which type of analysis applies to which specific market.

### 2.1. Diffuse market interests

Standardization may not easily arise when decision-making in a market is diffuse -- i.e., when a market has many buyers and many sellers, none of whom is responsible for a large percentage of economic activity. This is disturbing since diffuse market structures are typically very competitive and tend to allocate scarce resources efficiently through price mechanisms. Many policy issues would be simplified if diffuse market structures gave rise to desirable standards. Figure 1 summarizes the following analysis.

### 2.1.1. Too many hands and coordination problems

When decision-making is diffuse, the problems that arise are often called "coordination problems." This is not a statement about whether an economic enterprise coordinates its own employees around one objective. The main insight here is that all potential users and suppliers could benefit from as much technical interoperability as possible, but instead tend to go off of their own. The sheer number of decision-makers hinders adequate communication that would render the coordination problems solved. Even if all firms could communicate, differences of opinion make uniform consensus unlikely. Moreover, standards that serve as focal points are unlikely to arise very easily, because every potential supplier and user of a standard is a small part of the whole -- each decision maker has too little incentive to make the investments that will coordinate the design decisions of other users and lead to general interoperability.[2] Thus, due to market structure alone, network growth may be hindered because standardization does not arise, or it arises too late. The proliferation of slightly different Unix systems in the 1970s and 80s is an often cited example.

This observation immediately leads to one disturbing prediction for the growth of private telecommunications networks: if standards are unsponsored then different firm's networks will not likely work with one another without lots of adjustment. That is, private networks often develop according to internal imperatives. When these networks grow larger and brush up against one another, they may be unable to work together for the simple reason that no sponsor insured that they initially developed in a technically compatible manner. For example, after the introduction of the super market scanners it still took many years for suppliers to coordinate their delivery with the inventory management of grocery stores, if they coordinated them at all. Similar factors have slowed the introduction of scanners into the retail clothing sector.

When unsponsored economic networks develop and build capacity, they tend to grow and shrink for many reasons that may have only a minor correspondence with the long-term economic welfare of market participants. This is because standardization processes are often characterized by "bandwagons." For example, networks may be slow to start when they are small and many potential adopters "sit on the fence," waiting to make expensive and unrecoverable investments until a clear technical standard has been chosen by a large portion users. Networks may not develop at all if most participants are "lukewarm" about a new standard due to technical uncertainty, for example, even though all might collectively benefit from it. Alternatively, bandwagons may also grow remarkably quickly once a network's size becomes large enough to justify investments by potential adopters who, in the early phase of development, had delayed making commitments. The lack of communication between all the potentially affected decision makers exacerbates such bandwagons, though professional organizations can often provide communication channels to bridge some of the troubles (see discussion below).

### 2.1.2. Lock-in: Hand-cuffed by the past?

A very costly problem arises if most vendor and user capacity for a network becomes "locked-in" to a technical alternative, i.e. users and suppliers find it very costly to change fundamental technical specifications. Either hardware or software embodies technical features that cannot be easily changed, or humans cannot be retrained easily to work with a different technology, such as a software interface. These costs are especially high when a network must change (e.g., be upgraded, expanded, or replaced) and the network serves as an essential part of an organization's day to day operations. Change risks significant downtime arising from the costs of fixing the almost inevitable mistakes that any change produces. One recent example was the FAA's attempts in the 1980s to update their air traffic control systems across the country. The small margin for error (and the inevitability that a few mistakes will arise) made the upgrade especially difficult to plan and execute.

**Figure 1**
**Short-run analysis: trade-offs between different market structures**

|  | Unsponsored standard | Dueling sponsors | Single sponsored standard |
|---|---|---|---|
| **Decision making** | Diffused to many firms | Concentrated in a few firms | Concentrated in a single firm |
| **Severity of coordination problem** | Difficult to reach agreement between all interested vendors and users | Depends on willingness of vendors to design components that mix and match | All decisions internalized by single firm -- depends on management of firm |
| **Pricing** | Typically very competitive -- pricing close to cost | Oligopolistic pricing -- typically some markup over cost | Monopolistic pricing -- high markup over cost |
| **Primary distortion** | Decisions subject to band-wagons -- Society will not likely get optimal technology | Vendors strategy determine networks -- vendors will lock-in users and lock-out rivals | Monopolist will manipulate technology to own advantage -- blockade as much entry as possible |

Lock-in produces two related problems. First, a network may not become as large or as valuable as possible because users lock-in to a disparate variety of formats and each finds it costly to change later. The second problem is related. If many potential adopters wait for a "shake-out," then crucial choices between technologies may be made by early adopters. Thus, early adopters bear a disproportionate influence over standards. Technical designs may not easily be altered to accommodate the different needs of the later decision-makers.

It might be argued that the disproportionate influence of early users is justified because these same users bear a high risk for being intrepid, i.e., their investments in a network can become obsolete or "orphaned."[3] However, this observation does not really address the question of whether society gets an optimal technology or not, which is the central policy issue.

The issue is not solely that the hands of past investment influences future technical choices, which happens quite often and complicates choices, but it is a sober fact of life.[4] Much more of a concern is that society can be "locked-in" to the wrong technology ex post. That is, when viewed with hindsight, "society" could regret previous decisions. This occurs because, to reiterate the point by rephrasing it, even though past choices constrain future choices, future decision makers never have an opportunity to persuade previous decision makers about that choice. Hence, past choices will likely be short-sighted.

The most well known example of this is the QWERTY keyboard, which was explicitly designed to slow down the typists of the 19th century. David[5] argues that the interaction of uncoordinated decisions by typing schools, typewriter manufacturers, and early typists resulted in the adoption of the QWERTY keyboard and its persistence past it useful life. This is especially interesting because a superior alternative exists, yet market participants have never coordinated a switch. A more contemporary example of the lock-in due to intertemporal links is the MS-DOS operating system for PCs. Because it was designed for 8-bit microprocessors, it poorly uses the available RAM on today's 32-bit micro-processors. Similar examples from information technology markets, if perhaps less dramatic than QWERTY, include the development of AM stereo, FM stereo, micro-processor designs, and, as noted, Unix operating systems.

Perhaps the most unsatisfying feature of the analysis of unsponsored networks to date is its use of a stricter concept of irreversibility than is warranted due to the realities of typical technological and economic evolution. Are some features of a technology more mutable than others? Are there degrees of lock-in? Economic analysis has yet to fully understand how these notions can be properly modified for situations where interoperability for components evolve in constant flux, as suppliers update and revise them for applications. Later sections will discuss the growing analysis of converters and options, which partially addresses this issue.

## 2.2. A few vendors: Hand to hand combat?

Diffuse decision making leads to situations where (1) communication and sponsorship are unlikely and (2) coordination problems are likely. Thus, it would seem to follow that market structures with few vendors may not suffer as much from coordination problems. However, such a conclusion is hasty if it is not qualified properly. In markets with few vendors, the proprietary interests of the vendors leads them to take strategic actions designed to produce outcomes they favor. While this reduces the severity of some types of coordination problems, it instead induces other types of distortions.

The situation that best illustrates these concerns is "dueling sponsors" -- each sponsor has proprietary interests in an array of components that perform similar functions but competitors employ different technical standards. The VHS/Betamax duel in the VCR markets is a well-known and interesting case. Such battles are common today in high-tech industries (IBM v. DEC in minis, MS-Word v. WordPerfect in word processing, FDDI v. ATM in network communications), where the duels may start as multi-firm contests but quickly reduce to a handful of dominant participants. Sometimes a fringe of niche market suppliers follows the leaders, while two or three technical standards dominate all choices. Network duels also commonly arise as sub-plots to related larger product market duels. For example, different banks may belong to incompatible automatic teller machine networks, and United Airlines and American Airlines sponsor different airline reservation systems. If recent experience is any guide, this type of market structure will likely characterize many, if not the majority, of private economic networks in the future information infrastructure.

### 2.2.1. Problems with dueling

Economists are of two minds about dueling. On the one hand, an important distortion from dueling is that it may prevent the economic network from becoming as large as it possibly could be, even if all users would benefit from a larger network. Unlike an unsponsored network, dueling encourages a vendor to lock-in buyers. This is because dueling sponsors have incentives to design incompatible systems if incompatibility raises the costs to users of switching to a rival sponsor's system. Similarly, the sponsor of a system would like nothing better than to raise the costs to the experienced user from switching vendors, since it makes a user reluctant to change networks.

Vendors like to be the exclusive provider of a technology to a locked-in buyer for several reasons. First, it provides the sponsor with market power during any repeat system purchase. Second, it guarantees a stream of related business. In computing networks, for example, locked-in buyers will purchase CPU upgrades from their system sponsors, and often they continue to purchase a majority of their peripherals and software from the same vendor. Third, locked-in users can be manipulated for competitive advantage. For example, in the case of computer reservation systems, the sponsoring airlines were accused of locking in travel agents and then manipulating the screen to favor the flights of the system sponsor. Similar factors, as well as several pricing issues, prevented automatic teller machine networks from working together as one large network for many years.

Notice that a vendor may desire to lock-in their buyers, but a vendor's competitors will desire the opposite. While a vendor may try to raise the cost of switching, a rival may be working equally hard to lower those costs. From society's standpoint much of this activity is a waste. Wouldn't society be better off if lock-in was just ignored by all competitors and all energy were directed at making better products? Yes, but this will rarely occur because of the strategic importance of standards in a competitive dual.

As with unsponsored economic networks, the market's choice between dueling systems retains the sensitivity to small events, which is some cause for concern[6]. A well-researched example comes from the early history of electrical power supply. Though engineering evidence seems to suggest that alternative current is probably superior to direct current for widespread use, David and Bunn's[7] study shows that many other factors, including "beauty contests" and the decisions of crucial industry participants, such as Edison and Westinghouse, and the character of the gateways between AC and DC, played a crucial role in the success of AC over DC. To appreciate the lengths to which both parties went, consider this example: Edison attempted to persuade the New York state government to use AC in its electrocutions in order to foster the perception that DC, which Edison sponsored, was a safer form of electricity (Incidentally, DC made for more efficient electrocutions, so Edison lost this particular skirmish). In a more current example, Cusumano[8] showed that the development of the VCR standard was sensitive to the relationship of Sony and Hitatchi Corporations, the seemingly minor (and temporary) ability of VHS to record longer, and, most crucially, the timing of the introduction of video cassettes, which occurred unexpectedly and rather randomly from the viewpoint of the major VCR manufacturers.

### 2.2.2. Dueling has its good points

Yet, economists are not uniformly pessimistic about dueling, which is where some confusion arises. Sometimes dueling sponsors will not design incompatible systems. When rival sponsors provide components that perform different functions or complementary functions, compatibility permits many "mix-and-match" possibilities between the components of rival systems. In turn, this raises the profitability of producing compatible components (despite increases in competition). The market for stereo equipment is a familiar example, as is the market for PC hardware clones and software applications under the DOS standard. Thus, dueling sponsors are likely to find it worthwhile to make investments to reduce interoperability costs when they do not produce every type of component, or if each has comparative advantage in the design and production of some but not all components, which is a common occurrence when markets participants have different technical capabilities. This is probably a good explanation for the willingness of many firms, AT&T and IBM increasingly so, to participate in markets with non-proprietary standards.

Dueling standards may also be economically efficient if a variety of standards is appropriate for a variety of potential problems. The crucial question is whether the market will permit entry of a new standard suited to a minority of users; this may depend on the strength of "lock-in" effects or the success of actions of system sponsors to foreclose or induce entry of complementary products, such as software (see discussion below). It is difficult to make any conclusion without careful analysis of particular industries.

Another reason for optimism is that competition and innovation counter balance some of the distortions from lock-in. Monopoly profits may be dissipated through competitive bidding between the rival system sponsors. Since many buyers anticipate that their vendors will later gain monopoly benefits from their exclusive sales of complementary products, they will demand compensation before they commit to investing in network capacity with proprietary features. Such demands can potentially elicit "promotional pricing" from sponsors. The good news is that the networks with long-run economic advantages are likely to provide bigger price discounts. In addition, competitive bidding for new customers may spur incumbent system vendors to innovate. For example, some observers argue that inter-system competition was a primary driver of computer system innovation in the 1960s and 1970s.[9] The bad news is that this benefit sometimes accrues only to new users and not necessarily to users with an installed base of equipment, who are already locked-in.[10]

One other fascinating features of duels is that dueling may induce actions that ultimately lead to the success of one economic network but possibly the loss of the sponsor's control over it. For example, a firm may broadly license a technology to establish it as a standard, but in so doing, sacrifice its control over the standard and much of the monopoly profits associated with that control. Sun Microsystems' liberal licensing strategy, combined with the relatively non-proprietary SPARC architecture, has some of these features.[11]

Another variant of this phenomenon is for a firm to design a product that does not contain proprietary technology. A non-proprietary system induces entry of more peripheral and software suppliers and hardware clones. This makes the hardware conforming to the standard more valuable to users, while the entry of more clones reduces the price. The development of software and peripherals for the IBM-compatible personal computer followed this pattern. Once the standard was widely accepted (partially as a result of all this entry), IBM no longer garnered much of the rent from being the original sponsor of the standard. Indeed, today IBM and a consortia of private firms are battling to determine the direction of the next generations of "IBM-compatible" machines. Perhaps the greatest weakness of the economic analysis of dueling systems is also its strength -- the long list of possible outcomes. Prediction is quite difficult, particularly in view of the multiplicity of pricing and promotional strategies typically available to firms in information technology markets. Thus, it is difficult to translate economic analysis into useful managerial advice that is pertinent to more than one specific market.[12]

## 2.3. Dominance: a strong hand (and maybe even an outstretched arm)

A very natural solution to coordination problems is to place a single sponsor in charge of a standard. All design decisions, upgrading and maintenance problems are internalized within the structure of a single firm. Unifying control within a single firm generally eliminates competing designers and provides users with certainty about who controls the evolution of standards and their ultimate compatibility. This potential benefit from single firm sponsorship cannot be de-emphasized, especially in markets subject to uncertain and rapid changes in technology. Many readers will recognize this as the traditional model of telephone networks under AT&T's pre-divestiture leadership and as IBM's vision for integrating computers and telecommunications under the System Network Architecture (SNA) model. Many other firms have also tried to adopt this model, though competition often forces them into duels.

### 2.3.1. The problems with dominance

Unfortunately, single firm sponsorship *by a supplier*[13] also brings much baggage with it. There is a general concern that large firms have disproportionate influences upon market processes and they manipulate them to their advantage at the expense of society's long term interests. Most of these concerns arise in the context of anti-trust economics or traditional regulatory economics.

Anti-trust and regulatory issues arise whenever a dominant sponsor competes with small plug-compatible component suppliers in some or all component markets. For example, IBM battled plug-compatible component suppliers from the later 1960s onward. Similarly, from the mid 1950s on (and growing thereafter) AT&T faced competition in customer premise equipment markets and long-distance. And today the Regional Bell Operating Companies are beginning to face competitive bypass to their services from non-regulated suppliers of fiber-optics. Antitrust concerns arise because the dominant firm always wishes to prevent the component firms from gaining market share (and may even want to drive them out of business), while society can possibly benefit from the added competition. Controlling and manipulating technical features of a product, or effectively raising the costs of interconnection, may enhance a dominant firm's strategies aimed at gaining competitive advantage over rivals.[14]

The essence of the problem is that a large system sponsor and small component supplier do not possess the same incentives to be interoperable, i.e., a small firm usually wants interoperability and a large firm does not. The benefits to vendors from accessing a rival network's users is counterbalanced by the loss of market power from facing competition from a rival vendor. Vendors with larger markets are less likely to desire compatibility with smaller rivals (than the smaller rival does with them) because larger firms gain less from selling to a few more customers and potentially lose more from facing more competition. An example of this behavior might be IBM's role in blocking the development of ASCII standards for mainframe computers[15] and allegedly in plug-compatible equipment markets as well.[16]

**2.3.2. Dominance and policy issues**

There are two difficult issues regarding competitive behavior to address. First, under what conditions will a dominant firm manipulate a technology to its advantage *and* to the detriment of potential entrants and consumers? Second, can and should such behavior be regulated, i.e., are the benefits from preventing inappropriate market conduct greater than the side-effects from imposing an imperfect legal or regulatory rule? Most analysts stumble on the first question, and even if observers clearly describe (in non-polemic language) a sponsor's strategies that are inappropriate for society, they may fail on the second set of issues. Policy rules that prevent inappropriate behavior will almost always also deter perfectly acceptable behavior as well.

As a result, many relevant debates are unresolved. Unresolved debate surrounds any analysis of "leveraging", for example, i.e. using monopoly power in one component market to gain competitive advantage in another. Most economists agree that courts have carelessly applied this concept, though few agree on an appropriate alternative definition. Definitions aside, this issue is fundamental to markets with complementary components. There is no question that a network sponsor can delay entry of complementary component suppliers, and possibly foreclose entry altogether. For example, AT&T's resistance to designing modular telecommunication connections delayed entry of competition for customer premises equipment. However, the unresolved policy question is whether such behavior should be or can be regulated to any good end. One big problem, though not the only one, is that if courts get in the business of second-guessing every innovation, especially those with exclusionary features, it may have a chilling effect on many firm's willingness to introduce any innovation, which normally is not in society's long term interest.[17]

The legacy of the IBM antitrust victories has left firms considerable latitude in the use of standardization for strategic purposes (and potentially exclusionary purposes). However, key legal rulings will probably be further tested by future cases. For example, the recent FTC/DOJ investigation of Microsoft and the recent anti-trust suits against Nintendo foreshadow such a trend. In addition, important legal standards are likely to come from several on-going trials that raise issues in intellectual property rights in computer software standards, and also in trials that attempt to modify Judge Green's restrictions on the Regional Bell Operating Companies.[18] Moreover, legislative attempts to deregulate and foster competition in the telecommunications and cable industries must also confront the same dominance and inter-connection issues.

In sum, there are obvious distortions and biases inherent in having a dominant firm. There are also gains from allowing a single firm to coordinate product characteristics and standards. No consensus on these trade-offs is likely to emerge soon in telecommunications or any other network industry. Issues regarding sponsorship are likely to remain controversial as long as there is no consensus regarding the proper role for monopolies in nascent industries.

## 3. LONG-RUN ANALYSIS: MAGIC HANDS?

The discussion until now has treated the growth of standards as the byproduct of initial market conditions. This is obviously incomplete for long run analysis: as network industries mature, standardization alters a market's structure. While this feedback is easily recognized, it is not well understood. Usually several factors may be at work at once in the long-run and they may pull/push in opposing directions. Figure 2 summarizes this discussion.

**Figure 2**
**Standardization and technical change: trade-offs between different market structures**

|  | A single firm sponsors a standard | Standards are unsponsored |
|---|---|---|
| **Systematic innovation** | All decisions internalized within single firm -- likely to be accomplished as fast as technically feasible | Firms must coordinate changes within SDOs -- likely to be administratively difficult and slow |
| **Component innovation** | Sponsor tends to resist cannibalizing rents on existing products -- component innovation is slow | Component vendors must frequently innovate to stay ahead of the competition -- component innovation is fast |
| **Coordination of technical change** | Firm's administrative process coordinates changes in the design of own products | No one is responsible for technical change -- is uncoordinated and uncertain |
| **Degree of lock-in the long-run** | Likely to be high because users have no alternative | Lock-in is as low as possible because competing vendors will try to keep lock-in low. |

### 3.1. Converters: Hands across the water?

Perhaps the most unsatisfying feature of the short-run analysis of economic networks is its use of a strict concept of "lock-in." In most markets, interoperability is in constant flux. The "standard bundle" changes frequently as suppliers update and revise products. Buyers potentially pay enormous costs trying to learn about the new possibilities and trying to integrate components from frequently changing sets of suppliers. The analysis of converters partially addresses this issue.

Converters (or "translators" or "emulators") bridge the gap between otherwise incompatible networks. These products, whether supplied by a system sponsor or third party, reduce the costs of interoperability. For example, a number of third party vendors today supply programs that enable Apple Macintosh computers to use IBM software. As another example, many software programs now come with simple utilities for translating text or data bases from the format of one software package to another. These bridges clearly have value to buyers, so they arise in virtually every economic network (and often "between" networks).

The interesting feature of converters is that vendors unequally share the costs and benefits from their introduction and refinement. Thus, at the very least, the incentives to introduce a converter will probably not match society's. For example, most of the benefits of the IBM/Macintosh converter accrues to users of a Macintosh system, so IBM has little incentive help in its development. Indeed, sometimes a product vendor may actively seek to prevent the entry of gateways and sometimes not, depending on the costs and benefits. For example, IBM was often accused of discouraging global compatibility between all computer languages.[19]

A related feature of converters is that conditions of competition can shift suddenly and asymmetrically due to their availability. This is because converters may lead to large discreet changes in the boundaries of competition. For example, David and Bunn[20] show that the introduction of the dynamo greatly influenced the AC/DC battle at the turn of the century, tipping the balance irreversibly towards AC.

The economics of converters defies easy analysis because these products are always changing shape and their impact depends on temporary windows of opportunity. In one year a converter may work only at great cost, and in the next the technology may work cheaply. In one year, users may be investing in "anticipatory converters" in order to reduce the costs of a future switch between incompatible standards. In the next a third party may enter with a new product that de facto standardizes switching. In one year, a system supplier may resist the entry of all converters. In the next de facto standards for conversion may be so well defined that no converter is needed any longer. Thus, outcomes and their analysis depend greatly on the context and inherently unpredictable events.

## 3.2. Technological Innovation and industry evolution

Since so few parts of the information infrastructure have reached the stasis associated with mature product markets, standardization lies at the heart of technical change. For example, standardization issues lie at the core of technical developments in digital cellular telephones, high-definition television, and large local area network communication protocols. However, because standardization may both encourage and discourage innovation in the types of products and organization of the industry, it is difficult to provide unambiguous conclusions.

### 3.2.1. Does standardization encourage innovation?

On the one hand, well defined technical standards may provide components suppliers a more secure set of interfaces around which to design a product and thus, may encourage research and development into the design of new components for a network. For example, secure telecommunication transmission standards were important in hastening innovation in customer premises markets, such as facsimile machines and modems. More generally, Noam[21] has observed that the success of a communications network sponsor, such as AT&T, comes from developing and standardizing the technology of its network. Ironically, the sponsor's success lays the seeds for later third-party component competition.

On the other hand, an installed base of users may also be an unintended hindrance for innovation on a mature network. An existing substitute network may hinder the growth of a new networks, because the technology embedded in much existing equipment may be inappropriate for a new application, raising its cost. In addition, minority interests may be burdened with higher costs on an existing network, but may not be large enough to justify establishing a new network. For example, Besen[22] argued that the existing AM network hindered the post-WWII growth of the FM network.

Whether or not a network is sponsored or unsponsored, however, network capacity investment decisions determine the ultimate capability of the network. Since vendors often do not have sufficient incentives to embed interoperable technology in their equipment, one can make a case for limited government intervention aimed at guaranteeing a minimal amount

148

of interoperability, at least to induce technical change and capacity investment. This is a frequently used argument for government regulation of electronic protocols in Internet, where there is a fear of widespread technical chaos in the absence of minimal standardization.

### 3.2.2. Does standardization encourage industry concentration?

Economists are equally ambivalent about the influence of standardization and technical change on a network's market structure. As noted above, the factors producing less concentration are strong: network sponsors may have incentives to license their standard as a means to induce development of new components. In addition, standards may encourage product innovation and new entry by reducing technical uncertainty. For example, the establishment of non-proprietary standards within the PC industry hastened the entry of multitudes of hardware, component and software suppliers, which makes the industry incredibly dynamic and competitive today.

However, the factors leading to greater concentration are equally as strong: buyers often have strong incentives to use a single economic network. If a firm has a proprietary right over the technically superior network technology, then through appropriate strategic actions (and a little luck) the sponsor may be able to mushroom its advantages into dominant control of several technically related market niches. IBM's early success in the mainframe market with the System 360 can be interpreted this way. Similarly, some observers claim that Microsoft is able to use its control of MS-DOS and Windows for advantages in related markets (though the U.S. Department of Justice did not quite make up its mind whether to believe these claims).

### 3.3. The evolution of the information infrastructure

Economists have intensively studied the long-run evolution of standards in a few industries. Microprocessor markets,[23] computing markets,[24] VCRs,[25] and broadcasting,[26] have sufficiently long and well-documented histories to point toward the following relationships between standardization and industry evolution:

First, different types of sponsorship are appropriate for different types of innovation. If a technology is sponsored by a dominant firm then it is more likely that the sponsor will innovate on a systemic level, i.e. on a level that influences many components at once. Typically systemic innovations are technically complex and more easily coordinated within a single organization. RCA's shepherding of the introduction of color television (through its ownership of NBC) is one example of sponsorship working "well."[27] One drawback to sponsorship, however, is that sponsors of networks tend to resist too much innovation because sponsors do not want to quickly cannibalize their own products, which embody old designs. AT&T's steady, but undramatic, introduction of digital switching equipment is an often-cited example, perhaps rightly or wrongly, for both the good and bad.

In contrast, economic networks with diffuse ownership, where competitive dueling is more common, tend to lead to greater innovation from suppliers of component parts. Component suppliers must cannibalize their own products with new innovative designs just to keep ahead of the competition. One need only examine many information technology markets today to observe this at work. However, diffuse ownership, even combined with established producer groups or standards-writing groups, does not tend to easily lead to systemic innovations, because of the difficulties of coordinating complex technical change across many organizations. Coordinating UNIX standards is an oft-cited example of the latter. In that case, many vendors and public researchers, starting from the same base, each modified the operating system a little bit for their own reasons, effectively balkanizing the UNIX community.

Second, there is a tension between the role of sponsorship in bringing about coordination and in leading to market power. When networks compete, there is a long-run tendency for networks to become less sponsored, because many users resist the market power inherent in such sponsorship. Users choose products with wider supplier bases whenever possible, taking actions to reduce the degree of lock-in. At the same time, many users also strongly desire that at least one market institution take on a central coordination role, which leads them to a dominant firm because a single sponsor can often do a better job at coordinating a network than producer groups or standards-writing groups.

The best example of both these tensions comes from the last thirty years of platform competition in the computing market, where users have gradually been moving from sponsored networks, such as those based on the IBM360/370 mainframe platform or the DEC VAX platform, to non-proprietary PC networks, such as those based on the Intel x86 chip and MS-DOS operating system. Intel and Microsoft have recently been taking on more and more of the functions typically associated with a system sponsor, while so much of the standardization in the peripheral and software market remains non-proprietary.

In any event, prediction about the long-run evolution of an economic network is almost impossible because the success of an economic network is so tied to the success of its underlying technology, which is inherently uncertain (which, of course, does not prevent futuristic technologists from making predictions). Some highly touted technologies gain wide acceptance and some do not, but it is often hard to pinpoint the causes of success or failure. In product markets that regularly undergo radical product innovation, it will not be clear at the outset how valuable a product or service will be, nor what costs each technical alternative may impose on later technical developments, nor how large the network will grow as new applications are developed. As a result, it is difficult to predict a market's dynamics after standardization.

For example, none of the important firms in the VCR industry in the late 1970s anticipated either the consequences for *hardware* competition from the development of the rental movie market, nor the power of the economic links between geographically separate markets. In a more current case, technical uncertainty makes it difficult to predict whether the technical requirements implicit in ISDN will limit or enhance competition. After all, ISDN will influence product design and network growth, which in turn may influence other factors such as tariff structures, network controls, plant investment, and other regulatory decisions.

In sum, the only predictable feature of many information technology networks is that they change. It is not surprising if two snapshots of any particular market niche taken sufficiently far apart in time may reveal different firms, radically different products and applications, and even different buyers. From an individual supplier's or user's perspective, this uncertainty complicates decisions with long-run consequences, since investment in physical equipment is often irreversible and personnel training is expensive in terms of time and money.

150

### 3.4. Lock-in and control of technical options.

Most buyers and sellers in an evolving industry know that change will come and that its character will be unpredictable. As a result, most product designers and users of compatibility standards associate potential problems with being locked-in to a narrow technical choice. One of the most interesting and least understood aspects of standardization processes is how attempts to avoid lock-in influences design decisions and market outcomes in dynamic settings.

One approach to understanding standardization activity emphasizes the value decision-makers place on having "strategic flexibility," i.e., having a choice among many future technical options.[28] Its starting premise is that much technology choice involves discontinuous choices among alternatives and an important determinant of an investment is the uncertain revenue stream associated with future technical alternatives. Product designers and technology users will expend resource today in order to not foreclose technical alternatives associated with potentially large revenue streams. The greater the uncertainty at one time, the greater the value placed on keeping technical choices open over time. The value of strategic flexibility may far outweigh the value of any other determinant of technology choice.

Standards may influence firm decisions on whether to design a new product for a given product line, delay introducing a new product, or invest in capacity for an existing product line. A firm may choose to expend extra resources to become part of the largest possible network (by designing a standardized technical platform) because it cannot be certain which of many future designs will best suit its customers. A firm may also expend extra resources to make its products compatible with a mix and match network in order to give buyers assurance that many applications may be available in the future. A firm may hedge its bet by simultaneously employing different technical standards that permit it to reverse its commitment to a technical alternative.

Buyers will also expend resources to leave open options affected by technical uncertainties. Buyers require evidence that their technical options will remain open. For example, the existence of many peripheral component suppliers assures that buyer that an economic network caters to a variety of needs. Alternatively, users may purchase general purpose technologies rather than an application-specific technology as a means to leave open their options for future expansion. For example, Greenstein[29] discussed how federal mainframe computer users in the 1970s telescoped future lock-in problems into the present and made investments in "modular" programming as a result.

Some of this anticipatory activity is in society's interest, but not all of it is. Much of it can be a nuisance and some of it is probably wasteful. From any viewpoint, it is quite frustrating to expend resources on anticipated events that do not necessarily occur. It is also quite easy to be blindsided by events that were not anticipated. This is the aspect of today's network development that many vendors and buyers see day to day, which may be one reason, perhaps, that the absence of standardization is so maligned in trade publications.

## 4. INVISIBLE ADVISORS: INNOVATION BY ORGANIZATIONS

As noted above, there are many situations in which all component suppliers have an interest in seeing the emergence and the growth of an economic network. Yet, structural impediments may produce coordination problems. The strong mutual interest all firms have in the emergence of an economic network can lead firms to forego market processes and attempt to develop standards in organizations that combine representation from many firms. How do these groups work and do they work well? Do these groups ameliorate some of the problems identified in the short run and long run analysis of unfettered market processes? Figure 3 summarizes the following discussion.

## 4.1. Consortia and mergers: lending a helping hand?

It seems as if every other day the newspaper announces the formation of another alliance or the merger of erstwhile competitors -- where the participants come together in order to play a large role in the next phase of development of standards for some aspect of the information infrastructure. Though consortia do not have a long and well documented history, a few examples have pointed out some of the economic strengths and pitfalls of developing standards through these groups. Many of the same factors influence the merger of two firms, but this discussion will narrow its focus to only consortia. The reader will easily see the implications for merger.

**Figure 3**
**The economic role of organizations: A comparison**

| | Consortia | Standards development organizations |
|---|---|---|
| **Motivation for formation** | Strategic alliances or outgrowth of joint research venture | Professional societies |
| **Primary benefits** | May accelerate development of complementary components | Forum for discussion of issue surrounding anticipatory standards |
| **Main hindrance to success** | Strategic interests of vendors override greater interests of organization or society | Strategic interests of vendors override greater interests of organization or society |
| **Coordination of technical change** | Will coordinate change only among the subset of cooperating firms | Administrative processes tend to be slow relative to the pace of technical change |

Consortia are becoming increasingly popular in information technology industries, partially as an outgrowth of joint research ventures. Most of these groups seem to be concerned with the future of technologies and anticipated changes in related standards. The consortia jointly operates an organization responsible for designing, upgrading, and testing a compatibility standard. The main advantage to consortia is that it allows the firms to legally discuss technical issues of joint interest, while ostensibly avoiding antitrust problems, but retain considerable independence in unrelated facets of their business.

152

### 4.1.1. Good points to consortia

The greatest economic benefit of these groups is that they may accelerate development of complementary components. Success is more likely when all the companies (who may directly compete in a particular component market) find a common interest in developing products that complement their competitive offering. Each of the companies may offer different types of engineering expertise, whose full value cannot be realized unless combined with another firm's talents. Each firm may anticipate specializing in one part of the system that the consortia sponsors. In this respect, the incentives for firms to come together in a consortium and jointly design a standardized bundle of components resemble the incentives for several firms to independently produce a "mix-and-match" set of components. However, consortia retain an interesting dynamic element. The consortia help induce other firms to produce complementary components because the consortia's existence act as a guarantee that a standard's integrity will be maintained in the future. Of course, there may still be insufficient investment in complementary products since no producer internalized the entire interest of the network. However, some investment is often better than nothing, which is enough to begin development.

### 4.1.2. The problems with consortia

Consortia are not a perfect solution to coordination problems. They can easily fall prey to some of the same structural impediments that prevented network development in their absence. The experience with the development of Unix standards in the 1980s amply illustrates these weaknesses.[30] Many firms perceived strategic alliances as tools to further their own economic interests and block unfavorable outcomes. As a result, two different consortia, OSF and Unix International, originally sponsored two different Unix standards. Industry participants lined themselves up behind one or another based on their economic self-interest. More recently, different consortia (and firms) have sponsored slightly different forms of Unix, confusing the market place once again. While two standards (or a few) surely is better than the multiplicity that existed before, there does not seem to be sufficient heterogeneity in user needs to merit two or more standards. Society would probably be better off with one standard, but supplier self-interest will prevent that.

The other potential danger with consortia, as when any group of competing firms cooperate, is that such organizations may further the interests of existing firms, possibly to the detriment of potential entrants or users. For example, consortia may aid collusive activities through joint pricing decisions, or may serve as vehicles to raise entry barriers, chiefly by stifling the development of technology that accommodate development of products that compete with the products of firms inside the consortia. More understanding of consortia will be needed before it is clear whether this is a common practical problem or an unfounded fear. After all, it may be difficult to both credibly invite development of complementary components and deter development of competing components.

### 4.2. Standards development organizations: A handy alternative?

One of the reasons private consortia are often unnecessary is that other well-established professional organizations serve similar functions. Many large umbrella groups that cut across many industries, such as CCITT, IEEE, and ASTM have a long history of involvement in the development of technical standards.[31] These groups serve as a forum for discussion, development and dissemination of information about standards. In the past, such groups largely codified standards determined by market processes. Today a whole alphabet soup full of groups are involved with anticipating technical change in network industries and guiding their design. Their role in designing "anticipatory" standards takes on special urgency in economic networks in danger of locking-in to technical standards.

### 4.2.1. Do SDOs work?

Standards development organizations play many useful roles in solving network coordination problems, especially those related to lack of communication. They can serve as a forum for affected parties to educate each other about the common perception of the problems to be solved. They can also serve as a legal means to discuss and plan the development of a network of compatible components, as well as document agreements about the technical specification of a standard and disseminate this information to interested parties.

Perhaps most importantly, SDO standards can serve as a focal point to designers who must choose among many technical solutions when imbedding a standard in a component design. In other words, these groups are most likely to succeed when market participants mutually desire interoperability, need to establish a mechanism for communication and need a mechanism to develop or choose one of many technical alternatives. The involvement of Grocer's groups in the development of bar codes for retail products is an example of this type of situation.

### 4.2.2. Problems with SDOs

One important feature of most of these organizations is that they are "voluntary."[32] Participating firms and individuals have discretion over the degree of their involvement. In other words, though most firms or individuals belong to the relevant umbrella groups, their contribution of resources (and time) to development can wax or wane for a variety of technical and strategic reasons. This can lead to either extraordinary investment in the process to influence outcomes or to "free-riding" off the activities of the organization. These biases are well-known, and can only be held in check by the professional ethics of the engineers who design standards.

Voluntary standards groups are also no panacea for the structural impediments to network development in some markets. They will fail to produce useful standards when the self-interest of participants prevents it in any event. In other words, designers must have some economic incentives for embedding a technical standard in their product, since use is optional. For example, a dominant firm need not follow the recommendations of a voluntary standardization group. Moreover, it is not likely to do so if it believes that it can block entry and successfully market its products without the standard. IBM's marketing of systems using EBCDIC rather than ASCII, which originated out of an industry group, is one such example.[33]

Similar impasses may occur in a market with dueling technologies, although a voluntary group can play an important role in a duel: if it chooses a particular standard, it could swing the competitive balance in favor of one standard rather than another. However, each sponsoring firm may try to block the endorsement of its rival's standard as a means to prevent this result, which may effectively prevent any standard from being adopted by the voluntary group. The strategies employed in such committee battles can become quite complex, ranging from full cooperation to selective compromise to stonewalling.

154

SDOs also must battle the perception that they are too slow. No administrative process may be able to guide the development of a network when a slow administrative process cannot keep up with new technical developments. When events become too technically complex and fluid, a focal point is easily lost. For example, this problem is already arising as private telecommunications grow and private groups attempt to coordinate interconnection of their networks based on the ISDN model. One objection to ISDN is that the value from anticipating developments (on such an ambitious scale) is reduced if, as parts of the ISDN standard are written, the character of technology has changed enough to make the standard inadequate. In other words, the standard does not serve as a guide to component designers if the standards organization must frequently append the standard. Since no government administrative process could obviously do any better, market processes will usually predominate instead, coordination problems and all.

Since the decisions of voluntary groups can influence economic outcomes, any interested and organized party will make investments in order to manipulate the process to its advantage. As a result, user interests tend to be systematically unrepresented, since users tend to be diffuse and not technically sophisticated enough to master many issues. In addition, large firms have an advantage in volunteering resources that influence the outcome, such as volunteering trained engineers who will write standards that reflect their employees' interests. Finally, "insiders" have the advantage in manipulating procedural rules, "shopping" between relevant committees and lobbying for their long-term interests.

Committees have their own focus, momentum, and inertia, which will necessarily shape the networks that arise. As a general rule, the consensus rules governing most groups tends to favor backward-looking designs of standards using existing technology. As with consortia, standards may serve as vehicles to raise entry barriers by stifling the development of components from new entrants. The suppliers that dominate standards-writing will want to further the interests of existing firms, not potential entrants or users. These biases are also well-known, and are often held in check by the presence of antitrust lawyers and, once again, the professional ethics of the engineers who design standards.

In sum, voluntary standards organizations can improve outcomes for participants and society, particularly when they make up for the inadequate communication of a diffuse market structure. They are one more avenue through which a system may develop and one more channel through which firms may communicate. They are, however, just a committee, with no power to compel followers. In highly concentrated markets, their functions can be influenced by the narrow self-interest of dueling firms or dominant firms.

## 5. EPILOGUE

Do decentralized mechanisms lead to appropriate standards? It is difficult to know. Neither blind faith in market processes nor undue pessimism is warranted. Because standards can act as both a coordinator or a constraint, many outcomes are possible. These dual roles of standardization engenders so much confusion, because both roles are not always recognized.

In the short-run, when market structure is relatively stable, standards coordinate contemporary and anticipated market behavior. Standardization reduces the costs of interconnection. Standards let component designers anticipate interconnection requirements. Standards permit system users to make investments in assets and be assured that the asset's value will not depreciate due to loss of connectivity. Yet, both users and vendors become locked-in to a set of technical constraints that they may change only at a high cost. Moreover, vendors recognize the strategic importance of locking users to a standard and spend resources on manipulating their development.

In the long-run, the ultimate importance of standardization comes through its impact on technical change. In this setting standardization also plays a dual role as a constraint and as a coordinator. Predictable standards can aid technical development in most markets. Yet, standards also lock-in users and suppliers. Lock-in is especially costly when technical possibilities change rapidly, removing previous costly technical constraints and imposing others.

In a broader context, the progressive decentralization of decision making in information technologies away from a few sponsors, such as AT&T and IBM, has to be good in the long run. This decentralization unleashed an unmanageable variety of entrepreneurial activity. There is a natural (and sometimes legitimate) desire to want to manage and slow down the massive changes that accompany such entrepreneurial activity. However, such desires should not dictate the pace of change. Dynamism leads to economic growth and development and fantastic technical possibilities. The problems associated with standardization (and its absence) are an unfortunate, but bearable, necessary cost associated with such change.

## REFERENCES

Arthur, Brian, "Competing technologies: An overview," in *Technical Change and Economic Theory*, Dosi et. al. (eds.), London: Pinter Publishers, 1988.

Baba, Yasunori, and Imai, Ken-ichi, "Systemic Innovation and Cross-Border Networks: The Case of the Evolution of the VCR Systems," in *Entrepreneurship, Technological Innovation, and Economic Growth: Studies in the Schumpeterian Tradition*, Frederic M. Scherer and Mark Perlman (eds.), Ann Arbor: University of Michigan Press, 1992.

Besen, Stanley M., "AM vs. FM: The Battle of the Bands," mimeo, Santa Monica, CA: The Rand Corporation, 1991.

Besen, Stanley M., "The European Telecommunications Standards Institute," *Telecommunications Policy*, 14, 521-30, December 1990.

Besen, Stanley M. and Johnson, Leland L., *Compatibility Standards, Competition, and Innovation in the Broadcasting Industry*, Santa Monica, CA: The Rand Corporation, 1986.

Besen, Stanley M. and Saloner Garth, "Compatibility Standards and the Market for Telecommunications Services," in *Changing the Rules: Technological Change, International Competition and Regulation in Telecommunications*, R.W. Crandall and K. Flamm (eds.), Washington, D.C.: The Brookings Institution, 1988.

Bresnahan, Timothy, and Chopra, Amit, "Users' role in standard setting: the local area network industry," *Economics of Innovation and New Technology*, 1(½), 97-110, 1989.

Bresnahan, Timothy, and Greenstein, Shane, "Technological Competition and the Structure of the Computer Industry," CEPR Discussion Paper No. 315, Stanford University, June 1992.

Brock, Gerald, "Dominant firm response to competitive challenge: Peripheral Equipment Manufacturers' Suits against IBM (1979-1983)," in *The Anti-trust Revolution*, J. E. Kwoka and L. J. White (eds.), Glenview, IL: Scott, Foresman, and Co., 1989.

156

Brock, Gerald, "The Regulatory Change in Telecommunications: The dissolution of AT&T," in *Regulatory Reform: What Actually Happened*, L. W. Weiss and M. W. Klass (eds.), Boston: Little, Brown and Co., 1986.

Brock, Gerald, "Competition, Standards, and Self-Regulation in the Computer Industry," in *Regulating the Product: Quality and Variety*, Richard Caves and Marc Roberts (eds.), Cambridge, MA: Ballinger Publishing Co, 1975.

Cargill, Carl F., *Information Technology Standardization: Theory, Process, and Organizations*. Bedford, MA: Digital Press, 1989.

Cusumano, Michael A., Yiorgos Mylondadis, and Richard Rosenbloom, "Strategic Maneuvering and Mass Market Dynamics: The Triumph of VHS over BETA," Working Paper 91-048, Harvard Business School.

David, Paul A., "Clio and the economics of QWERTY," *American Economic Review*, 75, pp. 332-336, May 1985.

David, Paul, "Some New Standards for the Economics of Technological Standardization," in *The Economic Theory of Technological Policy*, P. Dasgupta and P.L. Stoneman (eds.), London: Cambridge University Press, 1987.

David, Paul A. and Bunn, Julie Ann, "The economics of gateway technologies and network evolution: Lessons from electrical supply history," *Information Economics and Policy*, 3, 165-202, Fall 1988.

David, Paul A. and Shane Greenstein, "The economics of compatibility standards: An introduction to recent research," *Economics of Innovation and New Technology*, 1(½), 3-41, 1990.

David Paul A. and Steinmueller, W. Edward, "The Economics of Compatibility Standards and Competition," TOP Working Paper, Stanford CA, Stanford University, Department of economics, January, 1992.

David, Paul A. and Steinmueller, W. Edward, "The ISDN bandwagon is coming -- Who will be there to climb aboard?: quandaries in the economics of data communication networks," *Economics of Innovation and New Technology*, 1(½), 43-62, 1990.

Farrell, Joseph, "Competition With Lock-in," U.C. Berkeley, Economics Department, no. 8722, January, 1987.

Farrell, Joseph and Saloner, Garth, "Competition, Compatibility, and Standards: The Economics of Horses, Penguins and Lemmings," in *Product Standardization as a Tool, of Competitive Strategy*, H. Landis Gabel (eds.), North-Holland, 1986.

Fisher, Franklin M. and McGowan, John J., & Greenwood, Joen E., *Folded, Spindled, and Mutilated: Economic Analysis and U.S. vs. IBM*, Cambridge, MA: MIT Press, 1983.

Greenstein, Shane, "Invisible Hands and Visible Advisors: An Economic Interpretation of Standardization," *Journal of the American Society for Information Science*, 43(8), pp. 538-549, Sept. 1991.

Greenstein, Shane, "Lock-in and the Costs of Switching Mainframe Computer Vendors: What Do Buyers See?" University of Illinois, Faculty Working Paper 91-0133, Political Economy Series #48, 1991.

Hemenway, D., *Industrywide Voluntary Product Standards*, Cambridge MA: Ballinger, 1975.

Kahin, Brian, *Building Information Infrastructure*, New York, McGraw-Hill, 1992.

Kindleberger, Charles P., "Standards as public, collective and private goods," *Kyklos*, 36, 377-397, 1983.

Langlois, Richard N, and Paul L. Robertson, "Innovation in Modular system: Lessons from the Microcomputer and Stereo Component Industries," *Research Policy*, 21 (4), 297-313, 1992.

Lehr, William, "Standardization: Understanding the Process," *Journal of the American Society of Information Science*, September 1992.

Link, Albert & Tassey, George, "The Impact of Standards on Technology-based Industries: the Case of Numerically Controlled Machine Tools in Automated Batch Manufacturing," in *Product Standardization and Competitive Strategy*, Gabel, H. L. (Eds.), Amsterdam: North Holland, 1987.

Noam, Eli. M, "The Tragedy of the Common Network: Theory for the Formation and Breakdown of Public Telecommunications," p.51-64 of this volume.

Noll, Roger, and Owen, Bruce, "The Anti-Competitive Uses of Regulation," *United States v. AT&T (1982)*," J. E. Kwoka and L. J. White (eds.), Glenview, IL: Scott, Foresman, and Co., 1986.

OECD, *Information Technology Standards: The Economic Dimension*, Committee for Information, Computers and Communication Policy, Paris, France, 1991.

Owen, Bruce, and Wildman, Steven, *Video Economics*, Harvard University Press: Cambridge, MA. 1992.

Postrel, Steven, "Competing networks and proprietary standards: The case of quadrophonic sound," *Journal of Industrial Economics*, 39(2), December 1990.

Robertson, Paul L., and Langlois, Richard N., "Modularity, Innovation, and the Firm: The Case of Audio Components," in *Entrepreneurship, Technological Innovation, and Economic Growth: Studies in the Schumpeterian Tradition*, Frederic M. Scherer and Mark Perlman (eds.), Ann Arbor: University of Michigan Press, 1992.

Rotemberg, Julio, and Garth Saloner, "Interfirm Cooperation and Collaboration," *Information Technology and Organizational Transformation*, Michael Scott Morton (ed.), New York: Oxford University Press, 1991.

Saloner, Garth, "The economics of computer interface standardization: the case of UNIX," *Economics of Innovation and New Technology*, 1(½), 135-56, 1989.

Sanchez, Ron, "Strategic Flexibility, Real Options, and Production Strategy," Ph.D. Dissertation, MIT, Cambridge, MA. June 1991.

Spring, Michael B., "Information Technology Standards," in *Annual Review of Information Science and Technology*, Martin E. Williams, (ed.), Medford, N.J.: Learned Information for ASIS, 26, 1991.

Swann, G.M.P., "Product competition in microprocessors," *Journal of Industrial Economics*, XXXIV/1, 33-53, September, 1985.

Wade, James, "Battle of Network Standards: An Empirical Investigation of the Entry Rates of Competing Standards in the Microprocessor Market," Mimeo, Walter A. Haas School of Business, University of California at Berkeley, January, 1991.

158

# ENDNOTES

[1.] For more on government regulations of standards see OECD [1991], David and Greenstein [1990], and David and Steinmueller [1992]. See Besen and Johnson [1986] for an emphasis on issues in telecommunications.

[2.] At least since the writings of Hemenway [1975], it has been recognized that standards for networks have a "public goods" quality -- i.e., it is difficult to exclude anyone from using a standard and many economic agents can benefit from their use without influencing the costs to anyone else. As is generally the case with public goods, in the absence of actions by government or industry organizations, standards will be underprovided by unrestricted markets.

[3.] "In network industries, successful innovations often harm the installed base of a user who bought equipment and training before the new technology was available or recognized as the incipient standard. If I develop a new mousetrap and you choose not to buy it, I have not harmed you. If I develop a new computer operating system, incompatible with the old one you already own, and you choose not to buy it but millions of their users do, then you will find your network benefits much diminished as a consequence of the innovation. This stranding externality has no direct parallel in industries without network effects (Farrell, 1987)."

[4.] For example, the installed base of color television sets in the US today all use one set of standards that is incompatible with many of the new high-definition television (HDTV) standards possible. Many observers think it is too costly to abandon this installed base and, thus, recommend using a high-definition standard that is backward compatible with the installed base, even if doing so sacrifices some of the pictorial quality possible with HDTV technologies or raises its cost .

[5.] David, Paul A., Clio and the economics of QWERTY, *American Economic Review*, 75, pp. 332-336, May 1985.

[6.] It is also the source of considerable intellectual interest. Mathematical models of such processes tend to display highly non-linear results (e.g., see Arthur [1988]).

[7.] David, Paul A. and Bunn, Julie Ann, "The economics of gateway technologies and network evolution: Lessons from electrical supply history," *Information Economics and Policy*, 3, 165-202, Fall 1988.

[8.] Cusumano, Michael A., Yiorgos Mylondadis, and Richard Rosenbloom, "Strategic Maneuvering and Mass Market Dynamics: The Triumph of VHS over BETA," Working Paper 91-048, Harvard Business School.

[9.] Fisher, Franklin M. and McGowan, John J., & Greenwood, Joen E., *Folded, Spindled, and Mutilated: Economic Analysis and U.S. vs. IBM*, Cambridge, MA: MIT Press, 1983.

[10.] One critical issue is whether system sponsors can successfully "price-discriminate" -- i.e. identify separate groups of buyers and systematically charge them different prices *and* prevent one group of buyers from selling to the other. If price discrimination is feasible, then only new users benefit from system competition.

[11.] However, a sponsor will sometimes give away the standard in the hopes of dominating markets for components later on. Thus, not all monopoly rents are necessarily lost.

[12.] Rotemberg, Julio, and Garth Saloner, "Interfirm Cooperation and Collaboration," in Ed. Michael Scott Morton, *Information Technology and Organizational Transformation*, New York: Oxford University Press, 1991.

159

[13.]It is rare, but notable, to observe the opposite, a large buyer acting as a network sponsor. For example, the U.S. Department of Defense has sponsored a network of products using ADA. Another is the GM and Boeing sponsorship of the MAP/TOP standards.

[14.]The dominant firm can take actions like "refusing to sell the primary good to a rival; selling only complete systems and not their components; selling both system components but setting high prices for components if purchased separately; 'underpricing' components that compete with those sold by rivals; and 'overpricing' components that are needed by rivals to provide complete systems (Besen and Saloner [1988])."

[15.]Brock, Gerald, Competition, Standards, and Self-Regulation in the Computer Industry, in *Regulating the Product: Quality and Variety*, Richard Caves and Marc Roberts (eds.), Cambridge, MA: Ballinger Publishing Co, 1975.

[16.]Brock, Gerald, "Dominant firm response to competitive challenge: Peripheral Equipment Manufacturers' Suits against IBM (1979-1983)," in *The Anti-trust Revolution*, J. E. Kwoka and L. J. White (eds.), Glenview, IL: Scott, Foresman, and Co., 1989. Readers also may be tempted to site pre-divestiture AT&T's behavior in the customer premise equipment markets and long-distance markets, but that case is different because of the impact of regulation on AT&T's incentives: Noll, Roger, and Owen, Bruce [1986], "The Anti-Competitive Uses of Regulation: *United States v. AT&T (1982),*" J. E. Kwoka and L. J. White (eds.), Glenview, IL: Scott, Foresman, and Co.

[17.]Similar questions permeate debate about whether product innovation in systems of interrelated components is always beneficial or is "predatory" in some sense. Another issue is whether "controlling standards," which various writers define differently, can be used to a controlling firm's benefit at all if competition between systems limits the returns to such behavior.

[18.]Also important are many future regulatory decisions regarding interconnection and bypass on local telephone networks, as well as regulatory rules governing private and public boundaries on the data-transmission electronic networks of this country. These rules will arise out of an interdependent mix of FCC decisions, state PUC decisions, Congressional lawmaking, and court decisions. For example, see Kahin [1992].

[19.]Brock, Gerald, "Competition, Standards, and Self-Regulation in the Computer Industry," in *Regulating the Product: Quality and Variety*, Richard Caves and Marc Roberts (eds.), Cambridge, MA: Ballinger Publishing Co., 1975.

[20.]David, Paul A. and Bunn, Julie Ann, "The economics of gateway technologies and network evolution: Lessons from electrical supply history," *Information Economics and Policy*, 3(Fall), 165-202, 1988.

[21.]Noam, Eli. M, "The Tragedy of the Common Network: Theory for the Formation and Breakdown of Public Telecommunications," pp. 51-64 of this volume.

[22.]Besen, Stanley M., "AM vs. FM: The Battle of the Bands," mimeo, Santa Monica, CA: The Rand Corporation, 1991.

[23.]Wade, James, "Battle of Network Standards: An Empirical Investigation of the Entry Rates of Competing Standards in the Microprocessor Market," mimeo, Walter A. Haas School of Business, University of California at Berkeley, January 1991. Swann, G.M.P., "Product competition in microprocessors," *Journal of Industrial Economics*, XXXIV/1, pp. 33-53, September 1985.

[24.]Bresnahan, Timothy, and Greenstein, Shane, "Technological Competition and the Structure of the Computer Industry," CEPR Discussion Paper No. 315, Stanford University, June 1992.

160

[25.]Cusumano, Michael A., Yiorgos Mylondadis, and Richard Rosenbloom, "Strategic Maneuvering and Mass Market Dynamics: The Triumph of VHS over BETA," Working Paper 91-048, Harvard Business School.

[26.]Owen, Bruce, and Steven WIldman, *Video Economics*, Harvard University Press: Cambridge, MA. 1992.

[27.]The usual consensus is that RCA's technology was as good as society could get. However, it is hard to argue that these events went "well" from CBS's perspective, since they had a competing standard that ultimately lost.

[28.]Sanchez, Ron, Strategic Flexibility, Real Options, and Production Strategy, PhD Dissertation, MIT, Cambridge, MA, June 1991.

[29.]Greenstein, Shane, "Invisible Hands and Visible Advisors: An Economic Interpretation of Standardization," *Journal of the American Society for Information Science*, 43(8), September. pp. 538-549, 1992.

[30.]Saloner, Garth, "The economics of computer interface standardization: the case of UNIX," *Economics of Innovation and New Technology*, 1(1/2), 1, pp. 35-56, 1989.

[31.]More than 400 organizations have been estimated to be at work in this country developing, revising, and reviewing standards, though a few groups tend to dominate the development of information technology standards.

[32.]The major exception in the United States is when standards written by voluntary standards groups are required by law or administrative fiat, as with building codes. When governments get involved, it is often for the purpose of writing or choosing a standard directly. On occasion government bodies will also rely on those standards determined by an industry umbrella group. See the discussion below.

[33.]Note, however, that any advantages IBM accrued were strictly temporary. Bridges between the two standards are common place and virtually costless today. Also see Brock, Gerald, "Competition, Standards, and Self-Regulation in the Computer Industry," in *Regulating the Product: Quality and Variety*, Richard Caves and Marc Roberts (eds.), Cambridge, MA: Ballinger Publishing Co, 1975.

PRIVATE NETWORKS PUBLIC OBJECTIVES
E. Noam and A. NíShúilleabháin (Editors)
© 1996 Elsevier Science B.V. All rights reserved.

# Interoperability -- Technical

# Standards, Regulations and Private Decisions: A Framework for Analysis

Martin B.H. Weiss

## 1. INTRODUCTION

In this decade the information technology (IT) industry has witnessed two important trends that have affected the fundamental operation of the industry. On the one hand, the industry standards have increased in number and importance, and on the other, the telecommunications industry, an important sector of the IT industry, was deregulated. These phenomena have similar effects on private decision makers because of their fundamental effects on the marketplace for products and services. In this paper, I propose a single approach that can be used to explain these effects.

The concept of entropy provides a novel framework for analyzing these trends. Deregulation has the effect of increasing the product offerings of a previously regulated industry, resulting in increased consumer choices, whereas voluntary consensus standards have the effect of reducing the number of potential design outcomes.[1] When framed in this way, these two phenomena can be considered simultaneously under the unifying concept of entropy.

In practice, the number of common carrier offerings have flourished under deregulation. As the telecommunications and computer industry have changed, the number of voluntary consensus and *de facto* standards have also increased. In some cases, these standards were substantially competitive with each other,[2] or complimentary to each other.[3] The network managers for private firms have an extraordinary number of choices when constructing private networks under the present circumstances; so many, in fact, that they cannot reasonably optimize the structure of their network. In addition, these choices are changing continuously as carriers offer new services, as new standards emerge, and as firms enter and leave the marketplace. As a result, they frequently choose to set internal standards to complement the body of public standards and regulations that they face.

In the sense of statistical mechanics, entropy can be qualitatively defined to be a representation of the number of ways in which a system can be arranged.[4] Within this construct, deregulation can be seen as a mechanism or phenomenon that *increases* entropy, since consumers and producers have more choices. That is, there are more states in which the system can exist. Similarly, standards have the effect of *decreasing* the entropy of the market, since designers and consumers are faced with fewer products and services that can be designed.

It is particularly interesting that these two contradictory trends are occurring in the information technology industry at the same time. The telecommunications policies promulgated by the United States' Federal Communications Commission (FCC) since the late

1970s have generally been deregulatory. At the same time, this deregulatory trend and the erosion of market leadership in the information systems area have caused a virtual explosion in the development of voluntary consensus standards. In the context of entropy at a macro level, deregulation has occurred because the "entropy" of the market was too low, and standards because the "entropy" of the market was too high.[5] An entropy level that is too low suggests that a market is too "simple," meaning that insufficient choices exist for buyers. Likewise, an entropy level that is too high suggests that the market is too complex, that users cannot make appropriate choices because they are overwhelmed by the number and kinds of products available. Similarly, producers may be unable to extract sufficient revenues from products to recover costs and/or to finance the R&D on the next generation of products in under-standardized markets.

This view of markets might also suggest that a role of government is to act as an "entropy optimizing" agent. In this role, governments would intervene in markets where entropy is too low by stimulating R&D in the appropriate areas of technology or decreasing regulations; similarly, markets where entropy was too high could be subject to decreasing R&D expenditures, increased regulation, *etc.* Practically speaking, of course, the regulatory structure must have sufficient stability so that producers and consumers are able to make efficient economic decisions.

Since standards have been developed well in advance of products performing equivalent functions[6] in the last decade, this question of the optimal level of standardization becomes more critical. Firms invest substantial resources in the development of standards, so over standardization can lead to social welfare losses.

Anecdotal evidence suggests that users of information technology are overwhelmed with the choices available.[7] Due to competing services, traveling telecommunications users are also faced with a myriad of choices when calling from a hotel.[8] These examples suggest that the market entropy for users could be too high.

The objective of this paper is to develop a model for analyzing standards and regulation in a unified way. Several researchers have already developed economic models of standards, and much has been written about regulation, but none integrate both of these phenomena.

## 2. BACKGROUND

Considerable work has already been done on the economics of standardization and regulation, as well as notions of entropy. This section contains a brief review of the relevant literature.

### 2.1. Standards and Standardization

Standards have proliferated in recent years, particularly in the economic sector of Information Technology (IT).[9] Opinions among industry observers vary as to whether or not too few standards exist. Preliminary research[10] has shown a relationship between structure of a particular market and the incentives of producers in that market to promulgate standards. More specifically, the higher a market is concentrated, the more likely it is to have standards, because the producers who develop the standards are more likely to obtain sufficient benefits from them. Link's model is a profit model that examines whether the standards development process will be initiated for a particular market, based on aspects of the independent variables.[11] Lecraw also examined higher-level market aspects of standards,[12] using discriminant analysis to predict whether a market will have a standard or not based on the independent variables.[13]  Neither of these studies attempt to estimate, even at a macroeconomic level, how many standards are enough in a market given various independent variables.

Much of the previous research, taken collectively, predicts that markets not dominated by single firms will produce excessive standards early in a product life cycle, and that these standards are not necessarily socially optimal.[14] Anecdotal evidence generally supports this result. While researchers do not, as a rule, explicitly discuss the emergence mechanisms for standards (*i.e.*, the *de facto* and voluntary consensus processes), their work is at a sufficiently general level that this difference is not important.

## 2.2. Entropy

The concept of entropy emerged out of the study of thermodynamics and originally represented the amount of irreversible work that was inherent in a thermodynamic system. It has long been used to analyze thermodynamic systems in and out of equilibrium. Boltzman formulated entropy on a macroscopic, statistical measure that is dependent on the distribution of the microscopic states that a system can occupy, subject to energy constraints. Thus the entropy of a system is a macroscopic measure consisting of a sumulative sum of all microscopic states.

Entropy has wider implications, as was argued by Georgescu-Roegen.[15] Georgescu-Roegen reconceptualized economics and scientific thought based on statistical (*i.e.* entropic) principles as opposed to mechanistic ones.[16] In this view, economic actors feed on low entropy (*e.g.* raw materials) and produce high entropy (*e.g.* finished goods). Georgescu-Roegen attempts to explain many human endeavors and conflicts in these terms.

### 2.2.1. Entropy in Statistical Thermodynamics

Thermodynamics generally concerns thermal energy flows in physical systems. The Zeroth Law is the thermal equation of state, indicating that the temperatures of all bodies in equilibrium will be equal. The First Law is a caloric equation of state, which is used to calculate energy (*i.e.*, the quantity of heat) that flows among bodies in a closed system to achieve equilibrium. The Second Law of Thermodynamics is used to examine the reversibility of thermodynamic processes. It is in connection with the Second Law that the concept of entropy is introduced.

Attempts to define entropy on a less mathematical level have led to the notion of "disorder." To understand this, imagine a steam engine as a thermodynamic system, using coal to heat water to the boiling point. The steam generated by the boiling water is used to drive pistons that convert thermal energy to mechanical energy. Throughout this process energy is lost because of imperfect insulation of the steam pipes, friction in the steam engine, and other inefficiencies inherent in that particular method of converting thermal energy to mechanical energy. It is clearly not practical or even possible to fully reverse this thermodynamic process, which would require the regeneration of the coal that was used to heat the water, without using more energy. Thus, in thermodynamic terms, entropy was increased. One can observe that the system moved from a more orderly state of coal and water as distinct entities to a more disorderly state of ash and gasses, the water was converted to steam, some of which mixed with the atmosphere, and some of which condensed. It is this irreversible march to disorder that captured the interests of Georgescu-Roegen and Campbell.

While this view is interesting, a more detailed examination of entropy that is based on Boltzman's statistical characterization of the microscopic state that a system can occupy as needed. It was this characterization that made possible the connection between modern particle physics and classical Newtonian physics.[17]

Boltzman represented the entropy of a system as $S = k \ln W$, where $S$ is the entropy, $k$ is Boltzman's constant,[18] and $W$ is the number of possible microstates that a system can assume given a set of energy constants.[19] In statistical thermodynamics, a *macrostate* consists of a specific distribution of particles among possible energy levels for a given system energy level. The manner in which specific particles are distributed in a macrostate is called a *microstate* of the macrostate. Several microstates can exist for each macrostate, and a system can have several possible macrostates.

For example, if particles A, B, C, and D can occupy states P, Q, R, S, and T, the macrostate "two particles in P and two particles in Q" refers to six different possible microstates for that macrostate.[20] Another possible macrostate that satisfies the system energy constraint could be "one particle in P and three particles in R." This macrostate has four possible microstates.[21] Given these two macrostates, it is now possible to compute the probability of observing each of them. Between the two macrostates, 10 microstates are possible, 6 in the first macrostate, 4 in the second macrostate. Thus the probability of observing the system in macrostate 1 is 60%, and the probability of observing macrostate 2 is 40%. The entropy of the system is then found using Boltzman's equation, $S = k \ln W$. For the example described above, $W = 10$, and $k = 1.38*10^{-23}$, so $S = 2.3k = 3.17*10^{-23}$, a very small number indeed. It is easy to see, however, that entropy increases as the number of available microstates increases. Sonntag and Van Wylen[22] and Finkelstein[23] show how this measure can be related to the entropy measure of classical thermodynamics.

### 2.2.2. Entropy and Information

The relationship between entropy and information can be attributed originally to James Clerk Maxwell in connection with the discussion of Maxwell's Demon. Maxwell's Demon was a thought-experiment designed to test the notions of entropy in thermodynamics. The demon attempted to reverse entropy by allowing fast moving molecules of warm gas to pass through an imaginary door to separate them from slow moving molecules of cold gas in a closed system without consuming energy. If successful, the demon would lower the entropy of the system. In order to accomplish this formidable task, the demon would have to be able to distinguish fast molecules from slow ones, *i.e.*, he would have to acquire *information* about each of the molecules before deciding whether to let them pass through the imaginary door. This information requirement lies at the heart of the argument about Maxwell's Demon.

The notion of entropy with respect to information in the context of communications systems was fomalized and adapted by Shannon, who took advantage of the prior work of Hartley and Wiener. His formalization dealt with uncertainty (entropy) in the context of the communication of information across a channel.[24] Subsequent researchers have developed the notion of the information of an event, related to the likelihood of that event, such that the information is greater in events that are less likely. This representation is intuitively satisfying because we learn more from uncommon statements than from statements that we expect.

### 2.2.3. Non-Technical Applications of Entropy

The entropy measure has been used outside the fields of information science and thermodynamics since the 1950s. Premier examples of its use in psychology can be seen in the work of Garner.[25] Brooks and Wiley[26] have demonstrated the application of entropy to biological evolution. This application of entropy is of most interest here.

The entropy concept was first applied in the economic context by Theil.[27] Theil's was the first analytical application of information theory to economics. He focussed on macroeconomic issues such as optimal firm location, input/output analysis, and comparing economic data, such as wages, across multiple economies. Georgescu-Roegen also considered entropy in the context of economics. In contrast to Theil, he examined entropy from a very general, philosophical viewpoint, and then considered economic applications of this theory.[28] The application of entropy in economics were reviewed and criticized by Brumat.[29]

### 2.2.4. Standards, Market and Entropy

This section presents a more detailed discussion of how these concepts might be tied together. Earlier in this paper, it was asserted that standards have the effect of decreasing entropy. Since standards and regulations have the effect of limiting consumer and producer behavior, they reduce the number of choices that both designers and consumers have. In thermodynamic terms, the number of states that the "system" (*i.e.* the market) can achieve are reduced, resulting in a reduction of the entropy of the system.

Introducing another global measure for markets cannot be done without justification. Other methods that have been developed to characterize markets have been the four-firm concentration ratio and the Herfindahl Index.[30] These indices are measures of industrial concentration within markets. While these might be applicable to this purpose in some cases,[31] they do not always capture the market complexity abstraction that is the focus of this paper. Indeed, Stigler captured the intent of these measures when he stated that "the purpose of a measure of concentration is to predict the extent of departure from price (or, alternatively, of rate of return) from the competitive level."[32] Thus, these measures are intended for antitrust application.

Market complexity can be uncorrelated with measures of concentration because different manufacturers can dominate in different market segments. For example, the market for modems can be segmented into speed (*e.g.*, 1200bps, 2400bps, *etc.*) and application (*i.e.*, dialup or leased line). One manufacturer may dominate in the market for 1200bps dialup modems, and another in 9600bps leased line modems. Thus, a market of complexity is not necessarily the same as the concentration of the modem market.

### 2.3. Market Model

We assume that consumers have a need for a product. They formulate their product or systems requirement based on an examination of their situation or system and their understanding of the technology that is available to them in the market. They then proceed to search the market for solutions to their needs. When they find a product or system that best fits their needs, they purchase it.[33] Thus, a market can be viewed as a search space for consumers. This view of markets was first suggested by Stigler,[34] with improvements and enhancements suggested by subsequent researchers. Philips[35] presents a thorough review of the literature, and Wilde[36] discusses the results of the psychological literature with respect to various search rules proposed by economists. According to the model proposed by Stigler, consumers search over a known number of shops using various search rules (several have been proposed, the most common being a sequential rule) to find the lowest price. Since searching may not be costless, the model attempts to identify the number of outlets a consumer may search and to explain price dispersion among outlets, a phenomenon that is not explained by traditional microeconomics.

Markets that are "over-standardized" or "over-regulated" are likely to produce insufficient kinds of products to meet the range of requirements that users have. In the context of the previous work, consumers will have exhausted the possible search space before they have reached their "cutoff" level (*i.e.*, their reservation price). That means that they would have continued to search, had there been more alternates available. Two principle effects can occur in these kinds of markets: 1) competing standards can be developed that cover different cost, performance, or application ranges, or 2) some of the standards can be dissolved (as in the case with deregulation). Markets that exhibit excessive numbers of competing standards can begin to take on the characteristics of an under-standardized market because users become overwhelmed with the choices available. Markets that are under-standardized are likely to overwhelm users with choices, resulting in an increase of search costs or increases in user uncertainty due to the risk of being stranded when network effects are present.[37] Producers have difficulty extracting sufficient profits from products in under-standardized markets because of the intense competition to achieve lock-in among potential users. The potential source of the problem is the limited human ability to process large amounts of information, as suggested by Simon's theory of bounded rationality.

## 3. MARKET ENTROPY

The underlying hypothesis of this paper is that standards and regulations reduce the entropy of a market. The product selection process of a user (*i.e.*, a consumer) can be viewed as a search of the space of existing products. Standards and regulations can be viewed as mechanisms that reduce the space that must be searched. Since consumers are faced with fewer choices, the entropy must be lower (by Shannon's second requirement for the entropy measure).

The lowest entropy level of a market would occur when a single standard encompasses the entire search space of the user. This standard would be optimal if it also met all of the user's requirements. Multiple standards would increase the entropy of a market, and could be optimal if a single standard was incapable of meeting the entire marketplace demand. The lowest entropy levels of multiple standards would occur if they are mutually exclusive. Overlaps in the functionality and scope of standards increases the number of choices available to a buyer, and hence increases entropy. Thus, additional standards (*i.e.*, the search space will be divided) will be added to the market until all user demands are satisfied. Similarly, users will disregard standards if too many exist.

To illustrate how all this can be applied to a real market, consider that the market entropy measure can be defined as a function of the number of market segments. Under this formulation, markets are characterized by several distinct market segments, each of which may have a standard associated with it. In order to formalize the notion of market entropy, it is useful to create analogies with the atomic models that underlie thermodynamic energy. In atomic theory, particles, such as electrons, are distributed among different energy levels within the atom. The manner in which they are distributed are dependent on the atom itself and its energy level. The macrostate of a thermodynamic system (*i.e.*, collection of atoms) is defined as the manner in which particles in general might be distributed among the energy levels within the atom, subject to the constraints of the system. In economics, consumers are the equivalent of particles and market segments are equivalent to atoms. Thus, a macrostate consists of the ways in which consumer purchases of products can be distributed over all market segments so that all economic and technical constraints are met. A microstate is the way in which specific consumers are distributed over the market segments within a particular macrostate.

As stated above, Boltzman formulated entropy to be proportional to the number of microstates that can exist within a system.[38] Due to deregulation, decreased standardization, or an increase in competing standards, the market entropy increases because the number of microstates increases. Similarly, a market that has few market segments due to over-regulation or standardization displays lower market entropy. To make this concept more concrete, consider the market for long distance data communications in the US (LAN products are explicitly excluded from this example). Business users may choose from a variety of products and services, each of which could potentially address the need. They include:

- Analog dialup or leased lines with modems
- Digital Data Services (DDS), which is widely available at 56kbs dedicated or switched
- Fractional T1, at a typical rate of 384kbs (although other rates are possible)
- T1 at 1.544 Mbps
- T3 at approximately 45 Mbps
- New services such as Frame Relay and Switched Mulitmegabit Data Service (SMDS), which are being introduced in most localities and are available at a variety of rates[39]

These services are plotted in Figure 1 as a function of line speed and line type (dedicated or shared). Users can select one of these services for their needs. Users have more choices as more services are developed. These represent the "macrostates" that users could occupy. The entropy of the market would be computed by observing the distribution of users over these services. If services such as Frame Relay and SMDS had not been standardized, or if they had been proscribed by government regulation, they would not have been choices available to users. Users that would otherwise occupy these "states" would be forced to different states, presumably ones that most closely met their needs. This would have an entropy reducing effect, since it would force users to cluster more than they would in the current marketplace. If prices and multiple carriers are included, the number of macrostates multiplies, since each users could use a service from a carrier at a given price, whereas another could use the same service at a different price. Figure 2 illustrates this. In fact, anecdotal evidence from telecommunications managers indicates that they are not able to dynamically optimize their networks. As soon as a particular implementation of a network is completed the network manager might learn of a new service or a new price of an existing service.[40] Changing networks is not without costs, so network managers are forced to operate sub-optimal networks. The strategy adopted by some managers to cope with this

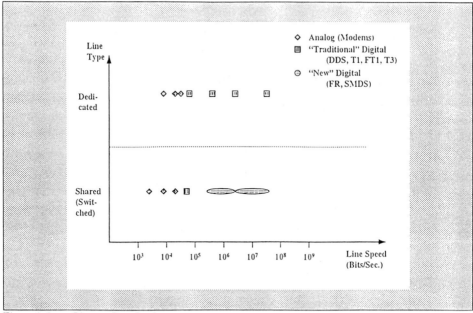

**Figure 1**: Long Distance Data Services

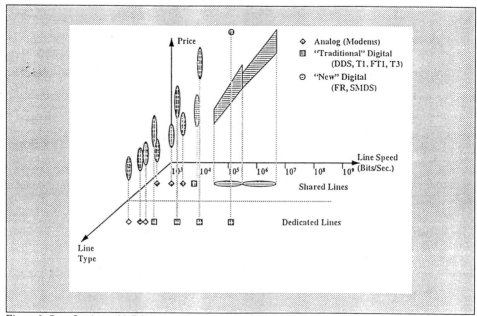

**Figure 2**: Data Services with Price

problem is to reduce the search space by adopting internal standards, such as identifying a preferred vendor, or selecting from a limited portfolio of available services. In this way, network managers reduce the perceived market entropy, even though the actual market entropy is much higher. The range of technology and price offerings is not without costs to vendors either, but these costs are normally viewed as a necessary part of doing business in the competitive information technology marketplace.

## 4. RELATIONSHIP TO PRIOR RESEARCH

While none of the previous research in standards has taken this particular view, this framework is not incompatible with some of the previously obtained results. Critical to most of the formal models developed above is the notion of technical externality that is a function of the number of compatible units in the market. In the entropic model, the externality is represented explicitly as the probability with which a particular product type is selected. Thus, non-standard products can be in the market, they just have a lower probability of being selected by a user. New technologies enter the model as new states that the market can assume, *i.e.*, they increase the entropy of the market.

### 4.1. Application to Private Networks

How does this theory matter to private networks? Consider the manager of a corporation with varying user needs. In principle, each of the users could contract privately to meet their needs. Corporations realize that economies can be gained by negotiating collectively, resulting in a private network for users. The private networks are economical for several reasons:

- Service providers are more likely to negotiate lower prices with a collection of users than with single users
- "Standard" internal products reduce the training requirements for network service personnel
- By developing a set of "standard" solutions to common problems, the corporation reduces the search space in under standardized markets, reducing the search costs for solutions to user's needs
- Users gain from the network benefits of internally standardized solutions

An ideal private network solution would be the superset of each of the individual's needs. It is possible that this superset will be smaller than the set of available products. In the context of the theory of market entropy proposed here, the entropy of the solution space is reduced, so firms gain economies by going to private networks. In fact, it is quite possible that the savings in going to a collective private network exceed the savings from collective bargaining for low cost.

Such a private network may be sub-optimal in several respects. First, since the public network service and equipment alternatives are changing rapidly, it is likely that the network is of a higher cost than it would be otherwise. Second, users' needs are dynamic; if the private network does not adapt to user needs with sufficient speed, than users will lose efficiencies that they might have had. Third, a collective decision to back a "losing" technology when standards rivalry occurs can have a larger net effect than if the decision were made individually, because some of the individual users would probably have backed the technology that was the winner, *ex post*.

## 5. CONCLUSION

A theory of standards and regulation has been proposed that is based on the concept of entropy. This theory was qualitatively demonstrated in a study of the market for long distance data services. This theory provides an additional factor influencing buyer behavior that traditional economic theory does not capture. The effect of market entropy that is too high is that buyers establish internal standards to which they adhere. While this means that they do not always purchase the optimal system for a particular application, it does result in a purchasing process that is less costly and more easily manageable. Similarly, a market whose entropy is too low would find users clamoring for other solutions, and potentially building systems privately that circumvent the overly restrictive marketplace.[41] This theory has some implications for policy-makers as well. While it is difficult to imagine an "entropy knob" that increases or decreases market entropy as needed, it is possible to imagine a deregulatory climate with lax enforcement when market entropy is too low, and a more regulatory and enforcement-oriented posture when market entropy is too high. In the latter case, one can even imagine lax enforcement of antitrust regulations so that market leadership could develop to reduce the market entropy. Since this measure can be used to determine the over- or under-standardization of a market, it can be used by the planning committees of standards development organizations as a strategic planning tool. For example, no new standards activities should be initiated in markets that exhibit low entropy and where user needs are being met. Instead, the standards development committees should concentrate on markets where the entropy is high, or on those markets with low entropy where user needs are not being met. While using this as a standards management tool, it is important to note that many factors affect the satisfactory outcome of a standards development effort. Just as product planning helps developers focus their activities, this notion of entropy may help standards planning committees focus their limited resources more effectively.

## REFERENCES

Brooks, Daniel R. and E.O. Wiley, *Evolution as Entropy: Toward a Unified Theory of Biology*, Chicago: University of Chicago Press, 1986.

Brumat, Carlos Maria, *Use and Abuse of Entropy in Economics*, Ph.D. Thesis, UCLA, 1976.

Campbell, Jeremy, *Grammatical Man*, New York: Simon and Schuster, 1982.

Cargill, Carl F., *Information Technology Standardization: Theory, Process, and Organizations*, Bedford, MA: Digital Press, 1989.

David, Paul A., "Clio and the Economics of QWERTY," *American Economic Review*, Vol. 75, No. 2, pp. 332-337, May 1985.

David, Paul A., "Some New Standards for the Economics of Standardization in the Information Age," in P. Dasgupta and P. Stoneman (eds.) *Economic Policy and Technological Performance*, Cambridge: Cambridge University Press, 1987.

David, Paul A. and Julie Ann Bunn, "The Economics of Gateway Technologies and Network Evolution: Lessons from the Electricity Supply History," *Information Economics and Policy*, Vol. 3, Num. 2, pp. 165-202, 1988.

Dragan, J.C. and M.C. Demetrescu, *Entropy and Bioeconomics: The New Paradigm of Nicholas Georgescu-Roegen*, Pelham, NY: Nagard Publishers, English Translation, 1986.

Farrell, Joseph and Garth Saloner, "Standardization, Compatibility, and Innovation," *RAND Journal of Economics*, Vol. 16, No. 1, pp. 70-83, Spring 1985.

Farrell, Joseph and Garth Saloner, "Installed Base and Compatibility: Innovation, Product Preannoucements, and Predation," *American Economic Review,* Vol. 76, No. 5, pp. 940-955, December 1986.

Farrell, Joseph and Garth Saloner, "Competition, Compatibility, and Standards: The Economics of Horses, Penguins, and Lemmings," In Gabel, H. Landis (ed.) *Product Standardization and Competitive Strategy*, New York: North Holland, 1987.

Farrell, Joseph and Garth Saloner, "Coordination Through Committees and Markets," *RAND Journal of Economics*, Vol. 19, No. 2, pp. 235-252, 1988.

Farrell, Joseph, "The Economics of Standardization: A Guide for Non-Economists," In Berg, J.L. (ed.), *How Standards Succeed, Proceedings of the International Symposium on Information Technology Standardization*, New York: North Holland, 1989.

Finkelstein, Robert J., *Thermodynamics and Statistical Physics*, San Francisco: W.H. Freeman, 1969.

Garner, W.R. and William J, McGill, "The Relation Between Information and Variance Analyses," *Psychometrika*, Vol. 21, No. 3, pp. 219-228, Sept. 1956.

Garner, W.R., "Symmetric Uncertainty Analysis and Its Implications for Psychology," *The Psychological Review*, Vol. 65, No. 4, pp. 183-195, July 1958.

Georgescu-Roegen, Nicholas, "Thermodynamics, Economics, and Information," in Marcelo Alonso (ed.), *Organization and Change in Complex Systems*, New York: Paragon House, 1990.

Georgescu-Roegen, Nicholas, *The Entropy Law and the Economic Process*, Cambridge MA: Harvard University Press, 1971.

Katz, Michael L. and Carl Shapiro, "Network Externalities, Competition, and Compatibility," *American Economic Review*, Vol. 75, No. 3, pp. 424-440, June 1985.

Katz, Michael L. and Carl Shapiro, "Technology Adoption in the Presence of Network Externalities," *Journal of Political Economy*, Vol. 94, No. 4, pp. 822-841, August 1986(a).

Katz, Michael L. and Carl Shapiro, "Product Compatibility Choice in a Market with Technical Progress," *Oxford Economic Papers*, Nov. 1986(b).

Kerr, Susan, "Cutting Through Network Control," *Datamation*, Vol. 35, No. 20, pp. 30-34, October 15, 1989.

Kwoka, John E., Jr., "The Herfindahl Index in Theory and Practice," *The Antitrust Bulletin*, Vol. XXX, No. 4, pp. 915-948, Winter 1985.

Lecraw, Donald J., "Some Effects of Standards," *Applied Economics*, Vol. 16, pp. 507-522, 1984.

Link, Albert, "Market Structure and Voluntary Product Standards," *Applied Economics,* Vol. 15, pp. 393-401, 1983.

Moriarty, Rowland T., *Industrial Buying Behavior*, Lexington MA: Lexington Books, 1983.

Nelson, Richard R. and Sidney G. Winter, *An Evolutionary Theory of Economic Change*, Cambridge MA: Belknap Press, 1982.

172

Phlips, Louis, *The Economics of Imperfect Information,* New York: Cambridge University Press, 1988.

Rifkin, Jeremy (w. Ted Howard), *Entropy: A New World View*, New York: Viking Press, 1980.

Shannon, Claude E. and Warren Weaver, *The Mathematical Theory of Communication*, Urbana IL: University of Illinois Press, 1949.

Sonntag, Richard E. and Gordon J. Van Wylen, *Introduction to Thermodynamics: Classical and Statistical*, New York: J. Wiley, 1982.

Stigler, George J., "The Economics of Information," *Journal of Political Economy,* Vol. 69, pp. 213-282, 1961.

Stigler, George J., "The Measurement of Concentration," in Stigler, Geroge J. (ed.) *Organization of Industry*, Homewood IL: Richard D Irwin.

Strauss, Paul R., "The Standards Deluge: A Sound Foundation or a Tower of Babel?" *Data Communications*, Vol. 17, No. 10, pp. 150-164, September 1988.

Theil, H., *Economics and Information Theory*, Chicago: University of Chicago Press, 1967.

Weiss, Martin B.H. and Marvin A. Sirbu, "Technological Choice in Voluntary Standards Committees: An Empirical Analysis," *Economics of Innovation and New Technology*, Vol. 1, No. 1, pp. 111-134, 1990.

Weiss, Martin B.H., "Compatibility Standards and Product Development Strategies: A Review of Data Modem Developments," *Computer Standards and Interfaces*, Vol. 12, pp. 109-121, 1991(a).

Weiss, Martin B.H., "Standards Development: A View from Political Theory," University of Pittsburgh, Department of Information Science Working Paper LIS042/DIS 91010, June 1991(b).

Wilde, Louis L., "Consumer Behavior Under Imperfect Information: A Review of Psychological and Marketing Research as it Relates to Economic Theory," In Green, Leonard and John H. Kagel (eds.), *Advances in Behavior Economics (Vol. 1)*, Norwood NJ: Ablex Publishing Corp., 1987.

Ziemer, R.E. and W.H. Tranter, *Principles of Communications: Systems, Modulation, and Noise*, Boston: Houghton Mifflin, 1976.

## ENDNOTES

[1] Weiss, Martin B.H. and Marvin A. Sirbu, "Technological Choice in Voluntary Standards Committees: An Empirical Analysis," *Economics of Innovation and New Technology*, Vol. 1, No. 1, pp. 111-134, 1990.

[2] For example, the V.22*bis* modem standard competes with the V.26*ter*, and the Ethernet LAN standard (IEEE 802.3) can be viewed as competing with the Token Ring LAN standard (IEEE 802.5).

[3] For example, the TCP/IP protocol suite can be thought to build on Ethernet; the X.25 packet switched network standard builds on HDLC.

[4] Campbell, Jeremy, *Grammatical Man*, New York: Simon and Schuster, 1982. Georgescu-Roegen, Nicholas, *The Entropy Law and the Economic Process*, Cambridge MA: Harvard University Press, 1971.

[5] There are many detailed explanations for the need for particular standards and regulations that are available. The use of entropy at a macro level is not intended to and does not void these explanations.

[6.]Cargill, Carl F., *Information Technology Standardization: Theory, Process, and Organizations*, Bedford, MA: Digital Press, 1989. Weiss, Martin B.H., "Compatibility Standards and Product Development Strategies: A Review of Data Modem Developments," *Computer Standards and Interfaces*, Vol. 12, pp. 109-121, 1991(a).

[7.]Evidence of this can be found in virtually every trade publication. Strauss, Paul R., "The Standards Deluge: A Sound Foundation or a Tower of Babel?" *Data Communications*, Vol. 17 No. 10, pp. 150-164, September 1988. Kerr, Susan, "Cutting Through Network Control," *Datamation*, Vol. 35, No. 20, pp. 30-34, October 15, 1989.

[8.]Weiss, Martin and Michael Lewis, "Telecommunications Pricing and Consumer Expectation: The Case of Alternative Operator Services," *Telecommunications Policy*, pp. 497-509, Dec. 1991.

[9.]Strauss, Paul R., "The Standards Deluge: A Sound Foundation or a Tower of Babel?" *Data Communications*, Vol. 17, No. 10, September 1988, pp. 150-164.

[10.]Link, Albert, "Market Structure and Voluntary Product Standards," *Applied Economics*, Vol. 15, pp. 393-401, 1983.

[11.]Link uses the following independent variables for his analysis: seller market concentration, technological complexity (which is a function of R&D), and the percentage of unionization.

[12.]Lecraw, Donald J., "Some Effects of Standards," *Applied Economics*, Vol. 16, pp. 507-522, 1984.

[13.]Lecraw's independent variables are Buyer Concentration, Seller Concentration, proportion of government sales, product safety role, elasticity of demand, advertising intensity, R&D intensity, product complexity, and producer good/consumer good. Note their similarity to the independent variables used by Link. Link, Albert, "Market Structure and Coluntary Product Standards," *Applied Economics*, Vol. 15, pp. 393-401, 1983.

[14.]David, Paul A., "Some New Standards for the Economics of Standardization in the Information Age," in P. Dasgupta and P. Stoneman (eds.), *Economic Policy and Technological Performance*, Cambridge: Cambridge University Press, 1987. Katz, Michael L. and Carl Shapiro, "Technology Adoption in the Presence of Network Externalities," *Journal of Political Economy*, Vol. 94, No. 4, pp. 822-841, August 1986. Katz, Michael L. and Carl Shapiro, "Product Compatibility Choice in a Market with Technical Progress," *Oxford Economic Papers*, Nov. 1986. Farrell, Joseph and Garth Saloner, "Standardization, Compatibility, and Innovation," *RAND Journal of Economics*, Vol. 16, No. 1, pp. 70-83, Spring 1985. Farrell, Joseph and Garth Saloner, "Installed Base and Compatibility: Innovation, Product Preannoucements, and Predation," *American Economic Review*, Vol. 76, No. 5, pp. 940-955, December 1986.

[15.]Georgescu-Roegen, Nicholas, *The Entropy Law and the Economic Process*, Cambridge MA: Harvard University Press, 1971.

[16.]Dragan, J.C. and M.C. Demetrescu, *Entropy and Bioeconomics: The New Paradigm of Nicholas Georgescu-Roegen*, Pelham NY: Nagard Publishers, English Translation, 1986.

[17.]Finkelstein, Robert J., *Thermodynamics and Statistical Physics*, San Francisco: W.H. Freeman, 1969.

[18.]Boltzman recognized the need for a constant to calibrate the model to the physical phenomenon. While this constant is required for physical interpretation in statistical thermodynamics, it is incidental to the *structure* of the phenomenon.

174

[19.] In the case of thermodynamics, it represents the number of energy states that the electrons in an atom could possibly assume. Sonntag, Richard E. and Gordon J. Van Wylen, *Introduction to Thermodynamics: Classical and Statistical*, New York: J. Wiley, 1982.

[20.] Microstate 1 - AB in P, CD in Q; Microstate 2 - AC in P, BD in Q; Microstate 3 - AD in P, BC in Q; Microstate 4 - BC in P, AD in Q; Microstate 5 - BD in P, AC in Q; Microstate 6 - CD in P, AB in Q.

[21.] Microstate 1 - A in P, BCD in R; Microstate 2 - B in P, ACD in R; Microstate 3 - C in P, ABD in R; Microstate 4 - D in P, ABC in R.

[22.] Sonntag, Richard E. and Gordon J. Van Wylen, *Introduction to Thermodynamics: Classical and Statistical*, New York: J. Wiley, 1982.

[23.] Finkelstein, Robert J., *Thermodynamics and Statistical Physics*, San Francisco: W.H. Freeman, 1969.

[24.] Shannon, Claude E. and Warren Weaver, *The Mathematical Theory of Communication*, Urbana IL: University of Illinois Press, 1949.

[25.] Warner, W.R. and William J. McGill, "The Relation Between Information and Variance Analyses," *Psychometrika*, Vol. 21, No. 3, pp. 219-228, Sept. 1956. Garner, W.R., "Symmetric Uncertainty Analysis and Its Implications for Psychology," *The Psychological Review*, Vol. 65, No. 4, pp. 183-195, July 1958.

[26.] Brooks, Daniel R. and E.O. Wiley, *Evolution as Entropy: Toward a Unified Theory of Biology*, Chicago: University of Chicago Press, 1986.

[27.] Theil, H., *Economics and Information Theory*, Chicago: University of Chicago Press, 1967.

[28.] Georgescu-Roegen, Nicholas, *The Entropy Law and the Economic Process*, Cambridge MA: Harvard University Press, 1971.

[29.] Brumat, Carlos Maria, *Use and Abuse of Entropy in Economics*, Ph.D. Thesis, UCLA, 1976.

[30.] Kwoka, John E., Jr. "The Herfindahl Index in Theory and Practice," *The Antitrust Bulletin*, Vol. XXX, No. 4, pp. 915-948, Winter 1985.

[31.] Link (1983) and Leecraw (1984) use these measures as independent variables in their macroeconomic studies of standards in markets.

[32.] Stigler, George J., "The Measurement of Concentration," in Stigler, George J. (ed.), *Organization of Industry*, Homewood IL: Richard D Irwin, 1968.

[33.] This model of purchase behavior perhaps fits corporate purchasing behavior better than consumer purchasing behavior. This model is consistent with the corporate purchasing behavior literature (Moriarty 1983). Similar models have been considered by several economists for other purposes, for instance Nelson and Winter (1982) used a search model to analyze economic change. Stigler (1961) discusses price search when consumers have imperfect information (See also Philips (1988)).

[34.] Stigler, George J., "The Economics of Information," *Journal of Political Economy*, Vol. 69, pp. 213-282, 1961.

[35.] Phlips, Louis, *The Economics of Imperfect Information*, New York: Cambridge University Press, 1988.

[36.]Wilde, Louis L., "Consumer Behavior Under Imperfect Information: A Review of Psychological and Marketing Research as it Relates to Economic Theory," in Green, Leonard and John H. Kagel (eds.), *Advances in Behavior Economics (Vol. 1)*, Norwood NJ: Ablex Publishing Corp., 1987.

[37.]For example, the choice of video recording format (VHS or Beta) made decision-making more risky that in would have been had a standard been agreed upon in advance. Most adopters of the Beta standard have since switched to the rival VHS format, losing any investment in Beta-based tapes and VCRs that they had made.

[38.]Boltzman's constant, $k$, is of no meaning here and can be dropped without loss of generality. Boltzman's constant is used to calibrate the entropy measure to the appropriate physical dimensions. This is not necessary in this application.

[39.]Integrated Digital Services Network (ISDN) services are deliberately omitted from this because they are not widely available in the US.

[40.]This is by no means unique to network managers. Buyers of personal computers and computer workstations also face this situation.

[41.]For example, if frame relay service were unavailable publicly, then a corporation could choose to construct a network privately by leasing lines and purchasing the appropriate hardware. In some cases, such privately constructed networks are more economical than purchasing a public service in today's market.

PRIVATE NETWORKS PUBLIC OBJECTIVES
E. Noam and A. NíShúilleabháin (Editors)
© 1996 Elsevier Science B.V. All rights reserved.

# Taking It All Apart: Principles of Network Modularity

David P. Reed

## 1.INTRODUCTION

When the Federal Communications Commission (FCC) acted to remove the regulatory barriers to entry to the long distance and customer premises equipment (CPE) markets, it sought to increase the number of suppliers in these markets so that consumers could realize the benefits of competition. In moving to deregulate these markets, the FCC reasoned that there were no inherent features to the structure of these markets, or adverse impacts on other policy objectives, which should preclude competition. Subsequently, consumers have arguably enjoyed lower prices and more innovative service offerings in these markets. The long distance and CPE markets serve as notable examples of the general policy direction taken by the FCC in the 1980s to reduce the traditional telephone monopoly into a set of competitive markets for the purpose of bringing the benefits of competition to consumers of telecommunications services. But while these two components of the monopoly have been stripped away in this process, the barriers to competition with the local access network--the portion of the public network which extends between the interexchange carrier's network and the end user--still remains in pre-divestiture form.

It now appears to be an opportune moment to re-examine the extent to which competition can be brought to the local access switching and transport markets. The proliferation of private network alternatives improves the prospects for facilities-based competition in the transport of communications services. These alternatives include cable television networks, wireless telephone networks, local area networks (LANs) and metropolitan area networks (MANs). Local exchange carriers (LECs) have indicated that they foresee their network evolving into a multimedia platform capable of delivering a rich variety of text, imaging, and messaging services. Many take this multiple service scenario a step further and imagine an "open" network platform--a network with well defined interfaces accessible to all--which would allow an unlimited number of entrepreneurs a means to offer services in competition with one another limited only by their imagination and the fundamental capabilities of the underlying network facilities.

In this context, the policy question of interest is the extent to which the local access network might be decomposed to stimulate competition in markets for local switching and transport. Could competition satisfactorily emerge by simply removing the regulatory barriers to entry or is some form of open access requirements needed to introduce competition into the market? If there are elements of a natural monopoly in the local exchange network, then policies which promote open access to these centralized network resources can be instrumental in promoting a competitive market in spite of its monopolistic nature. Indeed,

178

the FCC has already begun to consider what open access requirements are necessary in the local exchange network to insure open and equal access to the network in its Open Network Architecture (ONA) policy.[1] Likewise, the Europeans also have their own initiative, called Open Network Provision (ONP), for opening up access to their public networks.

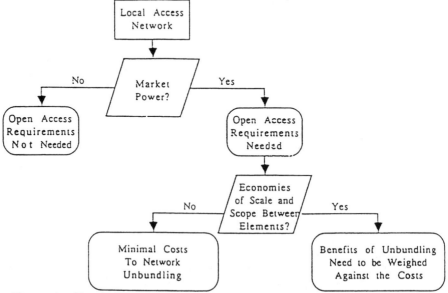

Figure 1: Simple Framework for Considering Open Access Requirements

The cornerstone of the ONA policy is the notion of unbundling network components to create open access to network resources.[2] Formally, network unbundling refers to the process of breaking the network into separate functional elements, or building blocks. Independent service providers could select only those unbundled components needed for their own service applications since the network operator cannot tie the availability of one element to subscription with another. If the price of the unbundled component exceeds what it would cost the service provider to provide this functionality on its own, the service provider has the flexibility to substitute its own private resources for the unbundled component.

Clearly, one could continue almost ad infinitum in this unbundling process, and one of the issues raised by this approach is the appropriate limit to this process. For example, network components can be classified into either logical or physical element categories. A logical element is a software defined network feature or capability, such as the number translations performed in a switch to establish a call; a physical element is the physical resource employed in the transmission or switching of the service.[3] Thus, a complete network service, whether it is offered by the network operator or a third party provider, would consist of a unique sequence of logical elements that are implemented by physical elements. But should open access requirements, in the form of network unbundling, apply to both physical and logical network elements? The FCC has just initiated a *Notice of Inquiry* into future network capabilities and architectures to investigate this question.[4]

An analytical framework which might be useful for considering these questions is shown in Figure 1. Given the local exchange network and local transport markets it serves, open access requirements should be considered if the LEC holds substantial market power to hinder the development of competition. If this is not the case, then the market should support some degree of competition and no open access requirements are needed. For the case where open access requirements are necessary, the next issue is to decide the extent to which unbundling is needed to open access to the network. When there are strong economies of scale and scope between the unbundled network elements, the process of network unbundling will make these economies unrealizable and therefore impose costs. To ensure that such a policy would be cost-effective, the benefits of the unbundled network components should be weighed against the lost economies arising from the unbundling process. Finally, if there are no large economies of scale and scope between the unbundled elements, then the costs of the unbundling process are less of a policy concern (although the actual costs of unbundling still need to be considered).

A full analysis of the questions raised in the broad framework of Figure 1 falls beyond the scope of this short paper, which seeks to investigate only a small subset of the issues associated with network unbundling. This framework does highlight, however, the difficult issues which should be carefully considered if network unbundling is to be applied broadly as a policy tool to open network access for the purposes of promoting competition:

- From a technical perspective, what are the basic network functionalities, both physical and logical, that could be candidates for unbundling?
- What is the appropriate framework for measuring the total benefits of unbundling? The benefits of open access to enhance the network platform are offset by the costs of the interface itself as well as the potential loss of economies of scale and scope across the interface. Is a quantitative measure possible to justify whether a network component is to be unbundled?
- To what extent should public policy mandate further network unbundling than might otherwise arise naturally through network evolution? What should be the criteria for imposing such a requirement?
- Will the pricing structure in place lead to a cost-based schedule of tariffs for the network components?

The focus of this paper is confined to the first issue listed above. Focusing upon this question, however, offers useful insight into the other issues by describing the technical context through which the process of network evolution and unbundling might have to proceed. To investigate this issue, the paper examines in a qualitative manner how a local exchange network could be unbundled in light of recent technological developments. The methodology taken in this paper is to investigate the prospects for unbundling network architectures which have been proposed by the LECs. This includes exploring how network elements might be separated using new technologies such as fiber optic transmission systems, digital switches, or intelligent network platforms. By selecting outcomes for analysis which might "naturally" occur through the process of network evolution, the paper implicitly identifies network components that could be unbundled at relatively low cost according to the LECs' strategy of network evolution.[5]

The resulting set of unbundled network components is important because it defines the set of options available to independent service providers. They have the option to offer any one of the unbundled components using their own resources. Thus, the extent to which a future network architecture provides a set of low-cost unbundled service elements also defines the flexibility afforded to independent service provider in building their own customized services.

This paper will show that it is likely that network unbundling requirements can be expected to impose costs by influencing how the LECs will build their networks. The upshot of this finding is to place added importance upon developing a framework for weighing these costs against the benefits of the open access requirements as the LECs incorporate new technologies into their network. Such a framework would be a useful, if not indispensable, policy tool for insuring that network unbundling does not impose undue costs by unbundling network elements from which telecommunications consumers derive little benefit.

To begin the analysis, the first section examines how physical unbundling might occur as digital optical transmission systems are introduced throughout the public network. Section II examines how logical unbundling might be possible using the advanced intelligent network (AIN) platform model as a guide. The final section synthesizes the results of these discussions and presents some general principles and consequences of unbundling physical and logical network components in this technological environment of the future.[6]

## 2. PHYSICAL UNBUNDLING

This section examines the prospects for physically unbundling the network transmission and switching technologies which appear likely to be incorporated into the local access network architecture over the next two decades. With regard to transmission technology, the paper focuses upon the increasing use of fiber optic cable in the subscriber loop. With regard to switching and multiplexing, the paper investigates the trend to a digital cell-based technique known as asynchronous transfer mode.

Before proceeding further, however, it would be useful to better clarify how network unbundling might occur with physical components. Unbundling network elements creates the opportunity for service providers to offer a service using a combination of LEC provided and private network components. Thus, one choice of an independent service provider is to provide any network component using its own private resources. If the service provider selects the LEC's unbundled component, it might be presented with two options. First, it could use the LEC elements to form a dedicated network to deliver a service independent of any other services on the public network service platform. In this case a service might be delivered partially, or entirely, to the customer over unbundled physical elements purchased from the public network operator for the exclusive use of the service provider. Second, unbundled physical components could be used to deliver a service which is integrated with other network services (although perhaps on a "virtual" basis). For example, the service provider might interconnect to the public network to receive dial tone by purchasing unbundled physical elements. Either application for unbundled physical elements may be considered depending upon the particular situation.

### 2.1. Unbundling Network Transport Using Fiber Optic Networks

A transmission link exists to transport information from one location to another in recognizable form. Three key functional attributes of this link are its capacity, location and quality of service. If network unbundling is a beneficial process, then it should somehow enhance one or all of these attributes of the transmission networks. That is, unbundling a transport network would presumably improve at least one of the following criteria: a) access to network capacity; or b) access to intermediate interconnection points along the transmission path.[7] The methodology taken in this paper is to use these two criteria to qualitatively evaluate the prospects for unbundling physical transmission elements of the existing copper and proposed fiber-based network architectures. If an unbundled network improves one or both of these criteria, then one outcome of this process would be to lower the cost of transmission by either allowing more efficient access to network capacity or the independent provision of some transport segments.

The current copper-based network presents limited opportunities for unbundling the transmission components using these two criteria as a metric of evaluation. First, for the transmission distances associated with the subscriber loop, the amount of bandwidth available over twisted wire pair is limited roughly to the DS1 rate of 1.5 Mbps. Thus, in a future where broadband services will become increasingly important, the copper network is severely constrained in the broadband services it can carry, and in the excess capacity available for use on an unbundled basis (unless there are spare pairs available). Second, the current switched-star architecture runs at least one dedicated twisted pair from a central switching node all the way to each customer without any intermediate locations available to unbundle the transport segment. Beyond the central office, there are generally no nodes which provide an opportunity for interconnection which would unbundle transmission segments in the subscriber loop. For these reasons, the current network does not appear well suited for physical unbundling.

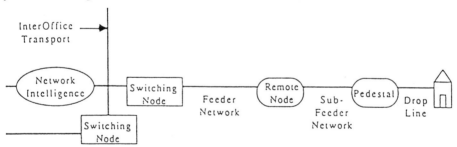

Figure 2: Local Access Network Architecture

While the current network may not be an attractive prospect for unbundling physical transmission components, fiber networks would appear to offer more opportunities. Figure 2 shows the local access network architecture that could be used by telephone companies to deploy fiber in the future. The figure indicates the customary central office switching node in addition to nodes at a remote site and the curb-side pedestal. These network nodes serve as network flexibility points where, depending upon the architecture, signals can be switched or multiplexed to the appropriate destination. The switched-star network architecture, which serves the great majority of telephone lines in the U.S., only includes one network flexibility point at the central office switching node. A small percentage of lines (less than 7% in 1989[8]) are served by digital loop carrier (DLC) systems which incorporate a second flexibility point into the architecture at the remote node. The third flexibility point at the pedestal has been proposed for fiber-to-the-curb systems in the future. The architecture of

Figure 2 also includes a central node for network intelligence, where the functionalities of the proposed advanced intelligent network are to be located.

How do fiber networks rate using the unbundling criteria? With regard to the first criterion, the fiber cable itself will effective impose no constraint in the amount of bandwidth available for unbundling. Indeed, LECs want to install fiber because of the enormous increase in bandwidth and the lower transmission losses it offers in comparison to metallic transmission lines. One fiber can transmit information at a data rate several orders of magnitude higher than what a copper wire pair can carry.[9] The bandwidth limitations of a fiber system are not due to the intrinsic properties of the fiber, but the limitations of the switching, multiplexing, and transmission equipment connected to the fiber.

In sum, because of the tremendous bandwidth potential of fiber optic cable, there is virtually unlimited bandwidth available for unbundling purposes. This simple observation must be accompanied with two important caveats. First, the abundant bandwidth that is theoretically available for unbundling on a fiber cable is not likely to be accessible for some time until the capabilities of the network equipment improve enough to utilize it. Second, this bandwidth is only available over the fiber links of a network. Because the adoption of a new technology is likely to be a gradual process, fiber will first be deployed in hybrid network architectures which continue to utilize existing portions of the copper network. As a result, until fiber is deployed all the way to the customer premises, portions of the network will continue to present the same limitations to physical unbundling as the current network.

While fiber systems may not present any intrinsic limitations to unbundling system bandwidth, the other important unbundling criterion against which they must be measured is the degree to which different transmission segments of the fiber network can be unbundled. To answer this question requires an understanding of the transmission elements of the local access network architecture, and the strategy of network evolution for incorporating fiber into the network.

The anticipated trend in the transmission technology of the telephone network is the deployment of fiber progressively closer to the customer premises.[10] Fiber was first used in long distance and interoffice portions of the telephone network where the large volume of traffic justified the additional cost and bandwidth of fiber links.[11] As the costs of optical systems have fallen, fiber may now be deployed in the feeder portion for DLC systems when the length of the feeder network is long enough to justify the higher costs of fiber, or the additional flexibility of a digital optical system is desired to accommodate the needs of more sophisticated business users. As the cost of fiber equipment declines further and more services are added to the network platform, the economics of deploying fiber will favor extending fiber closer to the end user.

The point at which the fiber portion of the network ends and the optical signal is converted to an electrical signal is called the optical network interface (ONI). As noted above, because the costs of fiber systems are declining, the location of the ONI has been gradually sliding closer to the end user as optical transmission technologies mature. Where the ONI is located at any particular time in the transition to a fiber network will depend upon the network architecture of the telephone network. For the vast majority of lines, the ONI is currently located at the switching node; for those lines served by optical DLC systems, it is located at the remote node. Future systems deploying a fiber-to-the-curb architecture would place the ONI at the pedestal, while a fiber-to-the-home architecture moves the ONI all the way to the end user's premises.

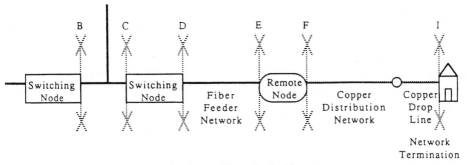

(a)    Near-Term  Network  Architecture

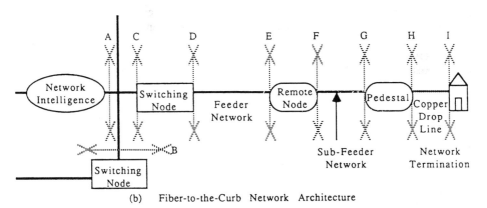

(b)    Fiber-to-the-Curb  Network  Architecture

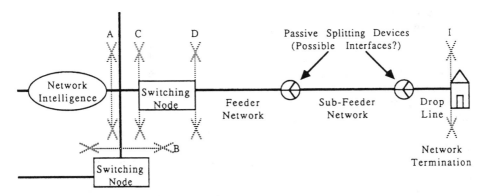

(c)    Long-Term  Passive  Optical  Network  Architecture

Figure 3:  Evolution of Network Architectures Using Fiber

The significance of the ONI with regard to the unbundling of network components is that it represents a natural flexibility point--or low-cost interface point--for the system where the local access transport segment can be broken into unbundled elements. As will be illustrated below, as the ONI moves progressively closer to the end user, the network platform will evolve to different network architectures, and new, or lost, opportunities for network unbundling. The current copper network, with its ONI essentially located at the switching node, was not an attractive architecture for unbundling network transport. This situation will change as fiber penetrates into the network through the gradual progress of network evolution.

Figure 3 illustrates three examples of how the location of the ONI can influence the extent to which portions of the local access transport can be unbundled at minimal cost. The first case considered in Figure 3(a) could be regarded as a near-term network architecture using an optical DLC system without an intelligent network service platform. The figure illustrates the possible network interfaces that could be available to unbundle local access transport. For example, transport could be unbundled using this architecture between interfaces B and C for interoffice transport, interfaces D and E for feeder transport, and F and I for transport in the distribution network. Thus, unbundling the local access portion of this architecture could result in two transport elements: a fiber-based feeder portion and a copper-based distribution portion of the network.

Figure 3(b) illustrates a more futuristic network architecture with a fiber-to-the-curb system and an intelligent network platform.[12] The fiber-to-the-curb system places another flexibility point into the network architecture which provides another level of unbundling local access transport. Under this architecture, transport could be unbundled between interfaces A and B for transport of network signaling, between B and C for interoffice transport, between D and E for feeder transport, between F and G for sub-feeder transport, and between H and I for the drop. As will be apparent with the next step in network evolution, this architecture may be the high-water mark for unbundling transport because of all the flexibility points in the architecture.

With the gradual deployment of fiber toward the end user, there is an accompanying trend to passive optical networks (PONs) which use some of the unique transport properties of optical signals. A PON places only passive components at the network flexibility points. Instead of electronic multiplexing and switching electronics at a flexibility point, a PON deploys optical couplers and splitters which take advantage of optical properties of the transmission signal to rout signals without the need for electronic equipment. PON architectures have fibers that fan out from the switching node via passive optical splitters similar to a tree and branch topology. In this way, PON networks can reduce costs by achieving a high degree of shared plant throughout the network. The lowest branch in the distribution tree connects to the individual homes.

Figure 3 is an example of a PON architecture where the remote node and pedestal flexibility points consist of passive optical components. As can be seen in the figure, if the passive nodes cannot offer access or interconnection services, then there are no low-cost interfaces in the local access portion of a PON. Passive nodes could provide interfaces like those described in Figure 3(b) if it is possible to inject or receive an optical signal using the passive components. In a PON system, the optical power budget determines the number of successive splitting nodes in the network. Larger bandwidth signals have smaller power budgets, so broadband services cannot be split as often as narrowband services. Thus, where a signal can be injected or removed from the network will depend upon the power budget as dictated by the PON architecture.[13]

The important point is that a different set of requirements arises when attempting to access a fully optical network as opposed to the current metallic or proposed hybrid networks. The bandwidth limitations of the metallic transmission media no longer exist, but they are replaced by concerns for the power budget and costs imposed by the network design. The margin of the power budget is set by the characteristics of the optoelectronics and the network topology. Expected advances in optoelectronics will increase the power budget, thus improving the flexibility of the network to accommodate unbundling of network capacity, and lower costs. Note, however, that one of the principal benefits of the PON approach is to eliminate "active" nodes in the network to avoid the high costs of providing power to these locations. Receiving or injecting an optical signal would require electronic equipment with power needs that might not be otherwise supported by the network operator.

Finally, with the continuing rapid advance in optical transmission technologies, an unresolved issue of great interest is the fiber-based network architecture most suited for the subscriber loop. While the strategy of network evolution presented above is consistent with many forecasts, there have been a number of alternative approaches proposed for installing fiber in the subscriber loop that vary depending upon the services carried by the network. The results of this section clearly demonstrate how the opportunities, and costs, for network unbundling can vary with network architectures. Thus, one would clearly expect both new and lost opportunities for low-cost network unbundling with each proposal.

## 2.2. Unbundling Digital Transfer Modes

The transfer modes of the network define the switching and multiplexing techniques that characterize the transmission structure of the system. The current network uses synchronous transfer mode (STM) techniques for switching and multiplexing digital signals.[14] Future networks will continue to assume a synchronous transmission hierarchy at the physical layer using the synchronous optical network (SONET) standards defined by the International Consultative Committee for Telephone and Telegraph (CCITT) standards group. The SONET standard describes a family of broadband digital transport signals operating roughly at multiples of 50 Mbps. As a result, wherever SONET equipment is used, the standard interfaces at the central office, remote nodes, or subscriber premises will be multiples of these rates.

Above the lower layers of the architecture, however, the network will probably not continue to be entirely synchronous, but will instead employ some asynchronous transfer mode (ATM) techniques. ATM uses packet switching and routing techniques to carry information signals, independent of their bandwidth, over one high speed switching fabric. For example, an information signal would be separated into fixed length cells, each consisting of a header for routing directions and an information field for data. These cells then combine with the cells of other signals for transmission to a common destination. In time division multiplexing (TDM) the position of the data channel in time is important, in ATM the label of the channel distinguishes it from another. The cells fit into the payload of the SONET frame structure for transmission. ATM promises to blur the distinction between switching and multiplexing on the cell level since an ATM switch is likely to integrate these two functionalities. There will, however, continue to be SONET multiplexers that combine and separate SONET signals carrying ATM cells.

What distinguishes ATM from a synchronous approach is that subscribers have the ability to customize their use of the bandwidth without being constrained to the channel data rates of the network transmission scheme. This characteristic, often touted as "bandwidth on-demand," allows variable data rate services to be easily combined by simply inserting the ATM cells into the SONET payload. In contrast, combining variable data rates using TDM can be difficult due to the different timing requirements of each signal.

For unbundling, the most important component of the transfer mode is the switching element (the multiplexing elements being unbundled by their very nature). An important trend in the current switching system is the move of network intelligence out of the switching software onto an intelligent network platform (see Section III for more on the logical functions of the intelligent network). Consequently, once the intelligent network is implemented, many of the logical network components will be separated from the physical switching element--where the physical component of a current digital switch consists of 64 Kbps (DS0) access to the network switch.

ATM techniques could improve the prospects for unbundling the physical switching elements of the network. The attribute of the ATM switch which could facilitate more modularity is the bandwidth flexibility it affords. Because each information signal is decomposed into cells, switching is performed in much smaller increments. Today, a digital switching element provides the capacity to switch a DS0 signal whether or not the user has the need for this much bandwidth. With ATM, the switching element resources can be much more efficiently matched to the bandwidth requirements of the user. By reducing the unit of access to switching resources, ATM can make more convenient increments of switching elements available on an unbundled basis. Access to the ATM switch will be specified according to the maximum data rate forecasted for the particular access arrangement, instead of specifying the number of DS0 circuits required as is the case today with digital switches.

## 3. LOGICAL UNBUNDLING

In addition to the physical components discussed above, logical network features might also be included in the network unbundling process. For example, one of the questions raised by the Notice of Inquiry initiated by the FCC into future architectures of the intelligent network is the extent to which a network switch could be programmed by an independent service provider as part of its service application software. In the same way that the personal computer has served as a platform to spawn a new industry of application software developers offering computer services, could the public network play a similar role as the public platform that stimulates a new application software industry for innovative network-based services? An essential characteristic of the public network platform, if it is indeed capable of assuming such a role, will be the extent to which the logical elements of network functionalities can be offered on an unbundled basis.

This section investigates what opportunities may be available for unbundling the logical elements of the network in light of the new technologies being developed for the operating system of the telephone network. Like the success of the applications software market for personal computers, the future success of service providers on an open network platform is certain to hinge upon the distinctive features incorporated into their own service software. In a competitive environment, service providers will place a high premium on being able to customize their services using unbundled logical elements combined with their own proprietary software functionalities.

Presumably there will be the most demand for those logical features which can most efficiently be offered by a centralized network resource. Otherwise, the logical function could be implemented through private software on a decentralized basis. Finding which logical features can indeed be offered best through a public network platform again requires an analysis of the costs of unbundling versus the benefits of the unbundled network, which is beyond the scope of the current discussion. As was the case when examining the physical unbundling of network components, the approach taken in this section is to look at the proposed direction of network evolution, and examine how this network architecture might offer inherently low-cost unbundling of logical components. Accordingly, the discussion begins with the capabilities of the advanced intelligent network (AIN), which the LECs are proposing to implement within the next decade.

## 3.1. The Advanced Intelligent Network

The LECs have been developing the AIN to provide themselves with the capability to rapidly create new services or customize current services. Today's switching system software contains most of the intelligence found in the network. The design of this software is such that the applications software for any particular functionality is fully enmeshed into the systems software. Consequently, whenever a new feature or any other software modification is necessary, the entire switching system software must be tested by the switch manufacturer. Eventually, the repeated addition of features and modifications can degrade the original switch architecture to the point where it becomes increasingly difficult to respond in a timely manner to the dynamic needs of the customers.

The limitations of this architecture became particularly apparent when intelligent services were deployed with functional elements that require a centralized network architecture. For example, the first network-wide intelligent service available over the public network was the 800 number service.[15] The network intelligence for this service resided in the switching software of the toll exchanges. Yet as the need increased for more intelligence in the service, maintaining the intelligence in a distributed architecture (i.e., in every toll exchange) became increasingly difficult and impractical. The LECs now want to develop a network architecture which enables more efficient and rapid network management on a centralized basis for the creation, provision, and deployment of services like 800 number service.

The AIN attempts to satisfy these criteria by defining a network architecture where the logical features are distributed from the switching nodes to intelligent network nodes (see Figure 2). By moving this intelligence away from the switching node, a LEC is able to concentrate logical functions at more centralized intelligence nodes instead of the more numerous local exchanges--assuming such a concentration is desirable from a cost standpoint.[16] For example, a new sequence of logical instructions, called the service logic, could be installed at the intelligent node without requiring software upgrades in all the switching systems. The degree of centralization that might be desirable for any particular service will vary, depending on service characteristics and the type of network. The important characteristic of AIN is that it offers the flexibility to configure the network according to the characteristics of the service. The modular architecture is capable of adding adjunct processors, such as voice processing equipment, data communication gateways, and alternative switching systems, to the platform, without modifying the application interfaces.[17] These adjuncts, which provide service logic and local customer data, have capabilities similar to centralized intelligence nodes but are situated at the local level (i.e., at the local exchanges). They are an attractive option for particular applications requiring local, transaction-intensive services as opposed to network routing services, which can be more efficiently supported at the central intelligence nodes. The functionalities of the adjuncts, however, are limited by the capabilities of the application interface to the switch.

At a more fundamental level, the difference between today's network architecture and one with the network intelligence unbundled from the switch lies in how the switching node processes each network connection request. When a call is placed on the current network, the switch executes the service logic according to the call model embedded in the switching software. The call model defines what steps, or check points, are executed during the call. AIN specifies a new call processing model with a new set of steps, or check points which depend upon external processors to operate. When a call is placed, the switch executes the call model and, depending upon the instructions, launches queries to the external processors of the intelligent network. Designing the call model in this way separates--or unbundles--the switching functions from the application functions residing in the intelligent nodes.

The basic architecture of the AIN takes these application functions and breaks them into a collection of function specific components that interact using a standard communication protocol.[18] The sequence of these unbundled logical elements, and the specific parameters within each logical element, distinguish one application from another.[19] Notably, the crucial technology necessary to implement this architecture is the operating system software which can support network services in this environment of unbundled logical components.[20] Ultimately, the objective of the AIN is to allow modifications to application software without having to alter the operating system of the switch. If any service provider is capable of developing application software to operate over the network, it is imperative that this software will function on top of the operating system of the switch without any modification. The ability for the network platform to accommodate new applications in this fashion is therefore an essential requirement of an open architecture featuring unbundled logical elements. The tool in AIN that creates and introduces new services in this manner is the service creation environment discussed below.

### 3.1.1. The Service Creation Environment

The objective of the service creation environment is to provide the necessary platform to create, debug, and test new services. Before it can be used, any new software (or service logic) must undergo extensive debugging and verification to reduce the probability that it will harm the overall operation of the network. The service creation environment would test whether any of the new features of the service would interact with existing services to cause the system to crash. When a new feature is introduced, there are three feature interaction categories which must be managed to insure operability:[21] 1) interactions between the new locally based feature with other locally based features; 2) interactions of a local based feature with remotely based features (either in a adjunct or intelligence node); and 3) interactions of the remotely based new feature with other remotely based features.

The most interesting question, of course, is the extent to which independent service providers could use this tool to create and test new software applications of their own on the network service platform. The expense of service verification, along with associated security issues, could preclude extending this capability directly to service subscribers.[22] On the other hand, it may be possible to design the system software to protect itself from network reliability and security threats while still offering open access to some logical elements.

Resolution of this issue will require balancing the benefits of open logical access against the costs of an open, modular architecture. In a special issue of AT&T Technical Journal on the intelligent network, AT&T seemed optimistic regarding the prospects for an open architecture when it states that services residing in the adjuncts and intelligent network nodes could be created "either by vendors, service providers, or enhanced service providers."[23]

One method to control network reliability and security is to design the operating system into logical layers. A layered architecture can isolate the service logic executing in a higher layer from lower layers and thus reduce the chances that it will affect the operations of the lower levels. In a local exchange network, a layered software structure would attempt to isolate the switching system core, which includes basic call control functions, from the application features. The basic system functions necessary to most of the application features would therefore be consolidated in the lowest level. In fact, the AIN architecture can be described in three layers.[24] If a design can be achieved which allows each layer to operate independently, with access to lower levels restricted according to access privileges, then the concerns for network reliability and security might be met. In one scenario, for example, the switch manufacturer could supply the platform software for the bottom layer, while the service providers design and operate service scripts on the top two layers.

In summary, this description of the AIN architecture portrays the possibilities that the future may hold for unbundling logical elements. As customers of the switch vendors, the LECs are seeking the means to unbundle all the functionalities of the service platform from the switch to obtain the flexibility they desire to create new services. For policy makers, the important question is whether the same flexibility afforded to the LECs through the logically unbundled AIN could be extended to independent service providers to open access to the network. The extent to which logical elements could be unbundled remains the subject of debate. The fundamental trade-off in this debate weighs the benefits of the modular logical architecture against the costs of unbundling and assuring network reliability and security.

## 4. FUTURE PROSPECTS FOR UNBUNDLING LOGICAL AND PHYSICAL ELEMENTS

The FCC is now considering how more competition can be brought to the local access switching and transport markets while still preserving other regulatory objectives. The FCC has already begun to impose open access requirements through a series of dockets on ONA, and is considering further actions in its recent Notice of Inquiry on Intelligent Networks and Expanded Interconnection. The cornerstone of these policies is the notion of unbundling network components to open access to network resources. This paper has presented a simple qualitative framework for considering the circumstances under which open access requirements might be considered, and the appropriate conditions for implementing network unbundling to achieve an open network architecture in light of new technological developments.

In general, the analysis showed that network unbundling of both physical and logical elements of new technologies can be expected to impose costs by influencing how the LECs will build their networks. With regard to unbundling the physical network elements of future network technologies, the paper concludes:

- Fiber cable offers virtually unlimited bandwidth for unbundling, but access to bandwidth is constrained by the limitations of the switching, multiplexing, and transmission equipment on each end of the fiber
- As the ONI moves closer to the customer premises through the normal process of network evolution, it presents LEC competitors with opportunities for low-cost interfaces to the local access network
- The number of unbundled transport elements (or interconnection points) in the local access network will vary with network architecture. A fiber-to-the-curb network architecture appears to offer the most low-cost unbundling opportunities, while a PON might decrease the opportunities for interconnection. Also, requiring continued service to old ONI locations as network interconnection points could hinder the most efficient strategy of network evolution by precluding new architectures
- Implementation of an ATM network will further unbundle switching by offering access to the switching function in smaller units

With regard to unbundling the logical network elements of future network technologies, the paper concludes:

- The flexibility the LEC's seek from switch vendors to offer their own services through the AIN is similar to the flexibility that regulators want to provide independent service providers through the process of network unbundling
- The trend to modular architectures using the AIN is through separating logical functionalities from the physical switching element and moving them to centralized network intelligence nodes
- A major concern with opening access of unbundled logical elements to independent service providers is the potential loss in network reliability that could occur as multiple service providers program the network to offer their own customized services. The network reliability and security concerns might be mitigated by layered architectures, which restrict access to core network functionalities

The threat to network reliability and security posed by open architectures is a complex technical issue. An open architecture increases the risks of intrusions, system failures, and potential privacy breaches by those predisposed to electronic vandalism. In addition, the operation of thousands of service applications on the network platform increases the chances of a system failure caused by incompatible software instructions. Because the network is a shared resource, the troubles of one application can send shock waves throughout the entire network. Nevertheless, whether in response to regulation or competition, at some point in time it seems likely that a new level of openness will have to be incorporated into the network, forcing new developments in software technology to reflect the reality of the changing marketplace.

The concern for network security should not, however, preclude the possibility of an open architecture. Advances in software technology are likely to offer opportunities for building an open network while still protecting its integrity. For example, one could imagine designing a network platform with a layered operating system requiring successively more verification to enter a lower level of the system. By designing the platform so that applications are not integrated with the operating system, concerns for network security and reliability could be addressed. The key point is that these concerns can be addressed on a technical level, but at some cost. Whether this cost would exceed the benefits of logical unbundling is the larger question which regulators must consider.

The implications of these developments to regulators suggest that a framework is needed for weighing such costs against the benefits of the open access requirements. If the costs of an open architecture are high, then an open architecture might only be economically viable if the LECs hold substantial market power. But if a number of competing transport suppliers, such as cable television operators, PCS suppliers, or alternative local access suppliers, emerge to compete for a share of this market, the monopoly power of the telephone companies will erode. Indeed, the additional costs of unbundling could actually hinder the LECs ability to compete effectively in the market. A competitive transport market could develop into a market analogous to computers where customers actively seek the lowest cost suppliers because there is no significant differentiation in the underlying functionality of the hardware.[25]

This paper has only delved into the rudimentary elements of the new technologies which could be implemented in future LEC networks. A more comprehensive review of the economics of unbundling and the associated policy issues remains to be completed. Nevertheless, this study does indicate the need for an analytical framework to consider how network unbundling should occur as new technologies are introduced into the network. Policies concerning open network access can directly affect the design of the network, as well as the long term strategies of network evolution for both LECs and independent service providers. These great stakes place an added weight upon policy deliberations. Any policy decisions made now can materially affect, for example, the design of the advanced intelligent network platform and how it will be deployed over the next decade. When a strategy of unbundling network elements is pursued, policy makers will necessarily be operating along a fine line regarding how much responsibility will be retained by the LECs to design and implement their own strategies of network evolution.

## REFERENCES

Arnold, E.C., and D. W. Brown, "Object Oriented Switching System Architectures and Software Development Processes," Proceedings of the National Communications Forum, 44: 795-802, Rosemont IL, 1990.

Lemay, John et al., "Prototyping Environment for New Service Creation," Proceedings of the National Communications Forum, 44: 544-550, Rosemont IL, 1990.

Morgan, Michael J. et al., "Service Creation Technologies for the Intelligent Network," *AT&T Technical Journal*, 70.3-4, 58-71, 1991.

Reed, David P., *Residential Fiber Optic Networks: An Engineering and Economic Analysis*, Boston: Artech House, 1991.

Russo, Ernest G. et al., "Intelligent Network Platforms in the U.S.," *AT&T Technical Journal*, 70.3-4, 26-43, 1991.

Sable, Edward G., and Herbert W. Kettler, "Intelligent Network Directions," *AT&T Technical Journal* 70.3-4, 2-10, 1991.

Vanston, Lawrence K. et al., "How Fast is New Technology Coming?" *Telephony*, September 18, 1989.

192

Wyatt, George Y. et al., "The Evolution of Global Intelligent Network Architecture," *AT&T Technical Journal*, 70.3-4, 11-25, 1991.

## ENDNOTES

[1] For the most recent FCC action regarding ONA, see *Memorandum Opinion and Order,* Filing and Review of Open Network Architecture Plans, CC-Docket No. 88-2; FCC 91-382 38309, Released December 19, 1991.

[2] An equally important role of ONA is to establish the tariff guidelines for the unbundled offerings to insure that access to the network is nondiscriminatory.

[3] The notion of classifying elements into physical and logical categories is not original to this paper. For example, Bellcore has described a future network architecture consisting of service and delivery segments, which correspond to the logical and physical elements described above. The goal of the Bellcore architecture is to offer the functionalities of the service segments independent of the capabilities or functions of the delivery segment. This technology independence could offer service providers more flexibility in using the network platform. See *Information Networking Architecture (INA) Framework Overview.* Bellcore Framework Technical Advisory FA-INS-001134, Issue 1, (August, 1990).

[4] See Notice of Inquiry, In the Matter of Intelligent Networks, CC Docket 91-346, FCC 91-383 38274, December 6, 1991. For another FCC policy initiative with implications for network access, see Notice of Proposed Rulemaking and Notice of Inquiry, In the Matter of Expanded Interconnection with Local Telephone Company Facilities, CC Docket 91-141, FCC 91-159 3259, June 6, 1991.

[5] The consequence of this assumption is that the analysis will not uncover any unbundled network components that do not arise logically from the proposed architecture. Of course, a LEC has an incentive to modify its network architecture to unbundle a particular component if sufficient demand existed to warrant its inclusion in the set of unbundled elements.

[6] The scope of this paper is limited to examining the unbundling of the subscriber loop components of the public telephone network. The discussion does not focus directly upon the impact of unbundling the components of urban networks such as the fiber-based metropolitan area networks (MANs) that are currently proliferating.

[7] The third possibility, not listed, is that unbundling the network could give service providers more flexibility in specifying the reliability or grade of service of the transmission path. This capability depends more upon the network operating system and transport protocols (i.e. logical features) then the physical transmission links, and therefore is not discussed in this section.

[8] Vanston, Lawrence K. et al. "How Fast is New Technology Coming?" *Telephony,* September 18, 1989.

[9] While comparing fiber and copper cable in relation to the total data rate they can carry demonstrates the large differential in bandwidth capability between the two, a more accurate description of the capacity of fiber in the future is likely to be the number of wavelengths that can be transmitted over a single fiber. Instead of increasing the data rate of the transmission link as demand warrants, the capacity of a fiber link could be expanded by additional new wavelengths.

[10] Reed, David P., *Residential Fiber Optic Networks: An Engineering and Economic Analysis,* Boston: Artech House, 1991.

[11.]One study estimated that in 1989, 84 percent of interoffice voice circuits in use were digital, with 41 percent of the circuits being carried by fiber links. The same study forecasted that the interoffice network will be essentially all digital by 1995, and all fiber by 1999. See Vanston, Lawrence K. et. al., "How Fast is Technology Coming?" *Telephony*, September 18, 1989.

[12.]This architecture is similar to what has been proposed by Bellcore as a the next step for using fiber in the local access network. See Bellcore Technical Advisory. *Generic Requirements and Objectives for Fiber in the Loop Systems,* Bellcore, TA-NWT-000909, December, 1990.

[13.]Of course the power budget could be adjusted (increased) at a cost. However, such a cost could be very high in the PON architecture if it required a new optoelectronics in every household ONI device.

[14.]Transmitting information in digital form requires a timing reference to control the transmission. Without a clock synchronizing the entire digital network, the system would not be able to determine when to sample a signal to receive the transmitted information.

[15.]Sable, Edward G., and Herbert W. Kettler, "Intelligent Network Directions," *AT&T Technical Journal*, 70.3-4, 2-10, 1991.

[16.]Wyatt, George Y. et al., "The Evolution of Global Intelligent Network Architecture," *AT&T Technical Journal*, 70.3-4, 11-25, 1991.

[17.]Lemay, John et al., "Prototyping Environment for New Service Creation," Proceedings of the National Communications Forum, Rosemont, Illionois, 44: 544-550,1990. Wyatt, George Y. et al., "The Evolution of Global Intelligent Network Architecture," *AT&T Technical Journal* 70.3-4, 11-25, 1991.

[18.]Arnold, E.C., and D. W. Brown, "Object Oriented Switching System Architectures and Software Development Processes," Proceedings of the National Communications Forum, Rosemont, Illionois, 44: 795-802, 1990.

[19.]Bellcore offers one example that demonstrates how different services can be built by linking basic features in different orders. A 800 service with interactive dialing requires four features, which in sequential order are: number translation, play announcement, collect digits, and route call. A 976 number with screening (using a personal identification number) also requires four features: play announcement, collect digits, then either route call or play announcement. Example taken from a presentation to the FCC by Elizabeth Ireland, "Advanced Intelligent Network: An Overview," September 19, 1991.

[20.]The programming language used to connect each building block is likely to be a object-oriented language which treats the system as a network of interconnected functional components or objects. In contrast, the traditional software approach has been to represent the system as a giant matrix of interacting functional activities.

[21.]Russo, Ernest G. et al., "Intelligent Network Platforms in the U.S.," *AT&T Technical Journal*, 70.3-4, 26-43, 1991.

[22.]Morgan, Michael J. et al., "Service Creation Technologies for the Intelligent Network," *AT&T Technical Journal*, 70.3-4, 58-71, 1991.

[23.]Page 8, Sable, Edward G., and Herbert W. Kettler., "Intelligent Network Directions," *AT&T Technical Journal*, 70.3-4 2-10, 1991.

194

[24.] Lemay, John et al., "Prototyping Environment for New Service Creation," Proceedings of the National Communications Forum, Rosemont, Illionois, 44: 544-550, 1990. Morgan, Michael J. et al., "Service Creation Technologies for the Intelligent Network," *AT&T Technical Journal*, 70.3-4, 58-71, 1991.

[25.] Some argue that the reason that PCs have become commodities is that Intel Corp. and Microsoft Inc. effectively have monopolies for microprocessors and operating system software and sell their technologies to practically all comers. As a result, there is little differentiation in the functionality of the computer hardware beyond the intrinsic speed of the devices. See *The Wall Street Journal,* Thursday, September 5, 1991. pA1.

Interoperability -- Economic and Legal

## Public Access and Closed Network Membership: Electronic Trading Networks in Europe

Robin Mansell

## 1. INTRODUCTION[1]

The term, Electronic Trading Networks (ETN) is used in this chapter to define networks which combine the collaborative aspects of electronic trading with the competitive advantages of electronic network-based markets. These networks may be designed to ensure openness or closure to various communities of users. The emergence of these and other related advanced network applications has implications for the long-term public accessibility of advanced information and communication services.

ETN are being designed to enable the ultimate transfer of all aspects of trade into the electronic sphere.[2] This chapter considers the implications of ETN in the light of the experiences and conflicting priorities of organizations involved in their development. Analysis of several case studies suggests that scenarios for telecommunication infrastructure development which favor greater accessibility for users may be being countered by the proliferation of network applications specifically designed to meet the requirements of closed communities of users.

The chapter draws on the results of research which has focused on factors creating demand for ETN.[3] This work considered whether a shift of traditional physical trading networks into the electronic sphere would encourage greater openness in the trading environment or, alternatively, whether it would encourage new forms of network closure as a result of technical and organizational barriers to control network membership.

As ETN mature and become established, the preferences of network operators and users for highly differentiated network configurations are becoming increasingly apparent. In order to achieve secure and reliable networks, some ETN operators move their services from the public switched telecommunication network to dedicated or internal corporate networks while others take the opposite route. Still others prefer to develop ETN based on hybrid combinations of the underlying telecommunication infrastructure. However varied the individual network strategies, organizations responsible for managing ETN exhibit a tendency toward the development of closed trading environments. This is often achieved technically through the use of proprietary standards at the service application level, but it also is visible in the design of standards for the operation and development of advanced telecommunication infrastructures.

There has been little public debate about the implications of trends toward closed networks of electronic traders. The result of a migration of trade and commerce onto closed networks could mean that international trade regimes come to favor those able to access and control these service applications as well as the underlying infrastructure.[4]  This chapter suggests that the key issue is not whether the underlying telecommunication infrastructure is subject to single or multiple ownership.  Rather, the main issue which should concern policy makers is the terms and conditions of access to networks operating both in support of users who require that access be limited to authorized membership communities and of the wider public.

Table 1 - Design Parameters of Trading Networks

| PARAMETER | DEFINITION | EXAMPLES |
|---|---|---|
| Trade Information | The dissemination of background information, possibilities and options which provide the knowledge base required to become involved in trade | Databases, e.g. Patents, Standards, Catalogues Information Feeds, e.g. Market Intelligence, News Agency reports |
| Trade Facilitation | The information and procedures concerning activities, actions and choices necessary to allow the free movement of goods and services | Legal Procedures, e.g. Customs Clearance, Health and Safety Financial, e.g. Insurance, Letters of Credit, Logistical, e.g. tracking and tracing service Trade Related Tasks, e.g. certification, authentication, storage, repackaging Administrative, e.g. electronic movement of information, instructions, documents |
| Trade Execution | The process of informing the relative parties that a binding contract has been consummated | Conditions of Trade, e.g. Private Treaty, Closed Market, Open Sale Mode of Trade, e.g. tender, auction, open outcry Type of Trade, e.g. procurement, futures, options |
| Clearing and Settlement | All information-related actions to move goods, funds etc. triggered by an executed trade | Information, e.g. title transfer, clearing house, documentation Physical, e.g. delivery, testing Financial, e.g. guarantees, margins, funds transfer |
| Trade Regulation | Information concerning all elements of trade required by voluntary or statutory organizations. May eventually be released as Trade Information | Telecommunication, e.g. transborder data flows, Access nodes Financial, e.g. capital adequacy, settlement periods Competition, e.g. access, biased markets International Trade, e.g. TRIMS, TRIPS quotas, non-tariff barriers |

Source: R. Mansell and M. Jenkins, 'Electronic Trading Networks and Interactivity: The Route to Competitive Advantage?' Case Study Report, SPRU, Brighton, 1992.

## 2. DESIGNING INFRASTRUCTURE AND SERVICES

Trends in the development of the telecommunication infrastructure and service applications which support electronic trading can be considered from the perspective of the types of 'design parameters' which they incorporate. For example, the trade cycle can be disaggregated into five distinct phases - trade information, trade facilitation, trade execution, clearing and settlement and trade regulation (see Table 1). Each phase involves the production and exchange of information. The phases embody logically separate and coherent sets of parameters such as levels of access, data quality, security, speed, network redundancy, application standards, gateway protocols, cross-border regulations and dispute settlement procedures. To achieve the levels of confidence and integrity required by users, networks must enable different levels of access for user communities.

The five key design parameters of an electronic trading network suggest that any subset of relationships can be examined with respect to the implications of network design decisions for the strategic advantage of firms, the accessibility of networks for users, and the restrictions imposed by regulatory arrangements. Each of these design decisions will have an impact on the production and use of electronic information, the technical characteristics required of the underlying telecommunication infrastructure, and the organizational structure of the industry.

Each ETN involves compromises with respect to the design specifications required by the different parameters shown in Table 1. These compromises create constraints for both network operators and users. ETN like other networks embody the technical and institutional compromises that are needed to support the various facets of the trade cycle. Braudel[5] suggested that the pace and ease of movement within a trading network (i.e. network integration versus fragmentation or openness versus closure) is conditioned, not by the maximum potential of the parts of the network, but by the minimum characteristics of the elements present across the network. He also observed that advances in technical systems (e.g. communication, road, rail transport) tended to be subject to uneven development patterns. The unevenness of these patterns also created constraints for the network users.

In the context of the emergence of ETN, Braudel's observation encourages us to look at the minimum conditions required to support open or, alternatively, closed electronic network markets. What are the bottlenecks or minimum characteristics of these interlocking technical and institutional networks? What do these minimum characteristics imply for the long term evolution of the underlying telecommunication infrastructure? What do they imply for the balance between private (restricted membership) networks and those which are widely accessible to the public?

## 3. DESIGNING THE INFRASTRUCTURE

A central issue for European Union policy is the management of a transformation from the traditional telecommunication infrastructure to an advanced telematics infrastructure capable of supporting services as diverse as 'plain old telephone service' and the sophisticated applications which may be involved in ETN.[6]

Projections for the rate of growth and diffusion of the telecommunication infrastructure give little indication of the likelihood of any particular development trajectory. For example, it has been forecast that by the year 2000, broadband telecommunication services could generate annual Public Telecommunication Operator (PTO) revenues in Europe of about 10 billion ECU. Over 1 million business sites could be equipped with fibre access to networks by the year 2000. A much smaller number will make use of this capacity for broadband services. Certain services such as high speed non-voice communication, including graphics and digital imaging, are expected to create demand for growth in higher capacity networks throughout Europe.[7]

However, if the telecommunication infrastructure is to be responsive to a wide range of economic, political, social and cultural aspirations on the part of users, technological advance and network designs will need to be coupled with policy measures. Open access to advanced services will need to be encouraged because of pressures to achieve closure on the part of service designers such as ETN. Many of these users require an 'intelligent' infrastructure platform which can support closed membership networks for selected communities of users. Networks designed to meet these users' needs will be characterized by 'closure.' If this becomes the predominant 'minimum' condition for advanced telecommunication network design, then policy measures will be needed to alleviate bottlenecks to access for the wider community of public users.

The European Union's policy framework for the telecommunication infrastructure has been taking shape since the mid 1980s. By 1988 the Commission of the European Communities had observed that 'to flourish, telecommunication has to have the optimum environmental conditions.' One aspect of Commission activity has been a drive to promote the development of telematics services in support of the competitiveness and cohesion of the Single European Market. Programs have been aimed at promoting the competitiveness of manufacturing industry and at changing the structure and operation of the European telecommunication infrastructure.[8] This has been accomplished through policies directed at areas such as harmonization of standards for services and equipment and improved network access.[9] The Union's Framework Programs have supported pre-competitive research projects on technologies and applications with the aim of encouraging investment in an open accessible network.[10]

Much attention has been focused on corporate requirements for advanced services. By the early 1990s, it was clear that these would need to include pan-European access to wide area networks; data functionality matching the performance of local area networks; a mix of technologies and services creating the conditions for experimentation with new applications.[11]

The consumers' interest in the telematics infrastructure have not been neglected. The lead time and riskiness of investment in consumer oriented services, the demand for interactive and other types of services, and the need for a redefinition of concepts of public (universal) service have all been taken into consideration.

Public policy aims to influence the balance between publicly accessible and closed membership networks. The main emphasis has been directed to strengthening the coherence and integrity of the underlying European telecommunication infrastructure. However, the predominant vision for the development of services such as ETN is one which favors increasing heterogeneity, complexity, and in many cases, restricted access to new services.

In Europe, as in other regions, the key infrastructure institution in the early phases of telecommunications was the universal monopoly PTO. The PTO had little competence in fields such as computing or software development and relied upon closely linked equipment manufacturers to develop innovative services. Applications beyond telephone, telex, and simple data transmission were left to other firms within the information technology field.

Today's vision of a telematics infrastructure in Europe makes several assumptions about the level of complexity, standardization, and scope for new entry that will emerge in the future. A 'stage-oriented' scenario is influential. An essentially linear metmorphasis of the infrastructure is expected in which national PTOs remain dominant at first and the terminal equipment market is liberalized bringing entry opportunities for peripheral equipment manufacturers. Competitive tendering is required of the PTOs and two, or perhaps three, public switch manufacturers become the preferred suppliers of the PTOs. Mobile service providers are licensed and their equipment manufacturers see their markets expand. In some cases, satellite operators are licensed to engage in service provision.

In subsequent stages, the market position of the PTOs becomes less dominant and interconnection of facilities and services begins to be a priority issue. Service providers increase their use of infrastructure facilities to support new applications. Ultimately, the PTOs must contend with one or more network operators who are given the right to provide service to the public. The final stage foresees many different PTOs providing intelligent platforms to support numerous applications. Whether each PTO has the same service obligations with respect to the availability and accessibility of its network services has remained an open question in most of the member states of the European Union.

In addition, the fact that there are many possible departures from the technical configuration suggested by this stage oriented scenario and that these have implications for the balance that emerges among open network applications and those tailored to meet the needs of closed membership groups has not been an issue at the center of telecommunication infrastructure policy debates. For users, the main issues concern the access and usage conditions that will enable them to make use of the functionality embedded in the infrastructure.

One class of users which places heterogeneous demands on the infrastructure is comprised of those engaged in electronic trading. The following section focuses on electronic trading as a special case of infrastructure use and on the trends in network design that are associated with ETN applications.

## 4. DESIGNING ELECTRONIC TRADING NETWORKS

Six Electronic Trading Networks (ETN) in the Netherlands, Sweden, the United Kingdom, and the United States are considered here. These networks involve some of the largest firms in the telematics sector as well as organizations with little prior experience in managing or operating telematics services. They include examples in the financial services, transport and distribution and agricultural sectors (See Table 2). This section considers the ETN design parameters in terms of the requirements imposed on the underlying infrastructure and the specifications for computing power and software.

### 4.1. Telecommunication infrastructure use

NORDEX ETN membership was open to professional brokers rather than to institutional investors. Users were provided with a dedicated telephone line connecting a workstation to a central computer in London. Connections were established using private leased circuits in Europe supplied by PTOs and competing third party suppliers. Operators

## Table 2: Electronic Trading Network Organizations

| Organisation | Functional Description | Ownership and Control |
|---|---|---|
| NORDEX<br>Case Study No. 1 | Nordex is a London based, cross-border electronic marketplace for global professional investors who trade in shares of companies based in the four Nordic Countries. Nordex operates via a central counterpart mechanism offered by Citibank and linked to the bank's Clearing and Settlement Services. Planned to extend the service to Holland and Budapest | Subsidiary of Kinnevik (privately controlled Swedish Holding Company) which has national and international interests in the Information Distribution Industry e.g. Telecom ( fixed and mobile), Credit Card Phones, Cable and Satellite TV, Home Shopping Services. |
| Chicago Mercantile Exchange (CME) Chicago Board of Trade (CBOT) and Reuters GLOBEX<br>Case Study No. 2 | 'After Hours' 24 Global Trading Network linking Members of National Exchanges to buy and sell Futures and Options Financial Instruments e.g. Stocks, Currencies (using CME/CBOT structures); Global Networking/Facilities Management to be provided by Reuters | Will operate as an accumulated structure<br>-the three principals (CME, CBOT, Reuters)<br>-the National Futures Association (USA)<br>-the national exchanges (e.g. Paris MATIF)<br>-the members; NB. The fees paid by the users will be split between the above parties |
| UK EDI Association Oil Industry Interest Section PRODEX<br>Case Study No. 3 | Inter-firm Product Exchange Reconciliation Scheme. Based on EDI messages developed by UK group for submission to UN/EDIFACT | Part of pan-European EDI user Group - The European Oil and Gas EDI Group - involves both EC and EFTA countries |
| Maritime Cargo Processing Plc. MCP<br>Case Study No. 4 | A trade facilitation organisation which allows users direct access to UK Customs data and inventory control system (DEPS) | Service Company jointly owned by the founder members of the Port Community<br>Port of Felixstowe majority owned by Hutchison (Hong Kong) who also own Hutchison Communications |
| Dutch Tele-auctions VABA<br>Case Study No. 5 | VABA is a computer bureau and consultancy to provide network based services over leased lines to fruit and vegetable auctions | Wholly owned subsidiary company of CBT (Central Bureau of Fruit and Vegetable Auctions). CBT owned by the provincial auctions |
| Dutch Video auctions Westland<br>Case Study No. 6 | Westland is a trading center for buyers and an auction complex for flowers and pot plants. Provides grading, certification, packaging and other trade related services to its members. The video auction is a local initiative which may be offered to other auctions | Grower owned co-operative with 3000 members |

Source: R. Mansell and M. Jenkins, 'Electronic Trading Networks and Interactivity: The Route to Competitive Advantage?' Case Study Report, SPRU, Brighton, 1992.

of the underlying telecommunication infrastructure established connections using conventional facilities. GEIS Co., for example, configured its network to handle traffic generated by the ETN and another operator incorporated a transLAN bridge to connect the ETN. Innovations were required to meet the technical requirements of the ETN operator using interoperable cross-border proprietary standards and protocols.

In the case of GLOBEX, innovations were required to make the system operational. The network connects Reuters' subscribers and hubs traffic in Hong Kong, London, Paris and New York. To meet stringent requirements for security, speed and reliability, the network needed to have a three second response time and 99.5 percent availability.

Those developing the PRODEX ETN failed to find a way of using the telecommunication network in a way that met their members' needs. To do so would have required equipment suppliers to upgrade the existing infrastructure and to agree standards to support X.500 directories and databases. At the time there was little commercial incentive to do so.

The MCP ETN was originally designed to support direct data input using dumb terminals connected to a mainframe computer via the public network and leased lines. To retain users, the network operator added features and services, but was forced to rely on external suppliers. This led to increased operational costs and the operator was required to establish gateways into its mainframe computer for users already established on other networks.

In the case of the tele-auction (VABA), network operators and telecommunication suppliers provided a centrally configured network based on leased digital circuits and the Dutch PTO's Packet Switched Data Network. In the case of the video-auction (Westland), an on-site fibre-based Local Area Network was required.

## 4.2. Information processing and software

At the heart of the NORDEX ETN was a central electronic order book into which dealers placed offers to buy and sell on the market. The software was written in-house and workstations were configured to support open systems. The system involved a moderately complex configuration of computer processing capability. From the users' perspective the software was user-friendly and required a relatively high degree of co-ordination between the network operator and the computer workstation and mainframe suppliers.

GLOBEX was designed to support order entries using terminals consisting of a keyboard, monitor and printer located in the offices of clearing and individual members. Administrative terminals in the offices of clearing members receive confirmation of trades. Since the system was introduced, the intention has been to provide more real-time screen based information than is available to traders on the NORDEX system. Reuters, the network operator, absorbed the development costs of the software.

PRODEX's reliance on the application of computer processing power and software was relatively low. However, the software involved a set of rolling files for each company containing internal transactions and no plans were made to exchange information electronically among members of the trading community.

The MCP application of computing and software to support the data entry system ensured that software development would be as user friendly as possible. The MCP system software resided on the company's computers and the network was star shaped offering dumb terminal type tele-emulation. Since no sophisticated front end features were available to end users the system encouraged proprietary software and systems development on the part of specialist software houses.

The two ETNs in the Netherlands (VABA, Westland) required greater use of computer processing capacity. In the case of VABA, the computers occupy a central position in a number of star shaped networks and a central computer runs each tele-auction. Nevertheless, despite a relatively lengthy computer and software development process, the tele-auction runs more slowly than the physical auction. At Westland, computers link terminals and printers via a Local Area Network. Two video-walls require sufficient network capacity to allow the screens to be refreshed in under a second.

In each of these cases a network operator selected technical configurations and took responsibility for combining telecommunication and computing functions. The telecommunication infrastructure, service attributes, computing facilities and software capabilities were designed to meet the trading parameters of each organisation with varying degrees of success. Different parameters of each network were associated with specifications for peak volumes of traffic, access, speed, reliability, security, cost, etc. The selection process reflected the variable skills present in the user communities, the availability of computer processing power, and the availability of underlying infrastructure capacity which met their specifications.

## 5. DESIGN CONSTRAINTS AND MINIMUM CONDITIONS

The technical constraints encountered during the development of these ETN were demanding because they required negotiation with disparate equipment manufacturers, ETN operators and authorized members of trading communities.

These technical designs did not require major innovations in technology. Nevertheless, the main design constraints were: the uneven availability, cost, and access conditions of telecommunications infrastructure and services in different geographical areas; the need for co-ordination across spheres of competence (e.g. PTOs, cable operators, third party network operators); and, most importantly, the need to agree to minimum standards without which these ETN could not be extended to the members desired by the network operators.

For example, at the time the NORDEX ETN was designed in the early 1980s, the ways in which software should be written to emulate electronic trading were little understood. The network operator responded by attracting developers from a local rival company who had undertaken the early pioneering work. By importing competencies some of the risks associated with software development were reduced, but this decision created other problems. The inherited software development hardware platform became the basis for the trading communication network for which it was not ideally suited. Additional time and effort had to be spent tuning the technical system to match the communication and processing requirements of this particular market.

The design parameters for GLOBEX as a global market were demanding. Ensuring there would be no degradation of the market service caused by technical problems was difficult. There were numerous delays as network designers struggled to ensure that the software algorithm could cope with surges in network traffic as members were trading.

The preferred technical strategy for PRODEX was to use an X.400 system based on the public switched telecommunication network. This approach needed the provision of an X.500 central directory containing the addresses of all potential users of the system. This service was not available.

The design for the original MCP ETN was constrained by the need to interconnect to the UK Customs Computer system. This was a videotex system with ports on the computer reserved for MCP's user base. This technical constraint set the tone for the entire MCP development. Being a small technically inexperienced company they contracted out the software development to programmers linked to a hardware company who used their own proprietary operating systems. Responsibility for network management was taken by a sister company. They too had preferred technical strategies. The main technical constraint for MCP was to optimize the technical preferences of unrelated competing suppliers. This shaped the development of message standards, user interfaces, etc., in ways that have made further progress difficult.

Initially the VABA ETN was started by a group of users who attempted to work with an independent software company. Once VABA became involved, software development was brought in house and most of the problems were resolved. As originally designed the system had a major shortcoming - it was slower than the existing system and the average number of traded lots completed per minute decreased by 25 percent.

In the case of Westland, the development of an analog video system to run on a LAN was not difficult. The main technical problem was to transfer the system to external off-site networks. The PTO could not provide the capacity.

## 6. PUBLIC ACCESS AND PRIVATE MEMBERSHIP

A major network design consideration in each ETN was the impact of organizational and regulatory constraints. Problems arose because of difficulties in gaining agreement among the major network users. For example, NORDEX was launched in 1989. The reaction of brokers to the system was positive but there was reluctance to accept the risk of trading on an anonymous system. The absence of a known counterpart stalled the launch for six months. Citibank agreed to act as the universal central counterpart and each participating broker was required to agree to separate contractual obligations. As a result membership of the network was closed.

The main organizational challenge to GLOBEX was to attract major exchanges to the system. The US Commodity Futures Trade Commission adopted a rule limiting the liability of parties involved in GLOBEX. This rule disclaims the Chicago Mercantile Exchange from liability related to the development of GLOBEX and from losses arising from failures and malfunctions in the system. The total liability in a single day for all claims is limited to US$ 100,000 and the ruling requires members to supply clients with customer information and risk disclosure statements. Members must therefore belong to a closed 'club' of traders. PRODEX members also had to agree standards and procedures. Wide inter-company variations existed in the ways that products or locations were described. Only those using the PRODEX standard can effectively utilize the system and there is no interactive network.

The challenge to the Dutch tele-auction (VABA) was to modify the attitudes of user organizations. The auctions insisted that only Dutch produce be sold on the ETN and that only Dutch buyers would be able to access it. The objective was to use technology to reduce transaction costs and to raise returns to the growers using the system. The technology was used as a barrier to competition and market access. The Dutch video-auction (Westland) operator understood the benefits of logistical and trading networks and the intention was to open the network to non-Dutch users. Members profit from using the market, not from sharing surpluses that are generated centrally and this has affected the users' willingness to let the ETN operator push toward opening the network to outsiders. In each case, the problems of conflicting economic interests were resolved by solutions at a technical level which were regarded by users as being non-threatening to their longer term competition position in the marketplace.

## 7. CONCLUSION

Where the primary design feature of an ETN in these case studies has been to achieve security, trading integrity, and membership closure, there have been pressures to adopt a closed network solution in support of this goal. Proprietary standards have been used to restrict access to a limited community of traders - and these standards are regarded by users as a positive development. The ETN operators have forged new interfirm relationships, often across the borders of nations. They have tended to locate in the most favorable regulatory environments and the heterogeneity and fragmentation of networks and national regulations have been used as tools to exert 'regulatory arbitrage.' Co-ordination has occurred in the development of ETN when member organizations in a trading community have not been likely to face direct competition in their product or service markets. But, where competition has been likely, both technical and institutional (regulatory) barriers have been put in place, or existing ones have been used effectively to ensure that the design of the ETN enables the control of information flows among restricted groups of traders.

These ETN illustrate the multiple design parameters that can become embedded in networks. Closed ETN networks are achieved using a combination of technical and institutional criteria concerning membership. These criteria guide the network design process even when there is an economic justification for the extension of an ETN to new members in order to build critical mass and generate new revenues for the network operator. ETN that succeed in moving a growing number of the parameters of the trading cycle into the electronic sphere will take time to diffuse widely, but pressures favoring the emergence of closed, proprietary networks will continue to be strong. These come to the fore whenever members' commercial interests need to be protected. The new generation of electronic markets will not, therefore, offer a panacea to the exclusionary biases of traditional trading markets. At the ETN applications level, the tendency toward network heterogeneity is likely to strengthen despite policies which favor greater homogeneity in the terms and conditions of network access via the implementation of open standards and network interfaces. The minimum conditions for ETN development are being driven by priorities in the trading environment and by the needs of ETN members. This is despite the fact that the technical capabilities of computing and software technologies and the 'intelligent' infrastructure which can, in principle, support open networks.

These tendencies should not come as a surprise. They are a reflection of the underlying economic incentive structure which affects the commercial decisions of network user organizations who frequently are engaged global competition. Their aim is to use ETN to their own competitive advantage rather than to that of all potential users.

As Braudel observed: 'The division of labor on a world-economy scale cannot be described as a concerted agreement made between equal parties and always open to review. It became established progressively as a chain of subordinations, each conditioning the other. Unequal exchange, the origin of inequality in the world, and by the same token, the invariable generator of trade, are long-standing realities.'[12]   The Commission of the European Communities, and especially the Directorates responsible for information technology and telecommunication and competition policy, have yet to address the implications of design closure in applications such as ETN.   Policies continue to rely on pressures by user communities to encourage open access to advanced network applications.

The case studies reviewed here suggest that such pressures are unlikely to be strong where they conflict with users' economic interests in achieving a high degree of security, confidentiality, etc.   There is a growing need on the part of policy makers to address the way contradictions in design parameters coalesce in various telematics service applications.   There are clear tensions in the access and membership conditions expected by competing and co-operating user communities and these cannot be expected always to be resolved in favor of open network access.   The parallel trend toward heterogeneity in the underlying telecommunication infrastructure is likely to exacerbate these trends toward network closure.

## REFERENCES

Benjamin, R., "Electronic Links create new Market Dynamics," *Computerworld*, p. 22., November 1990.

Braudel, F., *Civilization and Capitalism 15-18 Century: Vol.III - The Perspective of the World*, London: Collins, 1984.

Bressand, A. and K. Nicolaidis, *Strategic Trends in Services: an Inquiry into the Global Service Economy*, New York: Harper and Row, 1989.

Butler Cox Foundation, *Electronic Marketplaces*, London: Butler Cox Foundation, 1990.

Commission of the European Communities, "Council Regulation instituting a community programme for the development of certain less-Favoured regions of the Community by improving access to advanced telecommunications services (STAR programme)," 3300/86, OJ L305/1, 31 October 1986.

Commission of the European Communities, "Towards a Dynamic European Economy: Green Paper on the Development of the Common Market for Telecommunications Services and Equipment," COM(87) 290 final, 1987.

Commission of the European Communities, "RACE Phase I - Council Decision of 14 December 1987 on a Community Programme in the field of Telecommunications Technologies - Research and Development (R&D) in Advanced Technologies in Europe," 88/28/EEC. OJC 16, Vol. 31, 21 January 1988.

Commission of the European Communities, "Directive, 16 May 1988 on competition in the markets for telecommunication terminal equipment," (88/301/EEC), 1988.

Commission of the European Communities, "Directive, 28 June 1990 on competition in the markets for telecommunication services," (90/388/EEC), 1990.

Commission of the European Communities, "Perspectives for Advanced Communications in Europe: 1990," Volume 1, Summary Report, Commission of the European Communities, Brussels, February 1991.

Commission of the European Communities, "RACE Phase II - Council Decision of 7 June 1991 adopting a specific research and technological development programme in the field of communication technologies (1990-1994)," 91/352/EEC, OJC 192, Vol. 34, 16 July 1991.

Commission of the European Communities, "Telematics Systems of General Interest, Council Decision of 7 June 1991 adopting a specific programme of research and technological development in the field of telematics systems in areas of general interest (1990-1994)," 91/353/EEC, OJL 192, Vol. 34, 16 July 1991.

Commission of the European Communities, *Perspectives on Advanced Communications for Europe,* PACE 92, Brussels, 1992.

Council of the European Communities, "Directive 28 June 1990 on the establishment of the internal market for telecommunications services through the implementation of open network provision," (ONP)(90/387/EEC), 1990.

Cowhey, P., "The International Telecommunications Regime: the Political Roots of Regimes for High Technology," *International Organisation*, pp.169-199, Spring 1990.

Hootman, J., "The Computer Network as a Marketplace," *Datamation*, pp. 43-46, 1972.

Keen, P., *Competing in Time: Using Telecommunications for Competitive Advantage*, Cambridge MA: Ballinger, 1986.

Malone, T., J. Yates and R. Benjamin, "The Logic of Electronic Markets," *Harvard Business Review*, May-June 1989.

Mansell, R. and M. Jenkins, "Electronic Trading Networks and Interactivity: The Route to Competitive Advantage?" Case Study Report, Brighton: SPRU, 1992.

Mansell, R. and M. Jenkins, "The Policies of Integration: Telecommunication Policy in the Single European Market," *International Review of Comparative Public Policy*, Vol. 5, 1993.

Mansell, R. and M. Jenkins, "Networks and Policy: Interfaces, Theories and Research," *Communications & Strategies*, No. 5, pp. 31-50, 1er trimestre 1992.

Mansell, R., P. Holmes, and K. Morgan, "European Integration and Telecommunications: Restructuring Markets and Institutions," *Prometheus*, Vol. 8, No. 1, pp. 50-66, 1990.

Mansell, R., B. Holbrook and T. Darmaros, "Telematics Services for the Less Favoured Regions of the European Communities: A Political Economy of Development," in B. Mody (ed.), *Planning Communication Technology Development: Alternatives for the Periphery,* New York: Sage Publications.

Promethee, *Networked Markets*, Project Promethee Perspectives, No. 13, May 1990.

Turner, S, J. Epperson, and I. Fletcher, "Producer Attitudes towards Multicommodity Electronic Marketing," *American Journal of Agricultural Economics*, No. 65, pp. 818-822, 1983.

Woodrow, B., "Tilting towards a Trade Regime: the ITU and the Uruguay Round Services Negotiations," *Telecommunications Policy*, Vol. 15, No. 4, pp. 323-342, August 1991.

# ENDNOTES

[1.] The research for this paper was supported by the UK Economic and Social Research Council's Programme on Information and Communication Technologies. Michael Jenkins, Research Fellow, SPRU made major contributions to the research on Electronic Trading Networks. The views expressed in this paper are those of the author and do not reflect those of any institution.

[2.] See, for example, Benjamin, R. "Electronic Links create new Market Dynamics," *Computerworld*, p. 22, November 1990; Bressand, A. and K. Nicolaidis, *"Strategic Trends in Services: an Inquiry into the Global Service Economy,"* New York: Harper and Row, 1989; Butler Cox Foundation, *Electronic Marketplaces*, London: Butler Cox Foundation; Hootman, J., "The Computer Network as a Marketplace," *Datamation*, pp. 43-46, April 1972; Keen, P.,*Competing in Time: Using Telecommunications for Competitive Advantage*, Cambridge, MA: Ballinger, 1986; Malone, T., J. Yates and R. Benjamin, "The Logic of Electronic Markets," *Harvard Business Review*, May-June 1989; Promethee, *Networked Markets*, Project Promethee Perspectives No. 13, May 1990; and Turner, S, J. Epperson, and I. Fletcher, "Producer Attitudes towards Multicommodity Electronic Marketing," *American Journal of Agricultural Economics*, No. 65, pp. 818-822, 1983.

[3.] Mansell, R. and M. Jenkins, "Electronic Trading Networks and Interactivity: The Route to Competitive Advantage?" Case Study Report, Brighton: SPRU, 1992; Mansell, R. and M. Jenkins, "The Policies of Integration: Telecommunication Policy in the Single European Market," *International Review of Comparative Public Policy*, Vol. 5, 1993; and Mansell, R. and M. Jenkins, "Networks and Policy: Interfaces, Theories and Research," *Communications & Strategies*, No. 5, pp. 31-50, 1er trimestre 1992.

[4.] Cowhey, P., "The International Telecommunications Regime: the Political Roots of Regimes for High Technology," *International Organization*, pp. 169-199, Spring 1990; Woodrow, B., "Tilting Towards a Trade Regime: the ITU and the Uruguay Round Services Negotiations," *Telecommunications Policy*, Vol. 15, No. 4, pp. 323-342, August 1991.

[5.] Braudel, F., *Civilization and Capitalism 15-18 Century: Vol.III - The Perspective of the World*, London: Collins 1984.

[6.] The telematics infrastructure refers to the substantial degree of information processing capability that resides within the public network with the advent of software driven 'intelligent' switching capabilities. The telematics infrastructure offers an 'intelligent' platform which may be used to supply services which require information processing far beyond that needed for the simple conveyance of messages.

[7.] Commission of the European Communities, "Perspectives for Advanced Communications in Europe: 1990," Volume 1, Summary Report, Commission of the European Communities, Brussels, February 1991.

[8.] Mansell, R., P. Holmes, and K. Morgan, "European Integration and Telecommunications: Restructuring Markets and Institutions," *Prometheus*, Vol. 8, No. 1, pp. 50-66,1990; Mansell, R., B. Holbrook and T. Darmaros, "Telematics Services for the Less Favoured Regions of the European Communities: A Political Economy of Development," in B. Mody (ed.), *Planning Communication Technology Development: Alternatives for the Periphery*, New York: Sage Publications, 1994.

[9.] Since 1987 legislation in the form of Directives has included: Commission of the European Committees, "Directive, 16 May 1988 on competition in the markets for telecommunication terminal equipment," (88/301/EEC), 1988; Commission of the European Committees, "Directive, 28 June 1990 on competition in the markets for telecommunications services," (90/388/EEC), 1990; and Council of the European Communities, "Directive 28 June 1990 on the establishment of the internal market for telecommunications services through the implementation of open network provision (ONP),"

208

(90/387/EEC). Also see: Commission of the European Communities, "Towards a Dynamic European Economy: Green Paper on the Development of the Common Market for Telecommunications Services and Equipment," COM(87) 290 final, 1987.

[10.]Commission of the European Communities, "RACE Phase I - Council Decision of 14 December 1987 on a Community Programme in the field of Telecommunications Technologies - Research and Development (R&D) in Advanced Technologies in Europe," 88/28/EEC OJC 16, Vol. 31, 21 January 1988; Commission of the European Communities, "RACE Phase II - Council Decision of 7 June 1991 adopting a specific research and technological development programme in the field of communication technologies (1990-1994)," 91/352/EEC, OJC 192, Vol. 34, 16 July 1991; Commission of the European Communities, "Telematics Systems of General Interest, Council Decision of 7 June 1991 adopting a specific programme of research and technological development in the field of telematics systems in areas of general interest (1990-1994)," 91/353/EEC, OJL 192, Vol. 34, 16 July 1991.

[11.]Commission of the European Communities, *Perspectives on Advanced Communications for Europe*, PACE 92, Brussels, 1992.

[12.]Braudel, F., *Civilization and Capitalism 15-18 Century: Vol.III - The Perspective of the World*, London: Collins, 1984.

PRIVATE NETWORKS PUBLIC OBJECTIVES
E. Noam and A. NíShúilleabháin (Editors)
© 1996 Elsevier Science B.V. All rights reserved.

# Access Charges for Private Networks Interconnecting with Public Systems

Dale Lehman and Dennis L. Weissman

## 1. INTRODUCTION

Private networks have proliferated since the advent of competition in telecommunications. Recent technological advances especially in wireless technologies and further regulatory changes, to permit interconnection of private systems with public systems, offer potential explosive growth in the reach of private networks.[1] No longer the exclusive domain of large companies, private networks are gaining the capability to attract significant numbers of smaller residential and business customers to their networks. This paper addresses the question of how to design access charges for interconnecting these private networks with public systems.

Private networks come in a variety of types and sizes ranging from CPE (including PBXs) and a variety of bypass technologies, to large network facilities serving many customers (e.g., General Motors' network is reported to serve 250,000 lines). Included are Metropolitan Area Networks (MANs) which offer network facilities to large business customers at highly competitive rates, and the possibility of interconnection with the public network translates this capability into full competition with the public network. Interconnection would significantly increase the competitive appeal of MANs to ordinary telephone customers. It is the terms of this interconnection which will largely determine the market shares of private and public systems, and, to an extent, the size of the market itself. As Eli M. Noam has said, "Whoever controls the rules of interconnection controls the network system itself."[2]

Private Networks develop for a diverse set of reasons, including the desire for control, reliability, new services capabilities, and the ability to cut costs. These can be classed into price and nonprice motivations. Nonprice motivations are largely efficiency enhancing and are part of the benefits of a more competitive environment. It is the cost-cutting motivations which are more ambiguous. Private solutions which require less resources than are needed by public systems are efficiency enhancing. Private solutions which simply allow users to avoid tarriffs, with no rational basis in costs, of the regulated public systems, and which actually expend more resources to provide services, are inefficient. The task is to design tariffs which provide incentives for efficient private network development while keeping traffic and customers on the public network who can most efficiently be served by that network. We will not address the difficult question of how to set charges for interconnection of different private networks with each other. The assumption is that there is a network with special characteristics--the public network--with which private networks may wish to interconnect.

The paper proceeds as follows. Section II examines the present tariff structure and how it may provide for overdevelopment of, and oversubscription to, private networks. Overdevelopment is defined in terms of economic efficiency. Oversubscription may well be the more critical policy issue, since much of the private network capacity is already a sunk cost, regardless of its efficiency properties. Given the existing capacity of private networks (estimated to be sufficient for the current total volume of telecommunications traffic), do present tariff structures promote efficient subscription decisions? Section III sketches the possible scenarios for the public network of the future under existing tariffs. The public network has traditionally been the "carrier of last resort," in that it was required (in exchange for its franchised monopoly) to provide service to all that desired it, under regulatory oversight of tariffs. Will the public network become "the carrier of last resort," in that nobody will voluntarily subscribe unless they have no alternative options? Section IV explores alternative tariff structures aimed at meeting the goals of maintaining the viability and function of the public network, as well as promoting the benefits of competition and interconnection.

## 2. PRIVATE NETWORK DEVELOPMENT MAY BE SOCIALLY EXCESSIVE

Determining the economically efficient level of private network development is difficult, if not impossible. Whether or not parts of the networks possess natural monopoly characteristics is much open to debate, as well as which parts and for how much longer. The fact that private networks are not being discouraged, and perhaps even encouraged, indicates that telephone service is not generally considered a natural monopoly.

The most appealing theory to date for the formation and fragmentation of "the public network" is found in Noam.[3] The public network is viewed as a club, formed to take advantage of cost sharing. Eventually, the cost shares become redistributed to account for network externalities, and to accomodate the desires of a majority of subscribers to allocate increasing cost shares to the minority who value service the most. This leads to the demise of the single club, as coalitions break off forming their own clubs with their own sharing rules. Noam points out that the "universal service" goal is likely to be inefficient, as the network externalities are probably not sufficient to justify universality of access. The common public network disappears and is replaced by multiple interconnected subnetworks.

The efficiency of this transition is not clear. Subnetworks allow for heterogeneous demands of subscribers to be met more closely than by a common public network. Differentiated needs for quality, reliability, multiple services, and alternative cost sharing arrangements are promoted, but at the expense of some duplication of facilities and costs of the compatibility required for interconnection. The net result for efficiency is ambiguous. At the same time, NTIA[4] calls for an expanded notion of universal service ("Advanced USA") which calls for a continued and upgraded public network. The optimal number of clubs, given a universal service constraint on one club, has not yet been modelled--nor has the ability of the constrained club to finance itself. Research on this important question is warranted and will impact the "optimal" rules for interconnection of clubs. However, we will not pursue this model here, since much of the private network development is already a sunk cost. Additionally, there appear to be a number of competing social goals, none of which our society is yet willing to abandon.

We take as our point of departure the assumption that continuance of the public network, with its attendant universal service obligations, is socially desired. Otherwise, there is no special status accorded to the public systems, nor to interconnection of private networks with it. Given the desire for continued "public systems" what can be said about the efficient development of private networks and the terms of interconnection?

Mueller[5] provides an extreme view: "nonconnected networks will always offer access to different subscribers... once interconnected, networks behave more like complements than substitutes."[6] Accordingly, competition between networks is enhanced by banning interconnection. However, the costs of banning interconnection may well be too large. As Noam[7] responds, "for states to fight the principle of open interconnection is to tilt at windmills."[8] The costs of duplication of facilities and/or the welfare losses associated with noninterconnected networks appear to us to be too large to seriously consider this prospect.[9] Hence we also assume that interconnection is a desired policy.

We therefore wish to examine access charges for desirable interconnection of private networks with a public system which has a universal service obligation. We will assume that interconnection is technologically feasible and costless, and we examine the extent of private network development under current tariff structures. Forces which tend to promote inefficiently excessive private network development are isolated in this section, while the next section forecasts the resulting effects on public and private network evolution. Section IV addresses the question: can the terms of interconnection be modified to promote an efficient level of private sector development?

We proceed with a series of highly stylized models aimed at isolating the major inefficient forces in the existing tariff structure. Many institutional details of actual tariffs are omitted. We will return to these in section III, as the complexity of actual tariff and cost structures provide some mitigating factors for the inefficiencies identified in this section.

## 2.1. Option Values and Default Capacity

Originally identified as promoting inefficient levels of bypass, the carrier of last resort obligations imposed on public network suppliers also can lead to inefficient development of private networks more generally.[10] It is often the case that the users of private networks retain their original lines to the public network. This reveals that they are receiving value at least as large as the access tariffs associated with these lines. Given the growing importance of network reliability, the significance of the backup capability of the public network is not surprising.

Consider a private network subscriber paying P for access to the private network and a constant usage price/cost$=$p. Let the indirect utility function be $U(Y,p,I)$ where Y is income (if a business customer, then this could be profit) and I is an index indicating whether or not access to the public network is possible ($I=0$: no access; $I=1$: access). We assume that the decision maker is risk averse. There are $i=1,...n$ states of the world, each characterized by different utility functions and possibly different income levels. The associated probabilities for each state are $\pi_i$ ($i=1,...,n$) with $\Sigma \pi_i = 1$. Define option price, OP, to be the state-independent maximum willingness to pay for access to the public network, and let $CS_i$ be the state dependent compensating variation measure of consumer's surplus in state i. Then, $CS_i$ is defined by

$$U_i(Y_i\text{-}P\text{-}CS_i,p,1) = U_i(Y_iP,p,0) \qquad i=1,...,n \qquad (1)$$

and OP is defined by

$$\Sigma_i \pi_i(Yi\text{-}P\text{-}OP,p,1) = \Sigma_i \pi_i U_i(Y_i\text{-}P,p,0) \tag{2}$$

Option value, OV, is defined as the difference between option price and expected consumer's surplus (ECS), i.e.,

$$OV = OP - \Sigma \pi iCSi \tag{3}$$

It is well documented elsewhere[11] that whether or not $OV > 0$ or $OV < 0$ depends on attitudes towards risk, the sources of uncertainty, and the opportunities availiable to protect against risk.

Some intuitive motivation for the nonequivalence of OP and ECS is useful. OP is a state-independent measure of value; ECS is the weighted sum of state-contingent values. The sign of OV will depend on how dollars are valued in different states of nature, which, in turn, depends on both the sources of uncertainty and the individual's attitude towards risk. Risk averse individuals will generally be willing to pay a state-independent premium beyond their expected consumer's surplus in order to resolve or reduce the source of uncertainty. Indeed, this is the principle behind the demand for insurance.

The possible sources of uncertainty are myriad, including but not limited to: tastes, income, prices, supply; and the opportunties to insure against such risk are similarly varied. Consequently, the sign of option value is not unambiguously positive, even for risk averse individuals. For instance, if I am uncertain as to my future demand because my future income is uncertain, than I may prefer state-contingent payments to the state-independent option price as the vehicle for expressing my valuation of a future option. Such contingent payments would provide the opportunity to minimize payments in states of nature where my income turns out to be relatively low.

Although OV is generally indeterminate in sign, results are available for specific sources of uncertainty and attitudes towards risk. The two cases most pertinent to private networks are (i) risk aversion, demand certainty, and supply uncertainty of the form that the option guarantees the supply while lack of exercising the option leaves some nonzero probability of supply, and (ii) risk aversion with supply certainty and demand uncertainty arising from exogenous factors which do not affect the marginal utility of income across states of nature (strong seperability of the indirect utility function). Freeman[12] has shown that both of these cases imply that $OV > 0$.

The first case is relevant to a private network which may retain access lines to the public network in case of system failure. The second case would apply to the option to resort to the public network in orer to reach individuals not on the private network (it is assumed that the private network will connect the bulk of the subscrtiber's trafic, but that no attempt is made by the private network to carry occasional traffic to remote parts of the public network). In both cases, the insurance provided by access to the public network is worth something, and this value exceeds the expected consumer's surplus. This last observation means that attempts to extract this value through ex post usage payments will fall short of the full ex ante value of access. Private network users are receiving some benefits for which they are paying relatively little. This enhances the viability of private networks as well as generating less revenue than its value would indicate. Market failure is possible, wherein public network revenues are insufficient to maintain or upgrade the public network even under conditions where the social value exceeds these costs.

## 2.2. Public Network Usage Tariffs

We assume that the public network fixed costs = FC(S) so that default capacity retains the same fixed costs as regularly used capacity, i.e., that the fixed costs of the public network depend on the level of total traffic, S, and not only the traffic on the public network. This assumption is justified if the private network users retain access lines to the public network that were installed prior to the development of the private network. The public network incurs provisioning costs associated with the potential for these lines to generate traffic. Private network customers are not guaranteed that all of their default traffic will be accomodated on the public switched network, but it is likely that most such traffic will be provisioned for.

Default traffic may be blocked at any of three points in the network: the line-side connections to the central office, the central office switch, and the trunk-side connections to the remainder of the network. The need to adequately provision the public network reduces the last of these to negligible levels. The outside plant for the original number of lines remains regardless of whether the number of active lines is or is not reduced. Central office switch capacity is more complicated, since it is engineered on the basis of lines terminations and normal busy hour conditions. Depending on the fraction of line terminations from the private network customer, some switch capacity costs are generally recovered on a usage sensitive basis. Such costs are fixed (based on potential traffic), but are recovered from users. Since private networks are only occasional users of default capacity, they bear little of this cost burden. The access charge for the lines may or may not be compensatory, but it is clear that the option to use the line is worth its cost or these lines would be disconnected.

Assume that FC' > 0 and FC'' > 0 and that the marginal cost for public network usage is constant=c. The private network incurs provisioning costs = P(Q), P' > 0 and P'' > 0, and constant usage costs of c. The efficient level of private traffic is determined by:

$$\min_Q \{FC(S) + P(Q) + c(S-Q) + ĉ(Q)\}. \tag{4}$$

The first order condition equates the marginal cost of provisioning the private network with the marginal cost savings of using the private network, i.e.:

$$P'(Q) = (c-ĉ) \tag{5}$$

Since networks have a risk of failure, let $\alpha$ be the probability of private system failure. The total cost function is now:

$$FC(S) + (1-\alpha)c(S-Q) + \alpha cS + P(Q) + (1-\alpha)ĉQ + \alpha Q \tag{6}$$

This assumes that the public network will serve any default capacity from the private network when it is down. The first order conditions are given by:

$$P'(Q) = (1-\alpha)(c-ĉ) \tag{7}$$

Optimal private network traffic is smaller due to the possibility of network failure (of course, the public network can also fail, so that it is the difference in failure probabilities which is relevant--we ignore this, as we are interested in how the private network traffic will compare with this socially efficient level and not the absolute level itself).

The private network development decision is driven by private network costs relative to the public tariff. Assume the latter has an access charge of T and a marginal use charge of t. A representative private network provider will:

$$\min_Q ( T + \alpha t \, Q + P(Q) + \hat{c} Q (1 - \alpha)) \tag{8}$$

The first order condition is:

$$P'(Q) = (1 - \alpha)(t - \hat{c}) \tag{9}$$

Private network traffic will exceed the efficient level if $t > c$, i.e., $Q > (<) Q$ as $t > (<) c$. We assume that the public usage tariff is set to make the public network break even (in an expected value sense):

$$TN + t(S - Q) + \alpha t \, Q = FC(S) + c(S - Q) + \alpha c \, Q \tag{10}$$

where N is the number of public access lines. Rearranging and solving for the public usage price gives:

$$t = \frac{FC(S) - TN}{S - Q + \alpha Q} + \frac{c(S - Q + \alpha Q)}{(S - Q + \alpha Q)} = c + \frac{FC(S) - TN}{S - Q(1 - \alpha)} \tag{11}$$

Inefficiency of private network traffic depends on the term:

$$\Delta = \frac{FC(S) - TN}{S - Q(1 - \alpha)} \tag{12}$$

Private Network traffic will be inefficiently large provided that FC(S) > TN, i.e., if access line revenues do not cover the fixed costs of the network. Given the regulatory objective of universal and affordable access, access lines (in the aggregate) have been underpriced, and so this inequality is satisfied.[13]

Straightforward comparative static properties of $\Delta$ reveal that the inefficiency is larger: the more extensive the private networks ($Q$), the more reliable private networks are (smaller $\alpha$), the greater the divergence between fixed costs and access lines revenues (FC(S)-TN), the greater the fixed costs (FC), and the smaller the total number of access lines (N). Further, the private networks may be less reliable than efficiency would dictate, instead relying on the public network to provide reliability in the form of backup.[14]

In theory, this inefficiency can be removed by a "tax" $= \Delta$.[15] Applying a charge to each unit of private network traffic is tantamount to charging such traffic for the expected loss in contribution payments to the public network. Such schemes are currently being considered and/or implemented, e.g., in New York State and Switzerland.[16]

It is important to note that this inefficiency results from the distorted public tariff structure and not the default use of the public network: i.e., even with $\alpha=0$ this inefficiency remains. So the inflated public usage tariff gives rise to inefficiently large private private network development. Still, the default use of the public network is of interest, since the last discussion revealed that there is option value associated with the default use of the public network by private network users. It is worth asking whether or not the access tariff paid by the private network is compensatory--do access line revenues + occasional usage revenues cover the costs imposed by the carrier of last resort obligations to serve the private networks in a default capacity?

To consider this question, we compute public network revenues (R) and costs (C) due to the private network being serviced under the carrier of last resort obligations. Let $N_p$ be the number of access lines from the private network to the public network.

$$R = TN_p + \alpha t\, Q \tag{13A}$$

and

$$C = (\frac{N_p}{N})\, FC(S) + \alpha c\, Q \tag{13B}$$

We have assumed that the fixed costs attributable to private network lines are proportional to the fraction of total lines which service the private network. Such lines may be less costly than average due to their relative proximity to central offices, but this must be weighed against the heavier pre-private network usage on such lines for which the public network was already provisioned. The net contribution of the private network as public customer is given by (substituting the value for t from above):

$$R - C = TN_p + \alpha c\, Q + \frac{\alpha Q\,(FC(S) - TN)}{S - Q\,(1-\alpha)} - FC(S)\,(\frac{N_p}{N}) - \alpha c\, Q \tag{14}$$

$$R - C = (FC(S) - TN)\,(\frac{\alpha Q}{S - Q(1-\alpha)}) + (TN_p - FC(S)\,(\frac{N_p}{N})) \tag{15}$$

$$R - C = (FC(S) - TN)\,(\frac{\alpha Q}{S - Q(1-\alpha)} - \frac{N_p}{N}) \tag{16}$$

The first term is positive since we have assumed that aggregate access line revenues do not cover all nontraffic sensitive costs. The second term depends on the relative fractions of traffic and lines represented by the private network. Due to the occasional use of the public network (whether derived from private network failure or from default to the public network to reach lightly called and/or distant subscribers), we assume that Q is small relative to S compared with the ratio $N_p/N$. Under these conditions the revenue contribution of private networks will fall short of the costs of providing default capacity. The earlier discussion also reveals that this revenue is likely to fall short of the total value of private access to the public network. This provides a ripe ground for market failure and/or inequitable cross subsidies from regular public subscribers to private networks defaulting to the public network.

It may be argued that from a network perspective, this default traffic of the private network appears no different than the infrequent usage of an occasional user of telephone service who is a public subscriber. While this may be technically correct, the similarity in kind is surely dominated by the difference in degree. Usage patterns resulting from innate customer characteristics would also appear to call for different treatment than those resulting from a change in customer behavior due to distorted tariff structures.

Without formally defining a measure of equity, the large business customer who consciously designs a private network so as to utilize the public switched network on a default basis without compensatory payment is surely different in society's eyes from an individual whose infrequent use of their telephone results in a degree of cross subsidization. Pre-competition, the former situation could not arise and the latter was simply a de facto social transfer. Post-competition, the former situation is economically inefficient and the latter may be as well. But from a socially equitable position, we are hard pressed to argue that these situations are one and the same.

This section suggests that the desire to underprice access results in overpricing usage which gives rise to inefficient private network development. This might suggest that cost based pricing which removed this cross-subsidy will remove the inefficiency. However, the next discussion reveals that there is a further distortion which will still cause inefficient private network development, even if aggregate access tariffs cover the fixed costs of the public network.

## 2.3. Geographical Averaging of Access Tariffs

Usage tariffs would probably be geographically averaged to some degree in a competitive world (current long-distance tariffs seem to support this). Transactions costs and customer satisfaction may well require a degree of averaging. However, it is unlikely that access tariffs would be averaged to a similar degree. Different subscribers impose quite different fixed costs on network infrastructures. Farther removed and low density routes are far more costly to serve than dense routes located near central offices. As Sharkey[17] observes, "we see that it is the network configuration rather than the network size that is relevant in the determination of natural monopoly characteristics in the industry."[18] Yet part of the carrier of last resort obligation imposed on the public network is that it average the access tariff accross customers, at least to a greater degree than the variation in costs.

It is not necessary that the cost structure depend not only on the size of the network, but on the identity of its subscribers. We assume that there are two types of fixed network costs: those that are independent of the subscriber set, F, and those that are individual to each subscriber, $F_i$ ($i=1,...,n$). The former may be thought of as switching and transmission costs, while the latter are trunking costs. Trunking costs will increase with distance from the central office due to the costs of installing additional plant, as well as the need for signal repeaters (roughly proportional to distance). The marginal cost of usage is assumed to be constant, c, and usage is assumed to be fixed and constant per subscriber, Q. We will relax these assumptions later.

Assume that the customer specific costs are ordered so that $F_i < F_j$ whenever $i < j$. We will partition the total set of subscribers, N, into two groups--those on the private network, m, and those on the public network, N-m. We assume that the private network will choose those customers with the lowest connection costs, leaving the remaining higher cost customers for the public network to serve. As Mueller[19] has observed, "Current policy, in contrast, fosters competition in high-density business routes only, where markets are undersupplied or overpriced due to rate averaging. Increasingly open interconnection policies allow new companies to leave the task of providing universal service to the established network, thereby making it highly unlikely that the benefits of competition will ever reach the bulk of the population."[20]

Assume that the private network has a parallel cost structure, with fixed costs = P, subscriber specific fixed costs = $P_i$ (i=1,...,n), and constant marginal usage cost = ĉ. We partition the total subscriber base into public and private subscribers, on the assumption that there is some real cost advntage enjoyed by the private network (otherwise private network development would never be efficient). The condition which describes efficient partitioning is given by:

$$F_i - P_i > Q(c - \hat{c}) \quad \text{(for all i = 1,...m*)} \tag{17}$$
$$F_i - P_i \leq Q(c - \hat{c}) \quad \text{(for all i = m*+1, ... ,n)}$$

The left hand side is the connection cost savings for the private network relative to the public network. The right hand side is the per subscriber usage cost savings on the private network. This inequality states that the private network never includes subscribers for whom the connection cost savings are less than the usage cost savings. m* is the efficient coverage of the private network.

The private tariff structure will charge each subscriber an equal share of the common fixed cost, P/m, and the customer specific connection charge, $P_i$. We assume the private market is sufficiently competitive that the usage price = ĉ. The public network is assumed to average its access tariff across its subscribers. To isolate the effects of access tariff averaging, we will assume there is no cross subsidy from usage to access in this model. In other words, the public access tariff is a two part tariff = T+tQ, where:

$$t = c \tag{18}$$

$$T = \frac{F + \sum_{i=m+1}^{N} F_i}{N-m} \tag{19}$$

Individual subscribers will join the private network as long as:

$$T + t\,Q > \frac{P}{m} + P_i + \hat{c}\,Q \tag{20}$$

The equilibrium marginal subscriber, $\bar{m}$, is defined by:

$$T + c\,Q > \frac{P}{m} + P_{\bar{m}} + \hat{c}\,Q \quad \text{and} \quad T + c\,Q < \frac{P}{\bar{m}+1} + P_{\bar{m}-1} + \hat{c}\,Q \tag{21}$$

Assuming that the number of subscribers is great enough that the optimal conditions hold with equality, $\bar{m}$ is given by:

$$T - \left(\frac{P}{\bar{m}} + P_m\right) = Q(c - \hat{c}), \text{ i.e.,}$$

$$\left[\frac{F}{N-\bar{m}} - \frac{P}{m}\right]\left[\frac{\sum_{i=\bar{m}+1}^{N} F_i}{N-\bar{m}} - P_{\bar{m}}\right] = Q(c - \hat{c}) \tag{22}$$

The right hand side is the same as in the determination of the efficient m*. The second term on the left hand side is larger than $(F_m - P_m)$ due to the access tariff averaging. So, private network coverage will exceed the efficient level, provided that the first term on the left hand side is positive (or sufficiently small, if negative). Of course, this must be the case for the private network to be viable. The only cost premium potentially attributable to the private network is that its size may not be sufficient to enable cost sharing to make it cheaper than the public network. This is related to the conecpt of "critical mass" found in Noam.[21] We will assume that the private network has reached cirtical mass. Then, the above analysis reveals that it has grown beyond the efficient level, i.e., $\overline{m} > m^*$.

Note that the excessive private network growth is not assured. The private network must gain sufficient size to overcome the cost disadvantage of its smaller sharing group. At the same time, there are a number of considerations which will tend to reinforce the tendency to overgrow. If we allow usage to vary between customers and for elastic demand, the private network becomes more attractive. In fact, it is likely that the covariance between connection cost and subscriber usage will be negative, meaning that a relatively small number of subscribers stand to gain a lot by private network subscription. This is further enhanced by the analysis of the last section, wherein the tendency for the public network to underprice access in the aggregate also contributes to private network over-growth. The option values inherent in public network access would only exacerbate this picture.

## 3. PUBLIC NETWORKS MAY BE UNSUSTAINABLE UNDER CURRENT TARIFFS

We have identified three major factors which interact to cause excessive private network growth from the point of view of efficiency. These are:

> (1) option values for connection to the public network for default in the case of private network failure and/or extending the reach of the private network to the universe of subscribers, many of whom will only occasionally be accessed--such option values tend to be priced lower than their provisioning costs
> (2) inflated public network usage charges resulting from the social goal of decreasing the cost of access--these inflated usage charges provide incentives for heavy users to flee the public network in favor of private networks with more cost based pricing
> (3) geographically averaged public network access tariffs--this provides an incentive for subscribers with lower than average connection costs to seek alternatives with more customer specific pricing

In addition, the three sets of customers to which these incentives apply have significant overlaps. In this section we put these factors together to forecast the evolution of the public network vis a vis private networks which interconnect with it. To simplify matters, we will assume that the private network has precisely the same cost structure as the public network-- this eliminates any truly efficient reason for private network development assuming that nonprice motivations for private networks are ignored. Any remaining incentive to flee public network subscription in favor of private networks can than be regarded as efficient.

Subscribers are heterogeneous and their differences are important to our story. We distinguish between subscribers in two critical dimensions: their usage level, and their connection cost to the network. We seek to describe the set of public subscribers who would prefer to join private networks ("defectors") despite the identical underlying cost structures for both networks. Figure 1 provides a framework with which to examine the defector potential. The first quadrant is the scatterplot of the universe of public network subscribers, shown in terms of their two basic attributes: usage level and connection cost. The third quadrant shows the critical level of cost savings required for subscription to the private network rather than the public network. This critical level of cost savings is given by:

$$\bar{F} = ( \frac{F}{(N-m)} - \frac{F}{m} )$$ (23)

This represents the cost disadvantage of a smaller sharing group on the private network. Of course, once the private network has sufficient size, this term could become negative. The most relevant case at present is that usage access cost savings must be sufficient to overcome the disadvantage of the smaller sharing group. If there were additional fixed costs of enabling connection to the private network and/or costs associated with achieving compatiability with the public network, then these costs would be added to $\bar{F}$. Note that the critical level of cost savings in quadrant III extends into quadrants II and IV, as only the total cost savings count in predicting defection. Any cost savings combinations that lie to the southwest of the $\bar{F}$ line are sufficient for defection.

The connection cost savings (CCS) and usage cost savings (UCS) are shown in quadrants II and IV, respectively. Usage cost savings result from avoiding inflated public network usage tariffs. Connection cost savings result from avoiding the geographically averaged public network access tariffs. Each of these varies across subscribers according to their attributes, and are given by:

$$CCS = T - \frac{F}{m} - F_i$$ (24)

$$UCS = Q_i ( t - c )$$ (25)

We have assumed that the private network charges each subscriber their true connection charge and not a geographically averaged access tariff. Since the private network will need to connect to the public network on behalf of their subscribers, it would be expected that the geographically averaged public access tariffs would be passed on to private network subscribers. However, the private network need not maintain a connection line to the public network on bealf of *each* of their subscribers, since they can conecntrate traffic that would flow onto the public network. It is expected, for example, that MANs would meet the heavier traffic needs of their customers, needing far fewer lines to the public network than their number of subscribers in order to achieve universal connection capabilities. These cost savings are assumed to allow the private network to charge individualized connection costs to its subscribers.

We constrain the public tariff structure to allow the public network to just break even:

$$T(N-m) + t \bar{Q} (N-m) = F + \sum_{i=m+1}^{N} F_i + c \bar{Q} (N-m)$$ (26)

# Figure 1

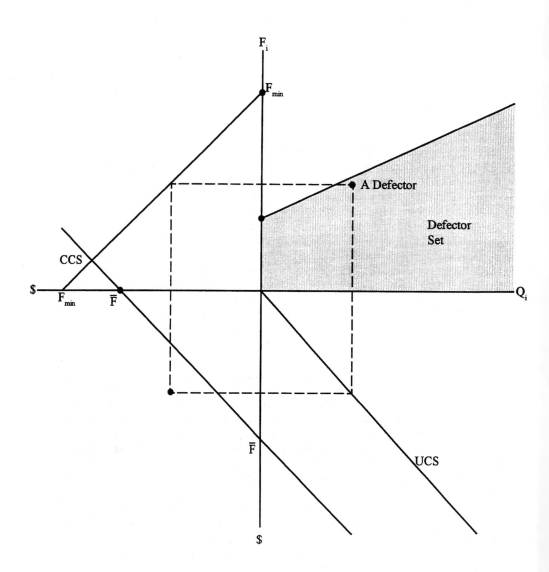

To simplify the analytics, we ignore default use of the public network and we assume that $\bar{Q}$ represents the average usage level for public subscribers.

In constructing Figure 1, consider the initial case where $t=c$ so that UCS$=0$. Define $F_{min}$ as the value of $F_i$ which gives CCS $\bar{F}$. All customers with $F_i<F_{min}$ will defect, but none with higher connection costs will. Consequently, the defection line in quadrant one is horizontal.

Now consider $t>c$. The UCS line is shown in quadrant IV. The breakeven constraint requires that T be lower than before, so that $F_{min}$ will be lower than before (CCS are decreased). The combinations of $(Q_i, F_i)$ which yield defections are now given by the upward sloping line in the first quadrant. Higher usage levels will induce defection, but for low usage levels, defection will require lower real connection costs than previously.

## 3.1. "Dynamics"

We mention only a few of the dynamic properties to Figure 1. The critical story is the evolution as private network subscribership increases. It is easily shown that $F_{min}$ increases since the remaining public subscribers are the higher connection costs individuals. The required cost savings for defection, $\bar{F}$, will decrease as the sharing group on the private (public) network increases (decreases). These are the effects if we assume that t is not adjusted in relation to c. The result is that the defector region is increased as private network subscribership increases.

Any attempt to lower t in response will serve to increase CCS, since T will be raised. Attempts to lower T will increase UCS, since t must be raised. Consideration of elastic demands and uncertainty will only exacerbate the problems. Elastic demands are tantamount to increasing UCS beyond what is shown, since we would add increased consumer's surplus to the cost savings. Option values are not related to actual usage levels, so the UCS line, if it included option values, would become an irregular surface including some $(Q_i, F_i)$ combinations previously not showing savings when option values were not considered.

The dynamic story would seem to indicate a dissolution of the public network, even in the face of assuming away any real resource savings in private networks. There are mitigating factors. Actual tariff and cost structures are quite complicated. Some business line access tariffs are compensatory, although the aggregate access tariffs almost certainly do not cover aggregate nontraffic sensitive costs. Actual connection arrangements to the public network for private network subscribers may vary considerably, only yielding connection cost savings in particular cases. Usage cost savings depends not only on usage levels, but on the entire usage structure. Time of day, distance, volume, etc. all matter. While the resulting pattern of defection is complex and requires empirical verification, we believe that the basic forces we have outlined will remain.

This paper has presented an extreme form of the forces for inefficient public network defection inherent in existing public tariff structures. There are mitigating considerations, but the forces will tend to force the public networks towards a minimal network, truly the "carrier of last resort." Existing tariffs provide incentives for private networks to pick off the more lucrative public subscribers, leaving only the more "undesirable," i.e., costly, subscribers for the public network to serve. The ability of technology to take advantage of these incentives will only increase with time. The situation will be exacerbated if the public network is to upgrade its infrastructure, incurring the modernization costs with no commitment on the part of its customers to repay these costs with public network subscription or usage.

This picture may seem extremist and/or unrealistic, but we hasten to point out that it already has a precedent in the health care industry. As documented in Leyerle,[22] Blue Cross-Blue Shield (BC/BS) was granted tax exempt status in exchange for carrier of last resort obligations. Its "community ratings" were required to equalize rates across people, regardless of health status (i.e., costs). Commercial companies (e.g., HMOs) had no such tax advantages, but utilized "experience ratings" which geared rates to the individual's actual experience (i.e., costs). The result was that the BC/BS market share of 61% in 1945 had dropped to 37% by 1969. In fact, BC/BS was forced to offer experience rating plans in competition with others. The community rating plans increased continually in price. The viability of BC/BS was further bolstered by a variety of government contracts (e.g., VA contracts). But the general policy of community ratings was abandoned in favor of experience ratings. Whatever community rating plans that remain are prohibitively expensive.

The health care industry presently has 37 million uncovered individuals. We doubt that universal telephone service will suffer the same fate where subscribership drops to some 75% of the households in the U.S. The cost structure for telecommunications is one of declining real costs as in health care. However, we believe there is a real danger of just such an outcome if we look at advanced telecommunications services. Indeed, we already are experiencing less than universal service for advanced services. The present tariff structure paints a bleak picture for the ability of the public network to offer advanced services on a universal basis in the face of significant competition from interconnected private networks.

We also raise the possibility that the current "infrastructure movement" may be socially excessive and/or biased. It may result in expensive modernization of the public network with little benefit to the mass of subscribers and facilities which are of value to a relatively small group--precisely those with private networks alternatives. With no commitment of the subscribers to pay its costs, i.e. no restrictions on exit, private networks need bear little of the costs of experimenting with new capabilities in the public network. Significant option values may be associated with such experimentation, but a free exit policy will allow private networks to realize the benefits of these experiments with no obligation to bear their share of the costs.

## 4. "SOLUTIONS"

We believe that the current set of social constraints on the evolution of telecommunications markets is untenable: the desire for public systems with universal service obligations; the desire for a degree of access charge averaging geographically; the desire to burden the heavier users of the public network with more than their share of its costs; the desire to significantly upgrade the technology of the public systems; and, the desire to foster private network development and competition. As Crandall points out:

"The lessons we have learned from the past two decades of reductions of regulatory barriers to entry into telecommunications are quite clear. Entry had proceeded much more rapidly than anyone would have expected from simply watching the new OCCs. The enormous rise in private communications systems ought to suggest to regulators either that there are diseconomies of scale and scope among the regulated telephone companies, that regulated institutions have created little incentive for efficiency among these telephone companies, or that regulated rates are substantially distorted. None of these possibilities would argue for a restoration of the status quo ante."[23]

We agree that all of these suggestions are true to an extent, but our focus has been on the last of these--the significant distortions in regulated rates. We have encouraged a vast social experiment with competition in telecommunications which has yielded, and should continue to yield, huge social benefits. However, as we seek to upgrade our infrastructure and continue to maintain universal service as a social goal, sitting on the fence between competition and regulated monopoly becomes increasingly precarious. It is critical that we enter the information age with an appropriate set of incentives in place, and not the vestiges of earlier regulatory structures.

Accordingly, we should outline what an efficient set of incentives for private network interconnection with public systems might look like. Unfortunately, it is far easier to state what efficient incentives *do not* resemble. We propose the following guidelines for public network tariffs:

1.  Eliminate as many cross subsidies in the current structure as possible. We view the dangers of distorting usage tariffs as more serious than distortions in access tariffs, so we should continue to move in the direction of lowering marginal usage prices. In fact, the flat rate usage tariff has much to recommend it, especially as the network becomes fully digitized. The desire to keep access universally affordable is better funded out of general tax revenues or some other more efficiency neutral device (this mirrors the suggestions of NTIA[24]).

2.  Actual usage is rapidly diminishing as a meaningful base for assessing charges. Most network costs are associated with access and *potential* usage, rather than actual ex post usage. We believe that option values are rising in significance and these cannot be recovered efficiently through ex post usage charges. Means need to be devised to recover costs, particularly the costs of new technology, through potential rather than actual usage. This would mirror the changes in the information structure of the industry. In the franchised monopoly era, the firm had better information than customers about usage patterns and was in a better position to forecast demand. Public networks bore this risk in the form of a usage dependent revenue structure. Private networks have shifted the information advantage towards the customer. Accordingly, users should now bear more of the risks associated with uncertain demand--payments should shift in the direction of independence from the state of nature.

3.  Given the large incentives for private networks to develop, *even in the absence of real cost efficiencies*, under existing tariff structures to the public systems. Compensation payments for lost revenues to the public systems could fulfill this, as being used in Switzerland or New York. Setting these compensation payments will be difficult and we would recommend erring on the low side rather than the high side. The payments could be adjusted according to the actual experience of public/private netowrk

evolution. The critical first step is recognition that such payments are appropriate in light of current market forces.

4.      We believe there is much to be gained from sharing of private and public networks. Efficiency would seem to call for sharing of such capacity jointly (i.e., bidirectional interconnection rather than unidirectional interconnection). Capacity at different times and in different places could be traded for excess capacity on private networks. The pricing recommendations above would facilitate such trades. Achieving the potential of bidirectional interconnection will require considerable compatability between networks and resolution of difficult network problems. Regulators have a key role to play in these areas. LECs may be in the ideal positions to be clearinghouses or brokers for excess capacity.

5.      A volume discount tariff structure might effectively collect the option values associated with public network access. The first price tier would have a high charge, with declining blocks thereafter. To regular public network users this would look like a two part tariff. For occasional users, it assesses high charges, as they would pay only when they use the public network. The advantage of this approach is that only a single tariff structure needs to be offered to all customers. There would be no need to differentiate between different classes of customers. The drawback would be that such charges on *all* occasional users may be inequitable.

6.      A final alternative is to tax some other input to telecommunications services which is used regardless of which network is subscribed to--e.g., CPE. This is the approach used to fund maintenance of the highway infrastructure. The primary revenue source is gasoline taxes. These taxes are levied on fuel without regard to what type of highway is traveled.

The above changes can ameliorate some of the potential dissolution of public systems posed by existing tariff structures. They would also send from regulators that private networks will not escape regulatory oversight. Part of the advantage of private network development is currently the ability to circumvent the regulatory process. The current regulatory paradigm regulates on the basis of the service being supplied.[25] Public welfare, on the other hand, derives more from the service than from the identity of the firm supplying it.

We are less optimistic that tariffs can be designed efficiently on the basis of existing knowledge and data. For instance, even if we accept that option values are significant and should be tariffed, we know of no adequate basis on which to determine the efficient levels for such tariffs. Elimination of all cross subsidies would go a long way towards providing efficient incentives, but we wonder about the political feasibility of the result. The transition to competition is frought with such problems, and asymmetric regulation during the transition only compounds these. We can recommend the above alternatives in order to buy time and prevent some of the grossest inefficiencies that might result from current market forces. However, we are concerned that we are headed towards a system of "managed competition." This system did not work well for the airline industry and tends to result in fixed market shares. In the rapidly changing telecommunications environment, fixed market shares does not strike us as a very efficient outcome.

# REFERENCES

Bishop, R.C., "Option Value: An exposition and Extension," *Land Economics*, 58:1-15, 1982.

Crandall, R.W., "Fragmentation of the Telephone Network," in *New Directions in Telecommunications Policy: Volume 1*, edited by P.R. Newberg, Durham NC: Duke University Press, 1989.

Egan, B. and Weisman, D.L., "The U.S. Telecommunications Industry in Transition: Bypass, Regulation and the Public Interest," *Telecommunications Policy*, 10:2, pp.164-176, 1986.

Freeman, M.A., "The Sign and Size of Option Value," *Land Economics*, 60:1-13, 1984.

Freeman, M.A., "Uncertainty and Environmental Policy: The Role of Option and Quasi-option Value," in *Advances in Applied Micro-Economics, Volume 4: Risk, Uncertainty, and the Valuation of Benefits and Costs*, edited by W.K. Smith, 1986.

Goldberg, V., "Regulation and administered contracts," *The Bell Journal of Economics*, 7:426-48, 1976.

Lehman, D.E. and Weisman, D.L., "The External Costs of Bypass," Presented at the TS Cost Recovery Conference, Bellcore, Seattle, 1986.

Leyerle, B., *Moving and Shaking American Medicine: The Structure of a Socioeconomic Transformation*, Westport CT: Greenwood Press, 1984.

Mueller, M., "Interconnection Policy and Network Economics," presented at the 16th Annual Telecommunications Policy Research Conference, Airlie, Virginia, 1988.

Noam, E.M., "Network Pluralism and Regulatory Pluralism," in *New Directions in Telecommunications Policy, Volume 1*, edited by P.R. Newberg, Durham NC: Duke University Press, 1989.

Noam, E.M., "The Tragedy of the Common Network: Theory for the Formation and Breakdown of Public Telecommunications Systems," pp. 51-64 of this volume.

NTIA, *The NTIA Infrastructure Report: Telecommunications in the Age of Information*, Washington DC: U.S. Dept. of Commerce, NTIA, 1991.

OECD, "Performance Indicators For Public Telecommunications Operators," Paris: OECD, 1990.

Schmalensee, R., "Option Demand and Consumer's Surplus: Valuing Price Changes Under Uncertainty," *American Economic Review*, 62:813-24, 1972.

Sharkey, W., *The Theory of Natural Monopoly*, New York: Cambridge Univ. Press, 1982.

Smith, V.K., "Option Value: A Conceptual Review," *Southern Economic Journal*, 49:654-68, 1981.

Southwestern Bell Corporation filing before the FCC on LEC interconnection, prepared by NERA, 1991.

Temin, P., *The Fall of the Bell System: A Study in Prices and Politics*, New York: Cambridge University Press, 1987.

Weisman, D.L., "The Proliferation of Private Networks and its Implications for Regulatory Reform," *Federal Communications Law Journal*, 41, 3: 331-68, 1989.

Woroch, G.A., "The Economics of Bypass in a Simple Model of the Telephone Network," presented at the Sixth Annual Conference of the Rutgers University Advanced Workshop in Public Utility Economics and Regulation, Bolton Landing, New York, 1987.

226

## ENDNOTES

[1] The NERA analysis filed by Southwestern Bell Corporation (1991) before the FCC indicates that there are significant revenues at risk from customer connections with MAN facilities rather than local exchange facilities. The analysis shows that private networks and MANs are no longer only for large companies--regular customers can also be served by such facilities.

[2] Comments of Commissioner Eli M. Noam, New York State Public Service Commission in FCC CC Docket No. 88-2, Phase I.

[3] Noam, E.M., "The Tragedy of the Common Network: Theory for the Formation and Breakdown of Public Telecommunications Systems," pp. 51-64 of this volume.

[4] NTIA, *The NTIA Infrastructure Report: Telecommunications in the Age of Information*, Washington DC: U.S. Dept. of Commerce, NTIA, 1991.

[5] Mueller, M., "Interconnection Policy and Network Economics," presented at the 16th Annual Telecommunicatios Policy Research Conference, Airlie, Virginia, 1988.

[6] Ibid. at 25-26.

[7] Noam, E.M., "Network Pluralism and Regulatory Pluralism," *in New Directions in Telecommunications Policy, Volume 1*, edited by P.R. Newberg, Durham NC: Duke University Press, 1989.

[8] Ibid. at 91.

[9] These welfare losses are self-evident to any highway traveller in the northeastern United States. Toll highways do not interconnect easily with the free interstate highway system (this is particularly a problem with the Pennsylvania and New Jersey turnpikes). Consumers' needs often require universal coverage of both sets of highway systems. The result is that innerconnection is accomplished, but with significant additonal travel times and congestion.

[10] For application to the case of bypass of the local exchange, see Weisman (1988) or Lehman and Weisman (1986). A rather different case for inefficient bypass, depending on unsustainability of a local exchange natural monopoly due to the different cost structure of bypass, is in Woroch (1987).

[11] Bishop, R.C., "Option Value: An Exposition and Extension," *Land Economics*, 58:1-15, 1982; Freeman, M.A., "The Sign and Size of Option Value," *Land Economics*, 60:1-13, 1984; Schmalensee, R., "Option Demand and Consumer's Surplus: Valuing Price Changes Under Uncertainty," *American Economic Review*, 62:813-24, 1972; Smith, V.K., "Option Value: A conceptual Review," *Southern Economic Journal*, 49:654-68, 1981.

[12] Freeman, M.A., "Uncertainty and Environmental Policy: The role of Option and Quasi-option Value," in *Advances in Applied Micro-Economics, Volume 4: Risk, Uncertainty, and the Valuation of Benefits and Costs*, edited by W.K. Smith, 1986.

[13] We will briefly address the case of elastic demand. The first order condition for private network traffic will now include an additonal term for the change in consumer's surplus resulting from the lower usage cost. Efficiency statements are more difficult, since any move in the direction of marginal cost is welfare enhancing, and the above inefficiency results from public usage prices which exceed marginal cost. Private network development will still be "inefficient" relative to the existing tariff, but possibly not in relation to the true cost structure.

[14] Lehman and Weisman (1986) investigate the possibility that bypass systems will be inefficiently unreliable due to underpriced option values. Similar reasoning applies here.

[15] Egan and Weisman (1986) discuss this option. Temin (1987, p.315) points out that there was a Congressional debate on taxing bypassers, which almost resulted in Congressional action in 1983.

[16] A 1/91 New York Telephone "actual collocation" tariff included a "Universal Service" rate element in which certain private line service components pay an access charge designed to offset the loss of contribution. This tariff was approved by the Public Service Commission in 5/91, the first of its kind in the country (NTIA(1991)). Switzerland has a similar tariff.

[17] Sharkey, W.W., *The Theory of Natural Monopoly*, New York: Cambridge University Press, 1982.

[18] Ibid. at 23.

[19] Mueller, M., "Interconnection Policy and Network Economics," presented at the 16th Annual Telecommunicatios Policy Research Conference, Airlie, Virginia, 1988.

[20] Ibid. at 31.

[21] Noam, Eli M., "The Tragedy of the Common Network: Theory for the Formation and Breakdown of Public Telecommunications," pp. 51-64 of this volume.

[22] Leyerle, B., *Moving and Shaking American Medicine: The Structure of a Socioeconomic Transformation*, Westport CT: Greenwood Press, 1984.

[23] Crandall, R.W., "Fragmentation of the Telephone Network," in *New Directions in Telecommunications Policy: Volume 1*, edited by P.R. Newberg, Durham NC: Duke University Press, 1989.

[24] NTIA, *The NTIA Infrastructure Report: Telecommunications in the Age of Information*, Washington DC: U.S. Dept. of Commerce, NTIA, 1991.

[25] Goldberg (1976) maintains that evaluation of regulation must begin with the nature of the service, or it will result in comparing imperfect regulation with perfect market environments. The reality is that the nature of the service being regulated often requires comparisons between two imperfect systems.

PRIVATE NETWORKS PUBLIC OBJECTIVES
E. Noam and A. NíShúilleabháin (Editors)
© 1996 Elsevier Science B.V. All rights reserved.

# Public and Private Constitutions for Private Networks

Michael I. Meyerson

## 1. INTRODUCTION

Law always lags behind technology. In part, this is inevitable for a profession based on precedent, where the common law still reigns after nearly 500 years. Of course, lawyers and judges who argue and decide the issues of technology and law are also somewhat to blame, as legal education does not include basic engineering and electronics courses. The result of this legal myopia has been a frequent misunderstanding of the promise of new technology.

In 1915, for example, the Supreme Court ruled that movies were not protected by the First Amendment, but were merely, "spectacles, not to be regarded ... as part of the press of the country or as organs of public opinion."[1] Similarily, one court in 1968 held that cable television was not sufficiently "affected with a public interest" to permit local regulation.[2] The court reasoned, "The public has about as much real need for the services of a CATV system as it does for hand-carved ivory back-scratchers."[3]

In this age of high-speed computer networks, the nation's legal system again seems unprepared. The rapid growth of computer technology has left the law far behind. Computers and communications have been improving at the extraordinary rate of 25% a year for two decades.[4] Meanwhile, computing costs have been cut in half every three years since 1950.[5] What began not long ago as just another ivory back-scratcher has suddenly become an omnipresent component of commercial and household existence. Ready or not, a legal framework must, and will, be created to respond to the introduction of computer networks into the fabric of everyday life.

There are three ways in which the behavior of networks of the future might be limited. First, the United States Constitution will control those networks that are considered "governmental." Next, for those networks characterized as non-governmental, legislatures and regulatory bodies may decide to impose a wide range of requirements and responsibilities. Finally, efficiency, necessity, and fears of legal liability inevitably will lead many networks to evolve their own "constitutions," to promote the general welfare of their users.

## 2. WHAT MAKES A NETWORK "PRIVATE"?

The determination of whether networks are governed by constitutional restrictions and how they should be regulated by the government cannot be answered in the abstract. There are simply too many types of networks. As Ithiel de Sola Pool noted, "Networks, like

Russian dolls, can be nested within each other."[6] The simple network that merely links a few computers together should undoubtedly be viewed differently from the super-networks that link all the smaller and mid-level networks together.

A second complicating factor will be the degree to which a given network is "private." For purposes of this discussion, a private network will be defined as one which is restricted to authorized members, as opposed to a "public" network which will operate akin to a classic common carrier, essentially open to all. Unfortunately, this definition of "private" (as perhaps would any definition of "private") leaves open many questions as to the "private" nature of a "private" network. The three major sources of confusion concern the issues of: a) whether or not government owns or controls the network; b) whether the actions of a non-governmental private network will be deemed to be "state action"; and c) when a non-governmental private network is truly "private," in the sense of not being open to all.

### 2.1. Ownership of the Network

The Constitution draws a sharp distinction between the actions of the Government and those of the private sector. Whether the requirements of free speech, equal protection, and due process, for example, will have to be obeyed will often turn on the ownership of a facility: is it owned by a governmental entity or by non-governmental parties? The government will often be constrained by constitutional requirements that simply do not apply when the government is not involved. A public (governmental) school library, for instance, will have far less discretion regarding decisions as to which books to discard than would a private (non-governmental) school library.[7]

Not all governmental facilities, though, are treated as public fora for open discussion. Governmental entities have been permitted to close off certain communication facilities to the public. For example, a public school could limit an interschool mail system to union messages, while excluding mail from a rival union.[8] As the Supreme Court has stated, "The State, no less than a private owner of property, has power to preserve the property under its control for the use to which it is lawfully dedicated."[9] Nonetheless, the freedom of government to control its own property is not unlimited. While the federal government can decide which charities are permitted to participate in a fund-raising drive among federal workers, it may not bar a charity due to, "a bias against the viewpoint advanced by the excluded speakers..."[10] Thus, even when the government acts in a "private" capacity, it is still limited by the Constitution. Because it is not a public forum, though, speakers can be excluded on a viewpoint-neutral criteria.

It is evident, then, that a publicly-owned network can still be regarded as "private," if access to the network is limited and restricted. Such a government-owned, private network would still face the constitutional restriction against viewpoint-based discrimination, but would otherwise have generally the same discretion to control the content of speech as would a privately-owned private network. A privately-owned network, such as AT&T or New York Telephone, though, can be considered a "public network," because it is open to all potential users. Such a non-governmental public network would have the general requirement of non-discriminatory access of a common carrier. Most networks will not fit these two categories. It is these privately-owned "private networks" that pose the newest, and perhaps most difficult, questions regarding the appropriate scope of limitations, if any, that should be imposed on network owners.

## 2.2. State Action

Further complicating this question is the concept of "state action," whereby certain actions of a non-governmental party are attributable to the Government, and hence governed by Constitutional mandates. The need for a theory of "state action" is based on the fact that the Constitution was only designed to restrict governmental behavior. Private parties are covered by laws passed by Congress or by state legislatures, but the Bill of Rights and the Fourteenth Amendment only apply to Government. Thus, a mob may prevent you from giving a speech, but they have not violated your First Amendment rights. A police officer who wrongfully pulls you off a podium, however, is an agent of the city and would be guilty of violating your constitutional rights. The issue of state action looks at the relationship between the Government and a private party to see if the actions of the ostensibly private actor should be attributed to the state. For example, a non-governmental school can discriminate based on race without violating the Constitution.[11] However, if a city permits such a discriminatory school to have "exclusive" use of municipal recreational facilities, such use would "significantly enhance the attractiveness of segregated private schools," and thereby violate the equal protection clause of the Fourteenth Amendment.[12]

If a private network were held to be a "state actor," its discretion over how to deal with users would be significantly restricted. The most important constitutional provisions would likely be the First Amendment's guarantee of freedom of expression, which generally prohibits content-based censorship, the Fourteenth Amendment's guarantee of equal protection, and the Fifth and Fourteenth Amendment's protections against loss of liberty and property without due process of law.

The relationship between privately-owned networks and the government is not only quite complex, it varies for different types of networks. The High Performance Computing Act of 1991 has further interwoven the Government and private sector.[13] In the Act, Congress established a super-network, the National Research and Education Network (NREN), to provide a "test bed" for the next generation of high-speed computer networks. NREN will be built on an existing network, NSFNET, which is run by the National Science Foundation. NSFNET is also the major backbone of the Internet. While only five percent of Internet's costs are paid for out of the federal treasury, a much larger federal outlay seems dedicated to NREN. Over the first five years of its existence, federal funding is to grow to one billion dollars per year. The actual operating structure of NREN is not mandated by the law which established it. Control over NREN is centered in the Office of Science and Technology Policy, which will coordinate the involvement of many other federal agencies.[14] It is also not apparent how NREN will relate to the private sector. The law specifies that NREN not be a competitor of private enterprises but instead be "designed, developed, and operated in a manner which fosters and maintains competition and private sector investment in high-speed data networking within the telecommunications industry." On the other hand, it is not clear whether there will be any private competitors for NREN.

By definition, everything NREN does is "state action" since it is governmentally created and controlled. The status of both the users of NREN and the super-networks, if any, that duplicate NREN's services, is far from clear. A changing technical enviroment makes predictions of legal conclusions speculative for the simplest legal issue. Unfortunately, the state action doctrine is a labyrinth of competing policies and analyses. Its complexities has led one scholar to conclude, "[V]iewed doctrinally, the state action cases are a 'conceptual disaster area.'"[15] One line of cases has held that only Government coercion or encouragement of a specific private act will lead to a finding of state action: "Mere approval of or acquiescence in the initiatives of a private party is not sufficient to justify holding the State responsible for those initiatives."[16]

Thus, in 1974, the Supreme Court ruled that a private electric utility's termination of service to a customer was not state action even though the state Public Utilities Commission had approved the general tariff containing the termination procedures.[17]  The Court explained that neither the existence of "extensive and detailed" regulation nor the P.U.C.'s approval of a general tariff would turn a private utility's acts into actions of the state.  The Court noted that the PUC had never discussed the specific provision and "[T]here was no ... imprimatur placed on the practice."[18]  The Court did note that:

> It may well be that acts of a heavily regulated monopoly will more readily be found to be "state" acts than will the acts of an entity lacking these characteristics.  But the inquiry must be whether there is a sufficiently close nexus between the State and the challenged action of the regulated entity so that the action of the latter may be fairly treated as that of the State itself.[19]

In a similar vein, the Supreme Court held that a private club could discriminate against African-Americans even though it received one of only a limited number of liquor licenses from the Pennsylvania Liquor Control Board, and was subject to detailed regulation.[20] Because the discriminatory policy was not mandated by the Board, the Court held that the State's general regulation, "cannot be said to in any way foster or encourage racial discrimination.  Not can it be said to make the State in any realistic sense a partner or even a joint venturer in the club's enterprise."[21]

Even receiving heavy state funding may not be enough to turn an enterprise public.  A private school which taught special-needs students and received more than 90% of its funding from the state was permitted to fire an employee for speaking out against school policies, even though such a firing might have been unconstitutional had the employer been a public school.[22]  The Court reasoned that the school's fiscal relationship with the State should be analogized to that of independent contractors performing services for pay, and thus not result in a finding of state action.

Under the reasoning of these cases, the vast majority of non-governmental private networks using NREN would maintain their private character unless their actions were either compelled by the federal government or induced by governmental encouragement.  The amount of governmental regulation and the degree of benefit received by the private networks would not turn otherwise private decisions into state action. Such an analysis, though, may understate the unique advantage given to certain private networks by the Government.  That special benefit, combined with an intermingling of governmental and private facilities, may be enough to support a finding of state action for at least some non-governmental private networks. A series of Supreme Court cases have stressed that, even without the government mandating or coercing activity, state action will be found when an interwining between the private and public entities indicates that the government, "has elected to place its power, property and prestige" behind a challenged private act.[23]  For example, a "private" restaurant, located in a municipal building, was held to have violated the Constitution by its racially discriminatory policies.[24]  The Court's finding that the restaurant's actions were "state action" was based on a number of factors, including the facts that the land and building were publicly owned, the building was "dedicated to 'public uses' in performance of the Authority's essential governmental functions," and the restaurant was a "physically and financially integral and indeed indispensable part," of the government's plan to operate as a self-sustaining unit.[25] What was probably most unacceptable to the Court was that under the lease agreement, the city benefitted from the discrimination, such that if found that "profits earned by discrimination not only contribute to, but are indispensible elements in, the financial success of a governmental agency."[26] The Court concluded that the local government had neglected its constitutional duties by failing to limit contractually the restaurant's discriminatory practices:

> [By] its inaction, the [government] has not only made itself a party to the refusal of service, but has elected to place its power, property and prestige behind the admitted discrimination. The State has so far insinuated itself into a position of interdependence with [the restaurant] that it must be recognized as a joint participant in the challenged activity.[27]

Like the restaurant in a public building, networks using NREN will be physically (or metaphysically) intertwined. Depending on the business relationship, the Federal government might well benefit financially from the actions of the "private" network. If such a network misuses its power, by, for example, banishing critics based on the content of their speech, it could be argued that the Government is putting its power, computing and otherwise, behind the misconduct. If so, the private network's actions might be characterized as state action. A similar concern led the Court to strike down restrictive convenants which barred the sales of homes to "nonwhites."[28] Even though the covenants were contained in contracts between private parties, the Court held that judicial enforcement of those contracts would be unconstitutional. Here, the State had, "made available to [private] individuals the coercive power of government" to deny buyers, on the basis of race, their right to purchase property.[29] Thus, the Court concluded, "It is clear that but for the active intervention of the state courts, supported by the full panoply of state power, petitioners would have been free to occupy the properties in question without restraint."[30] It is noteworthy that the actual covenant did not emanate from the state, nor was there evidence that the government encouraged the discrimination. It was enough that the government was making the discrimination possible. Likewise, Justice Anthony Kennedy, writing for the Supreme Court, stated that preemptory challenges of jurors by private civil litigants were state action because of the "overt, significant assistance," of state officials in the discrimination:

> [Without] the direct and indispensible participation of the judge, who beyond all question is a state actor, the preemptory challenge system would serve no purpose. By enforcing a discriminatory preemptory challenge, the court, "has not only made itself a party to the [biased act], but has elected to place its power, property and prestige behind the [alleged] discrimination."[31]

It could be argued as well that the federal government's infrastructure is essential for the larger, more powerful networks. The super-network provides "overt, significant assistance" which will undoubtedly enable these "private" networks to become economically viable. Thus, the government may find itself a party to challenged acts of such networks, even without active encouragement.

Certain private networks might also be analogized to company towns. The Supreme Court held that even though the streets of the town were privately owned, the First Amendment permitted Jehovah's Witnesses to leaflet on those streets, because: "Whether a corporation or a municipality owns or possesses the town, the public in either case has an identical interest in the functioning of the community in such a manner that the channels of communication remain free."[32] In language that could easily be applied to private network users, the Court stated that residents of company towns:

> are free citizens of their State and country. Just as all other citizens they must make decisions which affect the welfare of community and nation. To act as good citizens they must be informed. In order to enable them to be properly informed their information must be uncensored. There is no more reason for depriving these people of the liberties guaranteed by the First and Fourteenth Amendments than there is for curtailing these freedoms with respect to any other citizens.[33]

The reach of the company town concept was severely restricted when the Court held that there was no First Amendment right to petition in private shopping centers, and distinguished the company town because, unlike the shopping center, it "had all the attributes of a state-created municipality..."[34] Nevertheless, as networks develop, courts may find that they are far more essential for meaningful communication than shopping centers. Networks might carry all forms of electronic communication and deprivation of access to a network might indeed impair people's ability to be properly informed. For smaller networks, state-action will likely not even be an issue. If such networks are fungible, so that if one network is unsatisfactory, others are available, no single network would be essential. But if a private network involves a bottleneck, whereby one or only a few entities control access, this issue will become far more significant. After a finding that a private network has, "monopoly power, via economic, physical, or economic means, or via essential facilities."[35] the courts might be far more willing to conclude that its actions are state-action. As such, the constitutional mandates in favor of freedom of expression and against censorship and discrimination would govern the largest private networks' decisions.

### 2.3. How Private is Private?

The other major source of confusion over the term "private," can be seen in the concept of a "private" club. Normally, the First Amendment permits individuals to select those persons with whom they will and will not associate.[36] For instance, one court has held that parade organizers have a constitutional right to bar others form marching in their parade, and that the Government would violate the First Amendment if it tried to force them to permit others to march.[37] On the other hand, a so-called "private" club can be prevented from discriminating in its choice of membership when it is large enough to resemble a place of public accommodation. For example, it is constitutional for the Government to outlaw discrimination based on race, creed or sex in any club with more than 400 members that provides regular meal service.[38] As Justice O'Connor has observed, while an organization devoted solely to political or religious activity may have full constitutional protection against governmental interference, "there is only minimal constitutional protection of the freedom of *commercial* association."[39]

Thus, a "private" network, without unlimited access, might still be regulable by the government if it only involves commercial association [especially if multiple firms are involved] or is so large that it loses any plausible claim of intimacy and homogeneity. In sum, the "private" nature of a "private network" will not be resolved until we know the structure of the network system that is ultimately created and the path of analysis ultimately chosen by the Supreme Court. Until then, it is to be hoped that the court will strive to find the narrow pathway that both limits governmental interference and prevents private monopolistic abuses.

### 2.3.1. Whose Speech is it Anyway?

When a network owner establishes a forum for the speech of network users, by creating bulletin boards, for example, there is frequently wrangling over who has the right to determine what speech is communicated and who is responsible for speech that falls outside the bounds of the law. Without question, no party should ever be legally responsible for speech which it had no power to prevent. The harder question comes when a network owner tries to retain the right to bar speech it finds undesireable. The legal and policy problems are exacerbated when the network owner is unwilling or, as is the case with large networks, unable, to preview and evaluate all of the speech on the network.

As an initial matter, network owners do have right to define how their networks will be used. There is no sound reason why a company should be prevented from establishing a "family" network, as long as there are other networks freely available. An abundance of different types of networks would seem to further, not deter, free expression. There is a danger of hypocrisy seeping in, however, if corporate criticism is censored as if it were another form of sexually offensive material. Confusion, if not charges of false advertising, will also await a network that leads users to view bulletin boards as open fora, without ensuring that all know that the network considers all speech as "its" speech. Ultimately, though, the issue may be decided not on the basis of public or corporate policy, but by the dictates of legal rules determining who should be held responsible for network speech.

The first judicial decision on the issue of a computer network's liability for the communication provided by its users came on October 29, 1991 in *Cubby, Inc. v. CompuServe, Inc.*[40] CompuServe is a network that provides its subscribers with access to numerous information sources which including more than 150 "forums," such as electric bulletin boards, online conferences and databases. One forum, the Journalism Forum, is operated by Cameron Communications, Incorporated (CCI). CCI had a contract with CompuServe under which CCI, "agrees to manage, review, create, delete, edit and otherwise control the content of the [Journalism Forum], in accordance with editorial and technical standards and conventions of style as established by CompuServe." CCI, in turn, has contracts with many electronic publishers, including Don Fitzpatrick Associates (DFA), which publishes *Rumorville*. DFA's contract requires it to "maintain ... files in a timely fashion," and states that, "DFA accepts total responsibility for the contents of [Rumorville]."

On more than one occasion in April, 1991, Rumorville published unflattering statements about a competing service, Skuttlebut. The owners of Skuttlebut sued for libel, business disparagement and unfair competition. What raised this from the usual legal dispute was that they not only filed these charges against the head of DFA, which produced the material, but also against CompuServe, which carried it. The key issue, according to the court, was to decide which print model should be applied to computer networks. At common law, anyone who repeated or republished defamatory information, was as guilty as the original speaker.[41] Thus, if Anne said that Bob was a thief, and Carol's newspaper printed the charge, Bob could sue Carol for repeating the allegation.

Booksellers and newsstand operators, though, are not generally characterized as "repeaters" unless they know of the defamatory content.[42] Thus, if David sells Carol's newspaper at his stand, David is immune from liability as long as he is unaware of the defamation. The reason for this exemption is obvious. To make booksellers and newsstand operators libel for everything they sell is to require them to be aware of everything they sell. As the Supreme Court has stated, "It would be altogether unreasonable to demand so near an approach to omniscience... If the contents of bookshops and periodical stands were restricted to material of which their proprietors had made an inspection, they might be depleted indeed."[43]

The court in *Cubby* ruled that CompuServe should be viewed as an electronic newsstand rather than a high-tech newspaper. The court reasoned that CompuServe, "has no more editorial control over such a publication [as Rumorville] than does a public library, bookstore or newsstand, and it would be no more feasible for CompuServe to examine every publication it carries for potentially defamatory statements than it would be for any other distributor to do so." Accordingly, even though CompuServe could refuse to carry a particular forum or publication within a forum, "in reality, once it does decide to carry a publication, it will have little or no editorial control over that publication's contents." The legal result of the newsstand analogy is that CompuServe would be liable only if it "knew or had reason to know" of the statements. Because no such knowledge could be proven or implied, CompuServe escaped liability on all counts.

Of course, if the network is not responsible for the publication, focus will shift to the party who actually created the allegedly harmful material.[44] Such a ruling serves the interest of free communication. If networks are not held legally responsible for the other speakers' material that they carry, they will not have the same incentive to seek to control and censor the communications offered on the network. The court's decision, thus, helps to reduce the problem of bottlenecks facing electronic publishers, while maintaining individual responsibility for one's own remarks. Unfortunately, network owners and users may find that the court's decision does not go far enough to protect freedom of electronic speech. The dilemma is illustrated by the crisis that confronted another network, Prodigy, a joint venture of Sears, Roebuck & Co. and IBM. Prodigy offers its more than one million subscribers access to numerous services, including over 100 electronic billboards. In mid-1991, one of the billboards began displaying vicious anti-Semitic messages, including statements that stories about the Holocaust are "a hoax," and that the concept that Jews should be exterminated, "is a good idea." The Anti-Defamation League of the B'nai B'rith (ADL) complained to Prodigy and asked them to censor the offending items. At first, Prodigy refused, citing its policy of permitting free exchange on its bulletin boards. To many, this argument was insufficient. Prodigy, after all, had previously censored statements with which it disapproved. Prodigy in fact advertised itself as a "family-oriented" service, and vowed to screen messages both electronically and with a five-person crew and remove "offensive" statements.[45] Previously, Prodigy had removed not only statements of an explicitly sexual nature, but comments criticizing Prodigy for its actions. Apparently, the censors at Prodigy felt that corporate criticism was "offensive." With this background, Prodigy's acquiescence towards hate speech could easily appear as approval. As the Chair and director of ADL commented, because Prodigy both retained the ability to delete messages which it felt were offensive and permitted the anti-Semitic tirades to continue, "[W]e concluded that Prodigy did not regard them as offensive. However, we did."[46] Finally, Prodigy relented, and announced that "offensiveness" included statements, "grossly repugnant to community standards," including, presumably, those of bigots.

The Prodigy incident reveals the weakness in the *Cubby* decision's protection of networks. As long as a network preserves for itself the power to censor, it risks being treated, both legally and in the world of public opinion, as an electronic editor who concurs with all statements on the network. Since CompuServe only avoided liability because it was ignorant of the message, it presumably would have been reasonable for any repetition of the message once a complaint had been made. Its refusal to censor a statement would then be viewed as its adoption of the statement as its own. Moreover, once the network was informed of a problematic statement somewhere in its system, it might well be said that the network had "reason to know" of the possibility of future similar statements and thus should monitor the offending speaker.

Such a ruler would pose a grave threat to the free exchange of ideas on private networks. Owners would have to evaluate every communication about which they had received a complaint. And this problem is not limited to libel. Allegations of invasion of privacy, copyright violations and even obscenity would force the network owner to use their power of censorship. Worse, the determination of what is constitutionally protected speech and what is illegal speech is a complex and usually uncertain legal decision. Risk-adverse network owners will, undoubtedly "steer far wider of the unlawful zone," in keeping out questionable speech.[47] Since the speech being silenced did not originate with the network operator, the desire to communicate one's own thoughts, which sometimes can counteract the chilling effect of restrictions on speech, will not deter network "self"-censorship.

In defending its right to censor offensive material, Prodigy has stated that it had, by "using its editorial discretion, chose not to publish these submissions and other similar material... The First Amendment protects private publishers, like the New York Times and Prodigy, from Government interference in what we publish."[48] However, any network owner will eventually realize the impossibility of trying to catch all potentially damaging speech. Prodigy not only prescreens messages, it utilizes software to catch numerous expletives and otherwise offensive words and phrases.[49] Nonetheless, in early 1993 a Prodigy bulletin-board user was sued for libel and securities fraud for publishing negative statements about a small company in which he had previously invested and lost money.[50] Prodigy was not sued by the company, but could it have been? If a court took Prodigy at its word, then the offending comments were published as a result of Prodigy's editorial discretion and, like any private publisher, Prodigy should be held accountable for abuse of that discretion. Such a finding, though, would undoubtedly mean the end of bulletin boards and other network fora in no time.

There are two solutions to this dilemma. Congress could pass a law, clarifying the rule in *Cubby*, so that a network owner would not be legally responsible for any programming it did not produce, unless it had notice of actual illegality. That is, there would be no network liability for user speech until a court had found the speech to be beyond the protection of the First Amendment. Thus, the determination of the legality of the speech would be made by an impartial court, rather than the private network, while the party who produced the speech would bear the same responsibility as if a more traditional medium has been utilized. The most obvious weakness to this proposal is that legislative action is, at best, difficult to obtain, especially where lawmakers would have to resist the call for greater censorship of unpopular speech.

It is to be hoped that wise judges will make a similar ruling in the course of deciding litigation, but until cases are decided legal uncertainty will persist. Also, networks like Prodigy that choose to retain the power to exclude messages which they find offensive, may still be in legal limbo. It will not always be easy to discern the line between producing a message, which creates legal responsibility for the speech, and mere acquiescence in speech when one has the power to, but does not, prevent it.

The alternate solution, which may require nothing more than a published policy, is for a network to forego all ability to censor communication in exchange for freedom from liability for the communications of others. One example of such a tradeoff can be seen in cases freeing broadcasters from liability for programming they are required to carry. Federal law deprives a broadcaster of all "power of censorship" over material required to be broadcast under the "equal opportunities" law.[51] The Supreme Court ruled that this requirement creates, by implication, an absolute protection for broadcasters against state-imposed liability for the material carried.[52] As one court noted in relieving a radio talk-show host of legal responsibility for statements made by an anonymous caller: "The impact of the censorship [if liability was imposed] would not fall upon the broadcaster's words and ideas; instead, it would be applied to the opinions and ideas of those members of the public who elected to participate in this kind of open forum."[53]

To avoid repeated litigation and calls for network review of all information carried on billboard statements, E-mail, video programs, and more, networks may be willing to agree to carry messages without regard to their content. Thus, these networks will be more like public parks, or at least common carriers, than like private publications. Such an arrangement might be voluntary; to avoid legal uncertainty the choice probably should be embodied in legislation. This situation would replace one editor with thousands, and multiply the electronic voices heard. To paraphrase the Supreme Court, such freedom for networks from liability would help prevent the danger of shutting off "an important outlet for the promulgation of information and ideas by persons who do not themselves [control computer networks] -- who wish to exercise their freedom of speech even though they are not members of the press."[54]

A useful, if surprising, analogy can be made between this vision of modern private networks and the role of printers in colonial America. In those days, because printing was still an art that was both expensive and not widely mastered, printers performed a vitally different function than they do today. Like many contemporary networks, printers viewed their job largely as that of preparing for mass distribution the writings of others. Printers, therefore, would publish diverse points of view, and often received criticism for their willingness to publish undesireable material. In the 1730s, Benjamin Franklin was an influential Pennsylvania printer. On June 10, 1731, after enduring complaints about the writing he had printed, Franklin wrote his own defense, entitled "An Apology for Printers." In this essay, he argued that printers should be not be treated as proponents of all that they publish:

Printers are educated in the Belief, that when Men differ in Opinion, noth sides ought equally to have the advantage of being heard by the Publik; and that when Truth and

Error have fair Play, the former is always an overmatch for the latter: Hence they cheerfully serve all contending writers that pay them well, without regard on which side they are of the Question in Dispute....

Being thus continually emloy'd in serving both Parties, Printers naturally acquire a vast Unconcernedness as to the right or wrong Opinions contain'd in what they print; regarding it only as their daily lobor: They pring things full of Spleen and Animosity, with the utmost Calmness and Indifference, and without the least Ill-will to the Persons reflected on: who nevertheless unjustly think the Printer as much their Enemy as the Author...[55]

Franklin continued that printers should not be regarded as approving that which they printed, and then warned of the consequences of condemning printers for the work of the writers:

It is ... unreasonable what some assert, "That Printers ought not to print any Thing but what they approve;" since if all of that Business should make such a Resolution, and abide by it, and End would thereby be put to Free Writing, and the World would afterwards have nothing to read but what happen'd to be the Opinion of Printers...[56]

It would even more unreasonable for networks, carrying millions of messages, to carry only those they approve. If such a situation occurred, "an End would thereby be put to Free Electronic Communcation and the World would afterwards have nothing to read but what happen'd to be the Opinion of the Networks."

## 3. VIRTUAL CONSTITUTIONS

To a nation, a constitution serves many different functions. On its most practical level, a constitution describes the ways in which those in political control may exercise their power. Next, a constitution can provide the framework for the rights of the individuals living within the country. Ultimately, though, a constitution defines the very character of a nation, telling what sort of country it wants to be, and is likely to become. In many ways, constitutions for computer networks will operate in the same way. They will delineate the decision-making functions, outline the rights of users of the network, and both reflect and create a vision of what type of society we want within, and without, the universe of the network.

Assuming requirements are not imposed either by the courts or by the federal and local government, networks will need to create their own. Because of the variety of private networks, it is impossible to create any one-size-fits-all document. Certain fundamental principles can be ascertained, however, based on the current state of and future plans for private networks, coupled with a look back at the basic principles of a free society. One of the more overlooked aspects in current discussions of broadband networks is that a new technology does not always require new rules. Just as it is an invasion of privacy to read someone's mail delivered by the Post Office, it is an invasion of privacy to read their E-mail without permission. Just as a fast-food restaurant can prevent employees from receiving personal phone calls at work, an employer can keep employees from using a company network for personal affairs. Thus, some of the questions involving the next generation of private networks were answered long before there was a Silicon Valley. If a network is small

-- for example, an entirely in-house operation -- there seems to be no logical reason why the network should be viewed any differently from traditional workplace equipment. If an employer wants to limit the access of certain employees to parts of the network, he or she should be able to do so. Newsday, concerned that its reporters were using too much company time on E-mail, decided to alter its computer software to keep reporters from sending E-mail messages. Reporters were only able to receive messages, but their editors continued to have the ability to send E-mail if they so chose.[57] This may be a demeaning way to treat one's staff, but restricting reporters in this fashion is not analytically dissimilar from issuing a memo telling staff not to use copiers for personal items. What may require new thinking is what happens when technology poses new risks, or creates novel opportunities. For example, if an ever-increasing amount of personal information is carried over networks, the threat to personal privacy also increases. Moreover, if it is easier to tap into a computerized database than into the files inside a doctor's office, greater precautions are needed.

Networks must ensure privacy. All who use any network must be effectively informed as to the ability of others to learn of their communication. Any contractual agreement permitting a network owner, or other, to gather or disseminate personal information must be a knowing waiver. No "negative option," whereby a user waives privacy protection without affirmatively requesting it, should be permitted. As a matter of general principle, users should not be charged extra for routine privacy protection.[58] For those networks that include numerous participants, privacy must be guaranteed even further. Absent a significant threat to the network's viability or purpose, the right to send a message privately must be preserved. Encryption should be permitted. Each disseminator of information should have the right and ability to control who receives the messages. One area where individual autonomy may conflict with the public interest involves anticompetitive behavior. The desire to enhance one's own economic standing at the expense of one's competitors may lead to inappropriate, if not illegal, use of the private network. The danger of anticompetitive behavior increases, as does the likelihood of antitrust law violation, where multiple large firms use a network to the exclusion or detriment of their competitors. The antitrust laws view joint anticompetitive activity far more critically than unilateral anticompetitive action. The Supreme Court has held that concerted conduct violates the law if it merely restrains trade, while individual firm conduct is illegal only if it threatens monopolization.[59] In other words, an "unreasonable" restraint of trade may be permissible if imposed by a single firm, but not by two firms acting jointly.

In one of the first cases involving computer networks, airline computer reservation systems (CRS) were held not to violate the antitrust laws.[60] In this case, American Airlines and United Airlines had each created their own CRS (SABRE for American and Apollo for United), and, pursuant to federal regulation, charged competing airlines who used the CRS the same fee for any of their flights booked through the system.[61] The court found the arrangement legal because the CRS neither eliminated nor threatened to eliminate competition in air transport market. Moreover, each CRS was not treated as an "essential facility" because it was created by a single firm: "A facility that is controlled by a single firm will be considered 'essential' only if control of the facility carries with it the power to eliminate competition in the downstream market."[62] Such unilateral power is not often found. Only in extreme cases, such as the only local producer of electrical power refusing to sell to wholesalers in order to eliminate competition in the retail market, will there be the ability to eliminate competition.[63]

In the early 1980s, AT&T was found to have misused its control over an essential facility by refusing to allow MCI to interconnect with its local distribution facilities.[64] The court described four factors that determine if there is an antitrust violation by the unilateral owner of an "essential facility":

- It is controlled by a monopolist
- There is a practical inability to duplicate facilities
- The use of the facility to a competitor has been denied
- It would be feasible to permit use of the facility[65]

Another court has stated that a finding of "essential facility" requires a showing that "severe hardship" will result if the competitor is denied access.[66] In sum, one should only expect to find unilaterally-owned "essential facilities" if there is a showing that they involve, "natural monopolies, facilities whose duplication is forbidden by law, and perhaps those that are publicly subsidized and thus could not practicably be built privately."[67]

Certain of the larger networks, backbones or mid-level, may qualify as "essential facilities." This determination is always a case-by-case analysis, and courts will examine the practical reality as well as the theoretical possibility of constructing a competing network. As one court stated, just because Proctor & Gamble can bypass the local telephone loop, it hardly means that residential consumers have the same ability.[68] Any private network operated by more than one competitor will face the risk of numerous antitrust violations. The risks are high. If there are networks controlled by a few large players in an industry, anti-competitive network decisions may make the network owners liable for treble damages. Any action that is unjustifiable except as an attempt to harm competition, may be considered an "unreasonable" restraint of trade. If, for example, several banks combined to create a network for the purpose of clearing checks, any exclusion of competing banks might subject the network owners to liability. Similarly, rules that disadvantage disfavored competitors would also be suspect.

In terms of procedures, traditional constitutional notions of Due Process would not be applied (absent a finding of state action). Nonetheless, fundamental fairness in how the network treats its users would be necessary to prove "reasonableness." Procedures for resolving network disputes should be agreed upon, and made known to all users. Moreover, all similarly situated users must be treated equally. Before a small competitor is kicked off a network, the owners should be able to establish that a clearly enunciated, well-publicized rule was violated, that the offender was given a chance to explain its side of the story, and that similar previous violations have been similarly punished. By contrast, if a single bank creates such a network, it would have far greater leeway in how it treats its competitors. Unless it could meet the strict standards for "essential facilities," with the key inquiry being whether competitors could reasonably create a similar network, everything short of an attempt to monopolize would be permitted. On the other hand, blatantly anti-competitive action, especially if coupled with benign treatment of other competitors, might reduce the court's tolerance for unilateral action.

In the best of all worlds, the private constitutions of private networks will be created for the betterment of all the network users and will be decided well in advance of any crisis. Unfortunately, some private network owners will chose to assume that there is no need to make these decisions ahead of time, and that their discretion will be forever unlimited. But, like those who die without seeing the need to write a will, these network owners may find that decisions ultimately are made by a judge, and that the final dispositions are far from those that would have been preferred.

## ENDNOTES

[1.]*Mutual Films Corp. v. Industrial Commission of Ohio*, 236 U.S. 239, 245 (1915). This decision was not overturned until the middle of the century. *Burstyn v. Wilson*, 343 U.S. 493 (1952).

[2.]*Greater Fremont, Inc. v. City of Fremont*, 302 F.Supp. 652, (N.D.Ohio 1968), *aff'd sub nom, Wonderland Ventures, Inc. v. City of Sandusky*, 423 F.2d 548 (6th Cir. 1970).

[3.]*Greater Fremont, Inc.*, 302 F.Supp. at 665.

[4.]Dertouzous, "Communications, Computers, and Networks," *Scientific American*, September, 1991, at 63.

[5.]Tesler, "Networked Computing in the 1990's," *Scientific American*, September, 1991, at 88.

[6.]Pool, I. de Sola, *Technologies of Freedom*, Cambridge MA: Belknap Press, 1983, p. 199.

[7.]See *Board of Education, Island Trees Union Free School District v. Pico*, 457 U.S. 853 (1982)(holding that the First Amendment limits the discretion of a public school board to remove books from a school library).

[8.]*Perry Educators' Association v. Perry Local Educators' Association*, 460 U.S. 37 (1983).

[9.]*Adderly v. Florida*, 385 U.S. 39, 47 (1966).

[10.]*Cornelius v. NAACP Legal Defence & Educational Fund*, 473 U.S. 788, 812 (1985).

[11.]Such a private school may still be subject to statutory and regulatory limitations. *Cf. Bob Jones University v. U.S.*, 462 U.S. 574 (1983) (upholding I.R.S. denial of tax-exempt status to discriminatory private schools.)

[12.]*Gilmore v. City of Montgomery*, 417 U.S. 556, 569 (1974).

[13.]For an excellent summary of the Act, see "Information Superhighway Bill Sketches Outlines of Ubiquitous Computer Network," *supra* note 7.

[14.]Other agencies include the Department of Defense, the National Science Foundation, the National Aeronautics and Space Administration, the Enviromental Protection Agency, the Departments of Education and Energy, and the National Institute of Science and Technology.

[15.]L. Tribe, *American Constitutional Law*, at 1690 (2nd Ed., 1988) (quoting Black, "The Supreme Court, 1966 Term--Forward: 'State Action,' Equal Protection, and California's Proposition 14," 81 Harv. L. Rev. 69, 95 (1967)).

[16.]*Blum v. Yaresky*, 457 US. 991, 1004-05 (1982).

[17.]*Jackson v. Metropolitan Edison Co.*, 419 U.S. 345 (1974).

[18.] Id. at 356.

[19.] Id. at 350-51.

[20.] *Moose Lodge No. 107 v. Irvis*, 407 U.S. 163 (1972).

[21.] Id. at 176-177. The Court faced a somewhat similar inquiry in trying to determine whether broadcast licensees were state actors. There was no majority opinion but Chief Justice Burger wrote for a three-Justice plurality that a finding of state action would destroy broadcast journalism:
> [I]t would be anomalous for us to hold, in the name of promoting the constitutional guarantees of free expression, that the day-to-day editorial decisions of broadcast licensees are subject to the kind of restraints urged by respondents... Journalistic discretion would in many ways be lost to the rigid limitations that the First Amendment imposes on Government. Application of such standards to broadcast licensees would be antiethical to the very ideal of vigorous, challenging debate on issues of public interest."

CBS v. DNC, 412 U.S. 94, 120-21 (1973)(Burger, C.J., plurality). In the case of a common carrier, such as the post office, cable television as a provider of public and leased access, or computer networks, such constitutional standards would actually encourage free debate by enabling more to speak.

[22.] *Rendell-Baker v. Kohn*, 457 U.S. 830 (1982).

[23.] e.g., *Edmonson v. Leesville Concrete Co.*, 111 S.Ct. 2077 (1991)(holding use of preemptory challenge by private civil litigant to exclude jurors based on race was state action).

[24.] *Burton v. Wilmington Parking Authority*, 365 U.S. 715 (1961).

[25.] Id. at 723-24.

[26.] Id. at 724.

[27.] Id. at 725.

[28.] *Shelley v. Kraemer*, 334 U.S. 1 (1948).

[29.] Id. at 19.

[30.] Id. at.

[31.] *Edmonson v. Leesville Concrete Co.*, 111 S.Ct. 2077, ---- (1991).

[32.] *Marsh v. Alabama*, 326 U.S. 501 (1946).

[33.] Id. at 508.

[34.] *Lloyd Corp. v. Tanner*, 407 U.S. 551 (1972). See also *Hudgens v. NLRB*, 424 U.S. 507 (1976).

[35.] Hammond, "Regulating Broadband Communications Networks," 8 *Yale Journal on Regulation* 181, 234 (1981).

[36.] See e.g., *Board of Directors of Rotary Int'l v. Rotary Club of Duarte*, 481 U.S. 537, 548 (1987) (describing the "right to associate with others in pursuit of a wide variety of political, social, economic, educational, religious and cultural ends...").

244

[37.]See *N.Y. County Bd. of Ancient Order of Hibernians v. Dinkins*, 814 F. Supp. 358 (S.D.N.Y.1993) (permitting the long-standing sponsor of the St. Patrick's Day parade to exclude the Irish Lesbian and Gay Organization).

[38.]*N.Y.S. Club Assoc., Inc. v. City of New York*, 487 U.S. 1 (1988).

[39.]*Roberts v. U.S. Jaycees*, 468 U.S. 609, 634 (1984)(O'Connor, J., concluding)(emphasis added).

[40.]*Cubby, Inc. v. CompuServe, Inc.*, 1991 U.S.Dist. LEXIS 15545 (S.D.N.Y. 1991).

[41.]Restatement (Second) of Torts, sec. 578 (1977).

[42.]eg. *Lerman v. Chuckleberry Publishing, Inc.*, 521 F.Supp. 228 (S.D.N.Y. 1981).

[43.]*Smith v. California*, 361 U.S. 147, 153 (1959).

[44.]As of this date, there has been no resolution on the merits of Skuttlebut's charges against Rumorville.

[45.]Feder, "Toward Defining Free Speech in the Computer Age," *The New York Times*, Nov. 3, 1991 at E.5.

[46.]Salberg & Foxman, Letter to the Editor, *New York Times*, Nov. 15, 1991, at A30.

[47.]*New York Times, Co. v. Sullivan*, 376 U.S. 254, 275 (1964).

[48.]Moore, "The First Amendment is Safe at Prodigy," *The New York Times*, December 16, 1990, at Sec. 3., p.3.

[49.]Sugawara, "Computer Networks and the 1st Amendment," *The Washington Post*, October 16, 1991 at A12.

[50.]Harmon, "New Legal Frontier," *Los Angeles Times*, March 19, 1993, at A.1.

[51.]47 U.S.C. 315 (a) states that if a broadcast licensee permits a candidate for public office to use the station, equal opportunities to use the station must be made available to all competing candidates.

[52.]*Farmers Education & Cooperative Union v. WDAY, Inc.*, 360 U.S. 525 (1959).

[53.]*Adams v. Frontier Broadcasting Co.*, 555 P.2d 556, 567 (Wyo. 1976).

[54.]*New York Times Co. v. Sullivan*, 367 U.S. 254, 266 (1964).

[55.]"An Apology for Printers," *The Pennsylvania Gazette* (June 10, 1731), reprinted in L. Levy, *Freedom of the Press from Zenger to Jefferson*, at 4-5 (1966). Franklin, never one to hold himself to too high a standard, freely admitted that he had often refused to print material that would, "countenance Vice, or promote Immorality... [or] as might do real Injury to any Person..." Id.

[56.]Id.

[57.]Sproull & Kiesler, "Computers, Networks and Work," *Scientific American*, September, 1991 (p116).

[58.]"Untitled Article," *Common Carrier Week* (August 10, 1992) (discussing testimony of Marc Rotenberg, head of Computer Professionals for Social Responsibility at a forum conducted by the National Commission on Libraries and Information Science).

[59.]*Copperweld Corp. v. Independence Tube Corp.*, 467 U.S. 752, 774-77 (1984). In particular the section 1 of the Sherman Antitrust Act bars combinations in "restraint of trade," 15 U.S.C. 1, while section 2 prohibits any "attempt to monopolize." 15 U.S.C. 2.

[60.]*Alaska Airlines, Inc. v. United Airlines, Inc.*, 948 F.2d 536 (9th Cir. 1991), *aff'g sub nom In re Air Passenger Computer Reservation Systems Antitrust Litigation*, 694 F.Supp. 1443 (C.D. Cal. 1988).

[61.]14 C.F.R. 255.5(a). The Department of Transportation requires each CRS owner to charge its airline customers a uniform rate. In 1991, American Airlines charged $1.75 per booking.

[62.]948 F.2d at 544.

[63.]*Otter Tail Power Co. v. US*, 410 US 366, 377-79 (1973).

[64.]*MCI Communications Corp. v. AT&T*, 708 F.2d 1081, 1132-33 (7th Cir. 1983).

[65.]Id.

[66.]*Twin Laboratories, Inc. v. Weider Health & Fitness*, 900 F.2d 566, 569-70 (2nd Cir. 1990) (magazine not essential for sale of nutritional supplements).

[67.]900 F.2d at 569, quoting P. Areeda & H. Hovenkamp, *Antitrust Law* 680-81 (1988 Supp.).

[68.]*California v. FCC*, 905 F.2d 1217, 1234 (9th Cir. 1990).

PRIVATE NETWORKS PUBLIC OBJECTIVES
E. Noam and A. NíShúilleabháin (Editors)
© 1996 Elsevier Science B.V. All rights reserved.

Private Networks, Public Speech: Constitutional Speech Dimensions of Access to Private Networks

by Prof. Allen S. Hammond, IV

## 1. INTRODUCTION

The current multiple network environment -- broadcast, cable television, telephone, and computer networks -- in the United States is undergoing significant change. Network functions and the information they carry are merging as converging fiber optic, telephone, and computer technologies allow the integration of video, voice, and data information.[1] This integration has created opportunities for expanded access and speech activities in the workplace, the marketplace, and the home.

Regulatory distinctions between video distribution and public switched networks are disintegrating as the government increasingly allows inter-industry competition in the nation's video distribution, long distance, and local telephone markets.[2] Meanwhile, network video, voice, and data services are increasingly provided by private as opposed to public networks. The movement from public to private networks can be seen in two recent developments. For instance, in video distribution, the emergence of cable television represents a shift from "public/free" over the air broadcast television to "private/subscriber" driven cable television services. In telephony, public common carriers have begun to lose market share as large corporations and other sophisticated users demand more specialized services that private carriers are able to provide more efficiently. This is because private carriers have no obligation to serve the less profitable segments of the public. Thus network technology applications which facilitated broad public access to information and/or interactive speech are giving way to specialized private networks which may limit access based on market demand and profit maximization.

The shift in market reality has been mirrored by a shift in government policy regarding future networks. For example, the government is increasingly relying on private market driven investment to fund the building of the future broadband electronic super-highway. The Clinton Administration has made clear that they have resolved the question of who will build the electronic highways in favor of private industry.[3]

Administration reliance on private sector investment and privatization of network infrastructure is a pragmatic policy developed in a time of decreasing public revenues. However, sole reliance on pro competition policies will not adequately protect the individual and group speech and related activities potentially fostered by broadband intelligent networks or existing telecommunications networks. In the process of managing market entry and firm competition, current US competition policies run the risk of ceding creation and control of speech activities to private firms. This is particularly true to the extent the First Amendment is read as a negative bar to government action rather than an affirmative protection for speech activities.

Pro-competitive privatization policies do not directly address the need for preserving and expanding network access and electronic speech activities as an appropriate pro-social goal of American democracy because the policies possess no incentive structure to assure broad public access to the network. Under such policies, the provision of access [and subsequent speech "rights"] is a function of market demand for access and services which is, in turn, a function of the economic distribution of wealth and the network provider's perception of a market's desirability. Lack of wealth or lack of perceived desirability results in decisions to eschew deployment of infrastructure or the provision of services. The net result of such decisions in a broadband interactive network context is to deny access and speech opportunities.

The universal access and service debate addresses public policy concerns about how society may blunt the negative impact of pro-competitive network development policies on the economically disadvantaged. However, even this debate fails to address the impact of the provider's perceptions and assumptions about a potential market's or a potential user's desirability.

Because pro-competitive policies do not address the above-mentioned concerns, reliance on such policies creates a significant risk of losing opportunities for electronic speech and its related activities which might accrue to significant portions of American society. Consequently the definition, preservation, and expansion of electronic speech and its related activities must be elevated to a priority policy goal and incorporated within the broader policy framework of the government's network infrastructure policies.

At least one state has recognized the importance of elevating electronic speech policies to co-equal status with pro-competition policies. New York has recently published a document developed by the Governor's Telecommunications Exchange. The document, entitled "Connecting to the Future," identifies numerous policies which it is suggested the state pursue in acquiring the economic benefits of an advanced telecommunications infrastructure. Among the key recommendations is reliance on a competitive market to ensure greater consumer choice and higher quality service. However, unlike the federal government's NII report, the New York report acknowledges that the state retains an obligation to ensure a free flow of information and ideas accessible to all.[4]

As the movement from public to private provision of network services occurs, one of the critical questions for First Amendment theorists and scholars concerned with mass media and telecommunications is what access and speech rights will network owners and users have after the convergence and privatizing of the mass media and telecommunications networks?[5]

The growing reliance on network services provided by private as opposed to public common carriers, poses potential dangers to access and broad based speech opportunities. Privatizing the delivery of network services can lead to the concentration of control over access and content in the hands of private network owners. Because of the historic tendency to equate speech rights with ownership of the means of transmission, privatizing the merging of technology, network function and information streams could transfer control over access and speech activities from the current shared public/private constitutional arrangement to a private/contractual arrangements.[6]

Inherent in the status of ownership, is an underlying bundle of property rights which include control over who may have access to the network owners' facilities and/or services.

These rights are often referred to as rights to create, publish and/or distribute information. While the degree of control over access varies with the type of owner, ultimately, as long as ownership includes the right to decide access, some segment of potential users are likely to be excluded for a variety of oft-times unrelated reasons ranging from particular pricing or service configurations, to equipment requirements, information format, capacity needs, or discrimination based on economic or normative value considerations regarding identity of speaker or content of speech. This is so because private network providers may opt to act as publishers or distributors of information instead of carriers.

Such a result could be detrimental to the potential speech and access opportunities of existing and future network users of video, voice, and data network information services.[7] Private owners may not be motivated by public interest considerations of access and inclusion. Instead, where a private corporation is using an internal network, its major motivation to provide access and speech to their employees is utilitarian. A private network owner's major motivation to serve a particular individual or group of customers depends (in the most ideal sense) upon the desirability of that individual or market as a customer base and their ability to pay. Because these decisions about who to serve, what is said, and to whom, are private, there is arguably less opportunity to rest the justification for access and speech rights upon constitutional grounds given the alleged absence of state action.[8]

For instance, government regulation of broadcasting has not been deemed sufficient justification for finding that the editorial decisions of broadcasters constitute state action.[9] Recently, several circuit courts have held that decisions by regulated telephone companies to deny access or billing services to information providers of indecent communication do not constitute state action.[10] The weight of precedent would tend to support a conclusion that actions to deny access or speech conducted by regulated cable operators and telephone companies are constitutionally permissible, although they would be constitutionally proscribed if conducted by the government.[11]

Under such circumstances it is reasonable to ask, will privatizing the merged multi-function, multi-media networks result in speech rights only for network owners and those they employ or decide to serve? Who will serve people who own no network or are not selected as desirable markets? In an era of privatized carriage in the provision of network services, what ability will the government have to assure access and speech rights for the non-facilities based public?

This article begins the process of answering these questions. It defines private networks and closed user groups in relation to public networks and examines the current practices by which the owners of networks limit the access and speech activities of employees as well as potential and actual customers and subscribers on their networks. It then identifies and addresses some of the potential constitutional questions raised by such practices. In the process it identifies the current boundaries of the network access and speech continuum in the United States and addresses how these boundaries may change in light of evolving technology and government policy.[12]

The article concludes that a pragmatic balance must be struck between the speech rights of network owner providers and network users. In the area of employee access and speech rights, a three-way balance must be struck between the network owners' legitimate business needs; the employees' access, speech and privacy rights; and public policy concerns including the public's right to know. Ultimately, employee speech rights should not turn on whether they are employed by public or private firms. Rather, at minimum, employee speech "rights should encompass concerns regarding wages and working conditions, as well as safety and product quality issues about which the public may have interest.[13]

In the broader area of network access and service provision, the article concludes that current government efforts to rely on network privatization to assure the development and deployment of network infrastructure and services are problematic. This reliance, when combined with legislative and judicial decisions expanding network provider control over access and speech activities, may result in the loss of significant access and speech opportunities for network users and subscribers.

The government should acknowledge and protect the access and speech rights of network providers. There are a host of legitimate reasons why a network owner would deny access or speech to potential network users. However, the government also must act to ensure access and speech rights for potential public and private network users, whether they are subscribers or employees.

In addition, the government should use pro-active policies to discourage censorship by network owners. Network owners should have the right to speak but not the sole right to speak. Network owners should have obligations and incentives to be as inclusive and accessible as possible in what they carry and who they serve.

One way to accomplish these goals is to remove some of the liability network owners face for the speech of network users and subscribers. Network owners should be free to select the extent to which they will exercise editorial control without government requirement. Absent the assertion of editorial control by the network provider, responsibility and liability for speech should reside with the speaker.

Another way to encourage access and broad speech is to require interconnection among public and private networks. This gives all network users more potential access to a broader array of services and information, as well as to each other. As a result, the infrastructure does not serve to fragment the national polity or its discourse. Instead, it can be used as a positive tool for achieving an inclusive national and international dialogue.

Finally, incentives to insure universal access and services are needed. These incentives would include subsidies targeted to those subscribers who might not otherwise acquire access or needed services. They would also include active use of the anti-trust laws and structural safeguard policies such as open network architecture.

## 2. NETWORKS AND CLOSED USER GROUPS DEFINED

### 2.1. General Characteristics

In their most basic manifestation, networks are collections of interconnected users.[14] They can be defined in terms numerous characteristics, including: a.) technology [spectrum, wire, fiber]; b.) information [video, voice, data]; c.) ownership [private or public]; d.) control of content [editor, hybrid, common carrier]; and e.) control of network access and/or functionality. This article will discuss them primarily in terms of ownership of facilities, control of network access and/or functionality, and, ultimately, control of content. In the process, it will acknowledge the various characteristics as they apply in addressing the impact of owner control on the user subscriber and third parties.

## 2.2. The Network Lexicon

### 2.2.1. Public Switched Network: "Open Network"
The commercial common carrier network owners own the network facilities and retain control of all levels of network functionality.[15] There are no predetermined limits to who may or may not join the network. All who timely pay the subscription fee [tariff rate for the particular class and volume of service] may gain access and enjoy usage.[16] Because the network is available to virtually all potential users,[17] it may be defined as being "open.[18]" These networks are the long distance, regional, and local public switched networks.

### 2.2.2. Virtual Private Networks
In contrast to the public switched networks, virtual private networks (VANS), offer their customers access to reserved private line capacity on the public switched telephone network (PSTN).[19] VPN is essentially a long-distance service in the USA. In the case of VANS, the user manages network applications while the carrier manages all other levels of network functionality.[20] It is anticipated that by 1997, VPN services will account for 17 percent of the domestic service revenues of the three biggest US long-distance carriers -- AT&T, MCI, and Sprint.[21]

### 2.2.3. Private Networks
In the case of private networks, all telecommunications facilities are owned by an entity other than a government certified commercial common carrier, or, the user leases dedicated lines from certified carriers but maintains control over both ends of the communications channel. In the case of the latter, the user typically owns facilities on its premises [local area networks or private branch exchanges i.e. "intra-building private networks"] and leases from carriers anything that crosses public rights of way. For example, the company may lease a dedicated T-1 between two privately owned private branch exchanges (PBXs). Network usage is confined to the owner and its affiliates and is not usually shared or aggregated on a commercial basis.[22]

### 2.2.4. Closed User Groups
A private network may be open or closed. However, most closed user group networks are based on privately owned or dedicated facilities. Thus most closed user group networks are private.[23] Closed user groups are large volume users which tend to communicate with each other "intensely." They combine to form alternative network associations for much of their communications needs. Associations' networks may have specialized performance attributes related to group needs.[24]

### 2.2.5. Hybrid Networks
A large number of U.S. users have now opted for hybrid networks combining leased lines between particular locations with VANS. Users prefer to use private networks for sensitive business information (in the form of encrypted data) because these are considered more secure and upon occasion, cheaper than VANS.

### 2.2.6. Other Networks Distinguished

The preceding definitions are admittedly limited to switched telecommunications networks in some way related to the public switched networks. In contrast, video distribution networks include traditional broadcasting and cable television networks, which are non switched -- essentially one way distribution media which are not usually interactive.

### 2.3. Convergence and Metamorphosis: From Cable and Telephony to Broadband Networks.

However, it is argued that cable networks and local telephone networks likely will evolve into the switched broadband interactive networks of the near future.[25]   Should this be true, the resulting networks could span the gamut from private networks, virtual private networks, and hybrid networks, to public (common carrier) networks, and they could incorporate a potential range of access options from non-discriminatory access[26], mandated leased and/or tariffed access,[27] free access,[28] to private access by negotiated contract or ownership.  Speech options could range from owner control of a portion of available capacity with unrestricted user speech on the remaining portion, to owner control of all capacity and ultimately all speech allowed on the network.  This spectrum of alternative access and speech relationships is, in essence, the amalgam of access and speech relationships currently residing on cable (mandated leased or free access) and telecommunications (non discriminatory and negotiated contract access) networks.

In this context, litigation challenging the must-carry rules of the Cable Competition and Consumer Protection Act of 1992, and the telco-cable cross-ownership prohibition of the Cable Communication Policy Act of 1984, as well as several e-mail and electronic bulletin board service cases percolating through the judicial system, may establish much of the scope of access and speech rights network owners, providers, and users will have.[29]

### 3. THE CURRENT SCOPE OF NETWORK AND USER GROUP ACCESS AND SPEECH RESTRICTIONS

There are at least four levels at which a network owner or closed user group may control access and/or speech activities on their facilities.  Control may be exercised over actual speech or communication (content), over access to the network as configured by the owner (network access), over the ability to reconfigure network functionality (network software intelligence), and over the ability to set equipment standards for network provisioning and interfacing with the network (equipment standards and network protocols).  Current government policies affect the exercise of access and speech at each of the first three levels.

Legal sanction of the exercise of control varies depending upon the manner in which the network is used.  Where the network is merely one of many tools or assets used by a firm to conduct its business, the "network owner" enjoys wide latitude over each of the four levels.  Where the network and its related functions and services are the product the private or public firm sells to customers, the network owner's ability to control access has been subject to greater government restraint, depending on architecture, market power and traditional rights accorded networks having similar technologies and functions.

### 3.1. Owner Imposed Limitations on Access

### 3.1.1.Subscriber/User Initiated Access to Third Party Users and Networks

#### 3.1.1.1. Network Owner/Employer Restrictions on Outgoing Calls

Employers may be subscribers to the public switched networks, virtual private network subscribers, owners of their own networks or a collection or association of users forming a closed user group. They may be private or public firms. In any event, because of the utility of long distance and electronic mail (e-mail), as well as the growth in availability of 800 and 900 number services, employers often find it necessary to block access to certain networks and phone services to limit corporate expenses. Call blocking, for instance, is used to limit employee access to the above-mentioned services.[30] In the process, employees are denied access to the networks over which such services are provided, and to the information providers residing at the other end of the line. Federal and municipal government call blocking restrictions on access to dial-a-porn and long distance calls are well known examples.[31] Employers also engage in call monitoring as a means of policing their restrictions on network usage.[32]

Employers' justifications for engaging in these practices include the need to manage or reduce costs or fraud involved in unauthorized 900 number and e-mail calls which have cost companies hundreds of thousands of dollars. In addition some companies use computers to monitor customer service employees' performance, such as keystrokes per minute, time between phone calls, length of breaks, and number of errors.[33]

There are potential dangers inherent in call blocking and monitoring which raise significant public policy issues. Call blocking has been argued to implicate first amendment concerns because the employer's limitations on access to the network and hence on those an employee might contact, constitute limitations on potential speech activities in which the employee might otherwise engage. Call monitoring is said to raise issues of worker privacy, as the employee's expectation of privacy is infringed by periodic monitoring.[34] Call blocking and monitoring activities raise nettlesome problems for the public's "right-to-know" as well. For these practices may also be used to detect whistle blowers instead of individuals calling dial-a-porn providers and other unauthorized users.[35]

Some observers argue that employer/network owner control of access or usage of the corporate telephone or network affects employee's constitutional speech and/or privacy rights.[36] Such arguments have met with only limited success to date. The speech activities upon which the articulation of "new" employee rights are based nevertheless occur within the traditional confines of the work place, conducted over technologies which are owned and/or paid for by the employer. Even though e-mail and intelligent network technologies provide new opportunities for speech activities, the articulation of these activities as rights squarely pits them against the heretofore established and legally recognized property rights of the employer/network owner.

#### 3.1.1.2. Third Party Access to Private Network or VPN Facilities

Firms also attempt to limit third party access to their networks to protect against toll fraud.[37] Computerized telephone equipment such as voice mail, often help companies conduct business with greater efficiency and lower cost. However, they also often provide access to electronic thieves who steal thousands of dollars of long-distance telephone service.

Unauthorized entry can be accomplished by calling a company's toll-free 800 number or a voice mailbox and using a computer with an automatic dialer to break the security code and gain access to the company's telephone system and outgoing lines.[38] Electronic bulletin boards are sometimes used to exchange generic passwords which provide access company to maintenance ports; exchange programming instructions for various systems; or procure programming manuals for voice systems enabling unauthorized parties to gain operational control, including the ability to unblock restrictions on international dialing and turn off on-site call accounting equipment.[39] According to some experts, computer hacking, may cost U.S. companies between $ 2.2 billion and $ 4 billion nationally.[40]

In a less arcane realm, e-mail, voice-mail, and telephony systems may be used by union organizers, law enforcement authorities, friends, or family members to communicate with employees. However, efforts of union organizers to make use of the employer owned telecommunications systems and/or networks to communicate with employees under section 7 of the National Labor Relations Act (NLRA),[41] may prove unsuccessful. As a practical matter, recent precedent supports the employer's right to bar union access absent a showing that the union possesses no other reasonable means of communicating its organizational message to employees.[42]

### 3.1.1.3. Restriction on Membership in Closed User Groups: Control of the Jointly Owned Network Asset

Some firms cooperate to develop jointly owned networks (JONs). JONs can increase the efficiency and competitiveness of their owners.[43] In the process, JONs can adversely affect the relative market position of non-owners by creating new barriers to market entry and exit which are often controlled by the JON owners.[44] JON owners can raise barriers to network (and often, market) access for competitors by establishing, maintaining, and changing the network's pricing structure as well as applications, standards, protocols, and internal control procedures.[45] For instance, it is alleged that owners of major airline reservation systems have acted in anti-competitive ways by using their systems to minimize the bookings of competing non-owners.[46]

### 3.2. Network Owners' Exercise of Content Controls

Public and private firms also use call monitoring to manage employee communications to the firm's customers. Telemarketing and travel reservations services are two common examples.[47] There are also numerous content/subject matter restrictions. Computer networks such as Prodigy have asserted some control over bulletin board content in response to various user protests regarding speech on controversial subjects.[48] Some other bulletin board providers have no policy regarding what may or may not be said over their facilities. For them, the communicator of the information bears the ultimate responsibility for the content. Their position has met with judicial approval in one instance.[49]

Aside from firm business oriented restrictions on access and in house, on-line speech, there are the traditional limits on audience or subscriber access and speech in the realm of broadcasting, and the evolving limits in cable television and plain old telephone service (POTS). The First Amendment protects the exercise of speech and editorial control over programming decisions and transmissions by broadcast licensees from the assertion of access and speech rights by viewers and other programmers.[50] It protects the exercise of speech and editorial discretion by cable television operators,[51] but portions of the subscribing public and other programmers are afforded access and speech opportunities as well.[52] The First Amendment also has been held to protect subscriber and programmer access to telephone networks even where the voice communication is indecent.[53]

However, recent decisions in the area of telephony and cable may be harbingers of a revision of access and speech rights afforded network owners and subscribers. The First Amendment has been held to accord local exchange network operators the right to engage in video communication to their service area subscribers.[54] And, telephone common carriers are viewed by at least one Supreme Court Justice and two circuit courts as private speakers possessing the right to refuse carriage or billing services to subscribers seeking carriage of indecent programming the carrier deems undesirable.[55] The potential impact of these decisions is that common carriers which have heretofore been prohibited from exercising editorial control over the content of speech may do so either as constitutionally protected speakers,[56] or, under the guise of a refusal to transact business.[57]

By comparison, in a somewhat analogous case regarding the regulation of indecent programming on cable television access and leased access channels, a three judge panel of the D.C. Circuit did not adopt the Second and Ninth Circuits' private actor analysis as it was applied to telephony. It declined to view the cable operator as a private actor in the context of regulating indecency on access channels on cable television.[58] The D.C. Circuit noted that unlike the government-compelled offering of leased and public access channels in cable, the billing services provided by telephone companies were voluntary and therefore private.[59] The state action/private action distinction relied upon by the Circuit Court in Alliance, could have a profound effect on future regulation of customer access to the networks of forborne carriers.[60] They, like the local telephone companies' offering of billing services, offer their common carrier communications services on a voluntary basis. Thus, per the Alliance for Media analysis, they would free to engage in discriminatory provision of services.[61]

More important however, the dial-a-porn precedents have potentially serious and negative implications for network user access to common carrier telephone networks. Read broadly, these precedents allow telephone common carriers to deny carriage to speakers for private business reasons or because the carriers are able to classify the requested service as "non common carriage" despite the fact that denial of such service precludes viable access to the network.

When these precedents are combined with the recent holding that local telephone companies possesses constitutional speech rights, the constitutional construct of the content neutral common carrier is severely undermined. In the worst case scenario, telephone companies would be free to deny access and speech rights to others via the constitutional exercise of editorial control over their networks or by business fiat.

## 4. THE CONSTITUTIONAL DIMENSION

The above review, leads to the conclusion that network owner providers limit access and speech activities of employees, user/members and third parties to accomplish numerous tasks including: protection of property, assets, costs and market share, as well as to achieve competition advantage, limit or constrain dissemination of proprietary information, manage the communication of information and/or discourage the procurement or transmission of sometimes illicit information.

Under such circumstances when may we say that a user-member or a potential outside communicator is impermissibly constrained from gaining access or engaging in speech? Is it possible to distinguish between legitimate business needs and impermissible constraints on speech activities? At first blush, based on the prior discussion, one could suggest that permissible firm needs include all of those previously listed above.[62] By the same token, others might argue that impermissible firm needs include many of the same goals articulated as legitimate.[63]

One possible way to answer this dilemma is to examine the manner in which the law has addressed and apportioned access and speech rights in the varying relationships between network owner/providers and closed user groups on the one hand, and network users and third parties on the other. A critical distinction in the manner in which such rights are apportioned arises with the relative status of the network. Where the network is an asset established primarily for the internal use of the corporation or closed user group, the employees, closed user members, and third party communicators have very limited access and speech rights. Where the network is the product or service offered by the corporation or closed user group, subscribers and viewers have been accorded greater access and speech rights based on constitutional, economic and other public policy principles. But, in the latter area, the law is in substantial flux.

## 4.1. Network as Business Asset or Tool

### 4.1.1. Employer/Employee Relationships

As mentioned above, employers may be network owner/providers, closed user groups, or simply network subscribers. The nature of their status as public or private institutions, however, has a significant affect on the scope and expectations which an employee may have regarding constitutional protection of their arguable rights of access to company facilities and ability to speak on those facilities.

Recently there have been a spate of law suits filed by employees alleging that their constitutional rights have been violated when employers monitored their conversations over e-mail or telephone networks.[64] None of the suits appear to have been judicially resolved to date,[65] but there are some indications of the extent of protection afforded employee speech. For instance, most experts agree that while the Federal Electronic Communications Privacy Act of 1986 protects the privacy of electronic messages sent through public networks to which individuals or companies subscribe, it does not apply to internal E-mail.[66] Thus, to the extent that employees enjoy speech rights on company e-mail facilities, those rights are limited to communication over public e-mail systems. Employers retain the right to restrict access to, and monitor internal e-mail.

### 4.1.1.1. Public Employer/Employee

The courts have held that a public employee has First Amendment constitutional protection for speech about "matters" of public concern.[67] In cases where the employee is acting as a "whistle-blower," public policy and legislation in an increasing number of jurisdictions supports a public employee's right to speak.[68] It is clear that employees do not enjoy an unfettered right of speech, however. For instance, current cases allow the employer to deny such speech where it may disrupt the work place.[69]

#### 4.1.1.2. Private Employer/Employee

Under the National Labor Relations Act, an employee has statutory protection for speech concerning work related activities.[70] There are also "whistle-blower" statutes in many states which protect employee speech about company wrongdoing.[71] Otherwise, under the "work at will" doctrine, the employee ostensibly has no recognized speech rights in the face of legitimate company interests, aside from unionization related issues.[72] The scope of an employee's statutory license to use company e-mail and/or telecommunications facilities to realize their work related speech right is not established, however.[73]

#### 4.1.2. Closed User Group and Members (Actual and Potential)

Where firms or users associate via network facilities which they have acquired, they may exercise control over member and non member network access and speech.[74]

While the scope of a closed User Groups' [Private Network's] liability for actionable speech is unsettled, it seems intuitively appropriate that its liability track that of bulletin board sysops such as Compuserve and Prodigy.[75] The more extensive its control over the communication of content, the more extensive the liability for that content ought to be. At the same time, the more extensive the control of content, the less extensive individual user speech rights will be on that network.

### 4.2. Network as Product or Service: Relationships between Network Owner Providers and Users

#### 4.2.1. Network Owner Provider and Subscriber Users (Common Carriage)

The largest category of relationships between network owners and consumers exists in the provision of network transmission capacity and network related services. Telecommunications network owners may provide transmission between two or more points at varying speeds with a variety of ways to manipulate the various types of transported information. Services range from the provision of transmission capability for private networks, to virtual private and hybrid networks, 800 and 900 number services, billing, to plain old telephone service (POTS). The provision of network transmission, switching, billing and intelligence based services may be accomplished pursuant to regulated tariff, by contract or by a combination of the two.

As competition has increased, regulators have tended to afford network owner providers greater flexibility in providing services under contract.[76] Even where services are not provided pursuant to contract, network owner providers have been granted greater flexibility in providing many services under tariff.[77] Where the services are offered on a common carrier or quasi-common carrier basis, the network provider has tended to limit network access based on the type and class of service, network integrity, security, and capacity.

Aside from government mandated responsibilities to foreclose opportunities for harassing, indecent, or obscene speech to reach protected subscribers, carriers have tended to eschew control of information content thereby foregoing liability for customer communication. This practice has been sanctioned by federal and many state regulatory bodies. Also, carriers have traditionally sought to limit their liability for loss or damage to customer communications.[78] Until now, these efforts have been successful.[79]

However, a recent court decision has held that telecommunications network owners have electronic video speech rights as extensive as cable video distribution network providers.[80]

258

If the case is upheld on appeal, and if the telecommunications network providers exercise their speech and editorial rights by limiting the access and speech of users, attempts to limit speech related liabilities may, and increasingly should, prove less successful.[81]

For instance, in a related area, bulletin board/e-mail providers have the ability to control access and screen speech content on their systems.[82] While some do not actively seek to control access or more importantly, content, others do. As a result, while one provider has been successful in avoiding liability for libelous statements made by one of its users, it is not clear that others will fare as well.[83] Moreover, the decision to control content places the service provider in a difficult position when it either fails to prohibit offensive speech quickly or prosecutes other speech in a seemingly biased manner.[84]

### 4.2.2. Network Owner/Information Provider and Consumer/Subscribers

### 4.2.2.1. Telephony [POTS] and Telecommunications

The need for interconnection and the economies of scale inherent in provision of local telephone service led in significant part to the creation of government sanctioned telephone monopolies. Government then sought to assure the public access to the monopoly provider by requiring that the provider not discriminate between customers on the basis of facilities or the price paid for the services provided.[85]

As a further means of assuring non-discrimination, the telephone company was not allowed any control over the content of information it transmitted. More recently, however, telephone companies have been allowed to deny billing and collection services to dial-a-porn providers deemed undesirable by the carriers.[86] Also, government requirements that long distance common carriers may not engage in the provision of information services and local common carriers may not provide electronic video services within their local markets have been overturned. According to recent court opinions, local telcos now have video electronic speech rights.[87] Should the decision be upheld on appeal, there is still a question of how this newly articulated speech right will merge with the telco owner's property right vis a vis control of access and content.[88] Many potential competitors and customers of local carriers possessing essential facilities have voiced concern over the potential for unfair competition.[89]

In the area of switched, interactive telecommunications, the diverse set of relationships addressed above is expanding even farther as interactive video distribution capabilities come on line and user access to network functionalities increase via manipulation of network intelligence.[90] It is here that the greatest potential for increased access and electronic speech is to be found.[91]

As fiber optic, computer and switched telephony technologies merge, so do the heretofore separate network functions and information streams of telephony, broadcasting, cable and print.[92] As this occurs, there is a potential danger that the network owner as the transmission provider and as a potential speaker, may experience a conflict of interest between the provision of network related services to users who, like the network owner, are also information providers. Newspaper publishers, cablecasters and broadcasters have raised this potential for conflict of interest as a reason for continuing the prohibition against local telephone companies' entry into the information and video distribution markets.[93] While these arguments have found sympathetic ears in Congress, they have proved less persuasive before the FCC and at least one district court.[94]

Similar complaints have been raised in other instances where access to transmission and owner speech merge. These instances concern the exercise of access and content control by bulletin board service providers, and, the provision of access and speech related services by cable television media.[95]

### 4.2.2.2. Computer Networks

According to a number of legal commentators, individual subscribers to commercial or private computer bulletin board services have no access rights. Access is garnered by contract, and control of access and ultimately speech resides, in the first instance, with the service provider or the system operator (sysop). While there is very little information on the criteria employed for denying initial access, revocation of access is the ultimate sanction employed by sysops to discipline miscreant member users.[96] There are options short of denial of access which are also employed.

At base, the rationale for sysop control of access is ownership of the system facilities. With regard to sysop content control, the recent *Cubby v. Compuserve* decision provides some indication of the considerations militating against sysop exercise of content control.[97] The greater the discernable control which the sysop exercises over access and content, the greater its potential liability to users and third parties for damage caused by the information's content.

In *Cubby*, Compuserve, an on-line information service provider, was sued, unsuccessfully, for the alleged libel of a third party competitor of a bulletin board provided on the service provider's system. In determining that Compuserve was not liable for the alleged libel, the court established by implication that heightened control of the communicated content would have resulted in liability.[98] In another libel action ultimately settled out of court, Prodigy, another sysop, was sued for an alleged libel of a third party by a Prodigy subscriber.[99] Unlike Compuserve and many other sysops, however, Prodigy distinguishes itself based on the extent of control it exercises over transmitted content.[100] As a consequence, there was speculation that Prodigy might not have easily extricated itself from liability.[101]

### 4.2.2.3. Constitutionally Based Access and Speech Rights in Traditional Media: Broadcasting and Cable TV

Historically, market entry and technological considerations have affected the apportionment of access and speech rights between media owner-providers and the public. While, as a practical matter, electronic speech has been protected under the constitution regardless of whether it is in a print,[102] voice,[103] or video[104] format, traditional media owners in each industry have been accorded different First Amendment rights vis a vis users based on differing assessments of the ease of economic and technological entry into each market.

### 4.2.2.3.1. Broadcasting

The initial scarcity of broadcast frequencies relative to public demand for access resulted in the requirement that the broadcast licensee share its frequency with the public.[105] With FCC engineered deregulation of broadcasting, the fairness doctrine, community ascertainment regulations, and programming guidelines were abolished or seriously compromised.[106] Subsequent to deregulation and the abolition of the fairness doctrine, the scope of access sharing was ultimately limited to candidates for political office.[107] Even before the fairness doctrine was "abolished," its potential power to require access had been significantly limited by judicial decisions.[108]

The current scope of government-exercised content control over the broadcast licensee extends to the prohibition of speech which is libelous, indecent or obscene.[109] Users have a right to diverse information but no right to speak as individuals or information providers owner permission.

### 4.2.2.3.2. Cable Television

According to at least one legal scholar, government regulation of access to cable channels is justified because franchises are scarce due to the physical limits inherent in the use of public rights of way.[110] The physical scarcity is further exacerbated by the economies of scale inherent in the provision of cable service.[111] For these reasons, the cable franchisee is required to share his/her channels of communication with the public and other information providers. Concerns about the continued availability of local news and public affairs programming as well as economic market and anticompetitive constraints alleged to have been imposed by cable firms have been used to justify limits on the control cable franchisees may exercise over broadcaster access to the cable networks.[112] The leased access, must-carry and public access channels are an attempt by Congress to assure third party access to cable networks.[113] According to some scholars, the leased access rules have proved only moderately successful. And, due to recent litigation, the must-carry requirements are under a potential constitutional cloud.[114]

The cable franchisee's control of communicated content is constrained by legal sanctions which may be imposed for libelous, indecent or obscene speech.[115] In part due to the necessity to avoid government imposed sanctions, cable franchise owners are compelled to exert editorial control over matter provided by third party information providers which may be deemed indecent or obscene.[116]

## 5. REGULATORY SHIFTS IN THE AGE OF CONVERGENCE AND PRIVATIZATION: SOME PRELIMINARY ANSWERS

### 5.1. Network as Asset

### 5.1.1. Private Firms and Closed User Groups

Where the network is the private asset of the firm, employee and third party efforts to assert first amendment rights of access or speech over internal communications systems will be limited.[117] In the case of employees of private firms, the National Labor Relations Act may allow them to negotiate for speech rights provided the rights are exercised for the protest or discussion of working conditions.[118] All arguments for fairness and ethics aside, beyond the narrow entitlement of the NLRA, employees of private firms enjoy little real access or speech rights to corporate network assets. Ultimately, the company network owner may limit and/or control access and speech.[119]

### 5.1.2. Public Firms

Employees of public [government] firms are similarly limited. The First Amendment has been interpreted to afford such employees the right to speak on matters of public interest.[120] They, like their private brethren also receive some protection from a variety of state "whistle blower" statutes. Aside from these protections, however, public employees have no rights of access or speech to internal communications systems. At least one commentator has forcefully argued that private and public employees should enjoy the same scope of speech rights encompassing comment on work and product quality related matters.[121]

Access to the networks of closed user groups is also limited.[122] Here, absent a showing that the network asset is being used to unlawfully restrain competition,[123] the user group may exercise control over access and/or speech on virtually all aspects of the network. However, the exercise of control over access and speech carries a certain level of responsibility for actionable speech violations. The precise level of responsibility has yet to be measured, however, and may ultimately depend on the technology and the circumstances of each case.[124]

### 5.2. Network as Product or Service

### 5.2.1. Convergence and Change: The Evolution of Speech Regulation in Traditional Media and Telecommunications

While the traditional regulatory apportionment of network provider and user access and speech remains virtually intact in the broadcasting, it is under challenge in cable and telephony. Congress's decision to impose must carry requirements on cable franchisees has been upheld for the moment.[125] The statute authorizing franchising authorities to require cable operators to provide public, educational and government (PEG) access channels,[126] and requiring cable operators to provide leased access channels[127] were held to be constitutionally permissible.[128]

Congress's prohibition against local telco ownership of cable facilities in its service area and provision of video programming has been challenged and overturned in one district court. It too, is on appeal. Meanwhile, the cross-ownership ban is being challenged in other district courts as well.[129] The challenges to the must carry, PEG and leased access provisions as well as the telephone-cable cross ownership ban are significant because they provide several of the judicial pillars upon which regulation of the future electronic broadband networks will be built. This follows because the cases address the regulation of access and speech in cable and telephone, the two industries from which much of the broadband infrastructure is likely to emerge.[130] Thus, judicial pronouncements on the relative rights of network owners to provide information over their networks and to determine who may have access and speak over their facilities other than themselves, are critical to the evolution of speech rights on the new and evolving infrastructure.

A decision overturning the must carry rules is possible. Congress may have rested a significant portion of the justification for must carry on its desire to assure the continued broadcaster provision of local news and public affairs programming.[131] And, evidence of economic harm may, upon closer analysis and examination of prior history, prove insufficient to establish a sufficient threat to the government's interest in the retention of viable broadcast stations.[132] Moreover, Congress's efforts to establish evidence of broadcasting"s economic demise prove no less effective than prior efforts by the FCC and broadcasters.[133]

In 1984, Congress codified the FCC's telco-cable cross ownership rules in the Cable Communications Act of 1984.[134] The legislative history of section 613(b) of the 84 Act indicates that section 613(b) was intended to codify the then current FCC telco-cable cross-ownership rules prohibiting telephone companies from directly providing video programming to subscribers in their telephone markets.[135] The FCC subsequently reversed its earlier decision, and concluded that the public interest would be better served by partially lifting the cross ownership ban.[136] The Commission concluded that subject to safeguards, the public would receive significant benefits if telephone companies were allowed to provide cable television service. It tentatively concluded that "construction and operation of technologically advanced, integrated broadband networks by carriers for the purpose of providing video programming and other services [would] constitute good cause for a waiver of the prohibition."[137] However, Congress did not repeal its law.

In light of Congress's refusal to remove the prohibition, Bell Atlantic filed suit alleging that the 1984 Cable Act prohibition violates the First and Fifth Amendment rights of local exchange carriers as well as the First Amendment rights of subscribers. Bell Atlantic argued that video programming is a form of constitutionally protected speech which it is not allowed to present on its own network. According to the carrier, the statutory definition of video programming, the 84 Cable Act prohibition is a direct abridgement of Bell Atlantic's First Amendment rights because the company and its subsidiaries are prohibited from engaging in video speech.[138] Bell Atlantic has successfully plead its case before two courts.[139]

Thus it is possible that the rules may be overturned under the reading of the law espoused by the dissent or the majority in Turner.

The ban is a content neutral restriction which incidentally affects speech. It is narrowly tailored to meet the substantial government interests in preventing anticompetitive abuses by telephone carriers possessing monopoly power and maintaining a competitive environment for broadband communications. User control over access and speech on cable television and local telephone switched networks, will be revised to accommodate increased network owner control. The scope of user access and speech rights most likely would be established by contract and reflect the relative bargaining power of the parties.[140] In such a scenario, in the absence of state action,[141] small users and individuals would have access and speech rights solely at the sufferance of the network provider/owner, and the specter of private censorship unmediated by government, becomes quite real.

Should the must carry rules be upheld based upon economic market and anti-trust regulation and the telco prohibition overturned, at minimum, opportunities for access and speech would continue to incorporate the current statutory delineations of common carriage, leased access, public access and network owner access.[142] Opportunities for speech would be broadened to include telephone network owner/speakers and cable network speakers, as well as the merged cable-telco network owner speaker, and would continue to include unaffiliated information provider "speech" and user subscriber speech. Under this set of outcomes, the focus of access and speech policy arguably shifts to a government mediated inquiry into the extent and the manner in which the owner provider may limit or prohibit the exercise of access and speech rights by potential and actual user/subscribers. So long as owner providers and network users retain access and speech rights, the First Amendment is likely to be better served.

## 6. A SHIFT IN POLICY?

Regulating network owner control of employee and subscriber speech is problematic for all the reasons mentioned before. There clearly are legitimate and compelling reasons for employer and/or network owner limits on employee or subscriber speech in some instances. However, the potential for private censorship remains great and its negative impact is no less devastating to the individual or to groups than when engaged in by the government.

It is highly likely that convergence will continue as a market and technological reality and that privatization of telecommunications networks will continue as a preferred regulatory tool. The outcome of the Turner, Daniels and C&P cases will affect the scope of network owner control over access and content. However, until these cases are fully litigated, questions regarding the scope of access to networks and the extent of network control over content will remain unanswered. Indeed, they may remain even after the cases are decided. For instance, in the event Turner and Daniels are overturned and C&P upheld, cable operators would have no obligation to carry local broadcasters or make channel capacity available to public, educational, or government subscribers, or to competitive programmers. Cable operators would exercise nearly total control over their facilities. Local telephone companies would be allowed to exercise editorial control over at least a portion of their facilities. Should this come to pass, how may cable network owners and telephone companies establish criteria for access and speech on their networks?

Cable operators would make private decisions about who to serve based on their assessment of who would generate a high enough profit or what programming was desirable. If the dial-a-porn decisions are reliable precedent, telephone companies will be able to deny access and consequently, speech, based upon private business decisions and determinations that the requested service is not classified as a common carrier service.

In the event Turner, Daniels, and C&P are upheld, cable operators will continue to have the range of legislatively mandated access requirements they currently have. Thus, some local broadcasters would still enjoy free channel access, as would public, educational, or government subscribers; and, competitive programmers would still enjoy access for a fee. As in the first scenario, telephone companies would be able to deny access and speech, based upon private business decisions and determinations that the requested service is not classified as a common carrier service.

In either eventuality, how might the government seek to affirmatively ensure subscriber/user access and relatively unfettered speech, while avoiding inappropriate regulation of network owner speech?

### 6.1. Access and Scarcity

Access presents a particularly interesting set of problems. For instance, to the extent government regulation of network owner control over access is based upon technical scarcity, we may be approaching a time when technical scarcity will cease to be a credible concern.[143] Admittedly, however, an abundance of technical channel or switching capacity does not assure access to all potential users. Market place failures due to wealth distribution, limited network infrastructure availability and selective market competition still will play a significant role.

These questions of scarcity and access are doubly critical given the current proposed mergers of telephone and cable firms. To the extent that large telephone and cable corporations are allowed to merge, economic scarcity will remain a valid policy concern. Such mergers could reduce the number of potential local competitors while driving up the price for market entry. Also, the types of services made available and the manner in which they are priced by the merged firms would affect who would have access to network functionalities. If the post telco-cable merger economics follow the same trends as prior periods of merger in related media industries such as broadcasting, debt service demands will ultimately force the merged firms to cut costs, serve more lucrative markets and raise prices.[144] In such an event, some market segments may receive less service while other segments pay more. Such developments would certainly affect the cost of access. They may preclude significant segments of the market from having meaningful access. And they will affect the speech activities of those who acquire access and limit the speech opportunities of those who do not acquire access.

## 6.2. An Alternative Fix

Some scholars have argued that the nation's constitutional laws be changed to reflect the growth of speech related activity engendered by the convergence of computer, network switching and fiber optic technologies. For instance, at least one eminent constitutional scholar has argued for an amendment to the First Amendment to protect speech activities conducted over computers.[145] Other scholars have argued that the First Amendment in its current form, may be interpreted to protect access and speech activities conducted over computer augmented broadband interactive switched networks.[146]

Short of constitutional solutions, however, the government retains other regulatory tools for assuring "universal" access and relatively unfettered speech for network owners and users. These include use of: the antitrust laws, speech and tort liability, structural network parameters favoring distributed intelligence and switched interactive network technologies, and a universal service requirement to assure access and speech in the face of the above mentioned market failures. These regulatory choices affect the exercise of access and editorial control at the content, network configuration and equipment levels. The same levels at which network owners exert control.

### 6.2.1. Maximizing Access

#### 6.2.1.1. Choice of Technologies

For instance, given the extensive cost of deploying fiber optics to the home, federal and state regulators could allow private industry to continue to build network information delivery systems composed of one way, compressed channel technology (cable and video dial tone) rather than switched, two-way, interactive technology (ISDN/broadband). While this approach may be favored by portions of the industry, there is a significant danger that such a solution would postpone the advent of switched interactive multimedia communications. More important, however, it replicates the current regulatory difficulties which accrue when the government cedes control over distinct, clearly discernable transmission paths to network owners and then imposes liability for speech.

#### 6.2.1.2. Access via Market Regulation

Where the network owner exercises control over the network via access or content control to deter or forestall competition, the government can invoke the antitrust laws.[147]

Newspaper publishers, cable programmers and broadcasters which would comprise a significant portion of the potential information providers on a telecommunications carrier provided broadband network, have alleged that the local telephone companies will in fact engage in anti-competitive activities if they are allowed to vertically integrate into the market for providing information services. For instance, broadcasters and cable operators oppose limited local telephone company entry into the video distribution services market via FCC's video dial tone proposal absent significant structural safeguards.[148]

It is anticipated that some portion of the future broadband network infrastructure may be composed of essential facilities. If so, an antitrust violation will arise where such facilities are: 1.) extremely difficult, if not impracticable, for competitors to duplicate; 2.) owned by one or a group of firms; and 3.) not made available to competitors of the network facilities owner without an appropriate business justification or apparent efficiency, especially where the network owner is also an information provider.[149]

The FCC's structural safeguards policy was developed to address the concern that the RBOCs would use cross subsidies and accounting standards to compete unfairly in the competitive provision of enhanced and/or information services. In telecommunications, the term "structural safeguards" refers to the separation of a vertically integrated firm into corporate segments based upon whether they provided basic network services or enhanced services.[150] Enhanced services include data processing services as well as videotext, audiotext, database retrieval and other computer and communications technologies applications. The goal of open networks architecture policies[151] of which "structural separations policy" was a part, was to prevent the ability of the RBOCs to underwrite their provision of competitive enhanced and information services with monies garnered from their basic network monopoly. After a significant number of administrative hearings and judicial proceedings, there is still no agreement on how structural safeguards ought to be employed.[152]

## 6.3. Incentives Regarding Control and Liability for Speech

As privatization continues, the lessons learned in the Compuserve case as well as other recent cases regarding publisher liability should give would be private network editors pause. Where a network owner exercises control over access and content, they may not be able to avoid liability for that content when it is harmful to the public.[153] Similarly, network owners may be held liable for negligent or careless manipulation and control of subscriber/user information where such action results in injury to the user or to third parties.[154]

Certainly, the libel, obscenity, and indecency laws will remain, making control of content a cause for liability. Thus, even where network owners seek to eschew all content regulation, they are likely to be no more successful than telephone common carriers and cable operators who by statute must exert some control over obscene or indecent subscriber speech. Ultimately, however, self-preservation and protection of the bottom line may motivate firm efforts to curb libelous speech or avoid control of subscriber speech. But, forgoing editorial control over some content would remove a downside cost of doing business which may be preferable to the cost of maintaining the monitoring of subscriber and programmer speech and the potential liability which the exercise of editorial control brings.

### 6.3.1. Tort Liability

There is another way in which network owner control of speech may be tempered by government sanction, the imposition of tort liability. The exercise of control over access and content necessarily invites expectations that the network owner, in the exercise of its editorial discretion, has reviewed and sanctioned all information which it transmits. Moreover, should the network owner lose or damage customer information in storage, manipulation or transmission, or, negligently preclude the transmission of customer information entrusted to its care, it is reasonable to require that the owner compensate the customer to the extent of its legally recognized tort damages. A recent case in Illinois had so held based on state law.[155]

The removal of government sanctioned protections from carrier tort liability would encourage some network owners to eschew private carriage for the protection which public common carriage still affords. Tort liability would attach whenever the private carrier negligently handled subscriber information. Private carrier and closed user group attempts to exempt themselves from such liability via exculpatory contract clauses or tariff language would be deemed unconscionable and unenforceable as a matter of law where it could be established that the subscriber does not possess equal bargaining power.

At least one commenter has noted that in an era of deregulation, the reasons for continuing to limit the tort liability of non-dominant telecommunications common carriers cease to be applicable.[156] At least three reasons have been used by the courts to justify the continuation of exculpation clauses limiting common carrier liability. First, federal and state regulators may be held to possess the regulatory authority to establish such limits. Second, such limits, judgements paid by monopoly carriers would be passed on to subscribers having no alternative service providers. Third, limited liability provisions preserve national uniformity in the provision of services and avoid discrimination between like situated by geographically dispersed subscribers.

Today, however, such reasons retain little credibility. First, the Communications Act of 1934, does not authorize federal regulators to preempt state law tort remedies then existing at common law or by statute. Rather, such remedies as the act provides are in addition to existing state remedies.[157] In addition, courts have not automatically granted primary jurisdiction over state tort liability claims to regulatory agencies but often have found such claims to be within the purview of the courts.[158]

Second, in an era of convergence and expanding competition at all market levels in the telecommunications and ultimately, multi-media marketplace, many subscribers will have alternative sources of service. Finally, a growing portion of the telecommunications infrastructure is owned by a disparate number of private owners serving distinct "high-end user" sub-markets rather than the larger local or national markets of various subscribers. Under such circumstances, national uniformity appears to be less a function of government action and more a function of the relative market power of the service provider, the purchaser and market demand. For these reasons, government-sanctioned carrier-initiated limitations on tort liability should be abolished except where a carrier elects to serve all classes of customers via public switched multi-media networks.

A decision to remove the tort liability limitation except when applied to carriers serving the majority of all classes of users via a public switched multi-media network or providing significant interconnection between public switched networks, would serve as a financial incentive for some carriers to maintain service to a broad subscriber base, or to expand their service offerings to include other consumer groups or, at the very least, assure sufficient compatible interconnection.

### 6.3.2. Subscriber Protection via the Theory of Unconscionability

Where the non-dominant network provider or providers resort to contracts or tariffs as the vehicle for the offering of services to subscribers, there may be instances in which the doctrine of contract unconscionability may be invoked. If the network owner, as provider of scarce network resources, leveraged its economic position by employing form contract language to limit its tort liability, it's attempt to enforce such restrictions might be denied by the courts on the grounds of unconscionability.[159] Moreover, as one public service commission has observed, given the increasing complexity of tariffs it would be "...'unconscionable' to assume that any telephone subscriber had consented either impliedly or expressly to broad liability waivers."[160]

### 6.4. Interconnection and Distributed Intelligence

Other than the use of these strategies, the government may pro-actively encourage access and speech by creating regulatory policies and tax incentives which favor the building of open, switched, interconnected networks incorporating distributed intelligence. For instance, the government has initiated regulatory proceedings aimed at equalizing user interconnection to the local monopoly public switched network architecture and increasing network service offerings by enhancing network flexibility through distributed network intelligence. These proceedings have yet to be concluded.[161] A resolution which favors distributed intelligence and shared user/network control over network functionalities would maximize speaker control over the process by which information is communicated.

Networks incorporating distributed intelligence and shared control, whether public or private, could provide the opportunity to engage in broadband multi-media interactive speech to large numbers of users.[162] They arguably would also provide a preferable alternative to multi-channel, uni-directional distribution systems in which network architecture and functionality preclude two-way, broadband interactive communications.

When combined with the regulatory strategies outlined above, selection of a switched network architecture would also ensure that neither network owners or users forfeit meaningful access or speech rights. For, in a switched broadband interactive network environment, the capacity for carriage of information is substantial and the notion of scarcity upon which the constitutional regulation of antecedent technologies is based, should become a less viable justification for limiting access and speech rights.[163]

Each of the above mentioned policies affects the incentive structure under which carriers would exercise control of access and speech on their networks. The proposed policies do not preclude network owner exercise of control over access and speech. They merely remove liability protections enjoyed by public common carriers, expand technical opportunities for user access and speech, and continue pre-existing economic regulation. As such, they should be adopted as regulatory policy regardless of whether constitutional law is changed.

268

## ENDNOTES

[1] The convergence phenomena arguably began with the merger of telephone network switching and computer technology. It has continued with the evolution of network transmission technologies from copper and coaxial cable to fiber optic cable along with channel/signal compression and the evolution of signaling system seven (SS-7) technology. Its most recent manifestation is the merger of fiber, telephone and computer technologies into broadband communications networks.

[2] The speed with which various industry firms seek to joint venture or combine to enter new markets underscores this fact. *See* Alan Deutschman and Joyce E. Davis, *The Next Big Info Tech Battle*, FORTUNE, Nov. 29, 1993, at 39; *Policing the Information Highway*, CHI. TRIB., Nov. 26, 1993, at 30; John Huey and Andrew Kupfer, *What That Merger Means for You*, FORTUNE, Nov. 15, 1993, at 82; Julie Solomon, *Big Brother's Holding Company*, NEWSWEEK, Oct. 25, 1993, at 38; John Greenwald, *Wired!; Bell Atlantic's Bid for Cable Giant TCI is the Biggest Media Deal in History*; TIME, Oct. 25, 1993, at 50; and Sandra Sugawara and Paul Farhi, *Merger to Create a Media Giant; $26 Billion Bell Atlantic-TCI Deal Is a Vision of TV's Future*, WASH. POST, Oct. 14, 1993, at A1.

[3] *See National Information Infrastructure: Agenda for Action*, INFO. INFRASTRUCUTRE TASK FORCE, Sept. 15, 1993, at 1-2, 4-16. *See generally* John Holliman, *Vice President Gore Press Conference on Info Highways*, Transript No. 267-1 of live rep., CNN News, Dec. 21, 1993; Ronald Brown, *Secretary Brown on Three Goals for Our New National Information Infrastructure*, ROLL CALL, Nov. 15, 1993; and Brooks Boliek, *U.S. Data Superhighway Project Short on Concrete*, HOLLYWOOD REP., Sept. 16, 1993.

[4] *See* CONNECTING TO THE FUTURE: GREATER ACCESS, SERVICES, AND COMPETITION IN TELECOMMUNICATIONS, REPORT OF THE NEW YORK'S TELECOMMUNICATIONS EXCHANGE, Dec. 1993, at xii, 18-21, 28-29.

[5] As fiber optic distribution and switching technology is introduced, the distribution functions and information streams of broadcasting, cable, and telephony are merging. As they merge, the access, speech and related activities which received varying degrees of constitutional protection when conducted over the antecedent technologies will come to reside on the merged network(s). However, because the apportionment of these constitutionally recognized rights was made in the specific context of antecedent technologies and relationships, the fate of such rights in an advanced, intelligent, broadband network context is unsettled. *See generally* Joshua Quittner, *Online To A Revolution: The Amazing - and some Say Ominous - New World of TV, Telephone and Computer Is Heading Your Way*, NEWSDAY, July 18, 1993, at 4; and *Electronic Media Regulation and the First Amendment: Future Perspective*, DATA CHANNELS, Feb. 3, 1992, at 4 (hereinafter Future Perspective). This uncertainty is exacerbated by the growing number of private networks.

Some scholars have begun to address this question. *See* EDGE, Dec. 2, 1991, at 6,7, *Special Report: Universal Telephone Service; Ready for the 21st Century?* 1991 ANN. REV. OF THE INST. FOR INFO. STUD. (A joint program of Northern Telecom and the Aspen Inst.) (hereinafter Special Report: Universal Telephone Service).

[6] Several scholars have criticized the current state/private dichotomy established by the Supreme Court in light of the continuing trend toward privatization in American life. *See* Rodney A. Smolla, *The Bill of Rights at 200 Years: Preserving the Bill of Rights in the Modern Administrative-Industrial State*, 31 WM. AND MARY L. REV. 321 (1990) (arguing that since restraints on human thought and action are the same whether applied by public or private entities, protection of constitutional freedoms should be maintained in the private as well as the public sector.); and Clyde Summers, *The Privatization of Personal Freedoms and the Enrichment of Democracy: Some Lessons from Labor Law*, 1986 UNIV. ILL. L. REV. 689 (1989) (arguing that as more public functions are performed by private entities there is a critical need to protect constitutional rights heretofore protected from government control in the public

sphere from private control in the private sphere).

7. Users may be divided into two major groups composed of those who own network facilities (facilities based users) and those who do not own facilities (non-facilities based users). The vast majority of users are non-facilities based. These individuals, firms or groups purchase access to some of the networks (telephone) over which they may interact. They are most often semi-passive recipients of information transmitted one way over other networks (broadcasting and cable). The communications needs of these users vary substantially, are evolving at different speeds and in multiple directions. For instance, many businesses already have significant needs for high speed, high capacity broadband communication networks. *See* Michael L. Dertouzos, *Communications, Computers and Networks*, SCI. AM., Sept. 1991, at 62, 64; Al Gore, *Infrastructure for the Global Village*, SCI. AM., Sept. 1991, at 150-51; Michael L. Dertouzos, *Building the information Marketplace*, TECH. REV., Jan. 1991, 28, 31-2; George Gilder, *Telecosm; the New Rule of Wireless*, FORBES, Mar. 29, 1993, at 96. By comparison, the general public has not yet generated needs sufficient to precipitate demands for greater network speeds and capacities. Customer-users include residential as well as business customers.

8. Generally, absent a showing of an independent nexus of involvement by the state, neither the chartering, funding, licensing, regulating or tax exemption of a corporation by the government constitutes state action. *See* Cohen v. Illinois Institute of Technology, 524 F. 2d 818 (7th Cir. 1975), *cert. denied*, 425 U.S. 943 (1976); Sament v. Hahnemann Medical College and Hospital of Philadelphia, 413 F. Supp. 434 (E.D. Pa. 1976), *aff'd mem.*, 547 F. 2d 1164 (3rd Cir. 1977) (charter); Aasum v, Good Samaritan Hospital, 542 F. 2d 792 (9th Cir. 1976); Manning v. Greensville Memorial Hospital, 470 F. Supp. 662, (C.D. Va. 1979); Trageser v. Libbie Rehabilitation Center, 590 F. 2d 87 (4th Cir. 1978), *cert. denied*, 442 U.S. 947 (1979) (funding); Moose Lodge No. 107 v. Innis, 407 U.S. 163 (1972) (licensing); Jackson v. Metropolitan Edison, 419 U.S. 345 (1974) (regulation); Weis v. Syracuse University, 552 F. Supp. 675 (N.D.N.Y. 1982); Narango v. Alverno College, 487 F. Supp. 635 (D.C. Wisc. 1980); and Stewart v. New York University, 430 F. Supp. 1305 (S.D.N.Y. 1976).

Where the private entity exercises powers traditionally reserved to the state, state action may be found. *See* Nixon v. Condon, 286 U.S. 73 (1932) (election); Marsh v. Alabama 326 U.S. 501 (1946) (company town); and Evans v. Newton, 382 U.S. 296 (1966) (municipal park).

9. *See* CBS, Inc. v. Democratic National Committee, 412 U.S. 94 (1973).

10. Sable Communications of California, Inc. v. FCC, 492 U.S. 115 (1989) (Scalia, J., concurring); Dial Info. Servs. Corp. of N.Y. v. Thornburg, 938 F. 2d 1291 (2nd Cir. 1991); Carlin Communication Inc. v. Mountain States Telephone & Tel. Co., 827 F. 2d 1291 (9th Cir. 1987); and Information Providers Coalition for the Defense of the First Amendment v. FCC et al., 928 F. 2d 866 (9th Cir. 1991) (hereinafter Information Providers).

11. Recently, however, statutorily required efforts by cable operators to limit or ban indecent programming on leased and/or public access channels have been deemed to constitute state action. *See* Alliance for Community Media v. FCC, 10 F.3d 812 (1993) (vacated upon granting of request for rehearing en banc, Feb. 16, 1994. The decision has since been reversed. *See* Alliance for Community Media v. FCC, (D.C. Cir. en banc), No. 93-1169, June 6, 1995).

12. At present, the network access/speech continuum is bounded at one end by public switched telecommunications networks (PSTN) providing a variety of services to the public on a common carriage non-discriminatory basis. At the other end of the continuum is the privately network (PN) functioning solely as a business tool providing services exclusively to the owner(s). In between public telecommunications switched and private networks are the cable television (CATV), broadcast (B/CAST) and virtual private networks (VPN). With the advent of recent court decisions regarding cable television-telephone cross ownership and dial-a-porn, the continuum will become shorter. It may be that the pure public switched common carrier may cease to be a category. Certainly the former common carriers will have greater flexibility to provide services on a non-common carrier basis. The new network owners

will have the option to provide common carriage, private carriage and/or engage in speech themselves.

[13.] *See generally* Cynthia L. Estlund, *What Workers Want? Employee Interests, Public Interests, and Freedom of Expression*, 140 U. PA. L. REV. 921, 925, 935-936, and 960-964 (arguing that the general public has an equal interest in the product quality and safety concerns of public and private employees, and that public employees have work place concerns similar to those of their private employee counterparts and ought to enjoy the same protections for work place related expression and association).

[14.] For the purposes of the paper, networks are defined as collections of interconnected users. NATIONAL TELECOMMUNICATIONS AND INFORMATION ADMINISTRATION, NTIA INFRASTRUCTURE REPORT: TELECOMMUNICATIONS IN THE AGE OF INFORMATION, Oct. 1991, at 13-20, 92. The type of transmission and the receive/send machinery employed varies. These points may or may not be capable of engaging in interactive communication. This definition acknowledges that cable and broadcast television systems may be deemed to be networks just as the public switched inter-exchange and local exchange systems constitute networks. This definition also facilitates the exploration of the broader array of access solutions presently employed and likely to be employed in the regulation of future networks.

The paper does not address directly the need for common languages, protocols and conventions, speeds, as well as procedures of machine interaction, all of which are critical technical issues involved in network interconnection. For an excellent lay explanation of network interconnection and nomenclature, *see* Dertouzos, *Communications, Computers and Networks*, *supra* note 7. These issues are addressed, if at all, solely from the perspective of the network facilities, pricing and service configurations which the network owner(s) may choose in providing services and the impact such choices may have on the potential user class. It is recognized that these choices in significant measure will determine the eligible class of users.

Finally, the range of services that a network owner may provide are assumed to include inter alia, transmission, switching and routing, storage and/or manipulation of user information, access to 3rd party and/or network provider information, and enhanced services. A network provider need not provide all of the functions listed above, or be limited solely to those listed.

[15.] A network's functionality is the combination of the various hardware and software defined functions the network performs. A network's functionality is determined by its hardware and software architecture and by the network standards or documents which specify network protocols. Network protocols allow hardware of various manufacture to communicate with one another. Peter Fetterrolf, *Connectivity: The Sum of Its Parts*, BYTE, Nov. 1991, at 197.

[16.] A tariff is a published set of rates charged and conditions under which various classes of service are offered by common and private carriers.

[17.] The notion of network and service availability is subsumed within the definition of universal service. Universal Service was a government and industry policy which encouraged AT&T [then a monopoly] to make telephones and service available to the American public at reasonable rates. Subsidies of less profitable [or unprofitable] provision of service to rural and poorer areas were built into the business and long distance charges. David Coursey, *Battle of the Bandwidth*, INFOWORLD, Jan. 14, 1991, at 34. The traditional goal of universal service was to assure that "all but the poorest Americans could afford to make and receive telephone calls, even if they lived in remote, expensive to serve areas." *Special Report: Universal Telephone Service*, *supra* note 5. As such, universal service operated as a kind of equality in access and likeness in service offerings. In the current era of increased competition and privatization, however, universal service may no longer mean likeness (or comparability) of service or equality in technical access. *Id.*

[18.] The term "open" as used here to describe essentially, non discriminatory access to communicate on the network as configured by the owner, should not be confused with the Federal Communications Commission's "open network architecture" policy. In theory the open network architecture policy is an attempt to provide enhanced service providers such as voice messaging, on line data, and bulletin board service providers the same access to the local telephone companies' transmission and features as the telephone company or its subsidiaries. *See* Dawn Bushaus, *Enhanced Services -- ONA and AIN on a Collision Course*, COMM. WEEK, June 17 ,1991, at 32L.

[19.]*See generally VPNs Set to Challenge Private Networks and PSTN During Nineties*, FINTECH TELECOM MKTS., Apr. 15, 1992, at 31; Mark Luzak, *Tapping the Hidden Savings in Virtual Networks; Hybrid Networks*, TELECOMMUNICATION, Mar. 1991, at 45; and Robert Violino, *A Network of Their Very Own*, INFORMATIONWEEK, Jan.14, 1991 at 16.

[20.]*See supra* note 14.

[21.]*VPNS Set to Challenge Private Networks and PSTN During Nineties*, *supra* note 19.

[22.]The networks typically are created to meet the needs of their respective users for transmission of high speed data, information processing, voice traffic and/or security. Consequently, they serve closed sets of users with relatively cohesive sets of needs, as well as eligibility, procurement and financing criteria. There are some firms which sell their excess network transmission capacity commercially.

[23.]This definition doesn't include closed networks established without the use of private or dedicated facilities.

[24.]Closed user group networks may be local, regional, national, or international in scope.  Examples of closed user group networks include those owned by: ad agencies, media firms, printers, insurance agencies, hospitals, record rooms, police, automobile manufacturers, parts suppliers, dealers, financiers, and computer networks.  See generally, James I. Cash Jr. and Benn R. Konsynski, *IS Redraws Competitive Boundaries*, HARV. BUS. REV., at 134 (Mar./Apr. 1985); Venkatraman, *IT-Enabled Business Transformation: From Automation to Business Scope Redefinition*, SLOAN MGMT. REV., Jan. 1994, at 73N.  *See also* John Helliwell, *Networks Provide a Critical Competitive Edge for Airlines*, PC WEEK, Jan. 19, 1988, at C1; Salvatore Salamone, *Airline Reservation Network Flies Into New Age of LANs*, NETWORK WORLD, Nov. 26, 1990, at 34; *More Shared Networks Approved Under §4(c)(8)*, Banking Expansion Rep., Aug. 1, 1983, at 11; Rita Marie Emmer, *Marketing Hotels Using Global Distribution Systems*, CORNELL HOTEL & REST. ADMIN. QUAR., Dec. 1993, at 80.

User groups' networks may be closed for numerous reasons including: specialized equipment, specialized features, transmission speeds, security, service pricing, or speech related restrictions.  For instance, the European Commission defines closed user groups as groups of companies with "similar business interests..." Such closed user groups may include "business associates -- wholly or partly-owned subsidiaries and suppliers of products and services -- as well as customers." *See Shortlist of five for European Super-Network*, FINTECH TELECOM MKTS., Dec. 9, 1993; and *Viatel Goes Cross-Border with Europe's First Voice Network*, FINTECH TELECOM MKTS., Nov. 25, 1993.

[25.]*See* Deutschman & Davis, *supra* note 2; *The Tangled Webs They Weave*, ECONOMIST, Oct. 16, 1993 at 21; and Sugawara & Farhi, *supra* note 2.

[26.]Non-discriminatory access in the common carrier context connotes holding out oneself to provide like services to like situated customers at equitable rates.

[27.]This access option is similar to the common carrier model except that the network provider has not held itself out voluntarily to provide access to the network but is compelled to do so by law.  The cable television leased access provisions are the best current example of this form of mandated access.

[28.]The public, educational and governmental access channels which are required under cable franchises as well as the must carry channels set aside for broadcasters which are required by federal law are an excellent example of this type of "negotiated" or mandated access.

[29.]*See* section 5.2.1 *supra* and accompanying endnotes.

[30.]Carl Warren, *Abuse of Company Facilities for E-mail Must Be Curbed*, NETWORK WORLD, Mar. 30, 1992, at 25.

[31.]For instance, many New York City agencies have configured their phones to prevent city workers from dialing long distance and calling specialty phone services such as dial-a-porn and sports information lines. See Jennifer Preston, *It's OK, As Long As It's A Local Call*, NEWSDAY, Oct. 26, 1989, at 5.

[32.]Ronald E. Roel, *Advances in The Campaign For Workers' Rights,* NEWSDAY, Jan. 10, 1988, at 84; and *Plan to Monitor Calls Made by Civil Servants Attacked,* L. A. TIMES, Mar. 10, 1985, at A11.

[33.]Roel, *supra* note 32.

[34.]*Id.* An examination of employee privacy rights is beyond the scope of this article.

[35.]*See Plan to Monitor Calls Made by Civil Servants Attacked, supra* note 32. *Also see* Tom Devine, *A Whistleblower's Checklist,* CHEM. ENG., Nov. 1991, at 207.

[36.]Carol Wolinsky and James Sylvester, *Privacy in the Telecommunications Age,* COMM. OF THE ACM, Feb. 1992, at 23.

[37.]Susan E. Kinsman, *Toll Fraud On Rise, SNET Says,* HARTFORD COURANT, July 29, 1992, at B1. "To frustrate casual hackers, net managers are adding password protection to private branch exchanges, voice mail systems, automated attendants, and the remote administrative ports used to manage them. They are thwarting the pros by blocking calls to certain locations and taking corrective action when call monitoring indicates they've fallen victim to hackers." *See* Annabel Dodd, *When Going the Extra Mile is Not Enough,* NETWORK WORLD, Apr. 12, 1993, at 49.

[38.]*See* Kinsman, *supra* note 37.

[39.]*See* Dodd, *supra* note 37.

[40.]*See* Kinsman, *supra* note 37.

[41.]29 U.S.C. § 157 (1988).

[42.]For instance, absent a showing by union organizers that: (1) they possess no other reasonable alternative means of communication to reach non-union employees, or (2) that the employer is discriminating against the union's access to facilities it otherwise makes available, the courts are unlikely to afford the organizers access to an employer's private e-mail or telecommunications facilities. The Supreme Court has held that reasonable alternative means of communication (RAMC) do not exist when the location of the employer's premises and the employee's living quarters place the employees beyond the reach of the union's reasonable efforts to communicate with them. Reasonable alternative means of communications include publicity, mail, letters, and person to person communication at employees' homes, by phone, or on the streets. *See* Lechmere, Inc. v. NLRB 112 S. Ct. 841, 848 (1992); Sears, Roebuck & Co. v. San Diego County District Council of Carpenters, 436 U.S. 180, 205 (1978); and NLRB v. Babcock & Wilcox Co., 351 U.S. 105 (1956). *See* Michael L. Stevens, *The Conflict Between Union Access and Private Property Rights: Lechmere, Inc. v. NLRB and the Question of Accommodation,* 41 EMORY L. J. 1317 (Fall 1992) (arguing that the Supreme Court's "reasonable alternative means of communication" standard first announced in Babcock and later affirmed in Lechmere is the appropriate standard).

[43.]Cash & Konsynski, *supra* note 24. Companies may participate in JONs on three levels. They may enter and receive information (content and access to the network as configured), they may participate in the development of software and network maintenance (network intelligence), and they may manage the network and control its configuration and provisioning (network management and control) At the first level, the JONs participant only has access to the network through restricted protocols and usually acts solely as an information entry-receipt node. The JONs system simply provides standard messages. For example, an independent travel agency may use one of the major airline reservation systems without possessing additional in-house processing capability. The majority of current JONs participants are operating at this entry level. *Id.*

Companies participating at the second level control the development and maintenance of the software used by the other JONs participants. Usually, these JONs developers have absorbed the cost of software development and maintenance in order to gain exclusive control over decisions on access, price, application design, and the network. In the airline reservation systems, American and United Airlines are second level participants. They are primarily responsible for developing their SABRE and APOLLO systems, respectively.

Participants at level three serve as the utility. They usually own or manage all the network facilities as well as the computer processing resources. The Regional Bell Operating Companies (RBOCs), The Source, and CompuServe are examples of such participants. *Id.*

[44.]*Id.*

[45.]This is an area that is receiving increasing scrutiny as telephone network users push for access to the network's functionalities and intelligence for purposes of reconfiguration.

[46.]*See* Dunstan McNichol, *Former NWA Exec Says Computer Monopoly Is Killing Airlines,* STATES NEWS SERV. *See also* Helliwell, *supra* note 24.

[47.]*See* Wolinsky & Sylvester, *supra* note 36.

[48.]Prodigy Services Co., an information services company owned jointly by Sears, Roebuck and Co. and International Business Machines Corp., has been involved in a number of controversies regarding speech over it facilities. It eliminated controversial bulletin board files such as "Health Spa" which precipitated a bitter argument between religious fundamentalists and gays because of discussions of gay sexuality. It also terminated the memberships of subscribers protesting Prodigy's increase in e-mail prices to Prodigy advertisers. *See* W. John Moore, *Taming Cyberspace,* NAT'L J., Mar. 28, 1992, at 745.

Prodigy maintains that its subscribers have no first amendment rights on its bulletin board services, nevertheless it does not want to be held responsible for the content of communications it allows to run absent an express endorsement or failure to disavow. For instance, Prodigy was uncomfortable with taking responsibility for bulletin board statements that the Holocaust never occurred. *Id.*

[49.]*See* Cubby v. CompuServe Information Service, 776 F. Supp. 135 (S.D.N.Y. 1991). The Cubby court held that CompuServe was not responsible for allegedly libelous statements made in a bulletin board called Rumormonger, that was carried on CompuServe's system. Liability was not forthcoming because CompuServe did not exercise editorial control over the bulletin board's content. *Id. See also* Moore, *supra* note 48; and Felicity Barringer, *Electronic Bulletin Boards Need Editing. No They Don't,* N. Y. TIMES, Mar. 11, 1990, at D4.

[50.]*See* Syracuse Peace Council, 2 FCC Rcd. 5043, *recon. denied,* 3 FCC Rcd. 2035, *aff'd,* Syracuse Peace Council v. FCC, 867 F.2d 654 (D.C. Cir. 1989), *cert. denied,* 439 U.S. 1019 (1990).

[51.]Leathers v Medlock, 499 U.S. 439, 444 (1991); City of Los Angeles v. Preferred Communications, Inc. 476 U.S. 484, 494 (1986).

[52.]For the moment, broadcaster access to cable television channels has been upheld in Turner Broadcasting Sys., Inc. v. FCC, 818 F. Supp. 32, (D.D.C. 1993), vacated 114 S. Ct. 2445, (1994); while public access to cable channels via public government and educational access channels and programmer access to cable leased access channels has been recently upheld in Daniels Cablevision, Inc. v. United States, 835 F. Supp. 1, (D.D.C. 1993).

[53.]Sable Communications Inc. v. FCC, 492 U.S. 115.

[54.]Chesapeake and Potomac Telephone of Virginia et al. v. U. S. 830 F. Supp. 909, (E.D.Va. 1993), aff'd, 42 F.3rd 181 (4th Cir. 1994) (hereinafter C&P v. US). *Also see* Edmund Andrews, *Ruling Frees Phone Concerns to Offer Cable Programming*, N.Y. TIMES, Aug. 25, 1993, at A1 (announcing the decision of the U.S. District Court decision overturning the telephone-cable television cross-ownership ban), and 47 U.S.C. § 533 (b), The Cable Communications Policy Act of 1984 (prohibiting local telephone companies from providing video programming to potential viewers in their service area directly or indirectly through an entity owned by the telephone company or under its common control).

[55.]Sable Communications of California, Inc. v. FCC, 492 U.S. 115; Dial Info. Servs. Corp. of N.Y. v. Thornburg, 938 F. 2d 1291; Carlin Communication Inc., v. Mountain States Telephone & Tel. Co., 827 F. 2d 1291 (9th Cir. 1987), *cert. denied*, 485 U.S. 1029 (1988); and Information Providers Coalition for the Defense of the First Amendment v. FCC et al. , 928 F. 2d 866 (9th Cir. 1991).

    In each of the Circuit Court cases, the issues concerned messages for which the telephone companies collected fees on behalf of the information provider. The information providers were allowed to provide messages which the telephone companies did not provide billing services for. However, the difficulties associated with collections absent the assistance of the phone companies rendered the information providers' businesses marginal at best. The carriers' provision of billing services was voluntary rather than required by law.

[56.]C&P v. US, 830 F. Supp 909.

[57.]Professor Jerome Barron has taken justifiable issue with the Circuit Court opinions. He argues that the courts, in upholding the decisions of telephone common carriers to refuse carriage or the provision of billing services to dial-a-porn providers, have allowed the telephone common carriers an unjustified measure of editorial control over the content of speech transmitted over their facilities. Jerome Barron, *The Telco, The Common Carrier Model and the First Amendment -- The "Dial-A-Porn" Precedent*, 19 RUTGERS COMPUTER & TECH. L.J. 371, 385-91 (1993).

[58.]Alliance for Community Media et al. v. FCC, 10 F. 3d 812, (D.C. Cir. 1993), *vacated upon the granting of request for reh'g en banc*, 15 F. 3rd 186 (D.C. Cir. 1994); *reversed* (D.C. Cir. en banc. 1995) No. 93-1169. In Alliance, the Court considered among other issues, the constitutionality of FCC regulations requiring in some situations that cable operators: (1) prohibit or segregate any programming on their leased access channels which they reasonably believes to be indecent; and (2) prohibit obscene or indecent programming as well as programming soliciting unlawful conduct. In response to the government's argument that cable operators operating under the regulations are not state actors, the court concluded that the statute significantly encourages the operators to ban indecent speech. Consequently, operator action is state action. *Id*. at *31. This reasoning was expressly overturned in the subsequent en banc opinion. However, the en banc opinion has been appealed to the Supreme Court.

[59.]*Id*. at *24-*27 and accompanying notes.

[60.]Foreborne carriers have the right to serve discrete segments of the market with minimal tariff reporting requirments. *See* In the Matter of Tariff Filing Requirements for Nondominant Common Carriers, 8 FCC Rcd 6752; Aug. 18, 1993; In the Matter of Policy and Rules Concerning Rates for Dominant Carriers, Part 1 of 3, 4 FCC Rcd 2873, Apr. 17, 1989; and MCI Telecommunications Corp. v. FCC, 765 F.2d 1186 (D.C. Cir. 1985). Until recently, the Commission maintained a permissive tariffing policy which allowed non-dominant carriers to elect not to file tariffs. The FCC's permissive tariffing policy was recently overturned, by the Circuit Court of Appeals for the District of Columbia. This result was much to the disagreement of at least one former chair of the FCC. *See Sikes in Parting Shot to Congress Wants Forbearance Restored*, REP. ON AT&T, Jan. 18, 1993.

Nevertheless, shortly after the circuit court's decision, the Commission has approached the line of absolute deregulation by allowing non-dominant carriers to file tariffs on one day's notice under the rationale that they do not possess sufficient market power to set rates for competitive service offerings. *See* In the Matter of Tariff Filing Requirements for Nondominant Common Carriers, supra note 60. The Circuit Court's decision was recently upheld by the Supreme Court.

[61.]Under a narrow reading of the applicable precedent, they would arguably be free to ban dial-a-porn from their networks by refusing to offer billing services to dial-a-porn information providers. For D.C. Circuit Court analysis of Dial Info. Servs. Corp. of N.Y. v. Thornburg, 938 F. 2d 1291, Carlin Communication Inc., v. Mountain States Telephone & Tel. Co., 827 F. 2d 1291, and Information Providers, *see* Alliance for Media et al. v. FCC, 10 F. 3d 812 (1993).

[62.]While the Electronic Communications Privacy Act protects users of e-mail and bulletin boards against the intentional monitoring of their messages by third parties, employers seeking to protect company information and assets can monitor employee messages on internal e-mail systems. Julie Bennett, *Firms' Rights Protected by Electronic Mail Laws*, CRAIN'S N. Y. BUS., Oct. 8, 1990, at 28. The Electronic Communications Privacy Act of 1986, also allows employers to read employee e-mail messages situated on company computer systems that permit third party access, provided the employee gives permission. Rosalind Resnick, *The Outer Limits*, NAT'L L.J., Sept. 16, 1991, at 1.

[63.]Some take the position that any monitoring of E-Mail or searching through personal employee files is ethically wrong regardless of the law. *See* Glenn Rifkin, *Do Employees Have a Right to Electronic Privacy?* N.Y. TIMES, DEC. 8, 1991, at C8. Aside from questions of ethics, others have argued that the use of monitoring is demoralizing to employees and therefore counter productive. Glenn Rifkin, *The Ethics Gap*, COMPUTERWORLD, Oct. 14, 1991, at 83.

[64.]*See* Linda Wilson, *Addressing E-Mail Rights*, INFORMATION WEEK, Feb. 15, 1993, at 54, ; *Electronic Mail Raises Issues About Privacy, Experts Say*, BNA DAILY LABOR REP., Nov. 17, 1992; *More E-Mail Legal Actions*, COMPUTER FRAUD & SECURITY BULL., Feb. 1992; Rifkin, *supra* note 63; Alice Kahn, *Careful - The Boss Might Be Reading Your Electronic Mail*, SAN FRAN. CHRON., Nov. 20, 1991, at 3E; Bennett, *supra* note 62; and Resnick, *supra* note 62.

[65.]Victoria Slind-Flor, *What is E-Mail Exactly?* NAT'L L.J., Nov. 25, 1991, at 3.

[66.]The Electronic Communications Privacy Act protects all electronic communications systems, including purely internal e-mail systems and public systems from outside intruders. It also protects the privacy of certain messages sent over public electronic mail systems like Compuserve and MCI Mail in much the same manner as telephone calls over public telephone systems are protected. *See* Future Perspective, supra note 5. *See generally* Wilson, *supra* note 64; and Rifkin, *The ethics gap, supra* note 63; *Despite growing attention, many IS managers say, 'It's not my job,'* COMPUTERWORLD, Oct. 14, 1991, at 83.

The Electronic Communications Privacy Act (ECPA) of 1986, for example, states that electronic mail messages on company computer systems that also permit access from outside can be read by the employer -- but only if the receiver or sender gives permission. *See* Resnick, *supra* note 62.

Also, to the extent that state constitutions afford an employee a right of privacy or speech, they may not be precluded by the ECPA. For instance, a recent attempt to argue federal preemption failed in California. *See* Slind-Flor, *supra* note 65 (discussing Alana Shores v. Epson America Inc., SWC112749 and Flanagan v. Epson America, BC007036).

[67.]Rankin v. McPherson, 483 U.S. 378 (1987). (Public employees may not be fired for making statements about matters of public concern.) *See generally* Estlund, *supra* note 13. However, the question of whether employees can make such statements over the company's e-mail and/or telephone systems has not been addressed to date.

[68.]*Id. See also* Matthew W. Finkin et al., LEGAL PROTECTION FOR THE INDIVIDUAL EMPLOYEE 284-286 (1989).

[69.]Whether a public employee's speech concerns a matter of public interest is determined by the content, form and context of the statement, gleaned from the entire record before the court. *See* Connick v. Meyers, 461 U.S. 138, 147-148 (1983). *Also see* Cynthia K. Y. Lee, *Freedom of Speech in the Public Workplace: A Comment on the Public Requirement*, 76 CALIF. L. REV. 1109, 1111 (1988). Even when a public employee's speech addresses a matter of public concern, an employer can restrict the speech in question if the employer perceives that the speech will disrupt the workplace. Toni M. Massaro, *Significant Silences: Freedom of Speech in the Public Sector Workplace*, 61 S. CAL. L. REV. 3, 4 (1987).

[70.]These include section 7 concerted activities for the purposes of mutual aid, such as union organizing, and striking to improve working conditions. They arguably also include protests and advocacy which predate cognizable collective efforts to organize. *See* Estlund, *surpa* note 13, at 924, n13; and Charles Morris, *NLRB Protection in the NonUnion Workplace: A Glimpse at A General Theory of Section 7 Conduct*, 137 U. PA. L. REV. 1673, 1677 (1989).

[71.]*See* Estlund *supra* note 13, at 924. *See also* Finkin, *supra* note 68.

[72.]One expert has argued that despite the fact that free speech is a constitutional right outside of the workplace, speech can be regulated in the workplace so long as there are legitimate business reasons for doing so. Also, there should be a clear corporate policy enunciated which sets forth the reasons for the restrictions. *See Electronic Mail Raises Issues About Privacy, supra* note 64. The arguable absence of legally sanctioned speech rights has not deterred those who view employee speech as a right. *See* Rifkin, *supra* note 63, at 83, 85. To date businesses have not authored many guidelines for internal corporate e-mail networks. There are, however, as many as 200 state statutes covering e-mail related issues. *See Electronic Mail Raises Issues About Privacy, supra* note 64.

[73.]Similarly, at least one scholar argues that employers are free to invade employee privacy on e-mail as well. Steven B. Winters, *Do Not Fold, Spindle or Mutilate: An Examination of Workplace Privacy in Electronic Mail*, 1 S. CAL. INTERDISCIPLINARY L.J. 85 (1992).

[74.]Other forms of control are used as well. For instance, on the internet, an amalgam of research oriented networks moving towards commercialization, group users sometimes "...gang up on abuses [by a particular user] in a form of citizens' arrests [sic] in which abusers are asked to stop disrespectful behavior." J.A. Savage and Gary H. Anthes, *Internet Privatization Adrift*, COMPUTERWORLD, Nov. 26, 1990, at 1. According to the Chair of the Internet Activities board, this form of censure has been effective and no one has been forced off the network. *Id.*

[75.]It is possible that a sysop may be held responsible for libelous information residing on its bulletin board systems. However, the current law remains unsettled. *See* Robert Charles, *Bulletin Boards and Defamation: Who Should Be Liable? Under What Standard?* 2 J.L. & TECH. 121, 134 (1993). *See also* David J. Conner, *Cubby v. Compuserve, Defamation Law on the Electronic Frontier*, 2 GEO. MASON U. L. REV. 227 (1993); and David R. Johnson & Kevin A. Marks, *Mapping Electronic Data Communications Onto Existing Legal Metaphors: Should We Let Our Conscience (and Our Contracts) be Our Guide?* 38 VILL. L. REV. 487 (1993). It is argued that if the sysop knows the statement to be false, or should have known, or they fail to delete libelous information once notified by the injured party, they may be sued for publication of libel. *See* Charles, *surpa* at 147-148; Johnson & Marks, *supra* at 497.

[76.]In re AT&T Communications, Contract Tariff F.C.C. No.[s] 2[-13]; and 15, 9 F.C.C.R. 6752 (1993) (affirming the FCC decision to allow AT&T to offer business services under contract tariffs). The Commission has permitted AT&T to offer services under tariff via individually negotiated contracts provided the contract tariffs are made generally available to similarly situated customers under substantially similar circumstances. *See* In re Competition in the Interstate Inter-exchange Marketplace, 6 F.C.C.R. 5880, 5869-97 (1991), *recon. in part*, 6 F.cC.C.R. 7569 (1991), *further recon.*, 7 F.C.C.R. 2677 (1992) (Inter-exchange Order).

[77.]In the Matter of Tariff Filing Requirements for Non-dominant Common Carriers, 8 FCC Rcd 6752, August 16, 1993. While the FCC has substantially deregulated the telecommunications industry, it cannot compel carriers to eschew the filing of tariffs if they so desire. MCI Telecommunications Corp. v. FCC, 765 F.2d 1186 (D.C. Cir. 1985). The Commission has approached the line of absolute deregulation by allowing non-dominant carriers to file tariffs on one day's notice under the rationale that they do not possess sufficient market power to set rates for competitive service offerings. *Id.* Prior to the Commission's initial foray into deregulation, carriers were required to file tariffs as much as 90 days in advance of their proposed effective date to allow Commission and public review of the proposed offerings.

[78.]*See* Phillip S. Cross, *Utility Liability Waivers: New Rules for New Technologies,* 129 PUB. UTIL. FORT. 34 (1992); and James Brook, *Contractual Disclaimer and Limitation of Liability Under the Law of New York,* 49 BROOKLYN L. REV. 1, 22 (1982). *See generally Liability of Telegraph or Telephone Company for Transmitting or Permitting Transmission of Libelous or Slanderous Messages,* 91 ALR3rd 1015 (1993). Telephone companies retain the right to refuse service where a subscriber uses obscene or profane speech. *See* Allan L. Schwartz, *Right of Telephone Company to Refuse, or Discontinue, Service Because of Use of Improper Language,* 32 ALR3rd 1041 (1993).

[79.]Carriers are often successful in limiting their liability for provision of service. M.R.C.S., Inc. v. MCI, 1987 WL 12813 (E.D.La.) (claims against carrier for poor quality transmission is limited to the terms of the tariff.). *See also,* Brook, *supra* note 78. However, there are numerous instances in which the courts have refused to allow exculpatory language in carrier tariffs to limit carriers' liability. *See* In Re Illinois Bell Switching Station Litigation, 1993 WL 323120 (Sup. Crt. Ill.) (1993), (carrier's exculpatory tariff language limiting liability for consequential damages is not controlling in the face of wilful violation of a state statute and regulations requiring utility to provide adequate and efficient, just and reasonable facilities); Source Assoc. Inc., v. MCI, 1989 WL 134580 (1989) (tariff does not limit liability for willful misconduct); D. Clarico, et al. v. Southwestern Bell Telephone Co. 725 S.W. 2d 304 (1986) (reasonableness of public utility's tariff limitation becomes an issue of fact where utility can but does not timely remedy customer's problem resulting in a loss which exceeds tariff limitation on liability); Lahke et al., v. Cincinnati Bell, Inc. 439 N.E. 2d 928 (1981) (carrier's exculpatory tariff language is not controlling in the face of violation of a state statute requiring utility to provide necessary and adequate facilities).

[80.]*See* C&P v. US, 830 F. Supp. 909.

[81.]*See supra* note 79. There are also a growing number of cases extending tort liability to providers of goods and services generated via the use of computer and information technologies. *See generally* Barry B. Sookman, *The Liability of Information Providers in Negligence,* 5 COMPUTER L. & PRAC. 141 (1989).

[82.]"...sysops have the right to run their systems any way they see fit. They have no 'common carrier' obligations, as do the telephone companies, to transmit everyone's messages." Brock N. Meeks, *As BBSes Mature, Liability Becomes an Issue,* INFOWORLD, Jan. 22, 1990, at S14. According to some, a sysop is a publisher with the corresponding right to edit or shape the bulletin board's message traffic as they see fit. *Id.*

[83.]*Id.* Because Compuserve exercised no editorial control over information on one of its bulletin board services, it avoided potential liability for libel. *See* Cubby, Inc. et al. v. Compuserve, et al., 776 F. Supp. 135 (1991). Also see William Jackson, *Compuserve Picked its Fight in Libel Case,* BUS. FIRST-COLUMBUS, Nov. 18, 1991, at 4.

[84.]*See* Stuart Silverstein, *Prodigy Services' Fee Set Up Under Probe,* L.A. TIMES, Apr. 16, 1991, at D1; Geoffrey Stone, *The First Amendment Is Safe at Prodigy,* N.Y. TIMES, Dec. 16, 1990, at 3-13.

[85.]Warren G. Lavey, *The Public Policies that Changed the Telephone Industry Into Regulated Monopolies: Lesson from Around 1915,* 39 FED. COM. L. J. 171 (1989).

[86.]*See surpa* note 55.

[87.]*See* C&P v. US, 830 F. Supp. 909.

[88.]*See* Andrews, *supra* note 54.(announcing the decision of the U.S. District Court decision overturning the telephone-cable television cross-ownership ban at 47 U.S.C. @ 533 (b), The Cable Communications Policy Act of 1984). *Also see* 47 U.S.C. @ 533 (b), The Cable Communications Policy Act of 1984, prohibiting local telephone companies from providing video programming to potential viewers in its service area directly or indirectly through an entity owned by the telephone company or under its common control. Waivers have been granted under statue and *FCC rule. See FCC Upholds GTE Cerritos Waiver, Grants Another,* BROADCASTING MAG., May 1, 1989, at 136.

[89.]The National Cable Television Association has gone so far as to intervene on the government's side in its efforts to deny the entry of the Regional Bell Operating Companies (RBOCs) into the video programming markets existing in the RBOC's service areas. See Edmund L. Andrews, *A Communications Free-For-All,* N.Y. TIMES, Feb. 4, 1994, at D1; and Comm.Daily, Feb. 11, 1993, at 8.

[90.]In a similar vein, the Regional Bell Operating Companies (RBOCs) are currently seeking modification of proposed legislation that would require them to unbundle their switching and transmission services to allow potential competitors to interconnect at lower cost. *Id.*

[91.]*See infra* discussion of 1st amendment impact of switched intelligent networks.

[92.]*See* Allen S. Hammond, IV, *Regulating Broadband Communications Networks,* 9 YALE J. ON REG. 181, 183-191, (1992).

[93.]*Id* at 196-198 and accompanying notes.

[94.]*See* C&P v. US, 830 F. Supp. 909.

[95.]Regarding restrictions on access to on line data systems, *see* Silverstein, *supra* note 84; Michael Schuyler, *Systems Librarian and Automation Review: Rights of Computer On Line Service Users,* SMALL COMPUTERS IN LIBRARIES, Dec. 1990, at 41; and Geoffrey Moore, *The First Amendment is Safe at Prodigy,* N.Y. TIMES, Dec. 16, 1990, at 3-13.
   With regard to discriminatory provision of leased access to cable television, see Donna N. Lampert, *Cable Television: Does Leased Access Mean Least Access?* A REP. OF THE ANNENBERG WASH. PROG. IN COMM. POL'Y STUD., 10-12, 15-16 (Northwest U. ed., 1991); Henry Gilgof, *Report Card on Cablevision: Mixed Signals: Programs Praised, Fees Criticized,* NEWSDAY, Sept. 10, 1990, at 2; Chuck Stogel, *Amid Cable TV Tangle, Is Viewer Being Served,* SPORTING NEWS, Aug., 27, 1990, at 45. The more recent leased access provisions have been upheld as constitutional. *See Most Provisions of 1992 Cable Act Survive First Amendment Challenge,* BNA ANTITRUST & TRADE REG. REP., Sept. 23, 1993, at 387.

[96.]It may be that due to the relative newness of these services and the necessity to have access to the appropriate telephony and computer equipment, access is controlled by economic and market demand factors.

[97.]Cubby, Inc. et al. v. Compuserve, et al., 776 F. Supp. 135.

[98.]Compuserve was deemed a distributor rather than a publisher based on several factors. Based on its determination that Compuserve was a distributor, the court held that Compuserve would have had to have knowledge or reason to know that the remarks of the Journalism Forum were allegedly defamatory. *Id.*

[99.]Medphone Corp., a small New Jersey company sued Peter DeNigris, a 41-year-old elections forms processor and amateur stock investor, from Long Island, NY, in federal court in New Jersey. Medphone alleged that DeNigris' comments on Money Talk, a bulletin board service operated by Prodigy, helped cause an almost 50% decline in the company's stock in the summer of 1992. Medphone also alleged that DeNigris engaged in libel and securities fraud. Amy Harmon, *Cyberspace: Millions of Americans Swap Information on Computer Bulletin Boards*, L.A. TIMES, Mar. 19, 1993, at 1.

[100.]Prodigy is not named as a defendant in the Medphone suit. However, its insistence on screening all electronic messages on its system has led some to argue it is a publisher and therefore should have some liability for libelous statements made over its facilities. *Id.* The $40 million suit filed against Denigris was settled for $1.00 in late November 1993. See Fred Volgelstein, *Computer Libel Suit Settled, But the Issue Isn't*, NEWSDAY, Dec. 28, 1993, at 7; and Kurt Eichenwald, *Medphone Blames Messenger for its Stock Price Troubles*, N.Y. TIMES, Dec. 28, 1993, at D8.

[101.]*See* Harmon, *supra* note 99.

[102.]Miami Herald Publishing Co., v. Tornillo, 418 U.S. 241 (1974).

[103.]Sable Communications of California v. FC, 492 U.S. 115 (1989).

[104.]Leathers v. Medlock, 499 U.S. 439 (1991) (cable) and Red Lion Broadcasting, v. FCC 395 U.S. 367 (1969) (broadcasting).

[105.]*See* Metro Broadcasting v. FCC, 497 U.S. 547 (1990); and Red Lion Broadcasting v. FCC 395 U.S. 367 (1969). In Red Lion, the Supreme Court recognized broadcasters as having a qualified constitutional speech right. However, broadcasters' editorial speech rights were held secondary to the rights of listeners and viewers to receive diverse information and ideas. *Id.* at 389-390.

[106.]*See* CBS v. Democratic National Committee, 412 U.S. 94 (1973) (broadcasters could not be compelled to accept editorial advertisements covering controversial issues); and Syracuse Peace Council v. FCC 867 F. 2d 654 (1985).

[107.]Over time, the broadcast licensee's speech right has been expanded. Broadcasters may not be compelled to accept editorial advertisements for broadcast when they are already adhering to an obligation to present controversial issues of public importance fairly. They retain the right to decide what controversial "issues are to be discussed and by whom, and when." *See* Columbia Broadcasting System, Inc. v. Democratic National Committee. 412 U.S. 94 (1973).

Most recently, the Federal Communications Commission was upheld when it abolished the Fairness Doctrine because it "chilled" broadcasters' exercise of their editorial discretion, caused a reduction in the coverage of controversial issues, and hence deserved the First Amendment interests of the public. *See* Syracuse Peace Council, 2 FCC Rcd. 5043, *recon.denied,* 3 FCC Rcd. 2035, *aff'd,* Syracuse Peace Council v. FCC, 867 F.2d 654.

The Commission rested a significant part of its rationale for advocating the repeal of the Fairness Doctrine on technological grounds: "We believe that the dramatic changes in the electronic media, together with the unacceptable chilling effect resulting from the implementation of such regulations as the Fairness Doctrine, form a compelling and convincing basis on which to reconsider First Amendment principles developed for another market." *Id.*

[108.]CBS v. Democratic National Committee, 412 U.S. 94 (broadcasters could not be compelled to accept editorial advertisements covering controversial issues).

[109.]Action for Children's Television v. FCC, 932 F. 2d 1504 (D.C. Cir. 1991), *cert. denied*,112 S. Ct. 1282 (1992); and FCC v. Pacifica Foundation, 438 U.S. 726 (1978).

[110.]*See* Michael Meyerson, *The First Amendment and the Cable Operator: An Unprotected Shield Against Public Access Requirements*, 4 Comment 1 (1981).

[111.]*See* Berkshire Cablevision of Rhode Island, Inc. v. Burke, 571 F. Supp. 976 (1983), *vacated as moot*, 773 F.2d 382 (1st Cir. 1985) (holding that mandatory cable channel access rules are constitutional based on theory of economic scarcity). CF Preferred Communications v City of Los Angeles, 754 F.2d 1396 (9th Cir. 1985), *aff'd*, 476 U.S. 488 (1986) (requiring cable operator to set aside mandatory and leased access channels diminishes the operator's freedom of expression).

[112.]*See* Cable Television Consumer Protection and Competition Act of 1992; and Turner Broadcasting System , Inc. v. FCC, 1994 WL 279691 (U.S. Dist. Col.) June 27, 1994.

[113.]*See* Cable Communications Policy Act of 1984, 47 U.S.C. §§ 531 (public, educational and governmental access channels), and 532 (leased access channels).

[114.] Although a majority of the Court in Turner found that the must carry rules are constitutional in the abstract, the Court remanded the case back to the district court. The Court found that the government's interests in promoting diversity of information from competing sources, preserving 40% of the society's access to economically viable broadcast stations, and promoting fair competition in the video distribution market are compelling. It also determined, however, that the government had failed to provide sufficient evidence to establish that broadcast stations are in economic jeopardy and that the must carry rules will actually advance the government's interests by materially alleviating the economic harm.

[115.]Alliance for Media et al. v. FCC, 10 F. 3d 812 (1993).

[116.]*Id.*

[117.]*See Electronic Media Regulation and the First Amendment: Future Perspective, supra* note --; *See generally* Wilson, *supra* note 64; and Rifkin, *supra* note 63.

[118.]Rankin v. McPherson, 483 U.S. 378 (1987). (Public employees may not be fired for making statements about matters of public concern. *See generally* Estlund, *supra* note 13. However, the question of whether employees can make such statements over the company's e-mail and/or telephone systems has not been addressed to date.

[119.]Rifkin, *supra* note 63.

[120.]A government employee cannot be fired for non-disruptive exercise of her First Amendment right to speak on matters of public concern, Connick v. Meyers, 461 U.S. 138, 150-51 (1983), provided, however, that the employer does not possess an interest in "effective and efficient fulfillment of its responsibilities to the public [which] outweigh the employee's interest in speaking."

[121.]Estlund, *supra* note 13.

[122.]While arguments for absolute access to the networks of closed user groups seem inappropriate, it is reasonable to require access where the network is an essential facility or is used for anti-competitive purposes. Similarly, it is reasonable to require some appropriate level of access where a compelling public interest in the information to be provided.

[123.]Information providers who find their access to network or their communication over the network constrained by the network owner, may be able to establish that an antitrust violation has occurred. United States v. Grinnell Corp., 384 U. S. 563, 570-571 (1966).

[124.]*See generally*, Henry H. Perrit, Jr. *The Congress, The Courts and Computer Based Communications Networks: Answering Questions About Access and Content Control, Introduction*, 38 VILL.L. REV. 319 (1993).

[125.]Sections 4 and 5 of the Act require cable systems of a certain size to carry, upon broadcaster request, the signals of certain licensed commercial and non-commercial broadcast stations in the cable operator's market. The legislation had been upheld as constitutional for the moment. Turner Broadcasting Systems, Inc. v. Federal Communications Commission, 114 S. Ct. 2445 (1994).

[126.]Section 7(b)(4)(B) of the Cable Television Consumer Protection and Competition Act of 1992, Pub. L. No. 102-385, 106 Stat. 1460 (1992), allows franchising authorities to require cable systems to provide public, educational and governmental access channels.

[127.]Section 9 of the Cable Television Consumer Protection and Competition Act of 1992, Pub. L. No. 102-385, 106 Stat. 1460 (1992), requires cable operators to make a portion of their channel capacity available for leased access by unaffiliated programmers.

[128.]Daniels Cablevision, Inc. v. U.S., 835 F. Supp. 909 (E.D. Va. 1993), *aff'd*, 42 F. 3rd 181 (4th Cir. 1994).

[129.]Challenges have recently been filed in Michigan and Illinois. *See* note 139 *infra*.

[130.]Cable television and regional telephone companies have recently proposed numerous mergers. Although many turned out to be short lived in the initial stages, many regulators and industry analysts expect this merger of industries and technologies to result in the provision of interactive, broadband, multimedia services. *See* Deutschman & Davis, *supra* note 2; *Policing the Information Highway, supra* note 2; Kupfer, *supra* note 2; Solomon, *supra* note 2; Greenwald, *supra* note 2; and Sugawara & Farhi, supra note 2.

[131.]The court in Turner concluded that to the extent the First Amendment is implicated at all by the must carry rules, it is a mere by-product of the fact that cable operators transmit video signals having no other function than the communication of information. As such, the must carry provisions are, in the court's mind, "unrelated to the content of any of the messages the cable operators, broadcasters and programmers have in contemplation to deliver." *Id.*

[132.]*See* Report and Order, In the Matter of Policies Regarding Detrimental Effects of Proposed New Broadcast Stations on Existing Stations,3 FCC Rcd 638; 64 Rad. Reg. 2d 583. (Nov. 24, 1987).

[133.]The must carry question is not the first instance in which economic harm to existing broadcast stations has been raised against new competitors. In the broadcast economic injury cases, the courts and the Federal Communications Commission concluded that an existing broadcaster could prevent the entry of a new broadcast competitor based on pleading economic harm unless its allegations of economic injury were supported by proof of a significant loss in news and public affairs programming occasioned by a loss of advertising revenues. And, it also had to establish that this loss in news and public affairs programming would not be alleviated by the new entrant. After years of litigation before it, the FCC concluded that no broadcaster had been able to successfully meet the public interest burden and abolished the economic injury objection. *Id.*

[134.] *See* the Cable Communications Policy Act of 1984 (84 Cable Act) 47 U.S.C. @ 613(b). Also see Common Carriers for Section 214 Certificates for Channel Facilities Furnished to Affiliated Community Antenna Television Systems (Final Report and Order), 21 FCC 2d 307, recon. in part, 22 FCC 2d 746 (1970), aff'd General Telephone Co. of S.W. v. United States, 449 F.2d 846 (5th Cir. 1971).

[135.] *See* H.R. Rep. No. 934, 98th Cong., 2d sess. at 56; and 130 Cong. Rec. H 10,444 (Oct. 1, 1984).

[136.] *See* Further Notice of Inquiry and Notice Proposed Rulemaking, 3 FCC Rcd 5849, Telephone Company-Cable Television Cross Ownership Rules, §§ 63.54-63.58, FCC 88-249 (released Sept. 22, 1988).

[137.] *See* 3 FCC 5849 (1988), *citing,* 69 FCC 2d 1110.

[138.] *See* C&P v. US, Complaint for Declaratory Judgement and Injunctive Relief (Bell Complaint), para. 13 at 5. *Also see Bell Atlantic Challenges Cable Act in U.S. District Court,* TELEPHONE NEWS, Jan. 11, 1993.

[139.] C&P v. US, 830 F. Supp. 909, *aff'd on partly different grounds,* 42 F.3d 181 (Nov. 21, 1994). One other Circuit Court and five other district courts have also found the cable-telephone cross-ownership ban unconstitutional on First Amendment grounds. *See* US West, Inc. v. United States, 1994 U.S. App. Lexis 36775; 95 Cal. Daily Op. Serv. 15, Dec. 30, 1994; GTE California, Inc. v. FCC, 39 F.3d 940 (Oct. 31, 1994); Ameritech Corp. v.United States, 867 F. Supp. 721 (Oct. 28, 1994); Bellsouth Corp. v. United States, 868 F. Supp. 1335 (Sept. 23, 1994); and *USTA, OPATSCO, NTCA Win Lawsuit to Lift Cable Phone Ownership Bank,* BNA MGMT. BRIEFING, Jan. 30, 1995.

[140.] *See generally* In the Matter of Competition in the Interstate Interexchange Marketplace Petitions for Modification of Fresh Look Policy, CC Docket No. 90-132, 8 FCC Rcd 5046 (July 26, 1993); and In the Matter of Competition in the Interstate Interexchange Marketplace, 6 FCC Rcd 7569, November 25, 1991. Also see Victor J. Toth, *To Tariff or not to Tariff - That's No Longer the Question,* BUS. COMM. REV., Jan. 1993, at 60.

[141.] *See* Smolla, *supra* note 6; and Summers, *supra* note 6. *See also supra* note 8 and accompanying text.

[142.] The statutory requirement that cable operators provide leased, educational and governmental access channels was upheld recently. *See generally* Daniels Cablevision, Inc. 835 F. Supp. 1 (1993).

[143.] At least one communications expert asserts that there is no shortage of available spectrum, only a shortage of current human ingenuity to harness it. He points to the history of spectrum development and management wherein new technology allows the use of portions of previously "unusable" spectrum as well as the more efficient use of available spectrum via compression techniques. *See* George Gilder, *What spectrum shortage?* FORBES, May 27, 1991, at 324. Similarly, digital, switched interactive telecommunications networks can provide another source of increasing capacity for the transmission of information to the home. Consequently, they too reduce scarcity. Rockley L. Miller, *Digital World Future Systems,* MULTIMEDIA & VIDEODISC MONITOR, July 1993 (quoting Mitch Kapoor, former chairman of the Electronic Frontier Foundation).

[144.] Andrea Adelson, *Radio Station Consolidation Threatens Small Operators,* N.Y. TIMES Apr. 19, 1993, at D1; Edmund L. Andrews, *Plan to Ease Rule on Buying Radio Stations,* N.Y. TIMES, Feb. 27, 1992, st D1; and *1985: A year like no other for the fifth estate; Changes in the broadcasting industry,* BROADCASTING, Dec. 30, 1985, at 38.

[145.]Speaking at a recent conference on computers, freedom, and privacy in San Francisco, Laurence H. Tribe, a professor of constitutional law at Harvard Law School, called for an amendment to the U.S. Constitution that would protect privacy, speech, and other constitutional rights made possible in part, but now threatened by, computer technology. The Tribe Amendment reads, in full:

"This Constitution's protections for the freedoms of speech, press, petition and assembly, and its protection against unreasonable searches and seizures and the deprivation of life, liberty, or property without due process of law, shall be construed as fully applicable without regard to the technological method or medium through which information content is generated, stored, altered, transmitted, or controlled." In Professor Tribe's view, the current constitutional amendments do not protect the rights of computer users adequately. *See* Resnick, *supra* note 62.

[146.]*See generally* Hammond, *supra* note 92; and Perrit, *supra* note 124, at 334-335.

[147.]Associated Press v. United States, 326 U.S. 1, 19-20 (1945).

[148.]*See* Harry, A. Jessell, *Video Dial Tone Advances at FCC*, BROADCASTING , Oct. 28, 1991, at 26; *Cable Attacks VDT*, TELEVISION DIGEST, Oct. 19, 1992, at 1; and Charles Mason, *Who Are the Real Monopolists?*, TELEPHONY, December 26, 1988, at 10.

[149.]*See* 38 Vill. L. Rev. 571, 575, 584-585 (citing City of Anaheim v. Southern California Edison Co., 955 F.2d 1373, 1380 (9th Cir. 1992); and MCI Communications Corp. v. AT&T, 708 F.2D 1081, 1123-33, (7th Cir. 1983)).

[150.]The FCC defined enhanced services as services "which employ computer processing applications that act on the format, content, code, protocol or similar aspect of the subscriber's transmitted information; provide the subscriber additional, different, or restructured information; or involve subscriber interaction with stored information." 47 C.F.R. § 64.702(a) (1990).

[151.]At least one court was highly skeptical of the ONA plan's efficacy whether in its Computer II form or its subsequent Computer III form. *See* U.S. v. Western Electric et al., 673 F. Supp. 525 (1987). Ironically, the same mechanisms of the ONA plans which Judge Harold Greene found so ineffective in 1987, are the very mechanisms the FCC proposes to implement under its post California v. FCC, modified Computer III regulations.

[152.]In the Computer III decision, the FCC determined that it would be sufficient for the RBOCs to provide enhanced services as integrated entities and offer their "unbundled" basic network functions to other enhanced service providers on a tariffed, nondiscriminatory basis. *See* Computer III, 104 F.C.C.2d at 964-65, 1063-66. See Filing and Review of Open Network Architecture Plans, 4 FCC Rcd. 1 (1988), *recon.*, 5 FCC Rcd. 3084, *amended plans conditionally approved,* 5 FCC Rcd. 3103 (1990). The FCC concluded that requirement to unbundle the network functions, combined with accounting and other non-structural safeguards would obviate the need to rely on the separate subsidiary requirement to prevent the RBOCs from engaging in access discrimination and anticompetitive cross subsidization which would favor their enhanced service operations. Computer III, 104 F.C.C.2d at 1007-12, 2 FCC Rcd. at 3039.

The U.S. Court of Appeals for the Ninth Circuit vacated and remanded the FCC's decision, ruling that the FCC had not provided sufficient support in the record for its conclusion. California v. FCC, 905 F.2d at 1238-39. In the FCC's Computer III proceedings subsequent to the court decision, the FCC quickly reinstated its ONA requirements including its waiver of the structural safeguards. It required that the RBOCs implement their plans to offer unbundled services regardless of its ultimate decision on structural separation. *See* Computer III Remand Proceedings, 5 FCC Rcd. 7719 (1990) and 6 FCC Rcd. 174.

284

153.For instance, Soldier of Fortune Magazine was recently held liable for an advertisement it published which the court interpreted as soliciting contract killing jobs. *See* Ronald Smothers, *Soldier of Fortune Magazine Held Liable for Killer's Ad*, N.Y. TIMES, Aug. 19, 1992, at A18.

154."...Providers of goods and services created using computer and information technologies face increasingly greater exposure to liability when things go awry." See Barry Sookman, *The Liability of Information Providers in Negligence*, COMPUTER L. & PRAC., at 141-146 (1989).

155.At least one state has limited the applicability of telephone carriers exculpatory language to ordinary negligence and does not allow disclaimers for acts of gross negligence, willful neglect or misconduct. *See State OKs Liability Disclaimers for Telcos,* 130 PUB. UTIL.FORT. 42 (Dec. 15, 1992) (discussing Re Inclusion of Liability Limitations, Case Nos. 90-774-T-GI et al., Oct. 30, 1992 (W.Va.P.S.C)).

The Supreme Court for the State of Illinois recently reached the opposite conclusion. It determined that parties' suffering economic injury totalling millions of dollars as a result of a severe fire at an Illinois Bell switch could not recover their losses. The court held that the parties' statutory claims for economic losses were not recoverable in a tort action and that the exculpatory language in Illinois Bell's tariff properly limited claims for disruption of service to compensation for the cost of the calls. *See* Illinois Bell Switching Station Litig. No. 73999, 1994 Ill. LEXIS 97 (Ill. July 28, 1994).

156.Christy Cornell Kunin, *Unilateral Tariff Exculpation in the Era of Competitive Telecommunications,* 41 CATH. L. REV. 907 (1992).

157.47 USC § 414 (1988).

158.Kunin, *supra* note 156, at 914-15, 926.

159.It has been aptly observed that "...the law, by protecting freedom to contract does nothing to prevent freedom of contract from becoming a one-sided privilege." *See* Kessler, *Contracts of Adhesion-Some Thoughts About Freedom of Contract*, 43 *Colum. L. Rev.* 629, 640-641 (1943) (cited in Summers and Hillman, Contract and Related Obligation: Theory, Doctrine and Practice, chpt. 5., p. 585 (1987)).

160.Re Equicom Communications, Inc., 109 Pur 4th 540 (1990), cited in Cross, *supra* note 78.

161.One of the current policy goals in telecommunications regulation is to shift local exchange telecommunications network architecture away from a reliance on centralized network switching systems with limited flexibility to accomodate the creation of new services. The intent is to build networks in which the software "intelligence" is distributed throughout the network and often created and controlled by users rather than switch vendors and telecommunications providers. This shift in network paradigms is the essence of the movement from current telecommunications networks to advanced intelligent networks (AIN).

Ultimately, the anticipated benefit of AIN is to permit telecommunications and enhanced service providers as well as their respective customers, to enhance existing services or create new ones to meet the customers' individual needs. Steven Titch, *The Pathway to Freedom; Local Exchange Carriers, Advanced Intelligent Networks,* TELEPHONY, Apr. 15, 1991, at 30.

There is significant disagreement over the speed and manner of AIN deployment, as well as the manner in which carriers and users may gain access to future AINs. *See* Richard M. Firestone, *Telecommunications Pricing Strategies for the 90s*, TELECOMM. REP., 1991 FCC Lexis 2332 (Apr. 19, 1991) (Firestone is the Chief of the Common Carrier Bureau of the Federal Communications Commisssion).

162.There is significant uncertainty regarding how the public may ultimately react to and use the broadband multi-media capabilities which may be provided by the electronic superhighway. Nevertheless there is also substantial concern that, left to the vagaries of discernable short market demand, industry will not provide an infrastructure capable of extending broadband, multi-media interactive capabilities and services to most, if not all, network users.

[163.]There are several arguments which have arisen with regard to the viability of scarcity as a justification for future regulation of communication and telecommunication media. Some argue that choice of the appropriate technology can enhance opportunities for innovation and obviate the need for regulatory responses to access concerns raised by the existence of scarce transmission capacity. Miller, *supra* note 143. For different reasons, one noted commenter argues that spectrum scarcity as well as the current inability to build fiber to the home is a political rather than a technical or economic problem due to poor regulatory policy choices. *See* Gilder, *supra* note 7.

One possible combination of the two above observations on scarcity is evident in the recent observations of Professor Edwin Baker. He emphasizes what Kapor implies and Gilder states explicitly, that government choices regarding structural regulation can create transmission scarcity. Baker goes on to note that the scarcity is then managed by use of other structural regulation which seeks to manage the impact of the scarcity consistent with first amendment values. *See* C. Edwin Baker, *Merging Phone and Cable*, REMARKS AT THE CITI CONFERENCE ON CABLE TELEVISION AND THE FIRST AMENDMENT (Feb. 21, 1994) (citing C. Edwin Baker, HUMAN LIBERTY AND FREEDOM OF SPEECH, 1989).

PRIVATE NETWORKS PUBLIC OBJECTIVES
E. Noam and A. NíShúilleabháin (Editors)
© 1996 Elsevier Science B.V. All rights reserved.

Interoperability -- Domestic and International Policy

Consumer Protection in the Decentralized Network

Rohan Samarajiva

## 1. INTRODUCTION

The problem addressed in this chapter begins from the phenomenon of "use privatization," described by Eli Noam,[1] more particularly from his concern that operators of private networks will exercise power over persons connecting to the public network through them.[2] Noam defines private networks rather broadly--"they are private in the sense of being separate from the public or general network, and they are not open to all in the way that the public network is."[3] This definition is not hardware or ownership based. It is based on access. Indeed, it suggests that access to the private network is dependent on membership in some social group or organization. When thought of in this way, the phenomenon loses some of its novelty. Organizations such as offices and hospitals used as illustrations have had "membership" criteria and also telecommunication systems governed by internal organizational rules for quite some time. At the simplest level, the household (the unit usually considered the "consumer" within the residential segment of the public wireline network) is an organization with its own rules about access to the telephone instrument and thereby to the network it connects to. A pay phone with its technologically embedded rules governing network access also affects user behavior. So, the phenomenon is actually more general, and more important, than Noam suggests. But the phenomenon has undergone dramatic changes since the liberalization of customer interconnection to the public network in *Carterfone*[4] and the proliferation of private networks is deserving of scholarly attention.

The principal modes of consumer access to the decentralized network are depicted in Figure 1. Of the four principal modes of consumer access to the public network, only one allows direct access--as sole occupant of a household, where the intervening layer of household social organization is absent. In all other situations, the consumer must go through some form of an intervening layer. In a household, it is the family or other social relationship. In the case of access via pay phone, the pay phone provider can constrain and enable the consumer's form of access. Where the consumer is connected to the public network through a private network, the provider of the private network can constrain and enable consumer access. This is in addition to the household layer, if applicable. The above discussion conceptualized the consumer as a "calling party." But almost every consumer is also a "called party." Access to the network is sought not only for the initiation of outgoing calls (faxes, computer messages, etc.);[5] the ability to receive incoming calls is equally important. Control of the interfaces between various networks, and the design of networks and abutting proximate environments can constrain and enable the initiation and the receipt of calls. A private network can be programmed to reject all calls from one or more prefixes

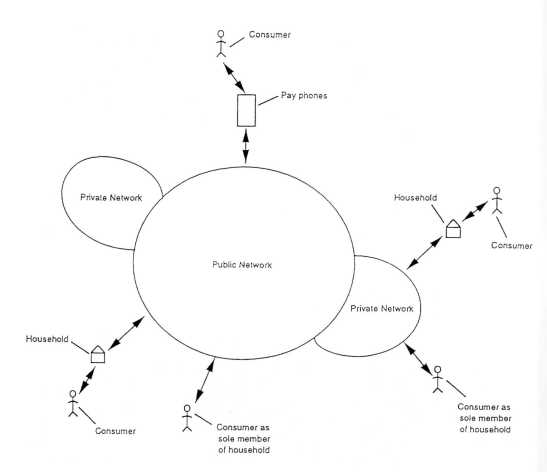

Figure 1: Consumer Access to the Network or Network of Networks

or numbers. In jurisdictions where the call reject service of the "call management services" package has been offered, a residential telephone system (many North American homes have more than one telephone) can be programmed to reject calls from specified numbers without the phone even ringing. Pay phones are frequently programmed to accept no incoming calls at all. This chapter discusses a taxonomy of forms of consumer access to the decentralized network. Secondly, a theoretical framework for analysis of policy implications of private control of such access is outlined. Finally, consumer protection implications in terms of research and policy are discussed.

## 2. A TAXONOMY OF FORMS OF NETWORK ACCESS

At the simplest level, entities participating in the network may be classified as individuals and organizations. Organizations do not actually make calls, individuals call on their behalf, even in this age of automatic dialing and announcement devices and computer-to-computer communication (it is possible to identify an individual responsible for these communications). Thus the classification actually refers to individuals *qua* individuals and individuals *qua* organizations. Given the chapter's focus on consumers, the taxonomy will exclude individuals *qua* organizations. Individual participants in the network are described as consumers, whether or not they have contractual relationships with network providers. That is, a homeless person using a pay phone would be included in the category of consumer.

Figure 2 shows the primary modes by which consumers are linked to the network. Consumers can be connected through the ubiquitous, predominantly wireline, public network. They can also be connected through currently non-ubiquitous, predominantly wireless, public networks, exemplified by cellular networks. The basic distinction between the wireline public network and the wireless public network is that the former was set up as a network connecting immobile physical locations (e.g., rooms in buildings) and that the latter was set up as a network connecting mobile physical locations (e.g., cars). If the inchoate moves toward personal telephone numbers on the part of wireline network providers and those toward truly portable cellular telephones and personal communication devices on the part of wireless network providers succeed, this distinction may begin to blur. Even if the two types of networks were to converge in terms of functionalities and ubiquity, their different institutional histories would still justify separate treatment.

Consumers may directly connect to the wireline or wireless public networks as sole users, or they may connect as household units. In the former case, there is no intervening social organization between the consumer and the network. In the latter case, the rules of the household enable and constrain the consumer's access to the network. An individual consumer's interests regarding network access may come into conflict with those of other individuals in the household or with the household's rules. It has been customary to conflate household and consumer. Perhaps because scholars and policy-makers writing on the subject did not occupy subordinate positions within households. But two recent policy controversies have highlighted the need to open the "black box" of the household.

The first controversy was regarding parental liability for portions of the telephone bill reflecting audiotex usage by minors.[6] Here, the affected parents claimed they were not liable for the high audiotex charges because they did not make the calls and/or the network provider's services had been changed in ways that made parental regulation of network access

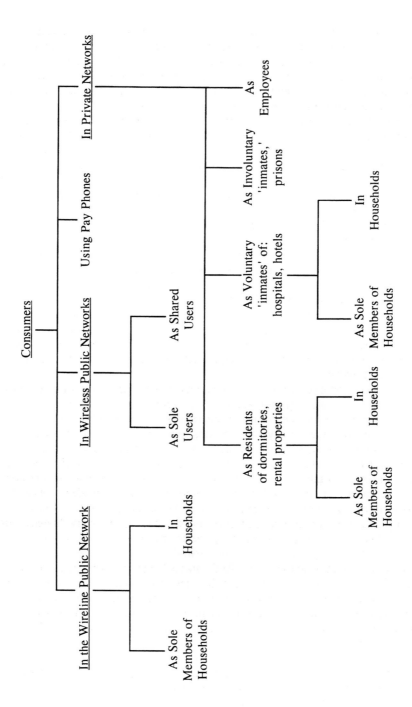

Figure 2: Forms of Consumer Access to Network

by household members difficult or impossible. These claims were taken seriously by regulators, legislators, and even by the Local Exchange Companies (LECs). Disconnection of complainants from the network, at least with respect to local exchange voice telephony, was generally prohibited and various methods of blocking access to audiotex services were devised and offered to parents. In many cases, the LECs forgave the payment due, especially if the appeal was regarding the first audiotex bill.

The second policy controversy was regarding "call management services." Calling number delivery (commonly known as Caller ID), the most controversial of these services, challenges the conflation of household and consumer. Contrary to telephone company puffery, the service does not truly identify a caller, but merely transmits the telephone number assigned to the location from which the call is being made. Should the called party wish to actually identify the caller by name, she must utilize some form of directory and make additional inferences. The assumption that the "will" of the household is identical to those of its members was challenged most poignantly by women's groups who intervened in "call management service" proceedings.[7] Instances of the abusive spouse disconnecting the telephone instrument from the wall jack and taking it when leaving the house (removing the abused spouse's ability to make and receive calls) were reported and the potential uses of the calling number display device and the call return service to monitor calls to the abused spouse were pointed out. Policy analysis premised on the conflation of household and consumer was incapable of addressing situations of coercive and abusive relations within the household.[8] Shared access to wireless public networks through cellular and PCN devices has many similarities with household access to the wireline public network. Current pricing policies that charge for incoming calls as well as outgoing calls further complicate the sharing of access to the wireless public network.

Even though pay telephones are considered by many to be part of the wireline public network, this taxonomy locates pay telephones in a different category. A pay telephone provides direct connection to the wireline public network like a telephone set in a household. However, its user's options with regard to interexchange carriers (and perhaps other features in the future) are affected by the owner of the physical location of the pay telephone facility or some entity drawing its authority from the owner. The recent decisions of certain pay telephone operators and city governments to remove incoming call reception and touchtone capabilities in the name of the "drug war" illustrate the point. The fourth mode of connecting to the network is through private networks interconnected to the public networks. Consumers can connect to private networks in four capacities--as residents, as voluntary "inmates" of institutions, as involuntary inmates of institutions, and as employees *qua* consumers.

(i)     Consumers may have to connect to the PSTN through a private network by reason of residency in more or less permanent housing with some form of common administration. Generally, they will tend to be renters, though some condominium owners may be included. Students living in dormitories or university-owned townhouses are a good example. The rental or condominium agreement will govern access to the network.

In the same way that administrators of these types of housing impose rules of behavior in physical space (e.g., no pets, no loud noise after a certain hour), rules of network access (or behavior in virtual space, discussed below) can be formally written into contracts or incorporated into the technical design of the private network[9] and enforced. The consumer has the choice of accepting the housing contract *in toto*, or finding other accommodation. The consumer's ability to make this choice or to negotiate the terms of access to the network (though this is extremely difficult if they have been embodied in the technical design) is dependent on factors other than telecommunication, namely the competitiveness of that particular housing market and the consumer's relative valuations of various elements of the housing package. Even this option may not be available to the consumer if the housing is a precondition of something else, such as enrollment in a university or employment in a factory. Here the exit option affects the consumer's education or employment, not merely his or her housing. Consumer options can be further constricted in situations where the rules of the private network are changed, by amendment of the lease or by changes in technical design, after the consumer has taken up residence. Here, the costs of moving or of breaking the lease further constrain the exit option. Family units or accommodation-sharing arrangements give rise to an additional layer of constraint/enablement.

(ii)     Consumers may have to connect to the PSTN through private networks as voluntary "inmates" of institutions, generally short-term. Examples are consumers in hospitals, resorts, camps, and hotels. Where the stay is long it may be more appropriate to consider the issues under the closely related sub-category (i) (residents), discussed above. As with residents, the voluntary "inmates" have greater or lesser exit options depending on their specific circumstances. Consumer sovereignty vis-a-vis telecommunication options has little relevance to a person being admitted to hospital following cardiac arrest. As in the previous sub-category, factors external to telecommunication such as the supply of and demand for hotel rooms in a particular location, and consumers relative valuations of elements of the bundled product offered by the institution affect the consumer's ability to exercise choice. Here too, "the household" may affect the terms and conditions of access by a consumer. Examples are a family sharing a hotel room and two patients sharing a hospital room and a phone.

(iii)    Consumers may be connected to private networks as involuntary "inmates" of institutions. An inmate of a prison, a suspect in a remand cell, and a juvenile offender in a place of corrections are examples. Depending on the circumstances, armed forces personnel may be placed in this sub-category or in that of residents ((i) above). A soldier in "boot camp" may be considered an involuntary "inmate," while a soldier living with family in armed forces housing may be considered a resident. By definition, consumers falling into this sub-category have no exit options. Therefore they have only the option of voice if the terms of access to the network are undesirable.[10] Not having the exit option weakens their voice. In addition, carceral institutions are pervaded by coercive power relations which affect both access to the network and negotiation over access. Yet it must be emphasized that power, even of prison administrators, is not absolute, and that inmates can and do exercise agency.[11]

(iv)     Consumers may connect to the PSTN via private networks from their places of employment. Here we have the use of the private network by an employee *qua* consumer. The employee is accessing the network on "company time" and using the organization's equipment, but for purposes different from those of the organization. Making a call from the office to a childcare center during office hours is an example. What the employee does outside "company time" falls into previously described categories, since those activities are of a consumer and outside the purview of the organization. What the employee does *qua* employee, is outside the purview of this paper.

In actual fact, the line between employee *qua* employee and employee *qua* consumer is not clear. To take the example of the call to the childcare center, what is the status of the call if the childcare center is a facility provided by the organization? What if the employee is working overtime (uncompensated), and calls the baby-sitter using the organization's equipment? What if the employee is on the road on the organization's business and routes a call home via the organization's network? Does it make a difference if that call was made during working hours, or when the employee was stranded in an airport due to bad weather? Many of these questions have been resolved, leaving little if any leeway for the employee, in blue-collar work settings. But the practices of white-collar workplaces have traditionally been more favorable to employees. Current perturbations in this area appear to be the result of efforts to increase productivity in white-collar work places using information and communication technologies. Some aspects of these delineation problems are likely to appear under the categories of consumers connecting to public networks (wireline and wireless) when their equipment and/or service charges are picked up by the organization because they work at home or on the road for the organization. This "spillover" is likely to increase with the blurring of the lines between work and leisure and between work place and home, driven in part by teleworking and personal communication technologies.

## 3. THEORETICAL FRAMEWORK[12]

The theoretical framework used in this chapter is a communication-laden reworking of Giddens' structuration theory,[13] with emphasis on time-space and the role of recursive practices in reproducing structure. Drawing from the burgeoning multi-disciplinary inquiry[14] centering on the concept of "cyberspace,"[15] this section seeks to rejuvenate Giddens' rather listless notion of locale. The proposed theoretical framework centers on the notion of "virtual space," reserving the Gibsonian sense of cyberspace--involving direct mind-network-mind communication--for applications more exciting than talking on the phone. Perhaps the most important idea taken from the cyberspace literature is the conceptualization of the network as a space, rather than as a conduit, or as a system of conduits. The framework introduces a cluster of related socio-spatial concepts--"space," "environment," "public space," "private space," and "virtual space." It is presented in greater detail in Samarajiva & Shields.[16]

Space can be understood as a terrain of human interaction. Space is produced, reproduced, and transformed by the same structural forces, social relations, and conflicts which affect social life more generally.[17] Space thus produced serves as a context or resource for action: "social space is what permits fresh action to occur, while suggesting others and prohibiting yet others."[18] In other words, as a social product, space is a material force which reflects back upon social processes. This is the essence of what Soja[19] calls the "socio-spatial dialectic." Proximate space can be distinguished from what Giddens describes as the "created environment" (e.g., pastures, national parks, offices, street corners, shopping malls) defined as "a manufactured series of settings, in which even the countryside is largely ordered in terms of social influences, rather than being a 'given' world of nature."[20] Humans draw upon and/or are constrained by aspects of the physical environment in the production of space. These abstract qualities of proximate space and physical environment also hold true for virtual space and electronic environment.

The simplest form of proximate space is constituted by the co-presence of human actors knowledgeable of each other's existence and relating in some way to each other. Aspects of an environment (e.g., the existence of walls, high noise levels) play an important role in the constitution of a proximate space. Potential for communication (e.g., Is vision obstructed? Does sound carry? Do actors perceive the environment as conducive for interaction?) is crucial. The design of physical environments provides a powerful vehicle for the exercise of power over actors. In his analysis of shopping malls, the modern exemplar of designed environment, Gottdiener argues that the function of mall design is "the control of crowds to facilitate consumption...to disguise the exchange relation between producer and consumer...and to present cognitively an integrated facade which facilitates this instrumental purpose by the stimulation of consumer fantasies."[21] Gottdiener's "socio-semiotic analysis" of control through architecture is important but overdrawn. The mall environment constrains and enables the behavior of the users in a broad sense (e.g., they cannot get out of the building without passing a lot of shops), but it does not fully "determine" specific behaviors (e.g., not every mall user forced to circumambulate shopping displays will make purchases). The mall environment only increases the probability of some of the users making shopping decisions they would not have otherwise made.

The specific relations between human actors in the environment determine the nature of the proximate spaces that can be created within it. These relations are shaped, in turn, by factors such as the comparative location of the interactants in social structure, the perceptions interactants have of these locations, the interactants' perceptions of their previous history with each other as well as their expectations concerning future relations. Depending on the nature of relations between co-present actors in a given environment, multiple proximate spaces can be created in one physical environment. The existence of other spaces in the environment affects the constitution of a proximate space as well, in the sense that one space is part of the environment of another. A prisoner who occupies a proximate space with his guard is constrained in the ability to create a new space with a third party, for example.

Another form of proximate space is produced when one or more actors are unaware of others who are physically proximate and very much aware of them. Environment properties are particularly crucial to the formation of this space. The space constituted by a voyeur utilizing the communicational properties of a one-way mirror is an example. A more complex spatial form is constituted when subjects behave as though others are potentially co-present. The production of this space is central to the disciplinary power discussed by Foucault.[22] Foucault uses the panopticon, an architectural device advocated by Jeremy Bentham in 1791, to exemplify the process which gives birth to the self-policing subject. The panoptic environment consists of a watch-tower surrounded by cells enabling a guard to supervise a multitude of individually segregated prisoners. The guard cannot be observed by the prisoners. Since no prisoner can be certain of when she is not being observed, she must assume constant surveillance. Panopticism forces individuals to self-police by exposing them to the examining gaze: "He who is subjected to a field of visibility, and who knows it, assumes responsibility for the constraints of power; he inscribes the power relation in which he simultaneously plays both roles."[23]  In the terms of the proposed framework, the subject is "locked" in a coercive space with a power-wielder, that is, the subject watches her own behavior so she can do what she thinks the power-wielder wants her to do.  Liberation from this space comes only when the absence of surveillance is established.  Foucault does not allow for this.  In his vision, subjects are never "alone."

Until the advent of electronic media, all significant social interactions occurred in proximate space.  At the present time, we are beginning to see the emergence of virtual space.  In virtual space, actors achieve conditions approaching co-presence via electronic communication media.  However, virtual space can never completely supplant proximate space.  Certain social relations such as procreation can occur only in proximate space.[24] Virtual spaces must be constituted from electronic environments and physical environments. In general, the possibilities of constraining and enabling space constitutive activities are greater in electronic environments than in physical environments.  Characteristics of producing and reproducing physical and electronic environments span a wide range.  In some cases, the up-front costs of producing the environment such as building the plaza or establishing the network are relatively high and the costs of maintaining it are negligible.  In such situations, there is a tendency to not charge for access on a per-use basis.  In other cases, where the costs of reproducing the environment are relatively high, the tendency is to charge for access on a per-use basis.  The latter type of pricing tends to reinforce the ability to control space constituting activities within the environment.  The ability to regulate access to features of the environment through price as well as "technical" design features allows for a more dynamic and continuous exercise of control than is possible only with design. Electronic environments also tend to allow for easier surveillance, in the form of network management software that tracks usage patterns and purposeful information gathering and dissemination features such as calling number delivery.   A distinction may be made between public and private space, within proximate and virtual space.  Erving Goffman, a preeminent theorist of face-to-face interactions, defined public spaces as "any regions of a community freely accessible to members of that community."[25]  A precise definition of public space must begin from physical public environments.  Physical public environments are those not marked out as private by permanent or temporary markers.  Highways, sidewalks, plazas, public parks, etc. would clearly fall within this category.  Public as well as private spaces can be created from public environments.  The range of possible spaces extend from the strongly private (e.g., lovers on a park bench) to the strongly public (e.g., police officer directing traffic), with most of the possible spaces occupying various points in the middle of the continuum (e.g., eye-contact and body signals between two subjects communicating the yielding of a right of way in pedestrian traffic).

In essence, public spaces are characterized by a relative openness to the initiation of communication by others, and private spaces are characterized by a relative closedness to the initiation of communication by others.  Openness or closedness must not be seen in terms of two well defined and mutually exclusive conditions, but as the extremes of a continuum.  The negotiation of the terms and conditions of communication is an intrinsic and continuing element of every communicative relationship.[26]

The definitions of electronic private and public spaces are similar to those of physical private and public spaces, except for the fact that they are constituted from electronic and physical environments.  The PSTN and the various e-mail capable computer networks of today constitute electronic public spaces. These networks offer the possibility of initiating dyadic or group communication links with millions of individuals, and of having one or more of these millions of individuals initiate communication with oneself. In terms of potential, the moment of "entering" virtual space by lifting the handset or logging on to a computer network is similar to entering a physical public space where one could initiate contact with any one of the multitude inhabiting that space, or having any one of those individuals initiate contact (but paradoxically, he is generally unreachable through the PSTN at the moment of dialing). In the case of virtual space, the possibility is that of initiating contact with a person or persons in that space at that moment (e.g., in the case of chatlines, or the "talk" mode in e-mail) or later when the person or persons log on (e.g., with conventional e-mail), or of initiating contact with those in physical private and public environments abutting the virtual space (i.e., a telephone subscriber at home or in a pub with a telephone, a physical public space). Generally, people do not establish contact with totally unknown persons in virtual space nor in proximate space. Such contacts are initiated infrequently in electronic as well as in proximate space, but the predominant pattern is for individuals to navigate their way through public space to establish contact with a known person or persons, at which point the dyad or larger group effects a complete or partial withdrawal from the public space into a private space. In both physical and electronic public spaces, the possibility of unintentional collision exists, bumping into a bystander in the former and dialing a wrong number in the latter. In both physical and electronic public spaces, the boundaries of these private spaces are defined by negotiation between the communicating parties. In both physical and electronic public spaces, the boundaries between public and private spaces are defined by implicit, and sometimes explicit, negotiation between the communicating parties, but also between them and third parties.[27] Infringements of these boundaries and/or the use of coercion in the negotiating process constitute violations of a basic ground rule identified by Goffman[28]:

> . . . in Western society, as probably in all others, there is the 'right and duty of partial display.' Two or more individuals present together have the right and duty to make some information generally available concerning their relationship and the right and duty to leave unsignaled other information about their relationship (p. 198).

Drawing on Goffman's work and subsequent scholarship on communication processes,[29] it is possible to define privacy as *the capability to implicitly or explicitly negotiate boundary conditions of social relations*. This definition includes control of outflow of information that may be of strategic or aesthetic value to the person and control of inflow of information, including initiation of contact. One thoughtful observer pithily described concerns over outflows as the "none-of-your-business" aspect of privacy, and concerns over inflow of information as the "leave-me-alone" aspect of privacy.[30]

The proposition that the PSTN (and e-mail networks) are virtual public spaces is challenged most by the apparent lack of co-presence between the inhabitants of the virtual public space. Many would find it difficult to accept the claim that the millions of potential called parties are co-present on the network at any given moment. They may be out boating, at lunch, or dead, for that matter. Anyone who has used the PSTN to talk to people will point to the frequency of "telephone tag" to refute the claim of co-presence. However, as discussed above, space is also constituted when one party believes the other is potentially co-present. Discovery that the other is not there terminates the (private) space. In a public space, the expectation is not that communication with a particular person is absolutely certain, but that the potential for communication with one of many individuals exists. The absence of a particular individual does not negate the entire public space. Indeed, the unanswered telephone/answering machine may not signify the called party's absence, but only the decision of that party to not communicate at that particular time.

If it is conceded that relationships can be established and/or sustained over electronic media, it would be necessary to accept virtual space, since space has been defined in terms of the underlying relationship. If relationships exist over asynchronous electronic media, then we must still concede the existence of the corresponding virtual spaces. All that has to be done is to take into account the accentuated time-spanning capabilities of virtual space. If virtual space is accepted it is possible to treat humans as existing in proximate and virtual space and to conduct research about interactions in both kinds of spaces, about how power in one kind of space is leveraged into the other, about how control over environment is translated into power in the resultant space, and how recursive practices of agents in these spaces produce and reproduce structural power.

It is also possible to utilize the framework for policy formulation. The conceptualization of telecommunication network platforms as environments, and social relations utilizing those platforms as spaces, can allow telecommunication issues to be reconceptualized as equivalent to proximate space issues, enabling the adaptation and adoption of value-based policy solutions developed for those familiar spaces. While this type of analogic reasoning is tempting (particularly for those suspicious of the never-ending, and possibly self-serving, chorus of "more research" from academics), it can be easily abused. For example, in the debate over the costs and benefits of calling number delivery services, many policy advocates rushed to draw an analogy between the proximate space situation of a stranger knocking at the door, and the virtual space situation of a telephone caller initiating a call. It was argued that refusing to allow number delivery was akin to wearing a paper bag over one's head when knocking at someone's door. Others pointed to the misleading nature of this analogy, emphasizing the negotiation of identification information release in proximate space and the inability of the parties to mechanically record the interaction and store and process the transaction-generated information. In virtual space, both these conditions did not hold.[31]

## 4. CONSUMER PROTECTION

This section assumes that direct access to the public network by the consumer is unproblematic from a policy perspective. This is far from true. First, the consumer protection regime that now exists in public networks is quite undeveloped. Second, the moves and countermoves of providers of public networks in response to private network operators, customer-premises equipment (CPE) vendors, and users, will destabilize the existing imperfect consumer protection regime. However, for the purpose of simplifying the analysis, consumer protection afforded to sole-occupant households directly connected to the public network is held constant and used as a yardstick against which the various other modes of consumer access can be measured. A complete analysis will have to relax this assumption and analyze the system as a dynamic whole.

### 4.1. The Household.

The household (or the family) is likely to continue to be a significant factor affecting consumer access to the public network for some time, despite industry initiatives in the areas of personal telecommunication numbers and devices tending to reduce the importance of collective and stationary access points to the network.  The dependence of minor children on their parents and the persistence of collective living arrangements due to psychological and economic benefits are likely to counter-balance tendencies toward non-shared network access. Inasmuch as most family homes in North America now contain telecommunication equipment unimaginable just a decade or two ago, it is reasonable to assume that more CPE will be hooked up to the network from the household, and that the household will increasingly resemble a private network.  The abstract similarity posited by this chapter between private networks and households will become a concrete similarity.

The implications of the household as a proximate space intermediating consumer access to the network may be illustrated in relation to a problem that has already reached the policy arena, that of parental control over children's access to services provided over the network.   As network access becomes more important to children, especially teenagers, parents will seek ways to control that access.  The network can be configured to assist parents (default blocking of the majority of network services) or to assist teenagers (non-availability of blocking, or blocking on request, or for fees).  Incentives of network providers may lead them in either direction:  the former because parents are present subscribers and capable of exerting political pressure; the latter because teenagers will spend money and are future subscribers.  Parents are likely to demand public policy intervention in various forms, as they have already done regarding audiotex and chatline access.

The problem may be conceptualized in terms of virtual and proximate space.  The household is a proximate space pervaded by power.  The power of the parent is never absolute, but for present purposes a power relationship skewed in favor of the parent may be assumed.  The teenager's location in the proximate space of the household constrains and enables her abilities to constitute other proximate spaces, e.g., hanging out at the mall with friends.  By methods including control of egress and ingress from the physical environment of the household the parent can control the teenager's constitution of external spaces.   In other words, the parent leverages control over the physical environment of the household to control the teenager's space constitutive activities outside the parent-dominated proximate space.  Changes in network technologies (electronic environment) that enable the child to constitute virtual spaces outside the household tend to be dealt with in the same way. Parental efforts to have the network designed in ways that enable the leveraging of power over family and household environment to control teenagers' outside activities are similar to ensuring parental control over access to the door keys.

The virtual space framework allows for the examination of privacy questions between members of households.  As the household's electronic network approaches the sophistication of today's private networks, its surveillance capabilities will also approach those of such networks.  Do parents have the right to collect and analyze their children's calling patterns, in the way that many business organizations analyze their employee's calling patterns using software built into their PBXs?  Do the protections against unauthorized wiretaps set out in the amended Omnibus Crime Control and Safe Streets Act of 1968 (18 USCA, Title III) apply to members of households, including minors?  The privacy question is integrally connected to parental or other control of access to the public network.  In almost all instances (except where certain forms of communication are precluded by network design), effective control of access and the enforcement of other rules requires infringement of privacy.

Once the problem is conceptualized in this manner, it is possible to either systematically investigate the implications of changing network access for the household, and thereby formulate policy, or directly frame policy based on values. Is the home a "castle" wherein the powers of the "lord"/parent are absolute, and unchallenged by government? This question has different answers in different cultures at different times. Whatever the answer is for proximate space, policy could apply it to virtual space (taking due care with the analogy). But this application is not simple. For those who think it is, a simple mental exercise is in order. Substitute the terms "abusive husband" for parent, and "abused wife" for child in the above discussion. How can policy, including policy on network design, accommodate values that privilege the needs of parents to control their children as well as values that privilege the needs of abused women?

### 4.2. Pay Phones

The basic issue of leveraging control over proximate space to control over virtual space runs through many of the private-public interface issues raised by Noam[32] and the conceptually similar, but more mundane, issues such as problems pertaining to pay phone interfaces with the public wireline network. In the case of many pay phones, the store owner or the airport operator controls the physical location of the facility. The value of this physical location as a pay phone interface depends on adjacency to a proximate public space and the amount of pedestrian or vehicular traffic within it. A part of the property rights pertaining to such a physical location is contractually assigned to the pay phone operator in return for payment. The pay phone operator utilizes this exclusive right to build an interface to the public network from that particular location with whatever design features she thinks will maximize returns. In other words, the pay phone operator leverages power over physical environment to create power over electronic environment. The consumer has an exit option, but in many cases there may be no other way to access the public network from the proximity of that particular physical location. Within the electronic environment provided by the pay phone operator, the consumer also can dial extra digits or whatever, and try to circumvent the technologically embedded rules imposed by the operator.

Generally, present-day pay telephones do not pose significant privacy problems since they do not identify the users and keep records of usage by specific persons. Of course, all pay phones pose privacy problems of a more mundane nature, in that conversations can be overheard by bystanders. Indeed, one of the most significant privacy cases in the US, *Katz v. United States* (389 US 347, 1967), involved the recording of a conversation in a phone booth by the Federal Bureau of Investigations. But the law in this area is settled. What is not settled is the status of information collected by credit-card and other magnetic card equipped pay phones that are becoming more common. Public policy concerns would be triggered if such features of the electronic environment provided by the pay-phone operator were to be used to collect information generated by users, and to process and utilize for purposes other than completing the calls.

Again, conceptualization based on the virtual space framework can lead to policy based on research or to purely value-based policy formulation. Research can examine consumer behavior at pay phones, the relative valuation of pay phone locations, etc. In the case of value-based policy formulation, the framework directs attention to how ingress and egress paths that bear bottleneck characteristics have been dealt with in proximate space. There is really not much of a difference between the basic issue addressed in 1877 in *Munn v. Illinois* (94 US 113) and the problem of delimiting the latitude pay phone operators have to constrain/enable consumer behavior. The fact that most, if not, all pay phones are located in public environments in the sense used by Goffman (i.e., public not because of government or other forms of public property rights, but by reason of more or less open access), distinguishes the pay phone problem both from the above discussed problem of household access and the problems of access to the public network via private networks, discussed below. It must, however, be emphasized that the location of pay phones in public environments does not imply a claim that the virtual spaces constituted by their users are public as well. As discussed in Section 3.0, private proximate or virtual space can be constituted from public environments.

### 4.3. Private Networks

Of the four sub-categories of connections to the PSTN through private networks outlined above, the resident and voluntary "inmate" categories can be dealt with together since the essential difference between them is duration of stay. Here, the basic problem is that physical environment (e.g., dormitory, hotel room) is being bundled with a particular form of electronic environment. Control over physical environments is being extended to electronic environments through the process of bundling. Generally speaking, antitrust law frowns upon the extension of market power from one market to another through bundling. But whether this is being done or not in cases falling under these categories is an empirical question. It is possible that there is really no market power in the hotel industry in a particular region, even if one hotel bundles network access with the hotel room in a particularly undesirable form. One problem in undertaking this type of analysis at the present time is that network access constitutes such a minuscule portion of the bundled package. But with the increasing importance of network access, it may become more commensurate with the other elements of the bundle of services offered by a hotel or similar institution.

Another way of coming at the problem is to identify situations where the exit option is severely limited, e.g., where accepting dormitory accommodation is a pre-condition of studying at a particular university. Public policy could identify a threshold of involuntariness beyond which certain safeguards for consumers would kick in. Hospitals where patients cannot make exit decisions due to medical or insurance factors, university dormitories where residence is compulsory, company towns where residence is a condition of employment, etc. would thus be subject to a different standard than the single hotel in an airport strip that prevents a consumer from calling a 900 number. The publicness of the institution, either in terms of ownership or in terms of publicness of purpose, may also be factored into the policy equation. Access to the public network via private networks by involuntary inmates of institutions poses a somewhat easier problem. These consumers have always had their proximate-space egress and ingress controlled. Extending that control to virtual space does not mark a radical change. The only problematic areas are where the levels of control in the two forms of space differ dramatically, or where the manner of control is inconsistent with contemporary standards for the treatment of incarcerated persons. The formulation of the problem as one involving two different forms of social space enables research to be conducted, or policy to be formulated based on value judgments. If the applicable values hold that solitary confinement for long periods of time is cruel and unusual punishment, it would not be unreasonable to infer that complete prohibition of access to the public network also constitutes cruel and unusual punishment. In the same way that prisoners are allowed different forms of interactions in proximate space, ranging from conjugal visits to guard-observed, no-physical contact conversations, prisoners may be allowed different forms of virtual-space interactions as well.

Conceptualizing incarceration as the coercive restriction of a person's ability to constitute proximate and virtual spaces leads to an interesting idea for releasing pressure on prison space. Why not punish certain kinds of crimes by restricting the ability to constitute virtual spaces only? The Secret Service and other law enforcement agents pursuing "hackers" and "crackers" appear to have hit upon this idea before anybody else, evidenced by their proclivity to "confiscate" all network interface equipment in the suspects' households. There is an apocryphal story about Kevin Mitnik (one of earliest "phreakers" to be apprehended) being served with an injunction not to go within five feet of a telephone. I have suggested on an earlier occasion[33] that obscene and harassing callers should be punished by having network privileges withdrawn or curtailed. I recognize that problems of enforcement and civil liberties must be carefully examined. Yet, the idea of meting out electronic punishment for electronic crimes, which could also affect recidivism, appears to be worth serious consideration.

The employee sub-category is quite complex. In legalistic terms, it can be argued that an employee cannot be a consumer on "company time" and using the employer's equipment. Most concerns about the attrition of employees' rights in relation to network access appear to refer to white-collar employees. Blue-collar employees have rarely enjoyed rights or privileges to engage in consumer activities on "company time" using company facilities, with the exception of certain customary rights built up in specific plants over the years. White-collar employees who enjoyed more flexible work conditions, and who usually do not differentiate between "company time" and personal or leisure time as clearly as blue-collar workers do, had built up a different set of rights and privileges with regard to telephone use, newspaper reading, and so on. The contemporary drive for increased office productivity has threatened some of these rights and privileges, including some relatively new practices such as playing computer games on office computers. So what is really at issue is not whether the formal legal rights of employees to free association and speech are being taken away by the new technologies. It is whether changes to customary practices within white-collar work places being implemented partly through technical design of information communication technologies (e.g., PBXs that monitor outgoing calls by number and duration, computers that count keystrokes), and partly through new work rules are justified. Again, the question ceases to be a purely telecommunication question, but instead becomes one of socially acceptable working conditions.

The problem of access to the network by employees for consumer purposes is somewhat tractable in standard work-places where distinctions between work-time and leisure-time, and between the employer's facilities and the employee's equipment are clearly demarcated. But more and more, these distinctions are becoming blurred in many employment situations. The truly difficult problems lie in these gray areas. Many employees, particularly those in creative or management positions, tend to work outside hours in work-places and/or take work home. Telework brings company computer and communication equipment into employees' homes. Employees on the move carry company communication equipment around with them on their persons or in their vehicles. The potential for dual uses of time and equipment is enormous. Preventing dual use by making demarcations between work-related space and personal space sharper is rather unrealistic at this stage. But the other solution of increasing the surveillance capabilities of the technologies runs counter to many contemporary social values. It appears that a different approach to the problem, perhaps one involving output-based performance criteria and disclaimer of all authority over how the work gets done and how the equipment is used, needs to be devised.

Surveillance and privacy issues are extremely important in relation to all forms of private networks. The control by private network operators that concerns Noam will be actually operationalized through surveillance-related practices. Using existing technological features, all these networks are capable of collecting detailed transaction records and of analyzing them in rather sophisticated ways (e.g., which employees called a particular number; the most-called number by employee; duration per call). In many cases, the private network operator will claim that such monitoring is required for billing purposes (residences, hotels, hospitals, etc.) or for control purposes (prisons, offices, etc.). They may even claim that such monitoring is required to fulfill legal obligations. In some cases, these rationales lead to the routine comprehensive or random taping of telephone conversations as such. Operators will exercise control over their networks by direct surveillance or by inducing self-policing through panoptical means. The latter could yield a form of control that is more pervasive, extensive, and economical than would be the case with direct surveillance.[34] Space limitations preclude a detailed discussion of these important issues here, particularly because much of the practice and law on this area is unsettled and problematic.

## 5. CONCLUSION

This chapter has developed a taxonomy of forms of access to the decentralized network, proposed a theoretical framework for analyzing the consumer protection implications, and examined the principal consumer protection issues in each of the forms of access. The taxonomy enables the extension of the scope of Noam's concerns regarding power of private network operators to a range of forms of access, unproblematic on the surface, but tending toward convergence with private networks in the near future. The application of the theoretical framework of virtual space to problems of consumer protection pertaining to access to the public network opens up a number of possibilities for framing research questions and for formulating public policy. While not yielding empirically testable hypotheses, the theoretical framework prepares the ground for empirical investigation. It focuses the researcher on the proper questions and relationships to investigate. It can guide research on the range of forms of access identified in the taxonomy, from the household to "private" use of corporate networks by employees. The research agenda derived from this framework would include ethnomethodological investigations of household and workplace behavior regarding telecommunication usage (including the identification of rules governing such usage) and analyses of market power in relation to pay phones, hotels, hospitals and other types of private network operators. The framework can also be utilized to guide policy formulation on the basis of values in conjunction with, and in even in lieu of, research findings. What is particularly interesting is how the application of the framework to consumer protection issues that are ostensibly within the province of telecommunication policy transforms them into family policy, competition policy, labor policy, and such general policy issues. This should not come as a surprise because telecommunication networks are utilized in the production and reproduction of social relations and are not a distinct and self-contained sphere of activity.

## REFERENCES

Benedikt, M. (Ed.) *Cyberspace: First steps*, Cambridge, MA: MIT Press, 1992.

Carterfone device in message toll telephone service, [In the matter of the use of the]. 13 FCC 2d 420 (1968), recon. denied, 14 FCC 2d 571 (1968).

Foucault, M., *Discipline and Punishment: The Birth of the Prison*, (A. Sheridan, Trans.), New York: Vintage, 1977.

Gandy, O.H., Jr., *The Panoptic Sort: A Political Economy of Personal Information*, Boulder CO: Westview, 1993.

Gibson, W., *Neuromancer*, New York: Ace Books, 1984.

Gibson, W., *Count Zero*, New York: Ace Books, 1987.

Gibson, W., *Mona Lisa Overdrive*, New York: Bantam Books, 1988.

Giddens, A., *Central Problems in Social Theory*, Berkeley: University of California Press, 1979.

Giddens, A., *A Contemporary Critique of Historical Materialism, vol 1*, London: Macmillan, 1981.

Giddens, A., *The Constitution of Society*, Cambridge: Polity Press, 1984.

Giddens, A., *The Nation-state and Violence: A Contemporary Critique of Historical Materialism, vol 2*, Cambridge: Polity Press, 1985.

Giddens, A., "A reply to my critics," In D. Held & J.B. Thompson (Eds.), *Social Theory of Modern Societies: Anthony Giddens and His Critics* (pp. 249-301), Cambridge: Cambridge University Press, 1989.

Goffman, E., *Behavior in Public Places: Notes on the Social Organization of Gatherings*, New York: The Free Press, 1963.

Gottdiener, M., "Recapturing the center: A semiotic analysis of shopping malls," in M. Gottdiener & A.P. Lagopoulos (eds.), *The City and the Sign: An Introduction to Urban Semiotics*, (pp. 288-302), New York: Columbia University Press, 1986.

Grieger, W., Testimony on behalf of the Manitoba Association of Women's Shelters, Inc., before the Public Utilities Board of Manitoba at the Public Hearing on the Application by the Manitoba Telephone System for an Order Approving a Trial of Call Management Services, 10 December 1991.

Hirschman, A., *Exit, Voice and Loyalty: Responses to Decline in Firms, Organizations, and States*, Cambridge MA: Harvard University Press, 1970.

Katz v. United States, 389 U.S. 347, 1967.

Lefebvre, H., *The Production of Space* (D. Nicholson-Smith, Trans.), Oxford: Basil Blackwell, 1991 (Original work published 1974).

Manitoba Association of Women's Shelters, Inc., Documentation of concern submitted to Manitoba Public Utilities Board on April 25, 1991.

Munn v, Illinois. 94 U.S. 113 (1877).

Noam, E., "Private networks and public objectives," In *Universal Telephone Service: Ready for the 21st Century? Annual Review of the Institute for Information Studies* (pp. 1-27), Nashville TN & Queenstown MD: Northern Telecom & Aspen Institute, 1991.

304

Omnibus Crime Control and Safe Streets Act of 1968 (18 USCA, Title III).

Péladeau, P., "The informational privacy challenge: The technological rule of law," in R. I. Chlewinski (ed.) *Human Rights in Canada: Into the 1990s and Beyond*, Ottawa: Human Rights Research and Education Centre, 1991

Petronio, S., "Communication boundary management: A theoretical model of managing disclosure of private information between marital couples," *Communication Theory*, 1(4), 311-335, 1991.

Samarajiva, R., Answers to cross-examination, following testimony before the Public Utilities Board of Manitoba at the Public Hearing on the Application by the Manitoba Telephone System for an Order Approving a Trial of Call Management Services, 19 December 1991.

Samarajiva, R., "Telecommunication privacy: Caller ID and customer information," presentation at the Washington Utilities and Transportation Commission, Olympia WA, June 12 1991.

Samarajiva, R., "The "intelligent network": Implications for expression, privacy, and competition," in W.H. Melody (ed.) *The intelligent telecommunication network: Privacy and policy implications of calling line identification and emerging information services: Proceedings of a CIRCIT conference* (pp. 34-60), Melbourne: CIRCIT, 1992.

Samarajiva, R. & Mukherjee, R., "Regulation of 976 services and dial-a-porn: Implications for the intelligent network," *Telecommunications Policy*, 15(2): 151-64, 1991.

Samarajiva, R. & Shields, P., "Emergent institutions of the 'intelligent network': Toward a theoretical understanding," *Media, Culture and Society*, 14(3), 397-419, 1992.

Samarajiva, R. & Shields, P., "Institutional and strategic analysis in electronic space: A preliminary mapping," paper presented at the 43rd annual conference of the International Communication Association, May 27-31, Washington DC, 1993.

Soja, E.W., "The socio-spatial dialectic," *Annals of the Association of American Geographers*, 70, 175-190, 1980.

Soja, E.W., *Postmodern Geographies: The Reassertion of Space in Critical Social Theory*, London: Verso, 1989.

**ENDNOTES**

[1] Noam, E., "Private networks and public objectives," in *Universal telephone service: Ready for the 21st century? Annual review of the Institute for Information Studies* (pp. 1-27), Nashville TN & Queenstown MD: Northern Telecom & Aspen Institute, 1991.

[2] ibid. Page 15-16.

[3] ibid. p.2.

[4] Carterfone device in message toll telephone service, [In the matter of the use of the]. 13 FCC 2d 420 (1968), recon. denied, 14 FCC 2d 571 (1968).

[5] This broad meaning is included in all references to "calls" and "calling" and "being called" in this paper.

[6.] Samarajiva, R. & Mukherjee, R., "Regulation of 976 services and dial-a-porn: Implications for the intelligent network. *Telecommunications Policy*, 15(2), pp. 151-64, 1991.

[7.] Manitoba Association of Women's Shelters, Inc., "Documentation of concern submitted to Manitoba Public Utilities Board on April 25, 1991." Grieger, W., Testimony on behalf of the Manitoba Association of Women's Shelters, Inc., before the Public Utilities Board of Manitoba at the Public Hearing on the Application by the Manitoba Telephone System for an Order Approving a Trial of Call Management Services, 10 December 1991. Also Samarajiva, R. & P. Shields, "Emergent institutions of the 'intelligent network': Toward a theoretical understanding," *Media, Culture and Society*, 14(3), 397-419, 1992.

[8.] Samarajiva, R., Answers to cross-examination, following testimony before the Public Utilities Board of Manitoba at the Public Hearing on the Application by the Manitoba Telephone System for an Order Approving a Trial of Call Management Services, 19 December 1991.

[9.] Peladeau, P., "The informational privacy challenge: The technological rule of law," in R. I. Chlewinski (ed.), *Human rights in Canada: Into the 1990s and beyond*, Ottawa: Human Rights Research and Education Centre, 1991.

[10.] Hirschman, A., *Exit, voice and loyalty: Responses to decline in firms, organizations, and states*, Cambridge MA: Harvard University Press, 1970.

[11.] Page 408, Samarajiva, R. & P. Shields, "Emergent institutions of the 'intelligent network': Toward a theoretical understanding," *Media, Culture and Society*, 14(3), 397-419, 1992.

[12.] Extracted from Samarajiva & Shields (1993).

[13.] Giddens, A., *A contemporary critique of historical materialism, vol 1*, London: Macmillan, 1981. Giddens, A., The constitution of society, Cambridge: Polity Press, 1984. Giddens, A., *The nation-state and violence: A contemporary critique of historical materialism, vol 2.*, Cambridge: Polity Press, 1985.

[14.] e.g. Benedikt, M.(Ed.), *Cyberspace: First steps*, Cambridge, MA: MIT Press, 1992.

[15.] Gibson, W., *Neuromancer*, New York: Ace Books, 1984. Gibson, W., *Count Zero*, New York: Ace Books, 1987. Gibson, W., *Mona Lisa Overdrive*, New York: Bantam Books, 1988.

[16.] Samarajiva, R. & P. Shields, "Institutional and strategic analysis in electronic space: A preliminary mapping," paper presented at the 43rd annual conference of the International Communication Association, May 27-31, 1993, Washington DC.

[17.] Lefebvre, H., *The production of space* (D. Nicholson-Smith, Trans.), Oxford: Basil Blackwell, 1991 (Original work published 1974).

[18.] Page 73, Lefebvre, H., *The production of space* (D. Nicholson-Smith, Trans.), Oxford: Basil Blackwell, 1991 (Original work published 1974). Page 202-206, Giddens, A., *Central problems in social theory*, Berkeley: University of California Press, 1979.

[19.] Soja, E.W., "The socio-spatial dialectic," *Annals of the Association of American Geographers*, 70, 175-190, 1980. Page 76-93, Soja, E.W., *Postmodern geographies: The reassertion of space in critical social theory*, London: Verso, 1989.

[20.] Page 280, Giddens, A., "A reply to my critics," In D. Held & J.B. Thompson (Eds.), *Social theory of modern societies: Anthony Giddens and his critics* (pp. 249-301), Cambridge: Cambridge University Press, 1989.

[21.]Page 293, Gottdiener, M., "Recapturing the center: A semiotic analysis of shopping malls," in M. Gottdiener & A.P. Lagopoulos (Eds.), *The city and the sign: An introduction to urban semiotics*, (pp. 288-302), New York: Columbia University Press, 1986.

[22.]Foucault, M., *Discipline and Punishment: The Birth of the Prison*, (A. Sheridan, Trans.), New York: Vintage, 1977.

[23.]Ibid. at pp. 202-3.

[24.]Benedikt, M. (Ed.), *Cyberspace: First steps*, Cambridge, MA: MIT Press, 1992. Gibson, W., *Neuromancer*, New York: Ace Books, 1984. Gibson, W., Mona Lisa overdrive, New York: Bantam Books, 1988.

[25.]Page 9, Goffman, E., Behavior in public places: Notes on the social organization of gatherings, New York: The Free Press, 1963.

[26.]Petronio, S., "Communication boundary management: A theoretical model of managing disclosure of private information between marital couples," *Communication Theory*, 1(4), 311-335, 1991.

[27.]Samarajiva, R. & P. Shields, "Institutional and strategic analysis in electronic space: A preliminary mapping," paper presented at the 43rd annual conference of the International Communication Association, May 27-31 1993, Washington DC.

[28.]Goffman, E., Behavior in public places: Notes on the social organization of gatherings, New York: The Free Press, 1963.

[29.]e.g. Petronio, S., "Communication boundary management: A theoretical model of managing disclosure of private information between marital couples," *Communication Theory*, 1(4), 311-335, 1991.

[30.]Rhodes, 1991.

[31.]Samarajiva, R., "The 'intelligent network': Implications for expression, privacy, and competition, in W.H. Melody (ed.) *The intelligent telecommunication network: Privacy and policy implications of calling line identification and emerging information services: Proceedings of a CIRCIT conference* (pp. 34-60). Melbourne: CIRCIT, 1992.

[32.]Noam, E., "Private networks and public objectives," In *Universal telephone service: Ready for the 21st century? Annual review of the Institute for Information Studies* (pp. 1-27), Nashville TN & Queenstown MD: Northern Telecom & Aspen Institute, 1991.

[33.]Samarajiva, R., "Telecommunication privacy: Caller ID and customer information," presentation at the Washington Utilities and Transportation Commission," Olympia WA, June 12, 1991.

[34.]For discussion, see Samarajiva, R. & Shields, P., "Emergent institutions of the 'intelligent network': Toward a theoretical understanding," *Media, Culture and Society*, 14(3), 397-419, 1992. And Gandy, O.H., Jr., *The panoptic sort: A political economy of personal information*, Boulder CO: Westview, 1993.

PRIVATE NETWORKS PUBLIC OBJECTIVES
E. Noam and A. NíShúilleabháin (Editors)
© 1996 Elsevier Science B.V. All rights reserved.

Towards a Public Metanetwork: Interconnection, Leveraging, and Privatization of Government-Funded Networks in the United States

Brian Kahin and Bruce McConnell

## 1. THE PARADIGM: PARTIAL PUBLIC FUNDING OF AUTONOMOUS INTERNETWORKS

Over the past twenty years the federal government has played a major role in the development of computer networks, initially in the development of the ARPANET under the Advanced Research Projects Agency of the Department of Defense (now DARPA), and subsequently in the development of the "National Research and Education Network" (NREN). Public funds, federal and state, have partially subsidized the creation of dozens of private, predominantly nonprofit, research networks over the past six years. These networks include state networks, multistate regional networks, metropolitan area networks, networks connecting supercomputer centers and their users, and other special purpose networks. These networks have been supported by a combination of revenue sources -- federal funding, state funding, user fees, and contributions from private industry.

As "enhanced services," computer networks have gone unregulated. Even after the Ninth Circuit determined that the FCC could not preempt state regulation of enhanced services,[1] few states have attempted to do so. However, the funding policies of the federal government and (to a lesser extent) state governments have played a major role in shaping a new computer networking environment. This environment has its roots in the packet-switching technology pioneered by the ARPANET in the 1970s, the nonproprietary TCP/IP protocol suite, the interconnection between the ARPANET and CSNET[2] in 1983 that "created" the Internet, and the NSFNET program launched by NSF in 1985. It has emerged as a decentralized quasi-public infrastructure of autonomous internetworks, no longer limited to the academic research community.

The public funding that supports this infrastructure has been characterized by proliferating policy objectives, including a growing embrace of traditional infrastructure rationales. At the same time, a distaste for government ownership and control has been combined with strategic leveraging of private investment. Despite the presence of public funding, this decentralized environment is not well understood by policy-makers and or even by many of the potential stakeholders. While the telecommunications carriers have supported the NREN legislation,[3] they have been slow to develop Internet-related services.[4] The Internet has been better appreciated and exploited by the computer industry, which has produced much of the driving technology, benefitted from the externalities of networking, and is accustomed to a decentralized multidimensional market environment. Public funds have supported research networking in the interests of increasing communication and cooperation among academia, industry, and government researchers. At the federal level, this funding has been aimed at basic research; but at the state level (where there is little public funding of basic research), the expressed goals often include economic development. State and regional networks have embodied a mix of public, private, and nonprofit investment, and have put forth a broader agenda than NSF and the White House Office of Science and Technology Policy have at the federal level. However, the High Performance Computing Act of 1991 reflected the growing political constituency for the NREN and growing expectations that it would help shape a universal information infrastructure.

The degree of direct public subsidy for research networks varies from zero (BARRNet in the San Francisco Bay Area, NEARnet in New England)[5] to 100% in the case of mission agency internetworks (ESNET, NASA Science Internet). Several networks received NSF subsidy at the outset but have since become self-sufficient. Some are organized as cooperatives; some are projects of private universities;[6] some are private, for-profit companies; some are owned by federal agencies but operated privately. Except for the agency networks, virtually all the networks of the Internet are private[7] and considered autonomous by the National Science Foundation and other federal agencies, even though the network may still receive public funds. Specifically, NSF does not dictate the acceptable use policy or other internal policies of grantee networks.

NSF prescribes an acceptable use policy only for the NSFNET backbone, which it makes available for all "mid-level" networks to use free of charge for qualifying traffic. According to the policy the purposed of the NSFNET backbone is "to support open research and education in and among US research and instructional institutions, plus research arms of for-profit firms when engaged in open scholarly communication and research."[8] By providing the backbone as free transcontinental trunk, NSF has greatly stimulated the growth of the Internet for research and education purposes. However, this policy has had the effect of segregating the commercial and noncommercial sides of the Internet and creating considerable confusion about the nature of the Internet.

In one sense, the noncommercial part is more "public" because traffic over the NSFNET backbone is restricted to the public purpose that is defined in the acceptable use policy (AUP). In another sense, the commercial portion is more public because use of it is virtually unrestricted, like the public voice network and the conventional public data networks (SprintNet and Tymnet). As we shall see, this division along with the NSF's cooperative agreement with Merit for the operation of the NSFNET has led to considerable controversy over the commercialization of the Internet and, in 1992, to hearings before the Subcommittee on Science of the House Committee on Science, Space and Technology.

## 2. CHARACTERISTICS OF THE INTERNET

The conceptual difficulties surrounding public and private characteristics are compounded by the technological characteristics of the network, which differ radically not only from the voice network but from more familiar fully private, centralized, or single-function computer networks. Indeed, the Internet is bedeviled by stereotypes. It is often perceived simply as an electronic mail network which public funding makes available free to universities.

In fact, the Internet is a generalized, multi-function, multi-protocol infrastructure, leveraged from three directions: 1.) enormous private investment in computers and internal networks; 2.) carrier investment in local and long distance fiber optic networks driven by the market for conventional voice and fax and special purpose data networks, as well as anticipated future demand for video services; and 3.) federal and private investment in very high-speed networking technologies, including federal support for high-end applications such as remote visualization.

These different leveraging forces give the Internet its unique character. 1.) It is a bottom-up *collaborative* enterprise, driven by the aggregation of demand at the institutional or campus level. Much of the technical design and development has been the product of volunteers working through the ad hoc Internet Engineering Task Force.[9] 2.) It is comprised of *overlay networks*, riding on leased lines and requiring minimal capital investment; its computer-based routing technology has benefited from rapid advances in microprocessor technology and the growth of LANs. 3.) Funding for high-end uses, statistical multiplexing, and low marginal costs for additional capacity result in *capacity-based pricing* at the wholesale level. Costs are allocated to end users at low flat rates or are simply absorbed into overhead at one level or another. Hence, the common but erroneous perception that use of the Internet is free.

The Internet is not a network but a *metanetwork* -- a functionally defined international set of interconnected, inter-operating, but autonomous networks. While the global telephone network is a homogeneous user-to-user metanetwork of 4 kilohertz voice channels, the Internet is a heterogeneous multi-object metanetwork of indeterminate links, which connect users to computers and information resources as well as to other users. The Internet extends to files that are readily addressable from the network, as well as users addressable from the network. It is defined by the interaction among several different types of "network objects" -- computers, applications, databases, other networks, as well as users and lists of users (enterprises).[10] In principle, each site on the Internet is accessible to any site on any interconnected network for a standard set of functions that includes file transfer, remote log-in, and electronic mail. Originally, the Internet was defined by the TCP/IP protocol suite, but protocol conversion makes it possible to include sites accessed through OSI and DECNET protocols. A user may gateway from one computer into another computer or another network, either transparently or by explicit direction, and the final destination may not be on the Internet in the usual sense of being directly addressable from the Internet.

Other definitional problems arise from the one-way nature of certain links. Corporate networks may be set up so that company users can Telnet and FTP out from the corporate network, but other Internet sites cannot FTP and Telnet into the corporate network. There is a more inclusive metanetwork, sometimes called the "Matrix,"[11] of more limited functionality. Sites in the Matrix, although not necessarily capable of real-time inter-operation through FTP, Telnet, and similar protocols, are nonetheless able to exchange electronic mail through common addressing and routing conventions. The Matrix includes a number of commercial services with mail gateways into the Internet -- MCIMAIL, AT&T Mail, Prodigy, and CompuServe -- as well as the cooperative dial-up networks, such as FidoNet. But because real-time interoperation is not required for mail, compatibility requirements are minimal. There is no central registry of addresses or institutional focus for the Matrix.[12]

There are a wide variety of unsubsidized commercial and noncommercial electronic mail services. There are also commercially available X.25 public data networks, such as SprintNet and Tymnet. However, the TCP/IP networks are distinct in that they support multiple services. They offer fast file transfer using File Transfer Protocol (FTP), which is the largest traffic component on the NSFNET backbone. (See table.) Using the TELNET protocol, they typically support much higher speeds of remote login and interactive use than the X.25 PDNs. (Most universities are connected at T-1 speeds (1.544 mbps); even small institutions are connected at 56 kpbs.) FTP, TELNET, and mail (SMTP) services are all available in a common network environment.

## NSFNET T1 Backbone Traffic Distribution by Service
### March 1992
Packet Total: 8,924,601,550
Byte Total: 1,641,789,183,650

| Service Name | Port | Packet Count | % Pkts | Byte Count | % Bytes |
|---|---|---|---|---|---|
| ftp-data | 20 | 2,345,582,650 | 26.282 | 828,850,604,950 | 50.485 |
| (other ports) | -- | 1,819,683,100 | 20.390 | 171,983,064,750 | 10.475 |
| telnet | 23 | 1,109,624,000 | 12.433 | 78,901,539,450 | 4.806 |
| nntp | 119 | 930,703,700 | 10.429 | 178,094,436,150 | 10.848 |
| smtp | 25 | 779,172,450 | 8.731 | 118,713,376,000 | 7.231 |
| nameserver | 53 | 616,370,700 | 6.906 | 62,653,762,550 | 3.816 |
| ftp | 21 | 210,861,050 | 2.363 | 15,199,203,900 | 0.926 |
| (other protocols) | --- | 187,167,800 | 2.097 | 15,913,880,450 | 0.969 |
| vmnet | 175 | 179,897,400 | 2.016 | 65,039,534,550 | 3.962 |
| irc | 6667 | 124,715,150 | 1.397 | 10,249,531,050 | 0.624 |
| who/login | 513 | 80,673,900 | 0.904 | 3,478,657,300 | 0.212 |
| ntp | 123 | 66,563,250 | 0.746 | 5,078,830,450 | 0.309 |
| (unknown) | 1023 | 64,405,950 | 0.722 | 9,733,875,200 | 0.593 |
| X0 | 6000 | 47,513,250 | 0.532 | 7,010,593,600 | 0.427 |
| syslog/cmd | 514 | 39,135,050 | 0.439 | 16,412,937,450 | 1.000 |
| talk | 517 | 35,336,300 | 0.396 | 3,623,556,450 | 0.221 |
| finger | 79 | 34,945,600 | 0.392 | 3,528,747,400 | 0.215 |
| snmp | 161 | 22,898,450 | 0.257 | 2,605,795,550 | 0.159 |
| (unknown) | 1022 | 22,293,750 | 0.250 | 3,844,914,900 | 0.234 |
| uucp | 540 | 17,925,000 | 0.201 | 3,929,692,550 | 0.239 |
| NSS-Routing | 159 | 17,281,650 | 0.194 | 1,413,335,700 | 0.086 |
| src | 200 | 13,387,100 | 0.150 | 783,693,150 | 0.048 |
| (unknown) | 1021 | 12,595,900 | 0.141 | 2,496,509,800 | 0.152 |
| ntalk | 518 | 8,396,300 | 0.094 | 902,138,400 | 0.055 |
| (unknown) | 1020 | 7,640,950 | 0.086 | 2,063,678,750 | 0.126 |
| tftp | 69 | 6,778,750 | 0.076 | 378,432,000 | 0.023 |
| router/efs | 520 | 6,282,700 | 0.070 | 3,003,212,200 | 0.183 |
| mdecnet | 700 | 6,127,900 | 0.069 | 1,509,414,900 | 0.092 |

Source: Merit, file= <NIC.MERIT.EDU> /nsfnet/statistics/1992/t1-9203.ports

NSFNET Backbone Traffic Distribution by Service
June 1994
Packet Total: 75,280,338,950
Byte Total: 15,350,480,259,500

| Service Name | Port | Packet Count | % Pkts | Byte Count | % Byts |
|---|---|---|---|---|---|
| ftp-data | 20 | 14,920,693,000 | 19.820 | 5,406,765,553,400 | 35.222 |
| (other_tcp/udp_ports) | 999 | 12,136,852,350 | 16.122 | 1,802,547,568,950 | 11.743 |
| telnet | 23 | 10,102,897,900 | 13.420 | 742,523,290,550 | 4.837 |
| nntp | 119 | 7,573,275,950 | 10.060 | 1,668,585,813,300 | 10.870 |
| smtp | 25 | 5,851,752,650 | 7.773 | 988,020,772,400 | 6.436 |
| ip | -4 | 4,014,654,250 | 5.333 | 1,204,497,949,900 | 7.847 |
| domain | 53 | 3,865,035,100 | 5.134 | 374,096,786,350 | 2.437 |
| www | 80 | 3,060,869,850 | 4.066 | 946,538,669,550 | 6.166 |
| icmp | -1 | 2,987,323,650 | 3.968 | 295,580,874,850 | 1.926 |
| gopher | 70 | 2,012,045,400 | 2.673 | 567,478,655,950 | 3.697 |
| irc | 6667 | 1,897,549,600 | 2.251 | 193,334,424,000 | 1.259 |
| ftp | 21 | 1,389,715,300 | 1.846 | 129,841,696,950 | 0.846 |
| talk | 517 | 889,821,500 | 1.182 | 92,412,534,800 | 0.602 |
| X0 | 6000 | 758,177,850 | 1.007 | 162,151,234,500 | 1.056 |
| login/who | 513 | 381,036,350 | 0.506 | 43,481,370,550 | 0.283 |
| vmnet | 175 | 351,185,300 | 0.467 | 142,147,311,950 | 0.926 |
| (unknown) | 1023 | 331,001,650 | 0.440 | 35,440,965,350 | 0.231 |
| snmp | 161 | 214,356,200 | 0.285 | 24,753,750,800 | 0.161 |
| unidata-ldm | 388 | 197,048,450 | 0.262 | 60,324,898,600 | 0.393 |
| ntp | 123 | 174,574,100 | 0.232 | 13,000,123,600 | 0.085 |
| finger | 79 | 163,632,900 | 0.217 | 20,579,482,950 | 0.134 |

Source: ftp://nis.nsf.net/statistics/nsfnet/1994/

The TCP/IP platform supports a wide variety of other services. See Table 1. showing the most widely used services on the NSFNET T1 backbone. There are nearly 200 "Well Known" services identified to ports 1 to 256. An additional like number are documented but used inconsistently across the Internet.[13] And there are unknown implementations using unassigned TCP ports (the sum of the "unknowns" equals the figure for "other ports"). Many of these services are experimental, but it is also possible to set up a virtual private network using common services on unassigned ports.

In effect, the backbone provides an open platform for the implementation of a wide variety of public and private networks supporting any combination of functional services in either an open or private manner. In this sense, it offers both a service platform for a wide number of applications in support of research, such as remote visualization, and a technology platform which offers opportunities for experimentation in computer-to-computer communication. In implementing a T-3 (45 mbps) backbone 1991-92, NSF pushed a particular technological envelope directly. On the other hand, the mail traversing the NSFNET backbone has probably had the largest impact on the greatest number of people. The multifaceted impact of the federal investment in research networking came to the fore in the rhetoric and debate that attended the high performance computing legislation introduced by Senator Gore.[14] The language on the NREN in the enacted High Performance Computing Act of 1991 reflects the variety of constituencies that took interest in the bill -- and the diversity of policy objectives that were read into it. These diverse but related objectives combine with the protean nature of the rapidly growing Internet to create a new policy environment where interaction among the sectors is accelerating dizzingly -- and where the tilt, size, and shape of the playing field are relative to perspective and the time of day. Before parsing out the policy objectives in plans for an NREN, however, we briefly review the history of federal funding for networks, beginning with its own voice network.

## 3. FTS TO FTS 2000 -- FROM NETWORKS TO NETWORK SERVICES

After the Second World War, Federal agencies individually satisfied their long distance telecommunications requirements by leasing circuits and services on an ad hoc basis from the Bell System. In 1961, traffic overloads during the Cuban Missile Crisis revealed weaknesses in the Federal government's communications systems and stimulated the development of a private, government-operated long distance telephone network, the Federal Telecommunications System (FTS). By 1980, AT&T supplied the Federal government, through contracts with the General Services Administration (GSA), a dedicated voice-grade network of 15,000 network trunks and fifty-two switching nodes. The network served 1.3 million Federal users at over 4,000 locations.[15]

Deregulation and rapid changes in telecommunications technology eliminated the cost advantages of FTS and strained GSA's limited technical resources. During the mid-1980s, GSA decided to replace the FTS with new contracts. Instead of a dedicated voice network, however, FTS 2000 would be a voice and data service offering, with pricing on a service usage basis. The decision to pursue a service offering instead of engineering a Federal network was grounded in practical and policy realities. GSA realized that it would be unable to keep pace with the rapidly changing technical and market environment. A government-built network would always lag behind the best private sector offerings. Strong pressure within the Reagan Administration to privatize government operational activities favored contracting out of network engineering and operations. Finally, key Congressional figures advocated Federal support of emerging competition in the provision of public switched network services, and for increased competition in contracting generally.[16]

GSA planned a winner-take-all competition in which the winner would be entirely responsible for engineering and operations, leaving GSA to manage the contract on behalf of all Federal agency users. By the time GSA had a request for proposals on the street in early 1987, however, only three firms (AT&T, MCI, and Sprint) remained which provided nation-wide telecommunications service. Although all three announced they would compete for the award, uncertainty in both the technical and business requirements of the government led Sprint to drop out of the competition in mid-1987. To increase the amount of competition (and thus increase pressure on the vendors to lower prices), the solicitation was restructured to provide for a two-vendor award, Sprint re-entered the competition, and along with AT&T, was awarded a ten-year contract in 1988 to provide voice and data telecommunications services to Federal agencies. By law, FTS 2000 is mandatory for Federal agency use, except for non-administrative Defense Department traffic.[17] Telecommunications between Federal contractors and grantees and their sponsoring agencies are generally not provided under the FTS 2000 contracts because these services are generally acquired under grant or cooperative agreements not subject to GSA's authority.[18] FTS 2000 is a private network in that it is privately owned, provided under specific contractual arrangements, and is accessible only to government officials or contractors conducting government business. Local access is provided by local phone companies and the regional Bells under subcontracts with AT&T and Sprint. Sprint's inter-LATA services are provided for entirely over its part of the Public Switched Network, whereas AT&T has installed dedicated switches to serve its FTS 2000 customers.

## 4. ARPANET -- A VERY DIFFERENT MODEL

Meanwhile, in 1969, the Defense Advanced Research Projects Agency (DARPA) established ARPANET, an experimental network connecting Defense agencies with their contractors and grantees. The network was designed to demonstrate the potential of computer networking made possible by packet-switching technology and the resource sharing it allowed. The DARPA-developed packet-switching technology was later successfully commercialized by private sector firms such as the Tymnet and Telenet services. DARPA sponsored several additional networks during the 1970s and developed the Internet protocols, which allowed messages to be interchanged across multiple interconnected networks. By 1983 ARPANET became congested and Defense split its military R&D traffic onto a separate network, MILNET. Defense shifted responsibility for civilian R&D networking to the National Science Foundation in 1985, and shut down the ARPANET completely in 1988.[19] The ARPANET experiment differed from FTS 2000 in several ways. First, it was an experimental network, not a production network. While FTS 2000 tried to give government users access to the most advanced commercial offerings, DARPA used its network to advance technology beyond existing offerings. Its experimental nature was recognized by the research community, which was thus willing to tolerate its idiosyncratic performance and arcane user interface. In accessibility and usability, ARPANET was more restricted than FTS/FTS 2000, although, unlike FTS it could be used by those outside the government. Second, ARPANET was a collaborative Federal-university-industry development effort, not a arms-length competition among private firms wishing to supply commercial services to a large customer.

Consequently, a large portion of the development funding came from the R&D budgets of the computer and communications firms involved in the collaboration.

## 5. CSNET

By the late 1970s the contribution of the ARPANET to research collaboration became apparent throughout the US computer science community. However the ARPANET connected only those university sites such as Stanford, Berkeley, and MIT, which had DARPA contracts. Computer science researchers elsewhere felt that the network was producing an unfortunate situation of haves and have-nots in terms of connectivity. In 1979, some university computer science researchers, including Larry Landweber, Dave Farber, and Tony Hearn, collaborated on a proposal to NSF to extend ARPANET technology to other university sites. After several rounds with the NSF Science Board, and with the assistance of Rick Adrian at NSF, a program was agreed to. The new network, dubbed CSNET, was to become self-supporting in five years. ARPANET protocols (both X.25 and what was then NCP/IP) would be used throughout, except for dial-up connections which only offered e-mail.[20] To achieve self-sufficiency, dial-up was charged on a per-minute basis, and dedicated access on a capacity basis.[21] A management committee, and later a university corporation,[22] managed the network as not-for-profit business. Operations were handled by BBN, and a memorandum of understanding was developed between NSF and DARPA to allow the exchange of traffic. The first CSNET sites came up in 1982, with 40 sites operational in 1983. In 1988, 200 sites were connected in 12 countries, including commercial sites where the business traffic was related to Federal research.

An important effect of CSNET was to train many people in internetworking technologies, sowing the seeds for the eventual development of today's regional network structure. Federal funding, which began in 1981 and ended in 1986, went principally for technology development and the acquisition of four VAX computers to serve the network. As the NSFNET began to develop, CSNET ceased to grow and eventually terminated in 1991.

## 6. NSFNET

In 1985, the NSF began to fund the development of the NSFNET, a national high-speed backbone with connections to six supercomputing centers, five of which had also just been established by NSF. Beginning in 1987, NSF funded the backbone network under a cooperative agreement with Merit, Inc., a non-profit arm of the University of Michigan, to operate the backbone. IBM and MCI contributed switching and transport technology in a cost-sharing arrangement. NSF also established two additional funding programs to support the NSFNET. The first was grants to networks, the first of which were organized around supercomputer centers. Others were designed to serve states or regions. Some of these became projects of existing cooperative organizations, like SURANET, formed by the Southeastern Universities Research Association. NYSERNet was created by the NSF-funded Cornell Supercomputing Facility to allow it to share its computing resources with other research institutions in New York state, as such it became a state initiative supported by the legislature.[23] SURANET covered fourteen states, while four networks made their home in California. Some regional networks developed on their own, including a few for-profit networks that connected commercial firms to the Internet. Although NSF sought to ensure that the entire country was served by research networks, none of the networks enjoyed any kind of exclusive monopoly, and some found themselves competing with each other, especially on their outer fringes.

The second additional network funding NSF provided was the "Connections" program, which offered grants of $20,000 to cover the costs of switches (called "routers") and initial dedicated circuit connection from universities to the regional networks. The Table below shows the funding of these programs during fiscal years 1988-91:

NSFNET BUDGET ($ millions)

| Fiscal Year | 1988 | 1989 | 1990 | 1991 |
|---|---|---|---|---|
| Backbone | 2.7 | 3.6 | 4.9 | 8.8 |
| Regional Grants | 3.6 | 7.1 | 7.1 | 7.3 |
| Connections | 0.2 | 0.5 | 0.7 | 1.4 |
| Other | 1.2 | 2.3 | 2.4 | 3.5 |
| Total | 7.8 | 13.6 | 15.0 | 21.0 |

Source: National Science Foundation

The contribution of Federal funds toward the total costs of developing and operating the NSFNET is variously estimated from 1/3 to 1/40, depending on how the NSFNET is defined, on the case that is being made, and what is included in the costs. Part of the reason for this high degree of leveraging is that the results of Federal research efforts in networking technologies can be transferred to the private sector faster and more completely than in some other research areas. Networking research is more like biotechnology research than like high energy physics. Access is much broader than with the ARPANET, for two reasons. First, as a part of the Internet, the NSFNET provides carriage to Internet users based on reciprocal agreements with other Internet networks. Second, the growing number of users on the NSFNET (currently over 1000 institutions are connected) mean that its "privateness" is lost.... A watershed decision during the mid-1980's was NSF's choice of the TCP/IP protocol rather than a proprietary protocol or X.25. As Mandelbaum and Mandelbaum observe:

> "It led almost directly to the establishment of the system of specialized private academic networks we have today, rather than to reliance by the academic and research community on the public, commercial networks that are the mainstays of the business world."[24]

## 7. MISSION AGENCY RESEARCH NETWORKS

As NSFNET developed, several Federal research agencies (principally NASA and the Energy Department) saw a need for reliable, uninterrupted IP connectivity with their principal research partners. These networks are interconnected with the NSFNET but are controlled directly by the mission agencies and dedicated to mission requirements. The autonomy of

316

this arrangement allows the agencies to shed or delay unessential messages during a critical mission such as a space shot. These networks are more like the original FTS -- dedicated, government-owned networks, although they may be operated by contractors. In addition, they are primarily production networks supporting ongoing research programs, not experiments in network technology.

## 8. INTERAGENCY INTERIM NREN

The National Research and Education Network was first described in 1989 as providing "high-speed communication access to over 1300 institutions across the United States within five years. . . . so that the physical distance between institutions is no longer a barrier to effective collaboration."[25] The concept had evolved (and continues to do so) from the national research network that the NSFNET represented. In 1989, it became one element of the President's High Performance Computing Program, which was renamed the following year as the High Performance Computing *and Communications* Program, in recognition of the importance of the network component. The HPCC is a Federal R&D effort made up of four elements, and is "designed to sustain and extend US leadership in all advanced areas of computing and networking."[26] A key issue for the HPCC initiative is the definition of the migration path from the existing NSFNET to the NREN. This migration is complicated by a lack of agreement among the principal constituencies of the NREN as to what the NREN actually is. Officially, it is "the future realization of an interconnected gigabit computer network system supporting HPCC--a network for research and education, not general purpose communication."[27] But there are expectations of a broader agenda. For example, the Computer Systems Policy Project, an affiliation of major US computer systems companies, sees the NREN as "the foundation for something broader and more exciting. . . . that will provide all Americans with access to unique resources, public and private databases, and other individuals throughout the country." CSPP recommends "expanding the activities under the NREN" initiative, and:

> "expanding the current vision of the HPCC initiative to include Grand Challenges motivated by social and economic needs in areas of interest to the government and general public, such as advances in the delivery of health care and services for senior citizens; improvements in education and opportunities for lifelong learning; enhanced industrial design and intelligent manufacturing technologies; and broad access to public and private databases, electronic mail and other unique resources.[28]

In recognition of the evolving understanding of the NREN's ultimate configuration and scope, the Administration in 1991 introduced the concept of the Interagency Interim NREN (IINREN) as an evolutionary step towards the gigabit NREN. The IINREN is an effort to upgrade the NSFNET backbone, assist regional networks to upgrade facilities, capacity, and bandwidth, and to interconnect the backbone networks of other agencies.[29] But the IINREN and NREN are elusive terms because, as for the NSFNET, there is no clear definition of their scope. Indeed, it is difficult to discern and define any institutional structures other than the individual autonomous networks. There is no central management for the NSFNET, the Internet, the IINREN, or the NREN. Language in the High Performance Computing Act specifying NSF as the lead agency for the deployment of the NREN had to be excised, despite the support of the academic community, because the Administration did not want its

HPCC program locked into a particular managing agency. Passage of the bill was threatened repeatedly by the interests of national laboratories within the Department of Energy seeking a leading role in the NREN and other components of HPCA. In the end, the HPCA more or less restates what the agencies are already and adds general goals without specifying how they are to be achieved.

Even the NSFNET, which has been in existence over six years, remains vaguely defined -- an ambiguous collection of networks. The NSFNET backbone is a special case, since it is provided under an a formal agreement and serves as a free transcontinental transport for the 25 or so networks that are authorized to use it for qualifying purposes. Beyond the backbone, it is not clear what the NSFNET includes. NSF only funds some of the mid-level networks connecting to the backbone, but it does not deny access to the backbone for any internetwork wishing to use in accordance with NSF's purpose and policies. Thus, NEARnet and PREPnet (Pennsylvania) were permitted to use the backbone although they did not receive direct funding from NSF.[30] PSInet and AlterNet were also authorized to the NSFNET backbone for qualifying traffic, although they are for-profit services with their own transcontinental backbones.[31] In effect, the NSFNET backbone has served as a wholesale carrier available without discrimination to any internetwork service -- for traffic that satisfied the purpose defined by NSF. Originally this purpose was to support "scientific research and other scholarly activities," then in 1990, "academic research and education," and, finally, in early 1992, "open research and nonprofit instruction" (see Appendix). The nature of the use is determinative, not the status of the user.

With this access to the backbone for qualifying uses, and their own transcontinental backbones for non-qualifying uses, AlterNet and PSI (Performance Systems International) were able to interest companies that were familiar with the Internet in an academic context but would also use it for proprietary research or other purposes. These for-profit services naturally focused their resources metropolitan areas with concentrations of high-tech industry -- San Francisco, Washington, DC, Boston.... They were joined in California by CERFnet, a project of General Atomics which had initially received NSF funding. In 1991, the three services formed an association, the Commercial Internet Exchange or CIX (pronounced "kicks"), which maintained a physical exchange of the same name in the Bay Area. The CIX, as an exchange for sharing traffic, was modeled after the Federal Internet Exchanges (FIX) (of which there were two, one on each coast) which connect the NSFNET backbone and the mission agency internetworks.

In addition to direct competition among network services, for-profit and nonprofit, there is pressure from resale of network connectivity. At one level, this problem is present in university-developed industrial parks, which may offer connections to the university's campus area network. At another level, guest accounts on university computers have long been given out freely, usually without charge. Mid-level networks initially resisted "resale" of networks, at least for corporate connections. The mid-level network's interest in maintaining its revenue base does not hold very well against efficiency and equity arguments (or common carriage principles), especially since connections are priced on capacity. It may be desirable for a state education network to connect as a single customer to a mid-level network -- or even to do so indirectly through a university.[32] Competition among commercial providers now appears to be encouraging a growing number of re-sellers. One example is the World, dial-up host in Boston which retails full connectivity to the commercial Internet through AlterNet. Internet access through the World costs $20/month for 20 hours plus $1/hr. for additional hours. Another example is Netcom, which began as a single host in the Bay Area but now has its own network and can be reached with a local telephone call in most California metropolitan areas and a number of major cities nationwide. Netcom offers *unlimited* dial-up access for $17.50/month. Note that these providers cannot offer interactive services (FTP, Telnet, etc.) across the NSFNET backbone because of the NSF's acceptable use policy (as opposed to mail, which is transported freely throughout the Internet without regard to origination or destination).[33]

The pricing of the unsubsidized commercial Internet services is worth noting because it suggests extremely low costs of operation. However, it must be emphasized that these are dial-up services (up to 9600 baud) and that occasionally all ports may be busy. Furthermore, at the lowest level of service, the user is only on the Internet as an account at the provider's address. A higher level of service is available using SLIP, Serial Line Internet Protocol. Instead of accessing the Internet by logging into a host machine, SLIP service enables the user's own microcomputer to act as an Internet host with its own Internet address. When connected through SLIP, the user can pull remote files directly, instead of transferring them first to the host and then downloading them into the user's microcomputer. For an additional fee, a user may secure a dedicated port on the host system, which assures on-demand access to the Internet. By leasing a line and dedicating equipment on a 24-hour basis, the user can provide on-demand access in the other direction -- i.e., from the Internet -- which is necessary if employees, agents, customers, or suppliers need to access the system at will.[34]

As demand grows and TCP/IP technology is commercialized, mid-level networks themselves are increasingly providing low cost services directly to individual users and small businesses. Thus there may be competition between networks and their own commercial customers, at least in the more competitive markets. For the nonprofit networks, the big stumbling block remains the acceptable use policy which while not binding on them has left them the product of a specific culture, clientele, and charter in a complex, unregulated, increasingly environment.

## 9. ANS AND THE "PRIVATIZATION" OF NSFNET

The hierarchical model, which has remained essential intact in the telephone world and in which the regional networks once had a clearly defined place, is collapsing -- even at the highest level. Since September of 1990, the NSFNET backbone has no longer existed as a distinct network but as a contract for services from Advanced Network and Services, Inc. (ANS). ANS operates the backbone as part of its own private network, ANSnet, which competes with other network services, commercial and nonprofit, in offering T-1 connections to institutional and corporate networks. ANS was formed as nonprofit corporation by IBM, MCI, and Merit and capitalized by a commitment of $5 million each from IBM and MCI over a three-year period plus $1 million from the State of Michigan Strategic Fund. It became a subcontractor for Merit who continued to hold the 5-year cooperative agreement with NSF that it had won in 1987. It provides network services to Merit, and in turn subcontracts back to Merit for the operation of the NSFNET Network Operations Center in Ann Arbor. This arrangement replaced the joint study agreements that Merit had with IBM and MCI directly in support of the original cooperative. IBM and MCI still contribute technology (as well as funds for ANS), but their contribution has been through ANS. The restructuring of the cooperative agreement with ANS proceeded with NSF's approval as plans were being made to upgrade the backbone from T1 to T3 speeds nearly three years ahead of schedule. This pushing of the technological envelope in a fully operational production network with "cost-sharing" from the private participants was consonant with the evolving federal strategy for a National Research and Education Network. NSF's annual bill for the backbone went from $3 million to $8 million, but its cost for capacity in mbps dropped twelve-fold at the margin.

The advent of ANS was heralded as a unique partnership in the national interest and the new arrangement was described by its President, Al Weis, a former Vice President of IBM, as the privatization of the backbone. The expectation was that restricted NSFNET traffic could be aggregated with additional traffic from companies seeking to market services to users in higher education.[35] It was hoped that commercial users would pay at least the average costs of using the network, while noncommercial use would remain subsidized -- or that noncommercial use could be priced at the margin, while commercial users covered the principal fixed costs.

The additional traffic to be carried by ANSnet was initially restricted by ANS's charter which was intended to qualify it as a 501(c)(3) charitable organization. This left ANS with limited opportunities, so it formed a for-profit subsidiary, CO+RE, Inc. (meaning "commercial" plus "research and education" but pronounced "core"), in May, 1991, as a vehicle for marketing unrestricted commercial use of ANSnet. This put ANS in direct competition (at least for T-1 connections) with the commercial Internet providers, PSI, AlterNet, and CERFnet, who had just formed the Commercial Internet Exchange. Along with the CO+RE subsidiary, ANS announced a plan for commercial services designed to involved the nonprofit mid-level networks connected to the backbone. The plan invited the mid-level networks to hook up commercial customers, either directly or through ANS CO+RE, with the expectation that these commercial customers would be contribute to "the network infrastructure," specifically ANSnet and, through a special fund, the mid-level networks. The plan included measuring traffic to and from declared commercial sites in "COMBits," an original unit designed as a compromise between bits and packets. Although the plan was developed in conjunction with many of the mid-level networks, its complexity was daunting. It presented the networks with three options -- a "Connectivity Agreement," a "Gateway Attachment Agreement," and a "Cooperative Agreement"[36] -- which challenged the networks to make difficult decisions about how commercial their operations would become. While the measurement of COMBits was intended only to provide a guideline to setting annual fees in advance, it was perceived as introducing metering within an environment where capacity-pricing was the established norm and usage-pricing was anathema for both practical and philosophic reasons.

The commercial IP networks, who had just formed the CIX, saw the ANS plan as an effort to dominate the commercialization of the Internet under a centralized, privately controlled model. These commercial providers were all spinoffs of non-profit network organizations in some manner,[37] and so shared with the mid-levels similar roots and perspectives, despite the difference in profit orientation. Although ANS was nonprofit, its self-perpetuating board made it appear more private than most of the mid-levels, most of whom had "members" and some degree of accountability to major institutional users. As a large organization with extremely large corporations behind it -- and as a direct competitor at the high end that was hiring away many of the highly regarded individuals in networking community, ANS was viewed with suspicion by some of the mid-level networks.

The cooperative agreement between NSF and Merit (which in turn subcontracts with ANS) was to expire late in 1992, but in November 1991, NSF announced a new project development plan for the NSFNET. Acknowledging tension between concerns for stability of the NSFNET backbone and competition, the plan announced that in the interests of stability the cooperative agreement would be extended for an additional eighteen months. However, the plan announced three changes for the next solicitation: 1.) The routing authority function would be awarded separately to ensure that tactical advantages would not accrue to a provider of connectivity services; 2.) The awards for connectivity services would not be limited to a backbone model -- so that an award could be made for an exchange or series of exchanges like the CIX and FIX exchanges. (This change was not explicit but was implied in the choice of the term "connectivity.") 3.) There would be at least two awards to provide connectivity. Like the FTS 2000 solicitation, the proposal to enter into at least two cooperative agreements reflected an awareness of the impact of the federal funding on a competitive environment.

The CIX viewed the unwillingness of ANS to join the CIX agreement as evidence of a monopoly position within the NSFNET that extended to providing commercial services through the NSFNET-connected mid-level networks. ANS claimed that the CIX agreement, which required interconnection without compensation or settlements in either direction, would not adequately recognize and compensate ANS for its investment in the T-3 backbone. This debate was clouded by conflicting claims about the T-3 technology and the implications of the cost-sharing upon which the cooperative agreement between NSF and Merit was premised.

These issues were aired in a March 12, 1992, hearing before the House Subcommittee on Science, chaired Representative Boucher. William Schrader, President of PSI, claimed that ANS had favored T-3 technology under development at IBM rather than further developed technology of established TCP/IP router vendors such as Proteon and Cisco.[38] Schrader questioned the fairness of major changes in the cooperative agreement (the ANS subcontract and the substantial increase in funding for the T-3 backbone) without any public process. The NSF Acceptable Use Policy for the backbone was also at issue in the hearings. Schrader and Mitch Kapor, founder and former CEO of Lotus Development Corp. and now Chairman of the CIX, claimed that the AUP operated to give ANS a monopoly over commercial traffic between the sites connected by the NSFNET backbone.

Eric Hood, President of FARNET, the association of (predominantly nonprofit) mid-level networks, also testified in opposition to the acceptable use policy and invited Congressional action to remove it. Boucher questioned whether there was in fact a legal basis for requiring an AUP for the backbone.[39] In the end, he successfully sponsored legislation that would explicitly permit NSF to fund facilities for unrestricted use if doing so would increase the value of the network for research and education.[40] However, the arrangement with ANS was left unchanged.

## 10. CONCLUSION

The Internet continues its dramatic growth. The Internet Society estimates that fifteen million Americans now have full access to the Internet. However, the vast majority of users have access only through institutional or corporate networks. Probably less than 3% have access direct through commercial Internet service providers or public access hosts. This will change significantly over the coming year as the consumer online services, America OnLine and CompuServe, begin to provide fully functional connectivity. Most of the new addresses registered each month are now commercial sites. Many of the regional networks have sold out to private entities or spun off commercial services. The Commercial Internet Exchange now has over 40 members. ANS agreed to interconnect on experimental basis in June of 1992 and finally joined the CIX.

The cooperative agreement between NSF and Merit (and ANS) has been extended a second time and is still in effect, although the transition to the new NSFNET is scheduled for 1994-95. The solicitation was later amended substantially to unbundle connectivity services into three components: a very high-speed backbone (vBNS), which would eventually be limited to experimental uses and specialized research; a number of Network Access Points, which provided access to the vBNS but also permitted the exchange of traffic between commercial networks and "research and education" networks; and grants to mid-level networks to support inter-regional connectivity through the NAPs.[41] In effect, NSF moved toward a policy that, like the regulatory policies of the time, by using unbundling to promote competition rather than dual award compromise of FTS 2000.[42]

## THE NSFNET BACKBONE SERVICES ACCEPTABLE USE POLICY GENERAL PRINCIPLE:

(1) NSFNET Backbone services are provided to support open research and education in and among US research and instructional institutions, plus research arms of for-profit firms when engaged in open scholarly communication and research.  Use for other purposes is not acceptable.

## SPECIFICALLY ACCEPTABLE USES:

(2) Communication with foreign researchers and educators in connection with research or instruction, as long as any network that the foreign user employs for such communication provides reciprocal access to US researchers and educators.

(3) Communication and exchange for professional development, to maintain currency, or to debate issues in a field or subfield of knowledge.

(4) Use for disciplinary-society, university-association, government-advisory, or standards activities related to the user's research and instructional activities.

(5) Use in applying for or administering grants or contracts for research or instruction, but not for other fundraising or public relations activities.

(6) Any other administrative communications or activities in direct support of research and instruction.

(7) Announcements of new products or services for use in research or instruction, but not advertising of any kind.

(8) Any traffic originating from a network of another member agency of the Federal Networking Council if the traffic meets the acceptable use policy of that agency.

(9) Communication incidental to otherwise acceptable use, except for illegal or specifically unacceptable use.

## UNACCEPTABLE USES:

(10) Use for-profit activities (consulting for pay, sales or administration of campus stores, sale of tickets to sports events, and so on) or use by for-profit institutions unless covered by the General Principle or as a specifically acceptable use.

(11) Extensive use for private or personal business.

This statement applies to use of the NSFNET Backbone only.  NSF expects that connecting networks will formulate their own use policies.  The NSF Division of Networking and Communications Research and Infrastructure will resolve any questions about this Policy or its interpretation.

# ENDNOTES

1. *People of the State of California v. FCC*, 905 F.2d 1217 (9th Cir. 1990).

2. CSNET = Computer Science Network, a multi-protocol network funded by NSF to enable resource sharing among computer science departments and research facilities. CSNET and BITNET were merged administratively in 1988 to form the Corporation for Research and Education Networking (CREN). Both ARPANET and CSNET were defunct by 1991.

3. The High Performance Computing Coalition is the lobbying group organized to support the legislation introduced by Senator Albert Gore, Jr., beginning in 1988 that eventually became the High Performance Computing Act of 1991.

4. The RBOCs have been less interested than the IECs, although a few operating companies have participated in state networks, such as NYSERNET and PREPnet, where their visibility has political benefits.

5. BARRNet was funded by NSF early on but has since become self-sufficient. NEARnet was started without federal subsidy, although at one point it received funding to connect to the new T-3 backbone. Both were acquired by BBN Systems in 1994.

6. NEARnet was actually a project of MIT with a steering committee that also included Harvard, Boston University, and BBN Systems. However, to receive service one had to pay a "membership" fee.

7. The occasional exceptions are state networks, such as NYSERNET or CONCERT (North Carolina), which are usually specially chartered by the state legislature.

8. From 1990 to February 1992, when the current AUP was issued, the stated purpose of the NSFNET was "to support research and education in and among academic institutions in the U.S. by providing access to unique resources and the opportunity for collaborative work." Prior to that, the purpose was "scientific research and other scholarly activities."

9. The Internet Engineering Task Force and the Internet Research Task Force comprise the Internet Activities Board (IAB). In 1992, the IAB was integrated into the Internet Society as the Internet Architecture Board.

10. Sophisticated users can leverage network objects with far-reaching consequences. Using *Archie servers* it is possible to locate any file posted using public directory conventions at any site on the Internet. Large files -- be they libelous, pornographic, or pirated -- can be retrieved and broadcast instantly and effortlessly to automated mailing lists of thousands of individuals. By combining such lists into a personal address file, the file can be sent to hundreds of thousands, congesting the network and clogging mailboxes.

11. John S. Quarterman, *The Matrix*, Digital Press, 1991; John S. Quarterman, "How Big is the Matrix?" *Matrix News*, Vol. 2 No. 2, February 1992.

12. Except, of course, for the amorphous Internet and its domain style of addressing. Some commercial bulletin boards misleadingly offer access to the Internet when, in fact, they only provide an Internet mailing address.

13. See "Port Numbers" in Joyce Reynolds and Jan Postel, *Assigned Numbers*, RFC 1060, Internet Activities Board, March 1990.

[14.]S. 2918, "The National High-Performance Computer Technology Act of 1988, introduced October 18, 1988; S. 1067, "The National High-Performance Computer Technology Act of 1989," introduced May 18, 1989; S. 272, "The High-Performance Computing Act of 1991," introduced January 24, 1991, which became Public Law 102-194, December 9, 1991.

[15.]Bennington, Bernard J., "Beyond FTS2000: A Program for Change," Appendix A, National Research Council, Washington, 1989, pp. 1-3.

[16.]Kettl, Donald F., "Sharing Power: Public Governance and Private Markets," Brookings Institution, Washington, 1993, pp. 67-98.

[17.]Treasury, Postal Service, and General Government Appropriations Act of 1994, P.L. 103-123, Section 620.

[18.]The Brooks Act, codified at 41 USC 759, gives the Administrator of General Services exclusive authority to procure computer and telecommunications equipment and services. The law exempts mission-critical Defense Department applications from the GSA authority. A recent Federal appeals court decision reaffirmed the exclusion from the Brooks Act for procurements conducted by Federal labs (US West Communications vs. United States, 940 F.2d 622 (Fed. Cir. 1991)).

[19.]Gould, Stephen, "The Federal Research Internet and the National Research and Education Network: Prospects for the 1990s," U.S. Congress, Congressional Research Service, 90-362 SPR, July 26, 1990, pp. 5-6. Reprinted in McClure, Appendix M, pp. 572-3.

[20.]IP did not support dial-up at that time, so modem protocols were used underneath the ARPANET protocols.

[21.]For a brief period, CSNET used commercial X.25 services, but the cost of hook-ups and per-packet charges proved prohibitive for computer collaboration.

[22.]University Corporation for Atmospheric Research (UCAR) in Colorado, which also runs the NSF-funded supercomputer center known as NCAR.

[23.]Ibid, pp. 60-61.

[24.]Mandelbaum, Richard, and Mandelbaum, Paulette A., "The Strategic Future of the Mid-Level Networks," in Kahin, Brian, ed., Building the Information Infrastructure, McGraw-Hill, 1992, page 62, fn. 6.

[25.]Federal Research Internet Coordinating Committee (FRICC), Program Plan for the National Research and Education Network, May 23, 1989.

[26.]Office of Science and Technology Policy, "Grand Challenges 1993: High Performance Computing and Communications," January, 1992. The four elements support development of hardware, software, networking and human resources.

[27.]Ibid. Section 102 of the High Performance Computing Act of 1991, offers less of a definition but paints a descriptive picture:
NETWORK CHARACTERISTICS.--The Network shall--
(1) be developed and deployed with the computer, telecommunications, and information industries;
(2) be designed, developed, and operated in collaboration with potential users in government, industry, and research institutions and educational institutions;
(3) be designed, developed, and operated in a manner which fosters and maintains competition and private sector investment in high-speed data networking within the telecommunications industry;

(4) be designed, developed, and operated in a manner which promotes research and development leading to development of commercial data communications and telecommunications standards, whose development will encourage the establishment of privately operated high-speed commercial networks;
(5) be designed and operated so as to ensure the continued application of laws that provide network and information resources security measures, including those that protect copyright and other intellectual property rights, and those that control access to data bases and protect national security;
(6) have accounting mechanisms which allow users or groups of users to be charged for their usage of copyrighted materials available over the Network and, where appropriate and technically feasible, for their usage of the Network;
(7) ensure the interoperability of Federal and non-Federal computer networks, to the extent appropriate, in a way that allows autonomy for each component network;
(8) be developed by purchasing standard commercial transmission and network services from vendors whenever feasible, and by contracting for customized services when not feasible, in order to minimize Federal investment in network hardware;
(9) support research and development of networking software and hardware; and
(10) serve as a test bed for further research and development of high-capacity and high-speed computing networks and demonstrate how advanced computers, high-capacity and high-speed computing networks, and databases can improve the national information infrastructure.

[28.]Computer Systems Policy Project, "Expanding the Vision of High Performance Computing and Communications: Linking America for the Future, Washington, 1991.

[29.]Office of Science and Technology Policy, Grand Challenges 1992: High Performance Computing and Communications, January, 1991, page 19.

[30.]NEARnet later received a grant to establish a direct connection to the new T-3 backbone.

[31.]They have sometimes been referred to as "peer networks" rather than mid-level networks. This reveals the fundamental illogic of the hierarchical model since it makes to no sense to discriminate between the two categories based on the exact geographic scope of the network.

[32.]Such is the case in Wyoming. The Wyoming Higher Education Computer Network provides community college users with university addresses and a connection to WestNet.

[33.]At the very low end, many commercial bulletin boards are now providing Internet mailing addresses and mail service at flat monthly or quarterly rates, but, again, users without interactive services are not properly on the Internet. Even these rates, $40-80 per year for unlimited e-mail, pale beside the per user costs attributable to university BITNET connections of $5-20 per year for full Internet functionality.

[34.]A dedicated SLIP port at 9600/14400 baud from Netcom is $160 month plus a setup fee of $750. Local loop costs (dial-up or leased line) are additional.

[35.]In fact, NSF's policies were fairly liberal. Commercial traffic was nominally precluded -- but could be approved if it was in support of research and education. NSF almost always approved such proposed uses, but on an "experimental basis." This was not very assuring to potential users, and ANS was able to commit equivalent use of the backbone on an ongoing basis.

[36.]See "A Mid-level's Guide to the ANS Agreements," Advanced Network and Services, Inc., August 14, 1991 (2pp.).

[37.]CERFnet was and is operated by General Atomics; PSI was a venture capital-funded spinoff of NYSERNET; AlterNet is owned by UUNet Technologies, which was originally set up as a nonprofit corporation.

[38.]The implementation of the T-3 backbone has in fact been fraught with technical problems. Although the transition to the T-3 backbone was scheduled to begin in December of 1990, as of this writing the T-1 backbone still carries most of the traffic.

[39.]NSF responded by referring to Section 3(a)(4) of the National Science Foundation Act of 1950, as amended, which directs NSF to "foster and support the development and use of computer and other scientific and engineering methods and technologies, primarily for research and education in the sciences and engineering," but concluded: "The AUP may be more restrictive than is legally required, and it is currently being reviewed for possible revision." It is worth recalling that no AUP is imposed on the NSF-subsidized mid-level networks.

[40.]P.L. 102-588, Section 217 (42 USC 1862(g)), which states ". . . the Foundation is authorized to foster and support access by the research and education communities to computer networks which may be used substantially for purposes in addition to research and education in the sciences and engineering, if the additional uses will tend to increase the overall capabilities of the networks to support such research and education activities." This change in law helped provide a sound basis for funding Network Access Points that would provide an AUP-free transfer point for exchanging traffic among networks under the future NSFNET architecture.

[41.]Program Solicitation: Network Access Point Manager, Routing Arbiter, Regional Network Providers and Very High Speed Backbone Network Services Provider for NSFNET and the NREN Program, National Science Foundation, Washington, DC, May 6, 1993.

[42.]Meanwhile, the follow-on to FTS 2000 is under study. See, "Post-FTS2000 Acquisition Alternatives White Paper," available on the Internet at post.fts2k.gsa.gov and from the General Services Administration FTS2000 Program Office, Room 6223, 18th and G Sts, NW, Washington, DC 20405.

PRIVATE NETWORKS PUBLIC OBJECTIVES
E. Noam and A. NíShúilleabháin (Editors)
© 1996 Elsevier Science B.V. All rights reserved.

# Information Technology, Private Networks, and Productivity

Steven S. Wildman

## 1. INTRODUCTION

There has been a widespread belief in the inevitability of a coming information age, at least since the publication of Daniel Bell's *The Coming of Post-Industrial Society: A Venture in Social Forecasting*, in 1973. Just as the widespread application of industrial technology leads to a many fold increase in the productivity of economic activities, and thereby to a dramatic improvement in the quality of life for members of industrial societies, so it was prophesized that pervasive applications of information technologies (IT) would take us to a yet higher plane of economic and social well-being.

Today, few would question that the pervasiveness part of that prophesy has come true -- at least for the world's advanced economies, where information technologies have become vital to the facilitation and coordination of economic activity. The growing centrality of information technology and information services to economic activity in general is reflected in the growth of information workers as a percentage of the total workforce in the United States (now well over fifty percent) and in the dramatic growth in the percentage of capital investments going to information technology. From 1972 to 1989, U.S. service sector spending on IT increased from about three percent of total investments in durable equipment to about forty percent. In the manufacturing sector the increase was from three percent to about twenty-five percent over the same period.[1]

Given the degree to which the transformation toward an information society has been documented, it does not seem too early to be looking for empirical evidence of the economic benefits that are supposed to accompany the information revolution. At the very least we might expect some solid theoretical work to tell us whether these expectations are justified. If measured by volume, the research community has been more than obliging. In what he characterized as a selective review of this literature, Brynjolfson[2] surveyed over 150 articles, books, and research reports on IT productivity. The results were disquieting. The overwhelming majority of studies found no significant payoffs to IT investments, although Brynolfson's own more recent econometric study[3] does find significant benefits. The inability of researchers to consistently document significant returns on IT investments, combined with disillusionment by many business leaders whose firms have not experienced sustained increases in profitability following major IT projects, have lead many to question the business wisdom of past IT investments and public policies that promote them.

This chapter looks at the productivity contributions of private networks. The linking of varied information processing devices to create networks with functional capabilities vastly exceeding the stand-alone capabilities of their components is a development that was not widely anticipated by the early prophets of the information age. In fact, researchers' recognition of the significance of networks as functional entities providing services other than transmission is too recent to have been the subject of much empirical investigation.

Private networks may contribute to productivity in two ways: (1) They may provide the same services as public networks but at lower cost. The comparative benefits of public and private networks, when private networks are viewed as alternatives for performing the same basic transmission-related services as the public switched network, are examined by other authors.[4] (2) Private networks may also contribute to productivity by making it possible to produce other goods and services more efficiently, which is the subject of this chapter. The empirical literature on IT productivity is briefly reviewed in the next section. I will argue that, for the most part, the empirical studies of IT reported to date have placed the empirical cart a considerable distance ahead of the theoretical horse. In part this situation reflects the inadequacy of current theory for addressing certain problems raised by IT, including private networks; but it also reflects the fact that in our rush to measure we have made inadequate use of the theoretical tools at hand.

Theoretical work that has been done on modeling the social welfare consequences of investments in new technologies shows that a wide variety of outcomes are possible.[5] Results are highly context specific, with both welfare gains and welfare losses possible. This suggests that further progress in developing a broader understanding of the benefits of IT investments will depend to a large extent on a succession of application-by-application and industry-by-industry studies. The productivity implications of several services and benefits associated with certain types of private networks are examined in Section III.

## 2. EMPIRICAL ASSESSMENTS OF INFORMATION TECHNOLOGY BENEFITS

Most of the attempts to empirically assess the benefits of information technology have lumped various types of information technology together. While private networks are components of the larger whole being examined, it is not possible to disentangle their contributions to productivity from the contributions of other IT investments. The fact that networks add capabilities not present in their component pieces alone is further complication. Nevertheless, at the conceptual level the same issues must be dealt with in assessing private network benefits as for assessments of IT benefits generally. Empirical studies of the benefits of information technology fall into four broad groupings: (1) Studies of the profitability of business investments in information technology; (2) Studies employing Bureau of Labor Statistics (BLS) productivity measures; (3) Production function studies; and (4) Studies of the economic surplus generated by information technology investments. The preponderance of these studies fall in the first two categories.

Profitability studies come in several varieties. For example, there are comparisons of the profits of firms employing different IT strategies across industries[6] and work comparing the profits of firms with different IT strategies in the same industry.[7] Whatever approach is used, however, the search is always for correlations between firm profitability and IT investments. Strassman's conclusion that there is no clear correspondence between IT investments and profitability at the firm level characterizes the findings of this branch of the literature in general.

While less numerous, studies employing BLS measures of productivity, have received by far the most attention, especially a series of studies by Stephen Roach.[8] In his widely cited reports, Roach compares trends in productivity indices for manufacturing industries and for service industries during the period, from the early 1970s to the late 1980s, when IT investments in both sectors rose dramatically. BLS measures of manufacturing productivity rose through most of this period while measures of service sector productivity were basically flat. This, Roach argues, showed that investments in IT in manufacturing industries had been reasonably productive, while the return on IT investments in service industries was been woefully inadequate.

In a widely cited working paper, Loveman[9] estimates a Cobb-Douglass production function for manufacturing firms that included information capital as a factor of production. On the basis of comparisons of output elasticities, he concludes that funds invested in information technologies would have yielded higher returns had they been invested in more traditional forms of capital instead. Brynolfson[10] applies this technique to a larger and more recent sample of firms and found significantly higher returns to IT investments than for other capital investments.

Bresnahan's[11] econometric study of investments in computer technology in the financial services industry measured benefits as the area under the industry's derived demand curve for information services. He estimated benefits at five times the cost of the technology. Hitt and Brynolfson[12] applied Bresnahan's methodology to a larger and more diverse data set covering the years 1988 through 1992 and estimated the surplus created by computer investments for their sample of 367 large (Fortune 500) firms to have been $4.1 billion per year.

Each of these empirical approaches is either theoretically flawed or based on theoretical assumptions that make their use for estimating IT productivity benefits highly suspect. The profitability studies can be dismissed on purely theoretical grounds. While long-term, supracompetitive profits are the objective of the business strategist, to the policy maker they are often taken as evidence of less than vigorous competition. In dynamic competitive markets technology innovators are often quickly imitated or leap-frogged by new innovators. This competition forces prices down toward costs and transfers the surplus made possible through productivity gains to consumers. Therefore, the complaint that the profits from IT strategies are not sustainable in the long run is really a complaint about the vigor of competition. As long as early IT adopters realize at least short term profits, the transient nature of these profits is evidence that productivity benefits are passed on to their customers in the end.[13]

Long recognized problems with the measurement of the outputs of various service activities have been the basis for criticisms of BLS measures of service sector productivity, and, because service industries have invested heavily in IT, criticisms of arguments like those advanced by Roach that IT investments have not been productive.[14] If businesses use IT to provide new services, for which there is no explicit charge, in conjunction with their traditional products or services, the value of the additional service does not show up in BLS measures of productivity. For example, a number of document and package shipping companies now use specialized networks to track the progress of shipments throughout the delivery process and let their customers use these network as a "free" add-on to their service. Because there is no explicit charge attributed to the tracking service, BLS productivity measures don't pick up the full contribution of private networks to these shippers' outputs. Similarly, the productivity benefits of a financial services firm using computer applications to create more sophisticated financial instruments for its clients may not be counted as a

330

productivity gain, given the way that financial services are measured. IT advocates point out that with the severity of the measurement problems in the BLS indices of services productivity, substantial IT productivity contributions may be going unmeasured.

Denison[15] points out that when there are unmeasured productivity gains in intermediate products and services, they may show up as measured productivity gains in an industry purchasing these inputs. Much of the output of the service sector is purchased by manufacturers. Therefore, a portion of the measured productivity gains in manufacturing may actually reflect IT contributions to service sector productivity.

Loveman's econometric production function study of the benefits of IT in manufacturing has been criticized by Baily and Chakrabarti[16] for relying on comparisons of estimated output elasticities, rather than on more meaningful marginal product estimates. It should also be noted that some of the output measurement problems inherent in the BLS productivity measures are also problems for the production function approach to measuring IT benefits, because customer benefits not captured by sellers will not be picked up. However, output measurement problems are less severe for manufacturing sector outputs, so these criticisms have less force when applied to the Loveman and Brynolfson empirical studies.

The theoretical basis for these production function studies merits further examination, however. Profit maximizing businesses should equate returns at the margin on all types of investment. Therefore, productivity studies should find higher returns for IT investments than for other capital investments only if the stock of IT capital is less than optimal. In other words, higher than normal returns to IT should be a disequilibrium phenomenon that can't persist in the long-run. As such, higher than normal returns on IT capital are a measure of prior ignorance regarding the true benefits of IT. Even the disequilibrium interpretation of production function estimates of IT productivity must be viewed cautiously, however. If we really are going through a period of disequilibrium and transition to a more IT intensive system of production, then the assumption underlying these estimates that production function coefficients are stable over time is hard to justify.

Bresnahan[17] developed a model of a perfectly competitive market in IT services to address the measurement problems just discussed. He used the model to show that there are conditions under which an industry's inverse demand function (derived from consumer demands) for information services can be used to estimate the benefits to consumers of investments in IT. In the process he provided the theoretically useful result that in some circumstances competitive markets can be relied upon to make social benefit-maximizing investments in information technologies.

In contrast with the production function studies, the recent findings of which make sense only if firms don't fully appreciate the benefits of information technology, Bresnahan's approach produces reliable estimates of IT benefits only if firms do fully understand the benefits of the information technologies they invest in. Because it estimates the area under a downward sloping demand curve, a finding of positive benefits is inevitable. Only the magnitude is in doubt. In other words, Breshnahan's approach doesn't allow for mistaken IT investments. If applied to U.S. nuclear power facilities, most of which are now known to have been mistakes, it would still show positive net benefits. Nevertheless, Bresnahan's model provides a useful benchmark for examining the extent to which the *understood* benefits of IT are likely to be internalized in market transactions.

The message of this brief review of the IT productivity literature is clear. The empirical techniques employed to date to estimate the productivity consequences of investments in information technology are not up to the task. Many of the claimed benefits of IT are intangible, which means they are not captured, or are captured imperfectly, in BLS productivity statistics. Bresnahan's approach is elegant and theoretically defensible, but only if the nature of the benefits is well-understood by firms investing in information technology. Brynolfson's estimates of substantial benefits, which imply that investments in information technology are not well-informed, and the fact that the "productivity paradox" is still a subject of intense discussion, suggest that for most industries Bresnahan's assumption, that firms fully anticipate the benefits IT will provide, is not satisfied. To make further progress in estimating the return on IT investments, we need to do a better job of modeling IT's benefits.

IT has many applications and the nature of the benefits should be specific to these applications. While less exciting than producing global estimates, clearly specifying and modeling the economic implications of the benefits that can reasonably be expected in specific IT applications seems to be the only way to make further progress. The next section of this chapter uses an economic perspective to examine the productivity implications of several of the observed consequences of certain types of private networks. Central to this analysis is the assumption that private networks provide services that are primarily facilitative. That is, they make it possible to carry out more primary economic activities more rapidly, or more accurately, or at lower cost, etc., than would be possible without them. Previously undervalued and/or unanticipated benefits of private networks are revealed. Once these benefits are better understood, the job of estimating their magnitude will be much easier. Besides making possible more accurate estimates of private networks' productivity contributions, this type of careful modeling of prospective benefits should lead to wiser and more productive investments in private networks and IT generally.

## 3. SEARCH FACILITATION: ANALYSIS OF AN APPLICATION OF PRIVATE NETWORKS

Economic actors often commit considerable resources to the gathering of information about their options before committing themselves to a course of action. In these situations, the net benefit associated with search is the realized (expected) increase in the value of the option taken relative to the value of the option that likely would have been taken with no (or less) search minus the value of the resources committed to the search processs. Private networks affect the cost side of this tradeoff by lowering the cost of search and they affect the benefits side to the extent that the quality of the option selected is affected. This is most obvious in the case of private networks used to facilitate buyer search, such as a real estate multiple listing service (MLS) or an airline computer reservation service (CRS). However, similar processes and consequences are to be observed in the manufacturers' and service providers' attempts to improve production practices and in the search for the inspirations for new products and services.

Consider the case of a private network used to facilitate buyer search. An optimal search strategy requires that the buyer continue examining new alternatives until the value of the best alternative examined so far is high enough that the expected improvement over that value from one more search is not large enough to justify the cost of the search.[18] The major attraction of certain private networks, such as MLS's and CRS's, is that they lower search costs. In both cases, buyers' direct costs of searching are reduced because they can compare significant attributes of different purchase options on-line. In the case of a CRS, enough information is provided to make a final selection -- at which point the CRS is also used to process the transaction. While the final selection of houses and other real estate properties are seldom made on a MLS, use of a MLS to screen options can significantly reduce the number of properties a buyer actually visits before making a selection.

The savings in buyer search costs are an obvious productivity gain from these networks, and one that may be recouped at least in part in buyer fees. However, the bigger benefit, especially in real estate markets, is likely to come from a better matching of buyer preferences with the options offered by sellers. An obvious implication of the search rule stated above is that buyers will examine more options if the cost of search is reduced. The benefit to the individual buyer of screening more options is that the best of the larger number of options considered with network search facilitation is likely to be better than the best of the smaller number of options that would be examined otherwise. In the aggregate, the benefit of search facilitation comes from a better matching of heterogeneous products with buyers with heterogeneous tastes.

To illustrate the nature of the benefits of buyer search facilitation, suppose that in the absence of network search facilitation home buyer A would end up with house 1, which she values at $100,000, and buyer B would settle for house 2, which he values at $100,000. With the aid of a MLS, A would find house 2, for which she would be willing to pay $110,000 and B would discover house 1, for which he would be willing to pay up to $110,000. In this case, network search facilitation would produce a reallocation of the existing housing stock among existing buyers worth $20,000 to the buyers.

Under a wide variety of circumstances, much of this gain would not show up in the prices reflected in BLS productivity statistics. As I showed in an earlier effort to model network search facilitation,[19] some of the benefits of better choices by buyers may be picked up by sellers who raise their prices when they realize that the prospective buyers who approach them are the ones who value their properties most highly. Prices could also fall, however, because buyers are now examining more options. In either case, the additional surplus retained by buyers does not show up in BLS-type productivity calculations because it is over and above the purchase price. Furthermore, because the same stock of houses is being sold, price increases due to better buyer-seller matches are likely to be discounted as price inflation in BLS statistics.

While not as easy to model, there are analogous benefits from the use of private networks to facilitate the search for solutions to the types of problems, which, while perhaps infrequent or even non recurring for the individual enterprise, must be dealt with by all enterprises engaged in similar activities. Typically there are a number of ways to address a given production problem or design problem, some of which are immediately apparent, others of which are not. The comparative advantages of alternatives are often hard to assess. Private networks are increasingly being used to facilitate the formation and operation of personal networks of experts and other interested parties who share information, perspectives, and the benefits of experience in dealing these kinds of problems. Examples are the bulletin boards that have emerged on the major on-line services, such as CompuServe, America On-Line, and Prodigy, on which computer experts post problems they are having difficulty solving and offer solutions to problems posted by others, and computer networks for physicians that post information about new medicines and procedures.

## 4. CYCLE-TIME REDUCTION: ANALYSIS OF AN OBSERVED EFFECT OF PRIVATE NETWORKS

Electronic data interchange (EDI) is probably the private network application that has received the most attention in the business press. EDI networks connecting buyers and sellers have made it possible for firms to dramatically reduce paperwork and implement just-in-time (JIT) inventory programs which, by making it possible for firms to place orders and receive shipments from suppliers on an as-needed basis, have dramatically reduced paperwork and the lapsed time from the placement of an order to the delivery of a part or product. Reduced order times, or order cycles, make possible smaller inventory holdings because the risks associated with stock outages are reduced. The savings from reduced inventories are obvious. Inventory has an opportunity cost equal to the cost of the financial capital tied up and there are the additional savings in storage costs and the costs of keeping track of inventory holdings. Substantial staff reductions are also often realized as various clerical functions are automated and the amount of paperwork falls.

With flexible manufacturing processes, the just-in-time philosophy is also being applied to production, which makes possible further savings in inventory holdings, paperwork, and personnel. Private networks have also been used to speed the flow of information between executive suites and the shop floor and to facilitate communication between product designers and product engineers and between product engineers and manufacturing operations. The aggregate effect of these applications of private networks has been an often dramatic reduction in the time required to move a new product or service from concept through design and into production.

The focus on inventory and paperwork reductions from JIT systems has obscured the fact that even without these benefits, there would probably be substantial, though more subtle, productivity benefits from the reduction in the time required to carry out various economic activities. Some of these are realized at the level of the firm while others reflect changes in entire production (or value) systems, the set of vertical relationships among firms at different stages in a production process. I want to examine two largely overlooked benefits of shorter cycle times: reduced opportunity costs associated with resource commitments and better matches of products and plans with market conditions.

One part of the resource commitments I am referring to is the expenditures on labor and other inputs that must be made at each stage of a product's transformation from raw materials and labor inputs to a finished final good in the hands of a buyer. Since the payoff to these expenditures is not realized until the end product is purchased by its ultimate buyer, the final cost of the product must include the opportunity cost of the expenditures on all inputs employed in the processes of producing, distributing, marketing, and selling of a product up to the moment it is actually sold. I will refer to this sequence of activities as the product provision cycle, or the provision cycle. The more drawn out are the processes making up the provision cycle, the greater the opportunity cost. Another way of looking at this is that the payments to labor and other inputs used to produce, distribute, market, or sell, the final product must be lower the longer is the product provision cycle, because the opportunity cost of funds tied-up must also be covered in the product's price, and price is constrained by the location of the product's demand function. In other words, longer production cycles reduce factor productivity.

In one respect this claim is pretty obvious. The length of the production cycle is partially determined by the speed with which labor works. Clearly productivity varies inversely with the pace at which the individual worker works. However, much of the delay in production processes is due to communication delays -- time required for acquiring, transmitting, and processing information. These delays occur independent of the rate at which individual workers (other than information workers) carry out their tasks. Therefore, using information technology to reduce these delays increases labor productivity even if the ratios of physically measured labor inputs to outputs stay the same, because consumption of the final product occurs much closer to the date the work was performed, and less opportunity cost of funds is included in the final price. Of course, this is also true for non labor inputs. The following example shows the magnitude of the productivity gains that might be realized from using information technology to shorten production cycles.

Consider a product that can be produced with an expenditure of $400 in direct payments for the labor and other inputs used in its production. Once produced, the product is purchased off the factory floor with no extra expenditures on distribution, marketing or sales. Suppose production takes place over a four year period, input expenditures are constant at the rate of $100 per year, and the annual interest rate is 10 percent. Then, at the end of the four year period the sum of direct payments to factors plus the opportunity cost of the funds tied up would come to approximately $487.31.

If the time required to move the product through all its stages of production is reduced to two years due to more efficient communication, the total of the opportunity cost of funds plus $400 in factor payments would be reduced to $441.00, a reduction of 9.5 percent from the four year cost. Halving the provision cycle again to a year would reduce the total cost to $420, a reduction of 4.8 percent from the $441 and a 13.8 percent reduction from the $487.31 four year cost.[20] Clearly the potential savings from shortening product provision cycles are quite substantial.

Ignored in the preceding discussion of product (or service) provision cycles were the costs of conceptualizing and developing new products and services and the costs of designing and setting up the facilities for producing them. New products and services are often years in development and in major industries like automobiles and prescription drugs, development costs may run to the hundreds of millions or billions of dollars. Private networks are now being used shorten product development costs by facilitating the flow of information among teams of marketing experts, design engineers, and the managers of manufacturing facilities. Given the financial sums involved, the potential opportunity cost savings from shorter planning cycles are clearly quite large.

Other benefits of reduced cycle times are similar in some ways to the benefits of better matching of buyers and existing products attributable to search facilitation, only the analogous benefits of shorter cycle times are reflected in smaller forecast errors and better matches of seller plans and buyer demands. Demand forecasts are always uncertain, and the magnitude of uncertainty grows the further into the future that demand must be forecast. Therefore a benefit of shorter cycle times is a better match of products available with buyer preferences. This applies to all three types of cycle times discusses. Shorter order cycles (often referred to as inventory cycles) mean a better match of goods retailers hold in stock with contemporaneous buyer preferences, given the range of options actually produced by manufacturers. Shorter provision cycles give retailers a better set of options (product options that more closely mirror buyer preferences) from which to choose than would be available otherwise. Finally, shorter planning cycles make a better range of production options available to manufacturers. Shorter planning and provision cycles also reduce costs by making it possible for manufacturers to incorporate more recent advances in production techniques and to select input ratios that more closely reflect factors prices at the time of production.

## 5. A MODEL OF CYCLE TIME COMPETITION

The model developed in this subsection is similar in many respects to that developed by Bresnahan.[21] An important difference is that the representation of the demand function employed here was chosen for its usefulness in modeling cycle time competition. The model follows Bresnahan in assuming that the productivity benefits of IT are manifest in direct consumer benefits rather in lower production costs.[22] However, the particular form of the model employed has little effect on the generality of the analysis.

We will consider an industry with n firms, indexed by $i = 1,...,n$ and employ the following definitions. Let $x_i$ be the measured output of representative firm i and let $d_i$ be i's cycle time (either product cycle or inventory cycle). Define $\phi(d_i)$ such that $\phi(0) = 1$, $\phi(\infty) \geq 0$, and $\phi' < 0$. $X = \Sigma \phi(d_i)x_i$.

Consumers' utility gross of expenditures on the industry's product is given by $U(X)$, with marginal utility increasing in X, but at a decreasing rate. That is, $U' > 0$ and $U'' < 0$. $\phi' < 0$ means that a longer cycle time reduces the value of a firm's output to consumers. (For example, longer product development cycles could result in product designs more out of date relative to current consumer preferences.) To illustrate what this assumption about the effect of differences in cycle times on preferences means in terms of the model being developed, suppose for firms i and k that $\phi(d_i) = .6$, $\phi(d_k) = .3$, and that $x_i = x_k$. Then, even though the unit measures of output for the two firms are the same, i's output contributes twice as much to consumer utility as k's (as long as the loss of neither has a significant impact on $U'$). Finally, let $p_i$ be the price for representative firm i, define $I_i$ to be per period expenditures on information services by firm i. Included in I are the rental value of investments in information technology and the ongoing costs of operating and maintaining the technology. The costs incurred by a firm with output x and information services purchases of I are given by $c(x,I)$.

We assume $d_i$ to be a decreasing function of $I_i$ only. This assumption, which is implicit in Bresnahan's model, is not totally innocuous, especially for the product cycle interpretation of the model. For example, it is not unreasonable to expect some of the market intelligence gathered by firm i in designing the next product model to be leaked to other firms in the market and vice versa. Nor is it unreasonable to expect that information acquired in this manner might be used to improve the "fit" of a firm's design to consumer tastes at the time of its release. Similarly, knowledge of advances in design techniques at one firm may eventually become common knowledge throughout an industry.

Our first task is to describe the configuration of the industry that maximizes consumer utility net of production and information services costs. In doing this we make the simplifying assumption that firms are selecting steady state values for all choice variables and that the discount rate is sufficiently low that we can ignore the fact that the effects of changes in a firm's level of I do not affect demand for its product until d(I) amount of time has passed. These assumptions should have no effect on the comparative static results while saving the notational clutter of discount factors that would appear in some first order conditions but not in others. With symmetry among firms, the problem can be written as:

$$\text{Max}_{x,I,n} \ U - nc(x,I), \tag{1}$$

where the unsubscripted x and I are values for these variables common to all firms. This gives us the following first order conditions for a welfare optimum, where $c_1$ and $c_2$ are the derivatives of c with respect to x and I respectively.

$$U'ø(d) - c_1 = 0 \tag{2}$$

$$U'ø'd'x - c_2 = 0 \tag{3}$$

$$U'ø(d)x - c = 0 \tag{4}$$

Let $\Pi_i$ be the profit of firm i.

$$\Pi_i = P_i x_i - c(x_i,I_i). \tag{5}$$

For firm i, $P_i = U'ø(d_i)$. In a standard competitive model, firms take price as parametric. In this model, it is U' that is taken as given. That is, each firm's output is a sufficiently small fraction of the market total that the effect of small variations in any $x_i$ on marginal utility is trivial. However, each firm can affect the price of its own product through its choice of I. The first order conditions for a Cournot competitor taking U' and the values of its competitors' information services purchases and outputs as fixed are given by (6) and (7).

$$P_i - c_1 = 0 \tag{6}$$

$$(\partial P_i/\partial I_i)x_i - c_2 = 0 \tag{7}$$

The zero profit condition for a free entry equilibrium is

$$P_i x_i - c_i = 0. \tag{8}$$

Substituting the utility function equivalents for the price expressions in equations (6), (7) and (8) shows them to be the same as (2), (3), and (4), which is Bresnahan's optimality result. What is not obvious are the cost function restrictions implied by a sustainable competitive equilibrium. The cost functions in turn imply restrictions on the types of information services that are compatible with a competitive equilibrium.

(6) in combination with (8) rules out cost functions in which I has a fixed cost component unless marginal cost is rising, since at most only variable costs could be covered otherwise. Thus, for example, a cost function of the form $c(x,I) = kx + I$, where I might be expenditures on a common information service available to all of a firm's customers is ruled out.[23] It is hard to envision a data base type service that would not be ruled out by this restriction.

For a firm's information expenditures to increase buyers' valuation of its product without adding a fixed cost component to a constant cost production function, the cost function would have to be of the form $c(x,I) = v(I)x$. This requires a separate expenditure on information inputs on the firm's part for each unit of the product sold, which seems unlikely. This possibility aside, for industries that do not have rising marginal costs, spending on information technology is incompatible with a classical competitive equilibrium. If IT spending adds a fixed cost component to an otherwise constant cost industry, a stable equilibrium requires that eventually enough firms exit the industry so that those remaining are sensitive to the effect of their output decisions on price. In general, it seems unwise to invoke Bresnahan's optimality result to justify IT investments in competitive industries unless careful attention is given to the nature of the contribution of IT to the value of the industry's product and the role of IT in firms' cost functions.

If the number of firms is taken as fixed, and we allow for positive spillovers from one firm's IT expenditures to other firms--perhaps the results of IT facilitated market research are leaked to competitors--then the model is formally identical to a model of R&D investments developed by Spence.[24] Such spillover benefits to competitors reduce the incentive to invest in R&D. Spence showed that in the presence of R&D spillovers an optimal policy would be to subsidize firms' investments in R&D. In fact, Spence shows that subsidies can be set to generate the optimal level of expenditure on R&D when the number of firms in an industry is fixed. By extension, these results would also apply to expenditures on information technologies such as private networks.

The fact that the spillover benefits of a firm's IT investments to other firms are not internalized in its derived demand for IT suggests that Bresnahan-type derived demand function estimates of benefits from IT investments might be used as lower bound estimates for actual benefits when firms understand the benefits of information technology and act as atomistic competitors. Dropping the assumption of atomistic competition in IT services can produce radically different results, as illustrated by the discussion of industry-sponsored search facilitation above.

The model still produces interesting insights into the nature of competition in information services and the implications of government technology policy, however, if we drop the restrictive assumptions that firms view price (or marginal utility) as constant and that competition proceeds to the point of pushing profits to zero; even though we lose the ability to make clean cut, comparative static welfare comparisons.

For example, assume a domestic market with the number of firms fixed at n, let s be the fraction of every dollar spent on IT that is rebated to IT purchasers by the government, and let $c(x,I) = kx+I$. These assumptions are reflected in equations (9) and (10), which are variants of the firm first order conditions, (6) and (7). The addition of the second term in (9), which is not in (2), allows for the possibility that firms are not price takers.

$$U'\phi(d) + U''[\phi(d)]^2x - k = 0. \tag{9}$$

$$U'\phi'd'x - 1 + s = 0. \tag{10}$$

Taking the total derivatives of (9) and (10) with respect to s, it can be shown that for a linear demand curve (which implies $U'''=0$), dI/ds and dx/ds are both positive. That is, IT investments and output both increase in response to an increase in the subsidy, which is intuitively plausible. These results do not generalize to all possible specifications of consumer demand functions,[25] but intuition suggests that they are likely to characterize most real-world situations. Given a fixed number of firms, $dI/ds > 0$ means that the industry as a whole increases its purchases of IT services if its own contribution to the cost of those services is reduced, which seems reasonable. $dx/ds > 0$ means that the physical measure of industry output increases as its cost for purchasing the IT inputs that make its product more appealing to consumers declines. This also seems reasonable.

Thus we would expect firms (or an industry) favored by IT subsidies to increase product quality and sell more units at higher prices than they would otherwise. More intriguing is the clear implication that a country providing larger IT subsidies to its domestic firms than its trading partners provide to their domestic manufactures could turn the balance of trade in the affected industries in favor of itself. This would happen because firms in the country with the largest IT subsidy would invest more in information technology and produce "higher quality" products[26] than their international competitors from other nations. While the firms with greater IT investments will also charge higher prices, their higher prices will be more than compensated for by higher quality. So their unit sales will be greater than competitors from other countries as well.

## 6. SUMMARY

Attempts to estimate empirically the benefits of information technology investments to date have either been theoretically flawed or have been based on theoretical assumptions (either implicit or explicit) that are hard to justify. What seems clear from the empirical evidence produced is that most firms have invested in information technology without a clear understanding of its prospective benefits. Theoretical considerations also suggest that, because both net benefits and net losses from IT investments are possible and the situations that generate benefits and losses are likely to vary among industries, attempts to directly estimate the aggregate benefits and costs of IT investments are not likely to produce useful results.

The fact that IT in general, and private networks in particular, are used primarily to facilitate the performance of more primary economic activities suggests that a careful study of the benefits of the types of facilitation provided by private networks (and information technology more generally) would be fruitful. This chapter examined the prospective productivity benefits that might be expected from the use of private networks to facilitate search and to shorten various economic cycles. The prospective benefits identified are potentially quite large and this identification lays the foundation for more meaningful productivity estimates. The clearer identification of prospective benefits itself should also further the goal of more effective IT investments.

A formal model of network-facilitated cycle time competition showed that the optimality properties of Bresnahan's[27] model are unlikely to be satisfied in most real world applications of information technology; however, his approach should be useful for calculating a conservative lower bound on the benefits of IT investments when firms are well-informed. An extension of the model showed that a country providing larger IT investment subsidies to domestic firms than its international rivals might be able to gain an advantage in international trade.

# REFERENCES

Baily, M. N. and Chakrabarti, A. K., *Innovation and the Productivity Crisis*, Washington, D.C.: Brookings, 1988.

Bresnahan, T. F., "Measuring the Spillovers from Technical Advance: Mainframe Computers in Financial Services," *American Economic Review*, September 1986, 76, 742-55.

Brynjolfsson, E., "The Productivity of Information Technology: Review and Assessment," Center for Coordination Science Technical Report #126, Sloan School of Management, MIT, December 1991.

Brynjolfsson, E., "Paradox Lost? Firm-level Evidence on the Returns to Information Systems Spending," Sloan School of Management, MIT, December 1994.

Denison, E. F., *Estimates of Productivity Change by Industry*, Washington: The Brookings Institution, 1989.

Dos Santos, B. L. and K. Peffers, "Rewards to Investors in Innovative Technology Applications: A Study of First Movers and Early Followers in ATMs," Krannert Graduate School of Management, Paper no 1014, Purdue University, November 1991.

Egan, B. L. and S. S. Wildman, "Investing in the Telecommunications Infrastructure: Economics and Policy Considerations," *A National Information Network: Changing Our Lives in the 21st Century*, Institute for Information Studies, December 1992, 19-54.

Fudenberg, D. and J. Tirole, "Understanding Rent Dissipation: On the Use of Game Theory in Industrial Organization," *American Economic Review*, May 1987, 77, 177-83.

Gilbert, R. J. and Newbery, D. M. G., "Preemptive Patenting and the Persistence of Monopoly," *American Economic Review*, June 1982, 72, 514-526

Hitt, L. and Brynolfsson, E., "Creating Value and Destroying Profits? Three Measures of Information Technology's Contributions," Sloan School of Management, MIT, December 1994.

Loveman, G. W., "An Assessment of the Productivity Impact of Information Technologies," MIT Working Paper 90s: 88-054, September 1990.

Panko, R., "Is Office Productivity Stagnant?" *MIS Quarterly*, June 1991, 190-203.

Roach, S. S., "America's Technology dilemma: A Profile of the Information Economy," Special Economic Study, Morgan Stanley, April 22, 1987.

Roach, S. S., "The Technology Trap," *Economic Perspectives*, Morgan Stanley & Co., December 15, 1989.

Roach, S. S., "Services Under Siege—The Restructuring Imperative," *Harvard Business Review*, September-October 1991, 82-91.

Roach, S. S., "Policy Challenges in an Era of Restructuring," Morgan Stanley, January 8, 1992.

Spence, M., "Cost Reduction, Competition, and Industry Performance," *Econometrica*, Vol. 52, No. 1 (January, 1984), 101-121.

Strassman, P. A., *The Business Value of Computers*, New Canaan, Connecticut: Information Economics Press, 1990.

Wildman, S., "The Economics of Industry-Sponsored Search Facilitation," in M. Guerin-Calvert and S. Wildman, eds., *Electronic Services Networks: A Business and Public Policy Challenge*, New York: Praeger, 1991.

340

# ENDNOTES

[1]Roach, "Policy Challenges in an Era of Restructuring," Morgan Stanley, January 8, 1992.

[2]Brynjolfsson, E., "The Productivity of Information Technology: Review and Assessment," Center for Coordination Science Technical Report #126, Sloan School of Management, MIT, December 1991.

[3]Brynjolfsson, E., "Paradox Lost?  Firm-level Evidence on the Returns to Information Systems Spending," Sloan School of Management, MIT, December 1994.

[4]Notably in the paper "Efficiency and Productivity of Public and Private Networks of NTT" by Oniki and Stevenson, delivered at the Private Networks and Public Objectives conferences at the Columbia Institute of Tele-Information during 1991.

[5]See, e.g., Gilbert and Newbery (1982) and Fudenberg and Tirole (1987).

[6]Strassman, P. A., *The Business Value of Computers*, New Canaan, Connecticut: Information Economics Press, 1990.

[7]Dos Santos, B. L. and K. Peffers, "Rewards to Investors in Innovative Technology Applications:  A Study of First Movers and Early Followers in ATMs," Krannert Graduate School of Management, Paper no 1014,  Purdue University, November 1991.

[8]Roach, S. S., "America's Technology dilemma:  A Profile of the Information Economy," Special Economic Study, Morgan Stanley, April 22, 1987, Roach, S. S., "The Technology Trap," *Economic Perspectives*, Morgan Stanley & Co., December 15, 1989, Roach, S. S., "Services Under Siege—The Restructuring Imperative," *Harvard Business Review*, September-October 1991, 82-91 and Roach, "Policy Challenges in an Era of Restructuring," Morgan Stanley, January 8, 1992.

[9]Loveman, G. W., "An Assessment of the Productivity Impact of Information Technologies," MIT Working Paper 90s: 88-054, September 1990.

[10]Brynjolfsson, E., "Paradox Lost?  Firm-level Evidence on the Returns to Information Systems Spending," Sloan School of Management, MIT, December 1994.

[11]Bresnahan, T. F., "Measuring the Spillovers from Technical Advance:  Mainframe Computers in Financial Services," *American Economic Review*, September 1986, 76, 742-55.

[12]Hitt, L. and Brynolfsson, E., "Creating Value and Destroying Profits? Three Measures of Information Technology's Contributions,"  Sloan School of Management, MIT, December 1994.

[13]Egan, B. L. and S. S. Wildman, "Investing in the Telecommunications Infrastructure: Economics and Policy Considerations," *A National Information Network:  Changing Our Lives in the 21st Century*, Institute for Information Studies, December 1992, 19-54.

[14]Panko, R., "Is Office Productivity Stagnant?" *MIS Quarterly*, June 1991, 190-203 and Baily, M. N. and Chakrabarti, A. K., *Innovation and the Productivity Crisis*, Washington, D.C.: Brookings, 1988.

[15]Denison, E. F., *Estimates of Productivity Change by Industry*, Washington: The Brookings Institution, 1989.

[16]Baily, M. N. and Chakrabarti, A. K., *Innovation and the Productivity Crisis*, Washington, D.C.: Brookings, 1988.

[17.]Bresnahan, T. F., "Measuring the Spillovers from Technical Advance: Mainframe Computers in Financial Services," *American Economic Review*, September 1986, 76, 742-55.

[18.]This is description of the optimal stopping rule that is the subject of a large body of literature on the economics of search.

[19.]Wildman, S., "The Economics of Industry-Sponsored Search Facilitation," in M. Guerin-Calvert and S. Wildman, eds., *Electronic Services Networks: A Business and Public Policy Challenge*, New York: Praeger, 1991.

[20.]Cost for a four year cycle was approximated as:

$$\$100(1+r/2)[(1+r)^3+(1+r)^2+(1+r)+1], \tag{19.1}$$

where r is the interest rate and set equal to .10 for this example. Similarly, the cost for a two year cycle is:

$$\$200(1+r/2)[(1+r)+1] \tag{19.2}$$

and the cost for a one year cycle is $400(1+r/2).

[21.]Bresnahan, T. F., "Measuring the Spillovers from Technical Advance: Mainframe Computers in Financial Services," *American Economic Review*, September 1986, 76, 742-55.

[22.]Spence (1984) shows for a R&D investment model, which is similar to the IT expenditure model developed here, that a cost reduction formulation is isomorphic with a consumer benefits formulation over a wide variety of circumstances.

[23.]This would also apply to informative advertising.

[24.]Spence, M., "Cost Reduction, Competition, and Industry Performance," *Econometrica*, Vol. 52, No. 1 (January, 1984), 101-121.

[25.]This is because U''', the third derivative of the demand function, appears in the expressions for dI/ds and dx/ds, and this term cannot be signed on purely theoretical grounds.

[26.]Higher quality in this analysis can refer to the greater likelihood that firms investing more in IT will have shorter planning, provision, and purchasing cycles, and thus will have product varieties that better match consumer preferences than their competitors' products.

[27.]Bresnahan, T. F., "Measuring the Spillovers from Technical Advance: Mainframe Computers in Financial Services," *American Economic Review*, September 1986, 76, 742-55.

# Network Security and Reliability: Emergencies In Decentralized Networks

A. Michael Noll

## 1. INTRODUCTION

The distinction between public and private networks has become quite blurred, as many of the papers presented in this volume, complied by the Columbia Institute for Tele-Information, have shown. Public and private networks are interconnected and use each other's facilities to create a transparent "network of networks." As opposed to the past when the long-distance network was the sole responsibility, and was under the control of, AT&T, today's "network-of-networks" is a decentralized network in terms of control and overall responsibility. The Bell operating companies, the former independent telephone companies, AT&T, MCI, Sprint, and a host of other network suppliers and operators, all have this responsibility. The entire telecommunication network is in a constant state of change as it is reconfigured to meet the needs of its users. The use of private branch exchanges has been on the decline as business customers return to Centrex service provided by local telephone companies. The truly dedicated private networks of large businesses are being replaced by virtual networks provided by the many common carriers.

All telecommunication users -- private and public, business and residential -- take telecommunication for granted. That is, until something goes wrong and the network goes down! Then suddenly we all again learn that telecommunication is essential to today's economy. Network failures indeed can have catastrophic results, and such failures must be prevented and minimized through adequate attention to the security of the network and the individual networks that comprise today's "network of networks." With competition, the reliability of tomorrow's network is at greater risk, according to a report of the National Research Council.[1]

This paper dicusses the issue of network security and reliability and how these topics relate to emergencies in decentralized networks. The technology of a modern telecommunication network is described. Emphasis is given to the role of common channel signaling and the extra vulnerability that it creates along with the means for protection and service restoration. Technological, procedural, and cooperative solutions to ensure the reliability of the network are discussed.

## 2. NETWORK FAILURES

Three major failures occurred in AT&T's long-distance network in 1991. These three failures resulted in lengthy outages, hours in duration, that disrupted telecommunication service in the affected major metropolitan areas and thus have focused attention on the reliability of today's telecommunication networks. All three of the failures in AT&T's network had a strong human component and were caused by management failures in procedures and policies. However, it is not only humans who cause network failures but technology as well; here, though, ultimately, human error is to blame.

Preceding years saw service failures caused by software errors and glitches in the signaling system that controls the overall operation of the network. One of these signaling system failures affected AT&T early in 1990. Other signaling system failures affected two local Bell companies on both the East and West coasts (interestingly, both local failures occurred on the same day). Long-distance carriers other than AT&T have also experienced various network failures, although the much smaller size of the total traffic carried by these carriers has resulted in much less impact and publicity.

These network failures serve to remind us that today's service and information economy is highly dependent on telecommunication, and any network failure of even a few hours strongly disrupts the conduct of business and even our personal lives. Two of AT&T's network failures in 1991 affected telecommunication service for two major airports thereby affecting airline service. Furthermore, today's technology has such a large scale that even a "small" failure has huge consequences. Over 30,000 telephone circuits are routinely carried over a single strand of optical fiber, one-tenth the diameter of a human hair. A single switching machine in a long-distance network can handle over 100,000 one-way trunks.

Network failures can occur for a variety of reasons. In most cases, the cause of a failure is accidental. However, network failure caused by deliberate acts or sabotage should not be ignored when planning for all contingencies. Deliberate acts of harm could come from either an external or an internal source, and a disgruntled employee could easily do much harm. The hardware could malfunction causing a network failure, although most key network hardware is duplicated and this redundancy greatly reduces hardware failure as a source of network failure. For example, the central processors and other key components in most switching machines are duplicated. Switching machines are operated by computer programs, or software, that is subject to a wide variety of errors, or bugs, when the software was written, ultimately by humans. Thus, even though hardware might be duplicated, usually the same software controls the hardware and thus a single software error could collapse the duplicated hardware. Hardware malfunctions can also affect software and lead ultimately to network failure.

Clearly, there are a wide variety of sources of network failure. The following tutorial is the basic architecture and workings of a modern telecommunication network in intended to help the non-technical reader to understand more fully these sources of network failure along with the means needed to protect against failure.

## 3. NETWORK TECHNOLOGY: A TUTORIAL

The network carries the signals generated by customer traffic from one place to another over a wide variety of transmission media, including optical fiber, microwave radio, and copper cable in the form of twisted pairs or coaxial. Various paths are switched together until a complete circuit between source and destination is formed to carry the signals generated by the customer traffic. The customer traffic usually consists mostly of speech signals generated by telephone instruments, but facsimile and data signals are also carried over the network.

Transmission and switching are the two major technologies involved in the switched telecommunication network. The various real and virtual paths that must be created to carry telecommunication traffic over the switched network must be set up and maintained during the duration of the call, and then dismantled at the completion of the call. Signaling is the aspect of telecommunication that deals with controlling the network to create, maintain, and dismantle these paths.

In the past, signaling was done over the same switched network that carried the customer traffic, and only when the complete end-to-end circuit was completed would the distant telephone be rung. Alternate routing to avoid congestion along the way was difficult. Costly voice circuits were connected even though actual talking had not yet began. This type of signaling was cumbersome, and the network could not be easily and quickly reconfigured. Call completion times were lengthy, and costly facilities that normally would carry actual telecommunication signals were being used to carry signaling information. Furthermore, fraudulent users could generate false signaling information to avoid being billed. Today's telecommunication network separates the transmission and switching of customer traffic from the network control functions of signaling, as depicted in Fig. 1. This separation results in increased network security, reliability, and efficiency while also giving a higher level of service to network users along with new "intelligent" services. Signaling today is accomplished over a separate data network that carries only the signals needed for signaling, namely, the data signals that control the operation of the network. Today's telecommunication network thus can be envisioned as two separate networks, as shown in Fig. 2: one that carries solely the data signals needed to assign the real and virtual paths that carry customer-generated telecommunication traffic and another that provides the actual paths over which the customer-generated traffic is carried. This approach to signaling is called Common Channel Signaling (CCS). CCS allows for more efficient operation of the network and also benefits the consumer through faster call set-up times and through novel network services, such as 900 and 800 numbers. At the local level, CCS allows local telephone companies to transmit information identifying the telephone number of the person calling, although the display of this information to the called party has become quite controversial because of the concerns of many consumers over the privacy of their telephone numbers. The specific standard for CCS used in the United States is called Signaling System 7 (SS7). The signals sent over the CCS network are packet switched. With packet switching, a short data message carries information about its source and destination. The destination information is examined by switches along the way, and the packet of data is stored and forwarded gradually to the final destination. This is unlike the circuit-switched network that carries customer traffic and in which individual circuits are maintained for the entire duration of a call. Packet switching is particularly appropriate for the short, bursty messages that comprise most data signals.

A block diagram of the basic structure of a modern long-distance telecommunication network is shown in Fig. 3.[2] Switching machines at Service Switching Points - SSPs (formerly called Action Control Points and now Action Points - ACPs by AT&T) assign and switch customer traffic over transmission paths between the SSPs. If a particular transmission path is fully occupied, alternative paths can be assigned dynamically in a non-hierarchical manner. The traffic carried over the network is usually digital, and a large number of such digital signals are combined together through time division multiplexing to share transmission facilities. A basic telephone channel in digital form requires 56 kbps or 64 kbps. Twenty-four such digital signals are multiplexed together to create a single DS1 (or T1) signal at 1.54

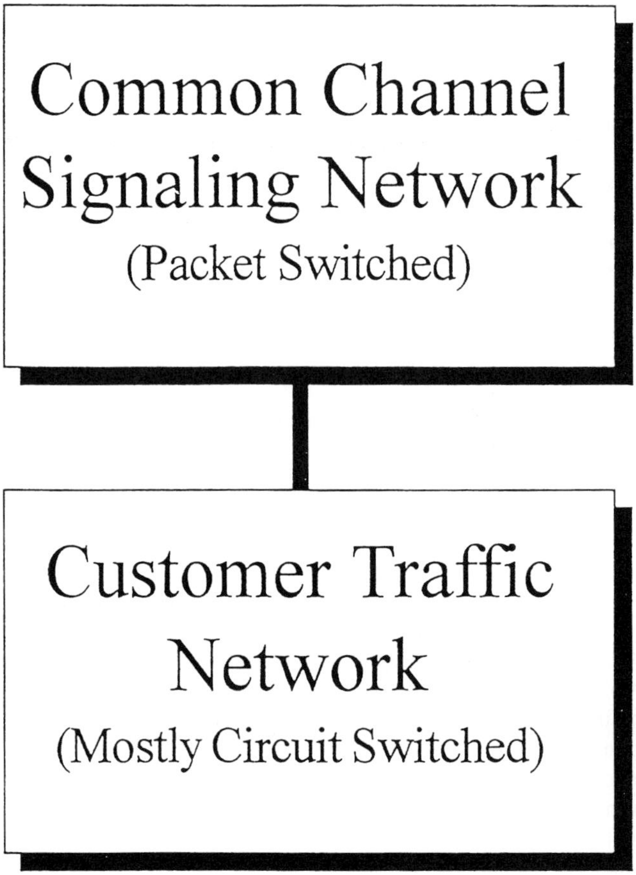

# Common Channel Signaling Network
## (Packet Switched)

# Customer Traffic Network
## (Mostly Circuit Switched)

## Figure 1

A modern telecommunication network can be conceptualized as two separate networks working together. One is the network that carries customer voice, data, and image traffic. The circuits carrying customer traffic are switched over this network. The other is a network that carries solely the signals needed to control the operation of the customer-traffic network. This control network is called the Common Channel Signaling (CCS) network and it carries short data messages that are stored and forwarded to their destinations in the network -- a technique known as packet switching.

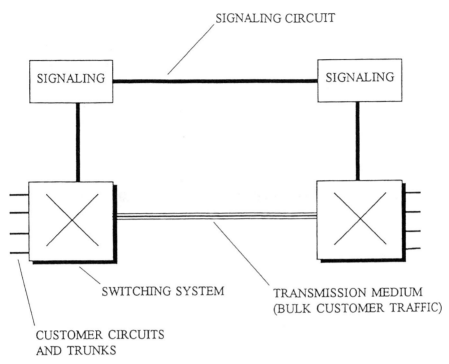

Figure 2

The switching systems responsible for switching the circuits carrying customer traffic are controlled by information sent over a separate Common Channel Signaling (CCS) network. The data sent over the signaling circuits is considerably less than the customer-generated traffic. The customer traffic in a long-distance network is carried in bulk over a variety of transmission media, including optical fiber, microwave radio, and copper wire.

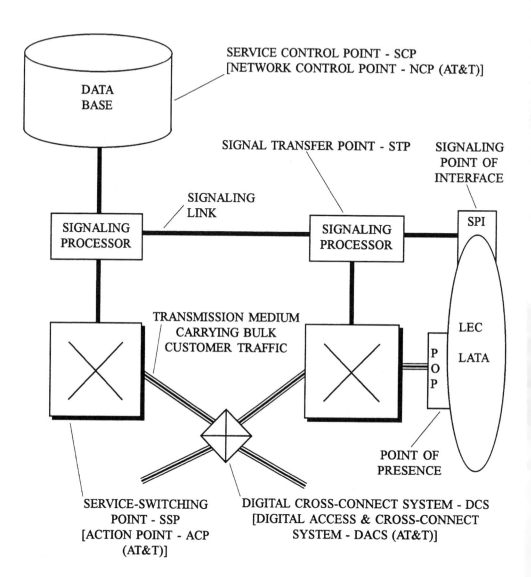

Figure 3

349

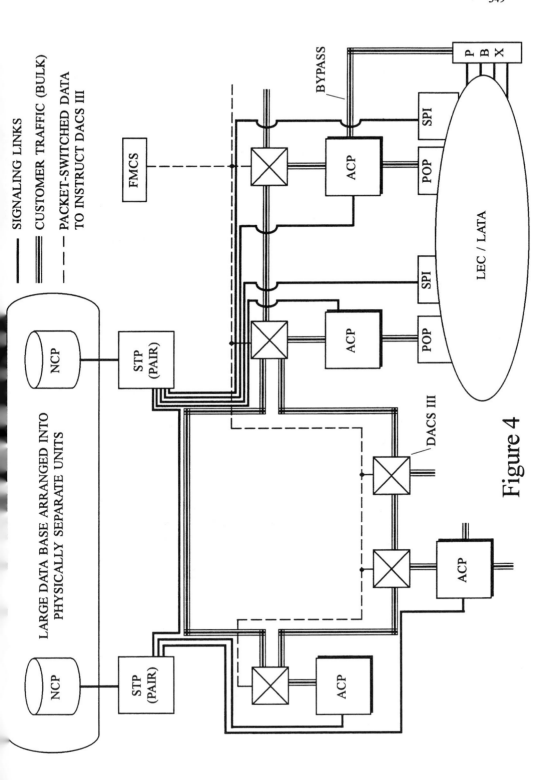

— SIGNALING LINKS
═══ CUSTOMER TRAFFIC (BULK)
--- PACKET-SWITCHED DATA
TO INSTRUCT DACS III

LARGE DATA BASE ARRANGED INTO
PHYSICALLY SEPARATE UNITS

NCP

STP
(PAIR)

NCP

STP
(PAIR)

FMCS

BYPASS

ACP

SPI

POP

ACP

SPI

POP

LEC / LATA

P
B
X

DACS III

ACP

ACP

Figure 4

Mbps. Higher-level digital signals are at the so-called DS3 (or T3) level, operating at a rate of approximately 45 Mbps and containing 672 voice channels. Only at the local level where customers are connected to their local serving office is the traffic mostly analog carried over twisted pairs of copper wire.

A separate network carries the signals needed to control the assignment of transmission paths so that customer signals can be carried from the calling party to the called party. This signaling network interfaces with the switching machines at the SSPs. The signaling signals themselves are switched through the signaling network at nodes called Signal Transfer Points (STPs). Customer and routing information is stored in the signaling network at nodes called Service Control Points - SCPs (called Network Control Points (NCPs) by AT&T). Signaling links connect STPs to each other and to the SSP switching machines.

Most long-distance networks carry vast amounts of digital traffic consisting of tens of thousands of mutliplexed digital channels over optical fiber. It sometimes is necessary to be able to reconfigure these higher-level digital signals. In the old days, such reconfiguring of telephone circuits would be done at patch-cord panels. The electronic version of such patch-panels for multiplexed digital signals are called Digital Cross-connect Systems (DCSs) (called Digital Access and Cross-connect Systems - DACS by AT&T). They are located in the transmission media so that higher-level digital signals can be re-routed from one transmission path to another. Such re-routing is performed for such purposes as an emergency, routine maintenance, or major network re-routing. The customer traffic carried over long-distance networks connects to the local networks operated by the Local Exchange Carriers (LECs) at so-called Points of Presence (POPs). The LECs are responsible for providing local service within Local Access and Transport Areas (LATAs). A Signal Transfer Point (STP) in the long-distance network connects to the local network at a Signaling Point of Interface (SPI).

### 3.1. An Example: AT&T's Network

The overall architecture of AT&T's long-distance network is depicted in Fig. 4. It is described as an example of a modern telecommunication network with advanced technological and service features and considerable use of technology to ensure reliability and fast restoration of service in case of a network failure. Fig. 4[3] shows that some large business customers could have their own direct access to the long-distance networks operated by the Interexchange Carriers (IXCs) and thus bypass the LECs for long-distance service. Most local networks are converting to CCS; AT&T's long-distance network was the first to use CCS.

AT&T operates a large, switched network providing long-distance service to residential and business customers. This network is controlled by software so that a wide variety of customized services can be offered. Such a software controlled network is quite flexible and can be configured to provide customized services that mimic the dedicated private-line services of the past. For those customers who demand dedicated facilities, AT&T offers "special services." AT&T's network supplies standard switched service, 800 service, 900 service, and a variety of customized business services. AT&T conceptualizes its network as having three layers: (1) bulk transmission at the DS3 level, including DACS III operating at the DS3 level to reconfigure the network as required; (2) a switching fabric consisting of No.4 ESS™ machines; and (3) the common channel switching network.

Considerable redundancy exists in the AT&T network as a means to achieve reliable service. Individual switching machines at the ACPs, CCS switches at the STPs, and databases at the NCPs all include duplicated multi-processors and other duplicated hardware to achieve redundancy in their internal operation. Some ACP switching machines operate in pairs so that one could handle the traffic of the other in case of an emergency. NCPs are paired in primary and back-up configurations. CCS switches at the STPs are also paired with each operating at no more than 50% capacity so that any one of the pair can handle all the traffic controlled by the other. Transmission paths are replicated to achieve redundancy, and three physically-separate routes carry East/West traffic across the country.

There currently are 22 STPs (operating in 11 pairs) and about 300 NCPs in AT&T's signaling network. Customer traffic is carried over a network consisting of over 100 No.4 ESS™ digital switching machines at the ACPs. Calls are switched in a dynamic non-hierarchical manner through no more than one intermediate ACP. The mainstay transmission medium of AT&T's network is optical fiber, and digital microwave radio is used to achieve redundancy and also to reach low-traffic locations. Nearly 140 million calls are handled each day over AT&T's worldwide network. AT&T's CCS network uses from one to sixteen 56 kbps data circuits to carry the CCS signals between STPs. Compared to the tens of thousands of circuits that carry customer traffic between ACPs, the CCS network is quite "thin." However, even so, AT&T states that its CCS network is the largest private packet switched network.

AT&T's digital cross-connect switch is called a Digital Access and Cross-connect System (DACS). There are in the order of 200 DACS IIIs in the AT&T network operating at the DS3 level. In case of an emergency, the DACSs can be commanded to switch and re-route traffic around faults in the network. Software, called RAPID, detects any failures, assesses the spare capacity needed to restore service, issues the appropriate commands to the DACSs, and tests the digital circuits both before and after the reconfiguration. The commands can be sent either over terrestrial fiber paths or, as a back-up, over a communication satellite and received at the DACSs by VSATs (Very Small Aperture Terminals). AT&T calls this automated system for the fast restoration of service FASTAR℠; presently, the first DS3 channel is restored in under one minute and additional DS3 channels are then restored every few seconds. So that there is more than one way to reach any location along the network, transmission routes in the AT&T network are configured in the form of large loops. DACSs are located at the points where one loop touches another and also in links from one loop to another.

## 4. LOCAL-INTEREXCHANGE DIFFERENCES

By their very name, long distance networks cover great distances and are very intensive in terms of costly transmission routes and facilities, particularly since these routes are usually duplicated to ensure redundancy. Common channel signaling was originally invented by AT&T as a means to ensure the more effective allocation of transmission channels. Long distance networks are relatively thin in terms of switching. Local networks are quite different. Local networks do not cover great distances but do have to switch many calls. Local networks thus require much more switching than long distance networks. Redundancy usually is less available at the local level; for example, there is only one local loop and one local office serving a customer. The problems of effective use of costly transmission facilities are much less of a problem at the local level and, not surprisingly, CCS has been much slower at being introduced at the local level. One motivation for CCS at the local level is the new "intelligent" services that it facilitates along with compatibility with interconnection to long distance networks.

## 5. THE SIGNALING SYSTEM: A NEW VULNERABILITY

We have seen how in the past the circuit for a long-distance call was connected progressively according to information sent along the lines. Today's telecommunication networks are controlled through a far better system: common channel signaling (CCS). We have seen how CCS sends data signals over a dedicated data network, and these data signals are received and interpreted by CCS computers and network switching machines that then allocate trunks and transmission facilities to carry the actual telecommunication traffic of the customers.

AT&T's and other carrier's networks use CCS, as do many local telephone companies, and soon the entire public telecommunication system of the United States will utilize CCS. Private corporate networks will want direct access to CCS to give them more direct access and control over various network features and functions. All this will certainly be to the benefit of the consumer and business users. However, there will also be a risk that some software glitch could transmit an erroneous signal or traffic indication that would collapse the entire network thereby bringing telecommunication to a total halt in the country. This situation is somewhat similar to what happened in the electric power industry. In the distant past each power station was independent and connected only to its local customers. Over time, power stations were connected to an electric power grid, or network. This interconnection created a situation in which some glitch could collapse the whole grid, as demonstrated by the Northeast power failures of the past. Computerized control systems with appropriate human intervention now minimize the risk of such catastrophic failures in the electric power industry.

## 6. NETWORK SECURITY AND RELIABILITY

Transmission media need to be protected. The cables that carry thousands of twisted pairs of copper wire in the local loop are pressurized both to keep out moisture and also to enable any leaks or breaks to be detected. Unlike copper wire, optical fiber is very difficult to tap and thus inherently offers security. Transmission routes are often duplicated to offer security in terms of alternate routing in time of emergency.

Today's telecommunication networks are switched and controlled by computers. These computers are a prime source of network vulnerability to failure. Although in most cases, the vulnerability is accidental, deliberate attempts to sabotage the computers in order to collapse the network can not be ignored. The security of these computers thus is essential. A fair amount of research effort has been developed over the past decades to the general topic of computer security, and the results of this research are applicable to the computer aspect of network security.

At the most obvious level of security, telecommunication gear and equipment facilities must be physically secured. Appropriate physical access safeguards must be installed. Without physical safeguards any person intent on harming the network need only "pull the plug" on a switching machine. At another level, the maintenance of appropriate audit trails is essential, both to determine when some deliberate attack is underway, and also to help in performing a "post mortem" to determine the causes of a specific network failure. The software that controls the switching machines and the signaling system is a major source of network vulnerability. Computer programs are designed and written by fallible humans and hence are subject to error. A simple software error might have catastrophic effects on the network and might even propagate through the network via the signaling system. Telecommunication programs are usually very large, and their production requires the considerable time and effort of many programmers. This human effort must be appropriately managed and all errors eliminated. However, errors will occur, either because of unanticipated situations or because of simple human fallibility. Automatic techniques to verify that a computer program does only what is intended and is free of error are being researched but are not yet foolproof. Meanwhile, the only real solution is to expect errors but minimize their effect through appropriate safeguards and testing.

## 7. SAFEGUARDS

The very technology that has increased the scope and impact of network failures also plays a major part in protecting telecommunication network. Computers monitor the operation of networks and automatically notify human network supervisors in the case of some abnormality. Presented with appropriate information, the human supervisors then instruct the control system to take appropriate action. Human intervention continues to have an essential role since otherwise the automated monitoring system might take inappropriate action and escalate the final harm to the network. Technology can only be trusted so far, in my opinion.

### 7.1. Gateways: Protection Against Outsiders
The existing common carriers at all levels -- local exchange and interexchange -- fully realize the essential importance of protecting their individual networks against failures from both accidental and deliberate sources. In essence, the existing carriers have created a security fence around their operations. As they interconnect their signaling systems, the security fence broadens to include others equally secure. The real threat is when others currently not part of the existing league want direct higher-level entry and access to the network and signaling system. Pressures from large business customers for such access are already starting. Large businesses and cellular operators want access to the customer databases stored at the NCPs. One possible solution to the potential threat posed by giving access to the signaling system to outsiders is the use of so-called gateways. All outsiders would be required to go through a gateway to gain access to the signaling system. A gateway would be a pair of STPs functioning as a boundary between the common channel signaling system and the outsiders. The gateway would be an overseer that would examine and monitor signaling messages sent by the outsiders to be certain that no inadvertent or deliberate harm to the network would occur. Clearly, research and development is needed to develop such gateways and to assure that they function as intended in protecting the network from harm.

### 7.2. Network Testing
The "network of networks" resulting from many interconnected long-distance, local, and private networks is a complex affair. Many of these networks are already controlled by Common Channel Signaling (CCS), and those that are not, are quickly migrating toward CCS. The "network of networks" thus will be interconnected not only in terms of the

transmission and switching of customer signals but also in terms of the signals that control the overall operation of the networks. This interconnection at the signaling level creates the need to be absolutely certain that any hardware and software additions or changes will not in any way harm any network to which it is attached.

Both intra-network and inter-network integrity must be assured. The Exchange Carriers Standards Association sponsors a Network Operations Forum with broad representation from the telecommunication industry. Guidelines are developed for the testing, maintenance, and installation of access networks and the interface between Local Exchange Carriers (LECs) and Interexchange Carriers (IXCs.) Bellcore developed an Internetwork Interoperability Test Plan for the Association's members to test and evaluate different network failure scenarios. In the first phase, test facilities at Ameritech, AT&T, Bellcore, Northern Telecom, NYNEX, and Sprint will be interconnected to test the response of existing systems to various failure scenarios.

Many interexchange carriers (such as AT&T, MCI, and Sprint), local exchange carriers, and vendors already have extensive testing programs before installing any new hardware or software. Cooperation between these bodies would make very good sense as a way to achieve an industry-wide testing program before any new hardware or software is installed in the network. Other than Bellcore, existing standards organizations or even the FCC might act as the facilitators to create the necessary forum for cooperation between competitors. Clearly, such cooperation will be challenging given the highly proprietary nature of any new product or system. Will a vendor be willing to release some new piece of hardware or software for testing by its competitors? Should some industry-wide neutral body be able to perform the needed tests and also safeguard the proprietary nature of a new product or system?

### 7.3. Procedural Solutions

In February 1992, a consortium of about fifteen major telecommunication carriers signed an agreement of mutual aid to restore service in the case of "critical disruption to their telecommunications networks supporting the New York City Metropolitan Region" (Agreement dated February 18, 1992). The agreement is the first of its kind and stipulates the procedure to be followed in time of a network emergency affecting high-capacity transmission facilities. The details of the agreement were determined by the Mayor's Task Force on Telecommunications Network Reliability, chaired by the Commissioner of the New York City Department of Telecommunications and Energy.

In the event of the loss of critical telecommunication facilities affecting New York City, the affected carrier notifies the Commissioner. If the failed facilities cannot be restored within two hours, the Commissioner is involved in declaring an "Emergency." The other carriers have then agreed to work with the affected carrier to make facilities available, for "reasonable and customary out-of-pocket expenses," to restore service. If more than one carrier is affected by an emergency and sufficient capacity is not available to restore the failed facilities, the Commissioner has the authority to allocate available facilities across the failed common carriers. The surviving carriers do not have any obligation to provide facilities if they do not have any excess capacity available. The Commissioner has no real authority to force cooperation, but the Agreement is a strong statement of intent to cooperate under the realization that a catastrophic network failure ultimately affects everyone and the common good of New York City is best served by cooperation at a time of emergency. The New York City Telecommunications Department also has published a catalog of various telecommunication services that may be useful to businesses in an emergency, such as call forwarding, or that may be used to create redundancy to avoid catastrophic failures or limit their effects.

At the Federal level, the National Communications System (NCS) is responsible for ensuring the integrity and responsiveness of telecommunications from the perspective of national security and emergency preparedness.[4] Military tactical transportable microwave radio gear, communication satellites, cellular phones, and high-frequency radio are some of the technologies that can be used in an emergency, such as an earthquake or hurricane to provide emergency communication until the public switched network and other conventional systems are restored. The Modification of Final Judgment gave Bellcore responsibilities related to National Security Emergency Preparedness (NSEP). In meeting these responsibilities, Bellcore serves as a central body to coordinate the efforts and activities of the BOCs related to NSEP. Service restoration, resource allocation, disaster response, the development of operational plans for NSEP, and joint government/industry planning are some of the specific activities coordinated by Bellcore.

## 8. CONCLUDING THOUGHTS

Private networks are today defined by software and rarely utilize dedicated facilities. Private and public customer traffic are carried together over one network. The network security requirements for different kinds of customers might very well be quite different. Should the network be designed to offer the highest level of security to all or is it possible to offer different levels to different customers on the same network? Might higher levels of security be offered to some customers at the expense of others? These and other interesting questions of public policy need not to be forgotten.

In the time before divestiture and telecommunication competition, AT&T had the sole responsibility for the operation and integrity of the Nation's telecommunication system. The administrative control of the network was centralized. However, the administrative control of today's "network of networks" is fragmented across many competing common carriers and is truly decentralized. One can only wonder whether some form of centralized administrative control and oversight over today's decentralized network is needed and, if so, who should perform that function. Some interexchange carriers have network operation centers where the entire operation of their networks can be instantaneously monitored. Displays of the status of various transmission routes and switching systems, of the traffic being carried, and of the signaling system are used to help human operators supervise the network and take appropriate action if needed in time of an emergency. Similar centers would help all carriers -- interexchange and local exchange -- monitor the status of their networks and assist restoration in time of emergencies. One even wonders whether some national center to monitor the entire network on a more global basis would be useful and whether the operation of such a center would be a meaningful role for the FCC -- particularly at a time when regulation is being reduced. The very technology that has made the network appear more vulnerable clearly can safeguard the network too. However, in the end, people and human error will most likely be the cause of most network emergencies and failures. The use of technology to protect against human shortcomings continues to be a challenge.

## REFERENCES

*A Guide to Contingency Services,* New York City Mayor's Task Force on Telecommunications Network Reliability, January 1992.

Bodson, Dennis and Eleanor Harris, "When The Lines Go Down," *IEEE Spectrum,* March 1992, pp. 40-44.

*Growing Vulnerability of the Public Switched Network,* National Research Council, Washington DC: National Academy Press, 1989.

Holste, D.J., "Creating A Network That Heals Itself," *AT&T Technology,* Vol. 5, No. 2, 1990, pp. 42-47.

Noll, A. Michael, *Introduction to Telephones & Telephone Systems (Second Edition),* Norwood MA: Artech House, Inc., 1991.

## ENDNOTES

[1.] *Growing Vulnerability of the Public Switched Network,* National Research Council, Washington DC: National Academy Press , 1989.

[2.] The switching nodes in a network are known as Service Switching Points (SSPs), or as Action Points (ACPs) using AT&T terminology. The signaling computers are at nodes known as Signal Transfer Points (STPs). A large data base containing routing, billing, and customer information can be accessed by the Common Channel Signaling system. This data base is known as a Service Control Point (SCP), or as a Network Control Point using AT&T terminology. The signaling information is sent over signaling links. The transmission media carrying customer traffic can be reconfigured using a Digital Cross-connect System (DCS), or a Digital Access and Cross-connect System (DACS) in AT&T terminology. The DCS is able to reconfigure digital circuits carrying 50 Mbps of customer traffic. A SSP connects to the local network operated by a Local Exchange Carrier (LEC) at a Point of Presence (POP); a STP connects to the local network at a Signaling Point of Interface (SPI).

[3.] The overall architecture of AT&T's long-distance network operates at three levels: (1) transmission media, that can be reconfigured by DACS IIIs carrying bulk customer traffic between ACPs; (2) No.4 ESS™ switching machines located at ACPs; and (3) a CCS network consisting of STPs and NCPs. In case of a failure in the network, the appropriate DACS IIIs can be reconfigured to carry traffic around the fault. The information necessary to reconfigure the DACS IIIs is sent over an AT&T packet-switched, terrestrial data network from a Facility Monitor and Control System (FMCS). A communication satellite system with Very Small Aperture Terminals (VSATs) at each DACS III serves as a back-up to this terrestrial data network. The signaling links in AT&T's CCS network consist of from 1 to 16 56 kbps, two-way, packet-switched data circuits. A business customer with a Private Branch Exchange (PBX) can bypass the LEC's network and connect directly to AT&T at an appropriate ACP. STPs operate in pairs so that any one of the pair can take over all the work of the other in case of an emergency. Transmission paths and processors in the No.4 switching machines are duplicated in AT&T's network to increase reliability. Local traffic enters AT&T's network at at least two POPs and two ACPs, again to offer alternative routes in case of an emergency.

[4.] Bodson, Dennis, and Eleanor Harris, "When the Lines go Down," *IEEE Spectrum,* March 1992, pp. 40-44.

PRIVATE NETWORKS PUBLIC OBJECTIVES
E. Noam and A. NíShúilleabháin (Editors)
© 1996 Elsevier Science B.V. All rights reserved.

International Studies -- Towards the Future

# Strategic Response to Competition by Public Network Operators

Aine M. NiShuilleabhain

## 1. INTRODUCTION

This paper analyzes the rapid adaptation -- as of mid-decade -- of private networking capabilities to the public network environment by telecommunications operators (TOs) which are either privatized or facing this certain destiny. This is viewed in terms of strategic response at the line-of-business level to reciprocally-generated competition, where (ex)-monopoly providers enter formerly-protected domestic markets.

At the line-of-business level, strategic choice involves pricing the product line; selecting technology for production, marketing, and distribution; and investment in capacity, advertising, and product development. This paper focuses upon the portfolio choices of public-network operators in their capacity as value-added network service (VANS) providers, and on developments sector-wide where true convergence of voice, data, and video capabilities is well underway.

At the corporate level strategic decisions hinge upon the firm's financial structure, its capital allocation among existing and new lines of business, and the acquisition and divestiture of business units. Elsewhere[1] we have developed an asset-pricing model for valuing providers both of private and public networking capabilities. This anticipates a future of virtually complete ownership-privatization and ongoing technological innovation; hence continuing product/service differentiation including flexibility of use-privatization.

## 2. WHERE AND HOW TO COMPETE: DOMESTIC (US) DEVELOPMENTS

### 2.1. The Emerging Asynchronous Transfer Mode (ATM) Market

ATM offers a unique range of capabilities applicable to each architectural segment of data networks: on the private network side, from workgroup to enterprise backbone; on the public front, from the access segment to the core backbone. Figure 1 illustrates this architectural segmentation and associated business and implementation issues. Deployed end-to-end, the synergies involve traffic control, network management, and the ability to add voice and video to existing data networks. Anticipated economies of scale associated with traffic-aggregation from separate and thus inefficient overlays onto a single broadband conduit mean that this sector is of considerable strategic significance both for network operators and suppliers.[2]

Figure 1
Types of Vendors Entering the ATM Equipment Market

| Vendor Segment | Interest in ATM Market | Vendors (Partial List) |
|---|---|---|
| LAN/WAN Networking Vendors | Offer customers new solutions for their growing bandwidth needs | • Bay Networks<br>• Cisco |
| Fast Packet Companies | Exploit technological expertise to open new markets | • Fore<br>• General DataComm<br>• Newbridge<br>• Cascade<br>• StrataCom |
| Public Network Vendors | Retain carrier customers as they migrate from TDM to ATM technology | • Alcatel<br>• AT&T<br>• Northern Telecom<br>• Fujitsu<br>• Siemens Stromberg-Carlson<br>• NEC |
| Computer System Vendors | Offer customers key networking technology as part of total solution for distributed computing enviroments | • Digital Equipment<br>• IBM |

*Source:*                                          *Northern Business Information*

## 2.2. Broadbanding Public and Private Network Components:

In the access segment, public carriers -- initially in the US but followed by some of their more aggressive European counterparts -- are deploying fast packet services (native LAN-interconnect, frame relay, ATM) to meet growing end-user demand as well as accelerate the shift from voice to more profitable value-added services. In 1995 US public network operators continued to trial multiservice switches supporting all cross service platforms and a limited number of supplier contracts were signed. As traffic increases on ATM overlay networks, carriers plan to add high-throughput core switches characterized by levels of redundancy and fault tolerance typical of traditional public network equipment.

On the private network side, LAN users of shared-media technologies (e.g. Ethernet, Token Ring) face increasing bandwidth constraints at the workgroup level. However, ATM to the desktop in the five-year timeframe is a niche market, because evolutionary technologies (LAN switching, Fast Ethernet) continue to extend the life of PC network-interface cards and other legacy equipment.[3] At the enterprise level and across the same (1996-2001) period, however, ATM deployment will be accelerated both by congestion problems on LAN backbones -- where fiber-distributed-data-interface (FDDI) technology is the norm -- and by cost-amortization across multiple desktops.

## 2.3. The US Private Line and Virtual Private Line Sectors

Wideband and emerging broadband services dominate the horizon in the world's most advanced domestic market. However, interexchange carriers (IXCs) and some of the Regional Holding Companies (RHCs)[4] focus increasingly upon developing low-speed data services as a prerequisite of end-to-end multinational service contracts. AT&T continues to dominate the hitherto robust, but intensely competitive, $6.5 billion domestic private-line market; 1994 revenues in this sector generated close to ten percent of total long-distance domestic income.[5] Nonetheless, this share is subject to continuing erosion by discount competitors and the proliferation of switch-based services (notably Switched 56, frame relay, and Fractional T services used for redundancy and videoconferencing).

Figure 2
Long Distance Private Line Revenues by Company, 1992-1997 ($1000s)

| Name | 1992 | 1993 | 1994 | 1995 | 1996 | 1997* | CAGR* |
|---|---|---|---|---|---|---|---|
| AT&T | 4,080,502 | 3,702,816 | 3,465,978 | 3,048,725 | 2,678,388 | 2,281,692 | -11.0% |
| MCI | 926,571 | 972,899 | 989,385 | 999,279 | 1,009,272 | 1,019,364 | 1.9% |
| Sprint | 685,254 | 706,590 | 718,998 | 726,188 | 733,450 | 740,784 | 1.6% |
| ALC | 47,961 | 48,154 | 48,194 | 48,047 | 47,976 | 47,978 | 0.0% |
| C&W | 167,831 | 166,478 | 164,800 | 162,767 | 160,788 | 157,572 | -1.3% |
| SP Tel | 55,479 | 56,913 | 58,051 | 58,972 | 58,835 | 58,236 | 1.0% |
| WILTEL | 389,317 | 412,756 | 422,859 | 431,316 | 430,886 | 424,229 | 1.7% |
| LCI | 55,647 | 54,534 | 53,218 | 51,716 | 50,052 | 48,452 | -2.7% |
| RCI | 30,086 | 30,524 | 32,209 | 33,506 | 34,859 | 36,269 | 3.8% |
| LDDS | 39,586 | 42,945 | 43,438 | 45,142 | 46,923 | 48,782 | 4.3% |
| Others | 396,542 | 384,781 | 374,061 | 363,908 | 354,317 | 345,281 | -2.7% |
| Total | 6,874,775 | 6,579,390 | 6,371,191 | 5,969,568 | 5,605,745 | 5,208,641 | -5.4% |

Source: *Northern Business Information*
*: Projected

During 1993-95 the market leader aggressively restructured private-line price tariffs and launched Fractional T-3 service. AT&T will continue to lose market share through the decade's close in the negatively-growing market (Figure 2). This pattern will be replicated in European, Asia-Pacific, and ultimately Latin American markets with lags ranging from five years (in the former case) to twenty (the latter scenario). Note that this trajectory distinguishes the typical domestic private-line business from the International Managed Private Line (IMPL) market, which must be characterized in terms of stability -- for reasons alluded to below -- rather than gradual decline.

The US domestic virtual private network (VPN) sector, on the other hand, remains the most dynamic of all IXC businesses. Market expansion during 1994 at over 20 percent -- on revenues exceeding $1.5 billion -- reflects massive promotional efforts combined with service enhancements. Today the domestic market is dominated by those public operators (AT&T, MCI, Sprint, Cable & Wireless) whose domestic and international strategies for logical use-privatization of existing public infrastructure combined with recently-introduced overlays are inextricably interlinked. Their international data-networking alliances -- ultimately the springboard for penetration of domestic voice markets across Europe, Asia, and Latin America, as detailed below -- provide for replication of revenue-generating programs overseas.

The intent and inevitable consequence of this activity is to supplant the historic bilateral accounting-rates system by alternative inter- and intra-group revenue-transfer practices: among network-operator alliances such as Phoenix,[6] Concert,[7] and WorldPartners;[8] and within each of these, among the domestic (typically former-monopolist) operators thus linked by joint equity-investment and revenue-sharing contracts. After more than a century of relative stagnation, the speed of the shift underway -- most clearly visible at the time of writing in Uniworld[9] -- is first a matter of internationalizing use-privatization. In the longer term, this development is more radical than ownership-privatization, and at least as significant as mobility, where growth-trajectory synergies will surely be exploited.

## 3. WHERE AND HOW TO COMPETE: THE GLOBAL DATA NETWORKING BUSINESS

### 3.1. Strategic Response

Here we focus on the corporate profiles and competitive strategies of dominant international (I)VAN service providers and their primary regional competitors in the shared (private) networking market.[10] By YE1994 the global VANS market had grown to US$15.3 billion, representing over a 14% increase in revenues generated during the preceding 12 months.[11] Eight entities contributing 35% of this figure[12] shared three conventionally-accepted strategic concerns:

- the establishment of alliance partnerships so as to expand operations -- as margins erode in horizontal services, scale assumes paramount importance
- strategic positioning to exploit already-cultivated installed base
- diversifying the risk associated with launching expensive technology overlays and/or migrating to increasingly-sophisticated technologies

### 3.2. Public Operator Alliances vs. Distributed-Computing Service Providers

The eight market leaders in global data networking belong to two core groupings. The first comprises three supercarrier alliances linking former voice monopolists: AT&T's WorldPartners and Uniworld constructions, the pending amalgamation of Atlas[13] with Phoenix, and comparatively advanced Concert (the latter two groups can be expected to add Asian partners).

The second defies easy classification since none involves the link-up of two or more sizable traditional telecommunications companies. Apart from C&W -- which fits the bill as a traditional operator but has not found a suitable partner -- these are the originators of global private shared networking. SITA[14] is perhaps the closest a VANS provider can come to full-fledged operator status (recall its history of near-monopoly service to a relatively stable customer base), but has likewise stayed independent. Other partnering arrangements will be developed by EDS and IBM Global Network[15] in the short term; the latter expects its STET alliance to be one of several. Infonet's[16] future clearly involves a change of ownership, though this is likely to be smooth so as not to alienate its customer base.

The market is evolving along oligopolistic lines, mirroring historical developments in the US long-distance market. However the well-established market-share balance among AT&T, MCI, and Sprint in US long-distance (64-17-9 percent; others 10%) cannot be expected to pertain in the more dynamic global VANS market.

### 3.3. Sector Overview: 1995 in Review

1994-95 was a year of partnering and reshuffling the main consortia. The year opened with AT&T talking to Deutsche Telekom and France Telecom about a joint venture with their jointly-owned managed data networking provider Eunetcom. AT&T ended the year by announcing it would form Uniworld with Unisource,[17] and advancing its WorldPartners concept. British Telecom and MCI were pillars of relative stability as they developed the Concert portfolio; the former focused its empire-building attentions anew on Continental Europe. IBM and EDS were speculatively linked with carriers, but all that came out of the talks was a broad IBM alliance with STET. Likewise, C&W concluded no major alliance agreements beyond a first step into the German market. GEIS was purchased in part (30%) by Ameritech, and SITA's highly-publicized alliance with Unisource unraveled amid bad publicity.

Progress was relatively slow in some traditional sectors (notably messaging and packet switching) as the new alliance partners began the slow process of rebranding and revitalizing the commodity end of the market. Nonetheless, new lower-level services emerged: dial-IP services designed to support information service providers and mobile employees; LAN connectivity, messaging (Lotus Notes, GEIS' Global Document Access); and online products (Microsoft Network connectivity) integrating so-called shareware and information processing across the globally dispersed organization.

Simultaneous technical challenges involved increasing the acceptance of frame relay -- a ready proposition because the technology clearly offers more at similar pricing levels than do leased-line/X.25 arrangements or combinations of these[18] -- and testing emergent ATM capabilities within the context of disparate installed data networking bases and highly divergent organizational capabilities. (Recall that Sprint International's Atlas partners still lie in public hands, although Deutsche Telekom can be expected to undergo fairly rapid transformation during 1996).

### 3.4. Market Developments, 1994-99

By 1999 the global VANS market is projected to increase to $33.5 billion, reflecting CAGR of 17.2% over the five intervening years.[19] Across this time period we expect a minor loss of aggregate market share by the eight global providers -- on the order of 1-1.5% -- with fastest regional growth in the Latin American (8.1%) and North American (5.1%) regions. Note that certain short-term shifts of global market power among providers (summarized as of year-end 1994 by Figure 3) can be anticipated. Although firms optimally invest at a common rate relative to capital -- and thus grow at a rate equal to that of their

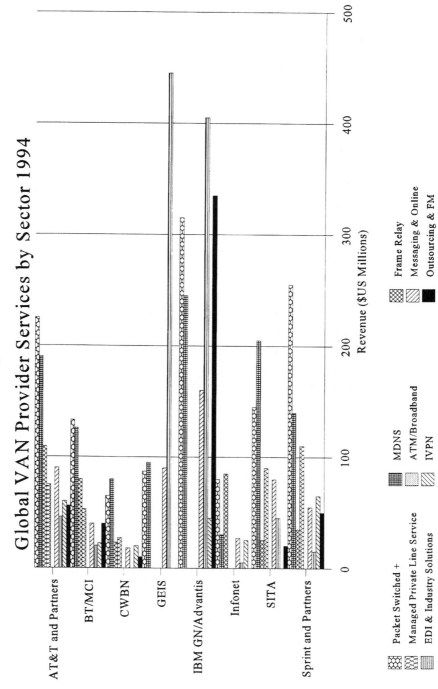

Figure 3

Global VAN Provider Services by Sector 1994

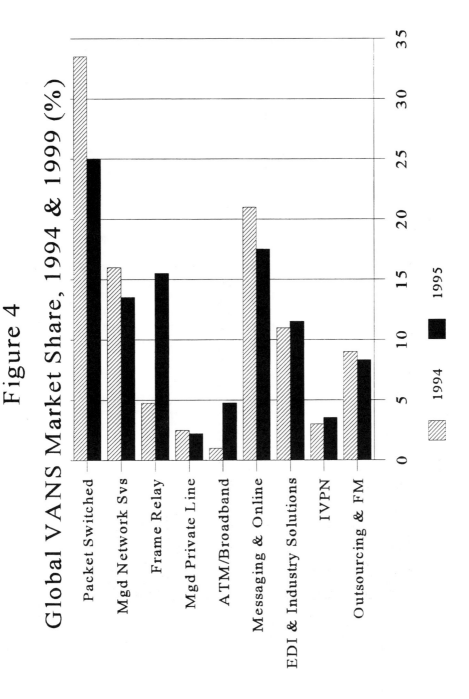

Figure 4

Global VANS Market Share, 1994 & 1999 (%)

(converging telecommunications, computing, and media) industries as a whole -- differences of strategic position, installed base, and geographic coverage can be expected to alter somewhat the current balance of power.[20]

Sectoral shifts will be more dramatic (Figure 4). For example, frame relay service -- which accounted for 5% of global VANS revenues at YE1994 -- should increase market share by 9.8% reflecting average CAGR across the North American, European, Asia-Pacific, and Latin American markets on the order of 47.2%. Growth in this sector, which has been slower to take off in the Pacific Rim and Latin American markets, will taper off thereafter. However, by the decade's close ATM and true broadband services will have supplanted this intermediate technology and assumed the dominant market-growth trajectory.[21]

## 4. A TAXONOMY OF VANS

### 4.1. Core and Periphery

As Figure 5 suggests, whereas core portfolio products change reflecting the latest technological developments, the migration path remains from data applications to voice, and from private- to public-usage environments. By 1994 64 kbps had become (even in Europe) the corporate standard access-speed in anticipation of 2 Mbps availability. Yesterday's generation of services -- and global managed data services (GMDS) by now have been relegated to this category -- moves from temporarily high added-value (with concomitant pricing potential) to permanent commodity. This dynamic is visible both in transport and application layers, and along the continuum extending from dedicated services to those provided on a virtual basis.

Figure 5
A Taxonomy of Value-Added Network Services

| Taxonomy | Transport | | | Application | | Virtual Services | Network Control |
|---|---|---|---|---|---|---|---|
| Portfolio Component | GMDS | Managed Bandwidth Service | Broad-band | Horizontal Services | Vertical Services | Virtual Network Services | Outsourcing |
| Service Sector | Public Switched and Related Services; Managed Network Services; Frame Relay | Managed Private Line | ATM | Messaging & Online Services | EDI & Industry Solutions | (I)VPN; (Intelligent Services, Int'l VPN) | All relevant |
| Medium | Data | Data | Data | Data | Data | Voice | Voice and Data |
| Service Availability | Public | Dedicated Private | Public | Public | Public | Virtual Public | Private |
| Economic Status | Commodity | Commodity | Value Added | Commodity | Value Added | Value Added | Value Added |

Source:                                                                                                    *author*

Virtual private network (VPN) services in particular highlight the private-public trajectory. Thus centrex and VPN services introduced to the North American market 5-7 years ago are increasingly common in Europe and Asia (Figure 6 details globally available VPN services) but all of the larger European and Asian operators offer domestic counterparts; and router networks considered *de rigeur* since the early 1990s are increasingly managed, supplied, or owned by VANS providers as publicly-accessible infrastructure. Thus during 1994-95 the process of branding so-called Managed Router Services -- an MDS subcategory -- began.

Both dynamics originate in the corporate (private) networking sector which determines their evolutionary path. Prior to full convergence the basic shifts underway as of mid-1995 are implicit in Figure 5. They involve: (1) the migration of corporate voice from dedicated- to virtual-private capability; and (2) the shift from private to public of corporate data transport -- (G)MDS at the lower end, emerging broadband capabilities at higher levels of required sophistication -- even as Managed Private Line services continue to generate revenues from so-called mission-critical traffic. This is the mid-term (through 2005) future of the oldest of applications dichotomies. Convergence under the ATM rubric notwithstanding, there is every reason to anticipate continued (albeit declining) physical segmentation at the international transport level in the longer term.

This is not simply a matter of installed base. It is also a question of longstanding commitments to separate international handling of high-security traffic within some industry sectors (the obvious cases are banking, financial services, oil, and petroleum products), where cultural and marketing pressures will counterbalance efficiency arguments. Hence the expected short-run stability of the international Managed Private Line (MPL) sector[22] -- valued at $370 million of a total international private-line market generating slightly over $1.3 billion in 1995 -- is documented by Figure 4.

## 4.2. Service Sector Trends

The strategic implications of developing experience curves, product life-cycles and portfolio balance within and among the various service sectors are essentially straightforward.

Basic network services undergo continuing commoditization although temporary niche markets exist. For example, Sprint International claims to handle 85 % of international Internet traffic. However since there are few (if any) artificial restrictions on the number of entrants to this market, there exists little potential for durable windfall profits. Likewise SITA's lock on the airline networking business, while undoubtedly strong, cannot be taken as a fait accompli.

Generalized horizontal VANS (here we include messaging, transactional, and online services) stimulate demand for basic infrastructure but margins are slim. On the other hand so-called Industry Solutions -- commodity products/services designed for vertically-networked markets -- leverage control over switching, transmission, interconnect arrangements, distribution channels, licensing agreements, and pricing. Such commodity-level provision is distinct from that of project-oriented firms who customize solutions on a case-by-case basis. Market leaders GE Information Services GEIS and IBM Global Network, as well as France Telecom and Deutsche Telekom together under the small but strategic EUCOM[23] rubric, are aggressively pursuing Industry Solutions revenues.[24]

## Figure 6

| IVAN | Packet Switched and Related Services | Managed Network Services | Frame Relay | Managed Private Line Service | ATM/ Broadband | Messaging & Online Services | EDI & Industry Solutions | IVPN | Outsourcing & Facilities Management |
|---|---|---|---|---|---|---|---|---|---|
| AT&T: BCS/IELS | CNCS, Accuenet Packet Services, Interspan Information Access Service | Accunet Spectrum; Accumaster | Interspan Frame Relay, | AT&T Managed Private Line | Interspan ATM srvcc | AT&T Mail, AT&T E-Fax, Mobile ms'ging, Infomaster, Invest ANALYST, AT&T FYI, AT&T Fax Solutions, AT&T Network Notes | AT&T EDI, FORMSolution, AT&T SALESolution, TradeSystem | | Accumaster, AT&T Customer Network Control Systems |
| AT&T: Uniworld | Unidata Packet Switched, Unidata LAN Interconnect, Unidata SNA/SDLC Service, Unistar, Unicast, Unilink | Unistream Mngd Bandwidth, Unmaster Private Ntwrk Provisions | Uniworld Frme Relay, Unidata Frme Relay, Interspan Frme Relay | PL-Standard PL-Switched Dig Backup PL-Hi Performance Svc | | UniPlus 400 Net, AT&T Mail, AT&T Fax Solutions, Infomaster, Invest ANALYST, AT&T FYI, AT&T Network Notes | AT&T EDI, FORMSolution, AT&T SALESolution, TradeSystem | Uniworld VNS* International Virtual Private Network | Unimaster Outsourcing, Unimaster Communications Facilities Management Service, Unimaster Network Operations Management |
| AT&T: World Partners | | GSDS | WorldSource Frame Relay Srvice | WorldSource Private Line | Interspan ATM srvcc | Mail400, Upfront 400, Custom Svcs, Message Handling Svc, NEWS-TAB, E-PUB, Cyclopean Gateway Svc, Videoconf. | AT&T EDI FORMSolution, AT&T SALESolution, TradeSystem | WorldSource Virtual Network Services | |
| BT | Global Connect Svc, Protocol Conv, GNS LAN interconnect | Managed Links, ExpressLANE | Concert Frame Relay | Concert Private Line | | Mail400, Upfront400, Custom Svcs, Message Handling Svc, NEWSTAB, E-PUB, Cyclopean Gateway Svc, Videoconf | EDI*Net, ETS, X.400 Gateway EDIPOST, Interbase PCTrans OFTP Int'conn | | Syncordia, Syntegra, Concert Data Manager |
| C&W | | Global Managed Data Service | GMDS Frame Relay | Global Managed Private Line, Global City Voice | ATM (trial) | SureFax, MultiMessage, ShipFax, Spectrum Infokey, Viewdata | | GVPN, GIVN | TFMS |
| GEIS | MARK 3000, MARK III, MARK 3000 Session Manager MARK*Net | Mgd Network Svc, High Performance Network (HPN) | | | | BusTalk-2000/OnLine Reader/FORMS, Internet Gateway Connector, QUIK-COMM, LAN Connect, Retail*Talk, Customized Svs, Bus Intelligence Portfolio, QuikNews Xp/Newsletter, SMCS | EDI*EXPRESS/CICS, BANCOR*EXP, CARGO*LINK, RETAIL*LINK, DESIGN-EXPRESS, Ordex, EDISWITCH, PRICE*NOTICE. POS*Intelligence, PETROLINE ECS | | |

| | | | Planned End 1995 | | | | | | |
|---|---|---|---|---|---|---|---|---|---|
| IBM IN/Advantis | AS/400 Comms, IBM Data Transfer Svc | Mgd Network Svs, NetView, End to End Network Mngmnt, SolutionPac NetView, LAN Interconnect | | | IBM Business Port | IBM Mail Exchange, IBM Info Exchange, Financial Info Svc, IBM IN Videotex | IBM ExpEDIe, Customized Svs/DataInterchange/Communicator Series/Interconnect, PC Quick EDI Professional, Consulting and Implementation Services, Electronic Marketplace, IVANS Quiklink, QuickResponse Service | | Enterprise Network Svs, Advantis |
| Infonet | IBM SNA/SDLC, Switched Access Service, LAN-WAN Connectivity | EDNS, PerspecXion Vision/Manager/Link | INFOLAN | | | EDMS, NOTICE/400/400PC/PC/Desktop/Private/Exchange/Soft-Switch Central Service/Internet, OSIWARE Messenger 400, Orion, PC COMplete, NOTICE edi/PC | | IGVN | Application Support Services, Development Support Services |
| Phoenix: Eunetcom | | Managed Bandwidth Svc | Private Network Services | Private Network Service (suite) | | | | | Global Outsourcing Services, Telecom Consultancy and Management Svs. |
| Phoenix: Sprint Int'l | Asyc Dial Svcs, DataCall Plus, MultiDrop Plus, Peer-Reach, Hybrid Nets, CLEARLINE | CustomLink Series, Basic Intl VPN, Global VPN, Frame Relay, Global Data Connection | Clearline (Suite of Services) | Clearline Private Line Global SprintLink | | SprintMail, Global SprintFax, SprintMail, FAX, Sprint InfoConnect, Sprint Info Connection, Sprint Meeting Channel | Sprint EDI | | Partner in Alcatel Data Networks, Insite, Sprint Network Systems |
| Phoenix: Transpac | LAN Interconnect | Corporate Network Svcs, Frame Relay | | | | ATLAS, ATLAS Poste, Teletel | ATLAS EDI | | Joint Marketing with DEC |
| SITA/Scitor | X.25 Direct Access, SITA Aeronet | Scitor MDNS, SITAVISION | SITA Frame Relay | | | SITATEX, Internail, SITAMAIL/Gateway, Scitor | SITAEDI, OTS, EDI Clearing House, EDI Software STX, SITA*EDI, Air-to-Ground Services, Computer Application Services | | SITAVISION |

Source:                                                                                                                                        Northern Business Information

Facilities Management, Managed Data Network Services (MDNS) and Outsourcing are three stages along a network-control continuum characterized by volatile demand and rapidly-expanding industry supply.

## 5. WHY PUBLIC NETWORKS CHANGE: EVOLUTIONARY DRIVERS

The general features shaping emergence of a global data networking business from prior domestic and regional entities[25] -- ownership-privatization, supply-side competition, public- and private-network demand for emerging broadband capabilities, increased user demand for corporate network services (notably global enterprise-wide capabilities on a shared or proprietary basis) -- continue to generate more specific tendencies accelerating the trend. These apparently counterposed pressures are best understood in the context of broader cyclical forces:[26] the dynamics of network specialization versus integration and their market-inflected counterparts (premium versus commodity pricing, although no one-to-one correspondence exists).

The first involves development of a core portfolio of competences common to all international VANS providers (notably the ability to provide one-stop shopping services, thus integration of the portfolio); the second is a matter of escalating need for market differentiation of contenders.  Both imply increased service heterogeneity as well as exploitation of software-defined use-privatizing capabilities.  The logic is one of falling costs, hence more flexible critical-mass parameters determining the thresholds of virtual but viable network groupings.

### 5.1. Ownership Privatization
Despite legitimate concerns that world equity markets during 1996-98 will be unable to absorb privatizations scheduled for this period, the reputation of former state-owned telephone companies as highly profitable cash-cows tends to entice investors (outside the US they also typically dominate domestic VANS markets).  By the end of this period all major European operators should be at least partly in private hands[27] whilst several Latin American TOs are the largest constituents of their local stock markets.[28]

This is a matter of becoming market-oriented with significant workforce-reductions despite union pressures[29] and (for governments) a question of maximizing returns in a one-period game; later branches are typically sold at prevailing market prices.  This in turn requires fine-tuning of regulatory environments prior to issuance (concrete assessment of the potential impact of competition is a precondition of investor interest) where the broader ground rules -- at least in Europe -- impose market liberalization.  Thus market-opening will be accelerated by ownership-privatization prior to 1998, when competitors will barrage national monopolies with lawsuits over the ritual anticompetitive behavior pervasive to most domestic markets.  Contemporaneously the ground rules circumscribing universal service obligations via proportional access deficit charges, social subsidies, and any number of other non-market distorting regulatory mechanisms will require national redefinition.

### 5.2. Technology Trends: Supply-Side Competition
Like mobility, ATM's long-term applicability across a broad range of markets (i.e. networking problems) erodes traditional market-segmentation criteria; this in turn positions equipment providers native to hitherto distinct information-technology sectors in direct

competition. Recall that Figure 1 summarizes the stakes involved in the US market, highlighting the distinction between vendors traditionally aligned with public versus private markets.

Traditional suppliers of transmission and time-division multiplexed (TDM) switching to the former group -- AT&T, Alcatel, Ericsson, Fujitsu, DSC, Hitachi, Nortel, Siemens Stromberg-Carlson, Tellabs -- aim to dominate the core-switch market as public carriers expand ATM overlay networks outward. In the short-term ATM switches offer high-growth revenues from the data-networking sector; in the longer term these will supplant existing central-office switches as public operators migrate voice networks from TDM to ATM over SONET. The interim challenge is to fund ongoing core-switch research and development but simultaneously exploit larger sales forces and budgets to develop a market-base in the more-competitive access market dominated by so-called fast-packet (i.e. ATM and frame relay) private network suppliers.

The latter group concentrated initially on early adopters -- private networkers deploying ATM at the wide-area network (WAN) level -- and enjoy important strategic advantages: faster time-to-market, superior technology, and the ability to establish relationships on both sides of the private/public network divide. Thus marketing has evolved to include public carriers as these expand their data networks and resell equipment to end-users. Similar technology deployment and vendors on both sides of the WAN link in turn erodes older private/public network distinctions, as does ATM's capability for network-wide - and independent of usage-parameters -- management and congestion-control routines.

## 5.3. Public and Private Fast-Packet Networking: Market Demand

In the less-regulated US environment, private users drive early adoption. The ATM Forum and Frame Relay Forum -- implementers' agreement bodies rooted in the private data communications community -- effectively define standards (which supplants traditional fora dominated by public network operators and suppliers) and redefine the process itself (advance shipments come with guarantees of retrospective software standardization).

However, early rollout of commercial ATM and frame relay services in the US contrasts sharply with market underdevelopment across Europe and Asia, where significant commercial service introduction is still hampered by pricing trade-offs with the impossibly lucrative leased-line business. In addition, European and important Pacific Rim operators are still wedded to the concept of ISDN. Having invested heavily in the technology over a decade for little return prior to 1993-94, they are in general reluctant to capitulate in favor of more advanced capabilities. British Telecom Concert (Figure 6) is one of the few European providers promoting frame relay; its ISDN investment cycle ended much earlier (not pushed by a national champion vendor), whilst heavy overcapacity on UK trunk networks exerts downward pricing pressure in the domestic leased-line business. Both ATM and frame relay have yet to penetrate the Asia Pacific market beyond international hubs; surely predictable, given the low level of penetration of basic telephony in several countries, and the managed industrial-policy bent typical of the remainder, excluding Hong Kong.

## 5.4. Global Enterprise Networking and Mass Customization

Emerging market availability of a range of multilateral VPN services is central to geography-independent enterprise-wide communication for the non-*Fortune 500* company. The size of a much-publicized European VPN Users Association (EVUA) contract awarded in 1995, intended to secure both reduced voice costs and significantly-enhanced cross-border functionality for members, is also an important precursor of future revenue-sharing agreements among IVAN alliance partners.[30]

However, most mission-critical traffic is data and multinationals appear increasingly unwilling to construct large networks of Cisco or Wellfleet routers. Thus the gradual and partial outsourcing of responsibility for enterprise-wide WANS is an inexorable trend. With reliability levels now guaranteed by the major VANS and cemented by fierce competition, few corporations claim a desire to supersede the standard 99% availability figure. This returns former dedicated infrastructure to availability on a shared public (e.g. where the outsourcer is Transpac) or (virtual) private basis (when IBM Global Network assumes control). Suggested examples notwithstanding, the network-access practices typical of both public operators and computing-services vendors under these circumstances are highly fungible. There are no obvious generalizations.

Beyond the large multinationals, enterprise-wide networking begins with group-level applications; hence Microsoft's recent commitment to joint-ventures with VANS as well as public network operators worldwide. Since PCs outside the US remain under-networked, the user interface presents a major barrier to expanded online-service usage. Thus such providers as Transpac -- experienced in developing relatively basic systems, with adequate functionality to meet short-term needs of the average consumer-user -- are beginning to translate these competencies into an expanded range of VANS products marketable across public data networks. At the same time traditional private-sector providers (IBM Global Network, EDS, GEIS) are increasingly oriented toward non-proprietary products, and masking problematic legacy (soft- and hardware) interfaces inherited from their own practices as well as those of competitors.

### 4.5. Core Portfolio Competencies
The ideal portfolio for a VANS supplier is still far from infrastructure-independence. The advanced public data-network operator requires five primary capabilities:

- end-to-end bandwidth control which remains a key differentiator (successfully exploited by MFS in Europe and London, and CWBN worldwide)
- network reach, which explains Scitor's success (Figure 3) in leveraging the SITA global network
- protocol-conversion, since the industry remains awash with multiple messaging and EDI systems notwithstanding the prevalence of X.25 and X.400 standards
- minimal competence in customer premises equipment (CPE) provision and maintenance[31]
- flexible marketing of shrink-wrap VANS. Customized applications targeting vertical markets will remain critical to the business of specialized providers (SITA, GEIS, IBM Global Network). However, public network operators in their capacity as basic VANS suppliers have rushed to market shrink-wrap packages such as Lotus Notes, because small and mid-sized users resist the steep learning curves preceding enterprise-wide implementation of customized (notably EDI) applications. As users migrate to richer versions of current LAN software, off-the-shelf functionality will be required network-wide. This is but one version of IBM's vision network-centric computing vision: a view tacitly endorsed by competitors seeking to sell more bandwidth-dependent services

The Internet model is another.[32] Core skills required to provide Internet access are broadly comparable to those required by other online services. Lead times are short (since service redefinition becomes a purely promotional affair) and market advantages based upon new technologies and networking concepts -- apart from the most radical -- are increasingly transitory. The Internet in its current form foreshadows a highly-evolved online service market, which refracts the notion of electronic commerce from its vertical-market origins (as conceived by GEIS) through the lens of mass consumerism.

## 6. MARKET DIFFERENTIATION OF GLOBAL SERVICE PARTNERSHIPS: THE THREE PUBLIC NETWORK-OPERATOR CONSORTIA

The short lead-time for launch of new data networking and so-called multimedia products diminishes opportunities for competitive advantage based on service differentiation.[33] Much of this has to do with technology availability: managed router services based upon Cisco components, and fast-packet services dependent upon Stratacom, N.E.T., or Newbridge Networks switches render these products *de facto* standards. This is not an area of strategic choice for service providers, since customers run in the opposite direction from anything which bears a proprietary tag.

This increases the significance of geographic coverage as a market differentiator (Infonet and SITA's reach to the Latin American market, for example, has been leveraged in marketing). Regional competencies are far easier to develop than global ones:[34] one of the reasons for consolidation in the data networking industry is that few companies can afford to develop the broad set of worldwide competencies required to compete in the first tier.

However, competition at the transport layer -- excluding broadband -- tolerates market differentiation only at the most demanding service levels. (There is no lock-in to use of one or another service provider's bandwidth.) Hence the increased focus -- even within the public-operator based consortia (Figure 6) -- upon developing products tied to vertical markets, where an installed customer base can be developed via customized applications.[35] Services such as Phoenix and Uniworld will have to move beyond cheaper bandwidth and faster connectivity to meet these market requirements. The same logic will deepen the vulnerability of VANs, software providers, and systems integrators lacking a strong infrastructure position: managing the network of networks at the required quality levels will become increasingly difficult. Thus further partnering between and among owners of network capacity and/or software competence is inevitable.

The strategic issues faced by the three main consortia at YE1995 in market differentiation can briefly be summarized.

### 6.1. AT&T and Partners (UniWorld/WorldPartners)

AT&T's difficulty in establishing long-term European alliance partners was rendered insignificant with formalization (August 1995) of an equity-investment joint venture with Unisource. Some distance is required by both sides even as portfolios and technology-base integration proceeds: an obvious prerequisite to better exploitation of existing and potential customer groups. AT&T has conventionally been viewed as aspiring controller in those operator-led consortia which it has attempted to catalyze to date. Similar caution will be needed in deepening the (largely Asia-Pacific based) WorldPartners' commitment to a more fully shared equity-based consortia.

Short-term market differentiation follows from developing access to the rest of the world via the Uniworld European base, Telefonica's Latin American links and the WorldPartners' Asian hubs. WorldPartners -- unlike non-AT&T Uniworld members -- are free to serve as distributors of global networking products marketed by competing consortia. They will optimize positional advantage by avoiding the regional profit-&-loss model which is Uniworld until the tripartite global alignment of public operators in networking consortia stabilizes.

Despite collective stakes by Uniworld members in Infonet which amount to controlling interest, the older organization in the interim will remain an independent vehicle providing custom network services and applications.

### 6.2. Phoenix

At YE1995 this is still (fundamentally) a marketing concept. Phoenix gains strength from the partners' market dominance at home both in infrastructure and service provision, but faces considerable hurdles in managing the regulatory environment. (Users must factor political risk alongside technical ability in selecting Phoenix over rivals.) A strong Asia-Pacific partner must be committed. Phoenix also faces basic challenges in network integration and developing one-stop shopping capabilities across three large organizations.

On the technical front, the problem of interworking equipment provisioned by disparate X.25 and frame relay suppliers is mitigated for the short term by common precommitments to N.E.T. IDNX switches. However this threatens to become a more thorny problem as Nortel, Siemens, and Alcatel compete to be future suppliers. The other issue to be resolved is managing the global business. In this area the reconciliation of multiple legacies and styles of account management will present more difficulties than those experienced by Concert. Uniworld profits from the level of internetworking established by Unisource partners to date, but the European account base is the smaller. The venture must assist both Sprint and Transpac in regaining marketplace differentiation lost as rivals have broadened their own offerings.

### 6.3. Concert

The BT/MCI joint-venture continues to differentiate itself based on a headstart in network integration and in portfolio rationalization: the dust has settled around Concert at a level unlikely to be accomplished by Uniworld or Phoenix before 1997 at the earliest. The group remains inexperienced with industry-specific applications, although British Telecom's experience in the retail, manufacturing and finance sectors is an asset. However, Concert claims service quality with excellent North America-Europe connectivity, high-profile marketing capabilities, and expanding presence (albeit local) in several European markets. In the short term Concert must aggressively market services to AT&T's Asia-Pacific WorldPartners, from whose perspective two global wholesalers are surely better than one.

### 7. THE FUTURE: DYNAMIC USE-PRIVATIZATION

As ATM is introduced in critical network components -- both public and private -- the synergies for adoption throughout much of the remainder will increase.[36] The erosion of former technical, marketing, and service-based distinctions between traditional public and private networking sectors -- by technological progress and those organizational realignments (documented above) -- combined with enhanced logical control extending across entire networks, bear important consequences. Among other properties networks of the future will be characterized by dynamic (re-)combination -- momentarily or temporarily -- of use-privatized and publicly-accessible components. Enterprise networking will extend mass customization to the desktop: individual users will be able to configure network interfaces with connectivity to other users as dictated by budget constraints. This offers briefly-interesting marketing angles well into the twenty-first century. (As historical materialism will record, it is a matter of ongoing refinement of the commoditization of time.)

This shifts the question of corporate strategy for telecommunications operators as well as other network-service and information technology providers to capital allocation among existing and new infrastructure components, to risk management in the face of geographic or line-of-business diversification, and the acquisition and divestiture of business units. By 2010 we can safely assume the emergence of a dynamic and relatively open market in service logic, with independent service providers developing subgroup-customized solutions. In such an environment, the dynamics of network development and virtual group formation will be increasingly difficult to predict. Part of the associated financial uncertainties will be reflected in stock-market returns as these reflect the expectations of more and less informed investors.

Measuring and forecasting volatility (intensity of random changes) of industry returns will thus underpin risk-management across the information technology sector which subsumes telecommunications. This positions it as a central component of future corporate strategy, nascent in the imperatives requiring AT&T's divestiture -- announced in September 1995 -- as well as France Telecom's financial modeling for the transatlantic Phoenix joint-venture with Deutsche Telekom and Sprint.

## REFERENCES

Arellano, M. and V. Mackall. *U.S. Broadband Equipment Market: 1995 Edition* New York: Northern Business Information/McGraw-Hill, 1995.

Copeland, T.E. and Westland, J.F.. *Financial Theory and Corporate Policy. 3rd ed.* Reading MA: Addison Wesley, 1988.

Cool, K. and D Schende. "Performance Differences Among Strategic Group Members," *Strategic Management Journal* 9:207-223, 1988.

Elton, E.J. and M.J. Gruber. *Modern Portfolio Theory and Investment Analysis. 5th ed,* New York: John Wiley.

Gort, M. and R. Singamsetti. "Concentration and Profit Rates: New Evidence on an Old Issue," *NBER: Explorations in Economic Research.* 3:1-20, 1976.

Hansen, G. and B. Wernerfelt. "Determinants of Firm Performance: The Relative Importance of Economic and Organizational Factors," *Strategic Management Journal* 10:399-411, 1989.

Jensen, M. and H. Meckling. "Theory of the Firm: Managerial Behavior, Agency Costs and Capital Structure," *Journal of Financial Economics*, 3:305-60, 1976.

McGee, J. and H. Thomas. "Strategic Groups: Theory, Research and Taxonomy," *Strategic Management Journal* 7:141-160, 1986.

Munroe, C. and M. Singh. *Long-Distance Markets: 1994 Edition.* New York: Northern Business Information/McGraw-Hill, 1994.

NiShuilleabhain, A. *Global VANS Markets: 1995 Edition.* New York: Northern Business Information/McGraw-Hill, 1995.

NiShuilleabhain, A. *An Information-Technology Capital-Asset Pricing Model.* Fontainebleau: INSEAD Working Paper, 1995a.

Noam, E. M. *Telecommunications in Europe.* New York: Oxford University Press, 1993.

Ravenscraft, A.D.J. "Structure-Profit Relationships at the Line of Business and Industry Level," *Review of Economics and Statistics* 65:22-31, 1983.

Rumelt, R.P. "How Important is Industry in Explaining Firm Profitability?" Unpublished Working Paper, UCLA, 1982.

Rumelt, R.P. "How Much Does Industry Matter?" *Strategic Management Journal,* 12:167-185, 1991.

Scherer, F.M., and D.Ross, *Industrial Market Structure and Economic Performance, 3rd ed.* Boston: Houghton Mifflin, 1990.

Weiss, L.W. "The Concentration-Profits Relationship and Antitrust," In Goldschmid, H. ed. *Industrial Concentration: The New Learning.* Boston: Little, Brown, 1974.

## ENDNOTES

[1.] *See* A. NiShuilleabhain, "An Information-Technology Capital-Asset Pricing Model," Fontainebleau: INSEAD Working Paper, 1995.

[2.] The market for ATM public network switches alone was worth approximately $41 million in 1994; Northern Business Information predicts market expansion to more than $320 million by 1999, *See* M. Arellano and V. Mackall, *U.S. Broadband Equipment Market: 1995 Edition,* New York: Northern Business Information/McGraw-Hill, 1995, page 16 and ff.

[3.] M. Arellano and V. Mackall, *U.S. Broadband Equipment Market: 1995 Edition,* New York: Northern Business Information/McGraw-Hill, 1995.

[4.] Recall Ameritech's 1993 acquisition of a 30 percent stake in GE Information Services.

[5.] US long-distance traffic in 1993 generated $65 billion, increasing to $68.3 billion the following year. Sectoral breakouts were roughly as follows: Message Toll Service (MTS) 63.8 percent, Outbound 14 percent, Inbound 9.7 percent, Other 2.5 percent, C. Munroe and M. Singh, *Long-Distance Markets: 1994 ed.* New York: Northern Business Information/McGraw-Hill, 1994, page 3 and ff.

[6.] *Phoenix.* In June 1994, Deutsche Telekom and France Telecom announced their intentions to invest approximately US$4.2 billion -- representing a collective 20 percent equity investment -- in Sprint over a two-year period. The partnership aims to market services worldwide via regional operating groups (home-country partners in the US, France and Germany); to compete in national long-distance markets where feasible; and to combine planning for global network facilities (existing correspondent bilateral relationships will remain in place). Phoenix anticipates merging most of the international assets of Deutsche Telekom and France Telecom (within the agreed scope of the Atlas global service portfolio), with most Sprint International assets. The option to add additional national partners -- notably in the Asia-Pacific region -- remains. Phoenix' launch awaits regulatory approval by the European Commission's Competition Directorate (DG IV, which is holding out on Atlas approval), the German Bundeskarllamt, and the US Department of Justice (DoJ).

[7.] *Concert.* Launched originally as a wholly-owned subsidary of MCI, which contributed $79 million to the cost of its establishment, MCI currently owns 25% of Concert. (In February 1994 MCI had announced the completion of its takeover of British Telecom North America's assets, which were integrated with MCI's Data Services Division.) Concert is responsible for managing both networks and their various capabilities, delivering seamless service. British Telecom and MCI serve as geographical distributorships covering Europe and North America respectively, market jointly-branded services and products, and handle all sales and marketing issues. Basic services continues to be handled through correspondent relationships. MCI leverages Concert assets (including the increasingly-sophisticated VNet) to develop the North, Central, and South America markets. British Telecom retains responsibility for business development in the UK, Europe, and the rest of the world (Asia-Pacific and Africa). Future third-party deals brokered by British Telecom and MCI are not expected to alter Concert's structural role.

[8.] *WorldPartners.* In May 1993, AT&T, KDD, and Singapore Telecom announced the WorldPartner association to provide WorldSource voice and data services to multinationals. The three founding members have equity investment and partner status. During 1993-94 membership expanded to include Telstra and the Telecom Corp. of New Zealand; in June 1994, Unisource acquired a 20% equity stake with European distribution rights to the WorldPartner portfolio and announced its intention to begin marketing WorldSource services. The Swedish-Dutch-Swiss joint venture company at that time was committed to invest US$350 million and employ 650 people in Europe during 1994-97 to develop and market customized voice and data services to multinationals. WorldPartners are committed to distribution of WorldSource, the global product portfolio marketed by BCS and its partners worldwide. As of September 1995, core portfolio components will be rebranded as Uniworld offerings for the European market. At YE1995 the North America/Pacific Rim component of the AT&T BCS global service partnership program comprises: AT&T, Unitel, KDD, Singapore Telecom, Telstra, Telecom New Zealand International, Hong Kong Telecom, Korea Telecom, Phillipines Long Distance Telephone Company (PLDT), and Telkom South Africa.

[9.] *Uniworld.* Announced in December 1994, this joint-venture company between Unisource (60%) and AT&T (40%) will provide liberalized voice and VAN services to multinational companies headquartered in Europe. The company will also supply direct communication via VSATs. However, as part of WorldPartners, Uniworld's reach will extend across North America and the Pacific Rim. After finalisation of definitive documentation and notification to the European Union, Uniworld is expected to be operational by 1 January 1996 with assets of approximately $200 million and over 2000 employees at launch. AT&T's Communications Services Group will manage AT&T's 40% shareholding. This group includes four dimensions: Consumer Communications Services, Business Communications Services, AT&T Universal Card Services (which markets consumer credit cards for general purchases and long-distance calling), and AT&T American Transtech (which provides telephone-based services such as lead generation and sales programs, facilitating businesses expand). Control by the Communications Services Group facilitates portfolio expansion to include consumer voice services -- and other businesses too -- as these become liberalized across Europe. This of course is the longer-term strategic intent.

[10.] Our analysis reflects interviews and revenue estimates from close to sixty service providers including the eight global market leaders whose fortunes are summarized in Figure 3.

[11.] At YE1994 IBM Global Network dominated with a 9.8% market share. The industry leader was followed by competing IVANs/global VAN service consortia in this order: AT&T and Partners (5.6%); GE Information Services and Sprint International with Partners (each of which controlled a 4.7% market share); SITA (representing a 3.9% worldwide share); and BT/MCI joint-venture Concert (3.4%). Each of these entities commanded worldwide revenues in excess of $500 million during 1994. Smaller global providers Infonet (1.7%), and Cable & Wireless Business Networks (1.5%) earned $252 million and $235 million (estimate) respectively in global VANS during 1994.

[12.] VANS service providers confined to the North American, European and Asia/Pacific markets in aggregate controlled 64.5%. Latin American VANS accounted for a mere 0.5% of this figure.

[13.] *Atlas.* In December 1993 France Telecom and Deutsche Telekom signed a Memorandum of Understanding (MOU) to co-operate in VANS market expansion, following with the nomination of Jean Arnould and Norbert Knoppik to lead the proposed joint venture from Brussels. The proposed service portfolio will be provided by a dedicated backbone network with unified network management across all operations. The joint venture will initially exploit existing France Telecom and Deutsche Telecom network service entities, notably Transpac's multinational capabilities, Datex-P and Eunetcom itself. From its inception the two partners had hoped that their co-operation be viewed as a contribution to Europe's overall economic development. Atlas was to operate in fully liberalized sectors and its activities would be pursued in complete uniformity with EC competition rules, i.e., would not involve the extension of a dominant position in one market to another. Following late-1995 approval by the European Commission's DG IV, a 1996 launch of X.25, frame relay, Internet Protocol, VSAT, international virtual private network (VPN), and international value-added voice is scheduled. However the challenges of launching Atlas cover considerably more ground: there are differing technical and operational systems to be integrated, and the two monopoly operator cultures will need to reconcile their approach to business development.

[14.]*Societe Internationale Telecommunications Aeronautique (SITA).* This cooperative venture involves 550 members, most of which are airlines. In April 1990, SITA established the value-added service provider Scitor to sell industry-specific solutions and resell SITA network capacity. Scitor effectively was formed out of ITS (International Telecommunications Services), the SITA subsidiary created in 1972 to provide total solutions to SITA members and others outside the airline industry. In 1989 SITA divested ITS BV to market VANS beyond the airline sector; this became Scitor (since 1992) which claims to market a full range of managed network offerings across target industries. In December 1994, the SITA board approved a change in structure which involved the establishment of a holding company in the Netherlands and the transfer of ITS, Scitor, and Novus into a single entity with a new commercial structure. The second phase of the restructuring will welcome outside investors, a process which had been intended to include Unisource, but will require a new set of alliance partners given its 1995 rupture with SITA.

[15.]*IBM Global Network.* The integration of IBM's intra-organizational corporate data and voice network with a backbone network connecting regional processing bureaus supported the introduction of commercial network service to the US beginning in 1982. European service followed four years later; in 1995 the IBM Infomation Network was renamed the IBM Global Network. Currently one of the world's largest dedicated data networks, the IBM Global Network is managed worldwide by Advantis, a joint venture with Sears.

[16.]*Infonet.* Established by Computer Services Corporation in 1970, the Infonet Services Corporation had 11 shareholders until 1993 (when MCI Communications Corporations' 25% share was redistributed following MCI's alliance with Concert). Late in 1994 Singapore Telecom sold its 7.1% shareholding. Following this sale, member shareholdings were: Deutsche Telecom and Transpac, 23.3% each; Telstra 7. 6%; Belgacom, Swiss PTT, PTT Telecom, Telefonica, and Telia International, 7.7% each; KDD 7.2%. During 2Q1995, a two-stage process of share redistribution began. The first phase involves reduction of Deutsche Telekom and France Telecom ownership - because of the Phoenix joint-venture with Sprint -- so that remaining shares are almost equally distributed among nine partners. The second phase during 1996 will involve the sale of remaining Deutsche Telekom and France Telecom shares in Infonet to new and/or existing owners.

[17.]*Unisource.* Originating in 1992 as a joint-venture partnership between PTT Telecom Nederland and Sweden's Telia (then Televerket), Unisource adopted PTT Swiss Telecom as a third and equal shareholder in mid-1993. Subsequent discussions led to the inclusion of Telefonica (noted below). In June 1994 Unisource bought a 20% stake in AT&T's WorldPartners -- jointly established with KDD and Singapore Telecom -- and thus earned exclusive distribution rights for WorldSource services in Europe. Thus was born Uniworld, a far-reaching market-sharing arrangement linking AT&T's European data-networking strategy tightly with that of the Unisource partners.

[18.]Most global providers claimed growth close to or exceeding 100% during 1994-95, and expectations for continued expansion at this rate through 1997.

[19.] A. NiShuilleabhain, *Global VANS Markets: 1995 ed.* New York: Northern Business Information/McGraw-Hill, 1995.

[20.] For example, by 2000 Cable & Wireless Business Networks should increase global market share to 2.9% based upon compounded annual growth (CAGR) on the order of 13-14%. Smaller increases - on the order of 0.3% and 0.1% respectively - should be recorded by BT/MCI and AT&T with its partners. For details, *see* A. NiShuilleabhain, *Global VANS Markets: 1995 ed.* New York: Northern Business Information/McGraw-Hill, 1995.

[21.] In the interim, Northern Business Information's *Global VANS Markets: 1995 Edition* database projects worldwide CAGR at 76.7% (on YE1994 North American revenues barely in excess of $90 million) and thus a VANS market share gain just above 4%. All eight global providers are working toward multilateral International Virtual Private Network (IVPN, but note that 'Intelligent' will also be coopted by marketers in this context); thus slight market share expansion (below one percent). Aggregating across regional revenue streams and by sector, these expansions should occur at the expense of the Packet Switched and Related, Messaging and Online, and Managed Network Services (MNS) service classes (see Figure 4). Worldwide these horizontal and fundamentally commodity sectors will lose significant market share (on the order of 7.8%, 2.7%, and 2.5% respectively). EDI and Industry Solutions will lose slight market share (below 1%) based upon a longer market-penetration trajectory. The Managed Private Line category can be expected to retain a 2% global market share based upon cannibalization of existing leased-line revenue streams linking the four geographic regions (thus a CAGR close to 14 percent through 1999).

[22.] This remains dominated by AT&T, Sprint, CWBN, and BT/MCI.

[23.] *EUCOM.* Launched by France Telecom holding-company COGECOM -- the umbrella under which all France Telecom subsidiaries operate -- and Deutsche Telekom in November 1988, this limited-liability company is incorporated under German law. The holding-company Logicels et Integration de Services (FTLIS) -- established by COGECOM in 1992 to control France Telecom interests in VANS, computer services, and facilities management -- owns the France Telecom share. COGECOM also controls 50% of the partners' outsourcing venture **Eunetcom** and (through FTLS) investment by Deutsche Telekom/France Telecom entities. Eucom initially targets the European market, seeking to pre-empt dominance of the industry-solutions sector by non-European service providers.

[24.] In contrast the Concert, WorldPartners/Uniworld, and SITA partnerships have yet to address this critical expansion path, intended by France Telecom/Deutsche Telekom (via Eucom) to exploit existing and committed future-network (SDH, GSM, B-ISDN, ATM) capabilities.

[25.] However transformed domestic entities appear to be continually replaced by new entrants to the national or sub-regional pool. The rate of introduction of new VAS providers in Europe is increasing -- albeit slowly -- in tandem with burgeoning growth of a regional internetworking sector. Pending effective infrastructure liberalization under European Commission (EC) guidelines, however, the possibility of rapid innovation characteristic of US hardware and software markets since AT&T's (1984) divestiture remains foreclosed.

[26.] See Eli M. Noam, *Telecommunications in Europe*, New York: Oxford University Press, 1993, and the same author's chapter in this volume.

[27.] The European process stretches back to flotation of British Telecom shares in 1983, followed by sales of Telefonica, STET, and SIP (now Telecom Italia), KPN in the Netherlands, TeleDanmark, and (in 1995), Telecom Portugal. The 1996 stock-market flotation of Deutsche Telekom (at YE1995 an incorporated entity wholly-controlled by the German government) will be Europe's largest equity offering to date.

[28.]Notable among successful Asian launches were those of Singapore Telecom (1994) -- briefly capitalized more highly than IBM -- and NTT (in 1995 the world's most highly-capitalized company).

[29.]In general this benefits both consumer/users and the privatized entities themselves. No longer a government department, there could be little of the traditional national champion justification for protecting British Telecom's interests. Despite the company's considerable market power, the level of choice afforded users in the competitive UK environment far exceeds that found elsewhere in Europe with the possible exception of Sweden. British Telecom itself has been a major beneficiary of this competition via efficiency improvements and operational streamlining. The Netherlands' PTT Telecom has emerged post-privatization as Europe's most efficient operator, benefiting in particular from exposure to new markets and partners via Unisource and Uniworld (the trans-Atlantic component of its alliance partnerships).

[30.]*EVUA.* This group of 40 multinationals (including founder members ICI and Rank Xerox) negotiated separate telecommunications services contracts in April 1994 with AT&T/Unisource and British Telecom for pan-European voice and data services. The EVUA final contract -- scheduled for renegotiation late in 1995 among several bidders ( including Cable & Wireless, Sprint/Eunetcom and Telstra) -- is worth an estimated 500 million ECU annually. AT&T/Unisource co-operation on this contract preceded Uniworld.

[31.]This stops short of a full outsourcing offering. Although EDS (for example) commands a powerful position with proven track-record in outsourcing as well as solving short-term employment problems for multinationals, this market is increasingly competitive. The former public monopolists have national market presence adequate to ensuring support-levels required by national and subregional businesses, and this in turn will boost confidence in outsourcing 'solutions' which they will inevitably introduce to market.

[32.]Revenues derived from providing Internet access are likely to be immaterial to international carriers excluding Sprint International, MCI Concert, and eventually AT&T. The wave of Internet access providers which emerged across Europe and Asia during 1993-95 will be followed by consolidation.

[33.]Whereas the US IXCs compete to claim the first or widest commercial introduction of ATM service to a given region, most North American VANS providers introduced frame relay service rapidly.

[34.]And few companies want to be in the position of trying to solve networking problems via a help-line call in Europe where the faulty node sits in Latin America or Asia.

[35.]Such is not the case with EDI software widely adopted across an industry, where competitors, suppliers, and customers perpetuate usage. It would be difficult to value goodwill developed by SITA within the airline industry, by GEIS in the retail sector, of even CWBN in important financial-services markets.

[36.]It is, of course, as a data networking technology that ATM finds first commercial application. Wide-scale deployment for voice and video will follow at several years lag in most markets.

PRIVATE NETWORKS PUBLIC OBJECTIVES
E. Noam and A. NíShúilleabháin (Editors)
© 1996 Elsevier Science B.V. All rights reserved.

# Private Networks in Japan and the Need to Secure Global Interconnectivity

Koichiro Hayashi & Richard Nohe

## 1. INTRODUCTION

Private Networks in Japan have not been deployed to the extent that they have in the US. This is due to the dramatic difference between the two markets and business systems. Because information is not available regarding the number of Private Networks (PNs) in Japan, it is necessary to derive the PN market size by looking at two sources: 1) the ownership structure of the New Common Carriers (NCCs);[1] and 2) the growth in the number of circuits leased from NTT.

Looking at such factors does not answer a fundamental question: Why has PN development in Japan lagged that of the US? Therefore, it is beneficial to examine the role played by the Japanese telecommunications infrastructure in the overall business environment. Even though this role is similar to the role played by the telecommunications infrastructure in the US, the marketplace in Japan has more strict boundaries for industry segmentation.

## 2. NCCs' ROLE IN PRIVATE NETWORKING

Large companies in Japan have not followed the lead of their US counterparts who have gone out to build their own networks. Instead, they have remained "faithful" to the public infrastructure, which was built and operated by the government and privatized in 1985. Until this time, the Japanese market did not experience the entrepreneurial spirit of NCCs. It was with the market entry of the NCCs that companies first started to move from NTT's network to others. Given the ownership structure of the NCCs, it can be argued that they are, in some ways, large private networks. As these networks were built, NTT customers shifted their traffic from what had historically been the only game in town.

There are three kinds of carriers in Japan. The first type are licensed facilities-based carriers and operate under the most severe restrictions imposed by the MPT. The second type are non-facilities-based carriers and operate without a license. These type of carriers are divided into special category which lease facilities from the first type of carriers and must obtain authorization from the MPT. Figure 1 shows how the market in Japan has developed around the Type 1 and Type 2 segments.[2]

One of the clearest distinctions between the US and Japan involves ownership structure of the telecommunications service providers. The ownership structure of the NCC market lends credibility to the assertion that NCCs can be categorized as PNs. Indeed, US companies that made huge capital investments in their own telecommunications networks are now moving away from such practices and back to the public carriers' networks. This phenomenon can be partly explained by two developments in technology — fiber optics and intelligent networks. Fiber created excess capacity in the long distance market and intelligent networks[3] allowed the interexchange carriers to provide private network functionality over their public network.

Figure 1
Number of Common Carriers in Japan

|         |         | 1985 | 1986 | 1987 | 1988 | 1989 | 1990 | 1991 | 1992 |
|---------|---------|------|------|------|------|------|------|------|------|
| Type 1  |         | 2    | 7    | 13   | 37   | 45   | 62   | 68   | 68   |
| Type 2  |         | 85   | 209  | 356  | 530  | 693  | 841  | 943  | 1036 |
|         | General | 85   | 200  | 346  | 512  | 668  | 813  | 912  | 1000 |
|         | Special | 0    | 9    | 10   | 18   | 25   | 28   | 31   | 36   |
| Total   |         | 87   | 216  | 369  | 567  | 738  | 903  | 1011 | 1104 |

Figure 2

| Company | Capital 100 mil | Major Investors |
|---------|-----------------|-----------------|
| Inter-City Carriers | | |
| DDI Corp | 108 | Kyocera: 25.1%; Sony: 5.0%; Ushio Inc.: 2.5%; SECOM: 2.5%; Mitsubishi Corp.: 2.5%; etc. Total: 225 companies |
| Japan Telecom Co., Ltd. | 243.79 | JR Eastern Japan: 19.6%; JR Western Japan: 15.1%; JR Tokai: 11.2%; etc. Total: 302 |
| Teleway Japan Corp. | 249.0 | Toyota Motor Corp: 6.9%; Road Facility Assoc.: 6.9%; Mitsubishi Corp.: 3.1%; Total: 289 |
| Regional Carriers | | |
| Tokyo Telecommunications Network Co., Inc. | 300 | Tokyo Electric Power Co., Inc., Mitsui & Co. Ltd. Mitsubishi Corp. |
| Lakecity Cablevision Corp. | 3.535 | Gyosei, Nikkan Shashin Tsushin, Sankyo Seiki, Chinon Int'l |
| Osaka MediaPort Corp. | 120 | Osaka-shi, Kansai Electric Power Co., Inc. |
| Chubu Telecommunications Co., Inc. | 120 | Chubu Electric Power Co., Ltd., Mitsui & Co., Ltd., Mitsubishi Corp. |
| Shikoku Information and Telecommunication Network Co., Inc. | 20 | Shikoku Electric Power Co., Inc., Mitsui & Co., Ltd., Mitsubishi Corp. |
| Kyushu Telecommunications Network Co., Inc. | 72 | Kyushu Electric Power Co., Inc., Mitsui & Co., Ltd., Mitsubishi Corp. |
| Hokkaido Telecommunication Network Corp. | 30 | Hokkaido Electric Power Co., Inc., Mitsui & Co., Ltd., Mitsubishi Corp. |
| International Carriers | | |
| International Telecom Japan | 200 | Mitsubishi Corp., Mitsui & Co., Ltd., Sumitomo Corp. |
| International Digital Communications, Inc. | 240 | C.Itoh & Co., Ltd., Cable & Wireless, Toyota Motor Corp. |

Figure 2 shows, among other things, that the ten main domestic Type 1 carriers are owned by over 800 companies. Of course these companies put at least some of their traffic onto these networks. It is more often the case that a company will participate in ventures such as this rather than build a PN strictly for their own use. Similarly, the international NCCs are primarily owned by *sogo-shosha* (trading companies).[4] On the other side of the Pacific, ownership of US-based telecommunications service providers is widespread, but companies do not typically support a new carrier through making a capital investment and then putting traffic onto the network. While there are exceptions to this in the US, it is the rule in Japan.

It has been suggested that major investors to NCCs are equipment suppliers, and it is the equipment suppliers that benefit most from the liberalization of the Japanese telecommunications market.[5] However, this is not necessarily true because it assumes that operating costs in the US and Japan are the same, or least more similar than they may actually be. If the costs were the same, then someone would benefit from the higher prices in Japan. But the costs and cost structures are not the same. This cost differential is a basic issue that should be considered when making economic-based comparisons between the US and Japan.

## 3. NTT LEASED CIRCUIT GROWTH

The second way to look at the size of the PN market in Japan is by focusing on the growth of leased circuits. Figure 3 shows that leased circuit usage is growing.[6]

Figure 3

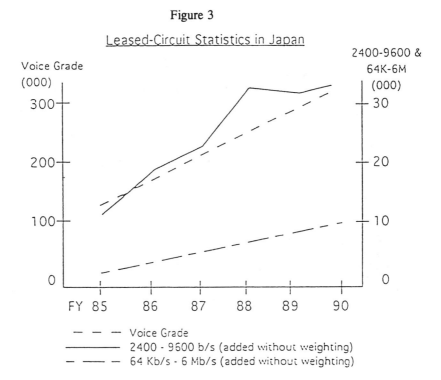

Leased-Circuit Statistics in Japan

The reasons why this trend is taking place in Japan are not similar to the growth seen in leased circuits in the US in the 1980s.

This type of analysis gets to a fundamental question: What is a private network? If the PN can consist of leased circuits from the "public" carrier, then the impact of PNs on the public infrastructure will be less than a definition whereby PNs only include separate physical networks. The response by the "public" carrier will be different in each of these situations. Historical background is necessary, in order to understand NTT's reaction to the growth of physically different PN (NCCs) and to leased-circuit PNs.

## 4. HISTORICAL PERSPECTIVE

Japan's telephone service began in 1890 with 237 subscribers in Tokyo and 48 in Yokohama. As the benefits of the telephone system were gradually recognized, the number of subscribers increased each year, reaching 1.5 telephones per 100 persons just before the second world war. However, the system was virtually destroyed during the war. Postwar operations began with the reconstruction of the network. This discontinuity of telephone-density growth can be easily seen in Figure 4.

### Figure 4

Telephone Density Growth Rate in Japan 1900-1990

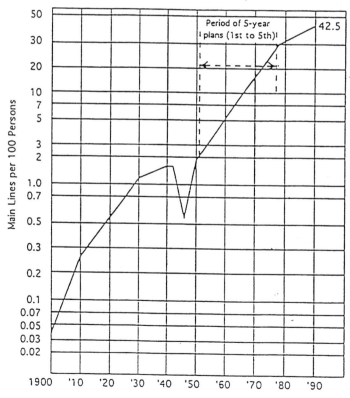

When telephone density had recovered to its pre-war level in 1952, Nippon Telegraph and Telephone Public Corporation (NTT-PC)[7] was established and established a series of five-year construction plans. This planning system rapidly increased telephone penetration, to about forty-four access lines per 100 population in 1991 — a level similar to telephone penetration of the world's leading industrialized nations. The organization responsible for providing telephone services was initially a government body, and its budget was part of the general account of the national budget. In 1950, only five years after the end of the World War II, the budget for telephone services was transferred to a special account making it somewhat independent of the general account.

In 1952, the operating body for telephone services was converted to a public corporation called NTT-PC, in order to achieve more flexibility of operations. At the same time, Kokusai Denshin Denwa[8] (KDD) was established to be the sole provider of international services. NTT-PC contributed to the improvement of telephone services in Japan.

The 100 years of telephone evolution in Japan has been characterized by the unique phenomenon of *sekitai* (backlog) and the associated "subscriber's bond system." Because the telephone business was profitable from the start, as in Europe, the Japanese telephone profits were used to subsidize the general account of the government budget, including the postal service deficit. The telephone operating body thus suffered both from shortage of construction money and from excess demand.

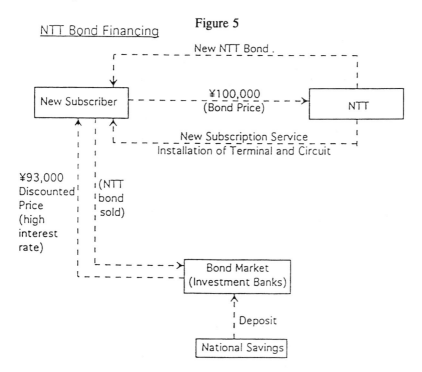

NTT Bond Financing    Figure 5

Figure 6
Raising Funds (in 1000s)

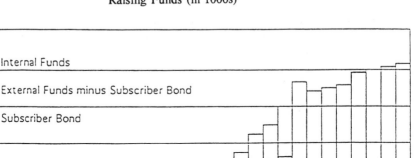

Therefore, it was natural that a kind of beneficiary-pay-system was invented as soon as the telephone system began. This system played an important role in financing construction. Even before World War II, the beneficiary payment was as much as 67% of the total construction budget.[9] By 1953, self-financing by the beneficiary-pay-system became more common with the introduction of the subscriber's bond system. This system contributed to NTT-PC's success in raising enough money to make substantial investments in the telecommunications infrastructure.

Each new subscriber was asked to purchase a subscriber bond that would be repaid after ten years. The bond price was equal to roughly half the cost of installing a new subscriber line and telephone set,[10] and in this way NTT-PC was able to finance the cost of accepting the new subscription. The subscriber had two alternatives — keep the bond and wait for its repayment, or sell it on the bond market to investment banks. At that time, only a small portion of new subscribers kept the bond, despite the attractive repayment rate promised. Most bonds were instead sold to the market at a discounted price. This meant that a very attractive investment, subscriber's bonds, were offered at a low price, allowing for a high rate of return to the investment banks. Consequently, private savings and other domestic and foreign funds were mobilized to invest in telecommunications. The point is that, by selling the NTT bonds, a new subscriber could in effect obtain a new line at a low fee. This can be seen in Figure 5.

The role of subscriber's bonds becomes more clear in Figure 6, which shows the source of funds used for construction of the telephone network. It is remarkable that nearly half of the total funds come from internal sources, which consist mainly of depreciation and profit. It is also apparent that subscriber bonds contributed very much to raising money until they were abandoned in 1983. Around 1965 subscriber bonds made up about a third of all construction funds. Of course such financing plans were not available to anyone. In fact, only NTT-PC had access to such devices. While companies were permitted to build their own telecommunications networks and bypass the government-sponsored monopoly, they were not allowed to interconnect until the liberalization of the market in 1985. Therefore, PNs were not an attractive option except to operations such as the government-owned railway system, or electric power companies, which did build its own network. This is similar to the situation in countries which operated PATS as government-owned monopolies, but it is in stark contrast to the development in the US.

## 5. INFRASTRUCTURE COMPARISONS

Of the many infrastructures supporting advanced economies, telecommunications has emerged as the most important. Despite this, very little concrete research has been done to evaluate the impact of telecommunications on economies and societies, in a quantitative way. However, a study[11] has been done concerning the impact of telecommunications. It was headed by Professor Hajime Oniki of Osaka University who did research to prove the following hypothesis: 1) the capacities of various infrastructures can be calculated and compared on a common basis; and 2) if we are really heading towards the information society, the telecommunications infrastructure should have developed faster than others.

Figure 7
Growth Rates of Japanese Infrastructures (1965-1985)

| Infrastructure | Total Capacity (annual growth rate) | Breakdown | |
|---|---|---|---|
| Telecom | 13.2 times (15.2%) | Subscriber Lines<br>Trunk Lines | 7.3<br>41.6 |
| Airways | 9.1 times (11.7%) | | |
| Railways | 4.5 times (7.8%) | New Bullet trains<br>Traditional Lines | 9.5<br>0.7 |
| Roads | 3.2 times (6.3%) | Expressways<br>Other Higways & Roads | 5.8<br>1.4 |
| Electricity | 4.0 times (7.5%) | | |
| GNP | 3.3 times (6.5%) | | |

Capacity was calculated in the same basic way for all infrastructures over the twenty years between 1965 and 1985. For example, in the case of railways, the maximum possible number of passengers in one car was multiplied by the total number of cars available. This number, n, was multiplied by the number of kilometers covered by all trains in a day. The result was around 6 billion people km$^2$/h in 1965 and around 27 billion people km$^2$/h in 1985 respectively. Therefore, the growth rate during these 20 years was 4.5 times or 7.8% per annum on average.

Applying this formula to telecommunications, it was found that the capacity of Japan's telephone network increased by a factor of 13.2 in the same 20-year period. This is an average annual growth rate of 15.2%, the highest among the five measured infrastructures.

NTT's performance in telecommunications infrastructure construction has surpassed that of any other infrastructures in Japan. Figure 7 shows the evidence in support of such an hypothesis. This implicitly indicates why private networking demand in Japan has been so weak.

It is also to be noted that all infrastructures studied in the Japanese market have exceeded or at least have kept pace with the GNP growth rate. Without this, the Japanese economy might not have achieved its astonishingly high growth after its recovery from the Second World War. One more factor in the growth of an infrastructure is that capacity tends to increase when a significant new technology is introduced. The most visible case is that of the railways. The capacity of the Shinkansen bullet train increased 9.5 times between 1965 and 1985, while that of conventional train lines decreased by 30%. Total railway capacity therefore grew about 4.5 times. The effect of new technology is also clear in telecommunications. The 13.2-fold increase in capacity is mainly due to the impressive 41.6 times growth in trunk lines over the twenty year period.

Figure 8
Telephone Network Capacity

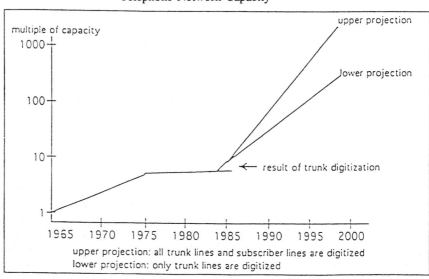

Time-serial development is shown in Figure 8. The vertical axis shows capacity on an exponential measure. It can be seen that capacity extended rapidly between 1965 and 1975. Just as capacity was maturing in the late '70s and '80s, the introduction of digital technology gave capacity another boost.

Professor Oniki's research team made a projection of trends to the year 2000, taking two scenarios. If both trunk lines and subscriber lines were digitized, total capacity would increase 140 times over the 1985 level. This is shown as the upper projection. However, if only trunk lines were digitized, capacity would increase 40-fold, lower projection. These projections were made in 1986 - 87, when 1985 date was the latest available. By 1990, actual capacity already exceeded the upper projection on Figure 8. Digitization in the late 1980s was faster and stronger than anyone expected.

Figure 9
Distribution of Subscribers in Texas

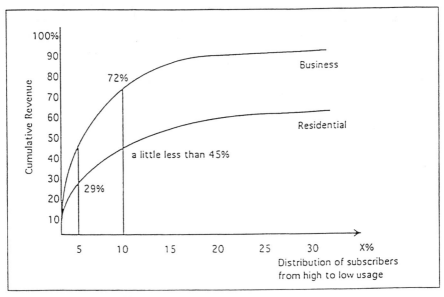

## 6. THE NEW ENVIRONMENT

Liberalization and privatization have already become world-wide trends. Especially in the developed countries, it may damage the whole national economy if this trend is not followed. This is because information technology has become the core of competitiveness and the telecommunications infrastructure is the essential platform for using this technology.

It is sometimes overlooked, however, that the potential power of leading-edge companies underlines this tendency. The leading-edge large corporations are the ones most affected by the tariff structure of the telephone industry. In other words, they have the most advanced technologies and return the benefits of these technologies to their customers. Because the telephone business in every country has long had a monopolistic nature, it is almost impossible to get public data for analyzing cost structures or customer distributions according to the usage of telephone calls. One exception to this is found in The Economics of Telecommunications by Dr. John T. Wenders.[12] It was found that only 10% of the high-usage customers contribute to 72% of total revenues from business customers in the State of Texas.

This implies that the high-usage customers are asked to pay more than the real cost under the universal tariff principle, where only one tariff is applied to every customer regardless of their level of usage. This situation is shown by Figure 10.[13] The telephone company earns much money from high-usage customers or routes and is able to compensate deficits due to low usage customers or routes. This is the essence of "universal services," and this kind of "cross-subsidization" has been traditional in the telephone industry. But it is now becoming a strong incentive for large customers to exit from the public telephone network.[14]

Figure 10
Cross-Subsidization in the Telephone Industry

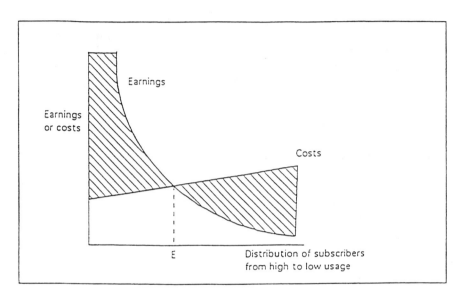

And from the standpoint of the common carriers, these larger corporations are their best customers because they pay more than the real costs. This enables the carrier to subsidize low-traffic customers and routes. The loss of these large customers is catastrophic for the public network.

As was seen by Figure 2, above, many of NTT's largest customers have invested in and become customers of the NCCs. This has caused a revenue loss for NTT, especially in the most profitable long distance corridor. This is perhaps the most dramatic impact on the modern NTT. The possibility that large corporations will leave is undoubtedly a threat to the public network and is the real driving force toward liberalization and privatization of telecommunications. Negotiations regarding trade in services are one of the most heated issues in the Uruguay Round of GATT. American Express is the most earnest promoter for trade in services, because of the great potential benefits it sees once the free flow of information is internationally secured.

## 7. EXPANSION OF COMMON CARRIERS ACTIVITIES

Globalization means that countries cannot afford to be isolated, and needs will grow to force a standardization of service menus and quality. The real driving force for such changes comes from Fortune 500 companies and other large users. They now prefer to outsource the telecommunications network.[15] These users are seeking One Stop Shopping (OSS) because they don't want to have to be concerned with receiving bills in eighteen different languages and currencies. OSS is one way in which common carriers can effectively serve their customers, by providing them with the convenience of a single contact point. The common carrier makes all necessary arrangements through cooperative agreements with friendly partners around the world. Another service of proven convenience is Joint Account Management (JAM), an advanced structure to support global customers, in which common carriers play the role of network system integrators (NSI).

Despite the moves to a multi-carrier environment, the need will continue for alliances to establish, operate and maintain networks. Syncordia,[16] originally proposed by BT, is an example of how an alliance proposal can become much more. Originally conceived as a cooperative agreement between BT, NTT and DBT, Syncordia, after failing at that goal has become part of the BT/MCI venture. But Syncordia differs from the OSS or JAM type of collaboration in three ways. Firstly, it leases private lines from common carriers at its own risk in order to anticipate the actual needs of specific customers. Secondly, its private lines are not simply raw cable, but a network management system (NMS). This may enable customers in the future to control their networks personally. Thirdly, even before the BT/MCI alliance, Syncordia had passed beyond the memorandum of understanding stage to become a physical entity, a joint venture which asks shareholders to take a certain amount of risk. With the activities of large telecommunications customers becoming globalized, in due course, multinational common carriers will begin to appear. As this occurs, we will see more mergers and acquisitions similar to the BT/MCI deal.[17] Carriers are now eager to look for beneficial alliances, regardless of the partner's nationality. Common carriers can move in one of two directions — either extend basic services or enhance their range.

## 8. SCENARIO FOR STANDARDIZATION

It may seem odd that common carriers are also seeking alliances regarding ISDN, because ISDN is fundamentally the most "basic" function of the network and Interconnectivity is to be secured by global standardization. But in reality, standardization includes certain amount of national options, and there are subtle differences of protocols between country A and B. Differences also occur in timing of implementation of specific terminals country by country. Thus, there will be alliances in relation to ISDN implementation. One unique fact to be noted here is that the US is fairly handicapped in this regard, probably because of the fragmentary nature of the network after the break-up of AT&T.

The choice for customers is expanding quickly, especially for high-volume users. This presents problems as well as opportunities, since network configuration inevitably becomes complicated in a multi-carrier environment.[18] It is beneficial to look at the players from the viewpoint of standardization. In the old regime, common carriers were solely responsible for end-to-end interconnection at any time and at any place. However, today they have already lost their sovereignty.

Equipment vendors and service providers are now also responsible for the end-to-end connection, because info-communication networks are a mixture of telecommunications networks, terminal equipment, and values added to this configuration. Without friendly cooperation and coordination among these three players, network connectivity could not be well maintained. These are of course the main players on the stage. But there are other important players, who do not appear on the stage but prefer to stay behind-the-scenes. One of them is the users. Users have long been accustomed to taking it for granted that there is no choice for terminals, for new services other than traditional voice telephony, or for carriers. Now users can enjoy freedom to choose equipment, service providers, and common carriers. They have acquired enough knowledge about network elements and the network itself. Their voices should not be neglected, but they are not yet formally involved in the process of discussing network-related issues. The United States runs a little bit ahead of other countries in terms of establishing users' organizations, and other countries have yet to succeed in this area. However, this does not necessarily mean that user's requirements are well fulfilled in the US either. The cynical point of view sees that the more frustrated customers are, the stronger their voice becomes. Therefore, it is modest to say that it is fairly difficult to represent users' voices without users' organizations.

Another player behind-the-scenes, is the government or regulators. Since the liberalization or privatization of telecommunications, regulatory functions and operational functions have been separated. In the old system, where common carriers used to have two different faces, everything had been decided by cooperative works among them. Now as these coalitions have been broken down, regulators are expected to play a certain role in this arena. But the regulators' role should be limited to specific items, since network issues should be decided mainly by market mechanisms. National security is one of the candidate items reserved for governmental intervention, and there are others.

Figure 11
Interconnection : Leveling / Bridging Map

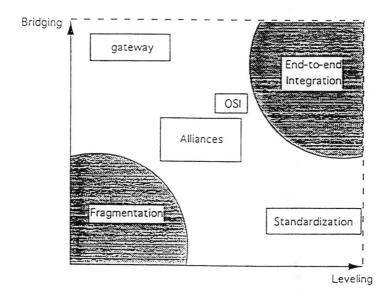

## 9. FOUR MEANS TO SECURE INTERCONNECTION

Figure 11 is the invention of Dr. Bressand of Promethee, a Paris-based think-tank. Dr. Bressand introduced and used this matrix in order to analyze and show where various strategies or means are located from a political point of view. For example, he tried to show where EC signal market or "mutual recognition" theory is located. But the methodology is also applicable here. The horizontal axis of this chart indicates the degree of leveling. "Leveling" means how flat and fair, or non-discriminatory, the platform or the fundamental condition is. On the other axis, there is shown the degree of "bridging." "Bridging" takes the opposite method or direction of leveling, because it takes for granted that "leveling" is difficult or unnecessary. Instead, "bridging" makes an effort to set-up interconnection among many different systems as widely and deeply as possible. Thus, various means for interconnection, including the way to insure network interconnection, are allocated in a proper position in this map. First of all, the most extreme cases: If the network concerned consists of several sub-networks, and they are lacking the interconnection function, these networks are completely fragmented. Therefore, "fragmentation" is put on the bottom left. On the contrary, if the networks consist of a single carrier, and that carrier can ensure end-to-end connectivity, both "leveling" and "bridging" functions are guaranteed. Therefore, "end-to-end" integration is put on the top right. In today's interconnected society, any means will be put somewhere in-between these two extreme cases. Here, four examples can be seen — standardization, gateway technologies, Open Systems Interconnection (OSI) and alliances.

Standardization is the traditional, popular method to ensure Interconnectivity, and is very useful for insuring network security. This is a typical method focusing on "leveling." But judging from an economic point of view, standardization suffers from several trade-offs: between prompt utilization of high technologies and economies of standards which require some time frame; between de facto standards and steady but complete standardization; between global standards and regional institution; between authorized, formal procedure and voluntary cooperation; between optional and strict standards, and so on.

A second solution is software conversion as one of the applications of gateway technologies. This is not necessarily standardization. Rather, it takes advantage of fragmented networks and finds business opportunities in setting up interconnection among them. As the down-sizing in computers progresses, it becomes both technically easy and economically feasible to introduce gateways at certain points in networks. That is the main reason why VAS attracts so much attention, not only in the telecom business but in every economic sector. But, regardless how easy it becomes, the introduction of gateways inevitably requires certain amounts of investment. Gateways are rationalized only when the investment costs are less than those of standardization or of any other means.

The third way of securing interconnectivity is to set-up a framework in advance for making software compatible. This is a kind of mixture of software conversion, as a gateway technology, and standardization focusing on software. The most famous and successful effort in this direction is OSI. Many software products are now being made under the scheme of the seven-layer OSI reference model. In this context, OSI is coming very close to the ideal of securing interconnectivity. In theory, it is closely located to the old regime of end-to-end integrity. But there are also problems. If OSI has such strength, it must be a very complicated and "heavy" software, not user-friendly and not easy to handle. On the contrary if OSI is only a basic concept and not so "heavy," it cannot contribute to implementing real software products compatible with each other. At any rate, OSI is not an absolute solution to secure interconnectivity.

Alliances among different methods go in the center of Figure 11. This is the forth way for interconnection. As the activities of large customers have been globalized, various kinds of alliances have been introduced. OSS (One Stop Shopping) provision under the collaborative agreements between the leading common carriers was the first step. It has now been enhanced to GAM or JAM agreements and even more formal equity investments. However, alliances may have two completely different faces. If a certain alliance is open to other members and flexible to invite them to join, it may become a public good and succeed in establishing universality, which may function just like standardization. But on the contrary, if a certain alliance is closed and reluctant to accept other members, it may remain a sub-network failing to set-up interconnectivity in a broader context. Judging from the principles of corporate behavior, the latter case is more likely to happen. Alliances tend to be a method for differentiation rather than universality. Therefore, alliances alone cannot solve the interconnectivity problems.

## 10. CONCLUSION

With privatization taking place globally, all networks are actually PNs. Computer technology is allowing carriers to make more efficient use of their networks by keeping their customers away from leased-circuit solutions. But this is taking place mainly in the US right now. There are still dramatic differences even between the US and Japan -- two of the most developed countries in terms of infrastructure. The impact of PNs on the public infrastructure in Japan, and other countries, depends on what defines a PN. Such a definition is very difficult to develop and will vary from country to country. An example of this is seen in the US/Japan comparisons made above. These two countries are similar in many ways, but political, economic, and financial differences are magnified when examined through the scope of the telecommunications infrastructures.

In the future, no single carrier will dominate the converging field of telecommunications and computing. And no single measure can assure world-wide interconnectivity between the variety of public and private networks. The sovereignty of the common carrier, which has lasted about 100 years, is now approaching the end. In its place is a new regime made up of subtle mixture of common carriage and contract carriage which may be the best solution for large customers. However, it is to be noted that simply combining multiple private networks does not necessarily assure interoperability or interconnectivity among private networks. The public network will always have its own advantages and features.

## ENDNOTES

[1] Large-scale and international Value Added Networks fall into this category.

[2] Information & Communications in Japan 1992, InfoCom Research, May 1993.

[3] Intelligent networks were first deployed on a large scale by Sprint with its Virtual Private Network (VPN) service offering; MCI and AT&T followed with Vnet and Software Defined Network (SDN) respectively. SDN became the platform for AT&T's Tariff 12 discount plan.

[4.]It can be argued that ITJ was established as a private network for the trading companies that own it. Mitsubishi, Mitsui, Sumitomo, and Matsushita each has a 9% ownership stake in ITJ. However, the same argument is more difficult to make about IDC. In March of 1984, Great Britain called upon Japan to allow foreign investment in competitors to KDD and threatened to impose sanctions if Japan refused. Ultimately, C&W was allowed to invest in IDC, but what lead to this had more to do with politics than business.

[5.]Noll, Roger G. and Frances M. Rosenbluth, "Telecommunications Policy in Japan and the U.S.: Structure, Process, Outcomes," Center for Economic Policy Research Publ. No. 349, Stanford University, May 1993.

[6.]NTT statistical data.

[7.]This is not to be confused either with the current NTT Corp. or with a subsidiary, NTT PC Communications

[8.]Kokusai Denshin Denwa literally means international telegraph and telephone.

[9.]see footnote 10 below for a fuller explanation

[10.]At the time, the central office-to-end cost for installing telephones was ¥350,000. However, ¥50,000 was charged directly to each subscriber as an installation cost, leaving ¥300,000 to be financed. This amount was divided by 2 so that each bond was valued at ¥150,000, and NTT would pay the other ¥150,000. Depending on the interest rate fluctuation and depreciation schedule, the bond system covered up to 67% of the total construction budget, as mentioned above.

[11.]Koichiro Hayashi participated in this study.

[12.]Wenders, John T. and Bruce L. Egan "The Implications of Economic Efficiency for U.S. Telecommunications Policy" Telecommunications Policy, March 1986.

[13.]Hayashi, Koichiro The Economics of Networking, NTT Publishing, 1989 (in Japanese).

[14.]Noam, Eli "A Theory for the Instability of Public Telecommunications Systems," in Cristiano Antonelli, ed. The Economics of Information Networks, New York: North Holland Press 1992.

[15.]This trend can be compared to the market segmentation structure in Japan, where companies prefer to stay in their own segment, see above.

[16.]Syncordia is apparently now to become part of the BT/MCI alliance and be managed by MCI out of Atlanta.

[17.]AT&T's WorldSource partnership alliance is an example of this trend. So far, AT&T, KDD and Singapore Telecom have announced a venture to provide customers with OSS. There have also been talks of expanding the Franco-German Eunetcom alliance or even making part of WorldSource.

[18.]This is even more of an issue when there are multiple PNs instead of multiple PTT-type configurations.

PRIVATE NETWORKS PUBLIC OBJECTIVES
E. Noam and A. NíShúilleabháin (Editors)

# End-User Networking In Asia

Ken Zita

## 1. INTRODUCTION

Telecommunications has become the strategic supply line for the modern corporation, but many firms have just begun to formalize communications strategies for the Pacific region. While the largest financial services, travel, and energy companies have had corporate networks in Asia for years, others have been less sure about their commitments. In the past, many companies regarded Asia exclusively for low-cost manufacturing and sourcing of materials, not as a group of individual mature markets. But as the boardroom view of the region shifts toward increased localization, alliances, and acquisitions, the corporate communications network must support and anticipate changes in the regional business strategy.

U.S. companies operating in Asia face many new challenges as the regional telecommunications industry undergoes profound change. Not long ago foreign firms were dumbfounded by impenetrable local telephone company bureaucracies, archaic infrastructures and extortionate circuit charges. Now competition is taking hold. Regional telecommunications carriers are leaping directly into the digital era and bringing local facilities in step with global networking standards. Regional GNP growth is forecast at about 5% for 1993, almost twice the world average. Nearly a third of worldwide information technology expenditures will be made in Asia this year. And market liberalization and telecommunications sector reform is redefining competitive trends in almost every major trading nation. Yet unlike the European Community, where economic planning and information networking developments are monitored by the European Commission, Asia has no common market, few similarities in industrial or political organization, and widely divergent values and expectations. Each country has vastly different rules and procedures regulating telecommunications policy, shaping both the scope and flexibility of end-user networking opportunities.

Complexity and composition of the Asian user networks naturally depends on the firm. Very large corporations typically have no choice but to build regional "private networks" consisting of high capacity lines leased from telephone companies. Smaller companies and those new to Asia still rely on dialing directly, which is expensive. Private networks provide considerable economies of scale in reducing the cost of telephone calls -- by as much as a factor of 10 -- as well as enabling data security and technological control. Private nets require field technical staff to manage the equipment, and not all companies can afford the privilege. Until recently, carriers did not have the expertise to manage complicated user networks, and were essentially oblivious to firms' real communications needs. Much of this is changing.   Carriers, traditionally stodgy, self-centered monopolies, are becoming increasingly market-driven.   The turnabout is not exactly altruistic:   with increased supply-side competition, profit margins on basic international telecommunications services are plummeting.   Service providers hope to make up the difference by charging a premium on specialized services such as customized care of high-volume accounts, a high-profile niche known as managed network services (MNS).   Communications managers designing and managing networks in Asia must address two critical questions.   Will the system be managed primarily as a private network, and if so, what are the optimal sites for regional network hubs?   And alternately, should users entrust their networks to carrier managed network service programs?

## 2. NETWORKING OPTIONS

Managed network services involve a global telecommunications carrier taking over some aspects of managing the corporate network, a role characteristically entrusted to in-house telecommunications departments.   Carriers argue that MNS allow users to focus on their core businesses, freeing them from the distraction -- and expense -- of running their own systems. By sharing the intelligence and common resources in the carriers' networks, staff and capital expenses can be cut.

Companies need to determine how much responsibility they are willing entrust to carriers.   MNS helps reduce technical salaries, which in some countries inflate by 15% or more per year.   At the same time, firing experts may seriously diminish the corporation's ability to plot and execute information management strategies into the future.   Similarly, by turning over basic communications operations to carriers, users lose commercial bargaining power.   The cost of high speed private circuits across the Pacific fell on average of 38% in 1992, and this drop will continue.   Companies can always provide cheaper solutions than MNS if they are willing to maintain investment in a private system.

Going it alone means users must decipher a barrage of idiosyncratic regulatory changes in each country in which they operate.   Since market deregulation first took hold in Japan in 1985, changes have been coming fast.   New competitors are proliferating (Australia, Indonesia, Malaysia), restructuring and privatization are pending (Korea, Singapore, Taiwan), and formerly hard-and-fast regulatory rules now shift with the political winds (China, Hong Kong, Thailand).   Keeping up isn't easy.   Users who maintain their own networks need specialists to stay current with market and political changes, or hire consultants who do.

New technologies for corporate networks are also eclipsing many systems in place today. Firms that have installed systems even five or six years ago must decide if they are prepared to make capital investments in the latest generation equipment to upgrade their network architecture.   Most have to do something.   In the 1980s, the Asian corporate network was engineered to send batches of financial and sales data from regional manufacturing sites back to the mainframe and data center in the U.S.   Applications have changed dramatically since then.   Corporate electronic mail and fax traffic is skyrocketing while the proliferation of PCs and "internetworking" of local area networks (LANs) means that companies are distributing computing processing power throughout the organization.   Bridging the gap between the old and new platforms is complicated.   The impending arrival of ATM could mean re-engineering everything in place today.

At issue is how much network self-sufficiency companies require in Asia. If trends in the U.S. market are any indication, the answer is less. U.S. carriers have pioneered "virtual private networks," a form of managed network service. AT&T, MCI, and Sprint all offer volume discounts of up to 22% on international switched calls, location-level billing, credit card calling and unified numbering plans, all consolidated on a single bill -- features too complicated for firms to do on their own. There are two drawbacks. Most companies don't trust virtual networks for anything but plain old telephone calls; data communications still get transferred on private networks. Second, placing voice calls to Asia on virtual networks siphons off traffic that would be used to cost-justify expensive dedicated circuits for data.

MNS offerings are growing increasingly powerful. New features over and above existing virtual services include private circuit monitoring, fault restoration to ISDN, one-stop shopping, outsourcing, on-site technical supervision, and soon, management "visibility" to LAN servers and desktop applications. Nevertheless, carriers expertise for operating regional user networks remains questionable. Carriers can manage circuits and data communications equipment well enough, but their ability to support higher protocol layers is suspect. Even as carrier value-added services grow more complex, emphasis is on connectivity and transport, not on applications interoperability and systems integration. Thus, users seeking comprehensive facilities and network management solutions in Asia -- that is, control and surveillance equal to what they would provide themselves -- rightly question if carriers are up to the task. Enterprise network management strategies seem to run in cycles, and the prevailing wisdom is that users are willing to entertain outsourcing and managed network services as a serious consideration -- to the carriers' delight, and possibly to the users' ultimate frustration. Many users would prefer to find a networking services company that can, as several Asia/Pacific network managers have said, "take the whole thing off our hands."

## 3. MANAGED NETWORK SERVICES

The big global carriers, especially AT&T and British Telecom, hope to convince users that virtual networks and other managed network solutions are ideal for the Asia/Pacific region. AT&T recently launched WorldSource, a $1 billion joint venture with Singapore Telecom and Japan's KDD, targeting corporate networks in Asia, and BT is extending the reach of Syncordia, its managed network services and outsourcing subsidiary. Both aim to take over day-to-day management of companies' "core" communications services: regular telephone calls and high volume private leased circuits, bot not actual applications such as accounting or internetworking between computers.

AT&T WorldSource president Simon Krieger says companies believe that the telecommunications network is a strategic resource that has potential for them to gain competitive advantage. But few companies are interested in merely handing over a strategic resource to someone else. "What they do want is to hand over the hassles of managing the network resources," Krieger says. These hassles include negotiating with foreign service providers and running humdrum operations like adding and deleting users, monitoring circuits and equipment and making sure communications are uncongested and static-free. The theory is that when companies are free of these burdens, network managers can concentrate on serving the corporate strategic vision, rather than get bogged down in managing operations. How much users are willing to pay for the convenience of managed network services remains to be seen. Approximately 1%-2% of a major multinational corporation's costs can be attributed directly to telecommunications, and carriers reckon that firms will spend more for the right services. Premiums could range from 8%-15% over standard tariff rates, depending on the features negotiated in the service level agreement.

## 4. REGIONAL PRIVATE NETWORKS

Despite the aggressive supply-side push by carriers toward managed network services, traditional private line networks still dominate corporate communications in Asia. Companies deploy a variety of private network designs to serve their Asia Pacific communications needs, reflecting regional presence, network applications, and business growth scenarios. Some firms are content with simple star configuration networks, sending regional low-speed data into a rudimentary network hub, and employing a single high bandwidth circuit across the Pacific. Other companies, dependent on transaction processing, heavy file transfer, or financial data management, are more inclined to duplicate domestic information systems architectures with complex, redundant network topologies. Often regional facilities have grown up in piecemeal fashion: circuits are added when new offices or factories require direct communications with headquarters, with little consideration for a regional plan. The result may be an inefficient, hodgepodge network. As traffic to and within the region increases, weaknesses in design quickly become apparent. To redesign the network, firms need to determine what degree of support and compatibility is required at Asian sites. Today many companies are installing global network platforms with consistent hardware and applications at all locations. This continuity comes at a cost. Creating a universal management environment may require significant upgrade of existing equipment, and a "highest common denominator" approach may not fit the traffic or business requirements in the region. For example, a company may be formalizing its domestic U.S. solutions for LAN/WAN integration, but in Asia, where PC and LAN penetration is limited, the bandwidth support and processing power may not be needed. The issue of network uniformity is complicated further by wide disparities in local infrastructure capabilities and competitive provisioning options. Private networks in Asia characteristically have two tiers, the "backbone" and the "outback." The backbone is the high-speed transit circuits connecting state-of-the-art facilities in the developed countries -- Australia, Hong Kong, Japan and Singapore -- while the outback, or poor quality networks, is almost everywhere else. (See Table 1.) Communications managers sometimes complain that 90% of their traffic is on the backbone circuits, but that 90% of their management headaches come from providing service to the region's developing countries.

Another important consideration in formulating the network topology is a firm's data processing strategy. Some companies, striving to achieve better MIS economies through consolidation of data centers, may attempt to harness "night MIPs" on home-office computers. For example, a subsidiary in Thailand may poll a mainframe in Texas during the Pacific business day when the machine is underutilized, thereby consolidating control at headquarters and reducing regional support costs. Harnessing U.S. or European processing facilities generally implies bigger network transport capacity, which is costly. It also demands a high degree of resiliency and reliability from international circuits and both factors tend to make communications managers nervous. Regional data centers, by contrast, require trained personnel -- a resource in acutely short supply.

Table 1

# Summary Regulatory Matrix
## First Tier "Backbone" Countries

| | PTT Restructured | Foreign Equity (Basic) | Competition in Voice | Competition in Data | Alternate Domestic Carriers | Private Network Interconn. | Shared Use of PLC | Private Satellite Earth Station |
|---|---|---|---|---|---|---|---|---|
| Australia | ○ | 49% | ○ | ○ | 1, (12) | ○ | ○ | ○ |
| Hong Kong | ● | 100% | ● | ○ | 1 | ○ | ● | ○ |
| Japan | ○ | 33% | ○ | ○ | 73 | ○ | ◐ | ○ |
| New Zealand | ○ | 49.9%* | ○ | ○ | 1, (6?) | ○ | ○ | ○ |
| Singapore | ○ | 20%? | ● | ○ | 0 | ○ | ● | ● |

Note: Australia and New Zealand allow resale.

## Second Tier "Outback" Countries

| | PTT Restructured | Foreign Equity (Basic) | Competition in Voice | Competition in Data | Alternate Domestic Carriers | Private Network Interconn. | Shared Use of PLC | Private Satellite Earth Station |
|---|---|---|---|---|---|---|---|---|
| Korea | ○ | 0% | ○ | ○ | 1 | ○ | ○ | ● |
| Taiwan | ◐ | 0% | ● | ○* | 0 | ● | ● | ● |
| China | ◐ | 0% | ● | ● | 0 | ● | ● | ○ |
| Indonesia | ◐ | 0% | ● | ● | 1 | ● | ● | ○ |
| Malaysia | ○ | 25% | ◐ | ◐ | 1 | ● | ○* | ○* |
| Philippines | ● | 40% | ○ | ○ | 50* | ● | ● | ○ |
| Thailand* | ● | 49% | ◐ | ○* | 2* | ◐ | ● | ○ |
| Vietnam | ● | 0% | ● | ● | 0 | ● | ◐ | ○* |

○ = Yes   ● = No   ◐ = Limited or In Transition   * = Restrictions Apply

## 5. SAMPLE NETWORKS

Companies develop unique topologies to support regional networks, and the following examples illustrate three basic designs. A simple and reliable network topology, in this case supporting a major hotel chain, is engineered for both high redundancy and maximum flexibility. The architecture is a physical ring (see figure 1), linking the U.S. with Japan, Hong Kong, Singapore, and Australia, and back again to the States. Redundancy is high because traffic can be routed in either direction on the backbone circuits. Under normal operating conditions, primary traffic from Singapore to points south flows through Australia, and primary traffic from Hong Kong north flows through Japan; the circuit between Singapore and Hong Kong is largely quiescent. All sites on this network have the same relative importance, and the probability of failure on a link is the same at each node. As designed, the system can tolerate any single circuit fault.

Flexibility was a central consideration in the design for two reasons: the locations of the reservation offices are subject to change, and the company's plans for new hotels are dynamic, with many projects pending. By establishing a stable backbone, adding or deleting sites is straightforward. Companies that cannot be certain of the full scope of business operations need to devise an architecture that allows flexibility without significant penalty.

Figure 1

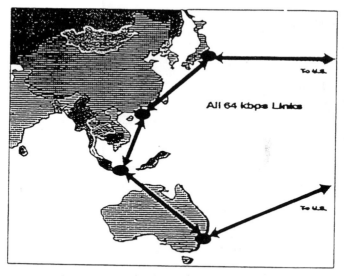

Another common network configuration is for firms to run dedicated circuits into Japan, which often has special traffic demands and applications support requirements, plus a separate star-hub network serving other areas in the Pacific.

Figure 2 below shows the network schematic for a large conglomerate. The Japan-U.S. traffic is routed over fractional T1 circuits (256 Kbps) to a site near the U.S. headquarters data center, and redundant routing is available between Japan and the southeast Asia network node in the event of a serious network outage. The Hong Kong-U.S. route terminates at a second site near the headquarters for security. Hong Kong is the primary feeder site for central and south Asia, funneling traffic from 13 countries on separate 64 Kbps circuits. Interestingly, because of the time zone differences between Asia and North America, peak daytime traffic within Asia -- for instance, between Japan and Hong Kong, which for this firm is a high volume corridor -- can be routed via the U.S. over the fast-packet (frame relay) network, more cheaply than though direct IDDD dialing. The reverse scenario from the U.S. to Asia applies as well, whereby routing domestic U.S. calls through the corporate network -- via Asia -- is in some instances less expensive than dialing over a domestic U.S. VPN. Some companies administer circuits to Japan as a discrete sub-network, with connectivity to a second, southeast Asian hub only for backup.

Figure 2

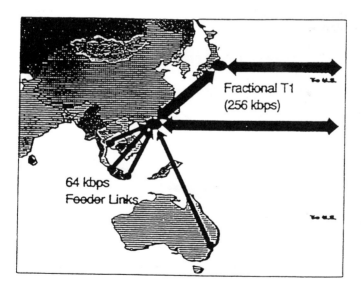

A third scenario, supporting extensive manufacturing, sales, and component sourcing operations, is engineered for high volume data and video conference, with diverse routing throughout. Trans-pacific circuits from Japan are twin 128 Kbps lines, terminating at separate domestic sites. Secondary circuits from Hong Kong and Australia use only 64 Kbps. The company believes that the 64 Kbps capacity will double by year-end 1993 (and that the 128 Kbps channels will grow to 192 Kbps or more), mainly because of increased traffic accelerated by the deployment of TCP/IP-based applications. The company has a number of data centers throughout the region, though Singapore acts as a client/server hub for terminal applications in four different countries: India, Indonesia, Malaysia and Thailand. Hong Kong is a hub for the Philippines and three locations in mainland China, which are triangulated with domestic leased lines -- a complex matter in the People's Republic. Most countries on the network have T1/E1 access domestically.

While each network has unique characteristics, some common themes are apparent. After analyzing the local competitive environment and internal traffic requirements, each firm identified the need for a physical ring, and the network topologies reflect their respective variations. The hotel's operations are distributed evenly throughout the region, the conglomerate has considerable traffic between its two primary hubs, and the manufacturer has immense requirements in Japan. The manufacturer added smaller backup circuits for key sites, while the hotel chain built in backup capability with a stable, reliable configuration.

Figure 3

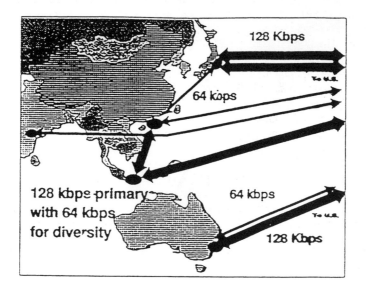

## 6. HUBBING OPTIONS

Selecting an Asian hub site has become a dark science. The options used to be simple, if only because they were so limited. Firms had facilities in Japan and, separately, a hub for the rest of Asia in Hong Kong. With the profound, consistent growth in Asia's economies, the dynamics of regional trade are shifting, and with them, the need for more flexible networking arrangements. Singapore is now the gateway to the vibrant ASEAN region, Australia is claiming its place in the Pacific Rim, and even the stalwart PATS in Korea and Taiwan have begun to recognize that the continued growth in national wealth depends on liberalization of telecoms solutions for large users. Competition among countries -- and not merely among carriers -- makes the choice tangled. Government tax concessions and R&D incentives are bandied about in the same breadth as leased circuit break-even economies and public data network (PDN) processable packet size.

Sorting through hubbing options is complicated, and no reliable rules apply. Likely hub sites may be management offices or large manufacturing facilities, though network hub technology sometimes resides at an entirely independent location. As the preceding section showed, companies will often use a hierarchical network of primary hubs (where multiple circuits or a regional data center resides), and secondary hubs (for redundancy, low volume traffic routing, or regions with new business development). Head office politics sometimes play a big role. The need to establish a local "showcase" office can outweigh traditional networking concerns such as traffic patterns, technical support, circuit costs, and so forth. Hong Kong is still the preferred hub location measured in terms of total regional network hub sites, with Singapore nipping after its heels; Japan and Australia are scrambling to expand minority shares. Assessing infrastructure fundamentals in each country is critical. A few general parameters that are especially important include competitive access and flexible interconnection. Users learn quickly which regulations are "real," and which can be stretched or broken. Only Japan and Hong Kong have direct fiber links and diverse fiber routing with North America. Singapore has just recently gained fiber connectivity via Brunei, and Australia added optical links only in late 1993. Additional considerations include terminal interconnection procedures and restrictions; direct access to satellite facilities, earth station ownership; and local definitions for "group VANs" and circuit reuse or resale.

Generally speaking, circuit pricing remains the weightiest concern in hub site selection. The cost of inter-regional circuits are characteristically equal to or only marginally less expensive than trans-Pacific Routes, and aggregate discounts have been a strong incentive for establishing a hub. Carriers in Hong Kong, Singapore, Japan, and Australia all offer volume and aggregate circuit pricing schemes. Most are encouraging migration to digital circuits and considerable economies can be achieved at higher line speeds; 64 Kbps DS0 channels have become the basic building blocks of regional enterprise backbone networks. Countervailing accepted logic (at least as it is espoused by the U.S. carriers), the U.S.-to-anywhere portion of an Asian network is not necessarily the cheapest leg of the journey. See Table 2 on the following page.

Table 2

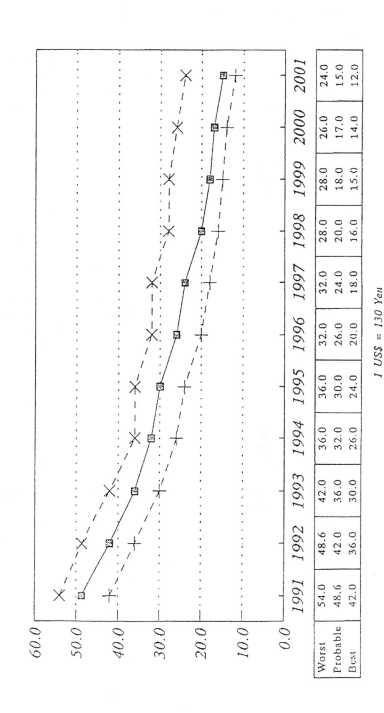

# JAPAN-U.S.
## T1 HALF CIRCUIT CHARGE PROJECTION
*(thousands $US per month)*

|  | 1991 | 1992 | 1993 | 1994 | 1995 | 1996 | 1997 | 1998 | 1999 | 2000 | 2001 |
|---|---|---|---|---|---|---|---|---|---|---|---|
| Worst | 54.0 | 48.6 | 42.0 | 36.0 | 36.0 | 32.0 | 32.0 | 28.0 | 28.0 | 26.0 | 24.0 |
| Probable | 48.6 | 42.0 | 36.0 | 32.0 | 30.0 | 26.0 | 24.0 | 20.0 | 18.0 | 17.0 | 15.0 |
| Best | 42.0 | 36.0 | 30.0 | 26.0 | 24.0 | 20.0 | 18.0 | 16.0 | 15.0 | 14.0 | 12.0 |

*1 US$ = 130 Yen*

☓ *Worst* ⊞ *Probable* ＋ *Best*

*Source: LYNX Technologies, Inc.*

### 6.1. Hub Choices

Hong Kong, still very much the Pearl of Asia, has long been the preferred regional networking center, and commands some 60% market share of Asian MNC hubs. Uncertainty over the Colony's political future after its June 1997, reunification with the PRC leaves some communications managers wondering if their investments will be safe. Several firms have pulled hubs out of Hong Kong, notably Reuters and Federal Express, but they are clearly the exception to the rule. Most China watchers concur that the changes pending in Hong Kong will be more cultural and political than economic: few believe that the transition of sovereignty will impact foreign business operations in a material way. Popular opinion actually maintains that because Hong Kong is the undisputed gateway to China, the importance of Hong Kong as a telecommunications hub will actually increase, as the economy on the mainland continues to boom.

More pressing problems for network managers in Hong Kong include soaring inflation (perhaps 13% in 1992), extremely high staff turnover, and escalating technical staff salaries and bonuses. At the same time, the advantages of Hong Kong remain: general business practices are highly efficient, and the local telephone company, Hong Kong Telephone, is highly responsive to MNC planning needs. Further, taxes are lowest in the region: 16.5% for corporations, 15% for individuals. Whereas Hong Kong is the gateway to China, Singapore is the window on ASEAN (Singapore, Indonesia, Malaysia, Philippines, Thailand, and Brunei). As such, many companies are designing networks to leverage the advantages of each site. Singapore is actively courting hubbing business, hoping to capitalize on the perceived political instability in China -- and the "dirty, disorderly and crime-ridden" qualities of Hong Kong life. Singapore seems intent on becoming the Switzerland of Asia, a manicured, tightly managed financial center with calculating government oversight. Of the four major hub sites, Singapore has by far the most aggressive government incentive programs for attracting business, coordinated by its Economic Development Board and National Computer Board. Firms can obtain generous tax holidays for committing to R&D and local investment. While Singapore Telecom has long shouldered a reputation for inflexibility, the tide may be changing. The recent corporatization of the carrier suggests that it has the potential to become more sensitive to the market, both at home and abroad. Like Hong Kong, Singapore has high technical staff turnover and fast rising salaries.

As the most powerful economy in Asia, the largest financial center, and the country with the highest volume of inbound and outbound traffic, Japan is also a critical hub site for Asia. The difficulty of establishing facilities is cost. While international tariffs out of Japan have become competitive with regional counterparts, the general costs of doing business locally has not. High real estate, technical support and labor rates far exceed any other region in the world. On the up side, Japan has extensive competition in services provision, and technical standards are unparalleled. Companies bound to Japan have begun to move data centers and network control centers to suburban locations, south along Tokyo Bay and to Yokohama, to defray exorbitant overhead expenses in Tokyo.

Australia has intensified its bid to become a regional hubbing anchor, underscoring the national commitment to the economies of the Pacific; Australia's trade with Asia now exceeds that with North America and Europe. The government offers modest tax and investment concessions, incentives which help mitigate the high standard corporate tax rate of 39% (the maximum rate for individuals is over 48%). Extensive fiber facilities into Australia will not be available until 1994, but good satellite coverage is in place today. Some user questions how Australia, some 4,500 miles distant from both Hong Kong and Tokyo, could serve as a hub. In the reality of information networks, however, regional physical distances are arguably irrelevant. Telstra is clearly the dominant carrier in Australia, though Optus, the newcomer led by BellSouth, will be sure to concentrate on attracting MNC customers from its home territory in the U.S.

Both Malaysia and Taiwan hope to become popular corporate network hub sites. Malaysia is situated strategically in ASEAN's "growth triangle" and government planners believe that Kuala Lumpur can rival Singapore as the local of choice for regional headquarters. Market liberalization is encouraging the emergence of a second national carrier, Time Engineering, and Telekom Malaysia is keen to capture international revenues it is losing to Singapore. Taiwan is poised for fundamental market restructuring in 1994, beginning with corporatization of the national carrier, the Directorate General of Telecommunications (DGT), and redefinition of network access parameters and opportunities for value-added services. With foreign reserves topping $80 billion, the world's eighth largest stock exchange, and a government eager to earn political recognition to match its economic might, Taiwan will soon cultivate a broader regional presence in telecommunications.

## 7. CONCLUSION

Users have no clear cut choice for networking in Asia. Firms inclined to trim staff or rely on outside experts might prefer an increased role for carriers through managed network services. But management must be convinced that agreements among several international telephone companies can do a better job running their communications than in-house experts can themselves. Other firms are keen to maximize technological control and to exploit falling circuits charges by continuing to manage their own networks. When the corporate business -- and the telecommunications manager's job -- depends on keeping things working, many are still reluctant to delegate core operations to a carrier. Because competition among countries is so intense, users are in an excellent position to negotiate for discounts and special treatment. In addition to pricing flexibility on published and group discount tariffs, users can bargain for circuit service level agreements, traffic engineering studies, tax concessions, facilities management terms and conditions and flexibility on terminal interconnection. By the mid-1990s, basic public networking facilities in Asia's largest information ports will be comparatively equal, and even variances in circuit pricing will cease to be a competitive variable. The real differentiating factors will lie in international alliances, networking management and outsourcing capabilities, customer service and local.

# The Viability of Policy Separation of Liberalized Value-Added Services From Monopoly Infrastructure

Richard A. Kramer

## 1. INTRODUCTION

The problem of policy separation of a liberalized upper layer of value-added services from a monopolistic infrastructure layer rests on political definitions of increasingly blurry boundaries. Liberalized VANs suppliers clearly benefit markets and the TOs with whom they compete. Infrastructure monopolies are more problematic, as they are clearly not sustainable in many network segments. To get effective and viable separation, one of two courses must be chosen. One is to reaffirm the infrastructure monopoly, divorced from the business of competing in VANs markets, to act as a unified bit carrier. This is unlikely to work. Technology advances such as ATM, INs, and desktop switching may help. Another choice is to rethink and strengthen interconnection policies, moving them in the direction of cooperative, rather than competitive efforts. This may, in the end, be too technologically complex. In either case, the incentives inherent in the system, and the information asymmetry between TO and market entrant must be addressed.

The rise of new regulatory bodies and new technologies have led to a significant rethinking of definitions of public and private networks, of added-value and infrastructure in the context of European telecommunications.

New and established players alike recognize that distinctions between public and private networks are arbitrary. All networks are "private": they are by definition closed systems. There cannot be an uncompleted link in an operating network. The "public" simply refers to the level of access granted to or ownership of such a network.[1]

As for infrastructure, the common transportation analogy should be abandoned: it is quaint to think of data files as trucks and voice traffic as (more numerous) cars, traveling through circles (switches), but almost anything can be a road for the right sort of vehicle. Roads are technologically far simpler (though perhaps as labor intensive); a much more limited range of environments can function as telecommunications networks. Road traffic does not imply a natural role for a systems integrator, a support for monopoly infrastructure provision.

The definition of infrastructure is central to the question of separation. If it consists only of physical network components: transmission conduit, switches and customer premises equipment, then the "value-added" layer begins with the addition of software to carry and switch traffic. This view implies that POTS, or simply switching should be thought of as adding value. (Value is added everywhere along the supply chain). Resellers of leased lines (such as the hundreds of "carriers" in the US) add value by dividing them among multiple users.[2] The service is the same--bandwidth between points--but value has been increased, measured by the excess revenues above the cost of facilities rental. Taking this minimalist approach makes things clearer but does not help. Viewing POTS as a value-added service is largely an anomaly of regulatory battles waged between IBM and AT&T in the 1970s and ongoing in the EC today. While the slippery slope argument (that it is impossible to functionally divide the switching of voice services from that of data service, and hence both represent value-added to the communications process) has meant the reality in a nation such as the UK is often *a shared, arguably instinctive understanding, of the boundary between basic voice services and value-added services.* That liberalized upper layer boundary is often set (with numerous exceptions) beyond basic voice services.[3] *This is where politics and confusion set in. Are we talking about a technical definition: point of software control; a regulatory definition: point of control over services; or a business definition: what level of control will users pay for?*

## 2. AGREEING ON LIBERALIZED VANs

A clear need for new products to replace telephone service as the main engine of growth provides incentives to encourage innovation to monopoly infrastructure and VANs providers, to invite competition (admittedly tightly managed, and at the margins) into the market. Some feel that "Technology has bred more ideas than the market can absorb...nowadays the industry could meet almost any presently conceivable need with technology already on the market or in the lab."[4] VANs suppliers play a critical role in conceptualizing these needed new products.

- VANs suppliers often target niche markets which TOs overlook. In contrast, TOs and their suppliers excel largely at conceiving and implementing technologies which improve price/performance of existing core products.[5] For example, they are driving customized corporate networking solutions.
- VANs suppliers stimulate demand for network services in the developing world near saturation. (And as the French have argued in promotion of the Minitel, a macroeconomic level competitive VANs supply provides entrepreneurial stimulus to economy.)
- So long as the infrastructure monopoly holds firm the scope of VANs competition can be limited by the cost of bandwidth or interconnection. And even if the market moves from monopoly to oligopoly, carriers have common incentives sell installed bandwidth at premium rates.

The arguments need not be taken to a greater level of detail to make a strong case for a liberalization. This case may be lost on TOs, who are more defensive about the associated costs. The TO mindset views customer specific networks as an imposition on the neat ideal of maximum economies of scale, via uniform generic service offerings. TOs fear competition in their core products at lower unit cost, which require special attention and disrupt their operations-intensive organizations.[6]

## 3. QUESTIONS OF SUSTAINABILITY

While the VANs market is far from perfectly competitive for the reasons mentioned in the preceding paragraph, there is substantial entry by rival suppliers. A monopoly over VANs is not sustainable, implying by extension, that fragmentation of an infrastructure monopoly cannot be prevented, even in the most rigidly controlled environments.[7] The benefits of simultaneous experiments with many approaches (for example, private networking) which follow a more rigorous cost-justification basis should not divert attention from the historical reasons for infrastructure monopolies: cost, complexity, and public service.

Networks support as a set of services, of highly differentiated commodities, not a single service or market. Network markets benefit from the presence of competitive VANs suppliers, (a relatively recent and limited phenomenon) as well as efforts of TOs.[8] In this broad spectrum, the TOs are the only ones with a (near-complete) picture of the costs and issues of all the disparate network submarkets.[9] The driving force behind models of network fragmentation, network tipping, or segmentation, is that the median network service cannot accommodate all users. But this view of centrifugalism, of traffic specialization, of the movement of networks away from a core service or center, focuses primarily on the specialization of providers, not the concurrent specialization of infrastructure monopolists. Users are returning to public network-based solutions as competition among VPN suppliers and bandwidth-on-demand promises reduce networking costs. (especially as the highly variable cost of a key component, leased lines falls). Hence, the *flexibility* of public systems (all too often absent from theories of network evolution) provides a clear path out of the specialization-generalization conundrum. Not all monopoly carriers are sluggish bureaucrats.[10] There is a countervailing trend of specialization *within* the public network, as CPE functionality migrates to the PSTN.

The liberalized upper layer is where the greatest profit margins and business development incentives are. Accordingly, the EC is backing off cost-based or cost-oriented tariffs as a hard and fast rule. Ramsey (value of service) pricing is needed to fund development of new applications for services like ISDN and to stave off competitors. Network economics are becoming three dimensional: tariffs are calculated in distance, time and also in bit rate--*new parameters of choice are emerging at the upper layers, which touch the infrastructure as well.* A world of pure bit carriage by comparatively dumb networks has already begun, though this direction may be reversed in the battle between ATM and intelligent networking decides.'[11]

TOs themselves can be as dynamic as entrepreneurial VANs suppliers, leveraging their resources and unique position from which to extend what entrepreneurs invent to the wider market. This has already happened where competition has galvanized TOs, (BT, and the French, Dutch, German, and Spanish carriers have shown tremendous progress). Moreover, TOs need not be the source of all creative ideas to be dynamic. External forces are pressing them to innovate alongside the VANs entrepreneurs. Other forces on the TOs include:

- **Equipment suppliers,** for whom the TOs represent by far the largest customers, need to sell new products and work through shortening product life cycles.
- **Regulators,** who by extending the like of the TOs historical mission have increased pressure for customer satisfaction and profitability.

- **TO's themselves,** who are in the midst of a dual cultural change which has profound implications for their future form - they are facing up to both liberalization of domestic markets and the necessary globalization of operations.[12]
- **Users,** whose increasingly sophisticated demands are finally receiving closer TO attention at the very point they are becoming a competitive threat to TOs.

The TOs view their market position as secure, as new configurations of hybrid networks still show a continued reliance on public infrastructure. How does one capture the dynamism of the liberalized upper layer - of the VANs providers, suppliers, users, etc.—in a monopoly infrastructure? Does one need to? There is clear reason for liberalizing the upper layer, despite TO objections yet there is still some hope for TOs. Now we examine the experience of *uniting* the layers, and whether bundling creates superior value for customers.

## 4. INTERCONNECTION AND INCENTIVES

An important point often lost in the debates over liberalizing infrastructure monopolies is the lack of a solid conceptual or legal argument for forcing a non-monopolistic firm to interconnect its competitors.[13]  Once monopolies are lost, interconnection becomes more difficult. Why should TOs be required to serve their competitors as customers, especially if they are not acting in part as public trustees? What kind of service can those competitors expect to get? Under ONA, those competitors have been given a choice of the status quo or paying higher tariffs to develop innovative offerings.[14] With ONP, the TOs have only just begun to price access in a more cost-oriented direction, and have slowed the implementation process through the ONP Committees and ETSI.[15]

The resistance to providing economic interconnection for rivals is understandably powerful and diffuse, coming from shareholders, government regulators, unions (protecting jobs) and often short-sightedly equipment manufacturers. New entrants pale in influence, and users straddle the fence because they cannot afford to be entirely hostile to the TOs, on whom they still rely. New entrants who still rely heavily on TO plant leave the TOs in control of market direction (BT is the Dutch PTT's largest customer). The difficulties of creating a web of interoperable systems, a network of networks, through interconnection

There is an added danger that interconnection may reduce competition by encouraging co-operative linkages -- suited to today's accepted business wisdom of specialization in "core" activities -- rather than end-to-end rivalry. The TOs are relatively happy to allow a competitive supply of VANs so long as they retain control over terms of network access and so long as there are only partial or specialized network solutions in the market, the separations process will rely on interconnect policies. Interconnection needs to be rethought. Can the process move from an extension of TO market power to progressive, cooperative effort not dominated by a single entity? Does this demand an industrial policy concerning access charges imposed from above. The political struggle over interconnection has not been pressed upon the main operators, nor has it been presented as beneficial and in their interest. *This is the starting point for the debate -- in the present system, separations are contentious because no one has an incentive for interoperabtlity.* This is partly due to capture of the regulators by the TOs, and also reflects the TOs aggregation of technical expertise about the network.

One recent paper from Cable & Wireless proposed a changing framework for interconnection, based on standard PSTN and leased line tariffs, indexed to the degree of service universality.[16] However, the authors admit that cost allocation problems are increasing, and suggest that the move to broadband networks may change the generally stable relationship between carriers, suppliers, and then customers. Following this line of thinking, there appears again to be two paths to making greatest use of the existing infrastructures. If interconnect policies can be established to encourage duplication, then the thorny policy questions of cost allocation are only temporary ones. Perhaps the Japanese approach? Or, if interconnect tariffs are set indexed to publish PSTN tariffs, there is probably less chance that benefits will be passed on to consumers (since incentives are increased for all parties to keep PSTN tariffs high) but a greater likelihood that the "public" network will be used.

## 5. LINES IN THE SAND?

What are the criteria for separate layers? One is whether services are infrastructure independent or transparent. If not, (as is usually the case) then their existence is determined by how networks are structured - standards, interfaces, architectures. The ability to define criteria for network access furthers the already tremendous market power of infrastructure prov. Even in the UK, where this situation is changing, new service providers still depend inescapably upon BT's technology decisions. This is the crux of a nasty dilemma. Guaranteed an infrastructure monopoly, the providers have little incentive to upgrade the network without competing for the value added portion. And as is well understood, the more it is allowed to provide, the less incentive it has to allow others to do the same. Standards interoperability, a common network architecture are all subject to political forces. Only applications for which there is a proven demand are exceptions to these rules. In Europe, political programmes such as RACE had to lead only where others would follow, and were shifted by political fiat towards funding applications experiments, after working to publicize the merits of advanced communications networks. The RACE example underscores the fact that regulation only poorly anticipates demand for services. Proactive standards in advance of investments in technology development, such as GSM, may lead to later problems. The dividing line will always be capricious, depending on the investment paths ahead of, and constituencies behind each service. This is so even in the much-heralded competitive UK market, where Oftel's pronouncements from on high show that the market is far from being "deregulated." Mercury's creation, RPI-x, the Duopoly Review decision, and so on were all products of intense political negotiations.

One possible solution is to have performance targets, such as a detailed schedule of infrastructure upgrades, which all providers would then refer to. Such attempts at forecasting have a mixed history at best.[17] An added danger highlighted by forecasting problems is the lack of applications developed to date to take advantage of the existing infrastructure. ISDN investments in France and Germany have shifted towards funding applications development. In the US CATV is the only broadband service which has interested the mass market. Most traditional telecommunications service providers have been criticized for standing too far from the needs of the user, but without taking the supply-side approach TOs may not be positioned to satisfy rapidly expanding and shifting user requirements. TOs need to anticipate market behaviors which have made ISDN slow to take off while increasing traffic and profitable installations dramatically through fax services. This is another old dilemma, which brings out the contradictions between complexity/uncertainty on one hand and system stability on the other. There is no way to accurately forecast the future evolutionary path of the network, and yet there are numerous parties with a tremendous investment in maintaining its stability and growth.

Had there been a massive investment in broadband in the last five years, the results would have been disastrous -- a platform with few applications to run over it, with users clamoring for lower tariffs and greater flexibility for their own specialized needs. Indeed, capital budgets have been falling. Users in Europe have not yet decided whether to be telcos themselves or to nudge TOs in a more efficient direction. As users win the freedom to pursue other options, mapping out long-term infrastructure investment will become even more problematic. They will want a secure public access network as a primary, not a secondary resource, as voice VPNs grow in prominence.

Many, if not most, firms already rely heavily on public networks alongside their own private systems, at least for backup. More efficient private networks would require fewer leased lines, (and reduce TO revenues), but using public network based systems, for shared backup facilities also provides cost savings. In many cases, the costlier status quo will be favored over the uncertainties inherent in new and less well tested systems.

Even where capacity is provided by two or more public access carriers, smaller carriers are often simply reselling lines leased from the dominant provider. Mercury's success has come as much from second sourcing for BT customer as from undercutting BT tariffs. While BT cannot prevent the former, indeed may not want to, (it gives them a backup as well) it has attacked the latter via rebalancing, shifting the burden onto rental and connection charges for residential consumers.

Private VANs providers cannot afford to pay more to TOs for enhanced functionality they do not need, or that replicates their own business; they need to mix and match network functionalities. More important rivals may prefer to share in the TOs economies of scope rejecting a separation which leaves them paying for every basic service element individually if a bundled, yet flexible service comes at a lower price. As flat growth in voice telephony leads TOs to search for new revenue streams, they become ever less likely to relinquish VANs opportunities to private suppliers. Unsurprisingly European TOs are eager to expand the definition of reserved or universal service to encompass more than basic voice telephony, to contain attacks from competitive access providers or regulators. But these political definitions poorly recognise the impact of new functionality in the network. For example, ISDN creates a problem in the integration of voice, a reserved service, and data, a liberalized service, on the same indistinguishable conduit. ONP is raising similar sticky problems. The advocates of unusual service regimes advance several powerful arguments:

- The public service goals of universality require a system of social subsidies Monopoly provision, it is argued, is needed to fund them. Any alteration of this arrangement raised the difficult issue of withdrawing "acquired advantages" from established players.
- Fragmentation of service provision saps the critical mass of revenues needed to fund development of advanced broadband infrastructures, which require long-range deployment schedules.
- Existing investments (funded by taxpayers) must be amortized. New providers are not eager to assume the cost burdens of serving all users who want access to their service.

- Infrastructure providers typically do not offer to rewire the nation. They look either to make use of existing facilities such as cable television networks, or to wire urban business corridors with MANs and WANs where concentration of users is greatest.

Eastern Europe provides an exceptional case: advanced services are being deployed with little reference to largely obsolete and unreliable monopolies, but again, no one provider can rewire over a dozen nations alone. A pure transmission infrastructure might be controlled by a number of relatively equal smaller specialized VANs suppliers, with a centralized firm offering basic voice services and selling bandwidth. Rival infrastructures seems less likely. Indeed, to put the debate in its proper context: most nations -- developed as well as developing -- cannot afford one viable infrastructure. The US and UK, embarrassment of riches, are talking about multiple infrastructure alternatives. (Note that the US market is unusual in the separation of TOs from CATV provision, (unlike Germany, France, Japan and so on). *Have we overestimated the benefits of alternative infrastructures, especially the cost savings over tried and true technologies and architectures? Is this a money pit, similar to the new technologies which were touted in the 1970s and 1980s?* The virtual invocation of the mystical benefits of competition so often heard in the US has not reached Europe, despite proselytisers of every stripe (most commonly the Union Jack). The costs of competition come down to the simple economics of constructing alternative infrastructures.

The Eastern Europe example highlights a critical problem: Where will the capital needed to construct alternative infrastructures come from? The myth of a recession-proof telecommunications sector is gradually showing its face: users are demanding action on inflated tariffs, which do not reflect productivity gains, and the recession is limiting spending on services, as well as forcing TOs to grow less dependent on national infrastructures, entering more speculative and competitive global markets. Suppliers' order books are always one year behind. What regulators approved cannot necessarily be extended in linear fashion into more turbulent and uncertain times (we see this reflected initially in the equipment industry, in the pressures faced by all the major CO vendors).

An added pressure is the sunk costs in plant, which suggests that changes in technology and markets cannot easily displace existing infrastructure. The lessons of the UK market, where infrastructure competition was introduced a decade ago, are highly instructive, and outline the fundamental economic reality of infrastructure provision. Barring any solutions as much delayed as discussed -- ISDN, IBN's, convergence, fiber-to-the-home, PCN, GSM, radio tails, DBS, cable telephony, and whatever else is on the horizon—local loop competition is developing only slowly, in pockets. Mercury has been building its network for ten years, yet still hands over 50% of its calls to BT. CATV telephony (where the UK is considered in the vanguard) also faces similar pressures. The teleports and CAPs in the US are targeting only high volume users which cost justify plant investments. This experience shows that VANs services which have mass market aspirations are likely to remain dependent upon lines leased from TOs. Competitive efforts in local loop provision are backed by a fraction of the investment already made in the current network. Some believe that a massive writeoff of existing plant is imminent, but this would cripple TO financing. Hence, TOs must protect infrastructure investments, and resist separation of layers, unless assured a role in both areas.

Another issue worth raising is whether today's infrastructure is already obsolete. The TOs are clearly not prepared for a rapid depreciation of existing plant; they cannot afford to absorb such losses as future returns become less certain, squeezed between the pressures of

414

global recession and technology advances (where workstations may soon replace CO switches). Is there a middle ground in deploying advanced functionality for preemptive cost-savings? Cost-savings are glimmers of such discontinuous changes which may make the task of separation easier. It is now possible to program a PC to perform the same function as a PBX, to switch traffic, such as providing public access to control over the switching function of the infrastructure. So long as that control is embedded in the CO switch, separation will never be complete. Part of the functional problem is that there are no dumb services or primitive systems. "Intelligence" has always been diffused, as various parts of telecommunications networks adopt and develop it. These are not developments which policy-makers can easily anticipate, and the linear quality of R&D and technology developments may prevent radical advances from being deployed.

An optimistic scenario, based on exponential improvements in computing technology, anticipates intelligent services which are infrastructure transparent by adjusting to the architecture over which it travels. This is beyond the current capabilities of expert systems, but might be simplified by flexible workstation-based switching. INs create a dilemma because they both simplify and complicate the issue of separation: the more logical functions embedded in remote locations, the more control needs to be exercised over the network by a single entity, (not necessarily a TO) to ensure interworking. This brings us finally to the third driver for INs; they are a "revenue protection investment strategy." Even if they bring greater devolution, there is still a natural role for a systems integrator, and that entity cannot simply provide pipes without having some expertise in plumbing. Indeed there is a strong argument for allowing TOs to provide liberalized services as an incentive to upgrade and deploy advanced networks.

Self-financing for new services is equally problematic. New entrants cannot drop usage charges too much since most traffic still terminates on the existing operator's lines, and hence incurs interconnection charges. Residential consumers are not ideal revenue generators: UK distribution circuits are used on average 10 minutes/day. This underscores the need to shift the focus on TO investments from new services to the cost savings rationale inherent in efficient network upgrades.

## 6. THE ROLE OF INDUSTRIAL POLICY

Industrial policy is a necessity as well as a reality for most nations.[18] Market fragmentation has its downside for innovation in services, and coordination is especially important during developmental phases. Of course, many innovations begin outside the public sector and are absorbed only when their scale becomes noteworthy.

This does not prevent VANs suppliers and private network managers alike from taking on an adversarial stance towards the TOs. INs, ATM and IBNs can all be portrayed as a plot to deprive large users of uncomplicated leased lines, interconnection rights and the ability to configure network solutions independent of the TO (though in reality they may provide the most cost effective networking solutions, depending on the scale economies).

Another problem comes from the often overlooked cross-elasticities of demand, which cloud purists' vision of broadband networks. Since before the ISDN concept was born in the 1960s, it has been taken as an act of faith that integrating services over a single transmission medium was beneficial (and indeed, the vanguard of corporate users are after voice and data integration today). Yet the virtues of chaos are not often presented alongside convergence scenarios, and economic models still view new service revenues without reference to loss of existing revenues. The assumption of a zero-sum game would shipwreck many a grand vision, such as the common 1991 prediction of 10 million UK PCB subscribers by decade's end.

## 7. COMPLEXITY AND NETWORKS

Complexity and stability are increasingly at odds in the modern network, which challenges the ability of engineers to hold together an increasingly untenable patchwork of technologies. Standardization is still problematic and politicized yet more critical than ever in maintaining a fragile interworking system with exponentially more points of risk.

*Vulnerability, survivability, reliability, quality--are these concepts anathema to modern telecommunications networks? Will our technical prowess outrun our ability to solve complex problems? Or are there new network architectures, solutions, technologies which can limit these risks? The breakdown of the cost-sharing coalition so eagerly celebrated by free-marketeers might be quickly reversed once the price of deploying a stand alone    quality service is realized.*

Are intelligent networks a solution? Based on modular software, INs will support decentralization and open more of the network to users, while at the same time protecting the physical infrastructure from intrusion by placing less secure software further from the digital CO switch. This evolution anticipates competition in software based services, viewing networks as enabling platforms which can be desegregated to individual software components. INs express a real need to simplify network switching software and services introduction, and to improve quality (a prime product differentiator of competitors).

Software complexity discourages experimentation with new services, given the time required to deploy new service concepts. It also skews investment priorities towards services which directly lead to new capacity of connections, as opposed to rationalization and improvement of internal facilities management. Another driver for INs is the need to offset rising data processing costs of TOs, now half of switching equipment spend. A prime asset of new operators such as MFS, Teleport, or WilTel is their manageable size. New services need close monitoring of profitability and technology, intrinsically difficult in TOs with many overheads and piecemeal billing systems.

Segmentation advocates often fail to recognize that both networks and users have little tolerance for complexity.[19] The convergence of interests--the TO's need to develop software engineering capability and their customers need more flexible software-defined systems-- must lead to simplified, more fault-tolerant networks, which allow faster services introduction.

Yet future network architectures represent quantum leaps in complexity. GSM requires tremendous amounts of data transmission alongside the voice signal. As seen in the UK, a single software error can ripple throughout the public access network and halt operations in seconds. Are multiple federations of networks prepared to handle these massive increases in complexity when the current system is struggling under the tremendous burden of performing a more limited task?

As the number of plant owning competitors--especially mobile operators--increases, the number of interfaces will grow more than linearly. The problem becomes more difficult still if several networks are used in sequence for a single call. (Interestingly, this is a problem which currently favors single-sourced panEuropean networks).

## 8. INFORMATION ASYMMETRIES

One issue which complicates not only competitive provision of infrastructure, but also the viability of a separate liberalized upper layer is the persistent information asymmetry between the main network provider and new entrants.

In the US, the decomposition of the local access network under ONA sought to stimulate competition in markets for local switching and transport. Unbundling encouraged more efficient and widespread use of scarce network resources. But this process is often seen as adversarial to the TO, demanding it relinquish what it has (and has invested in) to share its most profitable businesses with others. Any positive view of this process must include the carrier perspective, as they currently control the network resource. Without cooperation, unbundling, ONP, and competitive VANs markets will be gained only through a long uphill battle, and the opportunities for carriers to thwart the process are many and well-known. It is critical for new entrants to know the type and cost of functionality available to them. For example, European users have long complained about TO reticence to discuss and commit to long term network evolution plans. Private network deployment might be seriously altered if TOs were more forthcoming to large users about budgets devoted to broadband services. Yet it is unfeasible to mandate access to data on network development, given its commercial value.[20] Carriers cannot be required to file plans of modernization and technology deployment for any given time frame - and realistically be expected to follow them. And could a regulator penalize a TO for changing strategy midstream, preventing adoption of an unforeseen but beneficial new technology?

Under the current system, users have to check on TOs to follow present paths, but TOs restrict VANs suppliers via choice of protocols, technologies, etc. Indeed some TOs have only marginal incentive to develop strategies at all, or to reveal them to competitors. (This does not forestall them working in a proprietary manner with equipment suppliers, or service providers with whom they have alliances). In many cases, they have an incentive, often from the political sector, to develop certain strategies without regard for market conditions.[21]

Regulators also face a similar asymmetry, and are often handicapped as mediators. As one example, Oftel's information asymmetry may be small, but the administrative, rather than judicial system of policy-making does little to expand public knowledge about the British process. In the US, the asymmetry is lessened by data exposed in legal proceedings, but even the world's largest regulatory apparatus, the FCC, relies heavily upon the industry for critical data.

## 9. IS THERE HOPE FOR A PROGRESSIVE POLICY?

The larger question is, could (or would) the public network play a role as the platform which stimulates a new applications software industry? Can the PC model, with a single operating system supporting a host of applications, be applied to telecommunications networks? Much depends on whether the TOs are dragged kicking and screaming into this venture, or whether they see it as a strategic opportunity to further entrench themselves in the local loop transmission market, ceding some tightly managed competition in the value-added sector. (This also relies upon whether they see their infrastructure monopoly as sustainable. Most do.)

Liberalization of the VANs layer need not address the question of breaking the infrastructure monopoly - (*indeed, the argument here is that VANs providers have much to gain from that monopoly, depending on the terms of separationn and access - and vice versa).* With commercial or cost-oriented access charges, a shared monopoly system could be maintained, made easier by intelligent networking and variable bit rates.

Are there some regulatory or policy options which have been overlooked in achieving a viable separation? The basic thrusts behind separation are: 1) the need for VANs liberalization to unleash the benefits of a dynamic sector; 2) the economic logic of interconnection, though practical experience with it has not seen much progressive or cooperative effort, and 3) the treatment of the network as a huge and complex enabling resource, some of whose functions are best run by one entity, over which providers need fair and secure influence.

The main arguments presented thus far are: The infrastructure monopoly should not be defined even so broadly as to consist of all transmission paths. There is vigorous competition in toll networks in the USA and a clear demand for competitive LAN interconnect, MANs and WANs. It cannot even be confined to all local paths since there is ample competition in some areas, especially dense urban business districts, and radio access may help other areas. But duplication of plant is often inefficient, and new technologies unpredictable. A market test has its shortcomings. New entrants need regulation to provide effective interconnection, to subsidize if you will, their start-up costs. The information asymmetry and market power of TOs must also be addressed.

The viability question therefore concerns curbing monopoly power, to draw nearer to that platonic ideal, the level playing field. Two sets of solutions are presented here. The first continues the network monopoly, the second embraces fragmentation and non-sustainability. The monopoly ideas are geared towards divorcing infrastructure providers from service providers, and base the need for separation on the fair provision of capacity. The second set are based upon reforming the interconnection process, and achieving fairness through threats of exit and competitive entry.

### 9.1. Retail / Wholesale Separation

This proposal identifies a boundary between network operations and customer-facing activities. What is needed is a single network operator, not involved in services, to wholesale distribution plant on a fair basis to retailers. The wholesaler, freed from dealing with retail customers, can more readily embrace the principle of cost-savings and operational rationalization than TOs currently do.

This dichotomy plays to strengths in designing and building advanced networks on a mass scale and (still in Europe) weaknesses in marketing. It has the added advantage of focussing them on technology R&D than customer satisfaction. All retailers could hold a non-dominant share in the wholesalers providing joint incentives to deploy state-of-the-art technology. Obviously, this will not be an easy task, but the above dichotomy would free competitors from making the heavy investment needed to replicate TO plant.[22] The separation also reflects a boundary between low-labor intensity network deployment and maintenance (which will be largely through remote reconfiguration), and high labor intensive (and added-value) at the point of the customer interface.

### 9.2. Unified Bit Carrier Scenario

Advances in voice compression and increasing service integration suggest a scenario in which a common bit carrier could satisfy most user needs. Much like with the retail/wholesale separation, this carrier would only be allowed into the business of wholesaling distribution plant. This is the clearest path to an IBN if that is the policy goal. Arlandis[23] has noted that this can also shift functionality to CPE through Open Architecture Receivers, though cooperation is essential to make such a system work. If all providers do not agree to sustain the network, it will inevitably face competition and the process of disintegration will begin anew.

What are the practical dimensions of relegating the TOs to per bit carriers? Given the choice of providing profitable margin software-based services, or maintaining a physical infrastructure, operated on common carriage principles, who will choose the latter?[24] A physical infrastructure enterprise cannot be carved out without discussing who might be interested in running it. It would surely face stringent regulation, its tariffs closely monitored (especially as the service upon which all other providers would rely). Bit carriers, even one which can accommodate any service, offer only limited business opportunities: More bits may equal more money, but profit margins remain slim. For example, international carriers are having difficulty in profiting from underseas cables, as users simply lease bandwidth for in-house applications rather than purchasing higher profit VANs.

On the other hand, it offers a vehicle for a carrier, with public service aims, to stimulate the economy. Most European carriers remain state-owned. Such a carrier would get industrial policy support in the form of subsidies. However, the pure bit carrier solution implies a closed environment, as pieces of such systems cannot be removed if total costs are to be recouped. This latter argument is that of the US RBOCs, that greater entry into VANs (i.e. CATV and information services) markets is needed to cost justify the deployment of a broadband networks.

The interim step towards either of these proposals would likely be separate subsidiaries with stand-alone accounting through its history in the US should dissuade others. Until carriers are split from service provider, the viability of separation without anti-competitive behavior flourishing is at best doubtful, and Europe TOs seem especially unlikely to relinquish their historic role as service providers.

## 9.3. Interconnection

This solution begins by conceding that MANs, WANs, and radio tails all lead to full infrastructure competition. Since the argument goes, service providers cannot be easily split off from carriers (especially where the unified model has 150 years of institutional history and inertia behind it), the onus shifts onto those who determine and manage interconnection policy. It may invite wasteful duplication of resources, made all the more scarce by recession in key markets, but this market-oriented choice is implicit in interconnection policy.[25] As in other scenarios, the more effective system of protection needed would only work under a cooperative effort.

In Europe there is a unique opportunity to condition entry into new markets by offering a portion of network capacity for anyone else to use, gaining proportional access to TO networks. This would require some up-front investment (a goal of regulators) and also guarantee access for the new provider, overcoming TO objections. New providers have argued that reciprocal access is too onerous a burden, but it could be applied to players with domestic monopolies (or de facto monopolies) elsewhere, accepting the clear trend of a oligopoly. This puts the greatest barriers in front of the large players, but gives them a guarantee that investments will not go wanting for access. For those which can afford it, entry will have a clearly stated cost. Smaller flexible VANs providers have the edge in that they can piggyback on any carriers capacity so long as their service is differentiated enough not to threaten the carriers' revenues. Good examples are the service consortia like SWIFT and SITA, which could be opened to competing services but reach far more customers. They might also form alliances with larger carriers to jointly gain entry.[26]

### 9.4. Status Quo

The system we have is the easiest to criticize, and in many ways reflects the worst of both worlds. De facto infrastructure monopolies which also participate in liberalized upper layer services are the villains of a well-known and unsavory story. France Telecom's claims aside, in Europe at least they have not proved overly responsive. If infrastructure provision is only partly competitive, then the nature of interconnection tariffs will determine the scope for competition, and the story there is equally unpleasant. A choice is needed between support for a bit carrier, which provides and operates infrastructure on wholesale terms, and encouraging unlimited duplication of plant with a reliance upon rejuvenated interconnection policy and access charges to open access to competitive providers.

### 10. 10 YEARS ON: A PREVIEW OF THE NEW WORLD OF TELECOMS ORDER?

Whichever path is chosen, the nature of the process must change for separation to be viable. Instead of determining a monopoly through legislation, or tinkering with the present system of interconnection, a system must be devised to provide all parties with a common incentives to support a single network resource, rather than bemoan its shortcomings. This carrier will in turn have an incentive to serve as many parties as possible. Technology is bringing this possibility nearer. Users have shown a willingness to pay higher tariffs for similar services offered over competing networks. They would pay an even higher price (thought they might not have to) to keep an efficient, flexible and open network platform afloat.

- A unified bit carrier could be funded through access charges, based on the contributions of providers, who pay for carriage, and their rival networks who pay interconnection charges.
- This carrier could herald a return to the public service mentality which nurtured engineering excellence within the monopolies, within an organization run on competitive terms to serve all users of network capacity.
- Movement towards a broader oligopoly where the sharing of a few groupings of network resources is supported by cooperation for a monopoly infrastructure.

### REFERENCES

Arlandis, Jacques, "Convergence Between Telecommunications, Computing and the Media: Visions for the Future," Montpellier: IDATE, unpublished paper, 1992.
Barclays deZoete Wedde, *Research Report on BT*, London: BZW, September, 1991.
Elton, Martin, "Integrated Broadband Networks: Assessing the Demand for New Services," Unpublished Working Paper, New York: CITI, 1992.

420

Ergas, Henry, "France Telecom: Has the Model Worked?" Paper presented to the Royal Norwegian Council for Scientific and Industrial Research, 29 January, 1992.

Foster, C.D., *General Accounting Office, 1987, Telephone Communications: Controlling Cross Subsidies Between Regulated and Uncompetitive Services*, Washington: GPO, Oct. 1993.

Harper, John, *A 21st Century Structure for UK Telecoms: Competition Without Fragmentation.* London: CommEd Publishers, 1991.

Kramer, Richard, "Service Provider Strategies for Europe," (unpublished document), 1992.

Kramer, Richard and Aine NiShuilleabhain, "Monopoly Market Structure," from *Telecommunications, Limits to Deregulation: Proceeding of the 7th Conference on Eurocommunications Policy Research, 1992*; IOS Press, Burke VA, 1993.

Levine, Henry, "R.I.P. ONA," Unpublished paper, 1991.

Little, A.D., "Issues and Options for Telecommunications in Europe," 199G2010. Report prepared for the Commission of the European Communities, 1991.

Solomon, Jonathon and Dawson Walker, "The Interconnection Imperative," *Telecommunications Policy*, May/June, 1993.

## ENDNOTES

[1] Access need not move only towards publics. Many networks are designed to exclude. And public access to privately owned networks remains as a major stumbling block in EC debates over ONP; Europe's TOs argue that they should gain a reciprocal right of access to the network of any private provider for allowing access to their networks. This would clearly be a crippling blow to new entrants, and provide the same sort of disincentives to innovate as are imbedded in the tariffing policies under ONA.

[2] International simple resale reflects the fact that value can be added to a service without changing the actual nature of the service in the least. Fractional use of leased lines are another classic example.

[3] For example, ISDN systems which integrate data and voice complicate the liberalization of the former in the environment there the latter is considered a reserved, or monopoly service. This particular problem has been a driving force for voice liberalization in the EC as data over voice and ISDN services have been considered within the ONP context.

[4] Page 19, Harper, John, *A 21st Century Structure for UK Telecoms: Competition Without Fragmentation.* London: CommEd Publishers, 1991.

[5] Little, A.D., "Issues and Options for Telecommunications in Europe," 199G2010. Report prepared for the Commission of the European Communities, 1991.

[6] Service Grandes Comptes., Telekom Contact and Unisource all represent a massive cultural shift from where Europe's TOs stood five years ago. Even the BT-MCI alliance would have been unthinkable in that context.

[7] There is yet considerable reason for scepticism: the tremendous promise of today's new technologies bear striking resemblance to a similar "plethora of new technologies," the "alphabet soup" much heralded by the FCC and others throughout the mid-1980s in support of broadcast deregulation. How many of those services, besides CATV, have come to fruition? Even the most promising of technologies, such as DB, have had little impact on the market.

[8.]The TOs deserve some credit for their current status, whether attained through skillful manipulation of the regulatory and political process, or through internal engineering excellence.

[9.]See for example a 1987 GAO report which claimed that the FCC had the resources to audit local telcos only once every 16 years. The problem is even worse in Europe, where BT is perhaps the only European TO with a complete financial picture of its operation. Perhaps the strongest hope for changing this is the intense financial scrutiny of TOs by investment bankers assisting privatization's.

[10.]France Telecom's technology choices aside, they have shown that monopolists can mobilize resources to develop high-quality networks and services, though others question the wisdom of this strategy. Ergas (1992) argues that political imperatives often forced network deployment in an inefficient direction.

[11.]This is the battle of the big switch versus the smart box people. ATM allows users to customize their use of bandwidth without being constrained to the channel data rates of the network transmission scheme.

[12.] Kramer, Richard and Aine NiShuilleabhain, "Monopoly Market Structure," from *Telecommunications, Limits to Deregulation: Proceeding of the 7th Conference on Eurocommunications Policy Research*, Burke VA: IOS Press, 1992.

[13.]This of course presumes that one is largely following the neoclassical economic view which privileges unfettered competition. The reality, especially in Europe, is that state intervention is a first principle, therefore violating the "law" of perfect competition. Government can rarely avoid picking winners and losers in the marketplace.

[14.]Levine, Henry, "R.I.P. ONA," Unpublished paper, 1991.

[15.]Kramer,Richard, "Service Provider Strategies for Europe," unpublished document, 1992.

[16.]Page 278, Solomon, Jonathon and Dawson Walker, "The Interconnection Imperative," *Telecommunications Policy*, May/June, 1993.

[17.] Elton, Martin, "Integrated Broadband Networks: Assessing the Demand for New Services," Unpublished Working Paper, New York: CITI, 1992.

[18.]We should not forget that industrial policy and state intervention were part of the Founding Fathers' tradition, much in line with Colbertist thinking. As Alexander Hamilton wrote in 1791, "capital is wayward and timid in lending itself to new undertakings, and the State ought to excite the confidence of capitalists, who are ever cautious and sagacious, by aiding them to overcome the obstacles that line in the way of all experiments."

[19.]New applications also portend unforeseen usage patterns. France Telecom's Transpac network crashed in 1985 when Teletel services were introduced on a wide scale. The packet switching technology used by Teletel was designed for constant connections between mainframes, and the rapid shifting among services by users overloaded the software, causing network paralysis. Does a similar set of problems await GSM or PCNs, ATM and SOIKET; all largely untested on a mass market scale, creating a considerable burden on the unified network?

[20.]For an example from the US, see the discussion of the battles over the Customer Proprietary Network Information as described in Levine, 1991.

[21.]Ergas, Henry, "France Telecom: Has the Model Worked?" Paper presented to the Royal Norwegian Council for Scientific and Industrial Research, 29 January 1992.

422

[22] Page 22, Harper, John, *A 21st Century Structure for UK Telecoms: Competition Without Fragmentation.* London: CommEd Publishers, 1991.

[23] Arlandis, Jacques, "Convergence Between Telecommunications, Computing and the Media: Visions for the Future." Montpellier: IDATE. Unpublished paper, 1992.

[24] Even for the most bureaucratic of PTOs, international dissemination is where the interesting business questions, as the glamour and money, lie. Witness Belgacom's roll out of its Global VPN services, while domestic users go poorly served. The best hope there might be is to get POs to voluntarily jettison their carriage business as Pacific Telesis has proposed.

[25] This also reflects a  major difference between ONA and ONP, elaborated in Kramer 1992.

[26] Solomon, Jonathon and Dawson Walker, "The Interconnection Imperative," *Telecommunications Policy*, May/June, 1993.

PRIVATE NETWORKS PUBLIC OBJECTIVES
E. Noam and A. NíShúilleabháin (Editors)
423

Beyond Liberalization: From the Network of Networks to the System of Systems

Eli M. Noam

## 1. DOES LIBERALIZATION MEAN LIBERTARIANISM, WITH NO ROLE FOR REGULATION?

Suppose the telecommunications infrastructure keeps evolving towards institutional diversification and technological upgrade. What then? At present, the focus of attention is on restrictions -- technological, regulatory, political, and financial. Yet in the developed world, the day is approaching, historically speaking, when many of these bottlenecks will be overcome -- when entry by various service providers is wide open; fiber is widespread; radio-based carriers fill in the white spots in the map of telecommunications ubiquity; and global carriers operate beyond their home territory. In such an environment, what market structure can we expect? And what regulatory environment need we erect? It is time therefore to ask a fundamental question for future telecommunications policy: *After competition, what?*

The conventional scenario for the evolution of telecommunications, offered by traditional state monopoly carriers around the world as their vision of the future, was the *integrated single superpipe,* merging all communications infrastructure into a single conduit controlled by themselves and interconnected internationally with similar territorially exclusive superpipes. This scenario of integration took no account of the simultaneous organizational centrifugalism that was taking place, first in the U.S. and now increasingly in other countries. Instead of consolidating, the network environment kept diversifying.

Take as an example local transmission, the segment widely considered to be a natural monopoly's natural monopoly. Yet today, we can identify a wide variety of potential and credible participants for rival local transmission based on their entrepreneurial dynamism, and on economies of scope rather than on those of scale:[1] fiber-based metropolitan area networks; cable television providers; radio-based cellular carriers; electric utilities; long-distance companies extending their distribution plant; and other local exchange companies crossing territorial borders and invading each others' turf. Similar lists can be made for other physical segments of the network, whether they are in domestic, long-distance, international, mobile, or switching.

The emergence of new networks is not simply a matter of technology or politics, but of the dynamics of group formation. As the system expands, political dynamics lead to redistribution and expansion. This provides increasing incentives for some users to exit from a sharing coalition, and to an eventual 'tipping' of the network from a stable single entity to a system of separate sub-coalitions.[2] This view of success undermining its own foundations is basically Schumpeterian. From the monopoly's perspective, it is deeply pessimistic,

424

because it implies that the harder their efforts and the greater their success, the closer the end to their special status is at hand.

## 2. THE ROLE OF SYSTEMS INTEGRATION

Yet liberalization of physical entry is not the end of the story, only its beginning. Competition begets diversity; diversity begets complexity; and complexity leads to efforts at simplification. Thus, the challenge is how the actual user of telecommunications will handle an environment that is so different from the technologists' model of the single superpipe. How can the numerous network pieces be integrated into a usable whole? There are several ways to do so.

*1. Users' self-integration.* At a very basic level, this is today's system for American users, who arrange for their own long distance carrier and equipment. Large users often put together networks on their own, by leasing lines, buying equipment such as PBXs and LANs, and managing it. Self-integration gets complicated very quickly as the number of carriers, services, prices, and equipment options multiplies. A related technique has the user's terminal equipment incorporate some built-in intelligence which can make the right choices among carriers and services on a real-time basis.

*2. Carriers' integration by expansion.* Carriers could enter horizontally into new geographic markets or vertically into new services -- by expansion, merger, or acquisition. Realistically, it is hard to imagine today any company that is big and varied enough to offer all types of facilities and services, and to do it well, locally, domestically, internationally, across services, in telecommunications, computers, enhanced services, and equipment. This has led to a variant, namely *joint ventures* among carriers, where several companies specializing in different market segments link up with each other through institutionalized cooperation.

*3. Integration by systems integrators.* Perhaps the most promising way of putting together the various bits and pieces of networks and services is for a new category of "systems integrators" to emerge who provide the end user with access to a variety of services, in a one-stop fashion. They relieve customers from the responsibility of integration for which expertise is required, and yet are not captive to recover major investments as carriers are. These specialized integrators, whose predecessors are known as outsourcers or managed data services providers, might typically assemble packages of various types of services, equipment, etc, and customize these packages to the specific requirements of their customers. They could operate a least-cost-routing system, switching users around from carrier to carrier, depending on the best deal available for a given time and route. Likely to emerge is are domestic and international markets in transmission capacity, in which contracts in capacity are traded, with both consisting of future options and a spot market operating in real time.

The characteristic of "pure" systems integrators -- for there will be various hybrids -- is that they do not own or operate the various sub-production activities but rather select optimal elements in terms of price and performance, package them together, manage the bundles, and offer it to the customer on a one-stop basis. They resemble, in part, today's resellers, but they do much more. They relieve customers from the responsibility of integration for which expertise is required. To these customers, the identity of the underlying carriers and their technology might be unknown and transparent as transmission becomes a commodity.

Who will be the telecommunications systems integrators? They are likely to be a diverse lot. Some might be today's resellers and value-added providers, computer systems providers, defense contractors seeking diversification, and corporate networks with excess capacity. Others would obviously be carriers themselves, such as local exchange companies, long-distance and international telephone firms, cable television operators, and metropolitan area networks. Their integrator function, however, is very different from their carrier function, as will be discussed below. All are likely to compete and to collaborate vigorously with each other. Governments can also be system integrators, either directly by operating their own network systems, or indirectly by supporting new types of non-governmental integrated applications. The internet is an example. A public corporation for network applications could be the vehicle for such efforts.

Today, systems integrators already exist to some extent for large customers and customer groups. But tomorrow systems integrators may put together individualized networks for personal use, or *personal* networks. These "PNs" would offer individually tailored "virtual" and physical network arrangements that serve individualized communications needs and provide access to frequent personal and business contacts, data sources, e-mail, users groups, transaction programs, video and audio publishers, data processing and storage, bulletin boards, and personal information screening. A systems integrator is also likely provide to residential users with a *tele-mailbox* -- a customer's telecommunications node at or near their premise -- into which various communications flows terminate. As these integrator-provided networks develop, they access and interconnect into each other and form a complex interconnected whole sprawling across carriers, service providers, and national frontiers. In the process, the telecommunications environment evolves from the *network of networks*, in which carriers interconnect, to a *system of systems*, in which systems integrators link up with each other. The Internet is an early example.

This evolution has begun in the United States. The Rochester Telephone Co., a medium-sized independent telephone company, has proposed to separate itself into a carrier (R-Net) offering transmission to all, including its competitors, as well as a services operator (R-Com) which would offer the actual service to customers. Rochester couches this proposal in the language of "wholesale" and "retail". But clearly, R-Com will offer packages that contain much more than R-Net's services. Inevitably it will become a systems integrator.

## 3. REGULATION

Where does such an arrangement of customized networks and managed by systems integrators leave government regulation? How does it deal with real virtuality? Regulation had been essential to the old system, partly to protect against monopoly, partly to protect the monopoly itself. In the transition to competition, what was left of regulation was seen as temporary, shrinking reciprocally with the growth of competition. In time, it would diminish to nothing. Yet can one expect the "system of systems" to be totally self-regulating?

The notion of an invisible hand mechanism, the idea that out of numerous decentralized sub-optimizing actions there would emerge, without any central direction, some overall and beneficial equilibrium, is perhaps Adam Smith's major insight as a philosopher.[3] Its importance goes way beyond economics. Can electronic communications function in such a fashion, optimally arranging themselves in the absence of an overall plan or direction?

The mere notion is almost incomprehensible to telecommunications traditionalists. They argue that the more complex the technology and the network become, the more necessary it is to plan it in some centralized fashion. Yet the more complex and advanced an economy becomes, the more difficult it is to guide it centrally. Complexity is neither a necessary nor sufficient condition for justifying centralized control. On the other hand, there is the also the opposite and simplistic view that more advanced technology, merely by creating new options, makes all regulation unnecessary. But consider new chemical products or nuclear power generation -- complex technologies that are tightly regulated. Or airlines, whose actual operations are strictly controlled, even as their prices may be deregulated. Technology does not abolish negative externalities or market failures.

Why do we have regulation in telecommunications? To some it is merely an exercise in capture and rent-seeking by powerful interest groups. To others, it is based on underlying public policy goals, including restriction of market power. There is truth in both views, and they are not mutually exclusive. To assure various policy objectives, such as the free flow of information across the economy and society and technological innovation, regulators and courts instituted a variety of regulatory policies, such as universal service with rate subsidies, common carriage, interconnection rules, quality standards, and limited carrier liability. But in a system of system integrators, what forms of such regulation, if any, are still necessary? In traditional telecommunications, regulation by government existed partly to effect the balance of power between huge monopoly suppliers on the one hand, and small and technically ignorant users on the other hand. It inserted the political and administrative process to alter unconstrained market outcomes. In return, the dominant carriers, whether private or governmental, received protection from competition by other providers. In a system of systems, on the other hand, the imbalance changes drastically. Now, systems integrators, competing with each other for customers, act as these users' agents toward carriers. They can protect users against carriers' under-performance and power, and get them the best deal. This would largely resolve traditional problems of price, quality, privacy and market power. Thus, assuming that users have a choice among systems integrators and that systems integrators have a choice among non-colluding suppliers of underlying services, the need for government control declines drastically. On the other hand, not all traditional policy goals are fully resolved in a system of systems. Let us turn to them now.

*1. Universal Service.* The emerging systems of systems will exert competitive pressures on cost and therefore on many prices, thus making telecommunications more affordable to some. But it will be impossible to maintain the traditional redistributive system of generating subsidies and transferring them internally within the same carrier from one category of users to another category. Several things will disrupt this arrangement. With competing carriers, an internal redistribution is not sustainable once other carriers without redistributive burdens target the subsidizing users as the most likely customers. Furthermore, residential users may end up paying a proportionally higher share than large users, because cost shares in the substantial joint costs may end up allocated inverse to demand elasticity -- the Ramsey pricing rule -- and large users have more options and hence greater elasticity. Thus, the trend which at present is described as a "rebalancing" of prices towards cost would go much further than that, burdening the inelastic customers. Nor can one expect to continue to rely on a system of access charges to provide the source of subsidies, since these charges imply access into "the" network, which will be a meaningless concept where alternative transmission is easily available. Systems integrators, by aggregating the demand of many small customers, can provide them with a higher demand elasticity with respect to carriers, and thereby generate low prices and low shares in fixed costs. Systems integrators thus serve, in effect, as arbitragers in demand elasticity. This is also likely to increase their attractiveness to customers in comparison to staying as customers of carriers, and this accelerates the move to systems integration. On the other hand, those customers not able to obtain systems integrator service, perhaps because they are only reached by a monopoly carriers, would end up bearing a greater cost share. Also, systems integrators, absent some support mechanism, would de-average prices for their customers and charge, for example, rural customers a price that reflects the greater cost of serving them.

Yet this need not spell the end of support schemes. If, for various reasons of policy or politics, one wants to subsidize some categories of service or users, it is still possible to do so, only in different ways. One alternative mechanism might be a communications sales or value-added tax. The moneys raised might go to a "universal service fund" which would be used to support certain services or categories of users. Benefitted users could receive, for example, a 'virtual voucher' that could be redeemed at the various competing carriers, and which would make them, too, interesting to the new carriers. Such a system would replace the present hidden tax system and would make it accountable.

*2. Interconnection and Financial Viability.* The economic rationale behind the tension between the integrative and pluralistic forces is most pronounced on the front where they intersect: the rules of interconnection of the multiple hardware and software sub-networks and their access into the integrated whole. As various discrete networks grow, they must inter-operate in terms of technical standards, protocols, and boundaries. Yet interconnectivity is not normally granted by incumbent firms. That is the lesson of decades of American experience. Regulatory requirements such as open network architecture, comparably efficient interconnection, or collocation were part of the evolution towards competition, and towards an increasing unbundling of hardware and software segments. In effect, these provisions regulated in order to deregulate.

One problem here is technical interconnectivity. In a system of systems, integrators may well pick different standards and protocols, either for reasons of sub-optimization, or for strategic-competitive reasons. This can be exacerbated by vertical links. If they are part of equipment manufacturers, their standards may try to further their equipment vending strategies. And where the systems integrators are controlled by monopolistic carriers, standards may be set to provide advantages in integrator competition. Will market forces be sufficient for a convergence? Not always. Economic theory suggests that it is impossible to say in advance whether a convergence to compatible standards will take place. Where it does not occur one must weigh the cost of incompatibility against the benefits of flexibility. In some instances, the former would become too great, and interoperability may have to be instituted as a default standard, just as it is for other economic arrangements such as in the law of commercial transactions.

Assuring physical interconnectivity will be hard enough. But still harder will be financial interconnectivity. The first problem is that in a competitive environment systems integrators need to pay to compete carriers a price based only on the latter's short-term marginal costs, and can pass this low cost on to their customers. Yet the bulk of cost in a capital intensive industry such as telecommunications networks is fixed, and would not get compensated in such an arrangement. In a world of transmission as a commodity, carriers would not break even.

Interconnection rights accelerate this development. An initial investment is less likely if a loss were entirely borne by the first carrier while the benefits would have to be shared with other entrants who would be able to interconnect and thus immediately gain access to the critical mass created by the first carrier. The implication is that in an environment of multiple networks which can interconnect, less start-up investment would be undertaken. It pays to be second. A situation of market failure exists. The long-term result would be either a disinvestment in networks, the reestablishment of monopoly, or oligopolistic pricing. Because none of these scenarios is desirable, they would lead back to various regulatory schemes, and even to a direct outside subsidy for the early stage of a new network service.

*3. The Free Flow of Information.* In the traditional network environment, the granting of access and non-discriminatory content-neutrality is required of the general "public" networks by law, common carriage regulation, and even common law. But common carriage requirements do not apply to systems integrators. They can institute restrictions on their systems, and exclude certain types of information, subjects, speakers, or destinations.

One of the central observations of the "law and economics" school of thought has been the fundamental economic efficiency of the common law.[4] The implication is that common carriage, as the product of common law judges later codified by statutes, was an economically efficient institution. Among its purposes were reduction of market power; protection of an essential service; protection of free flow in good and information; promotion of basic infrastructure; reduction in transaction cost; and limited liability. The blows to traditional common carriage do not come from new rival telecommunications carriers, but from two new directions. The first is the increasing overlap between the common carrier system and well-developed mass media private contract carriers such as cable television networks. The other challenge to common carriage are the systems integrators we have discussed. As mentioned, common carriage does not apply to systems integrators.

In head-to-head competition between a common carrier and a private contract carrier or systems integrator, the former is at an inherent disadvantage, because, among several other reasons, it cannot use differentiated pricing due to its non-discrimination obligation, it cannot prevent arbitrage, and it cannot pick its customers. As a result, a systems integrator may provide services more cheaply, even though they use the carriers' underlying transmission facilities. It is unlikely that the common carriers will simply sit by in such a situation. They will operate their own systems integrators, and they will move to contract carriage themselves, such as price-differentiation of customers. And that is, indeed, what is already starting to happen.

What are the implications? The system of systems might have the technical capacity for a large number of voices, yet it may still result in a narrower spectrum of information, if systems integrators have gatekeeper powers. The need for the various systems to access each other, and for information to travel over numerous interconnected carriers, means that the restrictiveness of any one of the participants would require everyone else to institute content and usage tests before they could hand over or accept traffic, or they must agree to the most restrictive principles. Information travels across numerous subnetworks until it reaches its destination, and nobody can tell one bit apart from another bit. If each of these networks and systems integrators sets its own rules about which information is carried and which is not, information would not flow easily.

How do we deal with this problem? By establishing principles of common carriage or of "open platform" that provide for non-discriminatory service, neutral as to content, users and usage, and absence of liability for content. A decentralized network system requires some basic and fundamental rules of the road. This does not mean doing away with private carriage. But it might take the form of reciprocity: each service provider can elect to remain a private carrier; but if it accesses another carrier by way of common carrier *rights*, it must also provide, on at least part of its capacity, a reverse channel of common carriage. These channels can be called "common carriage rights-of-way."

## 4. NEW PROBLEMS

What other problems might be associated with "systems integrators"?

*1. Integrator Power?* If there are strong economies of scale and scope in systems integration, only a few large firms would survive. In theory, integrators with market power might sell only a full range of services to the end user, charge monopolistic prices, force a carrier to enter into exclusive arrangements, or control access to the "tele-mailbox." These are fairly standard problems of vertical extension of market power in one stage of production into other stages. Without such underlying market power no market distortion would be sustainable. Such problems, if real, could be dealt with through regular antitrust enforcement.

But in any event, is market power in systems integration likely? Sources of market power might be the ability of a large systems integrator to get advantageous rates from carriers or to set aside proportionately less spare and redundant capacity by averaging out demand spikes across its more numerous customers. On the other hand, any customized service operation requires close attention to and contact with customers, and this factor, does not favor large-scale firms. Generally, it is hard to imagine that the nature and shape of economies scale are similar for each layer of the OSI hierarchy of communications services, from basic transmission up to computer-based applications. Thus, integrator power is unlikely.

A more threatening potential for the exercise of power by a systems integrator would be if it controlled the tele-mailbox described above --the termination point for a variety of communications links to the user. To prevent this from happening, the operators of tele-mailboxes would have to grant equal access and interconnection to other communications providers. In other words, the tele-mailbox would have to be an open platform. Another issue of integrator power could be their hold over customers. For example, they might mislead unsophisticated users about performance characteristics and prices. Such issues of consumer protection can be dealt with by consumer protection or public service agencies.

*2. Carrier Power.* Carriers functioning as systems integrators could favor their own segments of service or equipment. Furthermore, their advantages include established customer relations, and the foundation of a major transmission element. However, this base is also a burden. In a competitive environment, it is more likely that independent integrators will have a competitive advantage over established companies who promote their own services over lower-priced independent offerers. To be truly competitive as a systems integrator, a traditional carrier's systems integration operation must be willing to compete against its own carrier and in effect become independent. While this might be conceivable, it might require significant rethinking. On the other hand, traditional carriers have some advantages. These include the coordination of planning, advance information, established goodwill, and reduced transaction costs for operations under one corporate roof. Carriers which strengthen these advantages might therefore establish themselves as competitors in systems integration. Yet what about advantages of size? We have to distinguish between economies of scale in systems integration, and in the underlying transmission elements. The latter would benefit independent systems integrators, too, as long as they could obtain capacity on the same terms as the carrier's integrator service.

Where monopoly power persists in any transmission segment, end-to-end competitiveness would have to be assured by the imposition of non-discriminatory access to these segments. But with such standby safeguards available, there should be no problem of having carriers operate as system integrators.

*3. International Asymmetry.* The system of systems works as long as it is competitive in each of its stages, or as long as regulation establishes non-discrimination. However, in an international setting neither of these conditions is likely to be met. Most countries lag the U.S. and Japan in the evolution of networks. The traditional monopoly carrier is usually firmly entrenched, and operating in all stages of communications. In consequence, systems integrators cannot truly compete against governmental or semi-official public telecommunications operators (PTOs) in systems integration, except in market niches. This might be considered to be an internal issue for these countries, except that it has a global anti-competitive impact. This is because some of these PTOs are aggressively pursuing international systems integration themselves, while at the same time holding gate-keeper powers over entry into their own home markets. Thus, the PTO of an important European country could restrict the ability of an American systems integrator to offer global services, while at the same time entering a liberalized environment in America.

Of course, other countries' PTOs can play the same game, and partly as a result, a new trend of international carrier collaboration has emerged in which major PTOs enter into joint ventures of systems integration. Potentially at least, these alliances of dominant national carriers could create international cartels, and barriers to competitive entry of other systems integrators, whether in their home countries or internationally. To prevent this it is essential to press internationally for non- discriminatory access, lease, and interconnection arrangements that are neutral as to the nature or the nationality of the systems integrator.

## 5. CONCLUSION

Telecommunications are moving from the traditional monopoly, by way of a "network of networks," to a "system of systems" in which users are served by systems integrators that access each other. This environment will not be the "end of history" as far as regulation is concerned, and government is not likely to disappear from this area. It would be naive to expect fewer regulatory tasks. Liberalization does not mean libertarianism. In the 1980s, telecommunications policy was centered on open entry. This was correct then and now. But in the 1990s, second-generation issues, or issues involving the integration of the various partial networks and systems, will be at the forefront. This means dealing with the impact of the systems integrators that will emerge, as this article has argued, as the central elements of the future telecommunications structure. Their influence will eliminate the need for many regulatory actions, but will keep some and add others. What will be left includes" responsibility for:

* Reform of universal service.
* Interoperability.
* Physical interconnection and access.
* Free-flow of information content.
* Prevention of oligopolistic behavior.
* Prevention of consumer and investor fraud.
* Network investments where market failure exists.
* International coordination.

None of the developments anticipated in this article will happen overnight, though some are already manifest. But policy wisdom meets the prepared. Opening telecommunications competition, painful as it is, will prove to be politically and conceptually the easy part. Dealing with the consequences will be the next and more difficult challenge.

## ENDNOTES

[1] For a view in support of economies of scale, see Peter Huber, *The Geodesic Network II*, Washington, DC: The Geodesic Company, 1992.

[2] Eli Noam, 'Network tipping and the Tragedy of the Common Network: A Theory for the Formation and Breakdown of Public Telecommunications systems', *Communications & Strategies*, No 1, 1er Trimestre 1991, pp 43-72.

[3] Adam Smith, *An Inquiry into the Nature and Causes of The Wealth of Nations*, 2 vols. Edwin Cannan (ed.). London: Methuen & Co., Ltd., 1904.

[4] See e.g., Richard A. Posner, *Economic Analysis of Law* (3d Edition), Boston: Little, Brown and Company, 1986; and Guido Calabresi, *Some Thoughts on Risk Distribution and the Law of Torts*, 70 Yale Law Journal 499, 1961.

434

Cellular: 21-5,32n,74,136,147,289,291,353,355, 423
Central Office: 12,22-3
Centrex: 79-80,114n,343
CERFnet: 317,319,325n
Chakrabarti, A: 330
Chicago Mercantile Exchange: 200,203
China: 396,399,402,405
CIA: 84
Cisco: 320,358,370
CITI: 31,68,113n,340n,343
Citibank: 67,200,203
CIX: 317,319-21
Clinton, Bill: 86,247
Collocation: 22-4,59,94,227n,427
COMBits: 319
Common Carrier: 42,45-6,65-6,68,78,161,230, 238,243n,247-8,250-2,255,257-8,262-3, 265-7,269-71n,274n,317,343,353,380, 388-9,392,426,428-9
Common Channel Signaling: 345-7,350-3,356n
Communications Act (1934): 3,266
CompuServe: 137,235-7,257,259,265,273n,275n, 278-9n,309,320,332
Computer III Inquiry: 5,283n
Computer Services Corporation: 376n
ConAgra: 73
Concert: 323n,360,369,372,374-8n
Congress: 85-6,159n,231,258,260-2,312,320
Constitution: 96,229-34,239,241,243n,249,253, 255-6,259-62,264,267,283n
Continental: 28
Cornell Supercomputing Facility: 314
Cornford, James: 47n
CPE: 12,76,80,177,209,224,297-8,370,409,418
Crandall, Robert: 65-6,222
CREN: 323n
CRIMNET: 84,87,92n
Crossbar Switch: 18
CSNET: 307,314,323-4n
Cubby, Inc: 235-7,259,273n

**D**

DARPA: 307,313-4
Darwinian Selection: 10,19,28
Data Packet: 12
Data Transmission: 2,16,42-5,66,68,72-3,78-81, 85,87-8,104,146,159n,167,170,187, 192n,197-8,231,247,249-50,270-1n, 344,375n,378n,407
Datex-P: 376n
DBS: 413
DDI: 380
DEC: 141,149

Defense Communications Agency: 85
DeNigris, Peter: 279n
Denison, E: 330
Department of Commerce: 65,70
Department of Defense: 6,86,135,159n,242n,307, 313,324n
Department of Education: 242n
Department of Energy: 242n,315,317
Department of Justice: 11,62n,145,148,374n
Deregulation: 28,103,113,161-2,167,266,275n, 312,426
Deutsche Bundespost: 62n
Deutsche Telekom: 361,365,373,374-7n,389
Dezalay, Y: 96
Digital equipment: 358
Digital technology: 3,18,22-3,43-4,79,88,136, 147-8,179-80,185,193n,198,200,350,395
Direct mail: 22
Distributed Systems Lab: 4
Divestiture (see also MFJ): 42,106,137,144,159n, 177,373,377n
DNA: 10,19
Don Fitzpatrick Associates: 235
Dresden Convention: 1,7n
DSC: 369
DS0: 186
DS1: 78

**E**

Eastern Airlines: 28
Eastern Microwave: 92n
Edison: 142
EDS: 361,370
Egypt: 52
800 numbers: 27,187,193n,253-4,257,345
Electronic Communications Privacy Act of 1986: 275n
E-Mail: 42,85,238-40,252-4,256-8,272-3n, 275-6n,280n,295-6,309,314,325n
EMPIRENET: 87,92n
Enviromental Protection Agency: 242n
Ericsson: 369
ESNET: 308
Ethernet: 358
ETN: 195,197-9,201-5,207n
Eucom: 365,377n
Eunetcom: 361,376-8n,393n
Euroclear: 117
European Commission: 374n
European Community: 62n,96,395,408-9,420n
Europeam Union: 197-9
EVUA: 378n
Execunet: 59